DATE DUE

LATIN AMERICAN LEGAL INSTITUTIONS:

PROBLEMS FOR COMPARATIVE STUDY

LATIN AMERICAN STUDIES
VOLUME 5

LATIN AMERICAN LEGAL INSTITUTIONS:
PROBLEMS FOR COMPARATIVE STUDY

KENNETH L. KARST

Professor of Law
University of California, Los Angeles

Translations and Editorial Assistance by
JANE R. TRAPNELL

LATIN AMERICAN CENTER

UNIVERSITY OF CALIFORNIA
LOS ANGELES, 1966

Published under the editorship of
JOHANNES WILBERT

Publication co-sponsored by Centro Latinoamericano de Venezuela

To Smiley, remembering a wooden sign in

Catamarca, and other milestones.

PREFACE

The two-part division of this book reflects a corresponding division in the objectives of my course in Comparative Law at the UCLA School of Law. The three chapters of Part One are designed to introduce the student to the civil law system, in the manner of what, in 1966, may be called the traditional comparative law course. Although such a course may serve many functions, I give greatest importance to that of providing the student with a new view of his own legal system. The emphasis, therefore, is not on foreign law, but on comparative study, and these three chapters include Anglo-American cases and commentary in abundance. Because I believe that it is not profitable to study comparatively without exploring some aspects of the foreign system rather deeply, the chapters of Part One concentrate on just a few persistent issues of civil, penal and commercial law. The student who objects to the cold-bath treatment of beginning Chapter I with problems may wish to begin with the historical note on page 112. In any case, at some point early in the course it will be useful for the student to read Professor John Merryman's excellent introduction to the civilian "style" of thought, *The Italian Style: Doctrine, Law and Interpretation,* 18 STAN. L. REV. 39, 396, 583 (1965-66).

The foreign law treated comparatively in Part One is not indigenous to Latin America. Most of it is transplanted from Europe, and from France and Spain in particular. A fair case can be made for the proposition that these subjects would be taught more effectively from European materials, which are richer and more fully developed. The decision to proceed with materials from Latin American sources resulted not only from my own regional preferences, but also from a wish to establish an institutional base for the subjects of Part Two.

The final two chapters are designed to take advantage of the fact that Latin America, as distinguished from other regions, has features that make the comparative study of legal institutions particularly rewarding: (a) a view of the role of law in the community that differs markedly from attitudes in the United States and Western Europe; (b) a degree of disparity between the written law and the law in action characteristic of the world's "developing societies"; (c) a varying social structure, ranging from the modern and highly "Westernized" to the semi-feudal; and (d) a rate of social change whose rapidity places serious strain on society's institutional framework. The public law issues of Chapters IV and V cannot be understood outside their social context; here, comparative *law* is only part of the subject. For this purpose the student should do some general reading relating to Latin America; one work which deserves particular mention is SILVERT, THE CONFLICT SOCIETY: REACTION AND REVOLUTION IN LATIN AMERICA (1961). The student who wants an entertaining refresher for his geography will find it in the paperback edition of KINGSBURY AND SCHNEIDER, AN ATLAS OF LATIN AMERICAN AFFAIRS (1965).

Although the materials of Part One derive largely from Europe, they provide a doctrinal foundation for the more distinctively Latin American subjects treated in Part Two. One theme which helps to unify the two parts is the role of the judiciary. To what extent have the civilian traditions considered in Chapter I influenced the development of the judicial protections against governmental arbitrariness which are treated in Chapter V? That question typifies the double purpose of this book: to explore the institutions and processes of decision-making as well as the substantive rules and principles that they produce.

KENNETH L. KARST

Los Angeles, California

June 1966

ACKNOWLEDGMENTS

These teaching materials, and the course for which they have been assembled, had their beginning late in 1960, when Frank R. Strong, then Dean of the College of Law of Ohio State University, generously offered his support for the project. Without that support, neither the course nor this book would have resulted; to say that I am grateful hardly makes the point, but he will understand. And so begins the usual list of persons and institutions "without whose help, ..." The reader trained in the art of skimming will go on to the Table of Contents, but I will not be deprived of the chance to make public my thanks, which are no less real for being recorded in a list.

My former colleagues at Ohio State gave me encouragement even when they did not know they were doing so; I am especially grateful to Professors Carl H. Fulda and Robert J. Nordstrom. The Ford Foundation and the Mershon Center for National Security Studies made possible the essential free time and travel. Professor Keith S. Rosenn used a tentative draft of these materials in his course at Ohio State, and I have liberally adopted his suggestions for their revision. A very large number of colleagues in Latin America have contributed in a hundred ways to this undertaking; to all of them, and particularly to my dear friend Dr. Ignacio Winizky of Buenos Aires, *un millión* . . . . Alan Buckner, of the class of 1966 of the UCLA School of Law, assisted in the revision of Chapter V.

Dr. Johannes Wilbert, Director of the UCLA Latin American Center, gave material and spiritual support to this project which made the difference between a scholarly exercise and a tangible product. Dr. William B. Stern, of the Los Angeles County Law Library, made available important institutional and personal assistance. The manuscript was produced in various early stages by Mrs. Gladys Paulin, Mrs. Marjorie Bishop and Mrs. Barbara Bidwell. Mrs. Elizabeth Scheib assisted in the preparation of the manuscript for the printer. Costs of publication were defrayed in part by funds from the International and Comparative Studies Grant of the Ford Foundation to the University of California, Los Angeles.

Jane Trapnell completely reworked all my translations; every translation not otherwise acknowledged is our joint product, negotiated at great psychic cost but with equal terminal satisfaction. Furthermore, she edited my prose —even this paragraph—and supervised the entire editorial process. This is her book, too, and she has my thanks and my esteem.

K. L. K.

TABLE OF CONTENTS

PART ONE

PART TWO

PART ONE

PART ONE

Chapter I

THE CIVIL CODES:

MISTAKE AND FRAUD IN THE LAW OF CONTRACTS

A. Some Argentine Solutions

Your first assignment is to analyze and decide five problem cases, using two sources which are printed immediately following the problems: (i) some eighty articles of the Civil Code of Argentina, and (ii) excerpts from a learned treatise dealing with some of the principles involved in the problems.

1. Arenas had two valuable sketches which he wanted to sell. He had talked the matter over with a friend who was an art dealer, and who had advised him that the sketch by Picasso was worth about 100,000 pesos, and the sketch by Goya about 200,000 pesos. Arenas made an error when he wrote to Barrios; his offering letter said: "I will sell you my Goya for 100,000 pesos or my Picasso for 200,000." Barrios telephoned his reply; he said, "I accept your offer of the Goya. May I send you the money tomorrow?" Arenas said, "Yes," and the next day Barrios' messenger appeared at Arenas' home with 100,000 pesos. Arenas refused to give him the Goya sketch. Is Barrios entitled to enforce Arenas' promise according to his offering letter? Would it make any difference if Barrios had been present during Arenas' conversation with the art dealer?

2. Quijote agreed in writing to buy from Repollo a 10,000-peso promissory note on which Repollo was the payee. Repollo endorsed the note to Quijote, but before paying for it Quijote learned that the maker of the note was insolvent at the time of his (Quijote's) agreement to buy it. Must he pay for the worthless note? Would your answer be different if the note were forged?

3. Chistoso wanted to sell some stock which he owned in Industrias Argentinas, S.A. The market price had recently hovered around 500 pesos per share. Chistoso wrote to Dorado: "I will sell you 100 shares of my I.A. stock for 52,500 pesos." Dorado agreed readily, by telegram: "Accept your offer 100 shares I.A. at 525 per share." Dorado thought that the reference in Chistoso's letter was to Iluminación Argentina, S.A., whose stock was then selling at around 550 pesos per share. When the mistake was discovered, each man insisted on going ahead with the deal as he had understood it: Chistoso's complaint demanded that Dorado accept 100 shares of Industrias Argentinas, and

Dorado's counterclaim demanded that Chistoso acquire and sell to him 100 shares of Iluminación Argentina. How should the court decide?

4. Galán told Holgado that Holgado's uncle had died, leaving Holgado a sizeable inheritance, including a large beach house. In fact, Holgado's uncle was still alive. Holgado then sold and transferred his own small beach house to Imperito, who did not know either Galán or Holgado's uncle, and who did not know of Galán's statement to Holgado. After making the transfer, Holgado chanced to meet his uncle at the club. What are Holgado's remedies, if any?

5. Jerez secretly hired a geologist to determine whether there existed a deposit of coal under Pandillo's farm, and the geologist reported that a large deposit, worth at least 5,000,000 pesos, was there. Without informing Pandillo of the report, Jerez offered to buy the farm for 2,000,000 pesos. Pandillo said that he was interested in selling, but that the farm was worth 3,000,000 pesos because the Ministry of Public Works had approved the paving of a road from the farm to a nearby market town. As Pandillo knew, the Ministry had not approved any such project. After a brief negotiation, Jerez and Pandillo agreed on a sale price of 2,500,000 pesos; with due formality, Pandillo transferred the farm to Jerez, who paid half the price at once and promised in the proper writing to pay the balance a year later. The year has not yet passed, and Jerez has discovered that the geologist was mistaken; there is virtually no coal under the land. He wants to annual the transaction and get back his initial payment; Pandillo refuses. What are the rights of the parties?

NOTE ON TERMINOLOGY AND TRANSLATION

The reader of translated foreign legal materials should be wary. The difficulties that beset the legal translator are considerable, but translations often fail to reflect the uncertainties which may have attended their birth. Any translation is likely to be an uneasy compromise between literal — *i.e.*, word by word — reproduction in another language, and the "true" sense of the original phrases as divined by the translator. The translations in these materials have sacrificed literalness in favor of readability; for research purposes, the reader is directed to the original sources.

One celebrated difference between civil law and common law languages relates to the terms "law" and "right":

> In many languages, such as Latin, French, Italian, Spanish and German, there is only one word for "law" and "right" (ius, droit, diritto, derecho, Recht). To avoid ambiguity, legal writers sometimes use this one word solely in the sense of "right," and employ the term denoting a code or statute (loi, legge, Gesetz [we may add ley — Ed.]) as synonymous with "law." In a code jurisdiction this usage is on the whole satisfactory for the everyday work of the lawyer; but it may lead the uninitiated to the inac-

> curate conclusion that statutory law is the only kind of law known in those
> countries. SCHLESINGER, COMPARATIVE LAW CASES, TEXT, MATERIALS
> 479 (2d ed. 1959).

Thus translation difficulties beget other difficulties of analysis which are more
serious.

To the ordinary hazards of translation must be added the differences in
legal context that may make even rough approximation hard, and worse, may
make the best possible translation misleading. Judge Frank has warned of the
"undetected pun," which is also found in domestic rules of law, and which may
be fruitful as well as dangerous in its ambiguity. Frank, *Civil Law Influences
on the Common Law — Some Reflections on "Comparative" and "Contrastive"
Law,* 104 U. PA. L. REV. 887, 920 (1956). Professor Schlesinger has referred
to a number of cases illustrative of what he calls "the maxim of caveat lector."
SCHLESINGER, *supra,* at 477-79. Any term draws meaning from its context;
definitions are made for purposes; when a civilian lawyer reads an article of
a code, he reads it against the background of his schooling, his legal system,
his culture.

> When we contemplate such a system from the outside it seems like a wall
> of stone, every part even with all the others, except so far as our own local
> education may lead us to see subordinations to which we are accustomed.
> But to one brought up within it, varying emphasis, tacit assumptions, un-
> written practices, a thousand influences gained only from life, may give to
> the different parts wholly new values that logic and grammar never could
> have got from the books. Díaz v. González, 261 U.S. 102, at 106 (1923)
> (Opinion of Mr. Justice Holmes).

Finally, there are civil law concepts which are not in any satisfactory way
translatable, because they have no common law counterparts which are close
enough to serve without creating more confusion than the translation is worth.
In the materials which follow, such concepts are either left untranslated or
given a literal translation. One example is the concept of *causa,* which serves
some purposes similar to those served by the doctrine of consideration in the
common law of contracts, but for which a translation as "consideration" would
be wholly unacceptable. The solution of Joannini in the translation which
follows has been to translate the term as "cause," a term which will not mislead because it has no common law (contracts) meaning. Others, such as Professor Lorenzen (see p. 87, *infra*), leave the term untranslated, to emphasize
the differences between it and analogous common law concepts.

Concerning the problems of this note generally, see Stern, *Comparative
Law: The History of the Language Problem and the Use of Generic Terms,*
55 L. LIB. J. 300 (1962).

CIVIL CODE OF ARGENTINA
(Enacted 1869) (Joannini translation 1917 *)

BOOK SECOND
OF PERSONAL RIGHTS IN CIVIL RELATIONS

SECTION I.   PART FIRST. OF OBLIGATIONS IN GENERAL

TITLE I.   OF THE NATURE AND ORIGIN OF OBLIGATIONS

495.   Obligations are: to give, to do, or to refrain from doing something.

496.   The right to demand the thing which is the object of the obligation, is a credit, and the obligation to do or refrain from doing something, or to give a thing, is a debt.

497.   To every personal right there corresponds a personal obligation. There is no obligation which corresponds to real rights.

498.   Rights which are not transmissible to the heirs of the creditor, as well as obligations not transmissible to the heirs of the debtor, are called in this Code: *rights inherent in the person, obligations inherent in the person.*

499.   There is no obligation without a cause, that is to say without being derived from one of the facts, or from one of the lawful or unlawful acts, of family relations, or of civil relations.

500.   Even though the cause be not stated in the obligation, the presumption is that it exists, unless the debtor proves the contrary.

501.   The obligation is valid even though the cause stated therein is false, if it is based on some other real cause.

502.   An obligation based on an unlawful cause is of no effect. A cause is unlawful when it is contrary to law or public order.

*   *   *

SECTION II.   OF ACTS AND JURIDICAL ACTS
WHICH GIVE RISE TO THE ACQUISITION,
TRANSFER OR EXTINGUISHMENT OF
RIGHTS AND OBLIGATIONS

TITLE I.   OF ACTS

896.   The acts of which this part of the Code treats are all those events susceptible of producing an acquisition, modification, transfer or extinguishment of rights or obligations.

897. Human acts are voluntary or involuntary. Acts are considered voluntary if executed understandingly, intentionally and freely.

898. Voluntary acts are lawful or unlawful. Lawful acts are voluntary actions not prohibited by law, from which some acquisition, modification or extinguishment of rights can result.

899. When the immediate object of the lawful acts is some acquisition, modification or extinguishment of rights, they shall produce such effect only in the cases in which they are expressly declared.

900. Acts performed not understandingly, intentionally and freely, do not produce any obligation whatsoever *per se*.

901. The consequences of an act which usually occurs, in the natural and ordinary course of events, are called in this Code *immediate consequences*. The consequences resulting solely from the connection of an act with a different event, are called *mediate consequences*. Mediate consequences which cannot be foreseen are called *incidental consequences*.

902. The greater the duty of acting with prudence and a full knowledge of matters, the greater is the obligation resulting from the possible consequences of acts.

903. The immediate consequences of free acts are imputable to the author thereof.

904. The mediate consequences are also imputable to the author of the act when he has foreseen them, and when, if he had employed the proper attention and knowledge of the thing, he could have foreseen them.

905. Purely incidental consequences are not imputable to the author of the act, unless they necessarily had to occur, according to his purpose in performing the act.

906. The incidental consequences of acts which are reproved by the laws are imputable, when the casualty of the consequences was prejudicial by reason of the act.

907. When damage is caused to the person or property of another by involuntary acts, the corresponding indemnity lies only if the author of the act has enriched himself by the damage, and to the amount whereby he has enriched himself.

908. Nevertheless, the rights of the aggrieved parties to enforce the liability of those who have under their charge persons who act without the proper understanding, are not affected.

909. In weighing voluntary acts, the laws do not take into consideration the special condition, or the intellectual faculty of a certain person, except in contracts which presuppose special confidence between the parties. In such cases the degree of responsibility shall be measured by the special condition of the agents.

910. No one can compel another to do a thing, or restrict his liberty, without a special right to do so having been constituted.

911.   No one can compel another to refrain from performing an act on the ground that such act might be prejudicial to the person performing it, except when a person is acting in violation of a duty prescribed by the laws, and the intervention of the public authorities cannot take place in time.

912.   A person who has the right under the law or a commission from the State to direct the actions of another, may employ force to prevent him from injuring himself.

913.   No act shall partake of a voluntary character, without an overt act whereby the will is manifested.

914.   Overt acts manifesting the will may consist of the execution of a material act which has been consummated or begun, or simply of a positive or implied expression of the will.

915.   The declaration of the will may be formal or informal, positive or implied, or induced by a presumption of law.

916.   Formal declarations are those the value of which depends on the observance of the formalities exclusively admitted as an expression of will.

917.   A positive expression of the will is so considered when manifested verbally, or in writing, or by other unequivocal signs, with reference to specific objects.

918.   An implied expression of the will arises from those acts whereby the existence of the will can be ascertained with certainty, in cases in which a positive expression is not required, or when there is no protest or express declaration to the contrary.

919.   Silence as to acts, or to an inquiry, is not considered as a manifestation of the will, as agreeing to the act or as replying to the inquiry in the affirmative, except in cases in which an obligation to explain oneself is imposed by the law or by the relations of family, or by reason of a relation between the present silence and previous statements.

920.   An expression of the will may likewise result from the presumption of the law in the cases in which it expressly so provides.

921.   Acts shall be considered acts done without understanding, if they are lawful acts performed by impuberal minors, or unlawful acts by minors under ten years of age; as also the acts of insane persons not performed during lucid intervals, and those of persons who are deprived of the use of their reason, by any accident whatsoever.

922.   Acts are considered to have been performed unintentionally, if performed through ignorance or error, under force or intimidation.

Chapter I
Of Acts Produced by Ignorance or Error

923.   Ignorance of the laws, or an error of law, shall in no case prevent the legal effects of lawful acts, nor excuse responsibility for unlawful acts.

924. An error as to the nature of a juridical act annuls everything contained therein.

925. An error as to the person with whom the relation of law is established is also a material [*esencial*] error, and annuls the juridical acts.

926. An error as to the principal cause of the act, or as to the quality of the thing had in view, vitiates the expression of the will, and avoids what has been provided in the act.

927. An error as to the object involved in the act, as when a thing has been contracted for, individually different from that regarding which it was desired to contract, or a thing of a different species, or a different amount, measure or sum, or a different act, also annuls the act.

928. An error as to some accidental quality of the thing, or as to some accessory thereof, does not invalidate the act, even though it had been the determining motive therefor, unless the quality erroneously attributed to the thing had been expressly guaranteed by the other party, or that the error had been caused by *dolus** on the part of such party or of a third person, provided it be established by the attendant circumstances that without the error the act would not have been executed, or when the quality of the thing, the thing accessory thereto, or any other circumstances have the express character of a condition.

929. An error of fact does not prejudice the act, when there was cause for the error, but it cannot be pleaded when the ignorance of the real state of things is due to culpable negligence.

930. In unlawful acts, ignorance or an error of fact excludes the liability of the parties only if it relates to the principal fact which constitutes the unlawful act.

CHAPTER II
Of Acts Produced by Fraud

931. Any false assertion, or dissimulation of the truth, any artifice, cunning, or machination employed to obtain the performance of an act, is a fraudulent action.

932. In order for fraud to be the means of invalidating an act, the attendance of all of the following circumstances is necessary:

1. It must have been grave.
2. It must have been the determining cause of the action.
3. It must have occasioned important damage.
4. Fraud must not have been employed by both parties.

933. A fraudulent omission produces the same effects as a fraudulent

---

* The translator has used the Latin form for the Spanish word *dolo*. The term often signifies what we call "fraud," but it also refers more generally to the intent to harm which is the basis for criminal responsibility. In Chapter II (articles 931-35) and in article 954, Joannini's translation has been modified, replacing "dolus" with "fraud." — Ed.

action, if the act would not have been performed without the fraudulent reticence or concealment.

934. Incidental fraud does not affect the validity of the act, but the person who employed it must give indemnity for any damage caused by him. Incidental fraud is that which was not the actual cause of the act.

935. Fraud affects the validity of acts *inter vivos* whether employed by one of the parties or a third person. If committed by a third person, the provisions of articles 941, 942 and 943 shall govern.

CHAPTER III
Of Acts Produced by Force and Fear

936. There is want of liberty in the parties when an irresistible force is employed against them.

937. There is intimidation when there is inspired by means of unjust threats in one of the parties, a well founded fear of suffering an imminent and grave injury to his person, liberty, honor or property, or to his spouse, descendants or ascendants, either legitimate or illegitimate.

938. Intimidation does not affect the validity of acts except when by reason of the condition of the person, his character, habits, or sex, it can be judged that it must have made a strong impression upon him.

939. There is no intimidation on account of unjust threats when the person who makes them confines himself to the enforcement of his own rights.

940. Reverential fear, or that in which descendants stand of their ascendants, that in which the wife stands of her husband, or subordinates of their superiors, is not a sufficient cause for the annulment of acts.

941. Force or intimidation make the act voidable, even though employed by a third person who does not take part therein.

942. If the force employed by a third person is known to one of the parties, the third person and the party aware of the force imposed are solidarily liable for all damages to the person the subject thereof.

943. If the force employed by a third person was not known to the party prejudiced by the annulment of the act, the third person shall be the only one liable for all damages.

TITLE II. OF JURIDICAL ACTS

944. Juridical acts are voluntary lawful acts, the immediate purpose of which is to establish between persons juridical relations, to create, modify, transfer, preserve or extinguish rights.

945. Juridical acts are positive or negative, according to whether the performance or omission of an act is necessary in order for a right to begin or end.

946. Juridical acts are unilateral or bilateral. They are unilateral, when

the will of a single person is sufficient to form them, as by a testament. They are bilateral, when they require the unanimous consent of two or more persons.

947.   Juridical acts, the force of which is not dependent upon the death of the persons from whose will they emanate, such as contracts, are called in this Code *acts inter vivos*. When they are not to produce any effect until after the death of the persons from whose will they emanate, such as testaments, they are called *dispositions of last will*.

948.   The validity or nullity of juridical acts *inter vivos* or of dispositions of last will, with respect to the capacity or incapacity of the parties, shall be governed by the laws of their respective domicile (Arts. 6 and 7).

949.   Legal capacity or incapacity, the object of the act and the material vices it may contain, shall be governed as to their validity or nullity by the laws of this Code.

950.   With regard to the forms and formalities of juridical acts, their validity or nullity shall be governed by the laws and usages of the place where the acts were executed. (Art. 12).

951.   The existence of acts *inter vivos* begins the day they were entered into, and if dependent for their validity on an instrumental form or any other form exclusively prescribed, from the date of the respective instruments.

952.   The existence of dispositions of last will begins the day of the death of the respective disposing parties, or on the date the law presumes that their death occurred (Art. 117).

953.   The objects of juridical acts must be things which are in commerce, or things which it has not been forbidden for some special reason to make the object of a juridical act, or acts which are not impossible, unlawful, contrary to good morals, or prohibited by the laws, or opposed to liberty of action or of conscience, or prejudicial to the rights of a third person. Juridical acts which do not conform to this provision are as void as if they had no object.

954.   Any act executed with the defects of error, fraud, simulation or [conduct in defraud of creditors] is void.

[Articles 955-60 deal with "simulation": the concealment of the "juridical character" of an act "under the appearance of another act," the use of "clauses which are not sincere," the use of false dates, etc. Articles 961-72 deal with acts in fraud of creditors].
        * * *

TITLE VI.   OF THE NULLITY OF JURIDICAL ACTS

1037.   Courts cannot declare other causes for the annulment of juridical acts than those established in this Code.

1038.   The nullity of an act is apparent when the law has expressly declared it void, or has made it subject to a penalty of nullity. Such acts are considered void even though their annulment has not been declared.

1039. The nullity of a juridical act may be absolute or merely partial. The partial nullity of a provision in the act does not prejudice other valid provisions, provided they are separable.

* * *

1044. Juridical acts are void when the parties have proceeded with simulation or fraud presumed by the law, or when the principal object of the act is prohibited, or when it does not have the form prescribed by the law to the exclusion of any other, or when the validity thereof depends on the form of the instrument, and the respective instruments are void.

1045. Juridical acts are voidable when the parties thereto have acted while under an accidental incapacity, as for example while they were deprived of their reason from any cause; or when their incapacity under the law was not known at the time of the signature of the act, or when the prohibition of the object of the act was not known owing to the necessity of an investigation of fact, or when the vice of error, violence, fraud, or simulation is present; and when the validity thereof depends on the form of the instrument, and the respective instruments are voidable.

1046. Voidable acts are considered valid as long as they are not annulled; and they shall be considered void only from the date of the judgment whereby they are annulled.

1047. Absolute nullity can and must be declared by the judge, even without the petition of a party, when it is apparent in the act. It may be pleaded by all persons having an interest in so doing, except by the person who drafted the act, knowing or being required to know the defect which invalidated it. His testimony may also be demanded by the government attorney, in the interest of good morals or the law. Absolute nullity is not susceptible of ratification.

1048. Relative nullity cannot be declared by the judge except on the petition of a party, nor can his testimony be demanded by the government attorney in the sole interest of the law, nor can it be set up by any persons other than those for whose benefit the laws have established it.

1049. A capable person cannot demand the annulment nor set up the nullity of the act on the ground of the incapacity of the other party. Nor can the person who made use of the violence, intimidation or fraud, demand the annulment on the ground thereof, nor can the person who caused the error on the part of the other party demand the annulment on the ground of such error.

1050. The annulment decreed by judges restores things to the same state or to a state similar to that existing prior to the annulled act.

1051. All real or personal rights in an immovable transferred to third persons by a person who became the owner thereof under the act annulled, are invalid and may be claimed directly of their actual possessor.

1052. The annulment of the act obliges the parties to return to each

other what they have received or collected by virtue or as a consequence of
the act annulled.

* * *

1056. The acts annulled, even though they do not produce the effects
of juridical acts, produce, nevertheless, the effects of unlawful acts, or of acts
in general, the consequences of which must be repaired.

1057. In cases in which it is not possible to enforce against third persons the effects of the nullity of acts, or to maintain an action against them,
a right of action to recover indemnity for all damages shall always lie.

1058. A relative nullity may be purged by the confirmation of the act.

[Articles 1059-65 deal with the manner of confirming voidable acts, and
the effect of confirmation.]

* * *

SECTION III.   OF OBLIGATIONS EX CONTRACTU

TITLE I.   OF CONTRACTS IN GENERAL

1137. There is a contract when a number of persons come to an agreement upon a declaration of common will, designed to regulate their rights.

1138. Contracts are called in this Code unilateral, or bilateral. The
former are those in which one of the parties only obligates himself to the
other without the latter becoming obligated to him. Bilateral contracts are
contracts in which the parties mutually obligate themselves to each other.

1139. It is also said in this Code that contracts are under an onerous
title, or under a gratuitous title: they are under an onerous title when the
benefits accruing therefrom to one or the other of the parties are granted to
such party only on account of a prestation * which he may have rendered, or
which he binds himself to render the other; they are under a gratuituous title,
when they assure to one or the other of the parties some advantage, independent of any prestation on his part.

1140. Contracts are consensual or real. Consensual contracts, without
prejudice to the provision relating to the forms of contracts, are perfected as
to the production of their particular effects, the moment that the parties have
mutually expressed their consent.

1141. Real contracts, in order to produce their particular effects, are
perfected when one of the parties has delivered to the other the thing which
is the subject of the contract.

---

* This is a little-used literal translation of the Spanish *prestación*, the payment of what is due,
or the performance of what is promised. — Ed.

1142. The class of real contracts includes *mutuum***, *commodatum****, the contract of deposit†, and the constitution of pledge and antichresis††.

1143. Contracts are nominate or innominate, according as to whether the law designates them by a special name or not.

CHAPTER I
Of Consent in Contracts

1144. Consent must be manifested by offers or propositions made by one of the parties, and accepted by the other.

1145. Consent may be express or implied. It is express when manifested verbally, in writing, or by unequivocal signs. It is implied when it results from facts or from acts which presuppose it, or which authorize a presumption thereof, except in cases in which the law requires an express manifestation of the will; or when the parties have stipulated that their agreements shall not be binding until after compliance with certain formalities.

1146. Implied consent is presumed if one of the parties delivers and the other receives the thing offered or asked; or if one of the parties does what he would not have done, or does not do what he would have done if it had been his intention not to accept the proposition or offer.

* * *

1157. The provisions of the Title Of Acts, of this Book respecting defects in consent, apply to contracts.

1158. The right to annul contracts on account of defects in consent, is vested in the party who has suffered them, and not in the other party, nor in the author of the *dolus,* violence, simulation or fraud.

1159. The right to claim that a contract is void ceases if after the causes of the nullities become known or have ceased to exist the contract is confirmed expressly or impliedly.

Dr. Luis De Gásperi, who authored the treatise extracted below, is a leading Latin American authority on civil law, and on the law of obligations in particular. Dr. De Gásperi is a Paraguayan, and his comments relate to the Civil Code of Paraguay. That Code, however, was adopted in its entirety from the Civil Code of Argentina, so that the comments apply equally to the Argentine law. Recently, Dr. De Gásperi has directed the preparation of a

---

** *Mutuo:* A loan of something which is to be consumed, the borrower repaying an equivalent. — Ed.
*** *Comodato:* A loan of something which is to be returned, analogous to a gratuitous bailment. — Ed.
† A bailment, gratuitous or for a fee, with return of the thing deposited upon demand. — Ed.
†† A "pledge" of immovables, in which the creditor receives the crops or other income as "interest" on the debt. — Ed.

projected new civil code for Paraguay. Some portions of that proposal are reprinted at p. 85, *infra.*

DE GASPERI, TRATADO DE LAS OBLIGACIONES (1st ed.* 1945)
Volume I, Chapter XXII.   Of Consent and Contract

§ 345.—WIDE AND RESTRICTED MEANING OF THE WORD CONSENT.

The word consent, in a broad sense, means a mutual concurrence of the wills of the parties concerning an act of which they approve, with full knowledge of it. In a restricted sense, it connotes the idea of adhesion of one party to the will of the other.

The first of these meanings is consonant with the etymology *(cum sentire)* of the word. It has been employed thus by Domat, Pothier, Duranton, Mourlon and other writers on French civil law.

For Domat, consent is a reciprocal psychological action of the parties through which agreements are made. He teaches that: "Agreements are contracted obligations formed by 'mutual consent' of two or more persons who reciprocally establish the legal obligations to perform what they have promised."

"An agreement or a pact," says Pothier, "is the consent of two or more persons to form an obligation among themselves, to terminate a prior obligation, or to modify it: *Duorum vel plurium in idem placitum consensus."* Nonetheless, the French Civil Code, in enumerating the essential conditions for the validity of agreements in art. 1108, does not require consent of the parties, but rather 'the consent of the party who is obliged.' This singularity is explained by interpreters of the French Code on the grounds that consent of the obligor presupposes that of the obligee.

Later writers, like Baudry Lacantinerie and Barde say: "I can will alone, but I cannot consent alone, because consent is a meeting of wills."

Influenced by this doctrine, Freitas composed the second part of art. 1833 of his projected Brazilian Civil Code: "There shall be no consent unless the promise of one of the parties has been accepted by the other."

Article 1104 of the Civil Code of Italy transcribed the text of the French Code's art. 1108, corrected it at the same time, and thereby required: "the valid consent of the contracting parties." The same doctrine is followed by the Spanish Civil Code, art. 1262, the Uruguayan, art. 1262, the Chilean, art. 1445, the Venezuelan, art. 1179, and so forth.

According to this conception, consent means that each of the parties transfers to the other a limited sphere of his will in regard to a particular thing or act, with the binding effect which in law is attributed to this accord of wills.

Consent is, thus, a juridical act that generates rights and obligations. It involves the reciprocal authorization to be bound to a given performance [*prestación*]. Josserand sees in it the contract itself, its fiber, its *substratum*.

Beudant, diverging from his predecessors, tends to attribute to consent the meaning of an adhesion of the parties manifested on one side by the offer and on the other, by the acceptance of this offer.

In this meaning, consent is an act of individual adhesion. Esmein understands that this adhesion does not necessarily involve the will to bind the other party. The adhesion or assent of the party who obligates himself would suffice, as art. 1108 of the French Civil Code says, because it is the most difficult adhesion to obtain. In unilateral contracts, it is made obvious that only the adhesion of the person who is obliged is necessary.

[Here the author describes a labor contract as a contract of adhesion in which the employer sets the terms and the employee simply binds himself to the employer's will. This description applies to contracts with big businesses, not those between a small artisan and his employers or workers; in the latter, there is a perfect accord, while in the former, only a pseudo accord. The contract of adhesion with which the students of this course are probably most familiar is the insurance policy.]

This restricted meaning gains all its importance when we speak of the defects of consent. In fact, when one alleges the defects of error, fraud, or duress, he does not refer to the defect in consent considered as a bilateral transaction, but rather refers to it in the individual adhesion to the act, whether in the offer or the acceptance.

The most common instance is for the defect to be suffered by the offeree who accepts.

Volume I, Chapter XXII.   Of Consent and Contract

§ 349.—DEFINITION OF CONSENT.

"Consent" is the name given to the concert of offer and acceptance. Thus, consent is essentially bilateral. Two volitions concerning two opposing interests unite with one another in a relation of justice or equality. Consent is "the reciprocal manifestation of complete accord between two or more persons, the object of each person being to oblige himself to a performance [*prestación*] in regard to the other party or parties; and consent is present even when it is the object of only one or some of the persons to oblige themselves to the other or others, without the latter assuming any correlative obligation."

§ 350.—CONSENT AND ITS EXTERIOR MANIFESTATION.

Consent thus conceived should not be confused with its manifestation. The latter need not be made in any prescribed form.

Some writers teach that consent is a matter of pure subjectivity. Others, on the contrary, say that as long as consent remains in the subjective sphere, as long as it takes no form and is not manifested to the outside world, it can acquire no binding force.

Thus, Beudant concludes that the important aspect of consent is intellectual and mental adhesion.

On the other hand, Dereux, with the second group, maintains that what is relevant to the law is not merely the act of willing, but the desire to be obligated. The latter cannot be known except through a manifestation of the will. In this respect, art. 913 of the Argentine Civil Code provides that: "No act shall partake of a voluntary character without an overt act whereby the will is manifested." It is inferred from this that a contract is not born at the moment when consent comes into being, but rather at the time when consent it manifested.

Manifestation of consent should not be confused with silence, which we have discussed elsewhere.

Volume I, Chapter XXXIII.   Of Error

§ 531.—Subjective Character of the Theory of Defects of the Will.

The second part of art. 897 of the Argentine Civil Code provides that: "Acts are considered voluntary if executed understandingly, intentionally, and freely." Art. 900 adds that "Acts performed not understandingly, intentionally and freely do not produce any obligation whatever *per se*." The presence of these three elements is thus required in order for the act to be considered voluntary.

In a legislative system founded on the principle of the autonomy of the will, one can understand the importance that the suppression or alteration of any of those elements may have on the binding force of the will, or rather, on the legal effects of lawful acts. This binding force can be destroyed or weakened by the so-called "defects of the will": intention, by error and fraud; freedom, by force and fear.

The theory of defects of the will thus acquires a subjective character. As we shall see later, in explaining error and fraud, traditional law conceives of them as subjective notions.

On the other hand, in German law, based on the theory of manifestation, error is seen only objectively, as "discordance between the true will, that is, internal will, and the declared will," according to the well known definition of Saleilles. It should be added that this discordance is "involuntary" in the case of error, as opposed to "intentional" discordance in the case of fraud [simulation].

§ 532.—Definition of Error.

Error is defined as the false idea that we have of a thing; and ignorance is defined as the absence of any idea. Although error and ignorance are not the same thing, there are occasions when they are confused, in that ignorance of a thing or act can lead to the supposition of the existence of another thing or another act. Error of law [*derecho*] is not merely ignorance of a statute [*ley*]. This explains why the Roman law treated them under the same heading: *De juris et facti ignorantia.* "From the moment when ignorance becomes the motive for an act," says Maynz, "it constitutes an error and, henceforward, naturally must lead to the same results in respect to juridical acts as an error would."

§ 533.—Error of Fact.

Thus conceived, error and ignorance . . . make the actor assume something that does not exist, or misinterpret a thing, and thus his "intention" is falsified or obstructed. The result is that his declared will may not be his true will.

Freitas was correct to link "lack of cause [*causa*]" of "false cause" with "error." In articles 1109, 1110 and 1131 of the Code Napoléon, the "cause" of contracts, says Freitas, appears as a separate element without reference to the subject of error, while for Freitas' own Brazilian Project the "lack of cause" or "false cause" is a defect derived from "error" and thus from "lack of intention." Such is the doctrine in which our Code is inspired, as we explained in [earlier sections of this treatise].

This ignorance and this error are not error and ignorance in general, but only about the particular act that must be judged, for which reason they are called "ignorance or error of fact." The formation of a legal relation demands an exact knowledge of the state of things. Persons gifted with discernment are in a position to know this state, but as Savigny observes, this is not always possible. Given its imperfection, the subject of law is exposed to error and there are occasions when it is impossible to avoid error. From this follows the importance given to error as a cause for annulment of an act that was executed "without the true intention" that determined its execution. The error must be of such a nature that blame for it cannot be placed on the one who is misled, although sometimes that occurs. If all error were excusable, there would be no juridical act free of this allegation. All debtors would be inclined to invoke it in order to remove the effect from their promises. Such a situation would be contrary to juridical order; so, since ancient times, care has been taken to distinguish excusable error from inexcusable error, or rather, error that does not injure from that which does, a distinction that is maintained in art. 929 of the Argentine Civil Code. Error of fact is considered inexcusable when it results from a substantial omission or great negligence. The difficulty lies in finding the criterion for weighing the degree of negligence to which the error is imputable, as error is a subjective phenomenon, variable from one person to another. . . .

Error of fact assumes, then, a concrete problem in which one must consider not only a particular act, but also the person who invokes it in his defense. That is to say, one must consider the actor and his diligence in arriving at a precise knowledge of the true state of things, for that knowledge is the principal motive in the determination of his will.

* * *

§ 540.—ESSENTIAL OR SUBSTANTIAL ERROR AND ACCIDENTAL ERROR.

"Error proper" is that which goes to the consent. If it invalidates the contract, it is "essential" or "substantial"; and if it does not invalidate it, it is "accidental" error or inherent *error concomitans.* The French jurists also call substantial error "voidness error" [*error nulidad*], because, as its name indicates, and as a defect of consent, it makes possible the voidability of the contract — it makes it voidable.

The expounders of the Code Napoléon, such as Baudry Lacantinerie and Barde, teach that error is substantial in two cases: 1) when it goes to the very substance of the thing, and 2) when it goes to the person with whom the contract was made, in contracts made in consideration of the person, *intuitu personae,* through application of art. 1110 of the French Civil Code.

Josserand, following Aubry and Rau, and Demolombe, adds a third case: error about the effectiveness of the cause, as when someone signs a document of obligation in favor of another, believing himself to be "civilly" obligated to the other when in fact he is obligated only morally [*naturaliter*].

This third case of error should not be confused with the hindering error that goes to the very existence of the cause, and which has its place in cases of false or erroneous cause.

In these three cases there is no failure of wills to meet, nor is there misunderstanding. On the contrary, there is consent, there is intention, but the "end" of this intention is falsified by error; for this reason the sanction for error consists only in a relative voidability [of the obligation].

* * *

§ 545.—CASES OF ESSENTIAL ERROR, ACCORDING TO THE CODE.

According to the Argentine Code, there are five cases of essential error: 1) error as to the nature of the juridical act; 2) error as to the person; 3) error about the object of the juridical act; 4) error about the substantial qualities of the thing, and 5) error as to the principal cause of the act.

* * *

§ 553.—ERROR ABOUT THE PRINCIPAL CAUSE OF THE ACT OR ABOUT THE QUALITY OF THE THING.

Art. 926 provides that: "Error as to the principal cause of the act, or as to the quality of the thing had in view, vitiates the manifestation of will, and avoids what has been provided in the act." Stated differently, this rule is also found in the first part of art. 1110 of the French Civil Code and in art. 461 of Freitas' Project.

Two criteria exist as to the interpretation of this precept: 1) that which distinguishes the idea of "principal cause" of the act from the idea of the "quality of the thing" held in view when the contract was made; and 2) that which reduces the idea of "quality" to that of "cause."

In Argentine law, the first system is followed by Machado, Llerena, Lafaille and Salvat, and the second is followed by Segovia.

* * *

§ 554.—OBJECTIVE THEORY OF THE CONCEPT OF SUBSTANCE.

It is well known that art. 1110 of the Code Napoléon provides that: "Error is not a cause for avoiding an agreement, except when it goes to the very substance of the thing which is its object," but without specifying the legal meaning of the word "substance." Because of this lack of precision, the doctrine has fluctuated between two different interpretations. The first, influenced by philosophical and scientific considerations and dominant until the first half of the nineteenth century, saw substance as resembling matter and understood this word [matter] not as the identity of the object, but rather as its elements, its attributes. The second interpretation, which began at the end of the first half of the nineteenth century and continues to the present, sees in the substance, not the object in itself, but the quality that was foremost in the minds of the parties when the contract was made, as something dependent on their will. The first of these concepts is known as the "objective theory" and the second as the "subjective theory."

Savigny [a 19th Century German scholar], in light of the rules of Roman law, finds that the expression *error in substantia* is an improper designation for the idea of error about an essential quality of the thing, that is, error capable of causing nullification of the consent. In fact, in the four cases that he cites, which are excerpted from the Roman texts, matter is not always the essential thing or the thing that determines the will of the parties. Thus, error in matter or in "substance" cannot be understood without some explanations.

Here are the cases, cited by the Roman jurisconsults, of error *in substantia:*
1. If someone buys an object of bronze, taking it for gold.
2. An object of lead, copper, and so on, or even of wood, that is taken for silver.
3. Vinegar thought to be wine.

4. A female slave who is believed to be a male slave.

In these cases, there is no consent on the part of the buyer.

The rule according to which *error in substantia* nullifies consent is applied exclusively to objects made by artisans, because in those objects the material is the principal thing; the rule does not apply to objects that are properly called art, in which the material is secondary. Thus, whether a statue by Benvenuto Cellini is of silver or gold is a secondary consideration. On the other hand, a table service of gold or silver is ordinarily purchased by weight, even though the metals are not without form. With respect to timepieces the question could be doubtful, because what is called a gold clock is nothing but a clock in a gold case. In an ordinary clock, an error about the material of the case would be an essential error, but not in a clock with a movement of extraordinary workmanship. In the case of a chronometer, for example, the value of the case is an addition of small importance.

In the example of the wine and vinegar, the essential error does not arise from the difference in price, since vinegar that is well prepared can be more expensive than a mediocre wine. In this case the essential error arises from the complete dissimilarity of the two goods.

In the example of the slaves, it would be foolish to seek the error in the *substantia* or "material," since the latter is the same in a male as in a female. Neither is the error in the money value, since a woman slave is ordinarily sold for a higher price than a man. The error is in the purpose for which each is purchased: the man will work at agricultural work and the woman at domestic tasks.

From such reasoning Savigny deduces the following general principle: "error about the quality of a thing is essential, since according to accepted ideas in the relationships of real life, a quality falsely assumed places the thing in a different class of object from its true one. A difference in material is not always a necessary or sufficient condition."

The doctrine of Savigny exercised considerable influence on later jurists [whose views are discussed at length].

   * * *

§ 555.—SUBJECTIVE THEORY OF THE CONCEPT OF SUBSTANCE.

The subjective theory of the concept of substance rests on a phrase of Pothier, who understood by that notion "the quality that was principally in the minds of the contracting parties."

And curiously enough, the example with which Pothier illustrates this case is the same used by Duranton to explain his objective notion of substance. That example is the one using a pair of candelabras of plated copper which I buy thinking them to be the pair of silver candelabras that I wanted to bu

Nevertheless, the doctrine of Pothier can be contrasted with the con of the so-called accidental qualities of the thing, as when a person h particular book in a bookshop, with the false persuasion that it is an excellent book, though it may be less than average."

In French subjectivism, not all error about the material substance of a thing is considered to be true error about the substance. The sale of copper candelabras that are believed by the buyer to be silver is not voidable if the consideration of material was secondary: the buyer could have bought the candelabras on the basis of their being antique or because they had belonged to a famous person: if their age or previous owner are proved, the sale will be valid. On the contrary, there can be an error about substance in the meaning of art. 1110, without any misunderstanding by the parties about the material of which the object is made. If the candelabras sold are of silver but of recent manufacture, the sale could be nullified if the purchaser had decided to buy them because of their antique value. Here there would be error about a substantial quality.

* * *

§ 556.—THEORY OF OUR CODE ON THIS MATTER.

Knowing these antecedents, we should note that art. 926 of the Argentine Civil Code does not use the expression "substance," as does art. 1110 of the French Civil Code. Rather, the Argentine Code uses the word "quality," which according to the foregoing explanations, implies the subjective considerations that were instrumental in the party's decision to make a contract. This word connotes the intentional, causal and final element of the will, which always outweighs the material, objective, and substantial element of the thing about which consent is given.

The Argentine jurists, with the exception of Segovia and Lafaille, are objectivists.

It may be stated further that, consistent with the subjective doctrine underlying the general theory of acts and juridical acts within our Code, we cannot subscribe to this interpretation, which has been superseded at present by the explanations of Josserand and Célice.

* * *

§ 564.—UNILATERAL NATURE OF ERROR OF FACT.

Another important question related to this matter is whether the error on which the nullification action of a juridical act is based must be unilateral or bilateral, that is, if it must be shared by all the parties who entered into the contract.

Our Code, inspired by art. 1865 of the Project of Freitas, provides in art. 1158: "The right to annul contracts on account of defects in consent is given to the party who has suffered them and not to the other party, nor to the author of the fraud, duress, or simulation."

Although this precept speaks only of contracts, it is applicable to all juridical acts, in conformance with the provisions of art. 1049, concordant with art. 1157.

The clarity of these provisions relieves us of all explanation.

Volume I, Chapter XXXIV. Fraud

§ 566.—METHODOLOGY.

Closely tied to the theory of error, fraud is an error provoked by the bad faith of the other party or by that of a third person, an error which, as such, overrides the intention of the actor in voluntary acts, invalidating his consent. With fraud thus conceived, its study forms part of the doctrine of intention, as a binding force of the will.

* * *

§ 571.—CIRCUMSTANCES THAT MUST COINCIDE IN ORDER FOR FRAUD TO BE THE CAUSE OF NULLITY OF AN ACT.

Law has an essentially moral content. The existence of a contractual situation creates in the parties duties that are closely related to that content. The parties, though they have opposing interests and pursue contradictory goals, have the duty to observe in respect to each other a moral conduct translated into respect for the juridical relation that binds them. They should act in good faith, that is to say, with strict loyalty and sincerity, proscribing lies, tricks, and artifice in the fulfillment of their obligations.

Doubtless this description is ideal. But between the ideal and reality there is a great distance. Regardless of the imperative of moral duty, we see daily that the parties, in their desire to carry out their juridical affairs, do not disdain unsuspected methods to persuade others to contract, for example, attributing virtues and effectiveness to the products of their industry that do not correspond to reality. The immoderate zeal of speculation, the extraordinary increase of business, the harmful effects of competition have ended by incorporating dazzling means for attracting clients into the practices and uses of business.

Doubtless, if the fate of contracts were to depend on these deceptions, there would be no juridical dealings left standing. We would risk nullifying all of them. And since this situation is also contrary to the general interest in the security of transactions, it has been necessary to seek a criterion by which to fix the limit between narrow [individual] morality and the morality of the Code, the latter being the only way of conserving a permanent and sure state of things in the world of contracts. From this reasoning it follows that the Code, inspired by the traditional doctrine, provided in art. 932 that: "In order

for fraud to be the means of invalidating an act, the attendance of all of the
following circumstances is necessary:

"1.   It must have been grave;

"2.   It must have been the determining cause of the action;

"3.   It must have occasioned important damage;

"4.   Fraud must not have been employed by both parties."

These are not all the requisites set forth by the consensus of writers on
the subject, but they are those set forth by the law, which is sufficient for the
time being. We shall presently study the other requirements.

§ 572.—GRAVE FRAUD AND TOLERATED FRAUD IN FRAUDULENT ACTIONS AND OMISSIONS.

It is surely difficult to characterize grave fraud by contrast with what it
is not. This is a point which has given rise to serious confusion. Larombière
gives the term "tolerated fraud" to a person's dissimulation of the weaknesses
of a thing, simulation of qualities that are missing from it, or diminution of
the defects that it may have, provided that his bad faith does not go so far as
to change the exterior of the thing through deceitful artifices and to impede
all inquiry, all discovery of the truth by the other party. These are, he adds,
the rather indelicate proceedings that we encounter in our fairs, in our markets,
in almost all commercial transactions. The scruples of fastidious honesty may
find them reprehensible, but the more tolerant scruples of the civil law leave
them unpunished because the damage that may result from them owes more
to the lack of prudence of the person who suffers them than from the maneuvers of those who gain advantage from them. Tolerated fraud is, therefore,
that which, because of the dullness of the deceived party or because of its
slight consequences, does not give rise to damages.

* * *

For Giorgi, the gravity of fraud must be considered from two points of
view: 1) whether the artifices and deceits are of such a nature as to affect a
prudent person, and 2) the fraudulent machinations must not be the sort of
dissimulation or reticence tolerated by civil law and generally practiced in
business.

These discrepancies show the size of the difficulties of the problem.

. . . There is no doubt that in our law, as in the French, fraud assumes
an illegal action characterized not so much by the method used to deceive as
by the elements of the illegal act itself: 1) the subjective element, the fraudulent intent; 2) the positive act contrary to the prohibition of the law, the
incitement to error, and 3) the damage.

French jurisprudence has always required a precise deceitful act, a material act, citing as examples the publication of a prospectus, circular, or poster
(*afffiche*), the display of written material distorting the performance of a
business, a false balance sheet, the announcement of distribution of a false

dividend, the presentation of a projected contract drawn up beforehand in obscure terms in order to deceive the contracting party about the extent of his obligations, the use of a false name or a false characteristic, the act of isolating the person to be deceived, keeping him away from his usual advisers, relatives, friends, and finally, from all those who might enlighten him.

On the other hand, fraud does not consist in exaggeration, by the promoter of a product, about the probable returns of a business enterprise. Nor is it necessarily found in the exaggerated manifestations of interested affection, and so forth.

Silence, the reticence dealt with in art. 933, does not constitute a fraudulent maneuver except when the person who is silent has a duty or obligation of conscience to speak. . . .

Ripert teaches to this effect: "In general it is said that simple reticence does not constitute fraud. Such an immoral principle cannot be established. What is true is that in the majority of contracts an opposition of interests exists between the contracting parties. Each is the guardian of his own interests and must, consequently, inform himself through his own efforts. There is nothing blameworthy in not giving to the other party hints that he would have been able to obtain for himself. But the outcome changes and reticence is culpable if one of the parties has the obligation of conscience to speak under pain of abusing the ignorance of the other."

As we see, neither doctrine [scholarly treatises, articles] nor jurisprudence [case law] furnishes a principle capable of eliminating the difficulties inherent in this material. The control of fraud is thus reduced to a question of fact that falls to the prudent appraisement of the judge.

The judge, in order to estimate the gravity of the facts that are alleged to constitute fraud, must especially study the probabilities of success of the maneuvers used. . . .

If it be a question of tolerated fraud, even though it be the determining cause of the decision of the other contracting party, the act will not be nullified, nor will there be indemnification of damages. This shows that the requisite of "gravity" should not be confused with that of being the determining cause of the act, which we shall now study.

§ 573.—CAUSAL RELATION BETWEEN THE DAMAGE SUFFERED AND ERROR RESULTING FROM FRAUD.

Art. 932, par. 2, requires as the second condition for the nullification of an act because of fraud that "It must have been the determining cause of the action."

Machado understands the determining cause of the action as the "cause of the contract," without explaining the significance of this expression. It can be believed, nonetheless, that this writer meant to refer to the cause of the contractual obligation, since the "cause of the contract," for our law, lacks meaning in this case. Obviously Machado is in error. The determining cause of the action as par. 2 of art. 932 states, means the "why" of the determination of will in the moment of the celebration of the act. Art. 1116 of the French Civil Code, referring to "fraud" as a cause of nullity, requires that the means used to persuade be such "that it is clear that without them the other party would not have entered into the contract." This phrase expresses the same idea found in the paragraph we are studying [of art. 932], dealing with fraud as the determining factor in the decision of the other party. . . .

This interpretation alone is in conformity with the illicit function of fraud, insofar as it is a means of invalidating consent. It would not vitiate consent if it were not, as Josserand says, "a factor of the determining motive, to which the victim agreed when he gave his consent."

      * * *

This causal relation between fraud and the act is the same as that which exists between the fault and damage caused, as a basis of the contractual and delictual responsibility. The fraud is not the direct and immediate cause of the injury, but the error caused by it is — error which decides the contracting party to perform a juridical act in conditions such that, had they not been present, he would have decided differently.

From the above it follows that the victim must show not only the gravity of the fraud, a requirement we have already studied, but also that his error is the consequence of the fraud. He must show also that this error is the one that made him decide to perform the juridical act in question.

      * * *

§ 574.—IMPORTANT DAMAGE.

      * * *

The importance of the damage is also a question of demonstration, the decision of which is reserved to the prudent discretion of the judge. There is no provision that fixes a criterion about this particular.

§ 575.—UNILATERAL AND MUTUAL FRAUD AND FRAUD COMMITTED BY A THIRD PARTY; FRENCH AND ARGENTINE DOCTRINE.

Finally, the article that we are studying demands as its last requirement that "fraud must not have been employed by both parties." The Code does not recognize mutual fraud as a cause of nullity and in this refusal it follows a universally accepted doctrine.

Consequently, the fraudulent maneuvers must be the work of the other party and this principle does not exclude those maneuvers originating with a third party. In this point, our Code departs from Roman law and from the French Civil Code.

In Roman law, fraud committed by a third party was not cause for nullity of the act unless one of the parties was an accomplice in the fraud. [The same doctrine appears in the Code Napoléon. Duress committed by a third person, however, is cause for nullity of the act in both Roman law and the Code Napoléon.]

The third person cannot be a party in the act. If the fraud was known previously by one of the parties, he and the author of the fraud will be jointly responsible for the indemnification of all damages of the party who suffered the fraud. If both parties to the contract were ignorant of the fraud committed by the third person, the entire responsibility will devolve upon the author of the unlawful act.

§ 576.—EFFECTS OF PRINCIPAL FRAUD.

Principal fraud produces: 1) the nullification of the act, and 2) the indemnification of damages.

§ 577.—INCIDENTAL FRAUD AND THE CRITICISM OF LAURENT.

Incidental fraud is that which leads to error on the part of the person who suffers it and causes him harm; but the error caused by that fraud was not the efficient cause of the act. Further, the damage, in order to lead in this case to indemnification, need not be "important" as when it is a question of principal fraud. We have already seen what Molitor says about this; for him, incidental fraud is the accessory fraud which decides a person to make a contract only on conditions that are so onerous as to be unacceptable, in the absence of the [fraudulent] maneuver.

* * *

Laurent understands that the distinction between principal and incidental fraud (if it must be defined traditionally), only serves to induce doctrinal error, because the distinction is false. Incidental fraud, according to traditional law, is that which may not have decided me to contract, but nonetheless induced me to do so on more unfavorable conditions or on such conditions that, having known them, I would not have accepted the contract. If this is so, incidental fraud, according to Laurent, becomes principal fraud.

* * *

§ 578.—PROOF OF FRAUD.

The last part of art. 1116 of the French Civil Code provides that: "Fraud is not presumed: it must be proved;" and although our Code contains no such provision, one should not therefore understand that this rule is excluded from our civil law. This is a question of an act classified as a civil wrong, which as such assumes "the intention" to harm or a wrongful state of mind. This subjective element of the unlawful act will usually be shown from the maneuvers used. The person who alleges it must prove it, which he can do with all the means of proof admitted in law, including those legal or judicial presumptions that are also used to prove contracts.

* * *

THE COVERAGE AND STRUCTURE OF THE CIVIL CODES

The Civil Code of Argentina is divided into four books:

> Of Persons
> Of Personal Rights in Civil Actions
> Of Real Rights
> Of Real and Personal Rights

All of the articles printed above are taken from the second book, which is the longest of the four. This book deals principally with the law of "obligations," most of which a common lawyer would describe as aspects of the law of contracts and torts. The substance of the Code is markedly similar to that of France's *Code Civil* of 1804, the code named for Napoléon. All the Latin American civil codes are principally derived from the Code Napoléon, although some, like the Argentine Code, differ somewhat in their organization. The following comments by Professor Tunc are thus instructive for the comparative study of Latin American civil law. They should be read with the foregoing articles of the Civil Code of Argentina in mind. Does this Code's structure support Professor Tunc's views of the differences between civilian and common law reasoning? Is he supported by the excerpts from Dr. De Gásperi's treatise?

TUNC, THE GRAND OUTLINES OF THE CODE
in THE CODE NAPOLEON AND THE COMMON-LAW WORLD*
at 19, 22-32 (Schwartz ed. 1956)

* * *

6.   The need for a Code as an instrument of unification of the law was a temporary one. What a French lawyer sees as the permanent basis of a Code, and what David Dudley Field sees in the same light, is the principle that was also historically its first justification: that the law should be clear and should be stated in written form, so that, as far as possible, every citizen may know

---

what his rights and his duties are. Only by such clarity can litigation be decreased, injustices avoided, and freedoms preserved. . . .

* * *

8. This justification of a code may explain the traditional French approach to codification. A code, a Frenchman thinks, should be complete in its field; it should lay down general rules; and it should arrange them logically. These are, in fact, three of the most important features of the Civil Code. We shall consider them separately. A fourth important feature should also be mentioned: viz., the fact that the Code is grounded on experience.

9. (A) A code should be complete in its field. There is no need to elaborate on this point. If the law should be clearly stated in a written document, this document should be complete, lest it be misleading.

10. From this point of view the Civil Code as enacted in 1804 was certainly satisfactory. The law of persons, including the law of the family; the law of property, including the law of mortgages; the law of torts and of contracts and the specific rules governing all the common contracts; the law of donations and the law of successions, were all encompassed within its 2,281 articles. Nor did any serious gap appear when the Code actually came to be applied. Probably one matter only had not been dealt with in the Code that should have been; the law of mines, which, only referred to in article 552, required a special statute as early as 1810. The Code was so complete that the legislature, when it sought to draft a rural code during the nineteenth century, could hardly find any matter not already contained in the Civil Code.

11. It should, however, be pointed out that revision of the Code — which has, in fact, been entrusted to a Commission since 1945 — now appears highly desirable because of the number of important statutes passed during the nineteenth and twentieth centuries and left outside the Code. . . .

12. (B) A code, in the traditional French approach, should also in the main state general rules. A well-drafted code should not contain too many detailed provisions or too many exceptions to the principal rules. . . . Such general rules are considered in France to be the best technical means of preventing litigation by stating to the ordinary citizen what he may and what he may not do, as well as the best means of resolving litigation when it does arise. Portalis [the "father of the *Code Civil*"] was even obliged to defend the draft of the Commission against the popular feeling that a code should not have more than a few hundred articles.

The justifications for this approach are aptly expressed by Portalis. First, a too bulky code would not be clear enough. Conciseness is a factor of clarity. More important, however, is the consideration that the legislature cannot reasonably hope to foresee all the applications of the basic principles it wishes to embody. If it tried to foresee everything it would probably foresee circumstances that do not arise, and thus leave the parties and the judge, for the decision of actual difficulties, with a bulk of details and exceptions very difficult to use. Of equal importance is a last consideration: the legislature should

not "bind the action of the future and oppose the course of human events."
Only in general rules can sufficient flexibility be found. That an American
scholar could write in 1940 that the Code "left open many avenues for growth
and change, as new pressures and new ethical standards emerged in French
society," should be gratifying to the memory of Portalis, for that was his express desire.

13.   These views may appear strange in the United States, where the
famous words of Justice Holmes, "General propositions do not decide concrete cases," are so often quoted to mean that a code is unworkable. Yet these
ideas represent daily experience for all civilians. The article requiring a man
to be at least eighteen years old and a woman at least fifteen before contracting marriage (Article 144) is a general rule that has governed all marriages
for one hundred and fifty years without the slightest difficulty. The article
preventing anybody from entering into a second marriage before the dissolution of the first (Article 146) is also as certain as possible if the time of the
dissolution of marriage is clearly defined in the law.

It is true that one can also find in the Code extraordinarily broad statements, such as the one in article 146: "There is no marriage when there is
no consent." Such statements can be found either as general explanations of
more precise rules — the law of duress, for instance, is made precise in articles 1111-1115 — or where the draftsmen felt that precision was impossible
and that decision should necessarily be left, in any concrete set of circumstances, to the courts. The rule of article 146, for instance, governs the marriage
of insane persons. But there are various mental diseases that alter the ability
to consent. These sicknesses are of various degrees. A person may have periods
of insanity alternating with periods of sanity of various length. All these particular circumstances cannot, it is true, be decided upon by general rules. But
neither can they be decided by detailed statutory rules or by precedents. Any
case of this kind raises a question of fact — whether there was consent — and
must be decided on the basis of its particular merits and only by remote application of a rule of law, whatever its form.

14.   Even if we disregard these exceptionally broad rules designed for
exceptional circumstances in which no authority can give the judge a reasonable ruling, the codification of law in general rules leaves the courts with a
specific responsibility, which Portalis feels obliged to stress at some length. The
Revolutionary trend was to strip the courts of any power except mere application of the statute. Portalis understood that this view was unrealistic, and he
tried to balance the task of the legislature and that of the courts.

In many cases, however, the application of the general rules to concrete
circumstances reveals a difficulty. The task of the courts is then to penetrate
the spirit of the rules in order to apply or to extend the proper one to the case,
so as to bring about the solution that would have been desired, or, if necessary,
the one that would be desired today, by the legislator. Such is Portalis'
view: . . . .
        *   *   *

17. (C) It would be unjust to the drafters of the Code not to stress their reliance on logic as an essential factor of the judicial process.

Again, this view may cause some surprise in a country in which the famous words of Holmes are nearly always quoted with approval: "The life of the law has not been logic: it has been experience."

The drafters of the Code would certainly not have challenged the dictum that the life of the law has been experience. In fact, some of them said it in so many words. But they would have been surprised by the contrast drawn between logic and experience. For they certainly considered life as having logic. This is, I think, the French approach to law and to life. You may remember the proof of the existence of God offered by Voltaire: "I cannot believe that such a watch exists and that there is no watchmaker." For him, the world clearly ran as logically as a watch. It may not be inappropriate either to recall the cult of Queen Reason that was celebrated during the French Revolution. For the Reason thus deified was not the reason of the reasonable man, but the cold Reason of clarity and logic. Most French people would still consider that there is no possible contrast between life and logic. The religious minds will agree on this point with Voltaire, Bergson with Broussais, the psychoanalysts with Condillac. The dissent that may be voiced by Jean Paul Sartre seems not to be a clear one; and the physicists, however fascinated by the apparently fortuitous internal life of the atom, will agree that at the human level life seems governed by logical rules. In the field of law the draftsmen of the Code certainly considered that the natural development of any legal system leads it to a point of logical consistency at which it can be codified. A code, to them, was not a mere collection of rules but a collection of rules with such inner consistency that logical reasoning could be a part of legal reasoning.

* * *

19. The French lawyer, it may be true, will give more importance to logic than the common lawyer. In very happy terms Dean Roscoe Pound has characterized the common lawyer's frame of mind as "a frame of mind which habitually looks at things in the concrete, not in the abstract; which puts its faith in experience rather than in abstractions; ... which prefers to go forward cautiously on the basis of experience from this case or that case to the next case, as justice in each case seems to require, instead of seeking to refer everything back to supposed universals; ... the frame of mind behind the sure-footed Anglo-Saxon habit of dealing with things as they arise instead of anticipating them by abstract universal formulas." The French lawyer, on the contrary, as Dean Pound has cogently stated in other writings, looks at the articles of the Code not as mere rulings, but a particular expressions of more general rules. Therefore, if no express answer to a certain problem is found in the Code, it is not improper to consider various articles in order to induce from them a more general rule and to apply this rule if it can give a solution, or, if not, to combine it with other rules to arrive at a solution. It has sometimes been said that articles of a code are not only law, but sources of law. This

is true, not only in the sense that the courts may, by deduction, decide on the implications of a certain article, but also in the sense that the courts may, if necessary, use induction to discover the general rules implied in the provisions of a code and then reverting to deduction, develop the full potential of these rules in the solution of the problem at hand. If all the rules were sound and no mistake was made in the reasoning, the result would be fortunate. If it fails to be so, the reason may be only that one of the rules is not in accord with social needs. But in that event it should be amended, not only in the particular circumstances of the case, but more generally. To respond to modern conditions of life the French courts may sometimes slightly distort the will of the drafters of the Code — although they will consider that the primary responsibility for amendment rests with the legislator — but they will always try to maintain the consistency of the solutions and the logical value of the body of law with which they are entrusted.

19. [sic] (D) No contrast, therefore, should be drawn, in the French approach, between logic and experience. And if the Code is a work of logic, it is also, and in the main, a work of experience. The draftsmen never meant to create a new law. They wanted only to restate the law, having to make a choice on the basis of experience when the Revolutionary law was at variance with the previous law. "Les codes des peuples *se font avec le temps,*" Portalis wrote in a passage already cited, "mais, a proprement parler, *on ne les fait pas,*" codes require time to be made, but, actually, one does not make them. . . .

SUPPLEMENTARY STATUTES AND CODE REVISIONS

In solving most legal problems — even problems of civil (non-commercial) law — the civilian lawyer in Latin America cannot be content with an examination and interpretation of the relevant portions of the civil code. He must also consult the provisions of a wide range of statutes which resemble, in their varied scope and subject matter, the products of legislatures in the Anglo-American world. In Uruguay, for example, a leading edition of the Civil Code contains a lengthy appendix in which may be found the complete texts of various statutes which modify or supplement the Civil Code, along with a ten-page index of similar statutory material which is contained in footnotes to the text of the Code itself. Some of the statutes which we might consider to be "supplementary" are sufficiently complete in their coverage as to be called codes: the Rural Code, the Mining Code, the Children's Code are examples.

The increasing complexity of legislation has brought about a more or less continual call for consolidation in new revised civil codes. In some Latin American countries (notably Venezuela, Peru and Mexico), civil code revision has taken place within the present century, but even the most recent revision

— that of Venezuela — is now more than twenty years old. (See p. 340, *infra*, for a discussion of Venezuela's recent efforts to revise the Commercial Code, with some corresponding effect on the Civil Code.) Typically, such a revision does not attempt to consolidate most of the vast amount of social legislation effective at the time it is made. Instead, such legislation remains set aside in separate laws or even separate "codes," such as Mexico's Agrarian Code.

Meanwhile, the demand for revision of the codified civil law continues. See, *e.g.*, De Gásperi, *El Futuro de la Codificación*, 29 TUL. L. REV. 223 (1955). In France, where the Code Napoléon's 2281 articles remain as they were first written, a commission has been appointed for the Code's complete revision in the light of the modifying legislation and jurisprudence (case law) of the past century and a half. See Julliot de la Morandiere, *The Reform of the French Civil Code*, 97 U. PA. L. REV. 1 (1948); Julliot de la Morandiere, *Preliminary Report of the Civil Code Reform Commission of France*, 16 LA. L. REV. 1 (1955); Houin, *Reform of the French Civil Code and the Code of Commerce*, 4 AM. J. COMP. L. 485 (1955). When and if the French revision — including its combination of civil and commercial law in a single code of private law — becomes effective, one may predict an increase in code revision activity in Latin America.

LATIN AMERICAN LEGAL EDUCATION

When a delegation of Latin American law students visits a law school in the United States, their North American counterparts tend to emerge from the encounter a bit bewildered. Here are these youngsters, some of them only 18, a great many of them girls, and the legal subject they want most to talk about is Kelsen's Pure Theory of Law. These are law students? Yes and no; they are undeniably students in faculties of law or juridical science, but many of them are there primarily for a liberal education. For such students, law school training is not aimed at entry into the legal profession, but rather provides the background for a career in government or business. Of course there are such students in our own law schools, but their proportion is far greater in civilian law schools, in Europe as in Latin America.

That may explain the girls (although lady lawyers are to be found in Latin countries, too), but does it also account for the youth of these students? The answer requires an acquaintance with the requirements of preparatory education and the curricula of the law schools. Starting at the end of the law student's educational career, we find five years of university study, the last three of which emphasize professional, or vocational training. In preparation for his work in the university, a student may have attended a specialized preparatory school upon completion of high school; there are separate *colegios* — preparatory schools — for each profession. In any case, the student will have attended five years of secondary school; some of them will have substituted work in a *colegio* for the last two of those five years. Since secondary school starts after six years of primary school (and up to three years of pre-primary school), the freshman law student is about as old as our college freshman. Typically, however, he has had a more intensive education; the graduate of a *colegio* (who is usually called a bachelor) has completed the equivalent of one or two years of college work in the United States. Latin American education, like its European counterpart, has been intensive at the cost of extensiveness. The great bulk of the child population does not know what a *colegio* looks like. The North American ideal of education for everyone is correspondingly achieved at some cost in intensiveness.

The law school curriculum is almost entirely required and not elective. After the first two years, devoted largely to such subjects as government, economics, history and sociology, but also including "perspective" courses in law (Introduction to Law, Roman Law), the law student has roughly the same educational background as does his North American cousin with a liberal arts A.B.

The traditional orientation of law study in Latin American has been theoretical. The professors lecture; while there may be a period set aside at the close of the lecture for discussion or questions, the discussion techniques of the kind used in North American law schools are used exceptionally rather than ordinarily. "Juridical science," in these schools, principally means the science of classification. Dr. De Gásperi's treatise, extracted at the beginning of this chapter, is typical of the manner of explanation of the law which is to be found in the classroom, even when the professor is a busy practitioner whose life is otherwise devoted to highly practical non-academic matters. Students are expected to master the most significant portions of the codes, and also the principles of the codes as expounded by the leading commentators. During examination periods, students may be seen in the corridors, reciting code provisions by memory. Examinations tend to be oral; since classes are large (there are 8000 students registered in the first-year class of the Faculty of Law of the University of Buenos Aires, and from 1500 to 1800 in the comparable class at the National University of Mexico), and professors are busy, half a dozen students may be ground through an examination in an hour, one at a time. As is the case in an increasing number of law schools in the United States, a major piece of written work is required for graduation. A student's thesis may not be completed until after he has taken all the required courses. When it is completed, he will often have it printed, at his own expense; the school will distribute it, and it is not uncommon for the visiting Latin American lawyer to walk into the Harvard or Columbia library and find his thesis listed in the catalogue. There may be a separate oral examination on the thesis, or a comprehensive examination at the time of completion of the required courses.

There is, however, no bar examination. The school issues the necessary certificate (in Mexico and in come other countries, it is even called a "license"), and the graduate is eligible to practice. The final three years of law school may include practice courses, moot court programs, apprenticeship programs and the like.

We said that the professors are busy. Doing what? Most of them are in the practice, and devote only part of their time to teaching. The full time law teacher is not unknown in Latin America, but he is still a rarity. Frequently a professor teaches only one course, and typically he has committed his teaching notes to print. If attendance is not compulsory, it may be low in proportion to the size of the class; why go to class when you can read the same thing sitting at home in a comfortable chair? What do students do, if they do not attend classes regularly? They may work in law offices, or write their theses, or engage in politics. Some students seem to be in school primarily in order to take part in student political activities; they are "graduated" into positions of leadership in the national political parties.

Because the faculties are mainly composed of part time teachers who may pursue their academic duties as little as three hours per week, they are large; the Faculty of Law of the National University of Mexico has around 350 members, of whom only a handful are full time teachers. Much of the administration of a law faculty must be turned over to a committee, on which there is normally some student representation. Students have an important voice in the administration; it is not unusual for a newspaper to carry a story of negotiation between student leaders and the rector (president) of a major university. Student strikes, while not unusual, are sufficiently infrequent that they make the newspapers; a strike in the spring of 1961 in an Argentine law school arose out of a dispute over examination procedures.

See generally Maxwell and Goldman, *Mexican Legal Education,* 16 J. LEGAL ED. 155 (1963); Mayda, *Problems of Legal Education in Latin America,* 12 J. LEGAL ED. 407 (1961); CUETO RUA, EL COMMON LAW 396-400 (1957); KATZ, REPORT TO THE COMMITTEE ON HIGHER EDUCATION IN THE AMERICAN REPUBLICS (mimeo 1961); Karst, *The Study of Latin American Law and Legal Institutions,* in SOCIAL SCIENCE RESEARCH ON LATIN AMERICA at 290 (Wagley ed. 1964). *Cf.* Riesenfeld, *A Comparison of Continental and American Legal Education,* 36 MICH. L. REV. 31 (1939).

SCHEMAN, THE SOCIAL AND ECONOMIC ORIGIN
OF THE BRAZILIAN JUDGES
4 INTER-AM. L. REV.* 44, 44-63 (1962)

* * *

In Brazil, in theory, no class or economic barriers bar the way to a judgeship. Within a few years after graduating from law school, the young lawyer

---

is eligible for competitive examinations which can result in the lifetime appointment as a judge. Aside from a law degree, no special qualifications are necessary. Thus, theoretically, a broad social and political spectrum with young men from all levels of society should be represented on the bench. This stands in sharp contrast to the system in the United States where a man enters the judiciary only after many years of law practice. Having been subjected to the rigors of public life, his ideas and thinking are known to conform to certain broad and accepted patterns. In Brazil there is no such prior knowledge. The young judge is an unknown entity in more respects than one. Accordingly, the possibility of having a politically daring or non-conforming judge on the bench is proportionately greater than the system in the United States. The question is — is this promise of broader representation fulfilled?

To probe this question, a survey of Brazilian judges was undertaken in 1960 as part of a comprehensive study of the Brazilian judiciary system. The data presented in this article are the product of that survey. The precise purpose of the survey was to focus upon the judge's social and economic background, to discover who he is and where he comes from. It is understood that any sociological survey attempting to define social and economic background is severely limited in utility and must be interpreted with great circumspection. It is not intended for prediction but merely to draw a rough sketch of an existing institution, and its use is only as a supplement to a broad understanding of the positive and living law of the society.

　　*　*　*

GENERAL STATISTICS

The 95 judges who constitute the subject of this analysis represent a good geographic cross section of the country. Eighteen of the twenty-one states were included, with only Amazonas, Paraíba, and Pernambuco, all in the northern geographic region, failing to provide any response. Only male judges replied.

　　*　*　*

A rough sketch of the average judge responding to the questionnaire indicates he is 50 years old, having served 17 years on the bench after practical legal experience of 6 years. The cross section of age groups was similarly broad in all geographic regions. ... It is noteworthy that in the northern states, where living conditions in the interior of the state are severer and consequently the attractions to the career magistrature less appealing, there is a noticeable tendency to enter the magistrature at an earlier age than in the other areas, and with a minimum of legal practice. Perhaps this can be attributed to the unattractiveness of the physical hardships of the judge's career once a young man has had a taste of legal practice and its greater financial rewards.

Cosmopolitan Origins and Geographic Migration

To a pronounced degree, the magistrature as a career was more attractive to young men born in the interior of the state, as distinguished from the capital cities. Of those responding, 75% indicated origins in the interior of the states, a pattern consistent for all geographic regions. Although the 25% who came from capital cities exceeds the 18% figure of the overall Brazilian population residing in the capitals, such a comparison is unreliable due to the fact that secondary and superior education is far more accessible to those in the capital cities. In the years that these judges attended law school, for example, 96% of the law schools were located in the capital cities, where even today 65% of the law schools are found.

Unfortunately, no statistics treating the distribution of law students between interior and capital cities are available for comparison. But it is known that significantly greater financial resources or strong motivation must be present to induce the trip from the interior, factors which were certainly more pronounced in the epoch that the judges attended university. Unquestionably, a closer investigation of the universities will reveal a far greater percentage than 25% of the student body to be comprised of students from the capital city. Thus, although a greater proportion of youth from the capital cities had access to training for the magistrature, a greater proportion of those who came from the interior cities elected to enter the career magistrature.

The reason for the fact that young men of the capital cities were less attracted to the magistrature was not elicited by the questionnaire. The demand that the career magistrature be initiated in the most primitive areas in the interior of the state, however, has been cited as a factor which tarnishes the [attraction] of the career to young men of city origin. The results of the survey tend to support this argument.

. . . 21% of judges, in choosing the magistrature, saw fit to migrate to another state. That the desire for self-improvement may have been a motivating force for the geographic mobility is suggested by the predominantly middle and lower class origin of those who migrated. . . . Furthermore, the greatest number of judges who chose to migrate came from the northern states, among the poorest in the country, ... The area most appealing to the judges was the eastern states, among the wealthiest, especially at the time many of the present day magistrates made their decision.

    * * *

Education of Parents

Although the differences between geographic regions were well-defined, the data relative to the education of the parents of the magistrates indicated the judges' origins in families having access to and having known the benefits of education. The unusually high percentage of magistrates who come from families where the father received higher education reflects the generally high level in the social structure of Brazil from which the judges are drawn.

29% of the magistrates had fathers who had superior education; 56% went beyond primary education. Only one judge replied that his mother was illiterate, and none stated that his father was illiterate. Totalled without the northern states, which were distinctly more provincial, these figures are even more imposing. Outside of the northern states, 40% of the remaining judges had fathers with university training and 71% who went beyond primary education.

. . . In the northern states only 10% of the magistrates came from families where the father had superior education. In contrast, the eastern states tallied 46% whose fathers received superior education while only 22% stated their parent went no further than elementary education. The divergence in educational levels is more striking than meaningful in relation to the social status of the families since, in the poorer northern states, education was notoriously weak and even those in the local upper classes had little access to formal learning. But the figures do unmistakably indicate the extraordinarily high percentage of the present magistrates from families which were well among the more privileged classes in their youth.

* * *

OCCUPATION OF THE PARENT

One picture quite clearly emerging from the survey was the roots of the judges in upper or middle class families of responsibility or independent means. Following a pattern consistent with the self-estimated predominantly middle class origins of the magistrature, 74% of the judges came from families where the father was either a professional man, businessman, farmer owner, or government official. . . . As expected, a sharp contrast was registered between the predominantly agricultural northern states and the other regions of the country. Whereas farming was the principal occupation in the north, the professional and business vocations were predominant in the eastern and southern states. In all, however, the percentages originating in families of substantial or independent means are roughly similar.

* * *

THE ECONOMIC REWARDS OF THE MAGISTRATURE

* * *

Clearly the judge is dissatisfied with his current earnings. What then is the salary which he considers appropriate for one exercising his function in society? The average wage which the judge indicated would be satisfactory was $3,420 per year (Cr\$ 57.000,00 per month) or an increase of 58% over their current earnings. All geographic regions were fairly consistent with this percentage increase, with the southern states registering the highest demand of $3,900 per year (Cr$ 65.000,00 per month).

* * *

CONCLUSIONS

The significance of this survey does not lie in any new or startling revelations but in the factual support it provides for what many Brazilians already assume to be true about their judiciary. While indicating that the process of social mobility and the representation of the lower classes in the judiciary are not so strong as had been supposed, clearly changes are taking place and a number of determined young men from lower class origins have been able to rise to the magistrature.

On the whole, however, in spite of the middle class not being a large one in Brazil, the magistrature is a preponderantly middle class institution with strong ties to the upper levels of the old social hierarchy and slight but increasing representation from the newly emerging middle class.

* * *

The judge comes to the magistrature with a minimum of practical legal experience and little direct experience with the various other economic means of livelihood. Few judges have any degree of experience in the world outside of their own native state. His business is judging, and it is around that which his life and experience have been oriented.

Of the various factors, some of them but vaguely related to intellectual capacity or dedication to a profession, which influence the choice of the career magistrature, this survey furnishes little information. To the magistrate himself the judgeship is obviously a position of social prestige. Although it brings with it some measure of financial security, economic appeal is not one of its strong attractions. At best, the judge lives a modest life on an income which he considers inadequate. Furthermore, he has generally come from families where at least as much, if not more, economic rewards were apparent in the economic activity of his parents.

In spite of great regional variations, the remuneration of the magistrate is far from sufficient to place him in a position of true independence. Economically strongest in the southern areas of the country, as evidenced by salary levels and the ability of the judges there to enjoy the fruits of their labor with travel abroad, nonetheless even here the vast majority of judges feel that their salary is inadequate to maintain the standard of living to which they feel entitled. On the other hand, the judge apparently demands little more than he currently earns to satisfy his economic demands.

[See also Scheman, *Brazil's Career Judiciary*, 46 J. AM. JUD. SOC'Y 134 (1962). — Ed.]

CIVIL PROCEDURE: A SKETCH

Latin American civil procedure differs from our own in two important respects: First, there is no jury. Second, and not unrelated, the adversary character of the procedure is subdued. Sharp clarity of issue, which motivated the technicalities of common law pleading, is normally absent. (It is also disappearing in pleading in the United States, under the influence of the Federal Rules.) There is no trial, in our sense; rather, there is an unhurried inquiry, in which the judge (or his secretary) takes charge of much of the fact-finding process.

What follows is an attempt at a capsule description of the principal stages of civil procedure in Latin America; this is a composite view, inaccurate in detail for any one jurisdiction but a fair approximation of a mythical "typical" jurisdiction.

1. *Initial shaping of issues.* The complaint *(demanda)* begins the action; it "interrupts prescription" just as the filing of the complaint in a United States District Court (absent the *Erie* question) begins an action for purposes of applying the Statute of Limitations. In the complaint, the plaintiff *(actor)* must state the name of the court in which he brings his action; his own name and his address for purposes of receiving notices concerning the action; the name and domicil of the defendant *(demandado);* the object which is claimed, and the value of what is claimed if the court's jurisdiction is limited to a certain amount; an organized and succinct statement of the facts on which his claim rests; the legal principles on which the claim rests and the kind of action brought. Only the last requirement differs from the practice in common law countries. One does not ordinarily plead law to a common law judge; nor is there any requirement that the action be labeled, although it is not unusual for a common law attorney to draft his complaint so that the judge is told what kind of case it is and the plaintiff's legal theory.

The judge may think that the plaintiff has not made himself clear, in which case he will tell the plaintiff to clarify the doubtful portions; once the judge is satisfied, he accepts the complaint and it is filed with the court secretary for the defendant to inspect it. A summons is issued to the defendant to appear and answer; the defendant is given a copy of the complaint. The defendant may be served either within the jurisdiction or outside it; personal jurisdiction (in the sense that forms the basis for a personal judgment) does not require physical presence within the jurisdiction, but may be based on other connections such as the performance of various acts within the jurisdiction, or even the location there of the intended performance of an obligation. See *In re Letters Rogatory out of First Civil Court of Mexico,* 261 Fed. 652 (S.D.N.Y. 1919), for a discussion of such a provision — since removed — in the Mexican Civil Code. (For the present Mexican rule, see article 149 of the Code of Civil Procedure of Mexico, resting jurisdiction on the familiar territorial principle.)

In the cited case, the late Judge Augustus N. Hand suggested that the former Mexican rule was "contrary to our own system of Jurisprudence," citing *Pennoyer v. Neff,* 95 U.S. 714 (1878). In the light of cases such as *Hess v. Pawloski,* 274 U.S. 352 (1927) (jurisdiction over non-resident motorist) and *International Shoe Co. v. Washington,* 326 U.S. 310 (1945) (jurisdiction over foreign corporation doing local business), is Judge Hand's sweeping statement still justified?

The defendant's answer *(contestación),* like the demand, pleads both fact and law; there is no counterpart to the common law separation between demurrer and plea. There may or may not be subsequent pleadings *(réplica* for the plaintiff and *dúplica* for the defendant). Then the judge may call the parties together for a conference at which he may (i) ask them to admit some facts or deny them clearly, and (ii) limit the points on which evidence will be taken; the parallel to our pre-trial conference is obvious.

2. *Proof.* The taking of evidence goes on over a period of time, called a "term for evidence." Because there is no jury, there is less need for focusing on one case at a time; as a consequence, the court will be receiving evidence for a number of cases at the same time. There is no trial, in the common law sense; rather, the court secretary maintains a file for each case, and adds evidence to a case's files as it comes in during the term for evidence. The *judge* does not study the evidence until it is all in, and he is about to decide.

Implicit in the foregoing is a recognition that the judge often does not receive the testimony of a witness until it has been reduced to writing. The parties may submit their requests for the examination of witnesses, along with questions to be asked. The judge may or may not screen the questions to eliminate questions he deems improper. In any case, he will not limit the testimony by any of the exclusionary rules with which we are familiar, for there are no such rules; only questions "contrary to law or morals" will be eliminated, if any are. The witness may be examined by the judge, or by the court's clerk. There is no cross-examination as we know it, but the parties may be permitted to submit interrogatories to the judge (or clerk), who may, but need not, put them (or his own version of them) to the witness. More often, a witness will just be allowed to make his statement, which is then reduced to writing, signed by him and certified by the clerk, and added to the case's file.

Documentary evidence is contained in either "public" or "private" documents. A public document — one which is issued by and recorded in a public office — is admitted without notice to the other party; he may attack its authenticity, but the issue is limited to a comparison of the certified copy in the file of evidence with the document in the official record. A private document is admitted when its authenticity is acknowledged by the opposing party or determined by the judge if there is a contest.

Burdens of proof are placed on the proponents of various propositions of fact, whether they be parties plaintiff or defendant. A court may be forbidden to accept testimonial evidence as sufficient to establish a fact unless there are two witnesses whose testimony concurs, or the parties stipulate that they will abide by the statement of a single witness. The codes of civil procedure spell out how a judge is to go about weighing testimony, specifying considerations such as the motivations for the testimony, its precision and clarity, the witness' capacity to perceive and communicate, etc.

3. *The decision.* The judge, after considering the evidence and prior proceedings, renders his decision in an opinion which must be clear and precise, and must expressly decide the object of the action. The opinion must state the legal grounds on which it is based. The opinion is unlikely to be published, unless the decision is appealed, in which case the opinion of the judge of first instance may be published along with the appellate opinion. The award of costs, in some countries, normally includes counsel fees.

4. *Recourse after decision.* (a) *Recourse other than appeal.* Either party may seek a clarification of the judgment *(sentencia);* the judge may clarify, but not modify the substance of his decision. If a party asks leave to appeal and the request is denied by the judge of first instance, he may interpose his "recourse from denied appeal," either to the superior judge of the same court or to a higher court (of second instance), which may or may not be the same appellate court to which the party seeks to appeal. Finally, a judge who negligently discharges his duties may be civilly responsible for harms he causes.

(b) *Appeal.* Appeal may be taken to a higher court (if allowed by the judge of first instance, subject to review as noted above), by a party who has lost (or who has not been given what he thinks is due), or by a third person who has intervened in the suit, or by other interested persons who are prejudiced by the decision — perhaps a branch of government. Sometimes the amount in controversy must be more than a specified jurisdictional minimum to ground an appeal. The appellate court, the court of second instance, is normally composed of three or five judges. It reviews the original file in the case, and may order the taking of additional evidence. It will affirm the decision below, or reverse it, or modify it; in any case it will issue its own judgment. The taking of new evidence in the appellate court makes it unnecessary to send the typical case back for further proceedings in the court of first instance. If the court of second instance affirms the decision of the court of first instance, the litigation terminates. If it disagrees, there is in some jurisdictions provision for a further appeal to a court of third instance, whose decision is final.

We shall consider some special aspects of commercial litigation, constitutional litigation and criminal procedure in later chapters. With respect to the foregoing sketch of civil procedure, consider these questions:

(a) How much of the difference between procedure in civil law jurisdictions and our own civil procedure is traceable to the absence of a jury? How much to the reduced role of the adversaries in directing the course of litigation? In what particulars?

(b)   How much of the difference is traceable to the structure of the civil codes, as compared with the sources of law in a common law jurisdiction? In what particulars?

(c)   Would common law courts profit by giving their judges greater control over the litigation and initiative in guiding their inquiry into the facts? Would such a change cause losses as well as gains? In what particulars?

SANTIAGO v. SZEINFAIN

National Chamber of Civil Appeals of the
Federal Capital (Division D)
1953-I J.A.* 108, 68 La Ley* 43 (1952)

1st Instance.—Buenos Aires, June 28, 1951.—*Resulting that:* a) The plaintiff demands the execution of title documents to real property at Otero 54/58, in this Capital. He says that on September 4, 1949, the defendant placed on sale at public auction the property to which reference is made, among others. The dimensions and price of the property were specified in the accompanying prospectus; the property has walls separating it completely from the neighboring houses. The auction was held on the property, and the plaintiff became the buyer for 41,000 pesos, the auctioneer Guglietti giving him the appropriate contract of sale, which is attached to the complaint and signed by both parties. In the contract it was simply stated that the measurements, stated in meters, were those to be found in the respective titles in the land registry; they were not copied in the contract. But it was added that the sale was *"ad corpus"* [Latin in the original], that is, that it should be understood to include everything enclosed by walls; this was also inferred from the prospectus to which the plaintiff alluded. The contract of sale also stipulated conditions relating to the form of payment and the granting of the deed.

All the preceding facts serve to designate the property that the plaintiff acquired in public auction, soon after visiting it, in the same way as other prospective buyers. Nonetheless, time passed without the deed's being delivered to him, and after the passage of the thirty days fixed by the contract of sale the notary office told him that in reality he had been sold a smaller part of the property, without any adjoining rear apartment. On the basis of this information, the plaintiff demanded by registered telegram the execution of the title documents and he received another telegram in reply, insisting that he accept title documents only for the smaller area, on penalty of the transaction's being

---

* J.A. is an abbreviation for *Jurisprudencia Argentina,* an unofficial reporter of the opinions of the leading courts in the country. The same publication also serves the function of a law review, carrying articles, book reviews, and annotations to some of the cases reported. *La Ley* is a competing publication of the same type, as is *Gaceta del Foro,* cited in this book as G.F. — Ed.

SANTIAGO v. SZEINFAIN
(Approximation)

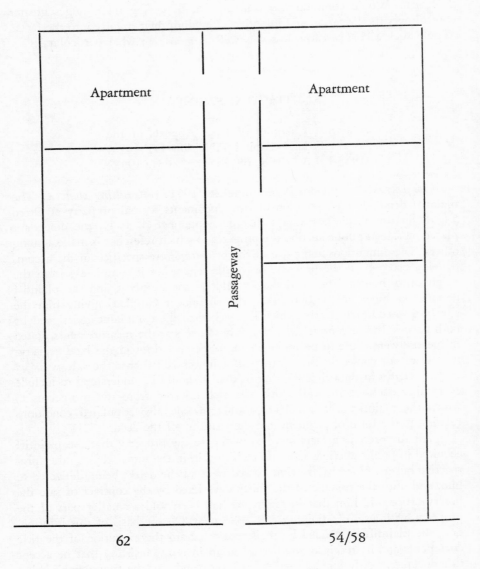

STREET
(Calle Otero)

considered rescinded and of the loss of the plaintiff's earnest money. The plaintiff repeated his previous demand in a second telegram, enumerating the true dimensions of the property. In view of this situation, in which the plaintiff has acquired one property, the defendant is attempting to give him a deed for another smaller one, and the seller, furthermore, has in his possession a sum of money given as part of the price, the plaintiff resorts to a court of justice in order to force the seller to execute the deed. As proof of the seriousness of his assertions, he deposits in court a bill of exchange to the order of the tribunal, for the balance of the price.

The complaint is based on arts. 1197, 1201, 1323 ff., Civil Code, and repeats what was asked at the beginning, with costs.

b)   The defendant, through his attorney, answers the complaint and counterclaims. He admits the auction, the sale price, and the accompanying bill of sale; nonetheless he stands firm on the terms of the prospectus, in which mention is indeed made of a piece of property with an adjoining rear apartment, but in which the following was also stated: "building, two rooms, bathroom and kitchen and one apartment: two rooms, bathroom and kitchen," so that there is one apartment and not two. He then explains that an error has arisen in the prospectus, which consists in attributing to lot 54/58 an adjunct that really is part of another lodging belonging to Otero 62. This is proved by the more or less equal prices paid for the four lots that he enumerates, a fact that would be inexplicable if Otero 54/58 had one more apartment. Thus, if the prospectus caused an error, it would be dissipated for anyone who attended the auction, as the plaintiff says he did.

There is, then, in the contract of sale a duality that confirms the mutual and reciprocal error of the parties, regarding all parties as good faith actors; this duality consists in speaking on the one hand of a sale *"ad corpus"* and on the other, of the measures and borders that the titles describe. The defendant considers, therefore, that an error has intervened which vitiates the consent of both parties.

The defendant counterclaims for rescission of the contract of sale, and to such an end he consigns to the court 4,100 pesos. Whether this sum be considered as returning the earnest money or returning part of the price, the act cannot be validated, nor can the deed be executed in favor of Santiago for what he did not buy, or for what the defendant on his part did not sell. He cites the articles of the Civil Code on which his argument is based and asks that the plaintiff's complaint be rejected and the transaction rescinded, declaring void the contract of sale, with costs.

c)   The attorney for the plaintiff asks for rejection of the counterclaim. He analyzes the supposed reciprocal error invoked by Szeinfain, which error surely did not exist. When the property was auctioned off, directly after all the prospective buyers had examined it, the auctioneer read the prospectus, with the measurements stated in it. Besides, the apartment spoken of is a very old building, appropriate only for demolition; and furthermore, when a piece of property is sold without specifying that the transaction includes only the land, it is understood that it includes everything built or placed on the land.

He studies the provisions of Civil Code articles 926, 927 and 928, which he considers inapplicable, since no error has intervened either as to the cause or as to the principal object or even the incidental object. Regarding the clause *"ad corpus,"* it was included in order to anticipate any small difference which might have existed between the registered titles and the property enclosed by the walls. The property Otero 54/58 constitutes an indivisible whole: it has two entrances (one for each number) and the entrance to number 58 would disappear if the property were reduced to the measurements that the defendant claims. A comparison of prices with neighboring houses also proves the plaintiff's argument, and is related to the small differences among their facades.

He adds that during a visit made to the notary, the latter offered the plaintiff 5,000 pesos for the rescission of the contract of sale, but this offer was not accepted since the plaintiff's purpose was not to make a profit but to construct a dwelling house.

In conclusion, he asks for the rejection of the counterclaim, as there has been no error at all and the plaintiff has acquired a piece of property the boundaries of which are very clearly defined; he also asks for the application of the principle that contracts be executed.

Considering: 1st. That the prospectus... as well as the contract of sale signed by the parties after the auction must be taken as admitted.

The question to be decided may be summarized in the following way: Santiago understands that since he has acquired in public auction a piece of property with specified measurements such as were announced in the prospectus and orally by the auctioneer, the execution of tittle documents should be ordered in the totality of the contracted purchase, that is to say, including the property Otero 54/58 and the adjunct that it forms behind number 62. For his part, Szeinfain considers that rescission is proper, since both parties have been in error: the plaintiff believed that he was buying more than Santiago understood was being sold.

2d.   That the existence of an error having been invoked, it is necessary to analyze this first argument opposing the progress of the complaint.

I have had repeated occasions to make known my opinion to the effect that error is not a ground for nullity of juridical acts. To enlarge upon this opinion now in such details would be a useless repetition of the arguments previously utilized ("Error de hecho y de derecho," 1st ed., 1946, pp. 87 ff.). And I say that it would be useless because in the present case it is evident that no error, of whatever nature, has existed, since, as will be demonstrated, the terms in which the transaction under consideration was concluded were clear and precise.

According to our Civil Code, in order for an error to cause the nullity of the act, it must devolve upon the nature of the act, its object, its cause, its substance or the persons involved. None of these hypotheses is that of the case at bar. Both parties have been completely in agreement about the thing sold. At most the defendant would be able to claim that there was an error in expression. This error results when a person means one thing and by mistake says another. For example: a merchant intends to offer a shipment of wheat at 35 pesos per *quintal* and through an error, of typewriter or pen, he offers it at 3.50. This hypothesis comes closest to what the defendant claims has happened; he would have wanted to offer equal lots and not the ones resulting from the measurements announced in the prospectus and by the auctioneer.

But the error of expression can lead only to the rectification of the offer — not to the annulment of the act — when such an error may be evident, either from the context of the declaration of will or from the irrational character of the stated offer. To the contrary, the declarant must suffer the consequences of his mistake, since it is not fair to make them fall upon the other party (In accord: Demogue, "Obligaciones," vol. 1, p. 423, number 256; Planiol and Ripert, vol. 6, p. 253, number 190; Carvalho, [and] Santos, "Código civil brasilero interpretado," vol. 2, p. 269; and my work "Error de hecho y de derecho," numbers 99 and 103).

Finally, the code requires that the error be excusable, in order for the code to be invoked (art. 929). And plainly, if an error existed on the defendant's part when he mistakenly announced the measurements of the lots put up for sale, that error is not excusable. He incurred it when he printed the prospectuses; it persisted when the auctioneer stated the conditions of sale; it was reiterated when the sale contract was drawn up and the sale stated as being *"ad corpus."* Plainly there has been the culpable negligence spoken of in art. 929, which prevents the invocation of that defect of consent.

3d. That such principles being settled, it is not difficult to resolve the case. There was an offer, clearly stated in the prospectus . . . . In it the property Otero 54/58 was spoken of, and precise measurements were given, which included the adjunct that has raised the question. Moreover, immediately thereafter the property Otero 62 was offered, also with its measurements, from which was excluded the rear apartment. It is true that in both offers, one house and one apartment were spoken of, which would appear to favor the defendant, but the truth is that the other circumstances make the fact of having mentioned the measurements more important. Thus all are in agreement that the measurements were read again at the very auction, before the auctioneer began receiving bids, so there could be no doubt in the minds of the interested parties as to the characteristics of the property.

Besides, the circumstance is very important that one can get to the apartments at the back only through the passageway of number 58. If the properties had been sold in the form that the defendant claims is correct, how could one enter the apartment situated behind number 62, which can be entered only through the passageway, if this passageway belonged entirely (this is not disputed) to the new owner of number 54/58? Perhaps in this question one should seek the reason for the subdivision made by the tax registry office. Neither the buyer of lot 54/58 nor that of lot 62 could retract the agreement, alleging fraud. The auctioneer gave the exact measurements and these measurements, coincident for the two lots, also took account of the actual necessities of the auctioned properties, since the passageway had to be sold joined to one of the two lots; and this passageway being the only entrance to the two apartments at the back, they logically had to be sold together with the lot to which the passageway was attributed (in this case, number 54/58).

[With respect to the statements in the contract of sale, the Code says that the contract is only executed in consequence of the auction, and cannot alter the terms of the auction agreement.]

It was also stated in the contract of sale, that the sale was *"ad corpus,"* that is, that this declaration should be interpreted to mean that independently of its measurements, there was taken into account a specified piece of property (in this case determined by the street number and other statements in the prospectus), its building and other characteristics (art. 1344, par. 1, Civil Code; Salvat, "Contratos," vol. 1, number 415). If number 58 was sold *"ad corpus,"* this means that included in the transaction were the two apartments at the back, which have this common single entrance. Then, it is not possible to formulate a claim now, saying that a smaller area was understood to be sold, which would be that area specified in the registered documents of title, as the defendant claims.

    * * *

In this case, as always, it must be the function of the interpreter [of the document] to extract the intention of the parties, not in an internal sense (which is not attainable to any judge), but insofar as it is made manifest, comes to the understanding of the other contracting party and, in turn, has been interpreted by the latter, to the point of deciding him to carry out a certain juridical course of conduct. For this reason, good faith requires that contracts be interpreted in accordance with what an honorable and correct person could reasonably believe himself obliged to do (see the article I published in the "Revista de la Facultad de Derecho," numbers 21 and 22 of December 1950, pp. 1175 ff.; Ennecerus, "Parte general," vol. 2, pp. 397 ff.; von Tuhr, "Derecho civil," vol. 4, pp. 222 ff.). Only in this way can it be determined what both parties, and not just one, took into account when they placed themselves under an obligation through a specified contract.

Therefore, it remains to allow the complaint, obliging the seller to fulfill the agreement (Civil Code, art. 1197) and to execute the title documents. The counterclaim is declared not allowable, inasmuch as it is based on error and such a defect of consent has not appeared, as has been seen.

    * * *

[The court then ordered execution of the title documents, with costs to the plaintiff.] *Guillermo A. Borda.* Before me: *Federico J. N. Peltzer.*

2d Instance.—Buenos Aires, August 12, 1952.—

1st.   Is the appealed decision void? *

2d.   In case of a contrary decision, is it according to law?

1st Question.—Dr. *Sánchez de Bustamante* said:

The alleged nullity of the decision is based on the fact that the judgment requires a performance the fulfillment of which would be impossible. As this does not indicate a formal defect and the matter is included in the appeal, I vote in the negative.

Drs. *Bargalló* and *Méndez Chavarría* adhered to the foregoing vote.

2d Question.—Dr. *Sánchez de Bustamante* said:

* * *

2d.   I should subscribe completely to the reasoning expressed in the distinguished decision of the court of 1st Instance, if, in accordance with the circumstances, the dispute should be resolved on the basis of the premises that serve as its foundation. It concludes that there was no error of any kind, since the terms in which the transaction was settled were clear and precise; because both contracting parties were completely in agreement about the thing; because, however much there might have been an error of expression, it is not just to make the consequences of such an error fall upon the other party; and because in conclusion if there was an error it was inexcusable.

In my opinion the fact assumption is different, since the facts of the decision convince me that the error alleged by the seller did exist, and that since it was manifest, it did not and could not pass unnoticed by the buyer, who is not free of the charge of bad faith or fault on agreeing to close the deal in such contradictory conditions as those in which the transaction was presented, without his even attempting to have them clarified at the auction.

3d.   It is true that in the auction circular the measurements of the property at number 54/58 are specified in accordance with the plaintiff's statement, and also that the auctioneer repeated these measurements out loud when he auctioned it off; but what the plaintiff does not mention — nor did he mention it when the purchase was made — is that in the said prospectus it is also definitely established that there are four contiguous pieces of property for sale separately, and that each one consists of a building and an apartment, each made up in turn of two rooms, bathroom and kitchen, and that all were placed on sale with the same beginning price of 16,500 pesos, as they are practically equal; .... [The court notes that the plaintiff visited the property.] He has not denied knowing the conditioning clause in the offer to which I have referred, nor could he truthfully deny it, given the preceding events that have been shown.

To me it is evident that the will of the seller has been poorly manifested, but that this discordance between the true will and that stated, was not hidden "in mente retenta," which is the only way in which the other contracting party

---

* The appeal of nullity, in ordinary Argentine procedure, is taken against decisions which violate formal requirements of the law, as distinguished from substantive errors. — Ed.

could have availed himself of a statement that was detrimental to the person who erroneously made it . . . . The error is serious, is evident, and goes directly to the object of the contract, because if one accepts the thesis of the plaintiff, the defendant would be selling something different from what he had decided to sell.

. . . I think that any buyer would have tried to ascertain what it was that was really being sold before making up his mind, notwithstanding that the description of the properties and the uniform price given to each indicated eloquently that there were no appreciable differences between them. The condition *"ad corpus"* appears in the contract of sale, and it should be kept in mind that it refers to the measurements of the registered title documents and not to those of the prospectus, which correspond to the plan in the property tax office. The explanation made by the plaintiff — that he was interested only in the surface of the property because the building on it was old, and that he bought in order to build — this explanation is not convincing, because the motive that may have induced him to buy does not bear on the validity of the contract nor does it make a difference in the offer. That it does not is due to the fact that the properties were not being sold as unoccupied and destined for demolition, but rather as income earning houses, it being observed that they were rented; and also because witnesses affirm that the buildings are habitable, although the construction is old.

[The court notes that the defendant justified his error respecting the sale of an apartment without an entryway on lot number 62 by stating that he recently acquired the property and he had not yet obtained possession of the title documents. The court notes that this error is inexcusable and thus of no benefit to the defendant.]

4th.   Nonetheless, although the seller has fallen into an error of this nature, I am of the opinion that the sanction of the Civil Code, art. 929, par. 2, should not be applied, since the circumstances in fact described do not favor the buyer, and thus the case does not fit into the supposition of the said rule.

In truth, when there is reason or sufficient motives for making a mistake, and for this reason the error is appraised as juridically excusable and the obligor is freed of the effects of the obligation (art. 929, par. 1), it is because he has not incurred fault and considering that no one is free of involuntarily making a mistake because of internal or external factors, the law authorizes one to invoke unintentional error as a defense, and takes good faith into account. If on the contrary the error arises from negligence or lack of attention and is the fault of the person who committed it, it becomes inexcusable. Then the law causes the contract to prevail, and considers that the security of commerce and good faith of the other party merit greater protection, assuming that the latter was ignorant of the error. But it would not be just to admit the validity of the agreement when the party who demands its fulfillment knew or could easily find out about the error committed by the other in the declaration of his will, applying normal or common diligence or attention to the matter. In such a case, there could be no contract, since there would not be a coinciding of wills, an essential element of the same (art. 1137), since the contracting party is warned that the declared will of the other party is not his real will, and because, in a different aspect, it would be to make bad faith prevail over a simple error, since in the interpretation of contracts, honest conduct is assumed and no one can affirm good faith except the person who is completely ignorant of any error on the part of the other party — good faith belief — not he who observes it and takes advantage of the other party. If the latter takes place, honesty disappears since good faith is likewise understood to include the loyalty of conduct between the parties.

[The judge reaffirms his devotion to the objective theory of contracts.]

Therefore, even if the error were inexcusable, the fraud of the contracting party is not necessary in order to deprive the act of its effects; the fact of its knowledge is enough, since the judge must interpret the contract as good faith demands. (Silence or omission can, in some cases, constitute fraud.) Whether the error of the declarant is known or knowable, one can no longer speak of his responsibility. If the recipient of the offer is apprised of the divergence between the will of the offeror and his declaration, how can be justify his conduct, which would mean the conscious exploitation of the error of the other party? It is worthy of addition that the possibility of knowing the error should be appraised in accordance with the usual attention of a common man (De Cupis, "La scusabilità dell'errore nei negozi giuridici," number 32). In the same sense, Messineo gives his opinion ("Dottrina generale del contratto," numbers 15 to 17) . . . .

On these grounds, I vote in the negative, and to allow the counterclaim, [with costs to be awarded as the judge of 1st Instance orders].

Drs. *Bargalló* and *Méndez Chavarría* adhered to the foregoing vote.

[The earnest money of 4,100 pesos was ordered returned to the plaintiff.] *Miguel Sánchez de Bustamante.—J. Miguel Bargalló.—César H. Méndez Chavarría.*

HORVAT v. EIROA
First Civil and Commercial Chamber of La Plata
1952-I J.A. 414 (1951)

2d Instance.—La Plata, October 19, 1951.

1st. Is the interposed appeal of nullity allowable?

2d. In the negative case: Is the appealed decision just?

3d. What decision should be given?

1st Question.—Dr. *Safontás* said: The appeal of nullity for defects in the form of judgments is not authorized by our procedural law (arts. 281 and 284, and report of the Compiling Commission).

Besides, the point in question is not stated in the statement of points on appeal (arts. 280 and 285, Code of Procedure).

I vote in the negative, that is, to reject the appeal.

Dr. *Valldeneu* adhered to the above vote, for the same reasons.

2d Question.—Dr. *Safontás* said:

Esteban Horvat demands of Manuel Eiroa execution of title documents and/or indemnification, based on a sale contract . . . .

Eiroa declares that the said transaction took place on July 2, 1948. It was subsequently noticed that an error had been committed when the land was designated as "lot 10 of block M," located in the neighborhood of Valentín Alsina with frontage on Paso de la Patria street, corner of Callao. This lot measures 10 *varas* [a vara is about 33 inches, corresponding roughly to an English yard] by 23.24 *varas* in depth, or 232.44 square *varas* of area. The verbal authorization given to the auctioneers Fernández Alonso Bros. was for "the lot of land number 10, block K, on Isleta street, corner of Chaco, which measures 10 *varas* of frontage (8.66 meters), 11.23 *varas* in back, 23.70 along the southwest side and 23.64 along the northeast side" (247.97 square *varas*). Because of this error Eiroa offered to sell the plaintiff lot number 10 on block K for the same price and with the same conditions (telegram . . .). The offer was not accepted and Eiroa then demanded that Horvat take back the earnest money within three days, warning that the sum of 1,000 pesos would be set aside for this purpose.

[A report from the Registry of Property showed that a stranger owned lot 10 of block M and that Eiroa owned lot 10 of block K.] . . . The declarations of the auctioneers . . . showed that the defendant entrusted them with the sale of lot number 10 of block K, and that when he did so he made the error of designating it as lot 10 of block M (arts. 172, 219 . . ., Code of Procedure).

In his answer, Eiroa counterclaims for rescission of the sale contract upon return of the earnest money to Horvat, affirming that "error is a cause for excuse from the contract and vitiates consent," and therefore "it is proper that the transaction be considered rescinded and that the buyer receive his earnest money."

I do not so understand the matter, because Manuel Eiroa signed the promise of sale . . . in his capacity as seller, . . . for which reason he cannot invoke art. 900 of the Civil Code in his favor. In the promise of sale the only item that coincides, in respect to the two properties, is the lot number, since the lots, the streets, and so forth, are different. All this demonstrates that there has been an error that cannot be alleged by the defendant to be an argument in his favor, because it is an inexcusable error (arts. 929, 902, 1145 et seq., Civil Code).

Salvat [a leading Argentine writer] instructs that the formula "when there was cause for the error" of art. 929 requires that the person have proceeded in his action with all prudence and that he have taken the care that is advisable in the circumstances of each particular case, since if he has done so the error can be considered, in a certain way, inevitable. Error of fact, on the contrary, is not excusable when ignorance of the true state of things results from culpable negligence, that is, when the error could have been avoided by employing the requisite prudence, in which case the person who incurred the error must bear the consequences and is not permitted to allege the error. The true thought of the law, he adds, is that in the first case the consequences of the error can probably be repaired; "the form of this reparation will be different according to the case, sometimes the nullity of the act, at others the return of what was unduly paid, at others the revision and rectification of certain acts, etc." But in the second case, "when the error is inexcusable, on the contrary, the party who committed it must bear all the consequences" ("Parte General," vol. 2, numbers 2334-2336).

And this last is, in my opinion, the legal solution applicable to the present case.

Things belonging to other persons may be the object of contracts, states art. 1177, Civil Code (and its correlative, art. 453 of the Commercial Code). But art. 1329 prescribes that "things belonging to others may not be sold," since in order to transfer validly a thing one must be the owner of it, while the sale contract is made for the purpose of transferring possession of the thing sold to the buyer ("*nemo dat qui nemo habet*," art. 3270; cf. Salvat, "Contratos," vol. 1, pp. 175 ff.).

Notwithstanding this, the rule that the sale of another person's things is null is not applied when the transfer of ownership is not immediate, for in such a hypothesis it is understood that the seller obliges himself to acquire ownership of the thing and transfer it to the buyer (Salvat, op. cit., vol. 1, number 381 et seq.; Rezzónico, "Estudio de los contratos," pp. 72-73, and authors there cited, etc.).

And in the present case we do not have a definite contract — with formal delivery and execution of the deed of ownership — but rather a promise made while contracting. Thus the only thing that follows for the present is to require the execution of title documents to the property to which the contract of sale refers. . ., within a reasonable time, and with the warning to discharge the obligation by payment of damages (arts. 1185, 1187, 628, 505, 1163 et seq.; Jurisprudencia Argentina, vol. 24, p. 461, etc.).

Therefore, I consider the points on appeal. . . to be unfounded and vote to affirm the decision of the 1st Instance.

Dr. *Valldeneu* adhered to the above vote for the same reasons.

3d Question.—Dr. *Safontás* said:

It remains to discharge the appeal of nullity and affirm the appealed judgment in the part that has been the substance of appeal . . . .

I so vote.

Dr. *Valldeneu* adhered to the above vote for the same reasons.

For the preceding reasons, the appeal of nullity is discharged and the appealed judgment is affirmed in the part which was the subject of the appeal; with costs of both instances.—*Simón P. Safontás.*—*Jaime J. Valldeneu.*

TURBEL v. MASEGOSA
Civil Chamber of the Capital (Division A)
1962-IV J.A. 138 (1961)

2d Instance.—Buenos Aires, September 12, 1961. — Is the appealed dicision just?

Dr. *Llambías* said:

1st. The plaintiffs, owners of the immovable property located at Rivadavia 1167, ground floor, apartment number 9 (horizontal unit number 10), ask the nullity of the contract of sale that they made with Berta Elvira Fernández de Masegosa, which is explained by the sale contract in the record.

The action is also filed against the husband of the named lady, Eduardo V. Masegosa, and it is based: a) on the error that the sellers would have suffered in contracting with Sra. de Masegosa, believing her to be the tenant of the apartment that was sold and, therefore, entitled to the [statutory] preferential right to buy that belonged to tenants during the time of the sale, ...; b) and on the incapacity of Sra. de Masegosa to purchase the said apartment without the permission of her husband.

On her part, the defendant affirmed the validity of the contract of sale and counterclaimed for execution of the title documents, which claim was granted by the court of 1st Instance.

[The plaintiffs appealed. The judge stated that there were three questions to be considered: 1) whether the alleged error was present in the impugned act and if so, whether the plaintiffs could invoke it; 2) whether the contract was invalid because of the incapacity of the buyer, a married woman; 3) whether the counterclaim for execution of the title documents was admissible, a demand that the sellers opposed, seven years having transpired since the sale without the contract's having been consummated. The decision of the court of 1st Instance was affirmed. Only the discussion of the first question is reprinted here.]

2d. Question of nullity by reason of error. This denial of the act's validity is based on the "error as to the person" of the buyer that the sellers would have suffered.

a) It is generally known that according to the prevailing doctrinal interpretation of art. 925 of the Civil Code, not every error concerning the person invalidates the act. The error must be of importance concerning the identity of the person or those qualities of his that were determinative of the act, since ordinarily "one contracts in view of a result, not a person" [citations to one French treatise and seven Argentine treatises].

In this case it would* be a question of error, not about the identity of a person but about the quality of the buyer as tenant of the apartment, which error constitutes a principal element, since probably the seller made the sale only because the other party had that quality. Nothing else is feasible, since the law obliges the seller to sell to the tenant, providing penalties for failure . . . .

As for the rest, in our legal system, as distinguished from the French, the one who impugns a juridical act that was performed through an error regarding a person need not prove anything except that failure of the will. It is incumbent upon the person who maintains the validity of the act to prove — to avoid nullification — that the consideration of the person was immaterial, and that the other party would just as well have completed the act if he had known the true identity or quality of the person. . . .

b)   Nonetheless, even when the hypothesis of invalidity invoked by the appellants fits within the scope of art. 925 of the Civil Code, it is still necessary to determine in an orderly fashion at the outset of the lawsuit whether the alleged error is excusable. For if it were not, art. 929, Civil Code, would hinder the effectiveness of the allegation of error.

It is very difficult to conceive an explicit formula more concrete than that of art. 929 for determining,. . . on the basis of the circumstances surrounding a mistake, whether "there has been cause to err." Giorgi provides an interesting guide in this respect, distinguishing between two possible situations: in the first, the error incurred arises from the very act of the person making the mistake or from circumstances that are accidental, extraneous, or common to both contracting parties, and thus the error must be considered inexcusable. In the second situation the error arises from acts of the opposite party or from circumstances relating to him, because of which it should be regarded as execusable (Giorgi, J., "Obligaciones," vol. 3, number 269, p. 273).

For Spota, "the excusability or inexcusability of the error must be judged in relation to whether or not it is possible that it may or should be recognizable by the other party in the juridical acts inter vivos" (Spota, A. G., "Tratado de derecho civil," vol. 8, number 1918, p. 564, ap. d).

These explanations help to show that the error that the sellers say they have suffered must be judged as inexcusable. The plaintiffs claim that their agents have sold the property in question to a person different from the tenant with the right to buy. But it is to be noted that they themselves were the ones who advised the [government agency concerned with urban tenancy regulation] that the defendant was the tenant of the apartment, which action led to Sra. de Masegosa's being notified by that agency to exercise in due time the preferential right to buy belonging to the tenant.

From the above it follows that the mistake — if there was one — originated in the very activity of the plaintiffs, who would have demonstrated their

---

* The judge uses this conditional form of expression when referring to the alleged error, because he determines ultimately that there was no error. See subparagraph (c), *infra*. — Ed.

negligence by naming as a tenant to the government agency a person who, according to them, did not have that quality. . . .

Therefore, I conclude that in this case there was no cause to err, the mistake held by the appellants being inexcusable.

c) Finally, I should say that in my opinion the asserted error did not exist. Error being a false notion about something — in this case concerning the character attributed to Sra. de Masegosa as tenant of unit number 10 — there is no indication of falsehood here since the evidence brought to the court of 1st Instance verifies that the defendant has been the tenant of the apartment in question from several years back until the present time.

[Dr. Llambías reviewed the evidence on this issue.]

d) From what has been shown up to now it appears that the claim of the appellants is unfounded, and my vote is that it be rejected.

[The court also rejected the argument that Sra. de Masegosa lacked capacity to contract.]

* * *

5th. By virtue of what is expressed, I vote to affirm the appealed decision. . ., with costs of the appeal to be charged to the appellants.

[The other two judges, including Dr. Borda, agreed. Dr. Borda took the opportunity to say once again, "As for error, I believe that it can never lead to the nullification of a juridical act, whether or not it is essential or excusable."]

As you read the following extract from the Kessler and Fine article, keep the *Santiago* case in mind. How might the courts have applied the doctrine of *culpa in contrahendo* to the case? Would such an application have made the result more just?

KESSLER AND FINE, CULPA IN CONTRAHENDO, BARGAINING IN GOOD FAITH, AND FREEDOM OF CONTRACT: A COMPARATIVE STUDY, 77 Harv. L. Rev.* 401, 401-05 (1964)

The doctrine of *culpa in contrahendo* goes back to a famous article by Jhering, published in 1861, entitled *"Culpa in contrahendo, oder Schadensersatz bei nichtigen oder nicht zur Perfektion gelangten Verträgen."* It advanced the thesis that damages should be recoverable against the party whose blameworthy conduct during negotiations for a contract brought about its invalidity or prevented its perfection. Its impact has reached beyond the German law of contracts.

In Jhering's view, the German common law of his day, the socalled

---

Gemeines Recht, was seriously defective in not paying sufficient attention to the needs of commerce. It did not adequately correct the will theory and the meeting of minds requirement. To give some of his illustrations: a slip of the pen, an erroneous transmission of an offer or acceptance, an essential unilateral mistake as to the identity of the other party or of the subject matter, however impalpable, fatally affected the validity of the contract. As a result a buyer, for instance, who inadvertently ordered 100 pounds instead of the intended ten was not liable to reimburse the seller for the costs of transporting the merchandise rejected. Furthermore, he argued, the prevailing view made it impossible for an offeree to rely on the perfection of the contract even if he had dispatched his acceptance because death of the offeror might have occurred or revocation of the offer might have been sent before the acceptance had become effective. Objective impossibility, finally, even if known to the promisor, brought about the invalidity of the contract. These and other instances where a party by "lack of diligence" had prevented the consummation of a valid contract persuaded Jhering to raise in a systematic fashion the question whether the "blameworthy" party should not be held liable to the innocent party who had suffered damages relying on the validity of the contract. His answer was in the affirmative. Of course, the party who has relied on the validity of the contract to his injury will not be able to recover the value of the promised performance, the expectation interest. But, he suggested, the law can ill afford to deny the innocent party recovery altogether; it has to provide for the restoration of the *status quo* by giving the injured party his "negative interest" or reliance damages. The careless promisor has only himself to blame when he has created for the other party the false appearance of a binding obligation. This is the meaning of *culpa in contrahendo.*

* * *

Of particular importance are the duties of disclosure imposed on negotiating parties in the interest of fair dealing and the security of transactions. Each party is bound to disclose such matters as are clearly of importance for the other party's decision, provided the latter is unable to procure the information himself and the nondisclosing party is aware of the fact. To illustrate: The owner of a house negotiating for its sale has made arrangements for inspection with a prospective buyer. He fails to give notice that he has sold the house to a third party and the prospective buyer makes a trip in vain. The seller of a house "negligently" fails to notify the buyer that the housing authority is planning to take over the rental of the house making it impossible for the buyer to move in. The action of the housing authority frustrates the purpose of the contract envisaged by the buyer and known to the seller. A party "negligently" discharging his duty to inform by giving erroneous information is equally liable. In all these instances *culpa in contrahendo* has been invoked and the blameworthy party held liable for the resulting injury. The victim is to be restored to the position he would have occupied had there been no violation of the duty of disclosure. Since in most situations where the duty to disclose was violated the other party, if correctly informed, would have abstained from entering into the contract, it makes good sense to measure liability, as a rule, on the basis of the reliance interest and not in terms of the benefit anticipated, the expectation interest.

BORDA, ERROR DE HECHO Y DE DERECHO* 90-91 (2d ed. 1950)

101. In our Tribunals a case was presented [Korinek v. Defossez, Commercial Chamber of the Capital, August 31, 1936, 55 J.A. 606] in which the principles stated in our previous paragraph would have found perfect application. Let us see, however, what was the solution given by the Commercial Camber of the Capital. A dealer in oils, Defossez, offered to Korinek an amount of turnipseed oil at 8.50 pesos per 100 kg., through the error of an employee who wrote 100 instead of 10. Korinek hastened to accept such an extraordinary offer; but when he demanded the fulfillment of the offer in its written terms, Defossez resisted, alleging that in reality the price was for 10 kg., and not for 100. In the action it was shown that 8.50 pesos was the current market price for 10 kg. at the time of the offer.

The matter thus outlined, the Chamber considered that in this case an error had taken place as to the cause of the obligation. It said the following: "If the sale is a synallagmatic [bilateral] contract, the performance [*prestación*] of each party is reciprocally the final cause of that of the other. The delivery of the thing purchased, which is the obligation of the seller, has as its final determining cause the price, which is the performance of the buyer. Then the price, the essential condition of the sale, is the principal cause of the obligation of the seller."

The argument of the Chamber seems to us to be totally erroneous. It is clear that there was no error about the price on Defossez' [the seller's] part. He knew very well how much the product was worth and how much he was asking for it. It is false to say there was an error about the price. The only error involved was a material error of expression.

It is evident that the Chamber pressed its argument in order not to have to recognize the validity of the offer, for such recognition would have given weight to an obvious injustice. But it could have arrived at the same solution by means that were much more logical, juridically proper, and true.

What prevents Korinek from being protected under the written terms of the offer is his bad faith. As a merchant in that business, he could not have failed to know that the market value of turnipseed oil was around 8.50 per 10 kg., and that Defossez could not have committed the absurdity of offering him 100 kg. at that price; to do that would have meant that he was not con-

---

* Copyright © Guillermo A. Borda, reprinted by permission.

ducting business, but foolishly losing money. The offer has the sort of irrational and extravagant character that was discussed [in a previous paragraph]. The acceptance of such an offer would suffice in itself to show the bad faith of the plaintiff, but in this case that bad faith was also evinced by the plaintiff's subsequent conduct. He departed from legal norms and business custom, trying to avail himself of the price before confirming that the acquired merchandise was of the agreed quality.

We have already said that declarations of will should be interpreted in good faith and that no one with a malicious purpose can be protected by an excessive term or a word that is obviously contrary to the spirit and intention of the person who spoke it. If the Tribunals were to accept the validity of agreements originating, like that in the present case, from erroneous offers accepted in bad faith, they would be converted into organs for protection of fraud and bad faith, sanctioning the validity of agreements which for that same reason are contrary to morality and good customs.

In our case, there was only a material error in the offer, so that when the figure is rectified and it is made clear that the price asked is not for 100 but 10 kg., the offer maintains its validity and its obligatory character for the person who made it. Consequently, Korinek would have had complete right to demand the fulfillment of the conditions that actually were offered and if, instead of asking in bad faith the delivery of 100 kg. of oil at 8.50, he had asked for 10 kg. at that price, Defossez would have been legally obliged to deliver them. All of which shows that the material error in this case did not give rise to nullity of the offer, but simply to its own rectification.

PROJECTED CIVIL CODE OF PARAGUAY
(National Codification Commission, 1964)

Second Book, First Section, First Part:
Of Acts and Juridical Acts
Title I, Chapter II.   Of Acts Produced by Error

521.   Ignorance of the laws [*leyes*], or error of law [*derecho*] shall in no case impede the legal effects of lawful acts, nor shall it excuse responsibility for unlawful acts except as provided by art. XI of the Preliminary Title [special rules for illiterates, etc.].

522.   Error of fact or law shall be the cause of voidability of the juridical act if the error be essential or substantial, and recognizable by the other party.

523.   Error is essential or substantial:

1st.   When it goes to the nature of the juridical act.

2d.   When it pertains to the identity or qualities of the person with whom the legal relation is formed or to whom it refers, whenever one or the other has been determinative of the consent of the mistaken party.

3d.   When it goes to the principal cause of the act or to the quality of the thing held in view as substantial.

4th.   When it goes to the object of the act, in the case where one party has shown a good [an item of property] that is individually different from that which the other wanted to buy, or when the error goes to a good of a different species, or to a different quantity, area, or amount, or to any fact which is not the one intended to be designated.

5th.   When it goes to facts which commercial good faith permits the victim to consider as necessary elements of the act celebrated.

524.   Error that goes to some accidental quality of the thing or to some accessory of it does not invalidate the act, even though the error might have been the determining motive for the act, unless the quality that was erroneously attributed to the thing had been expressly guaranteed by the other party, or unless the error were to arise from fraud [*dolo*] by the other party or a third party, provided that the circumstances of the case show that without the error the act would not have been executed, or when the quality of the thing, its accessory, or any other circumstances have the express character of a condition.

525.   The victim of error may not take advantage of it contrary to the rules of good faith. He shall be obliged to carry out the performance as he understood it, as long as the other party accepts the fulfillment.

526.   Error of fact does not injure the mistaken party when there has been a reason to err, but it may not be alleged when ignorance of the true state of things proceeds from culpable negligence. In this case, whoever invokes the nullity of the act, based on his own error, in order to escape the effects of the act, must indemnify the other party for the harm he has suffered, provided that the other party neither knew of the error nor should have known of it. This compensation shall not be permitted to be made by will. In unlawful acts, the actor shall be excused from responsibility only if the error goes to the principal act that constitutes the unlawful act.

527.   Error shall be considered recognizable when, considering the content of the error, the circumstances of the act, and the quality of the parties, a person of normal diligence could have noticed it.

528.   The provisions of the preceding articles shall apply also in any case when [an offer or acceptance or other similar communication] is transmitted incorrectly by the person or office in charge of conveying it.

QUESTIONS ON THE PROJECTED CIVIL CODE OF PARAGUAY

1.   In what respects has Dr. De Gásperi's proposal departed from the text of the Argentine Code?

2.   Do you detect evidence in this projected Code of a purpose to avoid some troublesome questions that have arisen under the Argentine Civil Code?

3.   How would the *Santiago* case, p. 69, *supra,* have been decided under this projected Code?

LORENZEN, CAUSA AND CONSIDERATION IN THE LAW OF CONTRACTS
28 YALE L.J.* 621, 632-43 (1919)

Many attempts have been made to find a general definition of *causa,* but none of them has met with approval. Baudry-Lacantinerie and Barde define it as "the immediate, hence the essential, purpose on account of which the contract is made." Great difficulty seems to be experienced by the French writers in distinguishing the *causa* of a contract on the one hand from its object and on the other hand from motive in general.

According to the [French] Civil Code a contract is invalid if it has no cause or if it has a false or an illicit cause. Illustrations may serve to indicate what is meant by these terms. A contract is deemed *without* cause if the parties did not have a serious intent to enter into a binding legal relationship, for example, if they were merely playing or joking. The transaction would be without cause also if the parties meant to bind themselves legally but the contemplated object of the contract failed. The obligation of the purchaser of a chattel which has perished prior to the making of the contract is regarded as without cause. An obligation is said to have a *false* cause if the parties believed that a certain legal foundation for the promise existed when it did not exist in fact. An agreement on the part of A to pay to B a certain sum of money which he erroneously believe that he owed B would be an agreement based upon a false cause. Not frequently the terms "without cause" and "false cause" are used interchangeably. A contract has an *illegal* cause if the object contemplated is condemned by law. Article 1133 of the French Civil Code expresses this rule in the following words:

> "The 'cause' is unlawful when it is prohibited by law, when it is contrary to good morals, or is against the public interests."

If the *causa* of the modern civil law has the above meaning, the question may be fairly raised whether it has a proper place in the law of contracts. May not the same results be attained through the ordinary rules governing reality of consent, legality of object, etc.? . . .

* Reprinted by permission of the Yale Law Journal Company and Fred B. Rothman & Company from the *Yale Law Journal,* vol. 28, pp. 632-643.

Planiol concludes that the doctrine of *causa* of the French Civil Code is both "false" and "useless."

The champions of *causa* seem to feel that the notion is necessary to explain the existing law in a number of situations. Suppose, for example, that A has sold to B a chattel which has been destroyed. They are ready to concede in this case that A's legal duty is void for want of an object; but they maintain that B's legal duty fails for want of cause, A's legal duty which was to be the cause of B's legal duty not having arisen. To these authors Planiol makes the reply that the legal duty of the buyer is a conditional duty, being subject to the condition that the seller becomes obligated to him. If this condition does not exist, the buyer's obligation likewise fails to arise.

Many of the French writers of the present day agree with Planiol. They regard the requirement of *causa* for the validity of contracts as an abstract and metaphysical notion calling for subtle distinctions, and creating confusion instead of serving a useful purpose.

* * *

A number of codes indicate specifically what they mean by *causa*. Art. 1274 of the Spanish Civil Code contains the following provision:

> "In onerous contracts the prestation or promise of a thing or services by the other party is understood as a *causa* for each contracting party; in remuneratory contracts, the services or benefits remunerated, and in those of pure beneficence, the mere liberality of the benefactor."

Art. 1467 of the Chilean Civil Code, after stating that pure liberality is a sufficient *causa,* gives the following definition:

> "By *causa* is meant the motive which induces the act or contract."

* * *

If we contrast for a moment the English doctrine of consideration and the continental doctrine of *causa* it is apparent that the doctrine developed by the English courts is narrower than that of the continental courts. Whenever there is a valuable consideration in the Anglo-American sense, except perhaps the peppercorn kind, the contract will be valid also under the doctrine of *causa*. But many agreements which cannot be supported in English law for want of consideration can be enforced under the broader doctrine of *causa*. Suppose, for example, that A gives to B a written guarantee without a valuable consideration and without any intention to make a donation to B, but merely from a desire on A's part to act fairly and generously by B in the execution of a contract which had previously been entered into between them. This would be a sufficient *causa* for the guarantee, but it would not constitute consideration in the sense of our law.

Again, if A should promise to B, the guardian of his illegitimate child, that he will contribute a certain sum toward the support of such a child, the natural obligation originally existing would make the agreement enforceable as one based upon a sufficient cause and would take it out of the class of donations.

The same result would be reached on like grounds if A should promise such a sum to his former wife, B, who had obtained a divorce from him owing to wrongful conduct on his part, or if he should agree to pay to B a legacy which is void.

Under the doctrine of *causa* there is no difficulty, either, in recognizing that part payment accepted in satisfaction of a debt will discharge the debt. Even an oral agreement to make a gift up to a fixed amount is actionable, the motive of liberality [*causa donandi*] being regarde das constituting a sufficient *causa*. Agreements conferring a gratuity are generally subject, however, under the modern codes to special requirements of form.

* * *

Assuming that Markby is right in regarding the doctrine of consideration, as it actually exists in England and in this country, as inconsistent and unjust, and that Planiol's criticisms of the actual French doctrine of cause are justified, the problem still remains whether the law of contracts can dispense with these notions in some form. The fundamental question is, what agreements shall be enforced? What operative facts must exist before the law will say that a party must perform? From what precedes, we find that the answer varies not only in the different systems of law that have reached the same degree of development but also in the different stages of the legal development of the same system. And this may be regarded as inevitable, because law is the expression of the *mores* of the times and must therefore to appear reasonable and just, satisfy the sense of the particular community. In all primitive law a legal obligation arises only from the use of symbols and forms which because of their connection with religion or tradition are regarded as sacred. In Rome the principal formal contract was the stipulation; in English law it was the deed. With the progress of civilization society regards it as reasonable that a legal obligation should also under certain circumstances result from the delivery of an article. Thereupon the notion of a *real* contract develops. Ultimately the idea gains ground that the law ought to attach legal consequences to agreements as such. In Roman law this idea never found a logical and consistent development. We have seen that in theory only four contracts were recognized as based upon consent as such, but that at the time of Justinian by reason of the recognition of enforceable pacts this theory was actually breaking down.

Under the influence of scholasticism there arose during the Middle Ages the belief in the power of the human will to create law. In the field of private law the doctrine of the omnipotence of the human will became on the continent a veritable dogma. The notion arose, therefore, that all agreements should be enforceable without reference to any form, from the very fact that the parties intended such a result. The earlier continental codifications of the last century still require, however, as an additional element, the presence of a sufficient *causa,* while the Anglo-American law to this day insists that the agreement must be supported by a valuable consideration or be clothed in a solemn form, that is, embodied in a sealed instrument.

But the dogma of the omnipotence of the human will, the development of which was powerfully assisted by the natural law jurists, survived on the continent of Europe until the present time, in spite of a reaction against it which has arisen more recently. The entire conception of the juristic act which plays such an important role in the theory of the civil law of the present day, is based largely upon the above doctrine. It is not strange, then, that the most recent civil codes — those of Brazil, Germany, Japan and Switzerland — omit all reference to the requirement of a *causa* or a consideration for the validity of contracts.

Meanwhile the complex and multiform business relations of modern times have increased the opportunities for fraud and error to such a degree that it has seemed advisable in the eyes of certain legislators to require certain contracts to be in writing. In England such a requirement was introduced as early as 1677 by the Statute of Frauds. In France also contracts involving a sum exceeding 150 francs cannot be proved generally unless they are in writing. In Germany, on the other hand, there is no similar requirement.

In other instances the legislator has prescribed particular formalities as a guarantee that the juristic act represents the deliberate will of the parties in question. Considerations of this kind have caused most countries to abandon the Roman rule concerning informal promises of gifts, and to require for the validity of all executory agreements of this character that they be authenticated by a notary or judge.

The dogma of the omnipotence of the human will overlooks, of course, the fact that the human will cannot have any legal effect without the sanction of law. It can in the nature of things operate only so far as the law permits it to do so. The question is, therefore, under what circumstances should a legal system give effect to the human will under the conditions prevailing to-day?

That the capacity to do a juristic act is determined finally and solely by law is not doubted. All would also admit today that the so-called doctrine of the omnipotence of the human will cannot be carried so far as to override positive and mandatory provisions of the law. It must yield whenever it conflicts with paramount general interests; any transaction which is prohibited by law or which is contrary to good morals or public policy is therefore void.

That the will in order to be legally effective must have in view an object that is physically possible is also self-evident.

Granted, however, that the parties have capacity and that they contemplate an object that is physically possible and legally permissible, should not the intent to create a legal relationship be regarded as sufficient to constitute a binding contract in every case in which that intent is so evidenced that it is reasonably susceptible of being understood, and of being proved before the court? . . .

Professor Lorenzen concludes (p. 646) that "Subject to certain qualifications relating to form, it should suffice for the formation of contracts that there exist: (1) capacity; (2) an intention to contract; (3) and a possible and lawful object."

Some of Professor Lorenzen's examples of "false *causa*" would be described by our own courts as "mistake" cases. *E.g.,* the payment of money by mistake. To what extent are the doctrines of error and *causa* interchangeable in the Argentine cases we have considered? If the Civil Code of Argentina had contained no reference to error, might the courts have elaborated similar doctrine, using *causa* as a starting point?

For a modern discussion of *causa,* see von Mehren, *Civil-Law Analogues to Consideration: An Exercise in Comparative Analysis,* 72 HARV. L. REV. 1009 (1959).

CECCHI v. CIA. DE COLONIZACION, MINAS Y CANTERAS (S.R.L.)
Civil Chamber of the Capital (Division B)
1960-I J.A. 459, 98 La Ley 398 (1959)

1st Instance.—Buenos Aires, April 11, 1957.

[The plaintiff buyers sued the defendant seller for nullification of a contract for the purchase of land in the Province of Mendoza. They also sued the notary who handled the documentary details of the transfer. Only the discussion of the action to rescind the sale contract is included here.]

2d.   Nullity of the sale contract because of error. According to the plaintiffs' statements, the codefendant Cía. de Colonización, Minas y Canteras (S.R.L.) misled them, "since the lands did not have the stated and publicized characteristics."

From what is alleged in the complaint and from the law invoked, it results that the plaintiffs claim to have been misled through the fraud of the selling company.

Therefore, the plaintiffs had the burden of proving the fraud of the defendant, since "they had to destroy the presumption that supposes every act to be serious, sincere, and indicative of the true intention of the actor, proof being required to establish the fraudulent action or omission, . . ." [citation to treatise of Aguiar].

* * *

None of the attitudes attributed to the representative of the seller tend to show that in order to sell the lands, he misled the buyers regarding the quality of the object of the contract. Rather, the plaintiff attempts to prove the real quality of the lands, whether or not they are suitable for cultivation, and so forth.

The witness Lanfranchi, who acted as intermediary in the sale, denies that when the sale took place he stated that the lands were cultivated and that there were minerals in them; he asserts that he informed the buyers that the lands were without water. I note that in the contract of sale. . . it is clear that the "sale is without water rights."

It remains to consider only if the statements in the offering circular regarding the location and quality of the lands for sale can be considered as fraudulent tricks that could have misled the plaintiffs . . . . All the declarations made in that circular are of a general character, with references to location, future possibilities, etc. The only concrete assertion made is that referring to the existence of minerals, along with the promise of the selling company to make holes for the construction of wells for drinking water; it should be observed that reference was made to access to the San Bernardo Valley and not to the lots offered for sale. Plainly, there would be only one concrete obligation contracted by the seller, which obligation would be to make holes for wells; the seller's failure to fulfill this obligation could never be a ground for an action to nullify the contract.

So it is that even though the display of the mentioned circular or the affirmations of the sellers may have induced the plaintiffs to go through with the act that they now seek to annul — might even be called shrewd or artificial tricks — they are not sufficient reason to classify the action as fraudulent. The reason they are insufficient is that the person who alleges the act to be fraudulent must not be, in a certain manner, culpable for having been misled or kept in ignorance. If one can arrive at the truth with greater attention or diligence, it means that the methods used were incapable of deceiving, and the law does not owe protection and security to a person who, being able to know, does not know it, because of his own carelessness or loquacity . . . .

3d.   In order for error to be the cause of nullity of the act, it must go to the principal cause of the act or to the qualities of the thing (art. 926, Civil Code).

In the complaint, error as to the principal cause of the act is not alleged; instead it is inferred from the context of the complaint that the error concerned "the qualities of the thing held in view," that is, error as to the substance.

The note of the codifier is explicit, in that it specifies that error as to the qualities of a thing refers to a quality which, not being a matter of more or less, places the object in one class or another, according to whether the quality is present or not.

It is inferred from the above that in the present case, there has been no error as to the qualities of the thing in question, and instead there could have existed an error only in regard to some accidental quality such as the location of the lots purchased, the extent of existing improvements, and so forth. Such an error does not proceed from the fraud of the other party or of a third person, which, as we have seen in the preceding paragraph, has been rejected. It has not been alleged that the quality erroneously attributed had been expressly guaranteed by the other party, nor has it been demonstrated that without the error the act would not have been completed; thus the act is not excusable (art. 928, Civil Code).

Besides, in accordance with art. 929, in order for the error to be excusable, it is necessary that there have been reason to err, that is, that in spite of the diligence employed to arrive at a real knowledge of the facts, obstacles that are impossible to overcome have been placed in the path to attainment of this knowledge . . . .

On the other hand, it is to be noted that the buyers, in June 1950, . . . were in possession of the lots, which fact implicitly signified their acceptance of what was acquired.

For the reasons expressed, the complaint should be rejected insofar as it seeks the nullification of the sale contracts.

[The decision was affirmed in the court of 2d Instance in Buenos Aires in December, 1959.]

LOPEZ v. LOPEZ
First Civil Chamber of the Capital
37 J.A. 1345 (1932)

1st Instance.—Buenos Aires, April 28, 1927.—Considering: [Upon the death of doña María Méndez de López Feito, proceedings were opened to distribute her estate. The heirs all agreed on a partition of property. Daughters of Sra. de López Feito later sought to set aside that agreement, on the ground that some of the land in the estate was worth more than the administrative accounts showed, so that they as heirs had been misled into agreeing that those lands go to other heirs. Although the question of valuation was contested vigorously, the judge accepted the proof offered by the plaintiffs.]

From the foregoing considerations, it is clear that the lands adjudicated to the defendants . . . were divided on the basis of a value less than the true one. Although it could be argued that the plaintiffs knew of this detail by reason of having ratified the proceedings and having taken part in them, it has not been demonstrated in this case that they knew it, especially if one keeps in mind that previous to this judgment they made claims for the modification of the bill of the administrator. . . .

On the other hand, it has been neither alleged nor demonstrated that the value ascribed to the property adjudicated to the plaintiffs was also false. Consequently there is a disparity of values that undoubtedly impaired the principle of equality that should prevail in such a division, and, therefore, also damaged the legitimate right of the plaintiffs.

By reason of these considerations, . . . and the provisions of arts. 922, 954 and 1045 of the Civil Code, I decide: Declaring null and without any value the statement of partition and adjudication of goods . . . in the proceedings to administer the estate of the decedent. The costs are charged to the losing party. . . . — Arriola.

2d Instance.—Buenos Aires, April 20, 1932.—1st: Is the appealed decision void?

2d.   In case of a negative answer: Is the decision in accordance with law?
* * *

Regarding the second question, Dr. Tobal said:

1st.   This cause should be examined in three aspects: a) Whether the valuation of the lands that were adjudicated to the defendant heirs effectively failed to show the true value of the lands; b) Whether in such a case the account of partition could be modified, despite its having been processed according to the procedure that is followed in such cases; and c) Whether the error of fact that the plaintiffs may have suffered does not entail negligence on their part that would impede the voidability of the agreement.

With respect to the first aspect, I believe that the evidence shows that . . . the expert who evaluated the lands in question departed from their real value. . . .
* * *

2d.   But even recognizing this inequality, may the partition accounting be modified? I discount the argument of res judicata. . . .

[The agreement of partition was a juridical act that complied with all the formal procedures established by law; thus nullity could result only from a defect regarding the substance of the act, such as error, fraud, etc. Although fraud had been alleged, the argument had since been abandoned. The judge found that the alleged error did exist.]

3d.   Such being the case, can this error invalidate the juridical act? The López daughters, the plaintiffs, claim there was an error of fact when they gave their consent, but although the error be recognized, the question remains: how are we to judge this error?

[The judge outlined the provisions of arts. 923-928 of the Civil Code, and noted in passing that Vélez Sársfield, the chief draftsman of the Code, could not accept the doctrine of *lesión*. For a brief explanation of the meaning of *lesión*, see the note that follows this case.]

4th.   . . . In respect to the error alleged in this case, one must ask in which of the hypotheses of art. 928 of the Civil Code it would have to be put. The point is basic, for the outcome will differ greatly depending on the path that is taken: if the error were judged to be accidental, the fraud of the defendant heirs not having been denounced at the appropriate time, the nullity that is sought would not be proper because the case would not fit in any of the hypothetical situations of art. 928; since what our law says about the "quality expressly guaranteed by the other party" (in art. 928, Civil Code) does not grant a guarantee against *lesión* suffered by some heirs in the partition, as the Code Napoléon does. On the other hand, in principle the outcome would be different if the error were placed in one of the hypothetical situations that for our law constitute cause for nullity.

5th.   Prima facie it would seem that the error invoked by the plaintiffs is accidental because it is a question of value ascribed to immovable properties, and in a new country such as ours, property prices are subject to fluctuations caused by a thousand factors. But after a moment's reflection one must conclude that here it is not a question (as it is in ordinary transactions) of an element — value — that is merely accessory, since that element is the principal thing about which the parties contracted. When the property of a decedent is partitioned, its evaluation acquires greater significance because it is on the basis of the establishment of that evaluation that the partition can be put into effect ... with equal parts going to the heirs. The Roman law itself, which remained faithful to the triple category of errors excluding consent ("in negotio," "in persona" and "in corpore"), could not, in special cases, avoid all psychological investigation of the will of the contracting parties. Even though, in accordance with this doctrine, error about the value of the object could not be a cause of nullity, the Romans nonetheless excluded some particular cases, considering that such an error as to an accidental quality could then be considered essential ... [citation to the Digest of Justinian].

6th.   Our code, although it may have followed the Roman tradition in order to accept error "in negotio" (art. 924), "in persona" (art. 925) and "in corpore" (art. 926), has found inspiration in Pothier to sanction art. 926 with greater flexibility. It establishes that error as to the principal cause of the act or about the quality of the thing under consideration vitiates the manifestation of will and leaves the act without effect.

But what is to be understood by "principal cause?" The note of Dr. Vélez shows us that he intended to follow Marcadé on the point, since he transcribes paragraphs of the brief commentary which this author made to art. 1110 of the French Code. But a comparison of the original work with that cited by the codifier shows us that although Dr. Vélez used quotation marks, he did not translate faithfully the paragraph with which the note begins. He interpolated something that was not in Marcadé; this something is in the text, precisely, "principal cause of the act." [The judge notes other errors in the translation of Vélez. He goes on to analyze the writing of Marcadé in some detail, particularly the criticism that Marcadé makes of art. 1110 of the Code Napoléon: its apparent willingness to invalidate transactions because of error even when the party who is not mistaken does not realize that a particular quality is crucial to the mistaken party.]

I have referred to Marcadé at some length because, without wanting to excuse Dr. Vélez from his inaccurate interpolations, I feel sure that his texts reflect his intention to avoid, in our code, the difficulties that Marcadé pointed out in the French Code. For this reason, Dr. Vélez inserted in art. 926 the material about the principal cause of the act, and about the quality of the thing had in view. In the same way he referred, further, in art. 928, to the accidental qualities erroneously attributed to the object by one party and guaranteed by the other. But what did he mean by principal cause?

... For me, as I said before, Vélez took into account the criticism of Marcadé and when he included in the text of art. 926 "the principal cause," he wanted to allude to the determining motive of the act. However, in the note he added more than the article said, because in the latter it is not stated that the principal cause should be made known to the other party. ...

I have lingered on this point because I believe that the present case may be included without violence in art. 926. It is unquestionable that the most usual thing about error is that it arises in contracts and that the texts, such as art. 1110 of the French Code, refer especially to contracts, ... But if Dr. Vélez deserved criticism for his casualness in this chapter on error, he also merits a double eulogy, in spite of the objections already noted. He is to be praised in the first place because he considered this defect of consent to be inherent in every juridical act and not merely in contracts. In the second place, in arts. 926 and 927 he did not use the word "substance," and thus avoided the criticisms that the use of the word may have merited in art. 1110 of the French Code, giving rise to the different meanings that divide the commentators as to whether the word should be understood in an objective sense, looking only at the material, or in a subjective light, which relies more on the intention of the parties. ... I believe that the present case can fit into the subjective concept permitted by the Code in art. 926, without forcing the content of the text. To my mind, when the heirs, through the partition, put an end to the estate created by the death of the decedent, the cause that prompts them to carry out this juridical act is not merely to seek the termination of the estate. It is rather the fulfillment of the original purpose of the law, which in this partition is the obtaining of equality of value. And for the code, the purpose to which that equality corresponds is so primordial, that on the basis of the equality, limitations of the will of the testator have been established, as well as an entire system regarding forced shares.

7th. But a new question presents itself now. Although the act might be considered annullable in principle, it would always be necessary to examine the error held by the plaintiffs according to art. 929, which prohibits the allegation of an error of fact when ignorance of the true state of things proceeds from culpable negligence.

Was there in the plaintiffs such negligence?
* * *
It is true that this case involved, as plaintiffs, women who with logical

confidence should have had faith in their brothers and who were not advised by their attorneys, to which is added the participation of the Ministry of Minors, which acted for the heirs who lacked capacity. But even so, since the hypothesis of fraud that was extemporaneously articulated is unacceptable, I do not believe that the plaintiffs can escape the sanction of article 929.

    * * *

Therefore, I consider that article 929 of the Civil Code bars the advancement of this claim. Consequently, I vote for the revocation of the decision, and that the costs in both instances be borne as apportioned, owing to the nature of the argued question and the family tie that binds the parties . . . .

[Dr. Barraquero wrote an opinion in which he agreed with the conclusion of Dr. Tobal, but on a different basis. He concluded that the equality of value in the adjudications was not a "principal cause" within the meaning of art. 926. For this reason, he would hold that the error did not permit the voiding of the agreement, since none of the conditions of art. 928 (concerning accidental error) were met. In addition, he agreed with Dr. Tobal that the plaintiffs were guilty of negligence, so that they should lose even though their error might be considered as an error concerning the principal cause.]

In accordance with the foregoing opinion, the appeal of nullity is declared improper, but the appealed decision is revoked and consequently, the action of nullity against the statement of partion . . . is rejected, with the costs of both instances apportioned.—Barraquero.—Coronado.—Tobal.—Grandoli.—Sauze.

LESION

In the opinion of Dr. Tobal in the *López* case, reference is made to the doctrine of *lesión*. Literally translated, the word means injury or wound. In law it means the disadvantage suffered by one party to a juridical act; in practice, the act is normally the agreement of sale. The buyer, for example, suffers a *lesión* whenever he buys at a price which is above the "real" value (market price, etc.) of the item bought. No jurisdiction makes *lesión*, by itself, a ground for annulling a contract. Some civil codes do, however, permit the nullification of juridical acts based on *lesión enorme* or *lesión enormísima* — great, or very great, *lesión*. A very substantial disparity between the contract price and the court's idea of the value of the item bought will, in such jurisdictions, justify rescission.

As Dr. Tobal indicated, the Argentine Civil Code makes no provision for relieving a party from the consequences of his juridical act because of *lesión*, however *enorme*. This omission was not an oversight. Vélez Sársfield, in his note to article 943 of the Code, made clear that he was rejecting the doctrine. A portion of that note follows.

VELEZ SARSFIELD, NOTE TO ARTICLE 943
OF HIS PROJECTED CIVIL CODE (Now Civil Code of Argentina)

Almost all the Codes and legal writings contain the rule that great (or very great) *lesión* nullifies juridical acts. The majority of the Codes and authors do not generalize the doctrine as it should be, but simply apply it to the contract of sale. In order for us to maintain that great or very great *lesión* should not nullify acts, and therefore to refrain from projecting Code provisions on the subject, we need only compare the various existing Codes. From the differences among them, it will be clear that they have shared no uniform principle in establishing that theory.

[The codifier cites the Roman and ancient Spanish law, a number of European codes and the Code of Louisiana. He notes that some of the codes have required that the *lesión* amount to half the value of the agreement, or as in the Code Napoléon, seven-twelfths of the sale price. He notes also that the various codes of commerce do not permit rescission for *lesión*.] Finally, we should cease to be responsible for our actions if the law permitted us to repair all our errors or indiscretions. Free consent, given without fraud, error, or duress, and with the solemnities required by law, should make contracts irrevocable.

SALVAT, TRATADO DE DERECHO CIVIL ARGENTINO
(Parte General), vol. II, p. 521 (10th ed., Romero del Prado, 1954)

Our Civil Code, the same as the English law and the German and Brazilian Civil Codes, does not establish *lesión* as a cause of nullity or rescission of contracts. From the economic point of view, this solution is perfectly justified. To consider *lesión* as a cause of nullity of agreements, equivalent to the defects of consent, it would have been necessary for the value of things to be exactly established. Now then, since value depends on innumerable economic and moral factors, this condition is little less than impossible to realize; what would be a just value for some would not be for others. The security of transactions would thus disappear completely. From the rational point of view, it is proper to keep two observations in mind: 1st, that in the celebration of the most frequent transactions in [daily] life, it is practically impossible [to avoid having] one party obtain advantages at the other's expense; each one, consequently, should know what he is doing and defend his own interests; 2d, that a will in which there exists none of the defects of error, fraud or duress, should be considered fully effective in law.

A QUESTION ON LESION

The Civil Code of Argentina contains these three articles, the first of which is taken from the Code Napoléon:

15. Judges cannot refuse to judge on the pretext of the silence, obscurity or insufficiency of the laws.

16. If a civil question cannot be resolved either by the words or by the spirit of the law, the principles of analogous laws shall be considered; and if the question still is doubtful, it shall be resolved according to the general principles of law, taking into consideration the circumstances of the case.

22. What is not explicitly or implicitly stated in any article of this Code can have no force of law in the civil law, although a similar provision may previously have been in force, whether in a general or special law.

Would it be possible to reintroduce the doctrine of *lesión* to Argentine civil law? Before reading the materials which follow, consider the various doctrinal alternatives open to a court which wished to do so.

MARANO DE PIETRAMALA v. GUFFANTI Y CIA.
Commercial Chamber of the Capital
66 J.A. 253, 16 La Ley 83 (1939)

[In 1925 the plaintiff negotiated to buy a Buenos Aires bakery from the defendant firm. The two parties executed a contract for the sale of the business, and the plaintiff paid 5,000 pesos as earnest money. The deal fell through, and the plaintiff sought to recover the 5,000 pesos he had paid, as well as interest and costs. He relied principally on two allegedly false and fraudulent representations made by the defendant firm: (a) that the business was producing 2,500 pesos per month and sometimes as much as 3,000, and that this amount could be increased with better administration; and (b) that the inventory value of the machines and fixtures was on the order of 49,000 pesos. The defendants denied both that any false representations had been made and that such representations had been confirmed later as essential conditions of the contract. As the sale price was to be 90,000 pesos and the earnest money was to be 10% of the price, the defendants counterclaimed for 4,000 pesos plus costs. In 1929 the court of 1st Instance rejected the complaint and found for the defendants on all important issues, ordering the immediate payment of the balance of the earnest money (4,000 pesos) to the defendants. Ten years later, the case reached the court of 2d Instance.]

2d Instance.— Buenos Aires, April 19, 1939. Is the appealed decision just?

Dr. Zambrano said: [The judge found that the inventory had been overstated as the plaintiff alleged; he also found that a member of the defendant

firm had stated orally to the plaintiff that the business had been producing a
net income of 2,500 to 3,000 pesos each month, and that this statement had
been confirmed in a letter written shortly after the contract was executed. In
fact, he found that the business had produced a monthly income during the
preceding three years that ranged from approximately 1,100 to 1,700 pesos.]

5th. Fraudulent action to bring about the execution of an act is — in
conformity with the definition given by the legislator — "any false assertion
or dissimulation of the truth, any artifice, cunning or machination employed"
to that end. In the present case, the defendant company ... affirmed to the
buyer the existence of earnings that vary greatly from the real ones, and in the
inventory the company stated an exaggerated value for the furnishings included
in the business. On the basis of that inventory the parties agreed on the sale.
These acts ... are included in the cited legal precept because of their nature
as well as their purpose and consequences, for they consisted of false affirmations that were used not only to complete the sale on the agreed terms, but to
simulate greater importance and efficiency of the firm than was the true case,
thus maintaining the plaintiff's interest in the transaction ....

This act is not simply the exaggeration of the excellent qualities of the
article or of the reasonableness of its price, which is commonly practiced to a
greater or lesser degree in the business world, as the appealed decision observes ....

This is a question of a singular act in the commercial life of the defendant, carried out apart from its work or ordinary professional trade, as it is
the sale of the business itself. For the plaintiff it is a question of an act that
was also exclusive, whose accomplishment was fundamental to his activity. ...

Neither is it possible to explain the commission of the fraudulent act as
a result of the negligence of the plaintiff, applying as an absolute norm for
judgment the abstract kind of foresight found in the "wise and prudent man,"
because a judgment so formed fails to consider the personal conditions of the
victim or the concrete situation in which he found himself. It tends, finally, to
eliminate as an element of fraud the deceit, artifice or machination that made
the fraud possible, that is, the various circumstances that have produced the
necessary state of confidence in the victim and that have led him to err and
kept him in error. Through such a judgment the fraudulent action would be
excused on the basis of the inexperience, ignorance, or foolishness of the person
defrauded; or bad faith would come to be accepted as the normal — not the
exceptional — state of things.

Salvat notes that fraud appears in infinitely varied and complex forms,
so that the legislator could do nothing but give us a general and elastic rule,
leaving its appraisement to the criterion of the judges; he then establishes that
the prudence of the latter has a wide field of application in this material. Salvat
continues, "It will be necessary to examine the intellectual conditions, the general grade of culture, and the habits of a victim of fraud, in order to decide

whether or not the fraudulent acts have been sufficiently grave to determine his will and lead him to complete the act in question. Acts that, with respect to a given person — for example, an inhabitant of this great city of Buenos Aires — would not be sufficient to constitute fraud, could be sufficient in relation to a rustic inhabitant of the countryside, who, recently in this city, falls victim to one of those clever and frequently practiced tricks."

One could object to this doctrine, he continues, that the law does not expressly establish our principle, as it did in art. 938 with respect to violence. But when the legislator said that fraud must have been grave and the determining cause of the act, it seems to us that he had in mind a practical concept in which it would not be possible to omit the personal conditions of the victim of fraud. To omit them would place us in a purely theoretical concept, within which the legal provisions about fraud would lose a great part of their importance and would have an increasingly rare application . . . . Thus we have a criterion that obviously implies an examination of the situation in which the victim may have found himself with respect to the actor and the act.

In the decision rendered on this subject by the 1st Civil Chamber in the case of *Correa v. Figueroa,* the doctrine of which is applicable in its fundamentals to the action examined in 3 J.A. 212 [1919], the tribunal said through the opinion of Dr. Giménez Zapiola, "It is true that the person who buys a house must be on his guard against any surprise in such an important transaction, which commonly is not carried out frequently or hastily. He must take the necessary precautions to make sure of the house's true value, but this does not authorize us to clothe with impunity and success the trickery and lack of scruples of the seller."

In this case the defendant put up for auction "a new house that had not been used," which he sold. The buyer could take precautions in order to find out whether the painting and retouching hid the truth, but he could also believe in the good faith of the seller. Moreover, he had the right to believe in that good faith, justified by the sound logic and assumption that neither law nor justice can have as an object the reward of trickery and shamelessness, punishing the credulity of the person who trusts in the honesty of others. It is for this reason that contracts must be interpreted according to the correct and probable intention that the parties meant to give them, and if deceit exists, the mere fact that the victim could have saved himself with a little diligence is not enough to avoid the effects of the deceit." [The court cites another decision to the same effect.]

[The judge notes that the circumstances were such that it would have been unusual for anyone in the plaintiff's position to suspect any trickery, and that the plaintiff suspected the defendants only when some of the former's business associates declined to join with him in operation of the bakery business.]

The account of the circumstances in which the defendants' action was

carried out demonstrates, as we see, that in the action all the requirements set forth by the legislator in art. 932 of the Code were fulfilled. . . .
* * *

On the grounds of the preceding opinion the appealed decision is revoked, giving effect to the complaint. Therefore, the contract between the parties is declared void . . . and the defendant firm is ordered to restore the 5,000 pesos in earnest money to the plaintiff, with interest and costs.—*Alfredo Labougle.—Santo S. Fare.—David Zambrano.*

In *Gutnisky v. Lusardi Monteverde,* 1951-IV J.A. 114 (1951), the plaintiff had bought at auction an immovable in central Buenos Aires. He asserted that the newspaper advertisements for the auction had overstated the rental income of the property, and that he had previously sought to rescind the contract. (Meanwhile, devaluation of the currency had made the price more attractive.) The court denied the plaintiff's demand for execution of the title documents, or, in the alternative, for rescission and return of his payment of earnest money. One of the grounds stated for the decision was that the error of the buyer, if any, relating to the past income of the property, did not go to a substantial quality of the thing bought, within the meaning of article 926. The court quoted with approval from Vélez Sársfield's note to article 926: "By substantial quality of the thing, we mean every quality which, *not being a matter of more or less,* places the object in one or another species, according to whether this quality exists or not, ..." (Emphasis added.) There was no citation to the *Correa* case or to the *Marano* case, perhaps because the present case was decided by the Civil Chamber, not the Commercial Chamber. (The court also disposed of the fraud issue — assuming for argument that the newspaper representation was fraudulent — by calling it a case of incidental fraud, for which the plaintiff would be entitled only to damages.)

IÑIGUEZ v. GRASSO
Commercial Chamber of the Capital (Division B)

1959-I J.A. 362, 95 La Ley 310 (1958)

[The plaintiffs bought a garage business in Buenos Aires from the defendants. During the negotiations preceding the sale, the sellers assured the buyers that the monthly gross receipts of the business had been approximately 15,000 to 16,000 pesos. After taking possession and making the down payment, the plaintiffs discovered that the gross receipts each month amounted only to some 10,000 pesos. The plaintiffs sued for damages in the amount of 198,000 pesos or whatever the judge might determine to be the proper amount, and also for fulfillment of the contract through transfer of various documents that had not yet been transferred by the defendants. The defendants answered by arguing that they had informed the plaintiffs of the true receipts of the business, but did not specify what they had said. Only those portions of the opinions dealing with the issue of fraud are reproduced here.]

1st Instance.—Buenos Aires, December 3, 1957.

* * *

3d. Damages: * * *

In this respect the contract contains a clause that says, "It is made clear that the gross receipts of the business are the same as those named on June 4, 1954 by Ernesto Grasso. . . ."

It is not disputed that the statement mentioned in the contract is the one contained in a document in the record, which says that the monthly receipts reach the approximate amount of 15,000 to 16,000 pesos.

The plaintiff asserts that the statement was made in bad faith, that the seller knew it was false and proposed to trick the buyer in order to get a higher price in the transaction. On the other hand, the defendants, without concretely denying that the income was really lower than the amount assured, understand the statement about it to be incidental, a mere illustration and lacking in relevance. Further, they understand that the subsequent taking of possession by the plaintiffs, without any reservations, completed the sale to perfection and precluded the allegation of facts such as those now asserted.

According to what is inferred from the above, the present case would be a compensatory action for the damages that would have been caused by the incidental fraud attributed to the sellers.

* * *

I understand that although there may have been a false assertion, that in itself would not be sufficient to characterize the fraud as a defect of the will. It would also have to be shown that it was an action designed to bring about the execution of the juridical act, or in this case the fixing of a higher price in the transaction. Further, it must be shown to have worked with such efficiency on the buyer that he was misled to the extent that one cannot believe his action was voluntary, in the aspect in question.

It is true that this purpose or bad faith does not exist only when the actor intends to injure or to produce error. It is sufficient that he simply know that the means used will induce the other party to err . . . .

But in the present case, I do not believe that from the facts one can deduce either the intention to deceive or knowledge of the consequence attributed to the means that are characterized as a fraudulent action.

The affirmation made by the sellers was not supported except in another statement, made in a former contract. It contained nothing that would lead one to suspect any machination, cunning, or artifice used in order to mislead.

nothing that would remove it from the realm of simple affirmation, the exactness of which, in all probability, could easily be tested.

The fact that Grasso might have been in a position to know . . . that the monthly income of the garage was less than that stated in the contract, . . . though of a certain value as a presumption, is not enough to prove an intent to deceive on his part.

As this is the principal proof brought forth to demonstrate that such was the defendants' intent, undoubtedly it is not sufficient for the purpose.

With regard to the defendants' knowledge that the consequences of the means used would inevitably mislead the buyers, it surely does not appear to be evidence of the sellers' bad faith, which would be a component of fraud.

In order to appreciate the foregoing, one must take into account the principles that enter into the determination of excusability of error of fact. In accordance with that, it seems that the circumstances of the case would indicate that if at any time there was an error as to the true state of things, at the same time there would have been negligence by the buyers, who could have escaped the error before bringing the transaction to completion.

In fact: the delivery of possession from one to the other was completed almost a month after the signing of the contract, and it was received in conformity with the contract by the buyers, who at that time made the agreed payments. These facts make one think that if the affirmation made by the sellers could mislead the buyers, in turn the latter, when they signed the contract, probably had time to extricate themselves from the same before making the payments and receiving possession.

This circumstance, further, would eliminate the gravity from the supposed fraud; gravity is a condition which, though not required by all authors in a definition of incidental fraud, . . . I consider to be properly used in such a judgment. Therefore, one cannot escape the conclusion that if the plaintiffs had acted prudently, they would not have been injured by such an error.

But, besides what has been said, this case would also lack any proof of damage caused to the buyer by the error into which he might have been led by the false affirmation attributed to the seller.

The plaintiff firm has not proved that it suffered any concrete damage. The estimate that it makes of the damage, asking that it be compensated by a proportional reduction in the purchase price, lacks foundation.

    *   *   *

[The complaint was rejected, except that the defendants were ordered to transfer all the documents necessary to complete the transaction.]

2d *Instance*.—Buenos Aires, October 1, 1958.—Is the appealed decision just?

Dr. *Halperín* said:

    *   *   *

5th. The plaintiff firm claims a reduction of the price, because they were told of an average gross income produced by the garage business and in reality the amount was 34% less than the stated figure.

The judge of 1st Instance rejected the action for damages on the ground that fraud had not been proved, and because the plaintiffs could have established the inaccuracy of the defendants' affirmation before completing the transaction.

[The judge refers to the statement concerning the monthly income figure of the business named by the defendants.]

The defendants maintain that the figure does not constitute a guarantee, but merely an accessory statement, which the plaintiffs could have and should have tested. Besides, they maintain that the plaintiffs cannot allege fraud after paying the price and receiving the thing sold.

The above-mentioned statement cannot be considered as accessory, because it concerns one of the principal elements that one has in mind in acquiring a business [since the value of such a business must be measured by its capacity to produce income].

And even if that statement could be deemed accessory, the inclusion of it in the contract as a "quality" of the property sold, makes it essential.

[On appeal the plaintiffs raised a new argument, that under Civil Code art. 2167, the sellers were required to make good any "concealed defect" in the property sold. The judge did not need to consider that ground, since he held for the plaintiff on the issue of fraud.]

But I believe — in disagreement with the judge of 1st Instance — that fraud did exist on the part of the defendants. . . .

[The judge reviewed the affirmations of the defendants, and also the statement by one of them in an earlier lawsuit, which took place two months before the sale now in question. In that lawsuit, the foundation of Grasso's defense was that he had bought the business on the assurance that the monthly gross income was between 16,000 and 17,000 pesos, and subsequently found that the actual amount was barely half what had been named to him. This incident demonstrates the defendants' subsequent bad faith.]

In view of the contractual clause, it was not incumbent upon the buyer to carry out any investigation of the property. On the contrary, he had the right to believe in the good faith of the seller; neither law nor justice can have as an object the reward of shamelessness . . . [citation to the 1919 case of *Correa v. Figueroa,* discussed at p. 101, *supra*].

The importance of this fraud must be judged keeping in mind that productive capacity is one of the fundamental elements in establishing value . . . and because of this, exaggeration of the income is the effect of fraud . . . [citation to the 1939 case of *Marano de Pietramala v. Guffanti,* p. 99, *supra*].

* * *

On the foregoing grounds, it is decided to affirm the appealed decision insofar as it rejects the defense of lack of a cause of action and requires the defendants ... to fulfill the contract by transferring the various documents mentioned above. It is decided to revoke the appealed decision regarding the indemnification for damages, which are found to be 140,000 pesos. [This figure was reached by deducting from the total sale price of 580,000 pesos the amount attributable to the tangible property sold, and multiplying the remaining amount (what we should call good will) by 33%, the difference between the gross receipts after the sale and those represented by the seller.] The costs of all the action are charged to the defendants.—*Isaac Halperín.*—*Alejandro A. Vásquez.*—*Carlos Juan Zavala Rodríguez.*

CLAGETT, THE ADMINISTRATION OF JUSTICE IN LATIN AMERICA *
123-126 (1952)

Perhaps one of the greatest differences existing between the common law and civil law systems lies in the weight and compulsion of the doctrine of *stare decisis* and judicial precedent. In the civil law countries, where codification is a scientific construction of legal provisions, generally the work of eminent jurisconsults, the members of the judiciary are required only to apply the law in accordance with the clear and precise terms in which it is set forth. In points needing interpretation, greater weight is given to *doctrina,* or what we may call "learned opinion," than to previous decisions of the court, although these are not altogether neglected.

The role of the judge, then, would seem to avoid the invasion of the legislative field. In Latin America if an alteration or modification of a law is necessary, should it become apparent during the hearing of a case this would be considered the duty of the legislator only. Thus all legislation can be kept up-to-date and in harmony with existing economic, social, and political development, as well as in the same form. If a judge were to be permitted to render a decision which would establish precedent and become binding on all lower courts, he would then be creating a new law or repealing an existing legal provision in what we call "judge-made law." This would constitute a direct violation of the prohibition in Latin American constitutions that two or more powers of the government shall not be united in one person or entity. Consequently, we find little or no "judge-made" law comparable in any sense to that of common law countries.

The courts in Latin America, however, are not completely indifferent to earlier decisions in point, particularly in the fields of administrative and constitutional law. Even though a decision is applicable by law only to the particular case in court at the time, yet the judges may study former judicial construction and interpretation as a persuasive guide in similar situations, particularly where a repetition in fact may fix a rule of law. The courts accord former decisions increasing respect, but with few exceptions they are not bound thereby, or even by a line of decisions. We do not find "precedent" listed in the civil codes as a source of law, although *"jurisprudencia"* may attain such a strong status through repetition as to be incorporated later in a statutory text, or cause the repeal of legislation.

A noted Mexican authority, Dr. Oscar Rabasa, has stated that the lack of observance of precedent and of the doctrine of *stare decisis* may perhaps be considered to be a defect of the civil law. He believes that in order to give firmness to the law in its interpretation and scope, it is necessary to establish a solid and compulsory body of case-law or *jurisprudencia* formed by a continuous link of cases. This would serve to round out and to complement the written law and the body of learned opinion, or *doctrina,* which up to the present time has been considered by far the more important sources. The writings of erudite commentators, generally European, emphasize the legal theory and philosophy rather than the practical side of the law and are generally used in the interpretation of some vague provision or in filling some vacuum in the law.

A growing tendency has been noted in a number of the larger American republics to recognize precedent of a sort, particularly when formulated through a long course of decisions and as enunciated by the highest court of the land. For example, in Mexico a provision has been incorporated in its law on *Amparo* of 1936 (Article 148) to the effect that a series of five decisions on a constitutional point, rendered by the Supreme Court of Justice of the Nation or by one of its four chambers, by a specified majority vote, which decisions are consecutive and uninterrupted by a contrary holding shall be held to constitute *jurisprudencia.* This type of ruling then becomes binding on all federal courts as well as state tribunals, and on courts of the Federal District and national territories. In Argentina, the recently amended Constitution (1949) [repealed after the overthrow of Perón — Ed.] includes in its Article 95 a broader concept than the former charter in this regard. It is to the effect that decisions rendered by the Supreme Court of Justice in the interpretation of the Constitution and of provisions of certain codes of law, when such cases come to it via extraordinary appellate channels or for review, shall create judicial precedent binding on all other courts and judges in the country. Colombia's provision on this point is limited to constitutional law decisions. By virtue of Article 4 of the Law 169 of 1893, three uniform decisions, rendered by the Supreme Court sitting as a court of cassation, shall constitute *jurisprudencia* and bind all other courts.

All of the Latin American countries issue official publications containing the decisions of the highest court of the land, but as a general rule there is very little official reporting, in published form, of the decisions of local courts or lower national tribunals, and no instance has been found of the reporting of trial courts of any country. In the federated countries we find occasional official reports of the highest local state or provincial courts, but this publication is generally a local matter and lacks uniformity and regularity to a great extent. A number of the larger Argentine provinces and Brazilian states issue excellent reports, but very few of the Mexican states publish their court decisions regularly. In addition, there are unofficial publications carrying either complete or selective reports of decisions, sometimes of several courts. Argentina, Brazil, Colombia, and Mexico issue the most comprehensive official and unofficial reports and digests of all Latin America. It must be stated, however, that official files are ordered to be kept by law in all courts, and decisions can be made available locally.

The principal reason for neglect and tardiness in reporting is easily explained by the unimportant status given to precedent, and the requirement that the law be strictly interpreted in each individual case.

To what extent do the foregoing Argentine decisions support Mrs. Clagett's description of the roles of precedent and scholarly doctrine as sources of law? In the *Santiago* case, p. 69, *supra,* Dr. Borda, the trial judge, seemed to feel quite free to apply his own rather unorthodox position on the law of error, despite the fact that he stands virtually alone in his interpretation. What is the explanation for this independence of attitude toward precedent? When the Argentine courts do refer to cases as precedent, do they make the same inquiry into the facts of earlier cases that we should expect from a common law judge? Does the law of error and fraud lend itself to the building of a body of case law?

See generally SCHLESINGER, COMPARATIVE LAW: CASES, TEXT, MATERIALS 311-17 (2d ed. 1959); Ireland, *Precedents' Place in Latin Law,* 40 W. VA. L.Q. 115 (1934).

RISOLIA, SOBERANIA Y CRISIS DEL CONTRATO EN NUESTRA LEGISLACION CIVIL* 142-45 (1946)

The return of *lesión* is a theme of our time. Vélez Sársfield proscribed it from our Civil Code and established his criterion in a note which transcribes the spirit of that body of law. The divergencies of [foreign] legislation, the difficulties in dividing *lesión* into degrees, are adduced by the Argentine codifier; but principally he makes a virtue of one essential argument, which de-

---

serves to be set out: "... we should cease to be responsible for our actions," he says, "if the law should permit us to make amends for all our errors or all our imprudences. Free consent, given without fraud, error or duress, and with the solemnities required by law, should make contracts irrevocable."

A progressive attenuation of the individualism which flows from those words now favors the return of *lesión*, with or without variations, respecting its classical [attributes]. . . .

[The author refers to examples in the Roman law, the pre-Code French law, the Code Napoléon and the German Civil Code, all of which relieve contracting parties from their bargains in some cases of *lesión*.]

The convenience of including a similar norm in all contemporary positive legislation has been overrated. It is argued that surely [such action] would not be incompatible with the principles of the liberal codes, since, logically, these cannot conceive of anything but sound, proper, efficient wills to govern juridical acts — wills which truly and not fictitiously realize that equality which is the soul of obligatory relations. The danger is — it is easy to warn of it — that such norms may be translated into an extraordinary extension of the powers of the judge, who would then be the arbiter of the situations which derive from acts, if *lesión* should not be graduated into degrees by the law itself. . . . Countries with an exalted cultural background, with a magistrature beyond suspicion, might run the risk. But the jurist should calmly measure that maturity and meditate whether, in [avoiding] the danger of patrimonial *lesión*, he does not provoke an enormous wound [*lesión*] in the juridical order, thereby achieving a certain stability by means of the convulsion of the whole regime supporting voluntary agreements.

Furthermore, it should be kept in mind that although the German Civil Code includes such an ample rule as its art. 138, it lacks provisions similar to those relating to cause and to the public order which appear in our Code. It is also proper to keep in mind that when establishing the juridical foundation of *lesión*, the majority of authors refer to defects of consent, to lack of cause, to public order, and to general concepts of equity and justice. We do not mean by this that [the other articles of] our Code fully replace the institution proscribed by Vélez [*lesión*], but we do mean that particular cases of notorious injustice will not find the judge disarmed, for (as has occurred in France) he will be able to use the concepts of fraud, error, duress, lack of cause or unlawful cause, and even the concept of public order, to give a sanction against evident abuse.

BORDA, TRATADO DE DERECHO CIVIL ARGENTINO:
CONTRATOS, vol. I, pp. 92-93 (1961)

[The author is discussing the contract of sale, and in particular the element of the sale price.]

The case of the paltry or base price [*precio vil*] is different. Here it cannot be said that the price is not serious, since both the buyer and the seller have proposed seriously to make the sale on that basis. Therefore, the base price does not change the nature of the act [as, for example, from a sale to a gift where the price of a house is stated to be one peso], nor does it prevent the formation of the contract of sale. Still this does not signify that the contract might not be impugned and that eventually a declaration of nullity might be obtained by reason of the defect of *lesión.* . . .

Although timidly, the jurisprudence has begun to [recognize] this motive for invalidity. Thus the Civil Chamber of the Capital decided that the sale for 50,000 pesos of an apartment which was worth 150,000 pesos permitted a declaration of nullity of the contract for *lesión*; the Chamber of Peace of the Capital annulled the sale of land for which a price of 800,000 pesos had been fixed when in reality it was worth 18,200 pesos, even though the existence of defects of consent had not been proved.

PEREZ v. COLOMBO
National Chamber of Civil Appeals of the Federal Capital (Division B)
1953-I J.A. 337, 68 La Ley 420 (1952)

1st Instance.—Buenos Aires, October 12, 1951.—Considering: 1st. Upon the death of Pedro Colombo, his brothers and heirs entrusted Juan Manuel Pérez with the administration of the succession and the carrying forward of the corresponding judicial proceedings, agreeing to pay him 5% of the total inheritance.

Based on this agreement, the plaintiff commenced an ordinary action for the recovery of money; but the defendants impugned the contract, maintaining that it was void, although they did not fail to recognize that Pérez had the right to be remunerated for his work as judicial administrator. . . .

The reasons invoked by the defendants in arguing for the nullity of the agreement are the following:

a)   That the agreed percentage included remuneration for professional tasks appropriate to a lawyer and *procurador,* qualifications which the plaintiff does not possess, from which it follows that the obligation contracted by the defendants is unlawful;

b)   That if that percentage has been agreed to with the sole purpose of compensating for administrative tasks, the amount of the remuneration would make the signed agreement immoral and contrary to good customs.

* * *

[The court agreed that Pérez was not entitled to any pay for tasks which would have to be performed by an attorney. That left the purely administrative tasks. The income of the administration amounted to approximately 94,000 pesos; 5% of the total estate came to over 423,000 pesos. The court agrees that such a remuneration would be entirely out of proportion to the benefits of the services for which the plaintiff is entitled to recover.]

If our tribunals have considered that an interest of 11 or 12 percent is immoral, and have reduced it to the maximum limit of 10 percent, then with much better reason a remuneration so far out of all proportion as that attempted here must be declared immoral.

* * *

Perhaps it will be said that our codifier has repudiated the theory of *lesión* in his note to art. 943; but apart from the fact that the notes to the Code do not have the force of law, and express nothing but an opinion of Vélez Sársfield, which may or may not be taken into account by the interpreter, it is evident that when the *lesión* reaches such limits that it is repugnant to morality, the act must be annulled (art. 953). In this sense, the French jurisprudence is very illustrative. As distinguished from our own, the French Code has expressly established the principle that *lesión* does not vitiate agreements (art. 1118), excepting the case of the sale of immovables. Notwithstanding this principle, the jurisprudence of that country has established that the fees of attorneys, notaries, bankers, and (with greater reason) business agents must be lowered when they turn out to be of an exaggerated amount. These limitations are justified by the inferior position of the client in the contract and the confidence which he has had to accord the other party. . . .

* * *

By reason of these considerations and the cited legal provisions, I decide that the defendants must pay to the plaintiff the sum of 6,503 pesos, with interest from the time of notification of the complaint.—*Guillermo A. Borda.* Before me: *Ranulfo J. González.*

[The court of 2d Instance agreed with Dr. Borda's decision, but increased the amount of the judgment to 25,000 pesos plus interest.]

ANOTHER QUESTION ON LESION

Was the *Korinek* case, discussed by Borda at p. 84, *supra,* a proper case for the application of the re-emergent doctrine of *lesión?*

In that case, the plaintiff buyer argued that the defendant must perform, since *lesión* was no part of Argentine law. The court of 2d Instance said that the case involved not *lesión* but error: ". . . *lesión* is applicable when a party who contracts at a determined price is in error, not as to the price, but as to the value of the thing itself in relation to the price, ..." Thus this was not a case of *lesión,* but of error as to the contract's principal cause.

Do you agree?

ERROR OF LAW: A LOOK AT THE SOURCES OF LATIN AMERICAN CIVIL LAW

No system of criminal justice can give consistent exculpatory effect to an accused wrongdoer's claim that he did not understand that his conduct was wrongful; in this sense, "ignorance of the law is no excuse." When a party *contracts* on the basis of mistaken assumptions about the state of the law, however, the considerations ought to be different; many of the reasons for relieving mistaken parties from their obligations are equally compelling whether the error be of law or fact. Nevertheless, it is not surprising that the quoted slogan has been applied in some jurisdictions, at some times, to some cases involving contractual obligations, without a critical examination of the different interests at stake. This note's main purpose is to take the student lightly through two millenia of legal history in the civil law world. The discussion of error of law is instrumental to that purpose. The hope is that some historical generalities may become more real when they are tested against a particular substantive issue.

Apologies aside, here is the problem:

> Morales told López that he wanted to buy López' urban lot in order to build a two-family dwelling; he proposed, as López knew, to live in one of the units and rent the other. The transfer was consummated with all due formality, and Morales paid the full price. Unknown to both parties, and throughout the time of the negotiations and afterward, an ordinance prohibited the building of any structure other than a single-family residence in the zone which included López' lot. Upon discovering that the municipal authorities will not permit him to build a two-family residence, Morales sues to rescind his contract with López and to get his money back. Will he succeed, (a) on the basis of the Roman law? (b) on the basis of the Code Napoléon? (c) on the basis of the Argentine Civil Code?

The first two questions are easy; the third is not. To relate the three questions, it may be helpful to look first at the key provision of the Argentine Civil Code, article 923:

> Ignorance of the laws [*leyes*], or an error of law [*derecho*] shall in no case prevent the legal effects of lawful acts, nor excuse responsibility for unlawful acts.

The chief draftsman of the Argentine Code, Dr. Dalmacio Vélez Sársfield, published his Projected Code with annotations designed to explain some of his vocabulary and to identify his sources. His note to article 923 includes long quotations from Savigny, the great 19th century German commentator on Roman law, and from various other jurists, principally French. It also includes these notations:

L. 20, Tít. 1, Part. 1ª.—L. 31, Tít. 14, Part. 5ª.—L. 24, Tít. 22, Part. 3ª.—Los arts. 1 y 2 del Título preliminar de las leyes.—L. 1, Tít. 6, Lib. 22, Dig.—L. 12, Tít. 18, Lib. 1, Cód. Romano.—Véase Cód. Francés, art. 1110 — Sardo, 1196 y 1197 — Holandés, 1357 — de Luisiana, 1813.

When this note is decoded, it means that Vélez Sársfield regarded as relevant authorities three references to the *Siete Partidas,* an old Spanish compilation; the first and second articles of his own draft code (the Civil Code now in force), which deal with the observance of the laws; a portion of Book 22 of the Digest of Justinian; a portion of Book 1 of the Justinian Code; and the specified articles of the Civil Codes of France, Sardinia, the Netherlands and Louisiana.

This Argentine Code was adopted in 1869, seven years after the achievement of political stability, 53 years after the proclamation of Argentine independence, and 350 years after Cortés proclaimed Spain's sovereignty over the region of the New World which is now Mexico. Spain had long since lost her political dominion in all America, save Cuba and Puerto Rico, but the legal institutions which the *conquistadores* brought with them had remained, along with some other things which they had brought, such as Moorish architecture, the horse, and various diseases. The Roman law, carried on the tides of conquest first to the Iberian Peninsula and thence to America, stayed on after those tides had receded — after Roman dominion over Spain had ended in conquest by the Visigoths, and after Spanish and Portuguese rule in the New World had given way to Independence.

The depth of the roots of the new Argentine Code is amply demonstrated by Vélez Sársfield's note: the *Siete Partidas* were completed in 1265, and the Digest and Code of Justinian were published in 533 and 534. It is no wonder that Max Radin was reduced to this kind of definition:

> The Roman law is the body of rules that governed the social relations of many peoples in Europe, Asia, and Africa for some period between the earliest prehistoric times and 1453 A.D. [the year Constantinople fell to the Moslems]. This date should perhaps be extended to 1900 A.D., or even to the present time, and we might include America in the territory concerned. RADIN, HANDBOOK OF ROMAN LAW 1 (1927).

Since definitions of such breadth do not really define, and since adequate substitutes are not likely to turn up, perhaps it is better simply to begin, keeping Vélez Sársfield's note as our reference point.

We noted earlier that nearly all the civil codes in Latin America are principally derivative from the Code Napoléon. (Even the Civil Code of Brazil, which in broad outline more closely resembles the German Code, borrows liberally from France in its details of coverage and style.) But to start with the Code Napoléon would give away too much of the story.

Rome

In any case, it is traditional to start with Rome; our predecessor scholars had little data concerning earlier legal systems, but the Romans had the helpful tendency to commit everything to writing. We do not need to go back to the earliest prehistoric times, but only to 450 B.C.

That is the approximate date of the first known Roman code, the Twelve Tables. This was a crude sort of compilation of customary law and previous legislation, which — like our Restatements — could not resist the temptation to make a few changes. It was short; Cicero reports that the schoolboys of his day customarily memorized it. (It doesn't seem *that* short; it contains over 120 laws, or articles.) This code's planning and adoption, its structure, its interpretation and application — all of these resemble the experience with later codes.

The code was drafted by a commission of ten patricians over a period of about a year. (The agitation for a code had come primarily from plebeians, not patricians, but the patricians had no intention of turning over the rules of law to a debtor class.) A code of ten major parts was drafted; two further Tables were added a year later by a new group of commissioners. (The commissioners, by the way, also administered the government in rotation, a day at a time, while they were in office; in this respect they are not typical of code drafters!) The legislative bodies duly adopted the code, which thereafter formed the core of Roman law for centuries, and which was the only comprehensive code to be enacted for a thousand years.

The first three of the Twelve Tables were devoted to what we should call procedural law.* The explanation for this curious fact lies in the plebeian origins of the demand for a code. The judicial machinery and the law itself were in the hands of the patricians, who tended to be creditors; the tribunes (the plebeians' special governmental representatives) could not protect the plebeians' interests if the patrician magistrate could dredge up some old rule of law to suit the needs of the moment. The plebeians — most of them debtors — wanted some public statement of the limits on the discretion of the magistrates in devising legal remedies, and the first three Tables were apparently designed as such a statement. Thus, "In the case of an admitted debt or of awards made by judgment, 30 days shall be allowed for payment." That does not mean that the code was soft on debtors. It was quite harsh enough: "In default of settlement of the claim, the debtor may be kept in bonds for 60 days. In the course of this period he shall be brought before the praetor in the *comitum* [like a public square] on three successive market days, and the amount of the debt shall be publicly declared. After the third market day the debtor may be punished with death or sold beyond the Tiber." "After the third market day the

---

* This description of the Twelve Tables is adapted from HUNTER, ROMAN LAW 15-22 (4th ed. 1903). Hunter's translations of the fragments available seem very English in legal terminology, spirit and structure; their clarity may thus be misleading.

creditors may cut their several portions of his body; and any one that cuts more or less than his just share shall be held guiltless." That such a law should be regarded as an improvement shows the high store set on certainty by the plebeians, or perhaps the depth of their legal status before.

The Tables continue: parental authority, inheritance and guardianship, contract, ownership, possession, real property law, torts and crimes, some public — we should say constitutional — law ("No laws shall be proposed affecting individuals only"); all are covered, along with detailed regulations for funerals and burial. But some of these subjects are "covered" only in the most generous sense of the word. We have been concerned with the law of error in contracts; there is nothing at all on the subject in the Twelve Tables, unless we include: "The legal effect of every contract . . . shall rest upon the declarations made in the transaction"; and "anyone that refuses to stand by such declarations shall pay a penalty of double damages."

With so little statutory guidance, how could our problem case have been decided? After a couple of centuries, there had already appeared professional experts on law — the jurisconsults. They interpreted the code, and "by their process of interpretation, they extracted out of the XII Tables a good deal that was never in them." HUNTER, INTRODUCTION TO ROMAN LAW 7 (1909). The magistrates themselves issued edicts declaring the law, helping to fill the gaps in the Twelve Tables. In time, and by custom, the same judges exercised a power to decide various questions on a more or less discretionary (we might say equitable) basis, and finally these additional bodies of law became crystallized, just as English Equity later evolved from flexibility into formality.

We said that there was no further codification for a thousand years. A little calculation places the date of the next code in the middle of the 6th century A.D. — the Justinian Code. During the intervening years, Roman law did not stagnate: "The real source of new law was the rising science of jurisprudence" — i.e., the writings of legal scholars. RADIN, supra, at 58. The Republic was replaced by the Empire under Augustus, whose rule straddled the great division of our calendar, from 31 B.C. to 14 A.D. Imperial constitutions (statutes) continued the pattern established by the republican statutes: they were ad hoc legislative responses to current needs, dealing with narrow subjects such as money lending, or a child's right to inherit from his mother, or a new kind of tax. Still, there were some efforts to be more systematic. As early as the 2d century, various private efforts at compilation of imperial legislation were made. And one great treatise was written: the Institutes of Gaius. Gaius was virtually unknown during his lifetime; we do not know his surname. His treatise is in the nature of an introduction to the study of Roman law, and it has been pieced together under difficult circumstances by hundreds of scholars over the years. As the title suggests, it was an institutional treatise, arguably designed as a practice manual, but in any case highly systematic, stating the main principles of Roman law.

Gaius gave Europe its three-part division of private law: Persons, Things and Actions (procedure). (He may have borrowed the idea from earlier writers, but in any case it was his treatise which had great influence in later years.) Within the heading of Things, Gaius treats of ownership, inheritance, and obligation. A look at the table of contents of the Argentine Code discloses that the modern civil law still uses a similar classification structure, some 1,800 years later. Although Gaius lived in the 2d century, his work focused on the Twelve Tables and on their elaboration by intermediate writings.

"True" codification, however, was not undertaken before Justinian's time. The Theodosian Code of 438 was instead a collection of imperial constitutions (statute law), rather like the United States Code, and did not purport to be a comprehensive codification of all private law. It remained for the Emperor Justinian to undertake the task of systematic arrangement and modernization of the whole body of private law. Even in the 6th century that was a monumental job.

The *Corpus Juris Civilis* of Justinian is unquestionably the most influential piece of legal scholarship the Western world has known. Justinian took the throne of the emperors at Constantinople half a century after the Western Empire was overthrown. The Empire had lost its hold on the northern frontier; the Germanic tribes could not be kept from entering the Roman domain. The tribes had, at first, recognized the formal authority of the emperors, but eventually had cast aside even the pretense of subjection to Rome. The Visigoths (western Goths) had taken control of what is now Spain around 400, under Alaric I. The 5th century had seen the gradual dismemberment of the Empire in the west, ending in the displacement of the last Roman ruler of Rome itself in 476. Justinian's great wish was to re-establish the power and unity of the Empire "under one emperor, one church and one law." WOLFF, ROMAN LAW 163 (1951). He had partial success militarily, retaking Italy and northern Africa, and even some of southern Spain, nearly all of which were lost again after Justinian died.

In addition to a reduced domain, Justinian inherited a legal system in bad disrepair. The Theodosian Code of a hundred years before had been supplemented by numerous imperial constitutions. Various private compilations (such as the Gregorian and Hermogenian codes of the 4th century) formed a new layer above the ancient praetorian edicts and the writings of the classical jurists. In all, the Empire was in a state of legislative confusion.

It had two outstanding law schools at Constantinople and at Beirut, however, in which scholars had been making exhaustive studies of the classical law. Their first task as codifiers was the consolidation of the old law. After a year's work by a ten-man commission the *Codex Vetus* (Old Code) was promulgated in 529; it brought together the law of the private compilations, the Theodosian Code and later imperial legislation. Then the scholars concerned themselves with the writings of the jurists; the result was the publication, over a four-year period, of the *Quinquaginta Decisiones* (Fifty Decisions) settling a number of points of dispute over the law of the jurists. These two tasks were largely preliminary to the main work; they are not included in the label *Corpus Juris Civilis*.

The *Corpus Juris* itself was prepared in a remarkably short time; the whole job took only four years. It was directed by Tribonian, the leading legal advisor to Justinian, and carried on by various committees of scholars and practicing lawyers. Three major works were produced: the Digest (or Pandects), the Institutes, and the Code; together, they formed the *Corpus Juris Civilis*.

> That collection would have been about as difficult to use as could be imagined had it not included the Institutes, a school book founded on Gaius's *Institutes* which sets out the elementary principles of the law in remarkably perspicuous order. But the Institutes form only between one thirtieth and one fortieth of the entire work and would assuredly not have made the fortune of Roman Law had they alone survived. The other portions are the Digest—the most important—which consists of extracts from the writings of the classical jurists, mainly of the second and third centuries A.D., and much altered by the compilers three hundred years later; the Codex, which is a collection of imperial enactments starting from about 120 A.D. but belonging mainly to the fourth, fifth, and sixth centuries; and the Novellae Constitutiones, or Novels, a string of Justinian's own enactments, which were afterwards added to the collection. The extracts from the classical jurists which form the Digest are almost all comments on the words of enactments or solutions of actual or hypothetical cases, supported at best by only so much reasoning as will connect them with other cases or with acknowledged principles of law.
>
> The Digest is, in fact, so far as its contents go, not at all unlike the digests of case law which are so familiar a feature of the Common Law on both sides of the Atlantic and of the Pacific. It is, however, not only casuistical in method, but extraordinarily ill-arranged. The titles, which are the main units, are in an order appropriate to a system of remedies existing in the classical period but hardly intelligible to the lawyers of Justinian's day, and not at all to those of the Middle Ages. It is very much as if we still arranged our legal encyclopaedias according to the order of the old Register of Writs. Within each title, the order of the extracts gives little or no help to the student in search of his law. The imperial enactments in the Codex are anything but comparable to a modern code with its clear and complete enunciations of principle: they are for the most part decisions of cases, greatly inferior in quality to the opinions of jurists contained in the Digest, but otherwise hardly differing from them except that they rest on the authority of the emperor and not on conformity to a pre-existing system of law. For practical purposes, their arrangement is perhaps even worse than that of the extracts in the Digest.
>
> The Digest is the core of the *Corpus Juris,* and it is a world in itself. Of the same order of size as the Bible, it has meant different things to different ages, and is almost as inexhaustible. LAWSON, A COMMON LAWYER LOOKS AT THE CIVIL LAW * 10-12 (1953).

How would the problem on p. 112 *supra,* have been decided under classical Roman law? It will be recalled that the Code and the Digest were mentioned in Vélez Sársfield's note to the Argentine Civil Code's article on error of law. The Code provision cited was Law (section) 12, Title XVIII, Book I; this was a constitution (statute) given in 391 by the emperors Valentinian, Theodosius and Arcadius to Flavian, a praetorian prefect, and reads as follows:

> We do not permit anyone to be, or pretend to be, ignorant of the Imperial Constitutions.

The Digest reference is from the writings of the jurist Paul. It begins, "Ignorance is either of fact or of law," and proceeds to state some examples illustrating the distinction. For example:

> (4)   We hold the same [that there is a mistake of law] where a man is appointed heir to an entire estate, but does not think that he has a right to demand possession of the same before the will is opened; but if he is ignorant that there is a will, he will be mistaken with reference to the fact.

That is by no means all the Digest has to say on the subject of error of law; four other jurists' contributions on the subject are also compiled, so that Title VI (of Book XXII), headed "Concerning Ignorance of Law and Fact," contains a total of ten articles. Some of these purport to be statements of a general rule of law (*error juris nocet,* error of law injures the one who is mistaken); some are applications of the general rule, and some are statements of exception to it. One is in the nature of a comment, an aside:

> It seems to be most unjust that knowledge should injure another than its possessor, or that the ignorance of one person should profit another. Dig. XXII, VI, 5.

Nevertheless, the severe rule that error of law did not excuse was carried over into contractual relations, with only a few exceptions: errors made by minors, women, soldiers who had been away.

In the Roman law, there was no generalized theory of the formation of obligations, or even of contracts. Instead, there were special rules for particular kinds of transactions, such as sale contracts, gifts, renting, mandate and the like. The law of error forms one exception to the usual lack of generalization; the writers speak of error in general as excusing or not excusing a party from the legal consequences of his acts; it is true that much of the discussion of error centers on error in contracts of sale, but not all of it. This generalization of the law of error is part of a larger generalization of the law of consent, which embraces the subjects of fraud and duress as well.

The characteristics of *emptio venditio,* the contract of sale (literally, purchase-sale, the source for the Spanish term *compraventa*), are those "common to the consensual group": first, that it *is* consensual, requiring no formality, and requiring no delivery of a *res;* second, that it is bilateral, in that "the liability of the one party depends on the other having discharged or being ready and willing to discharge his own liability." ZULUETA, THE ROMAN LAW OF SALE 7 (1945). Third, it is a contract of *bona fides;* this concept, like the common law concept of reasonable conduct, was fluid enough to permit variation as trade practices developed, and gradually took on certain standard characteristics. *Id.* at 9. The essential element in the formation of the contract of *emptio venditio* are: (i) a thing (*res,* or *merx*), which may be corporeal or not, but which must be an article of commerce (a free man, or religious property, could not be sold); (ii) a certain price in money (if it were not woney, the contract would not be *emptio venditio,* but rather *permutatio,* exchange or barter; note also that Roman law does not supply a "reasonable" price in the absence of an express agreement, as does modern Anglo-American law); and (iii) consent. The concept of error is defined for the purpose of determining the reality of consent — the freedom of the will, to use a later and typically French formulation.

Thus, Roman and later writers frequently say that there can be no contract of sale if there is an error of the "right" kind; because an essential element is missing, the contract does not come into existence. But even Roman law distinguished between *error in negotio* (error in negotiation, as when A means to offer to sell B his cow, but mistakenly says "horse") and *error in re* (error as to the thing, as where the wrong piece of real property is shown to the potential buyer) on the one hand, either of which would prevent the contract from being formed, and *error in substantia* (error as to the material, or substance of the thing sold) on the other, which merely made the contract voidable at the option of the mistaken party. Reflections of the Roman law's rules concerning error are apparent in the modern Civil Code of Argentina.

In the East, Justinian's legislation continued to be the principal source of law; theoretically it was *the* source, apart from later statutes. Justinian had forbidden commentary on the Digest, except within closely defined limits (more than a milennium later, when Napoléon heard of the publication of the first commentary on his Code, he is reported to have said, *"Mon Code est perdu"* — "My Code is lost"). In fact, the codification of Justinian survived the fall of Constantinople and the end the Byzantine Empire in 1453, and Roman law extended its influence even into the Slavic systems.

In the West, however, the *Corpus Juris* was virtually buried for centuries after its promulgation. An exception is Italy, where the legislation of Justinian was introduced at the time of reconquest. Even in Italy, however, the Digest was not of great importance; such influence as the *Corpus Juris* had was limited to the Institutes, the Codes and the Novels. When the Empire lost northern Italy again, the *Corpus Juris* faded from practical significance there. True, the West continued to be influenced by Roman law:

Yet the overall picture of Roman law in those centuries is one of progressive decay. The scanty literature of the period . . . shows us an increasing quantity of misconceptions, a complete lack of originality or ability to carry through doctrinal analysis, a further barbarization of institutions, and a greater mixture with elements of Germanic origin. However, from the standpoint of the historian of Roman law, the efforts of those centuries of decline are important, because they preserved the memory of, and respect for, Roman law until the revival of legal studies. WOLFF, ROMAN LAW* 184-85 (1951).

Why did the Justinian legislation fail to make headway in the West? (The earlier Theodosian Code, for example, had been adopted into the Visigothic legislation, although it had been published after the Visigothic conquests.) The answer probably lies in the breakdown of communication between East and West which resulted from the Moslem occupation of Spain, the islands of the Mediterranean, and northern Africa. With the trade routes closed, other forms of East-West intercourse virtually ceased. Western society became provincial and agricultural. The need for a law of sales, for example, was much diminished; one seldom bought anything unless he had a bad year and could not feed his own. See VON MEHREN, THE CIVIL LAW SYSTEM 3-5 (1957).

Still, legal learning did not die out altogether:

It survived to some extent together with other remnants of ancient culture, more especially through the agency of the learned classes of those days— the clerical and monastic orders. The survivals in question, however, are not only slight and incoherent, but, as a rule, hopelessly mixed up with the attempt of the early Middle Ages to effect a kind of salvage of the general learning of antiquity. There are no definite traces of organised schools of law. What legal learning there is remains connected with exercises in grammar, rhetoric, and dialectics. A striking example of the kind of work carried on in the course of the seventh and eighth centuries is presented by the Etymologies or Origins of the Spanish Bishop, Isidor of Seville. It is an *Encyclopaedia* embracing all sorts of information collected from classical sources—on arts, medicine, Old and New Testament topics, ecclesiastical history, philology, and law. The legal sections comprise, firstly, generalisations on subdivisions of jurisprudence, on the aims and methods of law, on legislators and jurisconsults; and, secondly, notices as to substantive law—on witnesses, on deeds, on the law of things, on crime and punishment, etc. All these matters are treated by excerpts from classical literature, from writings of jurisconsults, and from legal enactments. As is shown by the title, the author lays great stress on supposed etymologies for the explanation of institutions and rules. It is needless to say that the philological derivations compiled by him are sometimes fanciful in the extreme. VINOGRADOFF, ROMAN LAW IN MEDIEVAL EUROPE 27-28 (1st ed. 1909).

The invading barbarian kings had earlier divided the land among their military chiefs, who had made further divisions among their followers; personal loyalties thus had been reinforced by mutual rights and obligations arising out of the resulting military-agrarian relationships. In feudal society, political power had become associated with land holdings. If a king wanted to expand his own power, he had to diminish that of the feudal lords. It was natural for him to turn to the merchants of the cities, who were happy to give him financial support in exchange for protection from the barons. The king's protection in turn encouraged trade. Partly because of the impact of the Crusades, Moslem power waned in the Mediterranean, and trade routes were cleared. As trade expanded, so did cities and the power of the merchants, and therefore the power of the kings. Thus it was that the need for a more sophisticated legal system coincided with an improvement in communication. By the 11th century, the time was ripe for the revival of Roman law scholarship that took place.

Bologna became one principal center of these studies. Students came from all over Europe to study under teachers such as Irnerius, who made an examination of the text of a complete manuscript of Justinian's Digest, which had been discovered in Pisa. Irnerius and his followers concerned themselves with the text's "true" meaning — he was first a proffor of grammar — and did not go beyond interpretation in this rather narrow sense. But even this limited task required them to harmonize apparent conflicts, and to state the more generalized legal principles that seemed to be the basis for the rather specific statements of the Digest. Their method for making comments was to make marginal notes — "glosses" — on the manuscripts which they examined, and they became known as the "Glossators."

Being true medieval men, the Glossators were not motivated by any historical interest in Roman law. To their mind, Justinian's codification embodied the law of their own time; for they adhered to the theory that the Holy Roman Empire was the successor of the old Roman Empire, so that the law of the Byzantine emperor was conceived as the imperial law of their own period. Nevertheless, the *Corpus Iuris*—which was the almost exclusive concern of the Glossators (they did pay some attention to legislative acts of emperors of the Hohenstaufen dynasty)—was not the real law of their time anywhere. The law actually in force was largely based on native, i.e., chiefly Germanic, conceptions; in Italy it was a mixture of often degenerated Roman and of Lombard institutions. Canon law—i.e., the law of the Catholic church—was essentially Roman in spirit and followed the patterns of the late Roman law with regard to part of its institutions, such as court procedure; yet it was not the same as the legal system laid down in the *Corpus Iuris*. All this remained outside the orbit of the Glossators' interest. So did the rich crop of statutory law that in their own time was growing in many Italian cities, even though the teachings of the Glossators themselves found expression in these statutes. The attitude of the Glossators was not even changed by the fact that the professors of Bologna, through their own opinions on specific questions of law and through their graduates who went out into chancelleries and courtrooms of all Western Europe, exerted considerable influence on the development of the living law. The attitude of the Glossators was purely academic and their interest concentrated on only what they deemed worthy of scientific treatment. [Compare the note on Latin American Legal Education, p. 59, *supra.* — Ed.]

. . . The place of the scholars of Bologna as the leading authorities on Roman law was taken by other men who relied on the methods and achievements of the Glossators but approached their task from a different angle and with different problems in mind. . . .

The new school began in the thirteenth century, reached its peak in the fourteenth century, and continued into the fifteenth century. It is known as the school of the "Postglossators" or "Commentators." The latter name, nowadays more commonly used than the former, is derived from the fact that these men no longer contented themselves with interpreting the *Corpus Iuris* directly and in isolation. They wrote coherent treatises, or "commentaries," on specific topics and they took an important step forward by combining Roman law with the statutory law of Italian cities and with canon law. In this manner they succeeded both in adapting Roman law to the actual practical needs of their time and in giving the contemporary law a scientific basis through theoretical concepts derived from Roman law. The breadth of their interests enabled some of the Commentators to make truly original contributions and to set forth new theories which would have been unattainable from the narrower standpoint of the Glossators. To name a few examples, they founded the sciences of commercial law and of criminal law, and they laid the ground for what became the European theory of conflict of laws. The work of the Commentators is unthinkable without the previous achievement of the Glossators, but to the Italian Romanistic science of the fourteenth century—if judged as a whole and in its most outstanding representatives—goes the credit of being the real founders of modern legal science. WOLFF, ROMAN LAW* 188-90 (1951).

Spain

When the Romans ejected the Carthaginians from the Iberian Peninsula around 250 B.C., they brought their law with them. When the Romans in turn were conquered by the Visigoths some 650 years later, it might have been expected that the new conquest would result in a similar legal displacement. It did not; although the Visigoths had their own customary law (eventually codified in the Code of Euric in the late 5th century), they permitted the Roman law to continue as the binding law for Romans within their kingdom.

In fact, the Visigothic kings positively encouraged the Roman law, finally appointing a commission to codify the Roman law as it was practiced in Spain and Gaul. The result was the *Lex Romana Visigothorum* of 506, also called the Breviary of Alaric, since it was promulgated under the authority of Alaric II. This crude and rather disorganized code was dominated by excerpts from the Theodosian Code (which had been promulgated *after* the Visigothic conquest of Spain and Gaul), and also included an abridgment of the Institutes of Gaius, and other fragmented Roman sources.

The law of Spain was thus divided: part corrupted Roman and part Gothic (although the Gothic law itself often borrowed from Rome). After King Recared I was converted to Catholicism in 587, the unification of the nation became a primary order of business, and part of the process was legal unification. The new code, called the *Liber judicorum,* was first adopted in 654, and aimed at consolidation — political, social, even racial. The compilation was comprehensive, and overwhelmingly Roman; it amounted to some five hundred articles, and it underwent frequent revision until 694, when it was promulgated in its final form. The code has since become known as the *Fuero Juzgo,* a corruption of the Latin *Forum Judicum.* (The Spanish word *fuero,* in one of its legal senses, has come to mean statute law, or a compilation of laws.)

Very likely the reason why the *Fuero Juzgo* reached "final" form at the end of the 7th century was that there was no chance to revise it; Spain was overrun by the Moors soon thereafter. An exploratory invasion under a general named Taric was made in 710; it met so little resistance that the Moors planned a much larger one. The full-scale invasion began the next year with the fortification of Gibraltar, which took its name from Taric (Gebal Taric, or Mount Taric), and culminated in a battle in which 90,000 Goths were routed by a Moorish force one-fourth that size. The Moors stayed nearly 800 years.

The tenacity of Roman law was again demonstrated. The Moors applied their own law to their own people, but retained the old law — principally the *Fuero Juzgo* — for the Roman-Gothic population. The only substantive contribution of Islamic law which survived the expulsion of the Moors related to matters such as water rights and agrarian rights. The principal influence of the long Moorish occupation on Spanish law was its shattering of the national unity which had been attained at the close of the Gothic period. There was no Spain during this time, except as a geographical description; rather there was a multiplicity of small kingdoms and countries — all but a few subject to Moorish control, in varying degrees — each with its own legislative jurisdiction. The result was a legal diversity, against which various kings contended during the period of "reconquest." That period did not end until 1492, when the reconquest was complete.

The legislation of the reconquest period destined to have the greatest lasting influence was written during the reign of Alfonso X, *El Sabio* (the Wise). When Alfonso ascended the throne of León and Castile in 1252, the fragmentation of Spanish law begun under the Moorish conquest and accelerated by the operation of the feudal system was a serious obstacle to the unity of the kingdom. The local nobility was virtually, although not theoretically, sovereign in many areas; the cities and monasteries were also governed independently, by separate laws which tended to be Romanized because of the influence of the canonists and the increasing needs of merchants for a sophisticated law of trade.

Such kingdom-wide legislation as there was had dealt primarily with feudal relations, although there had been occasional abortive attempts to codify private law. The legislation of Alfonso the Wise represented a compromise between Spanish-Gothic sources and Roman sources, between codified custom and *ratio scripta* (written reason), between feudalism and the rising nation state.

The *Fuero Real* (Royal Code) of 1255 compiled the existing laws and customs of Castile. Its purpose was legislative unity, but it included many laws which were contradictory, and it did not succeed in supplanting local legislation. Attempts to discard some of this legislation and to create a coherent body of national law culminated in the *Siete Partidas.* This was in substantial part a Spanish translation of the *Corpus Juris* of Justinian, supplemented by the Glossators; it seems to have resulted directly from the studies of Spanish scholars at Bologna. The *Partidas* were not published as an official source of law during the lifetime of Alfonso X, but they represent his greatest legislative achievement.

The code takes its name from the fact that it is divided into seven books, or parts. Each part begins with one of the letters of Alfonso's name, making the document the world's outstanding legislative acrostic. The code contains much that is unrelated to what we now consider to be the business of codes: rules of chivalry (how to dress a knight, how to choose a horse, the knight's diet in peace and war); the desirable characteristics of leaders (the King should walk erect; his wife should be of good habits, beautiful and rich; he should eat and drink at the proper hour, and temperately); rules for the conduct of warfare (ships should carry salted meat, vegetables and cheese; leaders should be reserved or talkative as the occasion demands.) See Nichols, *Las Siete Partidas,* 20 CALIF. L. REV. 260, 266-73 (1932); Lobingier, *Las Siete Partidas and its Predecessors,* 1 CALIF. L. REV. 487 (1913).

This much of the *Partidas* is original; in fact, the code is said to be one of the most influential early documents in Spanish literature, coming as it did at the formative period of the modern Spanish language. But other parts are not new. The Third Partida deals with procedure and property, the Fifth with obligations and maritime laws. Both were cited in Vélez Sársfield's note to the Argentine provision concerning error of law, and both these Partidas were taken nearly word for word from the *Corpus Juris.* The First Partida, also cited in the same note, deals, as does the preliminary title of the Argentine Civil Code, with laws in general and their observance. It shows the influence of the canonists.

Roman law, as the underlying, supplementary — one might say common — law, filled in the gaps of the statutes. The Spanish legal system, even in feudal courts, was administered by lawyers and judges trained in the Roman system, who tended to interpret all law in the light of Roman principle. The cities thrived on the commercial law of Rome as elaborated by the Commentators. The unifying force of a single common law represented a threat to the local power of the nobility, and they resisted the *Partidas* with such force that they were not officially recognized until 1348, in the *Ordenamiento de Alcalá,* also of the Kingdom of León and Castile. Even then the *Partidas* were regarded as supplementary only; the old *Fuero Juzgo* and subsequent local and municipal *fueros* (charters) also supplemented the new codification. The *Ordenamiento* was the most successful Spanish codification, if success is to be judged by the unifying results of the various codes. But doctrinally, the *Partidas* have been dominant, as Vélez Sársfield's draft code suggests.

When Columbus proclaimed Spanish sovereignty in the New World, he represented a unified Spain. The marriage of Ferdinand and Isabella in 1469 had united Aragon and Castile; 1492 saw both the first voyage of Columbus and the Battle of Granada, which expelled the last of the Moors from Spanish soil. In time, the Spanish monarchs enacted a considerable body of special statutory law to govern their new provinces. But always underlying the statutes was the law of Spain itself, heavily Romanized, and increasingly unified — increasingly so but never completely unified, even in our own time. The pattern of royal encouragement of codification in order to achieve unification appears over and over in Spain, as elsewhere in continental Europe. In 1567, the *Nueva Recopilación de las Leyes de España* was published; it was badly organized, and made no effort to do more than gather together the most important laws, leaving earlier compilations in force. Despite this defect, the compilation was retained, going through ten editions over the next 110 years. Then in 1805, a similar effort was published, this time called *Novísima Recopilación,* etc.; this was, if anything, less satisfactory than its predecessor. Throughout this time, the Roman law of the *Partidas* continued as a supplementary authority to the statutory compilations. An official order of authority was established, which generally gave greatest authority to the compilation of the day, next greatest to the next-most-recent, and so on.

The Colonies of the New World

There was a similar need for gathering together the laws, orders, and administrative authorities governing the colonies. No such compilation appeared, however, for nearly 200 years after the discovery. Finally, after a number of attempts which failed to bear fruit, in 1680 there appeared the *Recopilación de Leyes de los Reynos de Indias,* the Compilation of the Laws of the Kingdoms of the Indies. This was not a code of private law; it was a collection of over 6,300 items which included regulations issued from the home authorities to the colonial viceroys, letters to individual ministers or churchmen, and the like. It is dominated by what we should call public law. The *Partidas* and the *Fuero Juzgo* remained important for the resolution of ordinary private disputes in the Spanish New World.

The Spanish New World does not, of course, include Brazil, which was settled by the Portuguese after some high-level politicking. Back in 1454, Pope Nicholas V had conferred on Portugal the exclusive right to explore the only known route to the Indies, around the Cape of Good Hope. Columbus, seeking an alternate route for Spain, remained convinced that he had reached the Indies — Asia — until he died. When his "new route to Asia" was discovered, Spain claimed the right to exclusive exploration of that route. Pope Alexander VI agreed, and conferred exclusive title to lands beyond the Western Ocean on Spain. Exactly one day later, the representatives of Portugal protested, and the same Pope amended his ruling. He gave to Spain all the lands west of an imaginary line, running north to south a hundred leagues west of the Azores and the Cape Verde Islands. Since those islands are not even close to the same north-south line, confusion resulted. By treaty, the two powers compromised on a line running 370 leagues west of the Cape Verdes, or across the mouth of the Amazon. (They did not know there *was* an Amazon then.) Portugal colonized around the northeast coast of South America, and Spain on the rest of the continent.

Within less than a century after the voyages of Columbus, however, Spain and Portugal were united under Philip I. (Portugal had become a separate kingdom in 1153.) During his reign Philip had Portugal's legal scholars begin a new codification of the Portuguese laws, which had already been codified and re-codified, beginning in the late 14th century. The new codification was published during the reign of Philip II, in 1603, under the title *Ordenaçoes Philippinas,* or more commonly the *Código Philippino.* This Code remained in force and was the heart of Brazilian private law until the adoption of the Brazilian Civil Code of 1917. Its sources include:

> the Visigothic code [perhaps an intended reference to the *Fuero Juzgo?*] and the decretals of the councils, the customary law, the *foraes* [*cf. fueros*] or the municipal charters and statutes, the Roman law, as found in the Breviary of Alaric [meant to be distinguished from the Visigothic code?] and its subsidiary sources, the *Siete partidas,* the canon law with its later concordias, and the general legislation which commenced in 1211. BOR-CHARD, A GUIDE TO THE LAW AND LEGAL LITERATURE OF ARGENTINA, BRAZIL AND CHILE 228 (1917).

In 1643, soon after Portugal again became independent of Spain, Philip's Code was confirmed by the new Portuguese king. Thus the background of Portuguese law on which modern Brazilian law rests is not different in essentials from the Spanish background of the law of the other republics of Latin America. Both were Romanized, and both were loosely codified. In Brazil as in Spanish America, atop the private law system there were layers of various royal decrees and administrative orders relating to the Portuguese colonies. But there is no Portuguese counterpart to the Spanish *Recopilación* of New World laws; the only compilations were unofficial.

The Code Napoléon

The Roman foundation for Latin American civil law, as exemplified by Vélez Sársfield's citations to the Justinian legislation and to the *Siete Partidas,* was thus established early. But Vélez Sársfield did not limit himself to Roman sources, nor did the other Latin American code builders. They all drew heavily on the modern codes of western Europe, and particularly France. The Code Napoléon (*Code Civil*) is not by any means a wholly Romanized body of law, nor is the later German code. Both of those codes are compromises, in many ways reminiscent of the eclectic legislation of Alfonso the Wise.

Taking the Code Napoléon as our example, we must recognize that the law of matrimonial property, the law of wills and succession, even the legal treatment of the *bona fide* purchaser, as codified, constitute a marked departure from Roman law. The chief draftsmen of the code were four in number: two from northern France, where customary law still prevailed, and two from the south, thoroughgoing Romanists.

> Only a compromise could be the result of such a commission. But this aura of compromise was exactly what gave the Code its strength. For the northern neighbors, the Belgians, the Dutch, the Rhenish, recognized in it their own customs; conversely, the southern countries of Italy, Spain, Portugal, and Roumania recognized in it their own laws so far as these were derived from Roman law. Limpens, *Territorial Expansion of the Code,* in THE CODE NAPOLEON AND THE COMMON-LAW WORLD at 92, 104 (Schwartz ed. 1956).

As described by Professor Lawson, the principal Roman elements in the civil codes of modern Europe, and thus in those of Latin America — apart from particular substantive rules — are their universality (they apply to all persons, and not only to various classes or localities); their preoccupation with movement and change (transactions, not status); their division of types of actions (similar to the English forms of action); and their "institutional, literary quality." LAWSON, A COMMON LAWYER LOOKS AT THE CIVIL LAW 75, 91-106 (1953). But the same writer goes on to show how various non-Roman elements dominate certain portions of these codes, as noted above, and how some of the Roman elements themselves have been heightened. In his chapter entitled "The Advance Beyond Roman Law" (pp. 138-74), he describes the changes in classification and structure of the law which resulted from the "movement from remedies to rights," and the corresponding increase in generalization of concepts.

The Roman law, as we have seen, did not include a generalized law of obligations, or even contracts; by concentrating on specific kinds of actions for the attainment of justice in narrow classes of cases, the Roman law achieved much of the advantage of particularity which we associate with the common law. It did, however, sacrifice some of the coherence which comes of generalization and abstraction. The Romans, says Lawson, gave the modern world the notion that men could be governed by rational rules; the modern civilians have erected on that foundation a conceptual structure which is far more generalized, and — they would surely contend — thus more rational. Is this conclusion of Professor Lawson's not amply demonstrated by the excerpts from the Latin American treatise printed above?

This "advance" beyond the Roman law did not occur overnight upon the adoption of the modern European codes; it was gradual, so that the period of "reception" of Roman law saw its modification as well. Then why did a new codification result, if an adaptation of Roman law had already been made? Professor Lawson is again instructive, and he adds a note of special interest to us:

> All the original codes have been in countries which have just undergone a revolution and wish to recast their law quickly from top to bottom, or in countries which had in the past suffered from a diversity of legal systems or had just found themselves in that position because they had incorporated new territories governed by different laws. . . . In the Republics of Latin America, the civil codes are the effects of revolution. Revolution not only makes the successful revolutionaries wish to secure and consecrate their victory by giving it dogmatic form in a code, not only are the forces of resistance weakened, but the lawyers themselves may find it less troublesome, and even more convenient, to accept a new and rational system than to pick up again the broken threads of their traditional law. LAWSON, *id.*, at 49-51.

The revolution which threw off Spanish domination in Latin America began in 1810, just six years after the enactment of the Code Napoléon. That Code was in some ways symbolic of the Revolution in France, but it was even more symbolic of the stabilization of the new imperial regime. In fact the Code's appeal is undoubtedly partly traceable to a yearning for stability, as well as the desire for national uniformity. The Code's newness, its rationality, its clarity of syle all recomended it to the new Latin American countries. The fact that it was heavily influenced by Roman thought and forms meant that its adoption would not require a complete break with the legal systems of the past; witness the fact that Spain itself adopted a new civil code modeled on the Code Napoléon in 1889, after most of her former American colonies had already done so.

How should the problem on p. 112, *supra,* be decided under the *Code Civil?* Article 1110 of that Code cited in Vélez Sársfield's note, relates to error in general, and not expressly to error of law. Articles 1109 and 1110 read:

> 1109.   There is no valid consent if consent was given by error, extorted by duress or procured by fraud.
> 1110.   Error is not a ground for nullity of an agreement [*convention*] unless it goes to the very substance of the thing forming the object of the

contract. Error is not a ground for nullity when it goes only to the person with whom one intended to contract, unless the identity of the person was one of the agreement's main causes.

Then what effect is to be given to an error of law on the part of one of the contracting parties? Arguing from the text alone, does the conclusion not rest on the meaning of the term "substance"? If the word be taken restrictively, as the material of an object, then error of law is no ground for nullity of the agreement; if, however, it be taken more broadly, as the essential facts which form the motivation for contracting, then one of those facts might as well be the state of the law as the state of a physical object. The text of the Code does not elaborate, but the leading modern French treatise, following the case law, states that error of law is not to be distinguished from error of fact; either may — if the error relates to "substance" — serve as a ground for nullity of the agreement. The rule that ignorance or error of law does not excuse, it is said, is confined to the criminal law. 1 PLANIOL AND RIPERT, TREATISE ON THE CIVIL LAW § 280 (12th ed. 1939) (La. State Law Inst. translation 1959).

If we accept that statement as an accurate reflection of the French "rule," developed in the absence of a clear statement in the *Code Civil,* what are we to make of article 923 of the Argentine Civil Code? Vélez Sársfield's note cites with evident approval a strong statement by Pochonnet, a French writer, reinforcing the Roman rule that error of law does not excuse. But the note also cites a seemingly contrary comment by another French writer, about which Vélez Sársfield says:

> Rogron, in a long note to Art. 1110 of the French Code, maintains that error of law can be invoked as a ground for nullity of an act, when the error has motivated it, or when the act has for its foundation an error of law, because then the obligation, the contract, or the act remains without a cause.

The "legislative history" of the Argentine article is thus cloudy. Does Vélez Sársfield mean to show us that he recognizes the departure which the French law makes from the Roman rule, and that he wants to return to the Roman rule? Or does he mean to tell us that the sweeping language of article 923 must be read with a qualification? The following is another except from Dr. De Gásperi's treatise. As you read this excerpt, ask yourself these questions:

1.   Does codification relieve a judge from making law?

2.   Does it diminish the discretion of the judge as to the decision of a case?

3.   Does it permit men to order their affairs with greater certainty as to the governing law?

4.   Does article 923 dispose of Morales' claim in the problem case?

5.   How would you redraft article 923? Suppose you wanted to adopt the Roman rule; what language would you use? Suppose you wanted to reject

the Roman rule in favor of the French solution; would you choose the language which Vélez Sársfield chose?

DE GASPERI, TRATADO DE LAS OBLIGACIONES (1st ed. 1945)
Volume I, Chapter XXXIII. Of Error

§ 536.—ARTICLE 923.
* * *

The codifier's note, in which a paragraph of the work of Ernest Pochonnet is transcribed, could mislead one regarding the true meaning and extent of this precept [art. 923]. It could make one believe that the legislator wanted to incorporate the Roman rule according to which an error of law never excuses. In spite of this possible confusion, the doctrine of our Code is different from the Roman rule. According to the precept that we are studying [art. 923], error of law by itself cannot be invoked in order to obstruct the legal effects of lawful acts, nor to impede the placing of responsibility for unlawful acts. Pedro, in the action that he brings against Juan, neglects to produce the evidence pertaining to the action; but noticing this omission later, he opposes the closing of the period for giving evidence, claiming that he neglected to produce the evidence through ignorance of the legal obligation to do so. In this case, the error of law would not be excusable and would not hinder the fulfillment of the legal effects of his neglect: the excuse of the defendant and a judgment against the plaintiff for costs. The following example appears in the same case: as the legitimate heir, I have accepted an inheritance purely and simply, and now I ask to be released from that acceptance, because I did not know that the heir is obliged to pay the debts attached to the inheritance *ultra vires haereditatis*. [Or again], I ask the nullification of a sale contract because as the seller, I did not know that the law made it obligatory for me to give a guarantee as to the thing sold. Pochonnet adds that the maxim, *error juris nocet,* is very clear in meaning: it is the rule used against the person who tries to avoid the application of a police law, against the person who attempts to escape the legal consequences of a regular and valid juridical act, and against the person who tries to avoid the consequences of an expired period of time.

Among Argentine jurists there is no uniformity of opinion about this delicate question. Llerena, following the French writers, distinguishes the following: 1) cases in which the error of law is the determining cause of the act, and 2), those in which the error of law is not the determining cause of the act. In the first kind of case, the error of law is excusable and the act is void; in the second kind, neither is true. Machado is obscure on this point. Nevertheless, one can say that basically he accepts the French doctrine. Salvat

---

teaches that the article's rule has as its basis the principle that laws, once promulgated, are supposedly known by all the citizens of a country; according to him, this principle serves as a foundation for all social order. If the inhabitants of a country, he adds, could invoke ignorance of the law in order to escape the consequences of their acts, no order, no guarantee, no right could last. Instead, insecurity and anarchy would reign.

It is obvious that Salvat did not comprehend this question, which is different from what he discusses, as one can see in the explanation of the French doctrinaires, now accepted by Bibiloni. The question is about error of law as determining the will, which even the most prudent can undergo, without any blame on his part.

Bibiloni, supporting the comparison of error of law with error of fact, expresses himself thus: "The proscription of error of law made by Roman law cannot be justified. It is a dead prohibition in modern law. French law, under the influence of the doctrines of d'Aguesseau, has rejected it. If we accept that error can influence the manifestation of will, it does so whether it be an error of fact or of law. It is false that the law should be known by everyone. It suffices to open a law book in order to see that all law is a topic of discussion, and that the most eminent authorities are the object of constant impugnations. If such occurs with the specialists, with those considered to be best prepared to deal with the most delicate questions, what is to be expected of the average man? How can it be maintained that he is not allowed to commit an error, if the foremost writers . . . do so at every step? No. The law is obligatory on everyone, but from that it does not follow that everyone knows it and interprets it exactly, without error.

"It is for this reason that the modern Codes, without exception, have followed the French. The Italian Code, art. 1109, admits error of law about the cause of the act as a reason for invalidity. The German Code, despite the influence of the great Romanists in the development of German national law, does not establish any difference between the two classes of error. The Swiss Code of Obligations, art. 23 and following, does not mention any such difference either. The most eminent writers of all countries recognize the precision of the principle adopted by the Code Napoléon. It is no longer possible to speak of the different effects of error of fact and of law upon the validity of acts formed under their influence. If the strict interpretation of the Code did not permit it, it would be necessary to reform the Code in order to erase the classical and unfair difference between the kinds of error."

The Commission of Reform has accepted these observations of Bibiloni, as can be seen on page 17 of its Report, and in arts. 141 and 142 of its Projected Code. Article 21 of the Mexican Civil Code contains thue Roman rule in principle, but immediately, keeping in mind the notorious intellectual backwardness of some individuals, authorizes the judges to excuse them from the sanctions they have incurred. This doctrine was embraced by Ossorio in art. 3 of his Preliminary Project for a Bolivian Civil Code, in 1943.

The expression "in no case," used in art. 923, is discordant with art. 20, according to which there are cases in which the law expressly authorizes the allegation of error of law. These cases are the following:

1. That of art. 784, which says: "A person who believes himself to be in debt because of an error of fact or of law, and who gives a thing or a quantity of money in payment, has the right to demand its return from the person who received it";

2. That of art. 858; which provides: [for the rescission of a compromise agreement the object of which is the transfer of a void title];

3. That of art. 3428 which says: "The possessor of an inheritance is acting in good faith when, through an error of fact or of law he believes himself to be the legitimate owner of the estate that he holds."

In all these cases the error of law affects the intention of the actor. The writers of traditional law call the intention "cause," and thus, in these cases, they say that there is "erroneous cause."

It may be seen that in these important exceptions to the Roman rule, the legislator established the rule of the excusability of error of law whenever this error was determining of the motive to contract. To this should be added the requirement that there be no fault on the part of the person who alleges the error, that is, by the person who claims to have been misled. In this manner the Code has incorporated in its provisions the foundation of the doctrine about error of law perfected by French jurisprudence [case law] because of the silence of the Code Napoléon about it. It should be stated further that even if the error of law determines the motive to contract, and even though there be no fault on the part of the person who suffers the error, error of law cauld not be invoked in order to nullify the application of a law of public order, such as the penal law or the law of civil marriage. The argument would be accepted, instead, in the case of a merely dispositive law.

In sum, the tendency of modern law is to compare error of fact with error of law, as one sees in the German Civil Code, in the Swiss Federal Code of Obligations, in the Brazilian Code, in the Chinese, in the Mexican, in the Italo-French Project of a Code of Obligations and Contracts, in the Preliminary Reform Project to the Argentine Civil Code and, finally, in the Bolivian Preliminary Project. [See also Arts. 521-22 of Dr. De Gásperi's projected new Civil Code for Paraguay, p. 85, *supra.* — Ed.]

[In addition to the citations in the text, see VANCE, THE BACKGROUND OF HISPANIC-AMERICAN LAW (1943); WALTON, THE CIVIL LAW IN SPAIN AND SPANISH AMERICA (1900); ASSO AND DEL RIO, INSTITUTES OF THE CIVIL LAW OF SPAIN (6th ed. 1805; Johnston translation 1825); SHERMAN, ROMAN LAW IN THE MODERN WORLD (3d ed. 1937); MACKINTOSH, THE ROMAN LAW OF SALE (2d ed. 1907); MOYLE, THE CONTRACT OF SALE IN THE CIVIL LAW (1892); SCHLESINGER, COMPARATIVE LAW CASES, TEXT, MATERIALS 168-98 (2d ed. 1959); PALMER, GUIDE TO THE LAW AND LEGAL LITERATURE OF SPAIN (1915); Lobingier, *The Modern Expansion of the Roman Law,* 6 U. CINN. L. REV. 152 (1932); SCHOENRICH, THE CIVIL CODE OF MEXICO iii-xii (1950); WHELESS, THE CIVIL CODE OF BRAZIL ix-xvi (1920). — Ed.]

B. Some Michigan Solutions

The materials which follow are a sample of the case law, in one substantive area, created by a single court over a period of one century. The subject matter is parallel to that treated in the foregoing Argentine materials; one useful way to review the preceding section will be to ask, with respect to each of these Michigan cases: How would this case be decided in Argentina?

Comparative analysis of that kind is only one of the goals of this section. An additional focus of analysis will be on a comparison of the sources of law and the decisional methods operative in Michigan and in Argentina. Because this section emphasizes the building of case law, the cases are presented in chronological order. The note cases, most of which are also listed in time sequence, do not necessarily relate closely (in a doctrinal sense) to the principal cases that they follow.

PICARD v. McCORMICK
11 Mich. 68 (1862)

Error to Washtenaw Circuit, where McCormick recovered judgment against Picard for false representations of the value of watches and other jewelry for which plaintiff had bargained with defendant at four hundred dollars, and paid in a horse at $160, and the balance in notes. The declaration and the objections made to a recovery under it are sufficiently stated in the opinion.

After the evidence was in, the Circuit Judge charged the jury as follows: "It is a rule of law that a mere assertion of value made by the seller, when no warranty is intended, is no ground of relief to a purchaser, because the assertion is a matter of opinion which does not imply knowledge, and in which men differ. Every person reposes at his peril in the opinions of others, when he has equal opportunity to form and exercise his own judgment.

"This rule applies only when the vendor and vendee rely upon their own judgment. But when the vendee expressly relies upon the knowledge of the vendor as to quality or value of the article of sale, the vendor is bound to act honorably and deal fairly with the vendee. When confidence is reposed in the vendor he is bound not to abuse it, and the rule of *caveat emptor* does not apply.

"When one piece of property is given for another, without regard to value, that is an exchange; but where one piece of property is sold at a price, and other property is by the same contract received in part payment at a price, and the balance in money, this is a sale and not an exchange.

"It is contended by defendant's counsel that the bill of sale is the evidence of the contract, and can not be contradicted by the parol evidence. Though the contract be in writing, if the defendant has been dishonest in the transaction, the plaintiff may disregard the writing and sue directly for the fraud."

CAMPBELL, J.:

McCormick sued Picard to recover damages on account of false representations whereby the former was induced to purchase of the latter watches and other jewelry to a large amount.

The declaration contains several different counts, and, inasmuch as it is claimed that all or some of them are fatally defective, it becomes necessary to refer to them.

The first count avers the ignorance of plaintiff concerning the value and quality of the articles sold, the defendant's knowledge of such ignorance, he himself being a skillful dealer in such goods, the application by defendant to McCormick to induce him to purchase, the refusal of McCormick to do so except in reliance upon Picard's representations, and a sale based on fraudulent representations of the value of the property, whereby the purchaser was damnified.

The second count is for a breach of warranty of value, by which Picard knowingly, falsely and fraudulently deceived McCormick.

The third count is for false representations concerning the value and quantity of gold in a necklace which Picard, knowing McCormick's ignorance, induced him to purchase by such representations.

The fourth and fifth counts are framed like the first, but upon different representations.

The principal objection alleged against these several counts (which is taken on assignment of error and not by demurrer) goes to the materiality of the frauds charged. It is claimed that an allegation of value, although false, can not be made the ground of an action.

It is undoubtedly true that value is usually a mere matter of opinion; and that a purchaser must expect that a vendor will seek to enhance his wares, and must disregard his statements of their value. But, while this is generally the case, yet we are aware of no rule which determines arbitrarily that any class of fraudulent misrepresentations can be exempted from the consequences attached to others. Where a purchaser, without negligence has been induced by the arts of a cheating seller to rely upon material statements which are knowingly false, and is thereby damnified, it can make no difference in what respect he has been deceived, if the deceit was material and relied on. It is only because statements of value can rarely be supposed to have induced a purchase without negligence, that the authorities have laid down the principle that they can not usually avoid a bargain. But value may frequently be made by the parties themselves the principal element in a contract; and there are many cases where articles possess a standard commercial value, in which it is a chief criterion of quality among those who are not experts. It is a matter of every day occurrence to find various grades of manufactured articles known more generally by their prices than by any test of their quality which can be furnished by ordinary inspection. Frauds are easily committed by dishonest dealers, by confounding these grades, and can not be detected in many cases except by persons of experience. In the case before us the alleged fraud consisted of false statements by a jeweller to an unskilled purchaser of the value of articles which none but an expert could be reasonably supposed to understand. The dealer knew of the purchaser's ignorance, and deliberately and designedly availed himself of it to defraud him. We think that it can not be laid down as a matter of law that value is never a material fact; and we think the circumstances of this case illustrate the impropriety of any such rule. They show a plain and aggravated case of cheating. And it would be a deserved reproach to the law if it exempted any specific fraud from its remedial action, where a fact is stated and relied upon, whatever may be the general difficulty of defrauding by means of it. The same reasoning will dispose of the objection that in the second count the representations are not set out as having been relied upon, or as having been made in deliberate breach of confidence. If value can be regarded in any case as a material fact, then it may be made the subject of a warranty. This count is in the usual from for breach of a fraudulent warranty, and is therefore good.

* * *

Upon the trial, one of the witnesses having detailed the false representations made by Picard to McCormick, concerning the watches, one of which was set with diamonds on the outside, was asked "what was said about the jewels?" This was objected to because the declaration alleged no representation about the jewels, but the objection was over-ruled, and the witness swore Picard said if the watch was smashed up the diamonds would be worth seventy dollars. The question was not improper. . . .

Exception was also taken to the charge of the Court upon the circumstances under which a vendor becomes liable for misrepresentation. We think the rule laid down remarkably clear and entirely correct. We also think the distinction between a sale and an exchange of property was properly taken. If property is taken at a fixed money price, the transfer amounts to a sale whether the price is paid in cash or in goods. The term *sale* is comprehensive, and embraces all transfers for a price named, whether confined to that class or not.

There is no error in the proceeding, and the judgment must be affirmed, with costs.

The other Justices concurred.

SWIMM V. BUSH, 23 Mich. 99 (1871): Bush, who lived in Pennsylvania, owned a farm near Owosso, Michigan; he had been negotiating for its sale with various persons. Swimm, who lived near Bush's land, went to Pennsylvania. He "gave Bush to understand that Owosso was not flourishing . . .; that property was declining, and that the farm itself was in very bad condition, as he described it; which was not a very great exaggeration. He, when asked concerning the value of the land, said it was not worth four thousand nor three thousand dollars, and that he had not expected to pay more than twenty-eight hundred dollars, but that he would give three thousand, as his wife was born on it and had an affection for it, ..." The last statement was false, as was the derogatory statement about Owosso's prospects. "The land was in demand and was worth more than four thousand dollars, and the purchaser knew this, and went down to Pennsylvania on purpose to prevent other offers from reaching Bush, ... He induced Bush to abstain from that deliberation which would have inevitably defeated the scheme." When Swimm sought specific performance, Bush defended "on the ground that the contract was obtained fraudulently and is unconscionable." A decree for the plaintiff was reversed, the court citing *Picard v. McCormick,* p. 133, *supra.*

WHITING V. HILL, 23 Mich. 399 (1871): Defendants bought a salt well, salt blocks, buildings and machinery from plaintiffs, giving a mortgage on the purchased property to secure the price. When plaintiffs sued to foreclose, defendants claimed damages in reduction of the amount due, for misrepresentation by plaintiffs "concerning the strength and quantity of the brine and its freedom from gypsum," which the court conceded to be known by the plaintiffs to be untrue. These representations were made sixteen days before the first payment was made; in the meanwhile, defendants had been in possession of the property, working it. The defendants "had abundant opportunity to verify the truth of whatever representations had been made of the conditions then existing." Held, for plaintiffs, reversing the trial court: " . . . however fraudulent and wicked a representation may be, if the innocent party, before being tied and while in a situation to retreat without prejudice, in any manner becomes acquainted with the truth, the misrepresentation will not be a ground of defense against the contract."

STEINBACH V. HILL, 25 Mich. 78 (1872): The purchaser of a lot in Detroit sought rescission of the executed purchase contract. "The alleged fraud consisted in representing the lot as embracing all that was enclosed by the fences surrounding it, when in truth it fell short on one side some seventeen or eighteen inches, and the rear part of the house extended a few inches over the line." The court held that the evidence established that the house was entirely on the lot. "We are not satisfied from the evidence that there has been any intention to commit a fraud in this case. Nevertheless if complainant had been deceived into a purchase by the acts or representations of defendants, however innocently done or made, and if the deception regarded the essentials of the contract, and worked a serious injury to the complainant, we might feel ourselves justified in affirming the decree, which set aside the sale. But it is not claimed that there was any special or peculiar value in the strip of four and a half inches which will be lost [instead of the 17 inches claimed by the complainant], and its value, estimating it in proportion to the price paid for the whole lot, would only be twenty-five dollars or thereabouts." Such damage is too insignificant to justify rescission; the bill must be dismissed, "but without prejudice to any remedy at law."

KOST V. BENDER, 25 Mich. 515 (1872): Defendant bought land from plaintiff, giving a note as part of the purchase price. In a suit on the note, defendant defends on the ground that plaintiff misrepresented "the surface indications that oil was to be found upon the land, the fact that it had been found in abundance, and that the land, even if not valuable for oil, would sell for a high price for farming lands. A judgment for defendant was reversed on several grounds. By way of dictum, however, the court made the following observations:

"It is alleged [by plaintiff] for error, that the court erred in giving a rule of damages to the jury which did not exclude from consideration the opinions expressed by the plaintiff, as to the value of the land, in the course of the negotiations. The position of the defendant is, that the plaintiff professed to have peculiar scientific knowledge, which enabled him to express reliable opinions as to the probability of the lands proving valuable for the production of oil; that the defendant relied upon these professions, and was deceived by the false opinions which the plaintiff expressed. If the defendant gave evidence tending to prove this case, we do not think the court erred in laying down the rule of damages. Perhaps some portion of the charge was not sufficiently guarded in language, but the liability of a party for a false opinion, under such circumstances, is well settled. *Picard v. McCormick*, [p. 133, *supra*,] 11 Mich., 68."

STARKWEATHER v. BENJAMIN
32 Mich. 305 (1875)

CAMPBELL, J.:

This action was brought to recover damages arising from alleged misrepresentations made by Starkweather to Benjamin, concerning the quantity of land in a parcel purchased from Starkweather and others for whom he acted, and which was bought by the acre.

The defense rested mainly on the ground that the purchaser saw the land, and was as able to judge of its size as Starkweather.

We do not think the doctrine, that where both parties have equal means of judging there is no fraud, applies to such a case. The maxim is equally valid, that one who dissuades another from inquiry and deceives him to his prejudice is responsible. It cannot be generally true that persons can judge of the contents of a parcel of land by the eye. When any approach to accuracy is needed, there must be measurement. When a positive assurance of the area of a parcel of land is made by the vendor to the vendee, with the design of making the vendee believe it, that assurance is very material, and equivalent to an assurance of measurement. In this case the testimony goes very far, and shows that the assertions and representations, which the jury must have found to be true, were of such a nature that if believed, as they were, a re-survey must have been an idle ceremony. They were calculated to deceive, and, as the jury have found, they did deceive Benjamin, and he had a clear right of action for the fraud.

It is alleged an error also, that the court should not have ruled out the common rumors concerning the size of the land, nor the instructions claimed by Starkweather to have been given him by the other owners, to sell the land as a parcel, and not by the acre.

It would be absurd to allow street talk about the size of a farm to rebut the conclusions of fraud arising out of positive untruths. It is certainly not presumable that others will know better than the parties interested; and even if such rumors had been multiplied and brought home to Benjamin, he would be justified in believing Starkweather's statements based on better knowledge.

If Starkweather was instructed by the other heirs not to sell by the acre, that fact would not affect the purchaser who bought in that way. If the sale was valid at all, Starkweather could not get rid of liability for fraud, by showing another and additional act of wrongdoing. It could not undo the effect of the falsehood.

There is no error in the record, and the judgment must be affirmed, with costs.

The other Justices concurred.

GIBSON v. PELKIE
37 Mich. 380 (1877)

GRAVES, J. The right Gibson asserts is based solely on an alleged special agreement entitling him to collect so much as he might of a specific judgment and to retain one-half of the sum collected. According to his own statement of his case, the judgment was the exclusive subject-matter of the agreement relied on. No other demand or form of demand entered into the bargain. The parties had nothing else in their minds. They did not assume to contract about an unliquidated claim or an unadjudicated cause of action, the enforcement of which in Pelkie's name might involve him in a much larger liability than would be likely to attend the collection of a judgment. It was a judgment which formed the subject-matter of the bargain. Such was the claim made by the declaration, and such was the case in issue. No other ground for recovery appears. Now, there was no proof of a judgment; but there was evidence concerning one, and it seems to have been in effect conceded that there was something which had been taken to be a judgment, but which was so defective that it could not avail any thing.

The case must be viewed as it is. It is not admissible to arbitrarily admit one part and reject another. If what there is to show that the supposed judgment was void, is rejected, then all there is to make out the existence of any such judgment will be stricken out, and if that be done there will be no proof whatever of the essence of the cause of action set up. There will be no showing that there was any subject-matter for the alleged agreement and no proof to maintain the actual averments of the declaration. The cause is presented here by both sides upon the theory that there was something which was intended as a judgment, but which was void and hence uncollectible, and the plaintiff in error cannot ask a more favorable view of the record. If then there was a proceeding which was meant to be a judgment, but which was void, there was nothing to which the actual bargaining could attach. There was no subject-matter. The parties supposed there was a judgment, and negotiated and agreed on that basis, but there was none. Where they assumed there was substance, there was no substance. They made no contract because the thing they supposed to exist, and the existence of which was indispensable to the institution of the contract, had no existence. *Allen v. Hammond,* 11 Pet., 63; *Suydam v. Clark,* 2 Sandf. Sup'r Court Rep., 133; *Gove v. Wooster,* Lalor's Supp. to Hill & Den., 30; *Smidt v. Tiden,* L.R., 9 Q.B., 446: 9 Eng., 379; *Couturier v. Hastie,* 5 H.L. 673; *Hazard v. New England Ins. Co.,* 1 Sumn. 218; *Silvernail v. Cole,* 12 Barb., 685; *Sherman v. Barnard,* 19 Barb., 291; Metcalf on Cont., 30, 31; 1 Poth. Ob. by Evans, 113; Benjamin on Sales, Sections 76, 77, Ch., 4; 2 Kent Com., 468. It is therefore the opinion of a majority of the court that the judgment in Pelkie's favor ought not to be disturbed.

Judgment is affirmed with costs.

COOLEY, C. J., and CAMPBELL, J., concurred.

NOWLIN v. SNOW
40 Mich. 699 (1879)

TRESPASS ON THE CASE by Nowlin, who declares that Snow represented to him that he wished to sell or exchange certain real estate in Kansas worth certain specified sums, and that Nowlin, relying on his representations exchanged for it some land in Dearborn, Wayne Country, Michigan, Snow agreeing to assume a certain mortgage, pay back taxes on the Kansas lands, and also to pay Nowlin $1,200; he further alleges that Snow's representations as to the value and local advantages of the land were false and fraudulent, and claims damages. The court charged the jury to find for defendant and plaintiff brings error.

[Counsel for plaintiff cited a large number of cases, including *Picard v. McCormick,* p. 133, *supra;* the dictum in *Kost v. Bender,* p. 137, *supra;* and *Starkweather v. Benjamin,* p. 138, *supra.*]

MARSTON, J. We are clearly of opinion that the court erred in withdrawing this case from the consideration of the jury. It is not very important whether we call the transaction between the parties a sale or an exchange, although we think the latter the more correct term. At the time the exchange was made, the parties did not stand upon an equal footing. The plaintiff had no knowledge whatever of the Kansas property except what he derived from the defendant, who claimed to have personal knowledge during the negotiations. The representations made could in no way be considered as mere matter of opinion as to the value of the land, or as to its location. The representations were distinct and important, and if found to have been made and that they were untrue in fact, and that plaintiff in making the exchange relied upon the representations made, then clearly he was entitled to recover. The case should have been submitted to the jury under proper instructions.

The judgment must be reversed with costs and a new trial ordered.

The other Justices concurred.

SHERWOOD v. WALKER
66 Mich. 568, 33 N.W. 919 (1887)

MORSE, J.   Replevin for a cow. Suit commenced in justice's court. Judgment for plaintiff. Appealed to circuit court of Wayne Country, and verdict and judgment for plaintiff in that court. The defendants bring error, and set out 25 assignments of the same.

The main controversy depends upon the construction of a contract for the sale of the cow.

The plaintiff claims that the title passed, and bases his action upon such claim.

The defendants contend that the contract was executory, and by its terms no title to the animal was acquired by plaintiff.

The defendants reside at Detroit, but are in business at Walkerville, Ontario, and have a farm at Greenfield, in Wayne Country, upon which were some blooded cattle supposed to be barren as breeders. The Walkers are importers and breeders of polled Angus cattle.

The plaintiff is a banker living at Plymouth, in Wayne Country. He called upon the defendants at Walkerville for the purchase of some of their stock, but found none there that suited him. Meeting one of the defendants afterwards, he was informed that they had a few head upon this Greenfield farm. He was asked to go out and look at them, with the statement at the time that they were probably barren, and would not breed.

May 5, 1886, plaintiff went out to Greenfield and saw the cattle. A few days thereafter, he called upon one of the defendants with the view of purchasing a cow, known as "Rose 2d of Aberlone." After considerable talk, it was agreed that defendants would telephone Sherwood at his home in Plymouth in reference to the price. The second morning after this talk he was called up by telephone, and the terms of the sale were finally agreed upon. He was to pay five and one-half cents per pound, live weight, fifty pounds shrinkage. He was asked how he intended to take the cow home, and replied that he might ship her from King's cattle-yard. He requested defendants to confirm the sale in writing, which they did . . . .

* * *

On the twenty-first of the same month the plaintiff went to defendants' farm at Greenfield, and presented the order and letter to Graham, who informed him that the defendants had instructed him not to deliver the cow. Soon after, the plaintiff tendered to Hiram Walker, one of the defendants, $80, and demanded the cow. Walker refused to take the money or deliver the cow. The plaintiff then instituted this suit.

After he had secured possession of the cow under the writ of replevin, the plaintiff caused her to be weighed by the constable who served the writ, at a place other than King's cattle-yard. She weighed 1,420 pounds.

* * *

The defendants then introduced evidence tending to show that at the time of the alleged sale it was believed by both the plaintiff and themselves that the cow was barren and would not breed; that she cost $850, and if not barren would be worth from $750 to $1,000; that after the date of the letter, and the order to Graham, the defendants were informed by said Graham that in his judgment the cow was with calf, and therefore they instructed him not to deliver her to plaintiff, and on the twentieth of May, 1886, telegraphed to the plaintiff what Graham thought about the cow being with calf, and that consequently they could not sell her. The cow had a calf in the month of October following. [We have it on the authority of DAWSON AND PALMER, CASES ON RESTITUTION 595 (1958), that the normal gestation period for a cow is nine months.]

[The court agreed with the trial judge that title had passed to the plaintiff.]

* * *

It appears from the record that both parties supposed this cow was barren and would not breed, and she was sold by the pound for an insignificant sum as compared with her real value if a breeder. She was evidently sold and purchased on the relation of her value for beef, unless the plaintiff had learned of her true condition, and concealed such knowledge from the defendants. Before the plaintiff secured possession of the animal, the defendants learned that she was with calf, and therefore of great value, and undertook to rescind the sale by refusing to deliver her. The question arises whether they had a right to do so.

The circuit judge ruled that this fact did not avoid the sale, and it made no difference whether she was barren or not. I am of the opinion that the court erred in this holding. I know that this is a close question, and the dividing line between the adjudicated cases is not easily discerned. But it must be considered as well settled that a party who has given an apparent consent to a contract of sale may refuse to execute it, or he may avoid it after it has been completed, if the assent was founded, or the contract made, upon the mistake of a material fact, — such as the subject-matter of the sale, the price, or some collateral fact materially inducing the agreement; and this can be done when the mistake is mutual. 1 Benj. Sales, Sections 605, 606; Leake, Cont. 339; Story, Sales (4th ed.), Sections 148, 377. See, also *Cutts v. Guild,* 57 N.Y. 229; *Harvey v. Harris,* 112 Mass. 32; *Gardner v. Lane,* 9 Allen, 492; S.C. 12 Allen, 44; *Hutchmacher v. Harris' Adm'rs,* 38 Penn. St. 491; *Byers v. Chapin,* 28 Ohio St. 300; *Gibson v. Pelkie,* 37 Mich. 380, and cases cited; *Allen v. Hammond,* 11 Pet. 63, 71.

If there is a difference or misapprehension as to the substance of the thing bargained for, if the thing actually delivered or received is different in substance from the thing bargained for and intended to be sold, then there is no contract; but if it be only a difference in some quality or accident, even though the mistake may have been the actuating motive to the purchaser or seller, or both of them, yet the contract remains binding.

"The difficulty in every case is to determine whether the mistake or misapprehension is as to the substance of the whole contract, going, as it were, to the root of the matter, or only to some point, even though a material point, an

error as to which does not affect the substance of the whole consideration."
Kennedy v. Panama, etc., Mail Co., L.R. 2 Q.B. 580, 588.

It has been held, in accordance with the principles above stated, that
where a horse is bought under the belief that he is sound, and both vendor
and vendee honestly believe him to be sound, the purchaser must stand by his
bargain, and pay the full price, unless there was a warranty.

It seems to me, however, in the case made by this record, that the mistake
or misapprehension of the parties went to the whole substance of the agreement. If the cow was a breeder, she was worth at least $750; if barren, she was
worth not over $80. The parties would not have made the contract of sale ex-
cept upon the understanding and belief that she was incapable of breeding, and
of no use as a cow. It is true she is now the identical animal that they thought
her to be when the contract was made; there is no mistake as to the identity
of the creature. Yet the mistake was not of the mere quality of the animal,
but went to the very nature of the thing. A barren cow is substantially a different creature than a breeding one. There is as much difference between them
for all purposes of use as there is between an ox and a cow that is capable of
breeding and giving milk. If the mutual mistake had simply related to the fact
whether she was with calf or not for one season, then it might have been a
good sale; but the mistake affected the character of the animal for all time;
and for her present and ultimate use. She was not in fact the animal, or the
kind of animal, the defendants intended to sell or the plaintiff to buy. She was
not a barren cow, and, if this fact had been known there would have been no
contract. The mistake affected the substance of the whole consideration, and it
must be considered that there was no contract to sell or sale of the cow as she
actually was. The thing sold and bought had in fact no existence. She was sold
as a beef creature would be sold; she is in fact a breeding cow, and a valuable
one.

The court should have instructed the jury that if they found that the cow
was sold, or contracted to be sold, upon the understanding of both parties that
she was barren, and useless for the purpose of breeding, and that in fact she
was not barren, but capable of breeding, then the defendants had a right to
rescind, and to refuse to deliver, and the verdict should be in their favor.

The judgment of the court below must be reversed, and a new trial granted, with costs of this Court to defendants.

CAMPBELL, C.J., and CHAMPLIN, J., concurred.

SHERWOOD, J. *(dissenting).* I do not concur in the opinion given by my
brethren in this case. I think the judgments before the justice and at the circuit
were right.

I agree with my Brother MORSE that the contract made was not within
the statute of frauds, and that payment for the property was not a condition
precedent to the passing of the title from the defendants to the plaintiff. And
I further agree with him that the plaintiff was entitled to a delivery of the

property to him when the suit was brought, unless there was a mistake made which would invalidate the contract; and I can find no such mistake.

There is no pretense that there was any fraud or concealment in the case, and an intimation or insinuation that such a thing might have existed on the part of either of the parties would undoubtedly be a greater surprise to them than anything else that has occurred in their dealings or in the case.

    * * *

There is no question but that the defendants sold the cow representing her of the breed and quality they believed the cow to be, and that the purchaser so understood it. And the buyer purchased her believing her to be of the breed represented by the sellers, and possessing all the qualities stated, and even more. He believed she would breed. There is no pretense that the plaintiff bought the cow for beef, and there is nothing in the record indicating that he would have bought her at all only that he thought she might be made to breed. Under the foregoing facts, — and these are all that are contained in the record material to the contract, — it is held that because it turned out that the plaintiff was more correct in his judgment as to one quality of the cow than the defendants, and a quality, too, which could not by any possibility be positively known at the time by either party to exist, the contract may be annulled by the defendants at their pleasure. I know of no law, and have not been referred to any, which will justify any such holding, and I think the circuit judge was right in his construction of the contract between the parties.

It is claimed that a mutual mistake of a material fact was made by the parties when the contract of sale was made. There was no warranty in the case of the quality of the animal. When a mistaken fact is realied upon as ground for rescinding, such fact must not only exist at the time the contract is made, but must have been known to one or both of the parties. Where there is no warranty, there can be no mistake of fact when no such fact exists, or, if in existence, neither party knew of it, or could know of it; and that is precisely this case. If the owner of a Hambletonian horse had speeded him, and was only able to make him go a mile in three minutes, and should sell him to another, believing that was his greatest speed, for $300, when the purchaser believed he could go much faster, and made the purchase for that sum, and a few days thereafter, under more favorable circumstances, the horse was driven a mile in 2 min. 16 sec., and was found to be worth $20,000, I hardly think it would be held, either at law or in equity, by any one, that the seller in such case could rescind the contract. The same legal principles apply in each case.

In this case neither party knew the actual quality and condition of this cow at the time of the sale. The defendants say, or rather said, to the plaintiff, "they had a few head left on their farm in Greenfield, and asked plaintiff to go and see them, stating to plaintiff that in all probability they were sterile and would not breed." Plaintiff did go as requested, and found there three cows, including the one purchased, with a bull. The cow had been exposed, but neither knew she was with calf or whether she would breed. The defendants thought she would not, but the plaintiff says that he thought she could be made to breed, but believed she was not with calf. The defendants sold the cow for what they believed her to be, and the plaintiff bought her as he believed she was, after the statements made by the defendants. No conditions whatever were attached to the terms of sale by either party. It was in fact as absolute as it could well be made, and I know of no precedent as authority by which this Court can alter the contract thus made by these parties in writing, and interpolate in it a condition by which, if the *defendants should be mistaken in their belief that the cow was barren,* she should be returned to them, and their contract should be annulled.

It is not the duty of courts to destory contracts when called upon to enforce them, after they have been legally made. There was no mistake of any such material fact by either of the parties in the case as would license the vendors to rescind. There was no difference between the parties, nor misapprehension, as to the substance of the thing bargained for, which was a cow supposed to be barren by one party, and believed not to be by the other. As to the quality of the animal, subsequently developed, both parties were equally ignorant, and as to this each party took his chances. If this were not the law, there would be no safety in purchasing this kind of stock.

I entirely agree with my brethren that the right to rescind occurs whenever "the thing actually delivered or received is different in substance from the thing bargained for, and intended to be sold; but if it be only a difference in some quality or accident, even though the misapprehension may have been the actuating motive" of the parties in making the contract, yet it will remain binding. In this case the cow sold was the one delivered. What might or might not happen to her after the sale formed no element in the contract.

The case of *Kennedy v. Panama, etc., Mail Co.,* L.R. 2 Q.B. 588, and the extract cited therefrom in the opinion of my brethren, clearly sustain the views I have taken. See, also, *Smith v. Hughes,* L.R. 6 Q.B. 597; *Carter v. Crick,* 4 Hurl. & N. 416.

According to this record, whatever the mistake was, if any, in this case, it was upon the part of the defendants, and while acting upon their own judgment. It is, however, elementary law, and very elementary, too, "that the mistaken party, acting entirely upon his own judgment, without any common understanding with the other party in the premises as to the quality of an animal, is remediless if he is injured through his own mistake." Leake, Cont. 338; *Torrance v. Bolton,* L.R. 8 Ch. App. 118; *Smith v. Hughes,* L.R. 6 Q.B. 597.

The case cited by my brethren from 37 Mich. *(Gibson v. Pelkie)* I do not think sustains the conclusion reached by them. In that case the subject-matter about which the contract was made had no existence, and in such case Mr. Justice GRAVES held there was no contract; and to the same effect are all the authorities cited in the opinion. That is certainly not this case. Here the defendants claim the subject-matter not only existed, but was worth about $800 more than the plaintiff paid for it.

The case of *Hutchmacher v. Harris' Adm'rs,* 38 Penn. St. 491, is this: A party purchased at an administrator's sale a drill-machine, which had hid away in it by the deceased a quantity of notes, to the amount of about $3,000, money to the amount of over $500, and two silver watches and a pocket compass of the value of $60.25. In an action of trover for the goods, it was held that nothing but the machine was sold or passed to the purchaser, neither party knowing that the machine contained any such articles.

[The judge distinguishes the other cases cited by the majority.]

* * *

In *Harvey v. Harris,* 112 Mass. 32, at an auction two different grades of flour were sold, and a purchaser of the second claimed to have bought a quantity of the first grade, under a sale made of the second, and this he was not allowed to do, because of the mutual mistake; the purchaser had not in fact bought the flour he claimed. In this case, however, it is said it is true that, if there is a mutual agreement of the parties for the sale of particular articles of property, a mistake or misapprehension as to the quality of the articles will not enable the vendor to repudiate the sale.

The foregoing are all the authorities relied on as supporting the positions taken by my brethren in this case. I fail to discover any similarity between them and the present case; and I must say, further, in such examination as I have been able to make, I have found no adjudicated case going to the extent, either in law or equity, that has been held in this case. In this case, if either party had superior knowledge as to the qualities of this animal to the other, certainly the defendants had such advantage.

I understand the law to be well settled that "there is no breach of any implied confidence that one party will not profit by his superior knowledge as to facts and circumstances" equally within the knowledge of both, because neither party reposes in any such confidence unless it be specially tendered or required, and that a general sale does not imply warranty of any quality, or the absence of any; and if the seller represents to the purchaser what he himself believes as to the qualities of an animal, and the purchaser buys relying upon his own judgment as to such qualities, there is no warranty in the case, and neither has a cause of action against the other if he finds himself to have been mistaken in judgment.

The only pretense for avoiding this contract by the defendants is that they erred in judgment as to the qualities and value of the animal. I think the principles adopted by Chief Justice CHRISTIANCY in *Williams v. Spurr,* 24 Mich. 335, completely cover this case, and should have been allowed to control in its decision. See, also, Story, Sales, Sections 174, 175, 382, and Benj. Sales, Section 430.

The judgment should be affirmed.

[In the *Spurr* case, cited by Judge Sherwood, an iron ore speculator had bought land believing it to contain some iron. He then sold it to others at a price in excess of the land's value for timber, calling it "iron land." The buyers made their own investigation and found a deposit of iron ore which made the land substantially more valuable than the seller realized. They said that they were buying only for the timber. This misrepresentation was held not to be sufficient to upset the transaction. — Ed.]

[With respect to the *Sherwood* case and the problem of "basic mistake," see PALMER, MISTAKE AND UNJUST ENRICHMENT, Ch. I (1962). See also Professor York's book review of the Palmer book, 11 U.C.L.A. L. REV. 653 (1964). — Ed.]

NESTER V. THE MICHIGAN LAND & IRON CO., 69 Mich. 290, 37 N.W. 278 (1888): The buyer of timber sued to compel the seller to accept less than half the agreed purchase price, on the ground that the seller's agents had represented the quantity of timber on the lands in question to be twice the true quantity. The evidence was strongly against the complainant's version of the representations; it seemed clear to the court that the seller had made clear that the buyer should not rely on the seller's estimates, which were only that. Sherwood, C. J. wrote for the court: "I hardly think counsel for complainant would think it equitable or just, if, when the timber was cut, it had been found to contain twice the number of feet either party had estimated, that the complainant should be held to pay defendant $54,000, instead of $27,000 as promised. ... We know of no case which will sustain the complainant's case upon the facts before us. That of *Sherwood v. Walker,* [p. 140, *supra,*] 66 Mich. 568 (33 N.W. Rep. 919), will come the nearest to it of any referred to. That is, however, somewhat different upon its facts, and the rule applied in that case can never be resorted to except in a case where all the facts and circumstances are precisely the same as in that." Morse, J. did not sit.

McKAY V. COLEMAN, 85 Mich. 60, 48 N.W. 203 (1891): Plaintiff sued to recover a $100 deposit, paid by him as the high bidder at an administrator's sale of land. When the deed was tendered, plaintiff refused to accept it, since he had discovered that a building on the land, "believed at the time of the sale to be entirely on the land advertised for sale," was in fact partly on another lot. Held, for plaintiff. "This case is ruled by the principles laid down in *Sherwood v. Walker,* [p. 140, *supra,*] 66 Mich. 568. There was a mutual mistake of fact as to the condition of the property. There was evidently a wide difference in value between the property as it actually was and as it was understood by both parties to be."

HOLCOMB v. NOBLE
69 Mich. 396, 37 N.W. 497 (1888)

CAMPBELL, J.   This action is on the case to recover damages for misrepresentation of the value and quality of certain lands. The plaintiff was shown to have been deceived, to his damage, concerning the lands, and there is no real dispute concerning it. The only defense which has any plausibility is that no actual fraud was intended.

The fact that the declaration contains charges of fraudulent and deceitful purposes does not in itself have any bearing on this question, or compel plaintiff to prove it. Such allegations were contained formerly in nearly every action on the case, and are of no more importance in pleading than the allegations of diabolical instigation in an indictment for misdemeanor. The forms of declaration in 2 Chit. Pl. upon torts exemplify this. It is probably true that, where fraud is not alleged, it cannot be proved, but the converse is not true, — that in all cases where fraud is alleged it must be proved.

It is admitted that in equity an actual design to mislead is not necessary if a party is actually misled by another in a bargain. There was abundant evidence in this case to authorize the jury to find that defendant, whether honestly or dishonestly, expected plaintiff to act on his representations of the reliableness of the reports which he produced, and that plaintiff did rely on them. There is no reason for a difference in action in such cases between courts of law and courts of equity. Where an equitable cause of grievance exists, it in no way differs from a legal one unless a different remedy is needed. A court of law cannot cancel a contract, and for such a purpose the equitable remedy must be sought. But where the relief desired is compensation for the wrong, the equitable remedy is much less appropriate, and an action in equity for mere damages will generally be denied, but denied only because the legal remedy is better. If there could be no legal remedy, there can be no doubt that equity would act. If the fraud is such that it creates a right of action anywhere, an action must lie on the case where a money judgment is needed.

Error is also claimed to exist in the reception of testimony showing representations that the land was represented valuable for farming as well as for timber purposes, this claim being rested on a failure to say anything about farming in the declaration. The declaration, in addition to what it says about timber, contains a distinct averment that the land was represented as of a certain value. This certainly would be proved by proof that it was said to be of that value for any purpose. A declaration might be made very prolix if all the talk swelling the value had to be averred. But in this case the allegations of value were all in one written paper, and closely connected, and it was impossible to show part without showing all. That paper, after describing the land, reads as follows:

"I had as good a judge of pine as there is in Michigan examine this land, and a good judge of pine, and he estimates that there is about five million pine on the land, — one-half of which is white pine, and the rest Norway; and he says that this is a very low estimate, and that the pine is of good quality. The white pine is scattering among hard wood, which usually indicates first-class pine. The land is worth, for farming purposes, $5 per acre after pine is off, and this is price of farming land in this locality. The land is close to logging stream which carries logs to Alpena. There are quite a number of good farms in same township. I hold lands at $12.50 per acre, and think there is enough pine on land to pay for it at that price.

Yours,

"B. R. NOBLE."

It is very plain that this paper was admissible as a whole, and could not have been received in any other way, and there could be no pretense of surprise at one part more than another. All of the elements set out in this letter were parts of the value, and it could not have been severed from any of them. It seems to me that there is no reason why any of them should be shut out from the consideration of the jury.

These questions are the only ones in the record calling for consideration. I think the judgment for plaintiff should be affirmed.

CHAMPLIN, J., concurred with CAMPBELL, J.

MORSE, J. I was strongly impressed, upon the argument of this case, with the theory of the defendant, supported by abundant authority outside of our own State, that unless the jury found that the representations relied upon by the plaintiff as false were made by the defendant, Noble, knowing them to be false, or he made the statements as facts within his own knowledge when he was ignorant of the truth or falsity of them, he could not be held liable in this action; that if he told plaintiff that he had never seen the lands, but that he had had the same examined by a competent landlooker, who said that there were five million feet of pine on the land, and made no representations as of his own knowledge, the plaintiff could not recover.

A subsequent careful examination of the case, and the authorities cited by defendant's counsel, has but confirmed me in the correctness and justness of his claim. I am satisfied that the law ought not to make a different contract for the seller than he sees fit to make for himself, and hold him, in effect, for warranties that he never made.

But an equally careful examination of the cases adjudicated in this State satisfies me that the doctrine is settled here, by a long line of cases, that if there was in fact a misrepresentation, though made innocently, and its deceptive influence was effective, the consequences to the plaintiff being as serious as though it had proceeded from a vicious purpose, he would have a right of action for the damages caused thereby either at law or in equity. *Baughman v. Gould,* 45 Mich. 483 (8 N.W. Rep. 73); *Converse v. Blumrich,* 14 Id. 109; *Steinbach v. Hill,* 25 Id. 78; *Webster v. Bailey,* 31 Id. 36; *Starkweather v. Benjamin,* 32 Id. 305; *Beebe v. Knapp,* 28 Id. 53.

I therefore consider the question foreclosed, and feel reluctantly compelled to concur in the result reached by my Brother CAMPBELL in affirming the judgment in this case.

SHERWOOD, C. J., concurred with MORSE, J.

[The rule of *Holcomb v. Noble* has been restricted to cases of privity. In the absence of privity, Michigan decisions have insisted on a showing of scienter. *E.g., Rosenberg v. Cyrowski,* 227 Mich. 508, 198 N.W. 905 (1924). — Ed.]

ROOT V. KING, 91 Mich. 488, 51 N.W. 1118 (1892) (facts simplified somewhat): Root bid in two lots at a foreclosure sale, paying $500 for each lot. In fact, both houses in the area were located on one lot, which was worth about $1,000; the other lot was vacant, and worth about $100. Root mistakenly believed that each house had one lot. King sought to redeem the lot on which the houses were built, paying the sale price of $500. Root sued to set aside the foreclosure, and to foreclose again. Held, for Root. "Defendant insists that there was no mutual mistake; that the mistake was that of complainant alone, and therefore he cannot recover. The mistake was not in the relative value of the lots but in their situation, and, under the circumstances, we do not think the complainant should suffer. Had he known the situation, and mistaken the value, the defendant's position would undoubtedly be correct. . . . [King] seeks to deprive complainant of the full benefit of his security on account of an honest mistake of fact."

WALKER V. CASGRAIN, 101 Mich. 604, 60 N.W. 291 (1894): Suit to enforce a vendor's lien under a land contract; defense: fraudulent misrepresentation. The seller's agent represented that the land was worth $4,500; in fact, says defendant, it was worth only $2,500. The sale price was $4,500. Held, for the seller: ". . . defendant Casgrain was not a stranger to real-estate transactions, ... A mere naked representation as to value, made under ordinary conditions, where the facilities for information are available, and no confidential relations exist, is not sufficient to avoid a sale. Some artifice must have been employed under such circumstances to aid the deception."

BEEBE v. BIRKETT
109 Mich. 663, 67 N.W. 966 (1896)

LONG, C. J. This bill was filed to compel the discharge of two mortgages upon the lands of the complainant. The bill alleges that complainant is the owner of certain lands in Livingston County, this state, and that on or about March 18, 1890, she mortgaged them to the defendant for $7,100. This mortgage was duly recorded. When it fell due the defendant commenced foreclosure proceedings, and, the complainant being unable to raise the money necessary to redeem the mortgage, on May 1, 1893, gave to defendant another mortgage upon the same lands for $7,280. This last mortgage was given to pay the first one, together with the interest and the expenses of foreclosure. Defendant, on receiving the second mortgage, agreed to discharge the first one without delay. About December 7, 1894, for the purpose of freeing her lands from the burden of the second mortgage, and supposing the first had been discharged, complainant entered into an agreement with defendant to obtain for him a deed of certain property in Wayne county. In pursuance of this agreement, complainant procured such deed and had the same delivered to the defendant, who accepted it and had it duly recorded. There was a difference in favor of complainant between the Wayne county lands and the amount due on the mortgage, and this difference was paid by the defendant. Complainant claims to have performed every part of her agreement with defendant, but insists, by her bill, that he refuses to discharge either mortgage. Defendant's contention is that the second mortgage did not cover the cost of the foreclosure proceedings of the first mortgage, and that the complainant agreed to pay the same, amounting to $35, and has failed to comply with that agreement. It is further contended by defendant "that, by the fraud of said complainant and her agents, the land so conveyed to him is not the land agreed to be conveyed by the said complainant, as alleged in said bill, but was land situated about two miles from the lands agreed to be conveyed, and two miles further out from the center of the city of Detroit, and has very much less value, being far beyond any settled or built-up part of the city of Detroit, and upon an open farm." Defendant also avers that he tendered a conveyance of the land, and demanded from the complainant the sum of $4,200, the amount paid her, but that she did not accept the conveyance, and declined to pay the money demanded. Proofs were taken in open court, and the court below decreed that there was due, for the costs of foreclosure proceeding on the first mortgage, the sum of $37, and that, on the payment of that amount, the defendant should discharge said mortgage. As to the second mortgage, the court decreed that it was fully paid and satisfied, and the court directed that it be discharged of record. Neither party was awarded costs. From this decree the defendant appeals.

It is unnecessary to set out here the testimony relative to the dealings between the parties in reference to the lands. The defendant, it appears, attempted to visit them, and was shown lands which, in an indefinite way, were pointed out as being the lands, or lands situated near those, deeded to him, though defendant was informed by the party who went to show them to him that he was not certain where the lands were situate. We think, upon the whole testimony, that the defendant made no such case as would entitle him to have the trade rescinded, and his money returned to him by the complainant. Had he exercised ordinary care, he could have at once discovered that the lands which he viewed were not the lands for which he was making the exchange, and we find nothing in the record which would warrant the assertion that the complainant or her authorized agents were responsible for his failing to discover the real situation of the lands deeded to him. The court below so found the fact to be, and, we think, very properly, under the evidence. The decree of that court must be affirmed, with costs of this court in favor of the complainant. The other justices concurred.

VALLEY CITY MILLING CO. v. PRANGE, 123 Mich. 211, 81 N.W. 1074 (1900): Defendant gave two notes for $200 each to plaintiff in payment for the privilege of removing gravel from plaintiff's farm. Although defendant told plaintiff that he intended to use the gravel to fulfill his contract to gravel and improve a street in Grand Rapids, plaintiff did not either represent or warrant that there was enough gravel of the proper quality on his farm to meet the defendant's needs. Judgment for the plaintiff on the notes was affirmed. "Counsel seeks to bring this case within the doctrine of *Gibson v. Pelkie* [p. 139, *supra,*] 37 Mich. 380. To bring the case within the rule there enunciated, it must conclusively appear that there was no subject-matter for the contract. The same principle is found in *Gribben v. Atkinson,* 64 Mich. 651 (31 N.W. 570), where the parties contracted with reference to the mutual belief that there was iron ore in the land. It was found that there was none. These cases, however, do not govern this. Here there was gravel suitable for one of the purpose for which it was intended. . . . Plaintiff refused to guarantee the quantity or the quality, but offered to sell the defendant the right to remove all the gravel upon the premises, if sufficient could be found for that purposes for which the defendant wanted it. He, through his agents, made an investigation. He was willing to assume the risk, and made the contract with the distinct understanding that the land might not contain gravel of the quantity and quality desired. There was no total failure of the subject-matter, such as constitutes a failure or lack of good consideration."

VAN NORSDALL v. SMITH, 141 Mich. 355, 104 N.W. 660 (1905): Mr. Smith died intestate, leaving some 94 acres of land, including his home; his heirs were his widow, two sisters and a brother. Mrs. Smith agreed to buy the other heirs' half interest in the land for $675. Before delivery of the deed, Mrs. Smith discovered that the husband of one of the sisters had a personal claim against the estate of around $700 (later allowed by the probate commissioner at $345); excluding that claim, the net estate, after deducting other claims and expenses, amounted to around $400 or $500. The presentation of the brother-in-law's claim would thus make the half interest in the land nearly worthless, since the land was subject to the decedent's debts and the expenses of administration. The trial court granted a decree of specific performance. Reversed: "Mere inadequacy of consideration, not accompanied by other elements of bad

faith, is not a sufficient ground for rescission of a contract or for refusing specific performance of it, unless so excessive as to furnish satisfactory evidence of
fraud. Fraud is always a sufficient ground for refusing specific enforcement,
and inadequacy of consideration may be, with other facts and circumstances,
convincing evidence of fraud .... [The brother-in-law, who negotiated the
sale agreement for the sisters and the brother,] concealed from [Mrs. Smith] a
matter of vital importance in the transaction between them, the effect of which
will be, if specific performance is decreed, to diminish materially the sum she
had the right to expect would remain to her as widow. ... Every unfair contract is in some measure unconscionable and hard. Courts withhold the peculiar
relief asked for here, as well where the hardship appears from external facts,
events, or circumstances as when it appears from the provisions of the contract
itself, and leave complainants to their legal remedy."

RICHARDSON LUMBER CO. v. HOEY
219 Mich. 643, 189 N.W. 923 (1922)

McDONALD, J. On the 16th day of September, 1916, the parties hereto
made following contract for the sale and purchase of a quantity of ties:
"Alpena, Michigan, September 16, 1916.

"Western Cedar & Lumber Company, City — Gentlemen: We will sell
you the cedar ties we now have on the Boyce property, Essexville, estimated to
be 11,500 at 42¢ on the ground, as they are, this to be for all. There are to be
no rejects. You are to pay us in cash as soon as the ties have been counted. We
have made this in duplicate and if you wish to purchase the same kindly sign
your acceptance to one copy and return it to us, when we will notify Mr. Mac-
Donald that you have purchased the same.

"Yours very truly,
        "Richardson Lumber Company.
            "By R. S. Richardson."
"Accepted this _____ day of Sept. 1916, by Western Cedar & Lumber
Company, by W. T. Hoey."

It is the claim of the defendants that when the acceptance was signed
Mr. Richardson said to Mr. Hoey, "You give me check for 11,500 ties and
you can load the ties any time you want to," to which Mr. Hoey replied that
he did not buy ties that way, but that he would make arrangements with plaintiff's Bay City office to count the ties and pay for them at Bay City; that
Mr. Richardson then said, "The ties are ours until you pay for them," and
that to this Mr. Hoey replied, "All right; I will take care of that. I wouldn't
touch the ties until I counted them and paid for them."

On the 19th of September defendants began to load and move the ties. They had taken out 1,721 when the remainder, not yet counted, were destroyed by fire. The defendants tendered plaintiff payment for 1,721 ties at 42 cents in full settlement of their obligations under the contract. The tender was refused, and this suit brought to recover for the entire quantity of ties named in the contract. Plaintiff had judgment for the full amount of its claim.

Defendants insist on three defenses to the action:

First. That the contract did not pass the title, and that, therefore, their only obligation is for the ties actually delivered.

Second. That the plaintiff, with knowledge of the facts, fraudulently concealed from the defendants that the ties were located in a place where there was imminent danger from fire.

Third. That there was a mutual mistake of fact in regard to the dangerous location and the liability of the ties being destroyed by fire, or that there was a mistake of fact on the part of the defendants while the plaintiff had full knowledge of it.

There are 67 assignments of error, and while we have carefully considered all of them, we will not discuss those which appear to be plainly without merit. . . .

* * *

The terms of the contract and circumstances of the case being undisputed, we think the court did not err in instructing the jury that they should find that the title to the ties passed at the time the contract was made, unless they found that there was a subsequent agreement by which the seller was to keep the title until they were counted and paid for.

It is urged that the court erred in his instructions to the jury with reference to defendants' claim of fraudulent concealment as to the dangerous location of the ties and the imminent danger from fire. We think that the instructions correctly stated the law applicable to this claim.

A more serious question is presented by the refusal of the circuit judge to submit to the jury defendants' claim of mutual mistake as to the danger from fire. The defendants claimed, and there was some testimony tending to support their claim, that at the time the contract was made fires were burning under the ground close to the place where the ties were piled, and shortly thereafter consumed them; that if this fact were unknown to the parties, that if they both believed that they were contracting for ties that were safe from fire, and could be delivered, it was such a mutual mistake of fact as would avoid the contract. The circuit judge was of the opinion that the mistake was not as to the identity or existence of the subject-matter of the contract, and therefore should not be submitted to the jury as a defense to the action. In this, I think, the court erred.

This is not a case of accident or something happening after the contract which destroyed the thing contracted for. If the defendants' claim be true, at the very time the contract was made the fire was near the ties underground, about to destroy them, thus making delivery within a reasonable time impossible. It was a present imminent danger which did, in fact, wipe out the subject-matter of the contract. If the fire were not present at the time, but originated afterwards, of course, it would have nothing to do with the contract, and would not affect defendants' liability. But that is not the claim here. It was an existing fact which continued until the property was destroyed. That the ties were in a safe place, and could be delivered, was a material element of the contract; it was one of the inducements which led to it. They would not have made it if they had known of the danger. They were mutually mistaken, and if defendants' claim as to the facts be true, it was a mistake that went to the entire consideration of the contract. If there was any evidence to support this theory (and I think there was some) the defendants were entitled to have it submitted to the jury.

I think it must be held that, if the ties were contracted to be sold in the belief and with the understanding by both parties that there was no imminent danger from fire, and if there was in fact imminent danger, and they were liable to be destroyed before the defendants could, by reasonable diligence, move them, the defendants would have a right to rescind the contract, and that if, after knowledge of the facts, the defendants had no time or opportunity to rescind before the ties were destroyed by the fire which threatened them at the time the contract was made, defendants would not be liable except for the ties actually delivered. This holding is in harmony with the principles enunciated in *Sherwood v. Walker,* 66 Mich. 568, 33 N.W. 919, 11 Am. St. Rep. 431, wherein it was said:

"But it must be considered as well settled that a party who has given an apparent consent to a contract of sale may refuse to execute it, or he may avoid it after it has been completed, if the assent was founded, or the contract made upon the mistake of a material fact, such as the subject-matter of the sale, the price, or some collateral fact materially inducing the agreement; and this can be done when the mistake is mutual."

The judgment of the circuit court will be reversed, and a new trial granted, with costs to the defendants.

BROWN LUMBER CO. v. CONSOLIDATED LUMBER CO., 255 Mich. 314, 238 N.W. 257 (1931): Plaintiff company agreed to buy all the timber in a certain tract at $6.50 per thousand feet of stumpage. "The amount of timber was to be determined by two cruisers, one selected by each of the companies, and, if they could not agree, a third cruiser should be named by the parties and the amount fixed by any two of them should be final." The cruisers evidently overestimated the amount of the timber by a factor of three. Plaintiff buyer sought to reform the contract to substitute the amount of timber which a later cruise (plus the amount cut) showed to be on the tract. The purchaser of plaintiff's purchase-money notes filed a cross-complaint for payment of the notes. A decree for the cross-plaintiff was affirmed. "It is seldom that two cruisers, although both have experience in such work, will agree upon the stumpage of a particular description of wooded land, and yet it is a well-known fact that men engaged in the lumber business have bought and sold many millions of feet of timber upon the estimates of cruisers. There is no other way in which the amount thereof can be determined before it is cut." There was no deliberate overestimate. When lumber prices are good, more timber is considered merchantable than when prices are bad. "The burden was upon the plaintiffs to establish the fact that there was fraud or such a mistake in the joint cruise . . . as relieves it from compliance with the [contract]. After due consideration of the facts disclosed in this record, we cannot so find. 'Courts do not make contracts for parties.' *Lee State Bank v. McElheny,* 227 Mich. 322, 327. The conclusion reached finds support in *Nester v. Michigan Land & Iron Co.,* [p. 147, *supra,*] 69 Mich. 290; [and other cases]."

PATTERSON, THE APPORTIONMENT OF BUSINESS RISKS
24 COLUM. L. REV.* 335, 355-57 (1924)

"Mutual Mistake as to an Essential Fact." The circumstance that rescission for mutual mistake developed chiefly in courts of equity should not obscure the fact that it is a doctrine under the guise of which risk-apportioning goes on. Some cases are put equally well under this head and under the head of impossibility, which was developed primarily in the law courts — as, for example, the case of the lessee who agrees to mine a minimum quantity.

It is frequently said that equity will allow rescission where the mistake is as to an "essential," a "vital" fact, but not where it relates merely to a "collateral" fact. Such expressions may possibly be useful as labels for conclusions, if they are not thought of as philosophical categories. There is some evidence that Anglo-American law has been influenced by the Roman law doctrines as to mistake. The Roman jurists developed some nice distinctions around such phrases as *"error in substantia," "error in corpore,"* etc. — distinctions which were developed from Stoic and Aristotelian metaphysics. For instance, it was said that if wine were bargained for and vinegar delivered, the buyer's right to rescind depended upon whether the vinegar had at one time been wine (in which case the *substance* was the same, in the eyes of the Stoic metaphysicians) or had been artificial vinegar, not made from wine. Perhaps a wine-buyer in the Stoic epoch would be satisfied with this explanation, but it is believed that a wine-buyer today would not accept this solution stoically.

Again, the attempt to develop an abstract conception of "mistake" or

---

* Copyright Ⓒ, Columbia Law Review, reprinted by permission.

"error" results in excluding the most significant factors in the phenomena which the general terms purport to describe. As Ihering long ago pointed out, the conception of *"error"* in general has no place in making practical decisions; it has significance only in particular transactions. On the other hand, discussions of the legal consequences of mistake have frequently been based upon the "will" theory of contracts, which went to the other extreme in attempting to individualize the process of attaching legal consequences to human behavior. Nor is this difficulty wholly avoided by taking the view that the external behavior is conclusive evidence of the mental state of the individual, for the emphasis is still upon introspection and the actual process of "constructing" legal consequences from external behavior goes on under the guise of "interpretation."

"Mistake" covers too many types of problems to permit of safe generalization. One type of problem may be pointed out in which, it is believed, clearer thinking is attained by stating the question as one of apportionment of risk, namely, where the person seeking legal relief (or resisting it) claims to have been disappointed in regard to some "material" fact. For example, one who purchases the promissory note of another as an investment or speculation has been denied a recovery of his payments where it was subsequently discovered that the maker was insolvent, while one who takes the note of a bank or of another person in payment of a debt may recover the debt upon subsequently discovering that the maker was, when the note was taken, insolvent. It is difficult to see why the fact of insolvency is not as "material," "intrinsic" or "essential" to the thing bargained for, or as "collateral" and "extrinsic" to it, in the one case as in the other. If, however, the results are stated in terms of risk-bearing, the purchaser of a note for investment or speculation takes the risk of prior insolvency of the buyer (apart from fraud, implied warranty, and the like), while one who takes a note as currency, as a medium of exchange, does not take this risk.

C. The Restatement of Contracts

The year following the *Brown Lumber Co.* case, p. 155, *supra,* saw the publication by the American Law Institute of the Restatement of Contracts, one in a series of unofficial codifications of the common law of the United States. These materials include excerpts from the Restatement's treatment of the subjects of fraud and mistake, followed by two comments comparing the Restatement to a "genuine" code. As you read these materials and the Michigan cases which follow, consider the following questions:

1. Does the Restatement accurately restate the Michigan law of mistake and fraud?

2. What are the similarities and differences, in substance and in orga-

nization, between the Restatement's provisions on these subjects and the comparable articles of the Argentine Civil Code?

3. To what extent does the Restatement justify Bentham's expectations for codification? Is the Restatement what Carter had in mind when he proposed his digest of the common law?

4. Can you discern any influence of the Restatement on the Michigan cases on fraud and mistake which were decided after 1932?

5. Does the experience with the Restatement throw any light on Professor Yntema's proposal for the enactment of a civil code?

RESTATEMENT OF CONTRACTS * (1932)

§ 1. CONTRACT DEFINED.

A contract is a promise or a set of promises for the breach of which the law gives a remedy, or the performance of which the law in some way recognizes as a duty.

    * * *

§ 3. AGREEMENT DEFINED.

An agreement is a manifestation of mutual assent by two or more persons to one another.

    * * *

§ 19. REQUIREMENTS OF THE LAW FOR FORMATION OF AN INFORMAL CONTRACT.

The requirements of the law for the formation of an informal contract are:

a) A promisor and a promisee each of whom has legal capacity to act as such in the proposed contract;

b) A manifestation of assent by the parties who form the contract to the terms thereof, and by every promisor to the consideration for his promise, except as otherwise stated in §§ 85-94 [pre-existing duty situation and "promissory estoppel"];

c) A sufficient consideration except as otherwise stated in §§ 85-94, and 535 [renewal of usurious bargain];

d) The transaction, though satisfying the foregoing requirements, must be one that is not void by statute or by special rules of the common law.

---

§ 20. Requirement of Manifestation of Mutual Assent.

A manifestation of mutual assent by the parties to an informal contract is essential to its formation and the acts by which such assent is manifested must be done with the intent to do those acts; but, except as qualified by §§ 55 [necessity of intent to accept offer for unilateral contract], 71 [the "Peerless" situation] and 72 [silence as acceptance], neither mental assent to the promises in the contract nor real or apparent intent that the promises shall be legally binding is essential.

§ 21. Acts as Manifestation of Assent.

The manifestation of mutual assent may be made wholly or partly by written or spoken words or by other acts or conduct.

* * *

§ 470. Definition of Misrepresentation; When Misrepresentation Material.

(1) "Misrepresentation" in the Restatement of this Subject means any manifestation by words or other conduct by one person to another that, under the circumstances, amounts to an assertion not in accordance with the facts.

(2) Where a misrepresentation would be likely to affect the conduct of a reasonable man with reference to a transaction with another person, the misrepresentation is material, except as this definition is qualified by the rules stated in § 474 [see *infra*].

§ 471. Definition of Fraud.

"Fraud" in the Restatement of this Subject unless accompanied by qualifying words, means.

(a) misrepresentation known to be such or

(b) concealment, or

(c) non-disclosure where it is not privileged, by any person intending or expecting thereby to cause a mistake by another to exist or to continue, in order to induce the latter to enter into or refrain from entering into a transaction; except as this definition is qualified by the rules stated in § 474.

§ 472. When Lack of Disclosure is Not Privileged.

(1) There is no privilege of non-disclosure, by a party who

(a) has previously made a misrepresentation, either innocently or without any intention or expectation that it would induce conduct and subsequently before a transaction has been in-

duced thereby is aware of the facts and intends or expects
that conduct will be induced by the mistake, or

(b) knows that the other party is acting under a mistake as to
undisclosed material facts, and the mistake if mutual would
render voidable a transaction caused by relying thereon, or

(c) occupies such a relation to the other party as to justify the
latter in expecting that his interests will be cared for, or

(d) is denied immunity for non-disclosure by any special rules
of law.

(2) Where non-disclosure is not privileged it has the effect of a material misrepresentation.

§ 473. PROMISE WITH INTENT NOT TO PERFORM.

A contractual promise made with the undisclosed intention of not performing it is fraud.

§ 474. MANIFESTATION OF OPINION AS FRAUD OR MISREPRESENTATION.

A manifestation that the person making has no reason to expect to be
understood as more than an expression of his opinion, though made also with
the intent or expectation stated in § 471, is not fraud or a material misrepresentation, unless made by

(a) one who has, or purports to have expert knowledge of the
matter, or

(b) one whose manifestation is an intentional misrepresentation and
varies so far from the truth that no reasonable man in his position
could have such an opinion.

§ 475. WHEN FRAUD OR MISREPRESENTATION MAKES A TRANSACTION VOID.

Where there is fraud or misrepresentation by one person likely to cause
and that does cause another, without negligence on his part, to believe that an
act that he does is not a manifestation of assent to any transaction or is a manifestation of assent to a transaction entirely different from that which would be
created if there were no mistake as to the facts, the act does not affect his contractual relations.

§ 476. EFFECT OF FRAUD OR MISREPRESENTATION THAT INDUCES ACTS AFFECTING CONTRACTUAL RELATIONS.

(1) Where a party is induced to enter into a transaction with another
party that he was under no duty to enter into by means of the latter's fraud or
material misrepresentation, the transaction is voidable as against the latter and

all who stand in no better position, subject to the qualifications stated in §§ 480 [offer to restore performance received], 481 [such an offer not required as condition to equitable relief], 486 [special rules for aleatory contracts], and with the exceptions stated in Subsections (2, 3).

(2) Where a transaction is voidable because of a misrepresentation innocently made and the facts become in accordance with the representation before notification by the deceived party of an intent to avoid the transaction, it is no longer voidable.

(3) Where a transaction entered into by an agent or by one who purports to be an agent is induced by his fraudulent misrepresentation of authority and he obtains authority before notification by the deceived party of an intent to avoid the transaction, it is no longer voidable.

§ 477. WHEN FRAUD OR MISREPRESENTATION OF A THIRD PERSON MAKES A TRANSACTION VOIDABLE.

Fraud or material misrepresentation by a third person renders a transaction voidable by a party induced thereby to enter into it if the other party thereto.

(a) has reason to know of the fraud or misrepresentation before he has given or promised in good faith something of value in the transaction or changed his position materially by reason of the transaction, or

(b) is affected by the fraud or misrepresentation under the law of Agency or of Trusts.

* * *

§ 479. WHEN FRAUD OR MATERIAL MISREPRESENTATION IS PRESUMABLY AN INDUCING CAUSE.

Where fraud or misrepresentation is material with reference to a transaction subsequently entered into by a person deceived thereby, it is assumed in the absence of facts showing the contrary that it was induced by the fraud or misrepresentation.

* * *

§ 484. LOSS OF POWER OF AVOIDANCE BY AFFIRMING TRANSACTION.

The power of avoidance for fraud or misrepresentation is lost if the injured party after acquiring knowledge of the fraud or misrepresentation manifests to the other party to the transaction an intention to affirm it, or exercises dominion over things restoration of which is a condition of this power of avoidance, except as stated in § 482 [after a reasonable time, the injured party if entitled to restitution can enforce a lien on what he has received].

* * *

§ 500.   Definition of Mistake.

In the Restatement of this Subject, mistake means a state of mind that is not in accord with the facts.

§ 501.   When Mistake Prevents the Formation of Contracts.

Mistake prevents the existence of a contract in accordance with the rules stated in §§ 51 [effect of delay in communication of offer], 71 [the "Peerless" situation], 456 [impossibility existing at the time of the promise]; and prevents the discharge of a duty or an effective assignment in accordance with similar rules.

§ 502.   When Mistake Makes a Contract Voidable.

Even though there is no such mistake as would deprive the acts of the parties of any effect on their contractual relations under the rules stated in §§ 49 [termination of offer by death (destruction) of essential person (thing)], 71, 456, where parties on entering into a transaction that affects their contractual relations are both under a mistake regarding a fact assumed by them as the basis on which they entered into the transaction, it is voidable by either party if enforcement of it would be materially more onerous to him than it would have been had the fact been as the parties believed it to be, except

(a)   where the welfare of innocent third persons will be unfairly affected, or

(b)   where the party seeking to avoid the transaction can obtain reformation or performance of the bargain according to the actual intent of the parties when the transaction was entered into, or

(c)   where it is possible by compensation to the party injured by the mistake to put him in as good a position as if the transaction had been what he supposed it to be, and such compensation is given.

§ 503.   Mistakes by Only One Party; Differing Mistakes of Both Parties.

A mistake of only one party that forms the basis on which he enters into a transaction does not of itself render the transaction voidable; nor do such mistakes of both parties if the respective mistakes relate to different matters; but if the mistakes relate to the same matter, the power of avoidance is not precluded because the mistakes of the parties as to that fact are not the same. [§§ 504-07 deal with reformation.]

* * *

§ 508. WHEN NEGLIGENCE DOES NOT PRECLUDE AVOIDANCE.

The negligent failure of a party to know or to discover the facts, as to which both parties are under a mistake does not preclude rescission or reformation on account thereof.

GOODRICH, RESTATEMENT AND CODIFICATION
DAVID DUDLEY FIELD CENTENARY ESSAYS* 241-45
(Reppy ed. 1949)

It is interesting to speculate upon the answers which the enthusiastic David Dudley Field and his withering critic, Mr. James Carter, would have made in 1923 to the American Law Institute's proposal to restate the common law. Would Mr. Field have thought the proposal for restatement a pale and bloodless substitute for his plan of codification of the law? Would Mr. Carter have asserted that an attempt at restatement, so far as it succeeded, carried with it all the evils which he felt inherent in codifications, or, as an alternative, that the plan was a futile gesture destined for failure? The answers we can never know. Certain it is that the elder statesmen in the Institute, like Mr. Root, Mr. Milburn, Mr. Wickersham, were alert to dispel the suggestion, which was not infrequently offered, that the proposed restatement was a plan for codification under another name. Perhaps they heard the echoes of the nineteenth century controversy still ringing in their ears and wanted to avoid the reopening of that battle. At any rate, the position they took was clear in their minds; they were not going to codify the common law. They were to improve and clarify it by restatement but what was to be done was not and did not look to codification.

* * *

Relationship of Restatement to Field Codes.—Just how far apart is this Restatement of the common law from the code proposed by Mr. Field? The question raised now is not the accuracy of the substantive rules contained in the Field Code as contrasted with the Restatement, but the theory of principle behind the job to be done. A code has been described as "an orderly and authoritative statement of the leading rules of law on a given subject." (Ilbert.) The object of the Restatement one may find stated by the then director, Dr. Lewis, in the preface he wrote to the first volume of Contracts, which was also the first volume offered as a finished product. It is there said: ". . . in order to clarify and simplify the law and render it more certain, the first step

must be the preparation of an orderly restatement of the common law . . . .
The function of the Institute is to state clearly and precisely in the light of the
decisions the principles and rules of the common law."

Note that there are at least two common assumptions made by codifiers
and the Institute.

One is that there are such things as rules of law. There are those who
deny this, or at least give the impression that they deny it, and insist, or give
the impression that they insist, that lawsuits are decided ad hoc, and that the
mouthings of the judges are but the ritual intoned while the real business is
done on considerations wholly apart from ritual. For such persons either codification or restatement could be regarded as a harmless if tiresome form of intellectual exercise, as far away from the business of life as the logic of medieval
scholasticism. This is not the place or occasion to thresh over this well-seasoned
straw. In law, as in life generally, either some assumptions must be made, or
some questions once critically considered and answered must stay answered for
a while at least. One cannot examine all the basic premises of life or law every
day and have time for anything else. We may, for purposes of discussion here,
assume the existence of general rules of law. If that assumption is erroneous, it
is at least a common basis of error for one who would restate as well as for him
tho would codify.

Second, codification assumes that some rules are more important than
others. It is, according to our definition, the "leading" rules which are to be
reduced to statement. The general principle that mental tranquility is to be
protected against intentional invasion in the form of threatened bodily contact may find expression as a code principle. The rule that one may be liable
for pointing an empty gun at a victim who does not know the thing is unloaded
may be left to the common sense of the court which is informed of the general
principle.

The same distinction will be found, in varying degrees of sharpness in the
various volumes of the *Restatement.* Principles or general rules (choose whichever term seems preferable if there is a difference) may be found in black-letter
statement; comment gives the explanation of why and how far they go; illustrations give the answer in concrete illustrative cases.

Now let us go back again to our definition. Codification is an "orderly and
authoritative statement." The adjective "orderly" need give us no concern. It
may not, with regard to a room in a home, mean the same thing to a sixteen
year old girl as it does to her mother, but it is not likely to raise differences
among those who would arrange the rules of law in systematic order.

The dividing word between the processes is of course "authoritative."
Upon whose authority is code or restatement to rest? It would be taken for
granted, would it not, that a code has the force of government behind it, whether that force be exercised by the emperor Napoleon or the legislature of the
state of Idaho. The authoritative source of the code is that of the lawmaking

body of the state where it is promulgated. The *Restatement* has no such backing. It was submitted to the legal profession on its own merits as a good piece of work, the merit vouched for by the professional standing of those who did it. If an advocate thinks the *Restatement* wrong as applied to his case, he can urge the court not to follow it, but to apply some other rule. If the court agrees, it will do so, but it will do so with the knowledge that the rule which it rejects has been written by the people who by training and reputation are supposed to be eminently learned in the particular subject and that the specialists' conclusions have been discussed and defended before a body of very able critics. The presumption is in favor of the *Restatement* and the course of decision since its appearance shows that the presumption is very seldom overthrown. Yet it can be overthrown, and that fact leaves *Restatement* acceptance to persuasion. It is common law "persuasive authority" with a high degree of persuasion.

YNTEMA, THE JURISPRUDENCE OF CODIFICATION
DAVID DUDLEY FIELD CENTENARY ESSAYS* 251, 255-64
(Reppy ed. 1949)

I refer to the Restatement as a code, despite the distinction which was drawn in defining its nature, since in substance and objective it bears the character of legislation; in John Austin's words, "It is not the instrument or means of deciding a specific case, but is intended solely to serve as a rule of conduct, and therefore to guide the tribunals in their decisions upon classes of cases." It differs from a proper code in two specific respects: it has not been enacted by a duly constituted legislature, but its authority depends upon approval of the Institute; and it is supposed to report, not to reform, the established law, a circumstance that has materially restricted its potentialities as a means to improve the law. Indeed, such has not been an object of the Restatement; it is a statement of the law as it is, or in other words a digest.

Effectiveness of Restatement.—The question naturally arises whether this conservative species of codification has or can adequately serve the purposes for which the Restatement was undertaken. Twelve years ago, I voiced the doubt whether the Restatement, albeit admirably calculated to enlist the members of the legal profession in a scientific study of the Common Law, had succeeded in alleviating the evils to which it was addressed, whether by reducing the mass of legal materials to be consulted, by simplifying their complexity, or more especially by diminishing the "turgid stream of judicial decisions." The doubt persists, as the stream of materials to be consulted by the lawyer rolls on in unabated volume; indeed, where is the reported case that has lost its formal effect by reason of the Restatement or the case unreported due to its existence? If there be such, and I have not heard of one, they do not affect the conclusion after a number of years that the Restatement has not relieved the public of the uncertainty and the expense attendant upon a system of case-law. Without formal enactment obviating recourse in ordinary cases to the existing decisions, it could scarcely be otherwise.

As stated in the illuminating Report of the Commissioners to codify the Common Law of Massachusetts of 1837, penned by Judge Story:

One great advantage, therefore, of a code, an advantage which in a practical view can scarcely be over-estimated, is, that it supersedes the necessity, in ordinary cases at least, of very elaborate researches into other books; and, indeed, it often supersedes in all cases, but those of rare and extraordinary occurrence, the necessity of consulting an immense mass of learned collections and digests of antecedent decisions.

* * *

Argument for Codification.—In the interests of brevity, the affirmative argument may be summarily epitomized, without endeavoring to define the necessary limitations of a codification of the Common Law, as suggested, for example in the admirable report of the Massachusetts Commissioners, in 1837, to which reference has been made. We note five principal considerations: superior economy in the ascertainment of law, clarity and conciseness in the statement of legal principles, correspondingly increased certainty in the law and reduction of the ex post facto legislation inherent in case-law, facilitation of reform, the diffusion among the people of a more accurate knowledge of their rights and liabilities. A further consideration, particularly urged by Bentham, namely that the uncertainty of "jurisprudential" law fosters unnecessary litigation, imputes a charge that no longer directly affects the juridiciary, now generally on a salary basis, but must remain a serious concern for the bar. In his inimitable language:

"By the uncertainty of the law, the partnership interest (viz. incident to the fee system) is served in three distinguishable ways: — 1. The number of suits is increased; 2. The quantity of business receives a further increase, from the quantity of advice which men are necessitated to purchase — advice before a suit, during a suit, and for fear of a suit; 3. In proportion to the degree of uncertainty, the judicial members are invested with a degree of power proportionably arbitrary, and thence applicable to the purposes of the partnership in all imaginable ways."

Before the logic of these considerations, the advocates of codification of the Common Law are convinced. In the words of David Dudley Field: "The question whether a code is desirable is simply a question between written and unwritten law. That this was ever debatable is one of the most remarkable facts in the history of jurisprudence. If the law is a thing to be obeyed, it is a thing to be known; and, if it is to be known, there can be no better, not to say no other, method of making it known than of writing and publishing it. If a written constitution is desirable, so are written laws."

James C. Carter's Objections to Codification.—Against this view was set the assertion of the distinguished committee of the Association of the Bar of the City of New York in their petition to the Legislature of May 1884, that the proposed adoption of Field's Civil Code was "the greatest misfortune that has ever threatened the State of New York." . . .

In Carter's paper, a fundamental distinction is drawn between the written and the unwritten law. The proper province of the former, i.e., of formal legislation, is defined as comprising those branches of law in which certainty is the paramount objective — constitution and public law, penal law, laws affecting social and political questions with respect to which there are variances of opinion that can only be resolved in this manner, and perhaps also judicial procedure and those parts of the law of property in which rigid technical rules respecting formalities are needed. On the other hand, in subjects appropriately governed by the unwritten law, embracing the usual relations and dealings of men with each other except as they are subject to statutory regulation, justice and not certainty is the prime need. For this vast area of ordinary human relations, codification is condemned as (1) unscientific in theory, (2) demonstrated by experience to have failed, (3) rejected by the preponderating weight of informed authority, and (4) if adopted, as the certain source of a host of seven evils from which the unwritten law is immune.

We may pass by the second and third items in the argument with the brief observations: First, the demonstration of the alleged failure of the codes of Rome, France, Prussia, and Louisiana to control the administration of justice or to produce superior judicial administration, as evidenced by the amendments and the judicial interpretations to which these codes have been subjected, apparently assumes the abandoned notion that such codes can be self-executing and so complete as to make amendment and judicial interpretation unnecessary. Second, the opinion evidence adduced oposing codification of the general private law is prejudicially selected, being drawn from the ranks of British jurists, without reference to the views entertained in countries where such codifications had been in use.

The first and basic point in Carter's argument, namely that codification of the Common Law is unscientific in theory, attempts to answer Field's observation that what is known can be stated and written. The gist of the answer is that rules evidenced by judicial opinions cannot be stated as true, because they are not absolute but only provisionally valid in reference to known facts. All *just* law, asserts Carter, "which consists in applying directly the standard of justice to human conduct, consists in applying that standard to *known* facts, and can have, in human apprehension, no existence apart from the facts." Therefore, the enactment of such rules in a code to cover future and unknown as well as past and known facts, is no law worthy of the name.

Defects in Carter's Argument.—The argument apparently is that, while Carter refers to established rules of the Common Law as controlling judicial decision, the limitations of human understanding preclude these rules being known or stated except in relation to past known facts. If so, if the rules do not justly apply to unknown future facts, however similar to facts known, it follows that there can be no general principles of the Common Law, defined by reference to classes of known facts, which may be assumed to apply to like situations in the future. And, if this be so, how can there be an unwritten law in any proper sense of the term?

The argument evidently turns on itself. Moreover, it is difficult on this theory to square Carter's approval of a digest of the Common Law with his general condemnation of codification. A digest, as distinguished from a code, of the whole unwritten law, in analytical and systematic form and expressed in accurate, scientific language, he asserted, "would be of priceless value to the world." Why of such value, if it were not a guide for future decision and advice? The truth is that this was an endeavor to import the mystical doctrine of Savigny, that law is an emanation of the national spirit, into the Common Law theory of precedents. "The whole administration of justice," states Carter, "consists in applying the national standard or ideal of justice to human affairs," whether such standard is to be found in the written or the unwritten law. He even admits that, apart from known facts, there is no law, "except the broad and empty generalization that *justice must be done.*" This conception tends to substantiate Bentham's charge that "jurisprudential law is sham law," a creature of the imagination. It was employed by Carter as by Savigny to oppose systematic legal reform.

* * *

Inadequacy of Judicial Formulation of Law in Modern Society.—The times press upon us in two major respects. In the first place the era in which we live is characterized by a prodigious expansion of industry and commerce, to the needs of which law has to answer. Consequently, in recent years the evolution of law has turned to a greatly increased and conscious employment of positive enactments both to provide certainty in the applicable rules and to control the effects of the extraordinary technological developments of this scientific age. The slow and uncertain response of customary law to current needs, appropriate to a more pastoral environment, is prevailingly supplemented by the more precise and prompt techniques of positive legislation. Thus, during the past century, the salient features of the law have come to be that it is distinctively composed of consciously prescribed enactments of the national states; that it has become vastly voluminous and complex; and that, to provide a modicum of coherence, continuity, and intelligibility within the incessant stream of regulations necessitated by the requirements of contemporary society, the basic elements of law are formulated more and more widely in relatively fixed codifications.

Modern Code to Respond to the International Commitments of the United States.—In the second place, it is no longer feasible, even in the administration of justice, to cherish isolationism. . . .

* * *

Feasibility of Codification at the Present Time.—It remains to point the moral of these observations, Codification is a practical matter; in application to the Common Law, it involves the question whether the existing melange of case-law and special statutes, covering the general private law, satisfies the needs of the United States in the modern world or provides a suitable basis for the adaptation of the rules governing the ordinary affairs of men to the needs to tomorrow. In 1923, the American Law Institute was founded in the conviction that substantial improvement in the system is imperatively required but, as has been observed, there is no evidence after twenty-five years that the magnificent, sustained effort organized by the Institute, the Restatement of the Law, has remedied the growing evils of the system of precedents to which it was specifically addressed. The effort, however, is by no means wasted; such a survey of the existing Common Law as the Restatement provides, supplemented by the projected Uniform Code of Commercial Law, is a necessary prerequisite for effective codification, or in other words scientific improvement of the general private law in technique, form, and substance. Also, the skill and experience organized in the American Law Institute is available to implement the grand enterprise.

Comparative Study Essential as Basis for Codification.—This is a large labor; it is not to be accomplished merely by slapping together the Restatement and the anticipated Commercial Code in a more compendious enactment. These would need to be reconsidered and restated in the light of modern conditions, the advance of legal science, and foreign experience. . . .

* * *

. . . In short, the prime vocation of legal science in the United States today is comparative law, without adequate attention to which, I believe, a codification of the general private law of the United States should now not be attempted. This is the most essential condition for the preparation of a civil code, appropriate to America.

VAN LOOYENGOED V. ALLENCREST GARDENS CORP., 265 Mich. 182, 251 N.W. 317 (1933): The plaintiff, a widow who was unfamiliar with the value of real estate, sought to rescind two contracts for the purchase of land, on the ground of fraud. Agents of the defendant had represented "that the purchase of the lots in question offered a wonderful opportunity for a safe investment and large profits; that she would double her money in five years if she bought the lots, which were well worth $1,300 each." The testimony at the trial concerning the lots' value ranged from $50 to $900 each. A decree of rescission was affirmed. "The general rule that an honest expression of opinion as to value in itself does not constitute actionable fraud is well settled; but we think the facts in this case present an exception to the general rule. If the plaintiff's testimony is true, there was more than expression of opinion. There was a concealment of facts bearing on the value. There was a misstatament of facts to one who was ignorant of land values in the vicinity where these lots were located. At the time the plaintiff purchased the lots there was no local market for them."

ACHENBACH v. MEARS
272 Mich. 74, 261 N.W. 251 (1935)

Bill by John A. Achenbach and wife against Thomas R. Mears and wife and Paul Murray for rescission of an exchange of property and other relief. Dismissed as to defendant Murray. Money decree for plaintiffs. Defendants appeal. Reversed.

POTTER, C. J.   Plaintiffs filed a bill to rescind a trade based upon a written contract, or alternatively, in case rescission was impossible, to recover damages for fraud.

Plaintiffs owned a farm in Allegan country, valued at $7,500, subject to an outstanding incumbrance of $2,300. October 5, 1933, they traded this farm with defendants Mears for a store in Fulton, Kalamazoo county, and gave back a chattel mortgage on the store building and fixtures in the sum of $2,300. Plaintiffs allege they were defrauded:

1.   As to the quality of the goods traded by defendants Mears to them;
2.   As to the value of the stock of merchandise;
3.   As to the value of sales of merchandise in the store;
4.   As to the value of the building used as a store.

(1)   It is not claimed there was any warranty of quality of the merchandise. Such merchandise was open to inspection and there could be no implied warranty as to its quality, fitness or condition. . . .

(2)   Value is usually a matter of opinion and statements of value can rarely be supposed to have induced a purchase, without negligence upon the part of the purchaser. False statements of value will rarely void a bargain. *Nowlin v. Snow*, [p. 140, *supra*,] 40 Mich. 699. Usually a person who has a store or other business to sell has a right to claim whatever value he desires for it, particularly when he is trading it for something else. Plaintiffs had an opportunity to examine the stock of merchandise and knew the manner in which

the value of this stock could be determined, by an inventory, examination and appraisal of the property by persons competent to fix a value thereon. They made no attempt to have such an examination made, to have an inventory prepared, or an appraisal made.

"No principle of the common law has been better established, or more often affirmed, both in this country and in England, than that in sales of personal property, in the absence of express warranty, where the buyer has an opportunity to inspect the commodity, and the seller is guilty of no fraud, and is neither the manufacturer nor grower of the article he sells, the maxim of *caveat emptor* applies. Such a rule, requiring the purchaser to take care of his own interests, has been found best adapted to the wants of trade in the business transactions of life. And there is no hardship in it, because if the purchaser distrusts his judgment he can require of the seller a warranty that the quality or condition of the goods he desires to buy corresponds with the sample exhibited. If he is satisfied without a warranty, and can inspect and declines to do it, he takes upon himself the risk that the article is merchantable. And he cannot relieve himself and charge the seller on the ground that the examination will occupy time, and is attended with labor and inconvenience. If it is practicable, no matter how inconvenient, the rule applies." *Barnard v. Kellogg,* 10 Wall. (77 U.S.) 383, 388.

There is no reason why plaintiffs should not have known, not only the quality of the merchandise for which they traded their farm, but also the value of the stock. They had ample opportunity to examine the merchandise and they could have had an inventory, examination and appraisal thereof.

(3)   Plaintiffs claim there was misrepresentation as to the volume of sales. The volume of sales depends very much upon the individual who has charge of the sale of merchandise. Plaintiffs claim there were certain misrepresentations made as to the volume of sales, which defendants Mears deny, contending that whatever representations they may have made as to the volume of sales were true and nothing was said about the volume of sales until after the deal was consummated. The trial court did not regard the testimony as to the volume of sales important. This was a general store located in a small hamlet. It is easy to acquire merchandise by mail and, with modern automobile transportation, buyers purchase where they please. Fraud may not be predicated on a falling off of sales after change in ownership and sales force.

(4)   It is claimed there were misrepresentations made as to the value of the building and the building was valued higher than it should have been. This building was being traded for a farm valued at $7,500 for the purpose of trading, and assessed at a smaller amount. Plaintiffs had an opportunity to examine the building; could have procured an estimate of its cost; were in a position to know as much about the value of the building as were the defendants Mears themselves, and we think no charge of fraud may be predicated upon any statement made in attempting to consummate a trade of the kind in-

volved here of the value placed upon the building which plaintiffs not only saw, but had ample opportunity to examine.

* * *

(7)   Plaintiffs recovered judgment upon the ground of fraud, the rescission not being possible by reason of the sale of the farm acquired by defendants Mears from plaintiffs. . . .

(8)   There was a provision in the written contract for exchange of property that the parties thereto relied solely upon their own judgment and not upon any representations made by one to the other. Plaintiff John Achenbach says he read and understood this agreement and that up to the time the agreement was made he relied solely upon his own judgment. The thing which he complained of was something which the defendants Mears failed to tell him. . . .

Decree reversed, with costs.

FEAD, WIEST, and EDWARD M. SHARPE, JJ., concurred with POTTER, C. J.

[Three judges dissented in an opinion which reviewed the testimony on the issue of misrepresentation of the value of the inventory.]

FARHAT v. RASSEY
295 Mich. 349, 294 N.W. 707 (1940)

BUTZEL, J.   Plaintiff filed a bill for the dissolution of a partnership and for an accounting. The case was submitted on the proofs in December, 1939, and on January 18, 1940, at about 9 o'clock in the morning, the trial court filed a written opinion in which he found that plaintiff was entitled to $3,933.33 as his share of the assets of the copartnership which totalled $11,297.68. On the same morning, the attorney for defendants called plaintiff's attorney and suggested that defendants would pay $1,400 to settle the case if an agreement could be effected that day. Plaintiff's attorney went to Flint, arriving there about 4 o'clock in the afternoon, and a settlement was made, reduced to writing, signed by the parties, and a check for the agreed amount of $1,400 was delivered to plaintiff's attorney. Immediately upon receiving the opinion of the trial court, plaintiff's attorney filed a motion to repudiate the settlement and for a decree on the findings of the trial court. The trial court declined to abide by the settlement, and a decree was entered in accordance with his opinion.

It is conceded that at the time the settlement was actually made, the trial court had already filed his opinion. It appears that defendants' attorney stated that the case had not yet been decided, which statement was in fact untrue; his good faith is unchallenged. We accept as true the statement in his affidavit that he had no knowledge of the decision at the time the settlement was consummated, and we shall assume that such knowledge on the part of defendants and their counsel was likewise wanting.

The trial court was correct in holding that plaintiff may avoid the settlement. The basic assumptions upon which the settlement rested were wrong in fact. The state of mind of all the parties was not in accord with the facts (Restatement, Restitution, § 6). The parties assumed that the case had not yet been determined and believed that a decision would not be forthcoming for several weeks. There can be no question but that these fundamental facts induced the compromise, and their absolute nonexistence was the starting point of the settlement contract. Having contracted on the faith of these assumptions not believed to have been doubtful, but which were in fact erroneous, the parties are to be relieved from their bargain. 5 Williston on Contracts (Rev. Ed.), p. 4332, § 1543; Restatement, Contracts, § 502; Restatement, Restitution, § 11, comment c; *Gibson v. Pelkie,* [p. 139, *supra,*] 37 Mich. 380; *Sherwood v. Walker,* [p. 140, *supra,*] 66 Mich. 568 (11 Am. St. Rep. 531); *State Savings Bank of Ann Arbor v. Buhl,* 129 Mich. 193 (56 L.R.A. 944); *Richardson Lumber Co. v. Hoey,* [p. 153, *supra,*] 219 Mich. 643; *Kutsche v. Ford,* 222 Mich. 442; *Grymes v. Sanders,* 93 U.S. 55. The situation before us is to be distinguished from cases where there is a mistake as to a doubtful, disputed, unassumed fact leading to the compromise. "With respect to any matter not made a basic assumption of the contract the parties take their chances." (5 Williston on Contracts (Rev. Ed.), p. 4332, § 1543.) In Restatement, Restitution, § 11 (1), it is said:

"A person is not entitled to rescind a transaction with another if, by way of compromise or otherwise, he agreed with the other to assume, or intended to assume, the risk of a mistake for which otherwise he would be entitled to rescission and consequent restitution."

See, also, *Lamb v. Rathburn,* 118 Mich. 666; *Kirl v. Zinner,* 274 Mich. 331; *Story v. Page,* 280 Mich. 34; *Welch v. Citizens Mutual Auto Ins. Co.,* 285 Mich. 82; *Mayor v. Sanders,* 286 Mich. 45. In the instant case, while the parties may have assumed the risk of any mistake in connection with the anticipated outcome of the proceeding on its merits and the time in the future when the decision would be rendered, they were acting under a basic mutual mistake in assuming that the case had not been decided at the time they negotiated and consummated their settlement. All mistakenly felt certain that the case had not yet been determined, and all joined in the belief that it would be several weeks before a decision would be rendered. They cannot be held to have assumed, or to have intended to assume by their compromise, the risk of being mistaken in these basic regards. For such mistake, the settlement, like any other contract, may be rescinded. Restatement, Restitution, § 11, comment c; 5 Williston on Contracts (Rev. Ed.) pp. 4332, 4333, § 1543. Knowledge that the case had already been determined would have put their negotiations on a different footing, if negotiations there would have been at all.

The decree is affirmed. Costs to plaintiff.

BUSHNELL, C. J., and SHARPE, BOYLES, CHANDLER, NORTH, McALLISTER, and WIEST, JJ., concurred.

Section 6 of the Restatement of Restitution, cited in the *Farhat* opinion, says: "Mistake means a state of mind not in accord with the facts." Comment c to § 11 says, in part: "Although a compromise is subject to the same rules as are other agreements, since it implies doubt as to the existence or extent of a claim, ordinarily the parties to a compromise intend that it shall be a final determination of the controversy between them irrespective of uncertainty as to facts. Nevertheless, even a specific statement by the parties that the transaction is final does not make it such, and it is not final if there is a basic mistake as to matters not believed by the parties to be doubtful."

In *Story v. Page,* cited above in the *Farhat* opinion, the court said: "Parties may not, after executing written releases in pursuance of a compromise of their claim, not free from doubt, promiscuously change their minds, and set aside the settlement, except where the proof of the fraud is clear and positive." Such conditions did not exist in the present case. The releases were binding on the parties. Compare *Welch v. Citizens Mutual Automobile Ins. Co.,* 285 Mich. 82, 280 N.W. 118 (1938) (release of personal injury claim not set aside; citing *Story v. Page*), with *Denton v. Utley,* 350 Mich. 332, 86 N.W.2d 537 (1957) (release of personal injury claim set aside in an opinion evidently intended to be a landmark opinion, describing *Story v. Page* as "contra in principle"; two other judges concurred in the opinion, and four others concurred in the result).

Is there any *law* that governs these mistake cases dealing with personal injury releases? See the comment of Mr. Justice Talbot Smith in *Denton v. Utley, supra:* "This case must be read with great care. We are upsetting the particular release here involved. We are not saying that all releases are vulnerable. What we are saying is that releases have no particular immunity of their own to attack on the ground of mistake or fraud. There is no form of words, there is no formula, no instrument, no transaction, that rises above the chancellor's scrutiny or resists his intervention. *'Fiat justitia ruat coelum.'* In the case before us Vernon Denton got into an automobile accident. . . ."

MESH v. CITRIN, 299 Mich. 527, 300 N.W. 870 (1941): Defendants subleased a gas station to plaintiff; plaintiff sues to rescind the contract of sublease, on the ground that defendants had fraudulently represented that the station had sold 29,000 gallons a month; that plaintiff would make a profit of $50 a week on the station, and that the station and equipment were in excellent condition. A judgment for plaintiff was affirmed (on condition of a remittitur by plaintiff): "We have often held that false representations concerning the past volume of business are actionable." After noting that fraud is never presumed, nor lightly to be inferred, the court added: "See, also ... *Achenbach v. Mears,* [p. 170, *supra,*] 272 Mich. 74; ...."

ESSENBURG v. RUSSELL
346 Mich. 319, 78 N.W.2d 136 (1956)

CARR, J. This is an action for damages based on a claim of misrepresentation in the sale of a grocery store and business in the city of Charlevoix. Prior to November 29, 1952, defendants were operating said store as proprietors under a contract of purchase from a third party. Following some negotiations between plaintiffs and defendants the former agreed to pay the sum of $25,000 for the property, including the merchandise on hand and the good will. The agreement was reduced to writing and signed by the parties. It is the claim of the plaintiffs that defendants stated during the negotiations that the cost price of the stock of goods and merchandise in the store was approximately $4,000. The contract referred thereto in specific terms, stating that "the said stock of goods and merchandise being of the value of approximately $4,000 cost price."

Plaintiffs went into possession of the store on the 1st of December following the execution of the agreement. It is their claim that they concluded after an examination of the stock that the cost price was less than had been represented to them by defendants. Accordingly they, with the assistance of other parties who were experienced in the grocery business, made an inventory which, as they claimed on the trial of the case, disclosed that the cost price of the stock of goods at the time of purchase was not approximately $4,000 but was in fact about ½ that sum. Plaintiffs complained to defendants immediately following the taking of the inventory, but no adjustment of the matter was made. Subsequently, under date of December 15, 1952, defendants by letter offered to rescind the transaction. Such offer was not accepted by plaintiffs, it being their claim, as found by the trial court, that they had altered their position by selling their home in Flint, removing to Charlevoix, and taking over the operation of the store.

* * *

It clearly appears from the record that the case was tried in circuit court on the theory of misrepresentation rather than of intentional fraud and deceit. In *Holcomb v. Noble,* [p. 148, *supra,*] 69 Mich. 396, it was held that:

"The doctrine is settled in this State that if there was *in fact* a misrepresentation, though made innocently, and its deceptive influence was effective, the consequences to the plaintiff being as serious as though it had proceeded from a *vicious* purpose, he would have a right of action for the damages caused thereby either at law or in equity. *Converse v. Blumrich,* 14 Mich. 109 (90 Am. Dec. 230); *Steinbach v. Hill,* [p. 137, *supra,*] 25 Mich. 78; *Beebe v. Knapp,* 28 Mich. 53; *Webster v. Bailey,* 31 Mich. 36; *Starkweather v. Benjamin,* [p. 138, *supra,*] 32 Mich. 305; *Baughman v. Gould,* 45 Mich. 481." (Syllabus 3).

       * * *

Counsel have directed attention to *Achenbach v. Mears,* [p. 170, *supra,*] 272 Mich. 74, in which a majority of this Court held that plaintiffs had not established their right to rescission of a contract involving an exchange of property. It was there indicated that the expresion of an opinion as to the value of property ordinarily is not actionable. In the case at bar, however, the misrepresentation made by defendants on which the judgment against them was based was not as to value but rather as to cost price. Furthermore, the facts involved in the cited case are not analogous to those in the case at bar. A controversy of the nature here involved must necessarily be determined in the light of the factual situation presented rather than by reference to other cases involving varying situations.

Appellants also argue that the proofs established that there was a mutual mistake of fact. We are unable to agree. Admittedly the plaintiffs were young and inexperienced in the grocery business and had not made any detailed examination of the merchandise in stock before closing the contract, nor had they procured others to determine in their behalf the cost price of the various articles in stock. They relied on the statements of defendants as to the matter in issue. This they had the right to do under the circumstances, and defendants are scarcely in position to claim otherwise.

We find no reversible error in the case, and the judgment of the trial court is affirmed. Plaintiffs may have costs.

DETHMERS, C. J., and SHARPE, SMITH, EDWARDS, BOYLES, KELLY, and BLACK, JJ., concurred.

LLEWELLYN, THE RULE OF LAW IN OUR CASE-LAW OF CONTRACT
47 YALE L.J.* 1243-48 (1938)

Ours is a legal system in which it is peculiarly difficult to reach agreement on what the Rule of Law is. I refer to the case-law portion of our law. Where we have a statute, we know at least what its words are, and we know that its language constitutes an authoritative direction to the courts, and we recognize that it can have authority as a rule, even when its language is flatly

* Reprinted by permission of the Yale Law Journal Company and Fred B. Rothman & Company from the *Yale Law Journal,* vol. 47, pp. 1243-1248.

at variance with anything which courts have said or done in the circumstance. Our legal techniques and our theories about them are indeed somewhat muddy as to statutes: cheek by jowl sit the principles about statutes in derogation and about remedial statutes, and it is a stout man who on any given issue can use both at once on the same statutory language.

But in the field of case-law which our general theory of rules of law has been most concerned, even the sureness about what the precise authoritative words are (which give the whole tone to a Continental discussion of rules) is almost wholly lacking.

To begin with, the verbal form of a rule of case-law is rarely fixed. The same judge who announces "a rule" as "long-established and clear" will often enough phrase "it" three different ways in the same opinion. In the very fact that this does not startle us lies a key to the degree of implicit fluidity of case-law rules. Similar troubles about fluidity and indefiniteness lie in the common practice of throwing make-weight arguments into an opinion after the "controlling" rule has been laid down.

The Protean Correctness of "The" Rule Based on Precedent

The fact is that there is not to be found in our system any clear and definite single relation between the cases and the Rule of Case-Law. We have instead a number of relations, any and each of which is authoritative and correct *if* the court chooses to use it. The correct doctrinal *possibilities* of case-law are hydra-headed, in the most settled field. It is the *probabilities* which move within a much narrower range, and which give guidance to counsellor and court. But the probabilities turn not on the fixity of doctrine, but on the relative predictability of courts' reactions to new cases. This is known to all of us, in our fingers. We *work* with the actual nature of case-law. But our technique of describing our goal and our work is not abreast of our working skills.

Let me set down a series of relations between the cases and "the" rule of case-law which judicial practice establishes as correct.

(1) The controlling rule of the precedent is the ground on which the court chose, explicitly, to rest the decision.

(2) The controlling rule is broad enough to include the theory of an institution laid down expressly in the opinion (as that a director is "a trustee").

(3) The controlling rule is any rule or principle "necessary" to the decision, whether or not explicitly laid down.

(4) The controlling rule extends, whatever the court chose to rest its decision on, no whit beyond what was "necessary" to the decision.

(5) The controlling rule is what some later writer has *said* it is — be he court or encyclopedia — and whether or not his statement is accurate.

(6) The controlling rule is anything a court has said, though in flagrant obiter.

(7)   Nothing can be the controlling rule which has not been phrased in quotable words.

Now it may be said, and I doubt not that it will be said, that at least the last three of these propositions are bad law, bad doctrine, and the mark of incompetence. To this I can answer only that they are part of the multiple *going ways* of case-law. If the fifth proposition does not have meaning, for instance, I cannot understand the indexing of opinions in which a case is said to have been "explained," nor the frequence of citation of Cyc. and Ruling Case Law as giving "the rule." If the seventh does not have meaning, I cannot understand the desperate search for quotable language for a brief, nor the pronounced feeling among good lawyers and poor lawyers alike that to set up new language, though it holds the actual decisions to perfection, is to buck extra danger in most courts. Where courts work under time pressure, or with limited library facilities, or both, these last three propositions will be potent parts of the available alternatives for determining "the Rule" from the cases.

In a word, if one is to see our case-law system as it lives and moves, one must see that the relation between the rule and the cases may move all the way from copying any words printed by anybody in a "law" book to meticulous re-examination of precise facts, issues, and holdings, in total disregard of any prior language whatsoever. And any degree or kind of operation within that lordly range is correct, doctrinally, if doctrine be taken to [be] a description of what authoritative courts are doing with and to cases and rules, and doing with effective authority.

Now it is not here urged that any one or more of these working relations between the rules in a case-law field and the prior cases in and around that field is The Correct Relation. *Each,* on authority, is *a* dogmatically correct relation. I do think certain of them more serviceable than others; but that is not at this point under discussion. It concerns me here to invite any lawyer or judge to canvass in his own mind *whether he has not used and is not now prepared to use* ANY ONE of these ways which may serve his need, in locating or building a rule based on case-law; and whether he is not aware, as he uses *any* of them, that his procedure is proper, and in accordance with the established authoritative tradition of our case-law scheme. Patently he cannot use all of the ways at once on any given precedent as to any given issue; but he can and will use several or most of them on any body of cases some of which have language which tends as he wants it, some of which have language which distresses him. He will "line these up." One piece of pure dictum will "admirably state the true theory," an opinion his way which quotes that dictum will become "the leading case;" two opinions with less happy language will buttress his present case by their facts and decision, but will not be quoted from; one case announcing a contrary rule be distinguished as not involving the point here at issue; another whose raw facts were almost identical will be pseudo-distinguished because the artifacts were different ("That was a case of an agency"); and any text that can be used, whatever it rests on, will be thrown in as showing the rule claimed to be "well-established."

In very sooth, there are a number of recognized authoritative relations which prevail between the rule of law which rests on case-law and the past decisions on which the rule purports to rest, and on which it is supposed to rest. And these recognized and authoritative relations are frequently semi-inconsistent, or wholly inconsistent with one another. Here lies the heart and juice of the matter: the various established and authoritative relations between the rule and the cases lead to *different* rules. These different rules, loosely formulated, or reformulated more precisely, or latent and never yet expressed, are in open or covert competition, and our going doctrine, both formulated and unformulated, about how to locate or build a rule gives no clear criterion at all about which rule is The Rule. There is one test, however, which in the long run we all use to determine the rule of law in a case law field. *That test is in first instance the test of how future cases will come out.*

If it is moderately clear how future cases will come out, then a statement of that clarity is the Rule of Case-Law, and it is the Rule, irrespective of whether it is a nice rule or a wise one or a just one. And it is also the Rule, irrespective of whether there are pseudo-rules lying around which purport to be The Rule, but are not. Doubt begins when it is not clear how future cases will come out; for instance, because the accepted formula does not effectively guide decision at all, or because the courts use it some of the time, but avoid its implications some of the time — situations which I hold to be more typical than non-typical of such fields of case-law as the law of Contract.

All or this leads to doctrinal difficulties. "Ours is a legal system in which" — on the case-law side — "it is peculiarly difficult to reach agreement on what The Rule of Law Is."

D.   The Field Code

A. VAN ALSTYNE, THE CALIFORNIA CIVIL CODE
WEST'S ANN. CALIF. CIVIL CODE* at 1, 3-33 (1954)

* * *

Although the civil law had its champions at the time, in the person of such influential citizens as Governor Burnett and John W. Dwinelle of the San Francisco Bar, the views of the Senate Committee prevailed over all opposition. Its recomendation that "in cases not falling within the Constitution of the United States, or the Constitution or statutes of this State, the Courts

---

shall be governed in their adjudications by the English Common Law, as received and modified in the United States; in other words, by the AMERICAN COMMON LAW," became law on April 13, 1850. Only nine days later, on April 22, all laws in force in California except those passed by the Legislature at the same session were (with certain minor exceptions), abolished. Other than the doctrines of community property law, which were retained, the substantive law was thus purged of all except an occasional indirect legacy from the Mexican-Spanish law. California, at the very beginning of its existence as a state, had joined the ranks of the common law jurisdictions.

The Movement to Codify the Common Law

Meanwhile at the other end of the continent David Dudley Field's prolonged struggle in behalf of codification was just beginning. The incomplete Field Code of Civil Procedure had been adopted by the New York Legislature in 1848; but the work of codification of the substantive law had broken down. The "Commissioners of the Code," first appointed for thus purpose in 1847, had made little progress by 1850, and, lacking Field as one of their number had displayed such a notable want of enthusiasm for their appointed task that the entire project had been abandoned in that year.

After a prolonged period of sustained agitation, Field managed to induce the New York Legislature to revive the defunct Commission in 1857. This second Code Commision, with Field now designated as a member, moved steadily forward with the task of codification. By 1862 a draft Civil Code was presented to the Legislature and to the bar, consisting of some 2,034 sections separated into four divisions relating respectively to Persons, Property, Obligations, and General Provisions. This first draft was largely the product of the personal labor of David Dudley Field himself, ...

Completion of the Civil Code was the occasion for an outburst of sustained and frequently vehement opposition to it from leading members of the bar. In a series of speeches, articles and committee reports, particularly by members of the Bar Association of the City of New York, the Code was attacked as dangerous in principle, unscientific in structure, confusing in terminology and inaccurate as an expression of existing law. The unceasing efforts of Field and his supporters in pointing out the advantages to be secured by adoption of the Civil Code, and in refuting the objections of his critics, has been ably chronicled elsewhere. These efforts however persistent, resulted in ultimate failure; and upon the two occasions when the Civil Code was in fact adopted by the New York Legislature, it was vetoed each time by the Governor. To this day, New York has never adopted the Civil Code, a failure described by one writer as "an indelible blot upon its escutcheon."

To understand the sources of the opposition to Field's Civil Code, one must appreciate the philosophic content of the juristic thinking of the times. Steeped in the traditions of historical jurisprudence, Field's critics, lad by James

C. Carter of New York City, declared that codification of the unwritten law represented an attempt to make certain that which inherently could not be made certain; that in the relations and dealings of men with one another justice, as reflected in the experience of a society and in the socially accepted standards of right conduct, was the essential goal, rather than certainty; and that the administration of justice as so understood was possible only under a system of unwritten law conceived with relation to specific fact situations and freely adaptable to changing circumstances. The only just law, proclaimed Mr. Carter, "which consists in applying directly the standard of justice to human conduct, consists in applying that standard to *known* facts, and can have, in human apprehension, no existence apart from the facts." To attempt to enact a system of rules developed with reference to past known facts but intended to be applied with reference to future unknown facts was thus, in the opinion of Field's critics, not only folly but a dangerous and undesirable deviation from legal tradition.

As Dean Pound as pointed out, Field's faith in codification put him in opposition to the juristic orthodoxy of the nineteenth century, which was against legislation in the field of the common law. To the lawyers of that day, who saw perfection in the capacity of the common law for adaptability and growth, the adoption of a Civil Code meant the introduction of error and rigidity, and supplanting of principle with cant, and the promotion of uncertainty and instability. Such a Code, they felt, would inevitably reflect the inadequacy of language and of human foresight to cover unknown future eventualities.

Although the influence of his critics carried the day in New York, Field's efforts to reduce the unwritten law to positive legislation were not entirely in vain. Codification offered a solution to the increasingly vexatious uncertainty, complexity, expense and confusion attendant upon a system of private law buried in a tremendous and ever-expanding body of judicial decisions. The prospect of a formally enacted repository of substantive principles gave plausible promise of increased economy in the ascertainment of law, greater conciseness and clarity in the statement of principles, and correspondingly more predictability leading to less litigation. Many felt that an authoritative restatement in compact and systematically organized form would, in addition, facilitate orderly reform of the law and permit of wider dissemination to the public of accurate information as to legal rights and duties.

Field's own convictions as to the desirability of the Civil Code were clear:

> "The question whether a Code is desirable is simply a question between written and unwritten law. That this was ever debatable is one of the most remarkable facts in the history of jurisprudence. If the law is a thing to be obeyed, it is a thing to be known, and if it is to be known, there can be no better, not to say no other method of making it known than of writing and publishing it. If a written constitution is desirable, so are written laws."

In the young and growing commonwealth of California, the basically practical views of Field commanded wider acceptance than the more theoretic and philosophic arguments of the jurists of the historic school. In 1872, the advantages of codification of the unwritten law, as well as of a systematic revision of statute law, loomed large, since that law, drawing heavily upon the judicial traditions of the older states of the Union, was still in a formative stage. The possibility of widely dispersed popular knowledge of basic legal concepts comported well with the individualistic attitudes of the early West.

* * *

The Civil Code, however, was not merely a reduction of the unwritten law to positive legislative form. It also constituted a revision of many pertinent earlier California statutes, which were retained as part of the Code after being redrafted to harmonize with its form and terminology. Such statutory precedent was interspersed where appropriate with related and complementary provisions based on common law sources. Among the major portions of the Code which were drawn primarily from previous California legislation were the numerous provisions relating to corporations, community property, apprenticeship, the execution and revocation of wills, the law of succession, fraudulent conveyances, mining partnerships, and the homestead provisions. In addition, the Code sections relating to marriage and divorce and to the recordation of documents relating to real property were greatly modified, in comparison with the New York draft, to incorporate the substance of prior statutes. . . .

* * *

In following Field, therefore, the California Commissioners did not hesitate to import into the law of California from the Field draft certain desirable but new substantive concepts previously unknown here. The rules governing accession to personal property, the provision authorizing the extinction of an obligation by deposit in a bank for the creditor, and the authorization of holographic wills, for example, were innovations, drawn by Field from the Code Napoléon and the Civil Code of Louisiana. . . .

* * *

By 1930 the Civil Code had grown to the most massive proportions it would attain. Excluding from consideration the initial revision of 1874, the Code had displayed a pronounced propensity to acquire new sections with but a slight ability to slough off the old. The process of amendment and accretion had resulted in a numbering system which was a monstrosity from both an esthetic and numerical viewpoint, as illustrated by a series of sections numbered from 653aa to 653xx, another bearing designations from 653ab to 653ag, and climaxed by a section carrying the fantastic number 453gg ½. The Code was by now a vast repository of miscellaneous substantive precepts, ranging from insurance to agricultural cooperatives, from the regulation of building and loan corporations to water rights, from the law of testamentary disposition to the rules governing the navigation of vessels on inland waters, from cemeteries to hydraulic mining, from divorce to bottomry and respondentia. Of even more significance, of course, is the fact that great segments of the statutory law relating to many of the topics touched by the Civil Code were not included therein, but were found only in the voluminous and much less accessible pages of the annual sessions laws, and the compilations thereof known as the "general laws." By 1930, therefore, the increasing tempo of Code amendment, the developing unmanageability of the Code itself, and the paradox of its heterogeneous scope but incomplete coverage, all were apparent and thoroughly justifiable grounds for reconsideration of the position of the Civil Code in the system of California statutes.

The first biennial report of the California Code Commission, dated December 15, 1930, attempted to analyze in some detail the position of the Civil Code in the system of codified law. Observing that "the law outside the codes is vastly greater than the law inside," the Commission pointed out that if all of the uncodified private law were introduced into the Civil Code, the "confusion would be almost inextricable" and the Civil Code "would be distorted beyond all recognition." The Commission generally proposed a complete recodification of the permanent substantive law according to cognate subject matter. In so doing, it recognized that if such restatement were carried through completely, "there would be nothing left of the Civil Code except those general statements of common law rules that in most states are left uncodified. It is submitted that the attempt to state these general rules in Code form is a mistake."

The Commission did not, however, propose to do away with the Civil Code as part of its recommended affirmative program. Instead, it recognized that there was some utility in its retention for limited purposes. Addressing itself to the problem of the Civil Code, the report states:

> "Logically, as we have said, and as an original matter, it has no place in our statutory law, but there are nevertheless strong practical reasons for retaining it. The lawyers are used to it. Many of its provisions have become embodied in our law. In many cases they have become rules of property. To alter these provisions, even to the extent of changing their positions and context, might result in unexpected disturbance of settled law and vested rights. Accordingly, the commission proposes to retain the Civil Code, but there will be taken out of it the provisions relating to:
> (1)   Corporations (the subject of Corporations was not included in the original Code as drafted by Field, except for a brief statement of general principles of organization, management and dissolution);
> (2)   Domestic Relations;
> (3)   Insurance;
> (4)   Mortgages and Liens;
> (5)   Partnerships;
> (6)   Wills and Succession (contained in the proposed Probate Code);
> (7)   A few miscellaneous provisions that more properly belong elsewhere. . . .
> This problem, however, of the future of the Civil Code should be left unsettled for the present, as its solution is not a pressing matter and can

be undertaken after the Code Commission has completed its work. The retention of the Civil Code, with the exceptions indicated, appears to the Commission to be the best policy for the present."

The work of the Code Commission had its first impact on the Civil Code in 1931 legislative session, when the Probate Code was enacted, taking from the Civil Code its extensive provisions relating to guardianship, wills, the interpretation of wills, and succession.

* * *

JUDICIAL DEVELOPMENT OF THE CIVIL CODE

The history of the Civil Code, however, is not merely one of growth and decline through the legislative process. The present role of the Code in the jurisprudence of California cannot be adequately appraised without at least a brief account of its judicial reception.

In 1873, the opinion of California's most distinguished jurist, Justice Stephen J. Field, pronounced the Civil Code and its companion works to be "perfect in their analysis, admirable in their order and arrangement, and furnishing a complete code of laws." By 1888, Commissioner Creed Haymond felt justified in reporting to David Dudley Field that the question of the advisability of codifying the unwritten law was "no longer an open one in California. . . . codification in that State is an accomplished fact, the propriety of which is no more discussed, than is the propriety of the written Constitution. The Codes have worked well in California. . . ."

Yet, as even its warmest supporters freely admitted, the Civil Code was far from perfect. The detailed work of the special Advisory Committee in 1872, and the further revisions promulgated in 1873 by the Commission to Examine the Codes, had removed a number of the more serious and glaring deficiencies. Nonetheless, major criticisms were still to be heard.

In 1884, Professor John Norton Pomeroy launched a heavy attack upon the Civil Code in the West Coast Reporter, of which he was co-editor. In a series of articles entitled "The True Method of Interpreting the Civil Code," he leveled a critical broadside against the terminology and form as well as the specific content of certain portions of the Civil Code. A great source of doubt, uncertainty and possible error had been created, declared Pomeroy, by the Code Commission's "constant, but wholly unnecessary practice, of abandoning well known legal terms and phrases, the signification, force and effect of which had long been settled and certain, and of adopting instead thereof an unknown and hitherto unused language and terminology"; by the incomplete and partial nature of the Code, which was limited on the whole to statements of general definitions and general doctrines, leaving unformulated the great mass of special rules applicable to particular circumstances; and by the "extreme conciseness and brevity" of expression uniformly employed by the codifiers — a technique which, to Pomeroy, "left it often very doubtful *what* doctrines and rules they intend to state." The absence of any amplifications, explanations, or illustrations of the various doctrines and rules "laid down in the most abstract manner" meant that "matters of the greatest importance are constantly left as inferences, and often as doubtful inferences."

Buttressing his position with references to numerous specific provisions of the Code, Pomeroy further stated that there was "hardly a definition, or a statement of doctrine in the whole work, the full meaning, force and effect of which can be apprehended or understood without a previous *accurate* knowledge of the common law doctrines and rules on the same subject matter." Indeed, the preoccupation of the authors with abstract doctrines to the exclusion of the special detailed rules obtaining in varied factual circumstances meant that "the great mass of actual, practical rules of law and equity which immediately guide the courts in their work of adjudicating" were not expressed in the Code and frequently were not even included by necessary implication in what was expressed. "For such rules," he proclaimed, "the courts must go outside of the Code, and must find them in the pre-existing and still existing common law or equity untouched or unaltered by the Code."

Pomeroy's articles were thus a powerful argument to the effect that the Civil Code was scarcely more than an outline of a complete code of private civil jurisprudence, and hence could not and should not constitute the primary source of the law of private rights. Rejecting the Continental system of code interpretation as wholly unsuited and unsuitable to a code whose heritage was based so largely upon common law precedents, Pomeroy urged the adoption of a uniform method of interpretaion of the Civil Code which would appropriately interrelate its text with its common law ancestry. He argued that as "decision after decision is made giving a construction to the language of the Code *without such a method,* members of the Bar will be wholly unable to advise their clients, with any certainty, as to the meaning of particular provisions which have not yet been expressly interpreted; and after the process has thus gone on for some few years, the whole law, based upon the Code, will have become a mass of uncertainties, inconsistencies, and contradictions, so that the welfare of the public will demand a complete repeal or abandonment of the Code legislation." The method advocated was simple: the provisions of the Civil Code "are to be regarded as simply declaratory of the previous common law and equitable doctrines and rules, except where the intent to depart from those doctrines and rules clearly appears from the unequivocal language of the text."

Prior to the publication of Pomeroy's articles, the California courts had not developed any consistent interpretative approach to the Civil Code. . . .

The uncertainty of the early cases is not surprising, since the Civil Code itself was somewhat equivocal as to its relationship to the common law. Section 4 declared, in part, that "The Code establishes the law of this State respecting the subjects to which it relates . . . ," while section 5 announced that "The provisions of this Code, so far as they are substantially the same as existing statutes or the common law, must be construed as continuations thereof, and not as new enactments."

The clear and explicit views of a highly respected jurist such as Pomeroy, being advanced before any firm decision had been reached in the courts as to the appropriate interpretative approach, were bound to command attention. The year following publication of the last of his essays on the subject, the Supreme Court took a long step toward adoption of the Pomeroy viewpoint when, after quoting section 4, it stated flatly that

> "this, of course, does not mean that there is no law with respect to such subjects except that embodied in the code. When the code speaks, its provisions are controlling, and they are to be liberally construed, with a view to effect its objects and to promote justice—the rule of the common law that statutes in derogation thereof are to be strictly construed having been expressly abolished here; but where the code is silent, the common law governs."

In a celebrated divorce litigation of 1888, a majority of the Supreme Court expressly adopted the views of Professor Pomeroy in considering the meaning of the phrase, "mutual assumption of marital rights, duties, and obligations," authorized by section 55 of the Civil Code as a mode for establishing a marriage in lieu of solemnization. Quoting extensively and with approval from Professor Pomeroy's articles, Mr. Justice McKinstry declared that when a Code section, or other statutory enactment "is so confused and uncertain that it can be given no intelligible meaning, we must consider the common law unchanged by it. . . . The common law underlies all our legislation, and furnishes the rule of decision except in so far as the statutes have changed the common law. When the common law is departed from by a provision of the code, effect is to be given to the provision to the extent — and only to the extent — of the departure."

Other cases followed the path thus blazed. It was soon settled, however, that the common law, of which the Civil Code was a continuation, includes only such portion thereof as "conforms to our institutions and form of government and is applicable to the habits and conditions of society." The fact that the provisions of the Civil Code were complete in themselves was held not to preclude their interpretation in the light of the common law rules on the subject nor to exclude variations and distinctions recognized by the common law in particular fact situations as to which the Code was silent:

> "The Civil Code was not designed to embody the whole law of private and civil relations, rights and duties; it is incomplete and partial; and except in those instances where its language clearly and unequivocally discloses an intention to depart from, alter, or abrogate the common-law

rule concerning a particular subject matter, a section of the code purporting to embody such doctrine or rule will be construed in the light of common-law decisions on the same subject." *

REPPY, THE FIELD CODIFICATION CONCEPT
DAVID DUDLEY FIELD CENTENARY ESSAYS ** 17, 29-30
(Reppy ed. 1949)

Thus forced to limit his codification efforts to a single state [New York — Field's Civil Code failed to be adopted by the New York legislature], Field found himself confronted with a second problem, to wit, that of choosing between the three recognized methods of codification, the gradual or partial, the philosophical or the historical.

If the gradual or partial method was to be used, then only specific subjects of the law could be codified. This method, far less scientific than the others, might have appealed to Field's practical mind, as it was more susceptible of realization. This was the type adopted in England as illustrated by the Bill of Exchange Act of 1882.

If the philosophical method was to be used, it presupposed an entirely new system of law, based perhaps on the experience or law of foreign countries, and completely unrestricted by the existing local law. The characteristic of this type of codification was careful classification and distribution of material, unity and coherence in development with reference to the whole body of the law, and consistency in language. It was best illustrated by Livingston's Penal Code of Louisiana.

If the historical approach, the best example of which was the Justinian Code, was to be followed, it would necessarily involve the digesting and restatement of the existing law, statutory and nonstatutory. Deviations from this conservative policy in the form of amendment of the existing law might be made if thought to be desirable, but subject to retraction if such changes proved unworkable.

As Field was not an iconoclast, or a destroyer of past traditions, as he had no desire to destroy the common law, but to preserve it by eliminating its defects and rendering it into language understandable to the people as well as the Bench and Bar, he naturally chose the historical approach, which merely involved the restatement of the existing law, cutting off its excrescences, amending it to meet modern conditions, then making it adaptable, not only in

---

* For further material on the codification movement in Anglo-American legal history, see KIMBALL, HISTORICAL INTRODUCTION TO THE LEGAL SYSTEM, ch. 7 (1966).

New York, but in the several states of the United States, and among all English-speaking peoples.

CALIFORNIA CIVIL CODE
of 1872, as amended

§ 1. TITLE AND DIVISIONS OF THIS ACT. This act shall be known as The Civil Code of the State of California, and is in Four Divisions, as follows:

    I.—The First Relating to Persons.
    II.—The Second to Property.
    III.—The Third to Obligations.
    IV.—The Fourth Contains General Provisions Relating to the Three Preceding Divisions.

    * * *

§ 4. RULES OF CONSTRUCTION. The rule of the common law, that statutes in derogation thereof are to be strictly construed, has no application to this Code. The Code establishes the law of this State respecting the subjects to which it relates, and its provisions are to be liberally construed with a view to effect its objects and to promote justice.

§ 5. PROVISIONS SIMILAR TO EXISTING LAWS, HOW CONSTRUED. The provisions of this Code, so far as they are substantially the same as existing statutes or the common law, must be construed as continuations thereof, and not as new enactments.

    * * *

§ 22.2. The common law of England, so far as it is not repugnant to or inconsistent with the Constitution of the United States, or the Constitution or laws of this State, is the rule of decision in all the courts of this State. [Added to the Code in 1951, based on a statute of 1850.]

    * * *

§ 1427. OBLIGATION, WHAT. An obligation is a legal duty, by which a person is bound to do or not to do a certain thing.

§ 1428. An obligation arises either from:
    One — The contract of the parties; or,
    Two — The operation of law. An obligation arising from operation of law may be enforced in the manner provided by law, or by civil action or proceeding.

    * * *

§ 1549.   CONTRACT, WHAT. A contract is an agreement to do or not to do a certain thing.

§ 1550.   ESSENTIAL ELEMENTS OF CONTRACT. It is essential to the existence of a contract that there should be:
1.   Parties capable of contracting;
2.   Their consent;
3.   A lawful object; and,
4.   A sufficient cause* or consideration.
* * *

§ 1565.   ESSENTIALS OF CONSENT. The consent of the parties to a contract must be:
1.   Free;
2.   Mutual; and,
3.   Communicated by each to the other.

§ 1566.   CONSENT, WHEN VOIDABLE. A consent which is not free is nevertheless not absolutely void, but may be rescinded by the parties, in the manner prescribed by the Chapter on Rescission §§ 1688 *et seq.*

§ 1567.   APPARENT CONSENT, WHEN NOT FREE. An apparent consent is not real or free when obtained through:
1.   Duress;
2.   Menace;
3.   Fraud;
4.   Undue influence; or,
5.   Mistake.

§ 1568.   WHEN DEEMED TO HAVE BEEN OBTAINED BY FRAUD, ETC. Consent is deemed to have been obtained through one of the causes mentioned in the last section only when it would not have been given had such cause not existed.
* * *

§ 1571.   FRAUD, ACTUAL OR CONSTRUCTIVE. Fraud is either actual or constructive.

---

* This section is virtually a direct copy of article 1108 of the Code Napoléon, except for the addition of the reference to "consideration." In Field's annotation to the corresponding section of the New York code which failed of passage, he cites both the Code Napoléon and the Civil Code of Louisiana. The California courts have read "cause" as the equivalent of "consideration." See Keyes, *Cause and Consideration in California—A Re-Appraisal,* 47 CALIF L. REV. 74 (1959). — Ed.

§ 1572.   ACTUAL FRAUD, WHAT. Actual fraud, within the meaning of this Chapter, consists in any of the following acts, committed by a party to the contract, or with his connivance, with intent to deceive another party thereto, or to induce him to enter into the contract:

1.   The suggestion, as a fact, of that which is not true, by one who does not believe it to be true;

2.   The positive assertion, in a manner not warranted by the information of the person making it, of that which is not true, though he believes it to be true;

3.   The suppression of that which is true, by one having knowledge or belief of the fact;

4.   A promise made without any intention of performing it; or,

5.   Any other act fitted to deceive.

§ 1573.   CONSTRUCTIVE FRAUD. Constructive fraud consists:

1.   In any breach of duty which, without an actually fraudulent intent, gains an advantage to the person in fault, or any one claiming under him, by misleading another to his prejudice, or to the prejudice of any one claiming under him; or

2.   In any such act or omission as the law specially declares to be fraudulent, without respect to actual fraud.

§ 1574.   ACTUAL FRAUD A QUESTION OF FACT. Actual fraud is always a question of fact.

                    *   *   *

§ 1576.   MISTAKE, WHAT. Mistake may be either of fact or law.

§ 1577.   MISTAKE OF FACT. Mistake of fact is a mistake, not caused by the neglect of a legal duty on the part of the person making the mistake, and consisting in:

1.   An unconscious ignorance or forgetfulness of a fact past or present, material to the contract; or,

2.   Belief in the present existence of a thing material to the contract, which does not exist, or in the past existence of such a thing, which has not existed.

§ 1578.   MISTAKE OF LAW. Mistake of law constitutes a mistake, within the meaning of this Article, only when it arises from:

1.   A misapprehension of the law by all parties, all supposing that they knew and understood it, and all making substantially the same mistake as to the law; or,

2. A misapprehension of the law by one party, of which the others are aware at the time of contracting, but which they do not rectify.

§ 1579. MISTAKE OF FOREIGN LAWS. Mistake of foreign laws is a mistake of fact.

§ 1580. MUTUALITY OF CONSENT. Consent is not mutual, unless the parties all agree upon the same thing in the same sense. But in certain cases defined by the Chapter on Interpretation, they are to be deemed so to agree without regard to the fact.

    * * *

§ 1688. RESCISSION EXTINGUISHES CONTRACT. A contract is extinguished by its rescission.

§ 1689. (a) A contract may be rescinded if all the parties thereto consent.

    (b) A party to a contract may rescind the contract in the following cases:

(1) If the consent of the party rescinding, or of any party jointly contracting with him, was given by mistake, or obtained through duress, menace, fraud, or undue influence, exercised by or with the connivance of the party as to whom he rescinds, or of any other party to the contract jointly interested with such party.

(2) If the consideration for the obligation of the rescinding party fails, in whole or in part, through the fault of the party as to whom he rescinds.

(3) If the consideration for the obligation of the rescinding party becomes entirely void from any cause.

(4) If the consideration for the obligation of the rescinding party, before it is rendered to him, fails in a material respect from any cause.

(5) If the contract is unlawful for causes which do not appear in its terms or conditions, and the parties are not equally at fault.

(6) If the public interest will be prejudiced by permitting the contract to stand.

(7) Under the circumstances provided for in sections 39 [unsound mind], 1533 [novation], 1566, 1785, 1789 [both dealing with sale of goods, and transferred to the Commercial Code], 1930 [use of thing lent for unauthorized purposes] and 2314 [rescission of ratification] of this code, [certain specified sections of the Corporations and Insurance Codes], or any other statute providing for rescission.

§ 1690. WHEN STIPULATIONS AGAINST RIGHT TO RESCIND DO NOT DEFEAT IT. A stipulation that errors of description shall not avoid a contract, or shall be the subject of compensation, or both, does not take away the right of rescission for fraud, nor for mistake, where such mistake is in a matter essential to the inducement of the contract, and is not capable of exact and entire compensation.

§ 1691.   PROCEDURE. Subject to Section 1693 [delay in notice of rescission or restoration of benefits], to effect a rescission a party to the contract must, promptly upon discovering the facts which entitle him to rescind if he is free from duress, menace, undue influence or disability and is aware of his right to rescind:

(a)   Give notice of rescission to the party as to whom he rescinds; and

(b)   Restore to the other party everything of value which he has received from him under the contract or offer to restore the same upon condition that the other party do likewise, unless the latter is unable or positively refuses to do so.

When notice of rescission has not otherwise been given or an offer to restore the benefits received under the contract has not otherwise been made, the service of a pleading in an action or proceeding that seeks relief based on rescission shall be deemed to be such notice or offer or both.

§ 1692.   RELIEF BASED ON RESCISSION. When a contract has been rescinded in whole or in part, any party to the contract may seek relief based upon such rescission by (a) bringing an action to recover any money or thing owing to him by any other party to the contract as a consequence of such rescission or for any other relief to which he may be entitled under the circumstances or (b) asserting such rescission by way of defense, counterclaim or cross-complaint.

If in an action or proceeding a party seeks relief based upon rescission and the court determines that the contract has not been rescinded, the court may grant any party to the action any other relief to which he may be entitled under the circumstances.

A claim for damages is not inconsistent with a claim for relief based upon rescission. The aggrieved party shall be awarded complete relief, including restitution of benefits, if any, conferred by him as a result of the transaction and any consequential damages to which he is entitled; but such relief shall not include duplicate or inconsistent items of recovery.

If in an action or proceeding a party seeks relief based upon rescission, the court may require the party to whom such relief is granted to make any compensation to the other which justice may require and may otherwise in its judgment adjust the equities between the parties.

QUESTIONS ON THE CALIFORNIA CIVIL CODE

1. Is this a code in the civil law sense?

2. What similarities and differences do you notice between the Code and that of the corresponding provisions of the Argentine Civil Code?

3. Is this Code an example of what Professor Yntema wants when he calls for the enactment of a civil code?

4. To what extent does the decisional method used by the California judges in the following cases resemble that of the Argentine judges in the cases printed above?

5. What light do these California cases throw on the codification controversy as outlined by Professor Yntema?

6. What is the *holding* of *Conlan v. Sullivan,* which follows?

CONLAN v. SULLIVAN
110 Cal. 624, 42 Pac. 1081 (1895)

APPEAL from a judgment of the Superior Court of Butte Country. J. C. GRAY, Judge.

The facts are stated in the opinion of the court.

Rearden & White, for Appellants.

The mere failure of consideration will not entitle the vendor to rescind the contract and recover back the land. (*Lawrence v. Gayetty,* 78 Cal. 134; 12 Am. St. Rep. 29.) The facts alleged are not sufficient to entitle the plaintiff to the relief demanded, because of inadequacy of consideration. (*Nicholson v. Tarpey,* 70 Cal. 609.) The facts stated do not entitle the plaintiff to relief upon the ground of mistake. Such a mistake must not be caused by the neglect of a legal duty on the part of the person making it (Civ. Code, sec. 1577; 1 Story's Equity Jurisprudence, sec. 195.) Having readily accessible means of acquiring knowledge of a fact, which might be ascertained by inquiry, is equivalent to notice and knowledge of it. (*Montgomery v. Keppel,* 75 Cal. 131; 7 Am. St. Rept. 125; *Board of Commrs. v. Younger,* 29 Cal. 176; *Champion v. Woods,* 79 Cal. 20; 12 Am. St. Rep. 126.) In order to entitle a party to rescind for fraud, he must show that some damage has resulted to him therefrom. (*Bailey v. Fox,* 78 Cal. 398.) One who rescinds must place the other party *in statu quo.* (*Collins v. Townsend,* 58 Cal. 608.)

John M. McGee, and *John Gale,* for Respondent.

The making of a promise without any intention at the time of performing it is of itself a fraud. (*Lawrence v. Gayetty,* 78 Cal. 126; 12 Am. St. Rep. 29; Civ. Code, sec. 1572; Bigelow on Fraud, 485, et seq.) If a man conceals a fact that is material to the transaction, knowing that the other party acts on the presumption that no such fact exists, it is as much a fraud as if the existence of such fact were expressly denied, or the reverse of it is expressly stated. (Kerr on Fraud and Mistake, 94.) Plaintiff was entitled to a rescission on the ground of mistake of fact. (Civ. Code, sec. 1577.) Equity follows the law as to title to improvements. (*Billings v. Hall,* 7 Cal. 8, 9; *Ferris v. Coover,* 10 Cal. 632.)

THE COURT.—This is an action of rescission. The findings of the court were in accord with the allegations of the complaint, and judgment went for plaintiff. The appeal is from the judgment, and the merits of the case will be determined by a consideration of the sufficiency of the complaint in stating a cause of action.

It appears substantially from the complaint that plaintiff owned a lot worth $700. By reason of a mistake of fact, he fully believed that it was mortgaged for $500, when it was another and different lot that was so mortgaged. He offered to sell the lot to appellants for $700, $200 to be paid in cash, the balance, $500, to be paid on the mortgage. The appellants, through their attorney, telephoned to the recorder and learned that respondent was mistaken, and that the lot was not encumbered at all. Then they agreed to buy the lot and pay therefor $700, to be paid as above stated. They did not intend to keep this agreement, but did intend to take advantage of respondent's mistake, and to obtain the property for $200, and to defraud him of the balance of the purchase price, $500. The $200 was paid, and the transfer made. Subsequently the plaintiff ascertained his mistake, and demanded that the $500 be paid to him, or his mortgagee, in satisfaction of the mortgage upon the other lot. Defendants refused so to do. Plaintiff thereupon tendered the $200 received, with interest, and demanded a reconveyance, which tender and demand were also refused. We think the foregoing statement of facts sufficient to justify relief by a court of equity, and that the contract should be set aside.

The court made a finding to the effect that defendants had expended $282 upon the property, but made no finding as to the increased value of the property by reason of this expenditure of money. The mere expenditure of money upon the property by defendants is not sufficient to justify a reimbursement of the amount expended. Perchance such expenditure did not add a dollar to the actual value of the realty. In addition, there is no allegation that such expenditures had increased to any degree the value of the realty.

For the foregoing reasons the judgment is affirmed.

HANNAH v. STEINMAN
159 Cal. 142, 112 Pac. 1094 (1911)

ANGELLOTTI, J. Plaintiff appeals from a judgment denying him any relief and from an order denying his motion for a new trial in an action brought by him to obtain a decree that a contract of lease had been rescinded.

Defendant is the owner of an unimproved lot of land in San Francisco, with a frontage of 90 feet on the northerly line of Geary street between Larkin and Hyde streets. On July 7, 1906, a contract of lease was executed by the parties, whereby defendant let to plaintiff and plaintiff hired from defendant said lot for a term of three years commencing August 7, 1906, for the sum of $9,000, payable in monthly installments of $250, and the privilege was thereby given to plaintiff to extend the lease for a further term of two years at a monthly rental of $300. It was recited therein that as the lessee contemplated erecting buildings on the premises he would hold the owner free of any claim of lien on account thereof, that all buildings or other improvements placed thereon by plaintiff should be plaintiff's property at the termination of the lease, that he would pay all taxes thereon and that he should have ten days free of rent at the termination of the lease in which to remove them. Up to the 5th day of July, 1906, the ordinances of the city and county of San Francisco were such that a permit could be obtained for the construction of a wooden building on this property, but on July 5, 1906, an ordinance was enacted that rendered it unlawful to erect or construct wooden buildings within certain limits prescribed therein, which included this lot. Neither plaintiff nor defendant knew of this change in the laws of the city and county at the time of the execution of the lease, each supposing that he knew and understood the law relative to such matters, and each apprehending the law to be that the erection of a temporary wooden building on said lot would be lawful. Plaintiff and defendant never met personally until long after the execution of the lease, all negotiations between them having been conducted through a firm of real estate brokers who acted purely as middlemen, and who were not the agents or representatives of the defendant. The finding on this question of agency is fully sustained by the evidence. About two weeks after the execution of the lease plaintiff, having already paid $250 rent, applied to the board of public works of the city and county for a permit to erect a wooden building on said property, and he then discovered that the law relative to fire limits had been changed and that no permit could be obtained. There was no attempt to question the positive evidence introduced by plaintiff to the effect that without the right to erect a wooden building upon this lot, the lease for three years only with the privilege of two years more at the prescribed rental was absolutely without value to a tenant and that plaintiff never would have entered into the contract had he supposed that he could not erect such a building thereon. It was impossible to use the lot to advantage without a building, and the cost of such a building as could be constructed in view of the building ordinances applicable would be so great as to render the lease in question valueless. The evidence compels the conclusion that it was within the contemplation of both parties that the lessee could use the lot to advantage only by constructing a wooden building thereon and that he was taking it for such use. ... Defendant refused to agree to a rescission, and this action was at once commenced.

* * *

A party to a contract may rescind the same if his consent thereto was given by mistake either of law or fact. Subdivision 1, § 1689, Civ. Code. We deem it unimportant whether the alleged mistake in this case be held to be a mistake of fact or one of law. The mistake was the belief of both parties that the lot was not within the limits fixed by ordinance wherein it was unlawful under the ordinances of the city and county of San Francisco to construct a wooden building — ignorance of the fact that an ordinance had just been adopted placing such lot within such limits. Unconscious ignorance of a fact material to the contract or belief in the present existence of a thing material to the contract constitutes a mistake of fact (section 1577, Civ. Code), and a misapprehension of the law by all parties, all supposing that they know and understand it, and all making substantially the same mistake as to the law, constitutes a mistake of law (section 1578, Civ. Code). Upon the facts of this case there was a mutual mistake either of fact or of law. Was it such a mistake as warrants rescission? Consent is deemed to have been obtained through mistake "only when it would not have been given had such cause not existed." Section 1568, Civ. Code. It cannot be doubted that plaintiff would not have consented to the lease but for this mistake. The principal question in this connection is whether it was "material to the contract" within the meaning of those words as used in our statute. That it was material in the sense that but for it plaintiff would not have considered for a moment the making of the contract we have seen, but that clearly is not enough. The same thing might be said as to mistaken expectations of both plaintiff and defendant as to plaintiff's ability to obtain tenants for the building he proposed to erect on the leased land, and, of course, a mistake in that regard would not furnish ground for rescission, although plaintiff never would have entered into the contract but for such mistaken belief. It is declared by Mr. Page in his work on Contracts that a mistake will not be operative to render a contract void, although in some cases is may render it voidable, if it merely affects some "collateral" though highly material matter, constituting merely a matter of inducement, but that it must affect the execution and the essential elements of the contract (sections 58 and 60), which elements are stated to be parties, the subject-matter, the consideration, and the offer and acceptance. We may assume for the purposes of this decision that our Legislature had some such idea as this in the use of the word "material" in this connection, but, so assuming, we are nevertheless of the opinion that the mistake here was not as to a purely collateral matter, but rather went to the essence of the contract. The authorities recognize the difficulty in determining whether a mistake applies to an essential feature of the contract or to a purely collateral matter. 1 Page on Contracts, § 71. It is thoroughly established that if the parties to a contract enter into it under the belief that the subject-matter or consideration is in existence, and in effect condition their contract thereon, and as a matter of fact, it is not in existence, the mistake will enable a party to avoid the contract. We are, of course, not speaking of cases where the parties are aware that the existence of the subject-matter is doubtful and contract with reference thereto. Thus, an ordinary contract of sale of property supposed to be in existence, but which in fact no longer exists, may be avoided. In such a case it is plain that the mistake is material and goes to the very essence of the contract. The assumed fact of existence is the whole basis of the contract. The same rule must necessarily apply where a material part of the subject-matter, as to which the parties supposed they were contracting, is not in existence at the time the contract is entered into. An example of this is the case cited by Mr. Page in section 72 of his work (Bedell v. Wilder, 65 Vt. 406, 26 Atl. 589, 36 Am. St. Rep. 871), a lease of property to be used for manufacturing purposes where entered into under a mistake as to water rights which were thought to be easements appertaining to the realty, and without which it could not be used for such purposes. See, also, Blakeman v. Blakeman, 39 Conn. 320; Champlin v. Laytin, 1 Edw. Ch. (N.Y.) 467. So, also, a material mistake as to the identity of the subject-matter or consideration may go to the very essence of the contract. A leading case in this regard is that of Kennedy v. Mail Co., 2 L.R.Q.B. 580, an action to rescind a contract of subscription for shares of the defendant on the ground of mistake. The prospectus of the defendant company stated that the shares were issued to enable the company to perform a contract for mail service entered into with the government of New Zealand. As a matter of fact the purported contract was invalid, but all parties believed it to be valid, and plaintiff had subscribed because of that mistaken belief. The value of the shares would have been greater had the contract been valid, but they were, nevertheless, of considerable value, the court in fact saying that the difference in value was not greater than "might very well be accounted for by the change of times, quite independently of the dispute about the contract." While relief was denied in that case, the court expressly recognized that if the invalidity of the mail contract really made the shares plaintiff obtained "different things in substance from those which he applied for" he would be entitled to rescission. The court said that "the difficulty in every case is to determine whether the mistake or misapprehension is as to the substance of the whole consideration, going, as it were, to the root of the matter, or only to some point even though a material point, an error as to which does not affect the substance of the whole transaction." It cannot be doubted that if the value of the shares had been entirely dependent on the validity of the mail contract the court would have held that the mistake was as to the substance of the whole transaction. The principles enunciated in this decision were applied in Sherwood v. Walker, 66 Mich. 568, 33 N.W. 919, 11 Am. St. Rep. 531, where a mistake as to whether a cow was barren and would not breed was held to avoid a contract of sale thereof, ... The case before us is very much stronger in favor of plaintiff than either of the cases just discussed. The evidence demonstrates that the parties negotiated and executed the lease upon the assumption that a wooden building could lawfully be constructed upon the demised land,

and that such was the use to which the lessee must put the land and was the main inducement of the contract. Without the right to construct such a building, it could be of no substantial value to any one holding a lease for only five years who was required to pay any substantial rent. While there was no mistake as to the identity of the land itself, without that right and viewed with reference to a lease for only five years the land was a substantially different thing from the land supposed to be contracted for. It is very analogous to a case of land bought and sold upon the mistaken supposition that an absolutely necessary way of ingress and egress is appurtenant to the land and passes by the conveyance, where, in fact, there is no such way. Without the right to construct a wooden building the tenant, so far as all practical considerations are concerned, was obtaining nothing. If an effectual prohibition against a wooden building on this lot had been imposed by the terms of a prior conveyance, and this lease had been given and received in ignorance of the existence thereof, it would probably not be questioned that the mistake would be of such a nature as to enable the lessee to rescind, the prohibition amounting to a practical and material impairment of the estate contemplated by the parties. Here we have practically the same result because of an ordinance of the city of which the parties were ignorant. We cannot believe that the equitable rules relative to mistake should be so narrowly construed as to require us to hold that this mistake did not go to the very essence of the contract between these parties. We have examined the cases cited by learned counsel for defendant on this proposition, but find nothing therein compelling a different conclusion from that at which we have arrived. It would unnecessarily prolong this opinion to discuss these cases. It is proper, however, to note that the quotation from 9 Cyc. 395, to the effect that where one buys land in the expectation of procuring a consent which is required for building on it, and fails to obtain such consent, his mistake will have no effect on the agreement, is not opposed to our conclusion. The connection in which this is said shows that the expectation there referred to is one not so regarded by the parties as to constitute an essential feature of the contract of sale, but as a mere expectation of the vendee as to what he may be able to obtain from another party in the future. In the case cited in support thereof (Adams v. Weare, 1 Bro. Ch. 567, 28 Eng. Reprint. 1301) it appeared that it was understood between the parties that the vendee assumed the risk of being able to get the consent, and that the sale was not conditioned upon his obtaining it. The trial court in this case concluded, as we have, that the consent of plaintiff to said contract was given and obtained by and through a mistake, and would not have been given had not such mistake existed, and its denial of relief to plaintiff was based purely on the ground of want of diligence on his part in rescinding the agreement.

Section 1577, Civ. Code, defining "mistake," declares that it is a mistake "not caused by the neglect of a legal duty on the part of the person making

the mistake." We find nothing in the record warranting a conclusion that the mistake was caused by the neglect of any legal duty on the part of plaintiff.
* * *

The judgment and order denying a new trial are reversed.

We concur: SHAW, J.; LORIGAN, J.; HENSHAW, J.; MELVIN, J.

TENTENMAN V. EPSTEIN, 66 Cal. App. 745, 226 Pac. 966 (1924): Mr. and Mrs. Kauffman owed some $461 to Epstein. In payment of their debt, they conveyed to Epstein four lots, believed by the parties to be worth around $100 each. In fact, the lots were worth about $500 each, because oil had been discovered in their vicinity. The trial court's judgment, in the nature of a reformation decree, was reversed. In addition, the Kauffmans argued on the basis of § 2224 of the Civil Code, "which provides that one who gains a thing by mistake is an involuntary trustee of the thing gained for the benefit of the person who would have had it." The court rejected the argument, holding that Epstein was entitled to the lots.

". . . If the mere ignorance as to the true value of property by one who sells it, where the sale is for a sum considerably less than its value, were a ground to set aside a deed, no transaction would be final until the validity thereof had been determined by a suit to quiet title. We are cited to no case holding that such ignorance or erroneous belief as to the mere value of property amounts to mistake of fact as defined in section 1577, Civil Code. In *Hannah v. Steinman, supra,* our supreme court, construing certain sections of the Civil Code, including section 1577, said: 'It cannot be doubted that plaintiff would not have consented to the lease but for this mistake. The principal question in this connection is whether it was "material to the contract," within the meaning of those words as used in our statute. That it was material in the sense that but for it plaintiff would not have considered for a moment the making of the contract we have seen, but that clearly is not enough. The same thing might be said as to mistaken expectations of both plaintiff and defendant, as to plaintiff's ability to obtain tenants for the building he proposed to erect on the leased land, and, of course, a mistake in that regard would not furnish ground for rescission, although plaintiff never would have entered into the contract but for such mistaken belief.'

"We have said that a contract may be rescinded where there has been a mutual mistake as to some collateral fact the existence of which constitutes the essence of the agreement. For example, in the case last mentioned, the mutual ignorance of the parties of the fact that the lot leased by the plaintiff had just been placed within the fire limits so that wooden buildings could not be erected thereon was held to be a mutual mistake of such character as to justify rescission of a lease contract where the parties understood that the lot was to

be used for the erection of wooden buildings. In the instant case the existence
or nonexistence of oil was not considered by the parties at any time. It cannot
be said, nor was it found, that they, under the mistaken belief that oil did not
exist in the vicinity of these lots, made this contract, and that such belief
served as an inducement, much less constituted an element thereof. The most
that can be said is that they gave no consideration or thought to the possibility
of oil being located near the premises."

BROWN V. KLEIN, 89 Cal. App. 153, 264 Pac. 496 (1928): Plaintiff sued to
rescind a contract in which he agreed to buy from defendant a one-third interest in a partnership. Defendant represented that the firm's liabilities did not
exceed $1,952.57; in fact, they amounted to some $3,300. A judgment for
plaintiff was affirmed:

"... It is the contention of appellants that plaintiff was an experienced
business man, was not free from negligence, and that having the means of
knowledge the law imputes knowledge to him.

"In view of the finding that the plaintiff did not make an independent
investigation and did not have the opportunity of doing so, we attach but little
or no significance to this part of the argument. While the testimony was conflicting, the finding of the court was amply sustained by the evidence.

"Appellants advance another theory, namely, that the adventure was a
speculative one and that for that reason the purchaser cannot be heard to complain. There is nothing in the point. The character of a business, if lawful, in
nowise softens the effect of misrepresentation.

"No question is raised as to materiality of the false representation, diligent
offer to return, or material change in the situation of the parties.
        "* * *

"A party to a contract may rescind if his consent was either given through
mistake or obtained by fraud. (Civ. Code, sec. 1689, subd. 1; *Canadian Agency
v. Assets etc. Co.,* 165 App. Div. 96 [150 N.Y. Supp. 758]; Story's Commentaries on Equity Jurisprudence, 13th ed., p. 213.)

"A late expression of this court on the subject is to be found in *Scott v.
Delta Land & Water Co.,* 57 Cal. App. 320 [207 Pac. 389], where it is held
that in a civil action the good faith of the party who procures the assent of
another to the making of a contract by material misrepresentations is of no
moment.

"In 12 Ruling Case Law, at page 343, paragraph 98, referred to in the
above decision, the principle is advanced that innocent misrepresentations of a
material fact are considered as constructive fraud because of its effect of imposing upon and deceiving the person to whom it is made.

"It is therefore clear that defendants' plea of innocent mistake rather than being available as a defense in a suit for rescission is itself a generally recognized ground for rescission.

"* * *

"Judgment affirmed.

"Koford, P. J., and Nourse, J., concurred."

SMITH v. ZIMBALIST
2 Cal. App. 2d 324, 38 P.2d 170 (1934)

HOUSER, Justice.

From the "findings of fact" made pursuant to the trial of the action, it appears that plaintiff, who was of the age of 86 years, although not a dealer in violins, had been a collector of rare violins for many years; "that defendant was a violinist of great prominence, internationally known, and himself the owner and collector of rare and old violins made by the old masters"; that at the suggestion of a third person, and without the knowledge by plaintiff of defendant's intention in the matter, defendant visited plaintiff at the home of the latter and there asked plaintiff if he might see plaintiff's collection of old violins; that in the course of such visit and inspection, "plaintiff showed a part of his collection to defendant; that defendant picked up one violin and asked plaintiff what he would take for the violin, calling it a 'Stradivarius'; that plaintiff did not offer his violins, or any of them, for sale, but on account of his age, after he had been asked what he would take for them, said he would not charge as much as a regular dealer, but that he would sell it for $5,000; that thereafter defendant picked up another violin, calling it a 'Guarnerius,' and asked plaintiff what he would take for that violin, and plaintiff said if defendant took both violins, he could have them for $8,000; that the defendant said 'all right,' thereupon stating his financial condition and asking if he could pay $2,000 cash and the balance in monthly payments of $1,000." Thereupon a memorandum was signed by defendant as follows:

"I hereby acknowledge receipt of one violin by Joseph Guarnerius and one violin by Stradivarius dated 1717 purchased by me from George Smith for the total sum of Eight Thousand Dollars toward which purchase price I have paid Two Thousand Dollars the balance I agree to pay at the rate of one thousand dollars on the fifteenth day of each month until paid in full."

In addition thereto, a "bill of sale" in the following language was signed by plaintiff:

"This certifies that I have on this date sold to Mr. Efrem Zimbalist one Joseph Guarnerius violin and one Stradivarius violin dated 1717, for the full price of $8,000.00 on which has been paid $2,000.00.

"The balance of $6,000.00 to be paid $1,000.00 fifteenth of each month until paid in full. I agree that Mr. Zimbalist shall have the right to exchange these for any others in my collection should he so desire."

That at the time said transaction was consummated each of the parties thereto "fully believed that said violins were made one by Antonius Stradivarius and one by Josef Guarnerius"; that preceding the closing of said transaction "plaintiff made no representations and warranties as to said violins, or either of them, as to who their makers were, but believed them to have been made one by Antonius Stradivarius and one by Josef Guarnerius in the early part of the eighteenth century; that plaintiff did not fraudulently make any representations or warranties to defendant at the time of said purchase"; that there was "a preponderance of evidence to the effect that said violins are not Stradivarius or Guarnerius violins, nor made by either Antonius Stradivarius or Josef Guarnerius, but were in fact made as imitations thereof, and were not worth more than $300.00."

The action which is the foundation of the instant appeal was brought by plaintiff against defendant to recover judgment for the unpaid balance of the purchase price of the two violins.

As is shown by the conclusions of law reached by the trial court from such facts, the theory upon which the case was decided was that the transaction in question was the result of "a mutual mistake on the part of plaintiff and defendant," and consequently that plaintiff was not entitled to recover judgment. From a judgment rendered in favor of defendant, plaintiff has appealed to this court.

In urging a reversal of the judgment, it is the contention of appellant that the doctrine of caveat emptor should have been applied to the facts in the case; that is to say, that in the circumstances shown by the evidence and reflected in the findings of fact, the trial court should have held that defendant bought the violins at his own risk and peril.

The substance of the argument presented by appellant is a recast of the decision at nisi prius in the case of Jendwine v. Slade (1797) 2 Espinasse, 572. The syllabus in that case is as follows:

"The putting down the name of an artist in a catalogue as the painter of any picture, is not such a warranty as will subject the party selling to an action, if it turn out that he might be mistaken, and that it was not the work of the artist to whom it was attributed."

It there appears that therein (as similarly in the instant case) "several of the most eminent artists and picture dealers were called, who differed in their opinions respecting the originality of the pictures."

Lord Kenyon (the nisi prius judge) said: "It was impossible to make this the case of a warranty; the pictures were the work of artists some centuries back, and there being no way of tracing the picture itself, it could only be matter of opinion whether the picture in question was the work of the artist whose name it bore, or not. What then does the catalogue import? That, in the opinion of the seller, the picture is the work of the artist whose name he has affixed to it. The action in its present shape must go on the ground of some fraud in the sale. But if the seller only represents what he himself believes, he can be guilty of no fraud. The catalogue of the pictures in question leaves the determination to the judgment of the buyer, who is to exercise that judgment in the purchase. * * *"

In the case of Chandelor v. Lopus (1603) 2 Cr. Rep. 4, 79 English Rep. 3 (Full Reprint), which in the state of New York for many years was relied upon as the leading authority in situations similar to that present herein, it was held that where one sold a jewel as a bezoar stone which in truth it was not, no action would lie, unless in the complaint or declaration it was alleged that the seller knew that it was not a bezoar stone, or that he warranted the stone to be such.

In Seixas v. Woods (1805) 2 Caines (N.Y.) 48, 2 Am. Dec. 215 (Chancellor Kent writing a concurring opinion), a sale of wood which both parties to the transaction supposed was brazilletto, when in fact it was peachum, in the absence of express warranty by the seller, was held binding on the buyer. It was also ruled that "mentioning the wood, as brazilletto wood, in the bill of parcels, and in the advertisement some days previous to the sale, did not amount to a warranty to the plaintiffs."

In the case of Swett v. Colgate (1822) 20 Johns. (N.Y.) 196, 11 Am. Dec. 266, it was held that where one, without express warranty, sold what he supposed was barilla, which he advertised as barilla, which he invoiced as barilla, and which prior to the sale thereof the purchaser examined "several times," but which after the sale was found to be kelp, the rule of caveat emptor, as announced in Chandelor v. Lopus, supra, would apply. And so in Welsh v. Carter (1828) 1 Wend. (N.Y.) 185, 19 Am. Dec. 473, which likewise involved the sale of an article known as barilla, but which in fact was a fraudulent imitation of it and entirely worthless, the contract was held binding on the purchaser who, before the sale, was told that he "must judge for himself," and who had a sample of the "barilla" analyzed.

* * *

But with reference to the first cited case (*Seixas v. Woods, supra,* in which Cancellor Kent wrote a concurring opinion), in 2 Kent's Commentaries, section 479, in part it is said:

"There is no doubt of the existence of the general rule of law, as laid down in *Seixas v. Woods;* and the only doubt is whether it was well applied in that case, *where there was a description in writing of the article by the vendor which proved not to be correct, and from which a warranty might have been inferred.* But the rule fitly applies to the case where the article was equally open to the inspection and examination of both parties, and the purchaser relied on his own information and judgment, without requiring any warranty of the quality; . . ."

Likewise, in 2 Blackstone's Commentaries, *451, the exception to the general rule is there noted as follows: "But with regard to the goodness of the wares so purchased, the vendor is not bound to answer; unless he expressly warrants them to be sound and good, or unless he knew them to be otherwise, and hath used no art to disguise them, or *unless they turn out to be different from what he represented them to the buyer.*"

     * * *

    In *Hawkins v. Pemberton,* (1872) 51 N.Y. 198 [10 Am. Rep. 595], where a sale by auction had been made of what was assumed to be "blue vitriol," after an extensive review of the authorities it was held that the contract was unenforceable. And in the same case, in referring to the case of *Chandelor v. Lopus* (1603) 2 Cr. Jac. 4, 79 English Rep. 3 (Full Reprint), upon the decision of which many of the former cases relied as an authority, in part the court said: "The doctrine (there) laid down is that a mere affirmation or representation as to the character or quality of goods sold will not constitute a warranty; *and that doctrine has long since been exploded and the case itself is no longer regarded as good law in this country or England.*" (Citing authorities.) To the same effect, see *Dounce v. Dow,* 64 N.Y. 411; *White v. Miller,* 71 N.Y. 118 [27 Am. Rep. 13.]

    A case which in its facts closely resembles those in the instant case is that of *Power v. Barham,* (1836) 4 Ad. & E., 473, 111 English Repts., Full Reprint, (K.B.) 865. Therein the early case of *Jendwine v. Slade,* 2 Espinasse, 572 (1797), to which reference hereinbefore has been had, is cited and "distinguished." The syllabus in *Power v. Barham, supra,* is as follows: "In *assumpsit* for breach of a warranty of pictures, it was proved, among other things, that the defendant, at the time of the sale, gave the following bill of parcels: 'Four pictures, Views in Venice, Canaletto, 1601.' The Judge left it to the jury upon this and the rest of the evidence, whether the defendant had contracted that the pictures were those of the artist named, or whether his name had been used merely as matter of description, or intimation of opinion, the jury found for the plaintiff, saying that the bill of parcels amounted to a warranty: Held, that the question had been rightly left to jury, and that the verdict was not to be disturbed."

    An American case which in principle is clearly applicable to the facts herein is that of *Sherwood v. Walker,* 66 Mich. 568 [33 N.W. 919, 11 Am. St. Rep. 531]. It there appears that the subject of the sale was a "blooded" polled Angus cow that both parties to the transaction assumed was barren and hence useless as breeding stock. In such assumed conditions the owner agreed to sell and the purchaser agreed to buy the cow at the market price of beef cattle, to wit, five and one-half cents per pound, or what amounted to about $80. Before the day arrived when the cow was to be delivered by the seller to the purchaser, it was discovered that the cow was with calf and consequently that the cow was worth at least $750. It was held that the owner of the cow had the right to rescind the agreement of sale. But to the contrary of such ruling on practically similar facts, see *Wood v. Boyton,* 64 Wis. 265 [25 N.W. 42, 54 Am. Rep. 610].

* * *

The governing principle of law to the effect that an article described in a "bill of parcels," or, as in the instance case, in a "bill of sale," amounts to a warranty that such article in fact conforms to such description and that the seller is bound by such description, has been applied in this state in the case of *Flint v. Lyon,* 4 Cal. 17, wherein it was held that where the defendant purchased an entire cargo of flour which was described as "Haxall" flour, he was not required by the contract to accept the same flour which in reality was "Gallego" flour, but which was of as excellent quality as "Haxall" flour. Therein, in part, the court said:

"What the inducement was to the defendant to purchase Haxall, we know not; but having purchased that particular brand, he was entitled to it, and could not be compelled to accept any other as a substitute. The use of the word 'Haxall' in the sale note amounted to a warranty that the flour was Haxall. (Citing authorities.) How, then, stands the case? The contract was founded in mistake, both parties supposing they were contracting concerning a certain article which had no existence, consequently the contract was void for want of the substance of the thing contracted for. Could then the acceptance of a different article than the one sold by Gorham, the sub-vendee, conclude the defendant? Certainly not! . . ."

In principle, to the same effect, see, also, *Burge v. Albany Nurseries, etc.,* 176 Cal. 313 [168 Pac. 343]; *Barrios v. Pacific States Trading Co.,* 41 Cal. App. 637 [183 Pac. 236]; *Firth v. Richter,* 49 Cal. App. 545 [196 Pac. 277]; *Rauth v. Southwest Warehouse Co.,* 158 Cal. 54 [109 Pac. 839]; *Brock v. Newmark G. Co.,* 64 Cal. App. 577 [222 Pac. 195]; *Brandenstein v. Jackling,* 99 Cal. App. 438 [278 Pac. 880].

Although it may be that by some authorities a different rule may be indicated, it is the opinion of this court that, in accord with the weight of the later authorities to which attention hereinbefore has been directed, the strict rule of *caveat emptor* may not be applied to the facts of the instant case, but that such rule is subject to the exception thereto to the effect that on the purported sale of personal property the parties to the proposed contract are not bound where it appears that in its essence each of them is honestly mistaken or in error with reference to the identity of the subject-matter of such contract. In other words, in such circumstances, no enforceable sale has taken place. But if it may be said that a sale, with a voidable condition attached, was the outcome of the transaction in the instant case, notwithstanding the "finding of fact" by the trial court that "plaintiff made no representations and warranties as to said violins," from a consideration of the language employed by the parties in each of the documents that was exchanged between them (to which reference hereinbefore has been had), together with the general conduct of the parties, and particularly the acquiescence by plaintiff in the declaration made by defendant regarding each of the violins and by whom it was made, — it becomes apparent that, in law, a warranty was given by plaintiff that one of the violins was a Guarnerius and that the other was a Stradivarius.

The findings of fact unquestionably show that each of the parties believed and assumed that one of said violins was a genuine Guarnerius and that the other was a genuine Stradivarius; the receipt given by defendant to plaintiff for said violins so described them, and the "bill of sale" given by plaintiff to defendant certifies that plaintiff "sold to Mr. Efrem Zimbalist (defendant) one Joseph Guarnerius violin and one Stradivarius violin dated 1717 for the full price of 8,000.00 on which has been paid $2,000.00. . . ."

Without burdening this opinion with the citation of additional authorities, it may suffice to state that, although the very early decisions may hold to a different rule, all the more modern authorities, including many of those in California to which attention has been directed (besides the provision now contained in section 1734, Civ. Code), are agreed that the description in a bill of parcels or sale-note of the thing sold amounts to a warranty on the part of the seller that the subject-matter of the sale conforms to such description. (See, generally, 22 Cal. Jur. 994; 55 Cor. Jur. 738 et seq.; 24 R.C.L. 171; and authorities respectively there cited.)

It is ordered that the judgment be and it is affirmed.

Conrey, P. J., and York, J., concurred.

A petition by appellant to have the cause heard in the Supreme Court, after judgment in the District Court of Appeal, was denied by the Supreme Court on January 17, 1935.

CLAUSER v. TAYLOR
44 Cal. App. 2d 453, 112 P.2d 241 (1941)

McComb, J.   This is an appeal by defendant from a judgment in favor of plaintiff after trial before the court without a jury in an action to rescind a transaction whereby plaintiff purchased certain real property from defendant.

These are the facts so far as material here:

Defendant owned two residential lots in Alhambra, California. These lots, as defendant knew, had been filled with debris in 1928, which, however, had been covered, and the fact that the lots had been filled did not appear from a casual examination of the property. Due to the fact that the lots had been filled, the cost of building on them was materially increased. In 1940 the lots were sold to plaintiff for $2,300. Plaintiff saw the lots but made no inquiry as to whether they were filled or not and neither defendant nor her agent made any representation concerning the lots. Upon discovering the fact that the lots had been filled, plaintiff tendered to defendant a deed to them and endeavored to rescind the transaction.

This is the sole question presented for determination.

When a vendor sells real property, which he knows has been filled and the value of which is materially affected by such filling, without disclosing to the vendee the fact that such property has been filled, and the vendee makes no inquiry relative to whether or not the property has been filled, may the vendee rescind the transaction upon learning the true facts?

This question must be answered in the affirmative. It is the law that, where material facts are accessible to the vendor only and he knows them not to be within the reach of the diligent attention and observation of the vendee, the vendor is bound to disclose such facts to the vendee, and upon his failure to do so, the vendee may rescind the transaction upon discovering the true state of facts (27 Ruling Case Law (1929) 367, sec. 67; 66 Cor. Jur. (1934) 575, sec. 124; see, also, *Conlan v. Sullivan* [p. 193, *supra,*] 110 Cal. 624, 626 [42 Pac. 1081]; *O'Shea v. Morris,* 112 Neb. 102 [198 N.W. 866, 867]; Restatement of the Law of Contracts (1932), vol. 2, p. 897, sec. 472, subsec. b.).

Applying the foregoing rule to the facts of the instant case, it is apparent that defendant was aware of the fact that the property which she sold had been filled, which filling materially affected its value. Since this defect was not apparent to the observer, which fact was also known to defendant, she was under a duty to disclose the information to the vendee, and, upon her failure to do so, plaintiff was entitled, upon learning the true state of facts, to rescind the contract.

For the foregoing reasons the judgment is affirmed.

Moore, P. J., and Wood, J., concurred.

VICKERSON v. FREY
100 Cal. App. 2d 621, 224 P.2d 125 (1950)

FRED B. WOOD, Justice.

Plaintiff appeals from the judgment rendered in an action in which she sought to rescind a contract for the purchase of certain real property from defendants and defendants sought damages from plaintiff for her asserted failure to perform that contract.

* * *

The issues framed by the pleadings embraced alleged fraud of respondents in obtaining appellant's consent to the contract by means of alleged misrepresentation by respondents' agents concerning the property. The asserted misrepresentation was that a part of the basement could readily be converted into a dwelling unit and produce a substantial revenue. The case appears to have been tried as if the pleadings also presented issues of mistakes of fact and of law. . . .

* * *

It appears that respondents listed for sale, at $22,000, a building in Oakland that contained two apartments and a partly finished basement. The front apartment was rented. The rear apartment was occupied by respondents and Mrs. Frey, Sr., mother of respondent Melvin Frey. In the basement there were three finished rooms; a bedroom for use as a guest room, and two rooms designated a laboratory and rented to a photographer. The remainder of the basement had a cement floor but was otherwise unfinished.

A Mr. Albert Bequette, salesman for a real estate broker interested in effecting a sale, telephoned appellant regarding this property, went to her home, and discussed it with her. They then went to the property and were shown through all of it, except the rented apartment, by Mrs. Frey, Sr. They returned the next day and, accompanied by Mrs. Frey, Sr., again examined the property, including the rented apartment. Upon each of these occasions they spent about one and one-half hours upon the premises, appellant spending the greater part of the time considering how the unfinished portion of the basement could be converted into an apartment to be rented for living quarters.

Appellant testified that at the very first discussion of this property, at her home, Bequette told her that there were two apartments finished and that she could finish a third which could rent at $40 a month; that the front apartment rented for $50; that the apartment occupied by respondents had no rent ceiling; that the photographic studio rented for $50 and the basement bedroom could be rented for $30; that that would mean an income of $220 a month and, for the price of $22,000, Bequette considered it a good deal; that Mrs. Frey, Sr., showed her where they had finished the bedroom in the basement, and where, as Mrs. Frey said, the roughed-in plumbing was, and that appellant could finish up the apartment; that, believing that an apartment could readily be finished in the basement, she signed the contract of purchase, but later discovered it could not be done because building regulations (Health & Saf. Code, § 16057) required a clearance of eight feet between finished floor and finished ceiling and this unfinished basement had a clearance of but seven feet six inches; that she would not have signed the contract had she known that the unfinished portion of the basement could not readily be converted into a dwelling apartment.

At none of these conversations was the height of the basement mentioned. Until appellant's discovery after the signing of the contract, neither she nor Bequette nor Mrs. Frey, Sr., knew or considered the basement height; nor was any of them aware that the applicable building regulations required (assuming that they did require) a height of eight feet.

* * *

Concerning mistake, as a ground for rescission, the trial court found that the agreement of sale was not obtained or induced by either mistake of law or mistake of fact. The evidence supports that finding.

Appellant when proposing and deciding that she would convert the basement into a living apartment, and Bequette and Mrs. Frey when concurring in that idea, assumed it could legally be done without lowering the basement floor. That was a mistake of fact ("An unconscious ignorance" of the basement ceiling height), as defined in section 1577 of the Civil Code, and a mistake of law ("misapprehension of the law by all parties, all supposing that they knew and understood it," a law which required a clearance of eight feet from finished floor to finished ceiling), as defined in section 1578 of the Civil Code.

But was this combined mistake of fact and law "Material to the contract" as required, for rescission of a contract, expressly by section 1577 and impliedly by section 1578? We think not.

This mistake bore upon the use of but a portion of the property under purchase, a contemplated use which, despite the mistake, was not impossible. As correctly found by the trial court, "it is possible to construct living quarters in the basement *** so as to provide the ceiling height required by law, provided the floor level in said basement is lowered." The contemplated conversion would merely be more difficult and costly than contemplated by appellant, and there is no evidence that the added cost would be prohibitive; indeed, no evidence concerning the contemplated or the increased cost of conversion, the sole testimony in that connection being that lowering of the basement floor would be a "major operation."

This mistake did not relate to the intrinsic nature of the bargain, did not vitally affect a fact on the basis of which the parties contracted. Appellant, despite the mistake, would acquire the very lot and building she examined and bargained for. It is not like a case where it develops that the seller had no title or that the thing bargained for had no existence, or other mistake concerning an essential matter.

It is a mistake pertaining to a collateral matter, a quality or characteristic of the thing sold, — the feasibility of converting the basement into living quarters. In such a case, the difference between the real and the supposed quality or nature of the thing must be so great, so extreme, as to make it virtually a different thing. Such was the nature of the mistake in Hannah v. Steinman, 159 Cal. 142, 112 P. 1094, upon which appellant chiefly relies. . . . [Description of *Hannah* case omitted.]

Similarly in Mineral Park Land Company v. Howard, 172 Cal. 289, 156 P. 458, L.R.A. 1916F, 1, which involved a contract by the defendant to take from plaintiff's land all of the gravel and earth needed for certain construction work. Defendant removed 50,131 cubic yards, taking the balance, 50,869 cubic yards, from another source. It appeared that plaintiff's land contained enough material to satisfy the balance under contract but that it was below the water level and the cost of extracting it would be ten or twelve times as much as the usual cost, and it would require drying at great expense and delay. In holding that these facts excused defendants' failure to extract the material that was below water level, the court said: "The parties were contracting for the right to take earth and gravel to be used in the construction of the bridge. When they stipulated that all of the earth and gravel needed for this purpose should be taken from plaintiff's land, they contemplated and assumed that the land contained the requisite quantity, available for use. The defendants were not binding themselves to take what was not there. And, in determining whether the earth and gravel were 'available,' we must view the conditions in a practical and reasonable way. Although there was gravel on the land, it was so situated that the defendants could not take it by ordinary means, nor except at a prohibitive cost. To all fair intents then, it was impossible for defendants to take it. 'A thing is impossible in legal contemplation when it is not practicable; and a thing is impracticable when it can only be done at an excessive and unreasonable cost.' 1 Beach on Contr. § 216. We do not mean to intimate that the defendants could excuse themselves by showing the existence of conditions which would make the performance of their obligation more expensive than they had anticipated, or which would entail a loss upon them. But, where the difference in cost is so great as here, and has the effect as found, of making performance impracticable, the situation is not different from that of a total absence of earth and gravel." 172 Cal. at page 293, 156 P. at page 459, L.R.A. 1916F, 1.

The instant case is neither of those cases. It is merely a case in which the planned alteration of a portion of a building proves more difficult and more expensive than contemplated. How much more expensive, there is no evidence; no evidence that the proposed alteration is "impracticable" within the meaning of the term as used in Mineral Park Land Company v. Howard, supra, 172 Cal. 289, 293, 156 P. 458, L.R.A. 1916F, 1.

* * *

The judgment appealed from is affirmed.

PETERS, P. J., and BRAY, J., concur.

EARL v. SAKS & CO.
36 Cal. 2d 602, 226 P.2d 340 (1951)

[Mr. Barbee and Mrs. Earl went to the Saks fur salon, where they saw a mink coat priced at $5,000. Barbee refused to buy the coat at that price, and offered to buy it for $4,000. When the Saks representative said he could not sell at that price, Barbee and Mrs. Earl left. "Unknown to Barbee, Mrs. Earl then asked Saks to pretend to sell the coat to him for $4,000, and stated that she would pay the difference between $4,000 and the price of the coat. Saks agreed to this." The transaction was consummated the same day. The next day Mrs. Earl returned the coat to Saks to be monogrammed; later that day, Barbee came to Saks and told them he had revoked the gift, perhaps "because Mrs. Earl had failed to live up to his expectations" (from the dissenting opinion of Traynor, J.). When Mrs. Earl asked for the coat, Saks refused to return it, offering to give her back her money. Mrs. Earl sued Saks, alleging conversion. Saks denied the conversion and interpleaded Barbee, claiming the full price from

Barbee or Mrs. Earl or both. Mrs. Earl had judgment in the trial court on the "Cross-Complaint in Interpleader" filed by Saks, as owner of the coat. Her conversion claim was rejected; in any case, she was not seeking the value of the coat so much as the coat itself. Reversed.]

SCHAUER, J. . . . [after holding that Barbee was entitled to rescind the gift].

* * *

Rescission of Contract

It appears from the findings of probative facts that Saks did more than merely fail to disclose its agreement with Mrs. Earl. In the circumstances, implicit in the finding that Barbee "was informed by Saks and Company's representatives that they would sell said mink coat to him for the sum of $3,981.25" is a finding that Saks actively misrepresented that the price had been reduced and that $3,981.25 was the full price. It is completely unreasonable to deny that a representation by a clerk in a reputable store that an article has a certain price, followed by the clerk's preparation and the customer's signing of a sales check showing purchase of the article for that price, amounts to a representation by the store that the *total* price and the *entire* sales transaction are as represented. This misrepresentation, it appears from the undisputed evidence, was made by Saks with knowledge that Barbee insisted on a reduction in price; from this it follows that such misrepresentation must have been made with intent to deceive Barbee and to induce him to buy the coat.

Although "Actual fraud is always a question of fact" (Civ. Code § 1574; see 12 Cal. Jur., Fraud and Deceit, § 82), and although findings of ultimate fact ordinarily cannot be controlled by findings of probative facts (see Cal. Jur., Trial, § 205), here the finding that Saks was not guilty of fraud is not controlling, for it was drawn as a conclusion from findings of probative facts which not only do not support it but which establish the contrary (see *LaMar v. LaMar* (1947), 30 Cal. 2d 898, 900 [186 P.2d 678], and cases there cited; *Robinson v. Raquet* (1934), 1 Cal. App. 2d 533, 541 [36 P.2d 821]) and it is contrary to Saks' own pleadings, to undisputed evidence and to all the evidence on the subject.

Saks' conduct was within the letter of the Civil Code definition of "actual fraud" which makes a contract voidable (§ 1572): "any of the following acts, committed by a party to a contract, or with his connivance, with intent to deceive another party thereto, or to induce him to enter into the contract: 1. The suggestion, as a fact, of that which is not true, by one who does not believe it to be true; . . . 5. Any other act fitted to deceive." Saks' conduct is also within the letter of the Restatement of Contracts definition of fraud which makes a transaction induced by it voidable (§ 471): "misrepresentation known to be such . . . by any person intending or expecting thereby to cause a mistake by another . . . in order to induce the latter to enter into . . . a transaction."

Saks relies on California cases which say that "fraud which has produced and will produce no injury will not justify a rescission." (*Spreckels v. Gorrill* (1907), 152 Cal. 383, 388 [92 P. 1011]; *Munson v. Fishburn* (1920), 183 Cal. 206, 216 [190 P. 808]; *Darrow v. Houlihan* (1928), 205 Cal. 771, 774 [272 P. 1049].) It asserts that a person is not injured by being induced to buy a $5,000 coat for $4,000. But the coat was neither sold nor bought for $4,000. Saks was selling the coat for the full price, and a person other than seller Saks and buyer Barbee paid a substantial part — approximately one fifth — of the full price. Furthermore, this "no injury, no rescission" formula is not very helpful, because of disagreement in the authorities as to what is meant by "injury." In a sense, anyone who is fraudulently induced to enter into a contract is "injured"; his "interest in making a free choice and in exercising his own best judgment in making decision with respect to economic transactions and enterprises has been interfered with." (See McCleary, *Damage as a Requisite to Rescission for Misrepresentation,* 36 Mich. L. Rev. 1, 227, 245.)

Also relied on by Saks is a definition of "injury" which has sometimes appeared in some California cases: "It may be conceded that it must be shown that [one who would rescind] ... by reason of fraud, suffered an injury of a pecuniary nature, that is, an injury to his property rights, as distinguished from a mere injury to his feelings, but it will be sufficient if the facts alleged show that material injury will necessarily ensue from the fraud, although the amount of pecuniary loss is not stated." (*Spreckels v. Gorrill* (1907), *supra,* 152 Cal. 383, 388.) The "concession" or implication that in every case there must be "pecuniary loss" is incorrect. (See *Hefferan v. Freebairn* (1950), 34 Cal. 2d 715, 721 [214 P.2d 386].) And the definition does not take account of the cases which allow rescission of a transaction induced by an agent's misrepresentation of his principal's identity, even though there was no economic reason for the unwillingness to deal with the principal. (See cases collected in 48 Harv. L. Rev. 480, 485; McCleary, *supra,* p. 246 of 36 Mich. L. Rev.)

The McCleary article, *supra,* suggests the following classification of the cases which have considered rescission for fraud:

1. The representee can rescind where he obtains the very thing that he expected but it is worth less than he was reasonably to expect. In most cases where rescission is sought the representee has received something of less economic value than he expected.

2. The representee can rescind where he obtains something substantially different from that which he was led to expect. If one is induced to buy a certain lot of land by misrepresentation that it contains a vineyard, he need not keep it when he learns that it contains instead an apple orchard; even though the lot of land is the identical lot of land and although the orchard may be more valuable than the vineyard which he expected to get, it is obviously unfair to require him to keep what he did not bargain for and did not want. The undisputed evidence describing the present sale would put it in this class. The coat bargained for between Barbee and Saks, within the knowledge

and belief of Barbee, as was known to Saks, was a coat fully paid for by Barbee, which Saks knew was to be used as a gift, but Saks intended to and did deliver something substantially different; i.e., a coat on which Barbee was charged only with a down payment and for which his intended donee had secretly agreed to pay in a substantial part. The seller was to receive approximately 25 per cent more for the coat than the buyer was paying and the element of a complete gift was being destroyed.

3. Where the representee obtains exactly that which he expects, although there was misrepresentation, the social interest in the stability of transactions may or may not out-weigh the social interest in not having one intentionally take advantage of another. Saks attempts to describe the present sale so as to put it in this class. It says that Barbee bargained for and expected to get a certain coat for a cost to him of not more than $4,000, and this is what he got. In the present situation, however, where the motives of Barbee were clearly noneconomic, the general social interest in stability of transactions is overridden by the interest in not having a seller make intentional misrepresentations which mislead a would-be donor into the erroneous belief that he alone is purchasing and that his donee is to receive from him a fully paid for gift, when the seller is fully aware of the effect which the misrepresentations may have and intends that they should have that effect. Again, it is important, the element of a complete gift by donor to donee is being destroyed through the misrepresentation and concealment.

Saks contends that Barbee has not rescinded, and cannot rescind, the sale because he has stated that he was willing to carry out the objectively manifested bargain to purchase the coat for $3,981.25. But at no time since Barbee's announced willingness to stand on the transaction which he believed he had entered into with Saks, did Saks offer to comply with the transaction and give Barbee what he bargained for: a coat for which he was paying in full, without Mrs. Earl, a stranger to the Saks-Barbee transaction, paying a portion of the price. Indeed, Saks, at the time of the rescission and mentioned offer by Barbee, was apparently unable to sell Barbee the coat in question as a fully paid for coat for $3,981.25 because Mrs. Earl refused to take back the $916.30 which she paid for the coat and which Saks had previously accepted. Barbee's counsel, at the trial, made clear his position; after the secret agreement, misrepresentation and payment of $916.30 were in evidence he said, "under the circumstances of this case we shouldn't be required to pay Saks and Company anything. ... [W]hen he [Barbee] learned all the facts he never would have approved that transaction and your Honor knows it ... [He] would do anything that could be done to repudiate that transaction and say it never was a real transaction." We are satisfied that the contract of purchase and the gift were voidable and were properly rescinded.

For the reasons above stated, the judgments are reversed.

Shenk, J., Carter, J., and Spence, J., concurred.

TRAYNOR, J.   Barbee received what he bargained for. *(Cf. Hefferan v. Freebairn,* 34 Cal. 2d 715, 721 [214 P.2d 386].) The mink coat that he examined and agreed to pay $3,981.25 for, was the one he received and gave to Mrs. Earl. He concedes that the fair value of the coat was $5,000. It was not unreasonable for the trial court to conclude that, since the coat Barbee received was actually worth more than he agreed to pay, he would not have rejected it because Mrs. Earl arranged to pay the difference. (See *Spinks v. Clark,* 147 Cal. 439, 444 [82 P. 45]; *Spreckels v. Gorrill,* 152 Cal. 383, 388 [92 P. 1011]; *Munson v. Fishburn,* 183 Cal. 206, 216 [190 P. 808]; *Darrow v. Houlihan,* 205 Cal. 771, 774-775 [272 P. 1049]; McCleary, *Damage as Requisite to Rescission For Misrepresentation,* 36 Mich. L. Rev. 1, 15, 23-24.) It was under no compulsion to believe his statement that he would have rejected it. (*Huth v. Katz,* 30 Cal. 2d 605, 609 [184 P.2d 521]; *Tingey v. E. F. Houghton & Co.,* 30 Cal. 2d 97, 102 [179 P.2d 807]; *Blank v. Coffin,* 20 Cal. 2d 457, 461-462 [126 P.2d 868].)

It was for the trial court to determine whether Barbee was a man of such temperament that he would have preferred having Mrs. Earl get along without the fur coat to accepting her contribution toward its purchase. He declared his love for her, expressing the sentiment several times that he wanted to give her a fur coat. She was "very much in love with the coat and wanted it badly." It was important to him that the woman he loved possess the coat; it was important to her to possess it. Her contribution enabled him to fulfill his wish and hers at a price he was willing to pay. Since they were both fur-coat-minded, it is a reasonable inference that he would not have risked disturbing the relationship between them by depriving her of the coat because she was willing to contribute toward its purchase.

Counsel at the trial made it clear that Barbee sought rescission of the sale because Mrs. Earl failed to live up to his expectations. This failure can in no way be attributed to Saks and Company. Its coat was of sound quality and came up to Mrs. Earl's expectations. The court properly rejected Barbee's offer of proof of his expectations and disappointment. Not only were they no concern of Saks and Company, but no issue was raised in the pleadings regarding his arrangements with Mrs. Earl. I would therefore affirm the judgments.

Edmonds, J., concurred.

Respondent's (Saks') petition for rehearing was denied February 15, 1951. Edmonds, J., and Traynor, J., voted for a rehearing.

BRUNZELL CONSTRUCTION CO. v. G. J. WEISBROD, INC.
134 C.A.2d 278, 285 P.2d 989 (1955)

[Plaintiff contractor sued defendant subcontractor for breach of a subcontract for steel construction on a contract to build a school building. Defendant had submitted an oral bid (by telephone) on the job for $37,700, excluding the steel decking. Plaintiff obtained bids on the decking work from another company. When defendant's office reduced its subcontract to writing in a confirming letter, the exclusion of steel decking was omitted. Plaintiff then asserted that defendant had agreed to do all the steel work, including the decking work, for $37,700. Defendant refused to perform under the contract as written; plaintiff awarded the subcontract for all the steel work to another subcontractor for $49,000, and sued defendant for the difference. The lower court found the facts essentially as stated, and entered judgment for the defendant.]

Plaintiff's fundamental contention is that "the court erred in ruling that [defendant] was entitled to rescind the subcontract agreement by reason of the discovery of certain alleged mistakes." Such contention is thoroughly refuted by the case of M. F. Kemper Const. Co. v. City of Los Angeles, 37 Cal. 2d 696, 235 P.2d 7, 10. There, plaintiff Kemper sued to cancel a bid it had submitted on a public construction project and to obtain a discharge of its bid bond. In submitting its bid, plaintiff inadvertently omitted an item amounting to $301,769 which had figured in its computations. The company discovered its error several hours after the bids were opened and sought to withdraw its bid. The Board of Public Works refused to permit this and passed a resolution accepting the erroneous bid. Section 386(d) of the City Charter of Los Angeles provides: "After bids have been opened and declared, except with the consent of the officer, board or City Council having jurisdiction over the bidding, no bid shall be withdrawn, but the same shall be subject to acceptance by the city for a period of three months ***" The trial court found, in part, that the bid had been submitted as the result of an honest mistake of a material character, that plaintiff was not negligent, that it had acted promptly to rescind, and that the board had accepted with knowledge of the error. It concluded that it would be unconscionable to require plaintiff to perform for the amount of the bid and that the city suffered no prejudice though it had to award the contract to the next lowest bidder.

In affirming the judgment, the Supreme Court expounded the law directly apposite to the case before us: "The city contends that a party is entitled to relief on that ground [rescission] only where the mistake is mutual, and it points to the fact that the mistake in the bid submitted was wholly unilateral. *** However, the city had actual notice of the error in the estimates before it attempted to accept the bid, and knowledge by one party that the other is acting under mistake is treated as equivalent to mutual mistake for purposes of rescission. *** Relief from mistaken bids is consistently allowed where one party knows or has reason to know of the other's error and the requirements for rescission are fulfilled. ***

"Rescission may be had for mistake of fact if the mistake is material to the contract and was not the result of neglect of a legal duty, if enforcement of the contract as made would be unconscionable, and if the other party can be placed in statu quo. *** In addition, the party seeking relief must give prompt notice of his election to rescind and must restore or offer to restore to the other party everything of value which he has received under the contract. ***

"Omission of the $301,769 item from the company's bid was, of course, a material mistake. The city claims that the company is barred from relief because it was negligent in preparing the estimates, but even if we assume that the error was due to some carelessness, it does not follow that the company is without remedy. Civil Code section 1577, which defines mistake of fact for which relief may be allowed, describes it as one not caused by 'the neglect of a legal duty' on the part of the person making the mistake. It has been recognized numerous times that not all carelessness constitutes a 'neglect of a legal duty' within the meaning of the section. *** On facts very similar to those in the present case, courts of other jurisdictions have stated that there was no culpable negligence and have granted relief from erroneous bids. *** The type of error here involved is one which will sometimes occur in the conduct of reasonable and cautious businessmen, and, under all the circumstances, we cannot say as a matter of law that it constituted a neglect of legal duty such as would bar the right to equitable relief.

"The evidence clearly supports the conclusion that it would be unconscionable to hold the company to its bit at the mistaken figure. The city had knowledge before the bid was accepted that the company had made a clerical error which resulted in the omission of an item amounting to nearly one-third of the amount intended to be bid, and, under all the circumstances, it appears that it would be unjust and unfair to permit the city to take advantage of the company's mistake."

The instant case falls squarely within the equitable principles announced in the Kemper case. The evidence shows that when defendant made its oral bid through Klamm, it specifically excluded the decking in its bid of $37,700. That plaintiff fully knew and comprehended this is reasonably to be inferred from a miscellany of evidentiary matters appearing in the record. First and foremost is the fact that in submitting its own bid, and in conformity with the requirement of section 4102 of the Government Code, plaintiff listed Walter Steyer, who had bid $9,300 for the decking job as the subcontractor for the steel decking. Secondly, as an experienced bidder on public projects, Brunzell must have clearly known that defendant's bid would be "in line" with other bids only if it excluded decking. This appears from the other bids — Apex Steel Company having bid $39,800 for the job without decking ($2,100 more than defendant's bid), and the Kyle Construction Company having bid $51,778 including decking (or $4,778 more than the combined bid of plaintiff and Steyer). Thirdly, after Brunzell received the confirming letter and before the contract was signed, Klamm and Brunzell discussed the arcade work, the only place in which the specifications called for decking. Brunzell emphasized the need for speed in constructing the arcade. Klamm replied that "furnishing the structural steel for this portion of the work is relatively simple. Completion will be dependent upon delivery of the metal deck by Mr. Steyer" — an indication that the parties recognized the decking would be Steyer's responsibility.

From all the foregoing evidence, the court was justified in finding that defendant had made a mistake in its letter of confirmation, that plaintiff knew that such a mistake had been made, that it took unfair advantage of this mistake to incorporate decking into the contract though the bid price was made exclusive of decking, and that defendant assented to the contract under an honest misapprehension which plaintiff was trying to exploit. Upon discovering the true facts a few days after the contract was signed and while it was still executory, defendant gave prompt notice of rescission "and no offer of restoration was necessary because it had received nothing of value which it could restore." M. F. Kemper Const. Co. v. City of Los Angeles, supra, 37 Cal. 2d at page 703, 235 P.2d at page 11. That some element of carelessness not amounting to " 'the neglect of a legal duty' " permeated defendant's mistake, will not of itself bar its right to relief where the mistake in question does not stem from an original error in judgment. M. F. Kemper, etc. Co. v. City of Los Angeles, supra, 37 Cal. 2d at page 703-704, 235 P.2d at page 10; Klose v. Sequoia Union High School Dist., 118 Cal. App. 2d 636, 641-642, 258 P.2d 515.

It follows that the court was therefore clearly correct in its implied conclusion that plaintiff could not enforce the contract asm ade. When a contract is still executory, and the parties can be put in statu quo, one party to the contract will not be permitted to obtain an unconscionable advantage through enforcement of the contract where he knows of the other's mistake, where such mistake is material and not the result of a neglect of a legal duty or an error in judgment, and the requirements for rescission are fulfilled. M. F. Kemper etc. Co. v. City of Los Angeles, supra, 37 Cal. 2d at page 701, 235 P.2d 7. That a mistake of which plaintiff was aware, and through which defendant seemingly agreed to perform a contract for a price of $37,700 calling for work reasonably worth at least $47,000, was of so essential and fundamental a character that the minds of the parties never met on the contract as executed, would scarcely seem to require discussion. And where, as here, one of the parties, through excusable mistake or neglect and not because of an error of judgment, has named a consideration that is out of all proportion to the value of the subject of negotiations, and the other party, cognizant of such mistake, takes inequitable advantage of it, the latter cannot under such conditions claim an enforceable contract.

* * *

The judgment is affirmed.

MOORE, P. J., and McCOMB, J., concur.

KESSLER AND FINE, CULPA IN CONTRAHENDO, BARGAINING IN
GOOD FAITH, AND FREEDOM OF CONTRACT: A COMPARATIVE
STUDY, 77 Harv. L. Rev.* 401, 432-37 (1964)

The civil law treatment of mistake, particularly unilateral mistake, as
worked out by the German law, has come in for a good deal of criticism
by Anglo-American writers in comparative law. Three arguments have been
made in the main: First, under the civil law, its critics tell us, no weight is
given to the "psychological effects of the promise and of its subsequent repudiation, upon the promisee, in cases where the promisee has done no overt prejudicial act in reliance upon the promise. The promisee may have made his
plans and even have altered his external conduct in innumerable ways in
reliance upon the promise, and yet such injuries go uncompensated. Noneco-
nomic . . . interests and mental injuries are not taken into account." Since it
is most difficult to prove and to evaluate the promisee's disappointed expectations, the common law courts justifiably were driven to adopt the other alternative, namely, to allow the promisee to recover the standardized value of his
bargain. Second, the common law cannot afford to adopt the civil law solution
of the mistake problem, since it has no *culpa in contrahendo* doctrine. Third,
by subjecting to liability the party responsible for the mistake, the objective
theory of contracts creates a powerful incentive to avoid careless manifestations
of assent. In short, the ideal of security of transactions demands an objective
theory of contracts and a confinement of operative unilateral mistake within
narrow limits. Thus, the impression of a deep cleavage emerges, at least on the
doctrinal level, between the civil law and the common law, the civil being
identified with the will theory, the common law with the objective theory of
contracts.

Indeed, there is the powerful authority of the *Restatement of Contracts*
which says that the mistake of only one party (as against mutual mistake
which is operative) does not of itself render the transaction voidable even
though it forms the basis on which the mistaken party enters into the transaction. But there is a widening countercurrent of case law which stresses factors
relevant under the *culpa in contrahendo* doctrine. Protection to the victim of
mistake has always been accorded when the mistake was caused by fraud or
misrepresentation of the other party. But the courts have increasingly come to
realize that the objective theory of contracts must give way whenever the
security-of-transactions principle comes into conflict with notions of good faith
and fair dealing. Protection, therefore, is no longer limited to the fraud and
misrepresentation situations. A party will not be permitted unconscionably to
profit at the expense of another who, as he knows, has made a "costly error";
and the domain of palpable mistake has come to include situations where the

---

mistake should have been known. Since many courts, to accomplish results which they have regarded as fair and just, have refused mechanically to apply the unilateral-bilateral mistake dichotomy, the line between hard bargains which are enforceable and those affected by operative mistake has become quite fluid.

Over the last decades notions of good faith and fair dealing have undergone a steady process of further expansion, particularly in the field of public construction contracts. By means of the notion of unconscionability, bidders for public construction contracts whose bids were based on "honest" errors in calculation or computation were granted relief provided the errors were "excusable," had serious financial consequences, and the nonmistaken party had not, acting in reliance, substantially changed his position to his detriment. The mere fact that an offer of a higher bidder had to be accepted has not been regarded as a change of position fatal to relief, particularly if due to statute or charter provision the other bids were still outstanding. Occasionally, relief has even been granted where the mistake was impalpable. Where relief was denied, the unilateral character of the mistake often has been regarded as only one of the factors to be considered. Stress has been laid on the absence of clear and convincing evidence as to the honesty and seriousness (materiality) of the mistake, the fact that the *status quo* could not be restored, and the "negligence" of the mistaken party claiming relief. An increasing number of decisions have even taken the position that a mere slight degree of negligence will not bar relief.

To be sure, many of the mistake cases where relief was granted involved public construction contracts in which plaintiff faced forfeiture of a deposit or bond statutorily required to secure a bid. But the liberalization of the objective theory of contracts has not been confined to these construction transactions. Nor has it been limited to releases. Relief has been granted for bona fide and material mistake of expression where the mistake concerned the essential terms of a writing; or where a buyer of land innocently bought the wrong piece, or was mistaken as to the availability of access roads.[146] Even in the field of sales of goods where one might expect strict adherence to the ideal of security, courts have accorded relief from mistakes as to substance (identity of the subject matter), as contrasted with mere quality, unless the risk of mistake was assumed by the party seeking relief according to the "intent of the contract." While miscalculations of prices or errors as to quantity bought or sold have often been regarded as inoperative, several of the decisions denying relief have emphasized the fact that the transaction was executed or a change of position had taken place. The significance of these statements qualifying traditional

---

[146] *E.g.,* Goodrich v. Lathrop, 94 Cal. 56, 29 Pac. 329 (1892), applying CAL. CIVIL CODE §§ 3407, 3408; Permutter v. Bacas, 219 Md. 406, 149 A. 2d 23 (1959) (seller not prejudiced beyond loss of bargain), *Contra,* Beebe v. Birkett [p. 150, *supra*], 109 Mich. 663, 67 N.W. 966 (1896) (buyer could have discovered his mistake by ordinary care).

mistake doctrine is difficult to assess. It is quite tempting to dismiss them as dicta gratuitously thrown in. And yet they may express an uneasy awareness of tension between the living law of contracts and case law. Unfortunately, we know far too little about the former. But there is enough information to indicate that the business community does not always regard a contract as a "steel chain" but often "only as a tentative arrangement, even after the legal requirements of contract have been satisfied." To the extent that the business community permits cancellation with impunity, or upon payment of reliance damages (reimbursement of expenses incurred), the strict rules of contract law with regard to unilateral mistake have lost some of their vigor. Unfortunately common law courts have generally felt that they had no alternative other than to enforce or deny a contract. Equity, on the other hand, has occasionally granted rescission or refused specific performance on payment of reliance damages.

To sum up, in attempting to find acceptable solutions mediating between the legitimate interests of both promisor and promisee, traditional doctrine in this country has been redefined by a body of case law too large to be ignored. In this process of refinement of our law of contract, *culpa in contrahendo* and notions of unjust enrichment have played a significant role. While in the civil law countries *culpa in contrahendo* has been used in large measure to mitigate the will theory, the common law starting from the other end has employed it as one of its weapons to soften the rigor of the objective theory of contracts. In this country the process of mitigation has found further manifestation in the notion that a mistaken party should be protected against oppressive burdens when rescission would impose no substantial hardship on the party seeking enforcement of the contract. Thus a link has been established between operative mistake and unjust enrichment. Here is an instance where the common law will look into adequacy of consideration. This variance from the general rule is not surprising, since the ordinary interest in protecting a price mutually arrived at is not present here.

VAN METER v. BENT CONSTRUCTION CO.
46 Cal. 2d 588, 297 P.2d 644 (1956)

Action for declaration of rights under a subcontract, reformation of the subcontract, recovery of reasonable value of services performed, and damages for false representations. Judgment for defendants reversed.

GIBSON, C. J. . . .

* * *

The general contract with the city required defendants [general contractors] to clear all of the reservoir basin below the elevation of 2,073 feet, and by the terms of the subcontract plaintiff [subcontractor] undertook to perform that part of the general contract providing for clearing the reservoir basin. Plaintiff has completed the work required of him and has earned the sum of $29,750 specified in the subcontract. When he entered into the subcontract he believed in good faith that the area required to be cleared was that portion of the reservoir basin below contour elevation 2073 which had been flagged by the city. Prior to the execution of the subcontract, defendants made untrue representations to plaintiff with regard to the extent of the area to be cleared. Defendants believed that flags had been placed around the entire contour, and they did not know that their representations were false, but defendants made the representations as positive assertions in a manner not warranted by their information. Plaintiff believe the representations, relied upon them in entering into the subcontract and was thereby caused to believe that by its terms he was to clear that portion of the reservoir basin lying below the lags which were then on the ground. A contractor of ordinary skill in the exercise of ordinary care should have known that the contract required that trees and brush be removed from both basins, and, had plaintiff made the inquiries reasonably suggested by the contract and an inspection of the premises, he would have discovered that it was intended that the entire reservoir basin be cleared. Plaintiff, who was an experienced contractor, failed to use reasonable care to ascertain the extent of the area involved.

The court concluded that because the fraud perpetrated upon plaintiff was not wilful and since plaintiff did not use reasonable care in ascertaining the extent of the work to be performed under the subcontract, he was entitled to no relief and that "The findings heretofore made are determinative of all the issues involved in this action and that it becomes unnecessary to make any further findings of fact."

In view of the positive misrepresentations made by defendants, the trier of fact could have found that plaintiff was not negligent, but we cannot say that there is no substantial evidence to support the finding that he failed to use ordinary care to ascertain the extent of the area to be cleared. All reasonable inferences must be drawn in favor of the findings, and it may be inferred that, although section H [of the contract] does not refer to a map, plaintiff was negligent in not examining the maps and drawings attached to the general contract to see whether one of them contained a description of the area to be cleared and also in failing to ascertain whether the flagged area covered one square mile.

In our opinion, however, the court erred in concluding that since the fraud perpetrated by defendants was not wilful, plaintiff's negligence precluded him from obtaining any relief and that it was unnecessary to make further findings. It is the general rule that the negligence of a plaintiff is not a defense where the defendant with intent to deceive has falsely represented as a fact something which he does not believe to be true. (*Hefferan v. Freebairn*, 34 Cal. 2d 715, 718-721 [214 P.2d 386]; *Seeger v. Odell*, 18 Cal. 2d 409, 414 et seq. [115 P.2d 977, 136 A.L.R. 1291]; see *California Trust Co. v. Cohn*, 214 Cal. 619,

626 et seq. [7 P.2d 297].) Although defendants were guilty of fraud as defined in subdivision 2 of section 1572 of the Civil Code, their fraud was not wilful since their representations were believed by them to be true and were not made with intent to deceive. Defendants contend that their conduct, though characterized by the statute as fraudulent, was merely negligent and that, by analogy to the rule in tort cases, plaintiff's contributory negligence is as a matter of law a complete defense. There is an element of carelessness in nearly every case of mistake, and it is obvious that the unqualified application of the principle urged by defendants would result in the virtual destruction of the equitable remedies for relief from mistake.

It is settled that, even in the absence of any misrepresentation, the negligent failure of a party to know or discover facts as to which both parties are under a mistake does not preclude rescission or reformation because of the mistake. (*National Auto & Cas. Ins. Co. v. Industrial Acc. Com.*, 34 Cal. 2d 20, 24-26 [206 P.2d 841]; *Los Angeles etc. R. R. Co. v. New Liverpool Salt Co.*, 150 Cal. 21, 25-28 [87 P. 1029]; *Mills v. Schulba*, 95 Cal. App. 2d 559, 564-565 [213 P.2d 408]; *Hanlon v. Western Loan & Bldg. Co.*, 46 Cal. App. 2d 580, 597-598 [116 P.2d 465]; see Rest., Contracts, § 508; McClintock on Equity (1948), pp. 246-247, 265-266; 3 Pomeroy, Equity Jurisprudence (5th ed., 1941), § 856b, pp. 340-341; 12 Am. Jur., pp. 624-625; *cf. M. F. Kemper Const. Co. v. City of Los Angeles*, 37 Cal. 2d 696, 702 [235 P.2d 7]; *Brunzell Const. Co. v. G. J. Weisbrod, Inc.*, [p. 214, *supra*,] 134 Cal. App. 2d 278, 286 [285 P.2d 989].) Some cases have said that a plaintiff will not be denied rescission or reformation because of lack of care unless his conduct amounts to gross negligence or the neglect of a legal duty. (*Los Angeles etc. R. R. Co. v. New Liverpool Salt Co.*, . . .; *Hanlon v. Western Loan & Bldg. Co.*, ...) These terms are perhaps unfortunate and have caused some confusion. The theory that there are degrees of negligence has been generally criticized by legal writers, but a distinction has been made in this state between ordinary and gross negligence. (See *Donnelly v. Southern Pac. Co.*, 18 Cal. 2d 863, 871 [118 P.2d 465].) Gross negligence has been said to mean the want of even scant care or an extreme departure from the ordinary standard of conduct. (See *Kastel v. Stieber*, 215 Cal. 37, 47-51 [8 P.2d 474]; Prosser on Torts (1941), p. 260.) A breach of legal duty may, of course, consist of either ordinary negligence or gross negligence (Harper on Torts (1933), p. 170), but it has been held that ordinary negligence does not constitute the neglect of a legal duty as that term is used in section 1577 of the Civil Code. (*Los Angeles etc. R. R. Co. v. New Liverpool Salt Co.*, . . .; *Hanlon v. Western Loan & Bldg. Co.*, ...)

There is even more reason for not barring a plaintiff from equitable relief where his negligence is due in part to his reliance in good faith upon the false representations of a defendant, although the statements were not made with intent to deceive. (*Cf. Shearer v. Cooper*, 21 Cal. 2d 695, 703-704 [134 P.2d 764]; *Fleury v. Ramacciotti*, 8 Cal. 2d. 600, 662 [67 P.2d 339].) A defendant who misrepresents the facts and induces the plaintiff to rely on his statements should not be heard in an equitable action to assert that the reliance was negligent unless plaintiff's conduct, in the light of his intelligence and information, is preposterous or irrational. (5 Williston on Contracts (rev. ed.) § 1512, pp. 4222, 4223.)

The court did not determine that plaintiff's conduct was preposterous or irrational or that it amounted to gross negligence or the neglect of a legal duty, and we are of the opinion that any such determination could not be supported in view of the findings that were made. The subcontract required plaintiff to perform the work described in section H of the general contract. The only provision in section H which describes the area from which trees and brush are to be removed states that the reservoir basin shall be cleared below elevation 2073, that contour 2073 will be flagged by the city during the bidding period, that the area of the basin is about one square mile and that the bidder shall make a visual observation before submitting a bid. When plaintiff made his inspection he discovered that the area flagged by the city was approximately coextensive with the lower basin, at the end of which the dam was to be located. Defendants, who as general contractors were in a position to know the facts, represented to plaintiff, both before and after he inspected the premises, that the area to be cleared was that which had been flagged by the city. Plaintiff's failure to make a more thorough investigation of the work required by section H was no doubt due in a large part to the positive representations made by defendants and to the circumstances under which they were made.

The court erred in concluding that, it having been found that plaintiff was negligent, he was precluded from obtaining any relief and that it was therefore unnecessary to make other findings. In the absence of findings upon all material issues we cannot determine what if any relief plaintiff would be entitled to receive.

The judgment is reversed.

Shenk, J., Carter, J., Traynor, J., Schauer, J., Spence, J., and McComb, J., concurred.

REID V. LANDON, 166 Cal. App. 2d 476, 333 P.2d 432 (1958): Defendant deeded to plaintiffs, as a gift, a half interest in a ranch, in joint tenancy; defendant kept a one-fourth joint tenancy interest, and gave a similar one-fourth interest to another lady, who died soon thereafter. Plaintiffs moved in with defendant and constructed a tearoom on the ranch; defendant agreed thereafter to deed to plaintiffs the portion on which the tearoom stood, in exchange for a deed to their interest in the remainder of the ranch. Plaintiffs then asked to buy one acre of land lying between the tearoom and the highway. Defendant did not want to sell, but agreed to give plaintiffs a right of first refusal, in exchange for a similar right of first refusal if plaintiffs should wish to sell the

portion of the ranch on which the tearoom stood. A letter agreement was prepared by defendant's attorney to effect the exchange. Before the agreement was
signed, plaintiffs went to the attorney, alone, and told him that they were supposed to have an option to buy the acre for $200 instead of a right of first
refusal. The attorney prepared an option letter agreement, along with other
documents. Defendant signed the documents, noticing the word "option," but
failing to understand that the term meant anything other than a right of first
refusal. Five years later, during which time plaintiffs and defendant continued
to live together, plaintiffs wrote to defendant, advising that they were taking
up the option; defendant refused to sell. Plaintiffs sued for specific performance
of the option agreement. Although one does not need to know any law to
know how this case must have been decided, the following doctrinal observations of the court are interesting:

"It is true that under section 1577, Civil Code, defining 'mistake of fact,'
not any and every mistake is remediable. Of whatever it might consist, the
mistake of fact claimed under this section must not have been caused by the
neglect of a legal duty on the part of the claimant. In determining what conduct will amount to a neglect of duty the courts recognize there is an element
of carelessness in nearly every case of mistake (*Van Meter v. Bent Const. Co.,*
[p. 220, *supra,*] 46 Cal. 2d 588 [297 P.2d 644]) and that which does not
amount to the neglect of a legal duty will not of itself bar rescission where the
mistake does not stem from an original error in judgment. (*Brunzell Constr.
Co. v. G. J. Weisbrod, Inc.,* [p. 214, *supra,*] 134 Cal. App. 2d 278 [285 P.2d
989]; *M. F. Kemper Constr. Co. v. City of Los Angeles,* [quoted at p. 215,
supra,] 37 Cal. 2d 696 [235 P.2d 7]; *Klose v. Sequoia Union High School
Dist.,* 188 Cal. App. 2d 636 [258 P.2d 515].) This rule is particularly applicable in a situation in which false representations were made to induce the
execution of the instrument, even though the person making them believed
them to be true. The Supreme Court so held in *Van Meter v. Bent Constr.,*
46 Cal. 2d 588, stating at page 595 [297 P.2d 644]: 'There is even more
reason for not barring a plaintiff from equitable relief where his negligence
is due in part to his reliance in good faith upon the false representations of a
defendant, although the statements were not made with intent to deceive. . . .
A defendant who misrepresents the facts and induces the plaintiff to rely on
his statements should not be heard in an equitable action to assert that the
reliance was negligent unless plaintiff's conduct, in the light of his intelligence
and information, is preposterous or irrational.'

"In support of their argument that no mistake of fact existed, appellants
place great reliance on defendant's testimony that before signing it she read
the letter agreement and observed the word 'option.' They urge that since the
term is unambiguous, defendant is presumed to have known its meaning. However, included in her testimony is her statement that although she now knows
the meaning of the word 'option,' she did not then understand it and thought
it had the same meaning as a right of first refusal. Although generally one is

presumed to know the meaning of unambiguous language and will be bound by the execution of a written instrument including it, the rule applies only in the absence of fraud, confidential relationship or circumstances indicating excusable mistake. (*Fraters G. & P. Co. v. Southwestern C. Co.*, 107 Cal. App. 1 [290 P. 45]; *Wetzstein v. Thomasson*, 34 Cal. App. 2d 554 [93 P.2d 1028].)

* * *

". . . We have before us a situation in which plaintiffs, unknown to defendant, had greater knowledge concerning the preparation and the terms of the agreement than she; a circumstance of intimate friendship bordering on a confidential relationship existing between defendant and plaintiffs, trust in plaintiffs, and defendant's reliance upon their false representations. Although the trial court found no fraud to exist, there was clearly an imposition by plaintiffs upon their friend. Had defendant known the agreement was not the same she had instructed her counsel to prepare and its terms were not in accord with her original agreement, she would not have signed it. The $200 consideration was wholly unreasonable and inadequate, the reasonable market value of the acre in July, 1951, being $550 to $800, the enforcement of which would have been unconscionable. It is clear that defendant's mistake was due to conduct that constituted neither a neglect of duty or an error in judgment and was not 'preposterous or irrational,' but a natural and reasonable mistake due largely to defendant's reliance on the plaintiffs' representations that the document reflected the terms of her original agreement. Having been told by plaintiffs the letter agreement had been prepared by her counsel, he never having advised her of the change; believing plaintiffs' representations that the document embodied the terms originally agreed upon and not understanding the difference between an 'option' and a 'first right of refusal,' defendant signed the option letter agreement in the mistaken belief that as a matter of fact she was signing quite another document. We conclude that the evidence justified relief from the terms of the agreement (Civ. Code, §§ 1577, 1689), and the court's adjudication of defendant's rescission thereof." [*Cf. Goldner v. Jaffe*, 171 Cal. App. 2d 751, 341 P.2d 354 (1959). — Ed.]

Section 2-302 of the Uniform Commercial Code provides as follows:

Unconscionable Contract or Clause.

(1) If the court as a matter of law finds the contract or any clause of the contract to have been unconscionable at the time it was made the court may refuse to enforce the contract, or it may enforce the remainder of the contract without the unconscionable clause, or it may so limit the application of any unconscionable clause as to avoid any unconscionable result.
(2) When it is claimed or appears to the court that the contract or any clause thereof may be unconscionable the parties shall be afforded a reasonable opportunity to present evidence as to its commercial setting, purpose and effect to aid the court in making the determination.

This section was originally drafted to apply only to contracts of adhesion — form contracts, with respect to the terms of which one side has little or no bargaining power. The language was broadened in successive drafts to cover all contracts for the sale of goods, although the official comment discusses principally cases of disclaimer of warranty. In its broad form, the section was rejected by the California State Bar committee, and then by the California legislature, on the ground that it gave too much discreation to a court to strike down contract terms. The worry was that there would have to be a renegotiation of the contract in every instance in which the parties came to disagree on the fairness of the contract's provisions. See the California Code comment to Section 2-302 in WEST'S ANN. CALIF. COMM'L CODE. There have been indications that some of the bar leaders and legislators who first opposed Section 2-302 now favor its adoption in California.

Was it wise for the Code's draftsmen to leave the term "unconscionable" undefined? Would it have been preferable to specify some percentage of value (less than one-half, five-twelfths, etc.) as a measure of unfairness, as in some civilian legislation on *lesión?* Is the Code provision necessary, or can courts reach similar results through other doctrinal media? Would the adoption of the provision promote greater certainty in commercial dealings, or reduce the security of transactions? Why?

BELLWOOD DISCOUNT CORP. v. EMPIRE STEEL BUILDING CO.
175 Cal. App. 2d 432, 346 P.2d 467 (1959)

Fox, Presiding Justice.

Plaintiff, referred to herein as Bellwood, seeks (1) to rescind a building contract that it had entered into with defendant, referred to herein as Empire, and (2) to recover its initial payment under said contract.

By the terms of this contract, entered into in March, 1956, Empire agreed to furnish all labor and materials to construct a tapered girder steel panel building on a parcel of land, owned by plaintiff, in the city of Indio, and "*** to furnish necessary engineering of structural steel and concrete block walls and foundation drawings *only*." (Emphasis added.) Under the heading *Work not included* was the following: "Any item not specifically mentioned, electrical, plumbing, concrete work, reinforcing steel, painting, or interior partitions." The contract also stated that the contractor "*** will obtain necessary permits covering *the work set forth in this contract* at the expense of the owner." (Emphasis added.) The contract price was $34,000, and the final ten per cent was payable "upon completion of Empire's *portion* of the work. ***" (Emphasis added.)

This building was to be the repair shop portion of a structure that Bellwood was erecting for use as an automobile agency. Bellwood's own architect was to design the showroom and the other facilities which comprised this development.

After the contract was signed, Empire prepared a set of plans for submission to the Building Department of Indio covering the structural details of the contemplated building and the concrete walls and foundations. These plans were submitted to and approved by Bellwood and then filed with the Building Department, Bellwood paying the filing fee. The Building Department returned the plans along with a "plan correction sheet" specifying certain additional information which had to be furnished before a building permit could be issued. Included were such items as plumbing, electrical facilities, an exhaust system, and other ordinary fixtures. Also listed were certain items required by the fire prevention provisions of the building code relating to the use of the structure as an automotive repair shop, which required either installation of automatic sprinklers or the division of the building into two parts by a proper fire resistant wall. The subject of a sprinkling system was not discussed between the parties prior to making the contract. Interior walls were not contemplated by the contract and Bellwood had expressly stated to Empire that no interior walls were to be used in the design of the building. After the Building Department pointed out the need for one or the other of these items, Bellwood served notice of rescission on Empire and demanded the return of its initial payment of $6,800, which had been made pursuant to the contract. Bellwood based its right to rescind the contract on the ground of mistake.

The trial court rendered judgment for Empire on the complaint,[1] ruling that Bellwood had no right to rescind. Further, the court held that Bellwood was not entitled to a return of any portion of the initial payment and awarded Empire attorney's fees in the sum of $1,500. From this judgment Bellwood has appealed.

Mistake, either of law or fact, as grounds for rescission of contract, must affect the execution and material elements of the contract and not merely some collateral matter. Civ. Code, §§ 1577 and 1578; Hannah v. Steinman, [p. 195, supra,] 159 Cal. 142, 112 P. 1094; Vickerson v. Frey, [p. 207, supra,] 100 Cal. App. 2d 621, 224 P.2d 126.

The trial court found, inter alia, upon substantial evidence, that: "It was never intended by the parties that the contract was to cover the entire project. The contract so provides. Work by others was intended. Defendant was to receive final payment upon completion of defendant's portion of the work. The contract expressly excludes 'any item not specifically mentioned, electrical, plumbing, or interior partions.' Defendant had no right or power to deal with any matter other than the building shell and the engineering thereof and the foundation drawings. All other matters were left to plaintiff. Plaintiff never sought from the defendant and defendant never offered advice regarding any

---

[1] Empire filed a cross-complaint for damages for breach of contract. However, it is not involved in this appeal.

phase of the project except that expressly covered by the contract. Defendant had *no such duty*. If plaintiff failed to consider the need for automatic sprinklers, partition walls, plumbing, ventilating or other matters not expressly covered by the contract it was of no concern of defendant and was a *collateral matter*." (Emphasis added.)

From the foregoing it is apparent that no provision for either a sprinkling system or a fire resistant interior wall was included in the contract and that Empire owed Bellwood no duty with respect thereto. These items were collateral to the agreement of the parties. Therefore, the court correctly held that plaintiff had no right to rescind on the ground of mistake. Civ. Code, §§ 1577 and 1578; Hannah v. Steinman, supra; Vickerson v. Frey, supra.

Bellwood also contends that it had a right to rescind the contract on the grounds of fraud, illegality and impossibility of performance. . . . [The court ruled against all these contentions.]

The judgment is affirmed.

ASHBURN and HERNDON, JJ., concur.

[*Cf. Elsinore Union Elementary School District v. Kastorff,* 54 Cal. 2d 380, 353 P.2d 713 (1960).]

GOLEM V. FAHEY, 191 Cal. App. 2d 474, 13 Cal. Reptr. 63 (1961): After defendant secured a 99-year lease of land from plaintiff, it was discovered that the property was zoned for agricultural purposes. "The lease clearly contemplated a commercial use of the property." Plaintiff lessor sued to recover rent due, unpaid taxes (required to be paid by the lessee) and a penalty for failure to construct improvements as agreed. Dedendant defended on the grounds of fraud and mutual mistake. The trial court found neither fraud nor mistake, and found for plaintiff; the appellate court agreed that there was no fraud, but said that the lease did result from a mistake. Held, the lease should be terminated as of the date of judgment, but plaintiff is entitled to the back rent. "Although our case comes within the mutual mistake principle of *Hannah v. Steinman,* [p. 195, *supra,*] . . . it is of no comfort to [defendant lessee] otherwise, since he failed to rescind the lease" under § 1691, Civil Code.

LAWSON, A COMMON LAWYER LOOKS AT CODIFICATION
2 INTER-AM. L. REV. 1, 4 (1960)

It is indeed quite obvious that no continental European lawyer works merely with his code. Ultimately his task is to interpret the code, but he makes use of several very important aids to interpretation which in practice enjoy almost as much authority as the code itself. The oldest of such aids are the great commentaries and other works written by professors. But it is quite a mistake to think that they alone enjoy authority. No decision of a court is binding on any other court; it is even possible for an inferior court to overrule a decision of a higher court. But in fact, as decisions have come to be efficiently reported, they have come to enjoy very high persuasive authority. Those of the [French] Cour de Cassation are in practice almost as binding as those of any court in a common law country. Thus, to differentiate between code countries and case law countries is in practice quite false. All advanced code countries have a great deal of case law and attach much authority to it, whereas most common law countries have partial codes such as the Uniform Sales Act. Thus, in a country like France it is always necessary to examine the ways in which the codes have been interpreted by the courts. The exact status of what the French call *doctrine, i.e.,* non-judicial writings, is said to be very uncertain at the present time, but it is undoubtedly quite great, probably greater than the authority of a book like *Williston on Contracts* or *Scott on Trusts.* Thus, if an American jurisdiction were to adopt a civil code, there would probably be little or no change in the use made of decisions or textbooks.

CUETO RUA, FUENTES DEL DERECHO* 71-78 (1961)

The great impulse observed in the West toward the adoption of a single normative body of harmonious and integrated laws, in order to regulate a particular sphere of the social activities of men — without leaving residual elements for other law to govern — has its origins in the French Code. That origin is seen, not so much in the intrinsic merits of the Code, which were many, but rather in the philosophical conception and world view that inspired it.

The Code Napoléon is the most complete expression of the rational optimism of the Age of Enlightenment. Man is considered a rational being and reason is the most potent and effective instrument to bring life into conformity with the great principles of equality, fraternity, and liberty. Intelligence is in a position to create and establish a perfect system of laws that will permit men to resolve justly all conflicts that can arise in society's bosom, without exception.

* * *

With this work the great movement toward private codification was begun in the West. The example spreads and hopes are shared. There is belief in the possibility of a closed system, which is endowed with perfection because it is the deliberated product of human reason, and which is to be applied to intrinsically rational beings. The power of intelligence is beyond doubt. Everyone will understand the Codes. The work of judges and lawyers will be simplified. The development of economic transactions will be facilitated and social life will be organized around canons that are completely obvious by virtue of their intrinsic rationality. Today we no longer share that optimism. We are aware of its exaggerations and we have experienced the difficulties resulting from its rigid adherence to the principles of enlightened rationalism.

Codes present obvious advantages. ... They provide a comprehensive conceptual system that facilitates the task of thinking and meditating on the phenomena of human conduct in their juridical meaning. ... The great juridical constructions, which reflect their origin in codification and its best expounders — constructions such as those concerning legal entities, goods, juridical acts, patrimony and succession — supply a series of positive concepts that permit us to work with multiple juridical phenomena, facilitating communication and putting into relief the unity of conceptual foundation in the Law.

The risk of codification is in the fact that one often loses sight of the instrumental character of the conceptual constructions, and because of a generalized tendency among jurists of Roman background (but foreign to the spirit and technique of the Roman jurisconsults themselves), those concepts are made sacred and detached from the reality described by them. The jurists focus their interest on the concepts, forgetting the human conduct to which they refer.

The great constructs and simplifications of the Codes are useful, but they are far from sufficient in themselves for the management of concrete social problems. This insufficiency was forgotten by the rationalist jurists when they studied and explained the French Code as well as those codes inspired by it. The judges and administrative functionaries, nevertheless, obligated as they were by their positions to decide the concrete conflicts within their jurisdictions, operated with great prudence and skill. They used the keen conceptual instruments they found in the Codes, but never lost sight of the particular needs of individual situations. They saw the distance between the generality of the juridical construction and the distinctiveness of the case before their eyes. And in this passage from generality to individuality, the considerations that guided their reasoning were not clearly logical and formal ones; rather, they were guided by the necessity for resolving the conflict in a positive way, accentuating the cohesion of the social group and strengthening the values shared by a majority of its members, and all this within the wide conceptual framework of codified legislation.

The great difficulty of codification is found, precisely, in its invitation to new and larger generalizations. In this continual process, the different articles that make up the Code are remodeled in relation to the conceptual construction, in order to satisfy the demands of logic and systematization, instead of the very concrete human wants which demand not coherent logic but rather order, security, peace, and justice.

In our countries one can observe illustrious jurists who have been dedicated for years to the task of strengthening texts, changing the placement of articles, polishing terminology, all with the exclusive object of attaining a greater degree of logical coherence. The questions that arose continually on their lips referred to the harmony of the texts, to their logical compatibility, and to their adequate classification, not to their justice or injustice. Those jurists were the geometricians of the Law, the theoreticians of refined and coherent form. It was left to the practitioners, the politicians or the judges to deal with the "secondary" task of resolving the conflicts of men in the best manner they could, always respecting the fundamental exigency of conceptual unity at the highest possible level of abstraction.

* * *

No doubt there is weight in this type of argument [i.e., for the creation of law by isolated legislation, custom, or case law, as opposed to codification]. The excess of generalization [in codification] has carried with it a divorce between the Science of Law and the reality of juridical experience, especially judicial and administrative experience. This divorce has resulted in nothing but injury to all, and in the discrediting of the speculative effort of the jurists. It is difficult to comprehend the value of an effort whose only destination is the specialists who are confined in libraries and removed from the command posts of social life.

On the other hand, it is also inconvenient for there to be an excess of casuistic legislation or to use custom as the principal instrument of social direction.

Custom is slow. It requires a prolonged process of adaptation and acceptance through the free play of a series of forces such as imitation, the prestige of the directive elites, and social inertia. That slowness can be the source of difficulties in an environment subject to profound changes by the play of external factors that are hard to control. Some impacts, such as a military defeat or the influence of a dynamic civilization, commonly have very profound dislocating effects, and the readjustment in these cases cannot be left to custom. To do so would demand a great deal of time and would require a high tribute in sacrifices, poverty, and frustrated attempts.

* * *

The jurist of rational formation prefers the Codes. The careful preparation of preliminary plans and of the projects themselves, their scrutiny from the logical and formal viewpoint, the availability of doctrinary material to assure their coherence and uniformity, provide the rationalist jurist a powerful sensation of security, not only because they satisfy his hunger for rationality to find consistencies, but also because he believes in the effectiveness of the Code, with its generality and conceptual rigor, to reduce judical discretion in the management of human problems. It is believed that the resolution of conflicts would be attained through the play of logical principles, the evidence of which is shown to all men. There would be no room for corruption nor for error.

Certainty and inevitability of the results would be the consequences of the logical perfection of the Code.

The empirical, pragmatic jurist prefers isolated legislation or the direct play of custom. Not logical consistency, but rather the usefulness of the solutions, is what interests him. The justification for a specific statute will not be found in its coherence with other laws or its perfect placement in the body of a Code, but in the concrete form in which it overcomes an obstacle arising in social experience. Here, then, are the two contrasted theses.

Three warnings are necessary to place the dispute in its proper perspective.

The first consists in pointing out that there is no universally valid answer to the problem. The two theses coexist and have greater or less validity according to the social group concerned. If one were discussing the juridical organization of a primitive tribe, there would be no doubt about the practical impossibility of codification, while custom would guide them securely, as it has done in the past, with its slow and effective adaptation to the tenuous and sometimes imperceptible changes in tribal life. On the other hand, if one were speaking of a nation such as Germany at the end of the 19th Century, with its extraordinary body of juridical doctrine developed by the pandectists, and with the efficient administrative and judicial organization of the Empire and the discipline of its people, a Code, concordant with that juridical doctrine through its structure and content, would be advisable.

The second warning refers to the level of abstraction and of casuistry characteristic of the Code and of ... isolated legislation, respectively. Of course, the dangers are to be found in exaggerations. A high level of abstraction may be useful to abridge a system and explain it in an abbreviated manner, but it can affect its efficacy as an instrument in the solution of social difficulties. Judges may feel perplexed, functionaries may show incompetence in their duties, and citizens may find themselves completely disconcerted in their eagerness to understand the meaning of codified norms. On the other hand, an excess of casuistry may be a cause of disorder and contradiction.

And the third warning is tied to the subject under discussion. There are sections of social life in which codification seems promising. These human relations have reached a high degree of settlement and consistency through long years of practice. Subjects such as civil obligations show little change through different times and countries. There are others, however, that show continuous change, such as those relating to matrimonial rules, labor relations, or the law of nuclear energy.

Therefore, a single answer is not possible in respect to the advantages or disadvantages of codification. It all depends upon the social group for which the legislation is being prepared, the degree of abstraction or casuistry that is present, and the content of the legislation.

QUESTIONS ON THE ROLE OF THE JUDGE IN LAWMAKING

The French Revolution not only produced the Code Napoléon, but also disclosed a popular distrust of judges, justifiably thought to have been instruments of the aristocracy. The position of the judiciary was deliberately lowered. The law was written in language thought to be clear and simple enough for everyone to understand; there would be no need for judicial interpretation. Judges were to be functionaries charged with applying policies made by others, and their main analytical problem was to be deduction. In contrast, the common law system from the first has required its judges to make policy; good legal analysis has always been forced into legislative considerations.

The writings of scholars such as Dr. Cueto Rúa make clear that there are powerful influences at work, bringing civilian scholarship closer to the kind of functional analysis that has been — with the exception of the late 19th and early 20th centuries — the staple of common law jurisprudence. The civil law system has steadily moved away from the tradition of the sterile judge and abstract scholasticism.

1. What evidences of this shift are there in the Argentine cases in this chapter?

2. Are there some characteristics of the problems of mistake (error) and fraud that tend to minimize the differences between common law and civil law techniques for determining the applicable law? See Sabbath, *Effects of Mistake in Contracts: A Study in Comparative Law,* 13 INT'L AND COMP. L.Q. 798, 828-29 (1964).

3. In a codified system, will case law be most important or least important in those areas where the code is least specific? Is it possible to create authoritative precedent in an area such as mistake? (Remember the words of Leon Green: "... we may have a process for passing judgment in negligence cases, but practically no 'law of negligence' beyond the process itself." JUDGE AND JURY 185 (1930).)

Chapter II

CIVIL RESPONSIBILITY FOR WRONGFUL CONDUCT: FRAUD AS A CRIMINAL OFFENSE

In the civil law as in our own, some kinds of disfavored conduct generate both criminal and civil sanctions. In Chapter I, we were concerned in part with civil remedies for conduct characterized as "fraud," which conduct is also an offense against the state. In this chapter we explore some of the relations, both substantive and procedural, between civil and criminal law, or, in the Argentine context, between the Civil Code and the Penal Code.

There are prominent differences between the criminal procedure found in most civil law countries and that of the Anglo-American countries. One difference commonly emphasized in the comparative literature relates to the "inquisitorial" nature of the civilian proceeding. While the typical civilian criminal proceeding includes a trial, the importance of the trial as a vehicle for producing evidence is vastly diminished in comparison to the common law criminal trial. Before the trial there is an investigation that superficially resembles our preliminary hearing, before a judge who serves as magistrate. In form, the judge also serves as director of the police investigation. While the normal practice is to leave the investigative work to the detectives, the judge nonetheless think of himself as an agent of the state, responsible for marshalling all the evidence relating to a case, and not as a neutral appraiser of evidence presented by the opposing sides. This investigation involves the interrogation of the accused and the witnesses (the accused is not treated as a "witness"), and has two purposes: (a) an initial screening of cases, so that no case goes to trial without a low-level judicial decision that there is sufficient evidence to convict the accused; and (b) the production of a file (in France, the *dossier*) that contains all available evidence concerning the alleged crime and the personal history of the accused.

Throughout the trial, this file is normally in the hands of the judge, so that his examination of the accused and the witnesses is based on full knowledge of their previous statements, and all the material in the file, including any statements by persons who were not witnesses.

From [the judge's interrogation, based on the file], uninformed observers have occasionally inferred that there is no presumption of innocence in civil law countries. The inference is, of course, nonsensical. SCHLESINGER, COMPARATIVE LAW: CASES, TEXT, MATERIALS 239 n.9 (2d ed. 1959).

It is less nonsensical to suggest that the file may affect the practical operation of the rule that the judge's decision must be based entirely on the evidence considered at the trial.

In any case, the presumption of innocence is just that, and no more. There is no special burden of proof on the prosecution, beyond that which falls to the proponent of a proposition of fact in a civil proceeding. In France, the trier of fact must have an "inner conviction" that the accused is guilty, which amounts in practice to the same as a preponderance-of-evidence test. In most countries, there is no jury. France is a partial exception, in cases of serious crimes.

The focus of this chapter is on another dramatic difference in the civilian criminal proceeding — the availability of a civil remedy for the victim, awarded by the criminal court at the same time the criminal sentence is imposed. We begin with short extracts from the two Argentine codes, which should be read initially for the purpose of drawing contrasts with the North American practice. The cases that follow raises issues concerning the substantive law of fraud. To what extent, and in what particulars, is the crime of fraud in Argentina congruent with the civil fraud which we considered in Chapter I? This chapter concludes by inquiring into the binding effects of various kinds of criminal court decisions in later civil proceedings. The resolution of these issues goes beyond the law of fraud, and so the cases are drawn from the whole range of wrongs that have both civil and penal consequences.

In the last two decades, considerable scholarly attention has been directed to comparative criminal procedure. Many of the sources are collected in SCHLESINGER, *supra,* at 237-39. Vouin, *The Protection of the Accused in French Criminal Procedure,* 5 INT. & COMP. L.Q. 1, 157 (1956), carefully outlines the French law and practice. See also Larguier, *The Civil Action for Damages in French Criminal Procedure,* 39 TUL. L. REV. 687 (1965).

ARGENTINE PENAL CODE of 1922, as amended
(González López translation,* 1963)

TITLE II
PUNISHMENTS

5. The punishments established by this Code are as follows: imprisonment,

---

   jailing,
   fine, and
   disqualification.

  6. Imprisonment for life or a period of time shall be served by compulsory labor in a penal institution intended for that purpose. The convicts may be employed in public works of any kind, excepting those contracted for by private corporations or persons.

   * * *

  11. The product of the convict's work in jail or prison shall be applied equally:

   1. to pay for the actual harm, and the pain and suffering caused by the crime, if not otherwise paid.

   2. to provide for alimony in accordance with the Civil Code.

   3. to pay for the convict's expenses in the penal institution.

   4. to form a special fund which shall be delivered to the convict on discharge from the penal institution.

  12. Imprisonment and jailing for more than three years entails total disqualification from holding public office and from exercising the right of suffrage for the term of the sentence, and this disqualification may last three further years, depending on the nature of the crime, as the court may provide. During service of the sentence, it also entails the convict's loss of his paternal rights, his right of administering his estate, and his right of disposing of his own property by inter vivos transactions. The convict shall be under the curator-guardianship provided by the Civil Code for incompetent persons.

   * * *

  19. Complete disqualification entails:

   1. Loss of any public position or office held by the convict, including those which are elective,

   2. Loss of his rights of suffrage,

   3. Incapacity to obtain public positions, offices or commissions,

   4. Loss of any pension or social security benefits to which he is otherwise entitled. If the convict has a spouse, children or old and indigent parents, the pension or the social security benefits shall go to them, and if not, the amount shall be applied to increase the fund provided for in Article 11.

  20. Limited disqualification shall entail the loss of the position, office, profession or any right specifically mentioned, and the incapacity to obtain another of the same kind for the duration of the sentence. Limited disqualification of political rights shall entail the incapacity to exercise rights mention in the sentence for the duration thereof.

  21. A sentence of a fine obligates the convict to pay the sum fixed by the sentence, in accordance with the general provisions mentioned in Article 40, and the financial status of the convict.

   If the convict does not pay the fine as prescribed by the sentence, he shall serve a term of imprisonment which shall not exceed one year and a half.

Before converting the fine to jailing, or imprisonment, the court shall try to levy execution for the fine on the estate, salaries or other assets of the convict. The convict may be allowed to pay the fine by free work whenever he has occasion to do so.

The convict also may be allowed to pay the fine in instalments. The court shall fix the sum and the date of each payment in accordance with the financial status of the convict.

22. The convict shall be discharged upon payment of the fine. The proportional part of the time he has spent in detention shall be deducted from the fine, in accordance with the rules governing compensation during detention.

23. Conviction of crime entails the forfeiture of the instruments with which it was committed and the objects which the crime produced, all of which shall be seized unless they belong to a third party not connected in any way with the crime. The seized instruments may not be sold and must be destroyed. The provincial governments or the arsenals of the nation are entitled to them.

24. Detention pending trial shall be computed as follows: for two days of detention pending trial, one day of imprisonment; for one day of detention, one day of jailing or two days of disqualification, or the amount of the fine which the court determines, between four and ten pesos.

* * *

TITLE III
SUSPENDED SENTENCE

* * *

28. Suspension of the sentence shall leave unaffected the duty of reparation for the harm caused by the crime and the payment of the procedural costs.

TITLE IV
REPARATION OF DAMAGES

29. The sentence may provide for:

1. Compensation for actual harm and pain and suffering caused to the victim and his family or to a third party. In the absence of evidence, the court may determine the amount within its discretion.

2. The restitution of the object obtained by the crime, and if restitution is impossible, the payment by the convict of the regular price of the object, as well as its sentimental value if it has such.

3. The reimbursement of the State for the procedural costs.

4. When the civil reparation has not been satisfied while the convict is serving the sentence, or if a judgment of reparation has been rendered in favor of the victim or his family, the Court, before paroling the convict, in case of his insolvency, shall determine the portion of his salary which shall be applied to the payment of such debt.

30. Reparation debts have priority over all other liabilities incurred by the convict after having committed the crime, and also priority over the fine.

If his assets are insufficient to cover all his liabilities, they shall be satisfied in the following order:

1. Reparation for harm and payment for damages;

2. Reimbursement of the procedural costs.

31. Reparation of damages is a joint and several liability of all parties to the crime.

32. Anybody who knowingly has profited from the crime shall be compelled to make reparation to the extent of his profit.

33. In the case of total or partial insolvency the following rules shall be applicable:

1. As to convicts sentenced to jailing or imprisonment, the reparation shall be as provided in Article 11.

2. As to convicts sentenced to other punishments, the Courts shall determine the portion of their income or salaries which they must deposit periodically until complete payment.

* * *

TITLE X
EXTINCTION OF ACTIONS AND JUDGMENTS

* * *

61. Amnesty extinguishes the prosecution and the sentence, as well as all its effects, excepting the compensation due to another party.

* * *

64. The right of prosecution of a crime subject to fine shall be extinguished at any stage of the proceedings by the voluntary payment of the maximum of the fine, imposable for that crime, and of the damage caused thereby.

65. The statute of limitations for crimes involving the punishments listed below shall be as follows:

1. imprisonment for life, after twenty years;

2. jailing for life, after twenty years;

3. temporary imprisonment or jailing, within a term equal to that of the sentence;

4. fine exceeding two thousand pesos, after three years;

5. fines of two thousand pesos or less, after one year.

* * *

70. Pecuniary liabilities incident to punishment can be enforced against the convict's estate after his death.

TITLE XI
EXERCISE OF PROSECUTION FUNCTIONS

71. All penal actions must be prosecuted *ex officio,* excepting:

1. those which require the complaint of the victim;

2. those which are only prosecuted by private action.

[Actions based on the various crimes of fraud do not require the complaint of the victim, nor are they prosecuted only by private action. — Ed.]

* * *

CHAPTER IV
FRAUDS AND OTHER DECEITS

172. Anybody who defrauds another by use of false name, position or title, or by the pretense of false influence, or by abuse of a confidence, or by pretending imaginary wealth, credit, commission, enterprise or negotiation or by any other kind of trick or deceit, shall be punished by jailing from one month to six years.

173. Notwithstanding the general provisions of the previous Article, the following special cases of fraud shall be punished under the previous Article:

1. Anybody who defrauds another as to the substance, quality or quantity of anything which he delivers to him by reason of contract or other lawful obligations.

2. Anybody who to the detriment of another, refuses to return or does not return when due, money, goods or any kind of movable thing which has been given to him in deposit, commission, management or any other means, which by legal obligation he must deliver or return.

3. Anybody who defrauds another by making him subscribe by deceit to any kind of document.

4. Anybody who defrauds another by use of the blank signature of another and thereby issues any document bearing such signature to the detriment of the person whose signature was so used or any third party.

5. Any owner of a movable thing who steals it from the lawful possessor to the prejudice of the latter or another.

6. Anybody who enters into a simulated contract or gives a false receipt to the detriment of another.

7. Any salesman, on commission, captain of a ship, or any

other representative who defrauds by altering his accounts, prices or conditions of the contract, or by simulating or exaggerating expenses he has made.

8. Anybody who defrauds by substituting, concealing or destroying any court, public or administrative file or record or any other document or important paper.

9. Anybody who sells or mortgages as free any property, the title of which is in dispute or which has been seized by a court order, or has an encumbrance thereon, or anybody who sells, mortgages or rents as his property that which belongs to another.

10. Anybody who defrauds another on the pretext of simulated remuneration to a judge or any other public official.

* * *

CIVIL CODE OF ARGENTINA (Joannini translation 1917*)

TITLE VIII. OF UNLAWFUL ACTS.

1066. No voluntary act shall have the character of an unlawful act if not expressly prohibited by the ordinary laws, municipal laws, or police regulations; and to no unlawful act can there be applied any penalty or sanction of this Code in the absence of a provision of law which has imposed it.

1067. For the purposes of this Code, there is no punishable unlawful act when no damage has been caused, or any other external act which could cause it, unless the parties thereto can be charged with dolus,** fault or negligence.

1068. There is damage whenever another person is caused an injury susceptible of pecuniary appraisal, either directly to the things belonging to him or in his possession, or indirectly on account of the damage done to his person, or to his rights or powers.

1069. The damage comprises not only the loss actually sustained, but also the profits of which the person damaged may have been deprived by the unlawful act, and which in this Code are designated by the word "damages."

1070. An unlawful act performed by insane persons in lucid intervals is not considered involuntary,*** even though they have been declared such in judicial proceedings; nor acts performed while in a state of intoxication, unless it be proved that such intoxication was involuntary.

1071. The exercise of a vested right, or the performance of a legal obligation, cannot operate to make any act unlawful.

---

* Copyright (c), Section of International and Comparative Law, American Bar Association, reprinted by permission.

** Here used to mean "fraud." See p. 35, *supra*. — Ed.

*** A typographical error in the printed version of the Joannini translation renders this word as "voluntary." — Ed.

1072. An unlawful act performed knowingly and with the intent to damage the person or rights of another, is called in this Code an offense (*delito*).

CHAPTER I.
Of Offenses (*Delitos*).

1073. An offense may be a negative act or act of omission, or a positive act.

1074. Any person who causes damage to another by any omission, is liable only when a provision of the law imposes upon him the obligation of performing the act omitted.

1075. Any right may be the subject of an offense whether it be a right in an extrinsic object, or whether it be confounded with the existence of the person.

1076. In order for an act to be considered an offense it is necessary that it be the result of a free determination on the part of the author thereof. An insane person and a person under ten years of age are not liable for the damage they cause.

1077. Every offense carries with it the obligation of repairing the damage resulting therefrom to another person.

1078. If the act should constitute an offense under the criminal law, the obligation arising therefrom comprises not only indemnity for damages, but also for the moral injury which the offense may have caused the person to suffer, either by molesting him in his personal security, or in the enjoyment of his property, or wounding his legitimate affections.

1079. The obligation to repair the damage caused by an offense lies, not only with regard to the person directly damaged by the offense, but also with regard to any person who has suffered therefrom, even though in an indirect manner.

1080. The husband and the parents may demand damages for the injuries committed against the wife and the children.

1081. The obligation to repair the damage caused by an offense rests solidarily upon all those who have participated therein as authors, abettors or accomplices, even though an act not punishable under the criminal law be involved.

1082. If one of them gives indemnity for all the damage, he shall not have the right to sue the others for their shares.

1083. Reparation for damages, whether material or moral, caused by an offense, must take the form of a pecuniary indemnity to be fixed by the judge, unless the restitution of the object which has been the subject matter of the offense should be made.

* * *

CHAPTER III.
Of Offenses against Property.

1091. When the offense consists of theft, the thing stolen shall be returned to the owner with all its accessories, and with indemnity for all the deterioration it has suffered, even though caused by a fortuitous event or *force majeure*.

1092. When the restitution of the thing stolen is not possible, the provisions of this chapter relating to indemnity for damages on account of the total destruction of a thing belonging to another shall apply.

1093. When the offense consists of the conversion of money, the delinquent shall pay interest at the current rate from the date of the offense.

* * *

CHAPTER IV.
Of the Exercise of Actions to Recover Damages *Ex Delicto*.

1096. Indemnity for damages *ex delicto* may be recovered only by a civil action independent of the criminal action.

1097. A civil action shall not be considered to have been renounced on account of the aggrieved persons not having brought a criminal action or having desisted therefrom during their lifetime; nor shall it be understood that they renounced the criminal action on account of having brought a civil action or having desisted therefrom. But if they renounced the civil action or made an agreement as to the payment of the damage, the criminal action shall be considered to have been renounced.

1098. An action to recover damages *ex delicto*, may be directed against the universal successors of the principals and accomplices, the provisions of the laws relating to the acceptance of inheritances with the benefit of inventory being nevertheless observed.

1099. When offenses are involved which have caused a moral damage only, such as *injuria* or defamation, the civil action does not pass to the heirs and universal successors, unless it was instituted by the deceased.

1100. An action for damages *ex delicto*, even though the offense be one punishable under the criminal law, is extinguished by the renunciation of the persons interested; but the renunciation by the person directly injured does not bar the exercise of the right of action which may vest in the spouse or his or her parents.

1101. When the criminal action has preceded the civil action or is brought while the latter is pending, no judgment [*condenación*] shall be rendered in the civil action before the conviction [*condenación*] of the defendant in the criminal action, except in the following cases:

    1. When the defendant has died before the rendition of judg-

ment in the criminal action, in which case the civil action may be brought or continued against the respective heirs.

2. In the event of the absence of the defendant, when the criminal action cannot be brought or continued.

1102. After the conviction of the defendant in the criminal action, the existence of the principal act constituting the offense cannot be contested in the civil action, nor can the fault of the party convicted be impugned.

1103. Nor shall it be permissible after the acquittal of the defendant, to plead in a civil action the existence of the principal act as to which said defendant may have been acquitted.

1104. If the criminal action is subject to pre-judicial[26] questions, which can be decided in a civil action exclusively, no judgment shall be rendered in the criminal action before the judgment in the civil action has acquired the force of *res judicata*. Pre-judicial questions are the following only:

1. Those involving the validity or nullity of marriages.

2. Those involving the classification of the bankruptcy of merchants.

1105. With the exception of the two preceding cases, or of others expressly excepted, the judgment upon the act rendered in the civil action shall have no bearing in the criminal action, nor shall it bar a subsequent criminal action based upon the same act, or on another act bearing a relation thereto.

1106. Whatever be the subsequent judgment in the criminal action, a previous judgment rendered in the civil action which has become *res judicata,* shall continue to produce all its effects.

TITLE IX.   OF OBLIGATIONS ARISING OUT OF UNLAWFUL ACTS WHICH DO NOT CONSTITUTE OFFENSES.

1107. Acts or omissions in the performance of conventional obligations are not comprised in the articles of this Title, if they do not degenerate into the offenses of the penal law.

1108. Articles 1070, 1071, 1073, 1074, 1075 and 1076 are applicable to unlawful acts, performed without the intention of causing damage.

1109. Any person performing an act, which through his fault or negligence causes damage to another, is obliged to repair the damage. This obligation is governed by the same provisions to which the offenses of the civil law are subject.

1110. This reparation may be demanded not only by the person who is the owner or possessor of the thing which has sustained the damage, or his

---

[26] *Pre-judicial:* Rom. Law. Of or pertaining to a judicial examination previous to a trial: applied to interrogatory actions for the determination of questions of fact or right, more particularly as regards status, generally with a view to further proceedings. (Standard Dictionary.) That which must be decided before judgment can be rendered on the main issue (Escriche).

heirs, but also by the usufructuary, or the usuary, if the damage causes injury to his interests.

It may also be demanded by the person who holds the thing with the obligation of answering therefor, but only in the absence of the owner.

1111. An act which would cause no damage to the person who sustains it, were it not owing to a fault chargeable to him, does not impose any liability whatsoever.

MERLO v. PARODI DEMARCHI
Criminal and Correctional Chamber of the Capital
11 J.A. 662 (1923)

[This is a *criminal* complaint by Merlo against Parodi Demarchi — notice the title of the action — arising out of the firing of a pistol by the accused, which resulted in a slight wound to Merlo. The judge of 1st Instance convicted the accused, and sentenced him to pay a fine of 200 pesos plus indemnity to Merlo in the amount of 635.85 pesos and costs.]

2d Instance.—Buenos Aires, September 7, 1923.—[The full court was called together to consider whether it was proper to award civil damages to the victim in a criminal proceeding.]

Dr. González Roura said: [Until the adoption of the Penal Code of 1922, it had been held, on the basis of art. 1096 of the Civil Code, that a criminal court had no jurisdiction to award damages to the victim in a criminal proceeding. The question is whether the new Penal Code made a change in this respect.]

In truth, admitting that the disposition of art. 1096 of the Civil Code could continue to be invoked in support of that theory (despite the obvious fact that the question of jurisdiction is foreign to the substantive law enacted by the Congress in that respect, because it is a subject reserved to the local legislatures by art. 67, par. 11 of the Constitution), the rule of that article [1096] is annulled by art. 29 of the Penal Code. The latter authorizes the exercise of a civil action for indemnification in the criminal court.

* * *

Dr. Frugoni Zavala said: Before voting in this case, I feel obliged to inquire into the scope intended by the legislator for art. 29, par. 1 of the Penal Code. This article states that in a criminal sentence the judge may fix the indemnification for moral or material damage caused to the victim, his family, or to a third person, and that he may establish the money amount at his discretion, in the absence of full proof regarding that amount.

That provision was included in the Executive branch's project [draft] of the Penal Code, and the [congressional] committee named to report on it said:

"It is indispensable 1) that the reparation of damage be imposed together with the punishment, and 2) that said reparation be extended to all offenses liable to produce damage."

"If the offense is a violation of the juridical order, and must cease and be replaced in the best way possible, it is evident that the social power should proceed to the re-establishment of the disturbed order, obliging the delinquent to compensate, etc. . . ."

"The reparation of damages caused to the victim of the offense must be, thus, as important an objective as the very application of the penalty."

* * *

Dr. J. H. Frías said: [Dr. Frías dissented. In a long opinion, he reviewed the history of the issue, both in earlier Argentine legislation (and projected legislation) and in foreign codes. His principal objection seems to have been that the Congress, in adopting art. 29 of the Penal Code, had done something that was conceptually messy. The following comment summarizes his position.]

From what has been expressed, it is clear that there has been a confusion of ideas which has been answered by the cited provision of the Penal Code concerning indemnification of damages caused by an offense. There has also been neglect, in the legislative process, of certain principles of a constitutional, civil, and procedural order embodied in our legislation. With it originates a juridical disturbance, which jurisprudence has to settle, seeking whatever harmony may suit the present state of the legislation.

[Dr. Frías went on to argue that the procedural law in force did not permit the exercise of civil jurisdiction by the criminal court, but that argument was also rejected by the other judges. By a vote of five to two, the decision of the court of 1st Instance was affirmed.]

QUESTIONS ON FRAUD IN THE CIVIL AND PENAL CODES

1.   In each of the following five criminal cases, consider whether the victim had any civil remedy (rescission, damages).

2.   Do the elements of the crime of fraud, as here elaborated, differ from the elements of fraud as it is defined by Civil Code arts. 931-35?

3.   Argentina's Constitution of 1949, which was scrapped when Perón fell from power, included the following provision, said at the time to be a codification of existing doctrine:

> The judges shall have no power to extend legal incriminations by analogy, or to interpret the law broadly against the accused. In case of doubt, the most favorable [interpretation] to the accused shall prevail.

If this be the law of the Constitution, are arts. 172-73 of the Penal Code constitutional?

Compare California Penal Code § 4: "The rule of the common law, that penal statutes are to be strictly construed, has no application to this Code. All its provisions are to be considered according to the fair import of their terms, with a view to effect its objects and to promote justice."

JOSE JORGE DOULING
Criminal and Correctional Chamber of the Capital
53 J.A. 799 (1936)

1st Instance.—Buenos Aires, October 1, 1935.—Resulting: a) Hrand Nikotian claims that on October 2, 1933, he signed a contract of sale ... in which the accused sold him the plot of land located at 1422-36 Vértiz Avenue free of all obligations, for which the seller collected the sum of 7,000 pesos on account of the price. As the accused did not deliver the appropriate title documents for execution, the complainant investigated, and ascertained that the seller was prohibited to sell, and that the property was attached, mortgaged, and in litigation; thus the seller committed the imputed offense [a violation of art. 173 (9)].

b) The accused acknowledges the act, asserting in this defense that he signed the contract by authority of his mortgage creditor.

c) [The prosecutor asks a sentence of one year and six months of imprisonment plus costs; defense counsel asks the acquittal of the accused.]

* * *

Considering: 1) That the unlawful act and the penal responsibility of the accused are completely demonstrated in the present case ... given that the accused hid the conditions of the property from the buyer, Nikotian, ... given the testimony of the mortgage creditors, ... and given also that, even if the accused had had the authorization of the mortgage creditor, ... he still concealed from the complainant buyer the fact that the property was attached and in litigation ....

2d. The crime falls within the provisions of art. 173, par. 9th, of the Penal Code, keeping in mind for the purposes of the penalty to be imposed, the amount defrauded, [the testimony of certain named witnesses,] and the police reports.

On these grounds, in accordance with the provisions of [the Code of Criminal Procedure], and after becoming acquainted with the moral personality of the accused, I decide condemning José Jorge Douling, as author of the crime of fraud, to the penalty of one year and six months imprisonment, and costs. The penalty shall be carried out in conditional [suspended] form by virtue of the provision of art. 26 of the Penal Code.—*Alberto Speroni.*—Before me: *Roberto Fernández Speroni.*

Opinion of the *Fiscal* of the Chamber.—On the grounds [stated in] the appealed decision, its affirmance is proper.—*Enrique J. Racedo.*

2d Instance.—Buenos Aires, March 13, 1936.—Considering: ....

As this is not a question of a sale but rather of a promise of such, ... the act cannot be placed within the terms of art. 173, par. 9, of the Penal Code.

It is proper to examine the acts of the accused, in order to establish whether his conduct is included in any of the provisions of art. 172. In this regard it should be noted that the quality of owner of the property, used by him to formalize the sale and to receive the earnest money of 7,000 pesos, is correct. He confined himself to ignoring the existence of the prohibition to sell, and of the attachment and mortgage on the property. There has been no simulation nor concealment through the use of maneuvers or acts tending to deceive the party interested in the transaction. Each and every one of the cases included in the text of art. 172, defining the concept of fraud, requires the exercise of an activity to defraud, that is, active artifice or deceit by the actor: a false name, a simulated quality, false titles, false influence, the abuse of confidence, appearance of wealth, ... or taking advantage of any other artifice or deceit. To be quiet when there is no legal obligation to announce certain circumstances that could hinder the success of the transaction (and in such conditions as those of this case, when the request for an easily obtainable report would have sufficed to find out the real situation of the property), though it may be incorrect or immoral, is not enough to be characterized as fraud, as the latter has been established by this tribunal in [two previous cases, dated 1933 and 1934].

Therefore the appealed decision is revoked, and José Jorge Douling acquitted of fault and charge.—*Francisco Ramos Mejía.—Lucas Luna Olmos.— Emilio C. Díaz.—Atilio Pessagno.—Roracio Vera Ocampo.*

GUILLERMO HERIBERTO DE LA PRECILLA
Criminal and Correctional Chamber of the Capital
1942-III J.A. 1023 (1942)

1st Instance.—Buenos Aires, April 20, 1942.—[The accused had obtained money from two agents of the National Lottery in the following manner: He had gone to the shops where lottery tickets were sold with tickets bearing numbers that had been drawn for prizes in the current lottery. These tickets were genuine lottery tickets, but they corresponded to other lotteries, not the current one. In each of two instances proved in the court of 1st Instance, the agent paid the prize money to the accused before discovering that the ticket did not correspond to the current lottery. The prosecutor asked a punishment of two years' imprisonment, suspended; the defense counsel argued that the accused should be acquitted, since he had made a mistake and believed that the lottery tickets referred to the current lottery. The court of

1st Instance found the accused guilty and sentenced him to one year and six months of prison.]

Opinion of the *Fiscal* of the Chamber.— ....

* * *

It is true that if the acts attributed to the accused were true, he would have told a lie upon presenting the tickets of another lottery for payment in the current one, in which the numbers of the tickets were prize winners. However, it is no less true that this single lie cannot, of itself, constitute the crime of fraud.

The lie, the artifice or the deceit referred to in art. 172 of the Penal Code must in turn be supported by other acts, intentionally misleading, all of which together may be capable of leading the victim into error. And such has not occurred in the present case. When the accused attributed an incorrect date to the tickets, he did not avail himself of any artifice to support his false claim, since the tickets he turned in had not been altered. If the agents who claim to have been injured were misled, that is attributable to their own negligence, for had they looked at the tickets and compared them with the proper date, nothing unfortunate would have happened to them.

Therefore, the acts charged by the victims do not constitute crimes, and it is proper for Your Honors to revoke the sentence of the court of 1st Instance, and consequently to acquit the accused Guillermo Heriberto de la Precilla of guilt and charge.—*Carlos M. Martínez.*

2d Instance.—Buenos Aires, July 24, 1942.— ....

* * *

A simple lie, that is, the mere affirmation of a fact that is not true, is not "per se" an element of fraud, but it will be so when it concurs with an artifice capable of deceiving.

In the present case the accused did not merely state that the tickets were prize winners, for the exhibition and turning in of the tickets was equivalent to such a statement .... With this procedure repeated in all the instances, the defendant affimed his apparent good faith. If the lottery agent did not observe the deceit, or understood it poorly, that circumstance does not exclude from consideration the effectiveness of the means used to cheat him, precisely because in the majority of cases his lack of understanding is caused by the faith that the criminal appears to display, exactly that "good faith" that the law wishes to protect.

In this regard Manzini ... adds that if one had to apply the Latin proverb "vigilantibus non dormientibus iura succurrunt" [the laws aid the vigilant, not those who sleep on their rights], there would never be a fraud that could be punished.

The means used by the accused to cheat were capable of achieving that end; this is established by the number of persons cheated. There would have been an even greater number [had not one of the victims warned his brother, who therefore was able to identify and detain the accused].

The penalty imposed is very appropriate and does not give the appellant cause to complain.

Therefore, the appealed decision sentencing the accused to one year and six months of imprisonment is affirmed, and the costs of both instances are charged to him.—*Raúl B. Nicholson.*—*Francisco I. Oribe.*—*Rodolfo Medina.*

DOMINGA REINOSO DE POSADA
Supreme Court of Tucumán
66 J.A. 1041, 15 La Ley 472 (1939)

Tucumán, May 23, 1939. Is the appealed decision in accordance with the law?

Dr. *Schreier* said:

Dominga Reinoso de Posada is accused of promising to transfer to the complainants a lot of land measuring 21 meters in frontage by 38 meters in depth, for which she received the price of 900 pesos. When the buyers went to the Registry of Ownership, however, they discovered that this transaction was not possible because Sra. de Posada could dispose of only 11 meters, having previously sold the rest of the lot to one Abraham Feldman.

The judge acquits the accused and there are no reasons for any other conclusion.

We have here a civil contract of sale for an immovable property, in the completion of which contract there was no trickery, artifice, or machination used capable of inducing the buyers to complete it. At least, there is no proof of such deceit, and the accusers themselves do not point it out.

The fact that the seller, an old lady of 109 years, may have offered for sale the property referred to by the complainants — themselves young people with mental qualities capable of avoiding any trickery — is not sufficient reason for the latter's having felt it necessary to pay for the property without taking the most elementary precautions to make sure that the accused had the right to sell it. She did not even show them title documents verifying her ownership of an area equal to or greater than that which she wanted to sell them, in order to make them believe in her trickery. Even that piece of deception would have been superficial and not determinative, however, since the buyers were obliged to take whatever measures the circumstances required to assure themselves of her right of ownership. If they did not do so, their monetary loss was caused by their own exclusive negligence, and any judge is obliged to declare the inexistence of a crime. Such is the decision of the tribunal in [a 1933 case, when this court said that] the somewhat suspicious conduct of the accused in the execution of a civil contract was not sufficient to justify a declaration of the existence of fraud, and the same is true of the conduct of the accused in the case at bar.

The simple failure of the accused to fulfill her obligation to transfer by legal means (art. 1184, Civil Code) the whole area of the property in question, will not be resolved by criminal procedure when, as in the case at bar, the suppositions of art. 172, P.C., are not present. Rather, it is to be resolved by the civil method in conformity with the provisions of arts. 1185, 1187, and 629, C.C.

Therefore, on the grounds of the appealed decision and in conformity with the recommendation of the *fiscal,* I vote to affirm.

Drs. *García Zavalía* and *de la Vega* agreed with Dr. Schreier and voted in the same way.

Because of the foregoing accord, the appealed decision acquitting the accused Dominga Reinoso de Posada of the crime of fraud is affirmed, with costs.—*Rafael García Zavalía.*—*Víctor Alberto de la Vega.*—*Román Schreier.*

JOSE HECTOR MOLINATTI
Criminal Judge of Bahía Blanca
1958-III J.A. 150 (1957)

1st Instance.—Bahía Blanca, October 28, 1957. [Molinatti entered a bakery owned by one Robles in the city of Tres Arroyos. Molinatti bought bread for 1.35 pesos, giving Robles a paper on one side of which was an imitation of a 1,000-peso bill. Robles gave Molinatti 998.65 pesos in change. The prosecutor asks a penalty of six months in prison, and defense counsel argues that the artifice employed was not sufficient to deceive the ordinary person.]

2d. We agree with the defense — and thus with the jurisprudence in general and the most authoritative doctrine — that fraud as a crime requires the use of sufficient artifice, that is, of reasonably deceitful means, to defraud a victim of average prudence. We also believe that the effectiveness of the stratagem may depend on the condition of the victim, to the degree that the latter may be known and exploited by the actor. Finally, we accept the doctrine that the effectiveness of the artifice is a question of fact to be considered by the judge.

3d. The paper [in the record] is an imitation of one side of a legitimate 1,000-peso note circulated by the government. It was not manufactured as counterfeit money but rather for advertising, the text of which is on the reverse side. Over the latter the accused pasted a piece of white paper that gave a rigid consistency to the supposed note and made it appreciably thicker than a legitimate 1,000-peso note. On the side that looked like currency the colors are very dull and the surface of that side, as well as the borders, are altered by small cracks and tears, features that are uncommon in notes of that size. In sum: we do not believe that a man of average caution could be deceived with this device. The accused himself — whose sincerity we have no reason to doubt in this case — did not believe in the effectiveness of his artifice, and tells us that he gave it "in case it passed" and if the baker refused it, he was going to tell him it was a joke. The baker, Robles, understood that he was the victim of a "dirty trick" [citation to the record].

Robles, the victim, is a mature man, and a merchant. He was not in a hurry when he took the "note," nor did he have to attend to other customers immediately. He was obviously careless, since it is uncommon to pay for 1.35 pesos' worth of bread with a 1,000-peso note. He took the "note" and put it in the cash box, without looking at it; he changed it; and when he put the money from the following sale in the box, he realized that the paper was not money.

It has not been demonstrated in this case that Robles is a man of inferior mental condition, and there is no reason to suppose that. And in any case, the accused was not trying to exploit such a condition, for [even if it were true], he did not know the baker well enough to be aware of it.

The accused acted "carelessly." He tried his luck to see if the phony note "passed." It could not pass a normally observant and alert businessman, but it could pass in the absence of observation [on his part]. We are not saying, of course, that the accused acted in a morally correct manner. He knew, when he was handed the "change," that it was money that did not belong to him. But his incorrect conduct is not viewed by the law as a crime of fraud. There was no theft, because the money was handed to him voluntarily by the proprietor. That delivery was induced, and induced by a trick that has no legal existence as a crime.

                            *   *   *

[The corpus delicti not having been proved], in accordance with the request of the defense counsel, I decide this case freely acquitting José Héctor Molinatti of guilt and charge, without costs (art. 68, C. Pr. Cr.).—*Juan J. Llobet Fortuny* (Sec.: Jorge A. Geddes.)

FRANCISCO OPPIDO
Second Criminal Chamber of Mar del Plata
1963-I J.A. 219 (1962)

2d Instance.—Mar del Plata, April 3, 1962.—1st. Is the appealed decision just?

2d.   What decision is proper?

1st. question.—Dr. D'Angelo said:

1st.   Francisco Oppido has been condemned to one month of imprisonment, suspended, for defrauding Juan Carlos Greco, in Mar del Plata on February 26, 1957; the sentence is agreed to by the prosecution and appealed by the accused and his counsel.

2d.   The offense for which he was sentenced consists in his having obtained from Greco the sum of 5,000 pesos for the transfer to the latter of a sale contract for a piece of immovable property belonging to another person. [The accused had owned this lot, but had sold it to another in 1944.]

3d.   In truth, there is no concrete objection about the proof of this act . . . .

[The court found that the prosecution's allegations were accurate.]

* * *

5th.   As the only argument of substance brought up, it is said that fraud (art. 172, P.C.) — such is the correct term as used by the judge of 1st Instance — could not have existed because there was no artifice adequate to deceive. The inadequacy of the means would rest on [the supposition] that, had the victim taken ordinary precautions, such as reading the sale contract and noting that it states in its text: "not transferable without the participation and consent of the seller, which when given, shall be noted on the same . . .," with such precautions the deceit would not have been successful.

I do not think so. This theory of the sufficiency of the artifice should not be exaggerated to the point where it leaves people helpless who are poorly advised, dull or unwary, and who are, paradoxically, the preferred victims. I admit that a simple lie, without anything objective to support it, cannot be considered "artifice or deceit," because "no one should believe easily in another's words, and if one believes them, he is himself to blame" (Carrara, "Programa," Nos. 2344 and 2345). But neither is it necessary to have a veritable *"mise en scène,"* with great preparation and complicated maneuvering (Soler, vol. 4, pp. 333, ff.).

In order to measure the effectiveness of the artifice, it is indispensable to observe the circumstances of the particular case, including the personality of the victim; and to remember that if the deceit turned out effective, that is a sufficient, if not a sure, presumption of its seriousness. In the present case the accused calls himself a "broker" by profession . . ., which makes one assume a certain degree of assurance and ease with words, while the victim is a mechanic. Further, they are tied by a certain degree of family relationship, since the victim is married to a niece of the accused, and this fact involves greater than usual confidence between the two. Finally, the lie was accompanied by the exhibition of documents that would be convincing to any average person . . . . I agree with the judge of 1st Instance that all this is more than enough to deceive, not merely a dull person, but also a man of average education, and even a university graduate who is not familiar with that kind of business. The average person trusts the good faith of others, given the apparent seriousness of those acts, and it is seldom that he attentively reads the text of such documents, or if he does, that he understands them well.

[The decision was unanimously affirmed, with costs.]

QUESTIONS ON THE EFFECT OF CRIMINAL CONVICTION
OR ACQUITTAL ON A SUBSEQUENT CIVIL ACTION
AGAINST THE ACCUSED

The availability of a civil action for damages within an Argentine criminal proceeding raises a tactical problem for the attorney for the victim of an action which may be a crime. Should he seek to have the actor prosecuted? If the actor is prosecuted, should the victim appear as an interested party in the criminal proceeding? These questions are more or less crucial to the protection of the victim's interest, depending on the degree to which conclusive effect will be given to the outcome of the criminal prosecution when it is raised in a later civil action arising out of the same events.

In which of the following cases should the determination of the criminal court be given the effect of res judicata? Should that effect take the form of a limitation on the civil court's decision? On the evidence which can be presented to the civil court?

1.   Defendant was convicted of a violation of art. 172, P.C., and sentenced to six months of imprisonment; no civil damages were asked or awarded. The victim now sues for damages caused by the defendant's fraud; the fraud alleged is that which was the basis for the conviction.

2.   Defendant was convicted of a violation of art. 172, P.C., sentenced to six months of imprisonment, and ordered to pay damages to the victim in the amount of 10,000 pesos. The victim did not appear in the criminal proceeding. He now sues for damages in the amount of 50,000 pesos, based on the fraud which was the basis for the defendant's conviction (offering to set off the 10,000 pesos already received). Would your answer be different if the defendant had appeared as a party to the criminal proceeding? Is the plaintiff entitled to a judgment rescinding his contract with defendant, to which he agreed because of defendant's fraudulent representations?

3.   Defendant was charged with a violation of art. 172, P.C., but acquitted, on the ground that someone else had made the fraudulent representations to the victim. The victim now sues for (a) damages and (b) rescission. If the defendant stands on his acquittal, will he succeed against both counts? Can the defendant now contest the finding of the criminal court that fraud was, indeed, committed by a third person? (See art. 935, C.C.) Does it make any difference whether the victim appeared as a party to the criminal proceeding?

VELEZ SARSFIELD, NOTE TO ARTICLES 1102-1103
OF HIS PROJECTED CIVIL CODE (Now Civil Code of Argentina)

The influence in a civil action of a sentence pronounced in a criminal action has been treated in several ways by French jurisconsults. Merlin ... maintains that, for example, when I claim reparation from Pedro in a civil court for an offense for which he was already condemned in a criminal court, the doctrine of res judicata applies to the existence of the offense and its imputation to Pedro. Thus the latter may not attempt to open the question again in order to show that he is not the author of the offense, because: 1) the *causa* in both decisions is the same, since the base of the two actions is the offense that was committed; 2) there is also an identical object, because in spite of the difference between the direct objects in the two decisions, both are judged to have the same fundamental object in the eyes of the law; 3) there are identical parties, because the Public Minister is the representative of the whole society and he has represented me, even though I may not have made the accusation.

Toullier ... refuted Merlin's system, demonstrating that there was no identity of parties, since the Public Minister could not ask for pecuniary reparation of the damage, and thus could not represent the injured party. He further showed that even if there were identity of parties, there was no identity of object.

French jurisconsults have been divided by these two opinions.

It may be said that in truth there is no identity of object. How can one say that to demand the payment of 20,000 pesos from Pedro, and to ask that he be condemned to death is to ask for the same thing and the same object? But even though there is no identity of the thing in the two complaints, how can we permit the accused to be brought before a civil tribunal later for the same act that a criminal court has decided never existed? Inversely, how can it be that after a defense freely made with all the guarantees provided by the law, a person who has been condemned as the author of an offense, can later in a civil tribunal maintain and even establish legally that the act did not take place, or that it is not imputable to him? This would be a juridical scandal, contrary to reason and to the truth that must be assumed in judicial proceedings that have been concluded.

The rule requiring the three conditions above to be present in order for res judicata to be established, is merely a rule of civil law given for questions of pure civil law. It is not given for those questions resulting from a comparison of civil law with criminal law.

... The mission of criminal tribunals is to decide whether the act attributed to the accused exists; whether the accused is the author and if that act is imputable to him according to the penal statute and as an offense in criminal law. If the victim does not join in the action, the criminal tribunal does not have to decide whether or not the act constitutes an offense in the civil law, or a quasi-offense. If then a criminal tribunal were to judge, when there is no individual complainant present in the action, that the accused's proven act is completely beyond reproach, and that it cannot lead to the application of a penalty nor to the payment of damages, the sentence would be without value in regard to this last point. The injured person could go to a civil court and raise the question of the existence of an offense in civil law or of a quasi-offense, this being a question that the criminal tribunal had no right to decide. Thus also, a person who may have been declared guiltless in the case of a fire in his own house could, nevertheless, upon the demand of an insurance company, be judged to have caused the fire through carelessness, and to have no right to any indemnity.

For res judicata to apply, it is also necessary that the point to be decided in the civil jurisdiction . . . be precisely the one decided by the criminal tribunal. Thus, when the criminal tribunal decides that the act attributed to Pedro does not exist, the person who claims to have been damaged by that alleged act cannot be allowed to try to prove the existence of the act in a civil tribunal, even though he may not have been a party to the criminal trial. If the criminal tribunal recognized the existence of the act and decided that Pedro was not the author, it is clear that the injured person cannot pursue Pedro for that act in the civil tribunal. The same is true if the criminal tribunal recognizes that the act exists and that Pedro is the author, but that he cannot be charged with it, and there is no criminal guilt on his part; this same guilt cannot be established against him in the civil jurisdiction. Reciprocally, if Pedro has been declared guilty of an offense and some civil consequence of that offense is claimed against him in the civil tribunal, . . . he would be unable to raise again the question of guilt. In these various cases the point that one would want to discuss again in the civil jurisdiction is that which was decided by the criminal tribunal. Although the second action may not have the same purpose as the first, although the claimant may not be the same and although there may be neither identity of object nor of parties, there is nonetheless res judicata. The civil jurisdiction cannot declare nonexistent the criminal act that was considered to exist by the criminal jurisdiction, nor can it judge innocent a person whom the other jurisdiction declared guilty . . . .

    * * *

AMORUSO v. CASELLA
Civil Chambers of the Capital (Plenary Session)
1946-I J.A. 803, 42 La Ley 156, 181 G.F. 457 (1946)

    * * *

Buenos Aires, April 2, 1946.—The judges of the 1st and 2d Chambers of Appeals (Civil) met in plenary session for the purpose of fixing the interpretation [of the two chambers] of the following point: "Does a definitive dismissal or a judgment of acquittal of the accused in a criminal proceeding constitute res judicata in a civil action for indemnification of damages?"

[This was a wrongful death action, arising out of an automobile accident which killed the son of the plaintiffs. The defendant had been acquitted of the crime of homicide in the federal criminal court. Nevertheless, the court of 1st Instance awarded damages in the amount of 4,000 pesos. The court of 2d Instance — the two civil chambers, sitting together — made no reference to the facts of the case. All of the opinions deal with the abstract question of law stated above. As the judge of 1st Instance noted in his opinion, there was no disagreement concerning the effect of an acquittal by a criminal court on a subsequent civil action when the acquittal was based on a finding (a) that the accused had not participated in the act, or (b) that the act alleged as a crime had not been performed. The judges differed with respect to the effect of an acquittal based on the classification of the accused's act as not wrongful. The word *culpa* means, in Spanish, guilt, blame, fault or even negligence. The question before the court of 2d Instance is whether a finding of absence of *culpa* in a criminal proceeding requires a similar finding of absence of *culpa* in a subsequent civil proceeding. Four of the judges in the court of 2d Instance were of the opinion that the two concepts are identical, and therefore that an acquittal based on absence of guilt — in the sense that the act of the accused was not criminally punishable — required the rejection of a civil action for damages based on the same allegedly culpable act. A majority of eight judges, however, took the position that the civil court might re-examine the question of the fault of the defendant who had been acquitted by the criminal court. Only brief excerpts of the two principal opinions are reproduced here. Dr. Barraquero wrote the main opinion for the minority, and Dr. Garriga was the principal writer for the majority.]

Dr. *Barraquero* said:

* * *

. . . A criminal acquittal, it has been argued, concerns only the penal guilt [*culpa*] of the accused, while his civil blameworthiness [*culpa*] is different, given the different nature, degree of guilt, and manner of proof in the penal and civil laws. So there is no res judicata with respect to an absence of civil responsibility of the actor resulting from his acquittal. This is the more true when the differentiation or assimilation of civil and penal guilt establishes a doctrinary question that "is not essential" for the solution of judicial cases in view of the provisions of art. 1103, C.C., which requires only that in a penal judgment one have proved the "materiality of the act" and the "participation of the accused" . . . .

The provision of the cited art. 1103, concerning acquittal of the accused, referred, as was previously shown, not only to the existence of the principal act, the materiality of the act, but also to the blamelessness — lack of guilt. Consequently, it is fitting to investigate "whether that lack of guilt," decided in the criminal court, is of a different juridical character from that which may be adjudged in the civil action for indemnification, arising from the offense envisioned in the P.C. It is also appropriate to see, in turn, whether there is a difference in degrees of fault and in the means of determining it in the two actions . . . .

* * *

It is a universal principle of doctrine that from every wrong in criminal law, there "is born," with the "penal" action, an action for "indemnification" of damages.

Art. 1096 of the Civil Code established as a rule the independent exercise of the two actions, penal and civil. But the new Penal Code has abolished that independence, for in art. 29 it permits the criminal judge to fix (on his own motion or on the petition of a party) the indemnification of material or moral [*i.e.,* nonpecuniary] damage caused to the victim, to his family, or to a third person . . . .

On the other hand, art. 29 has not created a new system for the civil action of indemnification, since it does not hinder the continued use of the Civil Code system, but simply [creates] the "legal possibility of pursuing the action" before the criminal judge. The latter, however, should apply the provisions of the P.C. first and only in a subsidiary manner those of the C.C. . . . .

Nonetheless, one should not conclude from the laws concerning this double system that the acquittal of the accused for "lack of guilt" does not constitute res judicata in the civil court. In both proceedings there is the same cause of action: the existence of the principal act that constitutes the criminal wrong.

In truth, we are dealing with the exercise of the action for the indemnification of damages caused by the criminal wrong, the "action of indemnification" which is the same in the field of penal law as in that of civil law. This identity in the cause of action is precisely the basis of the provision of the cited art. 29 of the Penal Code, which permits the action for indemnification in the criminal proceeding.

* * *

In view of that system in the present P.C., the acquittal of the accused "for lack of guilt," "extinguishes," *"ministerio legis"* the possibility of indemnification. It is not proper to revive it in a civil action, invoking the existence of precisely that same principal act — a criminal act — because, in accordance with "the unity and logic of penal legislation," that acquittal must govern "all the effects of the wrong," with obedience to its restrictive principles.

Consequently, if there is no penal responsibility, neither is there civil responsibility, since both actions are born of the same principal act, and a competent judge has declared that the accused did not incur "any blame."

* * *

Dr. *Garriga* said:
* * *

19. Given that the interpretation which I propose flows from the letter and spirit of art. 1103, in harmony with the doctrine expressed in the note [of Vélez Sársfield] and with the juridical system established by the other legal rules and clarified by their respective notes, as well as with the doctrinary and jurisprudential antecedents that served as their source, it would not be essential to show that the governing principles of juridical order accord with art. 1103. Nevertheless, it is convenient to do so in order to reinforce the argument.

a) Unlawful conduct — an action or omission transgressing the norms that govern juridical order — is divided into civil and criminal misbehavior, according to whether the transgressed rules refer to the relations of living together with others and of the compatibility of the activities of individuals among themselves, or to the relations involved with one's conduct regarding society as a whole .... Such a difference, which is tied to the means [employed by the one who commits a wrongful act], agrees with the difference between the consequences: a penal offense injures the interest of society while the civil wrong transgresses only an individual right. And although the distinction made between the two kinds of unlawful conduct, considering the form of the violation or the spirit motivating the actor, has been criticized because of the practical difficulties in establishing specifically when the social interest has been transgressed and when it is a question of an individual's interest, it is nonetheless true. The practical difficulty mentioned does not lessen the reality of the distinction between [the different kinds of offense]. Further, besides the objective and subjective elements, which are common to all unlawful conduct, civil unlawfulness is made up of another specific external element, which is the damage produced by the unlawful act, or any other exterior act that might cause damage. Thus, where there is no damage caused nor any other exterior act that might cause it, even though the damage were capable of being caused, unquestionably there is no civil misbehavior. For example: both an attempted crime that is not abandoned voluntarily, as well as the abuse of firearms (even if no one is wounded), are criminal wrongs (arts. 42, 43, 104 and 105, P.C.), and nevertheless, they do not constitute civil wrongs, since they have not caused damage nor can they cause it ....

b) Unlawfulness in the civil order arising from a breach of one's duty not to hurt another person unjustly, and in the penal order from the expressed rule of law. — Acts that make up civil unlawfulness are not strictly enumerated by the Civil Code, since it is enough that they be voluntary, imputable to the author by reason of his wrongful intention or his negligence and that they have produced damage; while there is no criminal unlawfulness if the act in question is not directly and specifically stated to be a crime: *"Nullium crimen, nullia pena sine lege."*

c) Criminal unlawfulness brings with it the application of a penalty to the aggressor, together with the obligation to repair the pecuniary or nonpecuniary damage that may have been caused. — Civil unlawfulness, exclusively, obliges only the reparation of the pecuniary damage that may have been caused, not as a penalty but as indemnification. If the act combines both civil and criminal unlawfulness, the application of the penalty is independent of the order to make compensation, because each has a different purpose. The purpose of the former is social defense, the correction of the criminal, the intimidation of his future imitators and even segregation from society when it is a case of an incorrigible. Indemnification, however, seeks only to re-establish the pecuniary situation of the victim as it was before the damaging act. A penalty, even when it is a fine, cannot go beyond the fixed limits of the statute, while the setting of compensation is left to judicial discretion. Indemnification is not a penalty; it is a simple compensation for the damage suffered by the victim. A penalty deals with a wounded social interest and the person who caused the injury; compensation, only with the pecuniary situation of the victim: one looks at society and the criminal, the other, only at the victim. In cases of criminal unlawfulness there must always be an absolute identity of the material or moral author of the act with the condemned person. In a case of civil unlawfulness the direct author of the act may be different from the person ordered to indemnify, and thus, for many reasons — individual or social — the law imposes on people the obligation to be responsible for the injurious consequences of the acts of others, and even for those of things that he uses or has in his care: No one, on the other hand, will be punished because his servant or his dog may have killed someone . . . .

* * *

[Dr. Garriga also reviewed some of the practical differences between civil and criminal wrongs, such as the inheritability of the civil action, the different ages of capacity of minors to commit wrongs, the fact that amnesty or pardon by the executive does not relieve the wrongdoer of his civil obligations, the different parties involved in the two actions, and so forth.]

* * *

As a consequence of the development of industry and the increase in automotive transportation, work and traffic accidents have multiplied. The victims and their attorneys ordinarily are not in a position to produce proof of the guilt of the author of the act. Legal presumptions, without violating reality, generally come to the victims' aid, and the author of the blameworthy act, who would have been acquitted in the criminal action for insufficient evidence, is convicted in the civil action.

Galli ["Culpa Civil y Culpa Penal," Anales de la Facultad de Ciencias Jurídicas y Sociales de la Universidad de La Plata, vol. 8, N° 509, p. 291], gives us an eloquent statistic. Of 666 criminal trials begun during 2 years in the criminal tribunal of Dr. Cañas, all for homicide or negligently caused injuries, and almost all involving traffic accidents, only in 58 of them was there a conditional conviction [suspended sentence]; 10 were absolved, 52 finally dismissed and 544 dismissed provisionally. That is to say, that not one sentence was executed.

* * *

Because of the foregoing opinions, it is declared that a definite dismissal, or a decision of acquittal of the accused in a criminal action, does not result in res judicata in the civil action. A definitive dismissal absolutely does not so result, and an acquittal does not when it is given in respect to the blameworthiness [culpa] of the author of the act, regarding his responsibility for damages caused. [Signed by all 12 judges.]

TENNESSEE ODIN INS. CO. v. DICKEY
190 Tenn. 96, 228 S.W.2d 73 (1950)

NEIL, CH. J.

This case was first tried in the circuit court of Maury County in which Sherman Dickey recovered a judgment against the Tennessee Odin Insurance Company upon a contract of insurance which insured a Dodge automobile truck against loss by fire, etc. The Bank of Columbia held a mortgage on the truck to secure a note due it, and for this reason the suit was brought for the use and benefit of the bank. There was also a recovery of the statutory penalty for failure to pay the amount of the loss within 60 days from the date of the fire. The Court of Appeals affirmed the judgment of the trial court, but held that there was no evidence to warrant a recovery for the amount of the penalty.

The defense interposed in behalf of the insurance company was that the insured, Sherman Dickey, fraudulently procured the truck to be burned. This was in fact the only defense of the company.

The insured was indicted and tried upon the charge of wilfully burning the truck for the purpose of defrauding the insurance company. He was acquitted. When the civil suit came on to be tried counsel for the insurance company gave notice to opposing counsel in open court that they would object to any reference being made to the judgment of acquittal of Dickey in the original court. Following Dickey's testimony in chief the counsel for the insurance company asked him on cross-examination if he did not procure certain persons to burn this truck to which he answered that he did not.

To rebut the defendant's proof, which pointed very strongly to Dickey's guilt, the trial judge over the objection of counsel permitted the introduction of the minutes of the court in the criminal case which showed that he was acquitted of the crime of arson. He instructed the jury that this proof could not be considered as evidence that the plaintiff did not burn the truck, but could only be considered as reflecting upon his credibility. The Court of Appeals held that the introduction of this evidence "did not constitute reversible error."

We granted certiorari to consider the question as to the correctness of the trial court and Court of Appeals in ruling upon the admissibility of this evidence. The learned Court of Appeals, in support of its opinion that there was no "reversible error," relied upon Code Section 10654 which provides that there should be "no reversal or new trial for errors not affecting the results of the trial."

It is urged upon us by able counsel that inasmuch as both the trial court and Court of Appeals have ruled that the alleged error did not "affect the results of the trial" that this Court should accept it as conclusive of the question. In most cases it would be highly persuasive, if not conclusive upon us. But not so in the case at bar for the manifest reason that the introduction by the plaintiff, Dickey, of the minutes of the court showing his acquittal of arson resulted in greatly impairing if not destroying the only defense which the insurance company had. Moreover it was an issue between the State and the plaintiff to redress a public wrong; while the present suit is to enforce a private right arising under contract. Ordinarily a witness may be asked upon cross-examination questions as to whether or not he has been guilty of certain crimes involving moral turpitude. His answers are binding upon counsel. Not so in the pending case, first because it was the sole and only defense to the plaintiff's suit and secondly the fact that the State was unable to prove *"beyond a reasonable doubt"* that Dickey was guilty of the crime of arson was wholly inadmissible upon the same issue in the civil suit in which his guilt could be shown by a *preponderance* of the evidence.

We are strongly convinced that when the minutes of the criminal court, showing Dickey's acquittal of arson, was offered in evidence the jury might well have concluded that the insurance company's defense was false, even though the court instructed the jury that it should go only to his creditability. In Massey v. Taylor, 45 Tenn. 447, 448, 98 Am. Dec. 429 it was held: "The acquittal of the plaintiff upon an indictment for embezzlement, is not entitled to any effect as evidence in a civil action, as an answer to the defense of embezzlement, or as tending to show, that, in fact, the plaintiff did not commit the embezzlement."

In Wigmore on Evidence, Vol. IV, Section 1346a, and Sec. 1671 there appears a conflict of authority as to the admissibility in evidence of a judgment of conviction or acquittal in a subsequent trial involving the same issue. But the weight of authority supports our own case of Massey v. Taylor, supra. We refer to the following cases appearing in the footnotes to Section 1346a (Wigmore). Shaw v. Glenn Falls Ins. Co. (Canada), 1 DLR 502, 12 Mar. Prov. 386, conviction of B for theft of an automobile, excluded. Mutual Benefit Health & Accident Ass'n. v. Neale, 43 Ariz. 532, 33 P2d 604. In Interstate Dry Goods Stores v. Williamson, 91 W. Va. 156, 112 SE 301, 31 ALR 258, a judgment of conviction in a criminal case was held to be inadmissible.

In Occidental Ins. Co. v. Chasteen, 255 Ky. 710, 75 SW2d 363 the suit was to recover for a fire loss; the plaintiff's prior *acquittal* of arson was *excluded*. To the same effect, Bobereski v. Insurance Co., 105 Pa. Super. 585, 161 A 412; Girard v. Vermont Mut. Fire Ins. Co., 103 Vt. 330, 154 A 666. In Alabama, Virginia and a few other jurisdictions, it is held that prior *convictions* of arson were binding in the civil case. See Fidelity-Phenix Fire Ins. Co. of New York v. Murphy, 226 Ala. 226, 146 So 387; Eagle Star & British Dominions Ins. Co. v. Heller, 149 Va. 82, 140 SE 314, 57 ALR 490.

The plaintiff's acquittal is not admissible as a means of rehabilitating his character as a witness in his own behalf, for, as said in Massey v. Taylor: *"it is not entitled to any effect."* It is not competent for any purpose. The defendant insurance company was entitled to have the issue of his guilt decided upon the preponderance of all the evidence, regardless of a verdict of acquittal in the criminal court.

The judgment of the Court of Appeals in holding that the recovery of the penalty was without sufficient evidence to support it is affirmed. In all other respects it is reversed and remanded for a new trial.

All concur, except Tomlinson, J., who did not participate.

NORTH RIVER INS. CO. v. MILITELLO
100 Colo. 343, 67 P.2d 625 (1937)

HOLLAND, Justice.

Militello, defendant in error, as owner, procured a policy of fire insurance from the North River Insurance Company, plaintiff in error, on an apartment house in Trinidad, Colo. On July 13, 1932, while the policy was in full force and effect, the building was destroyed by an explosion and fire. On the following day, July 14, an information, charging him with burning the property with the intent to injure, prejudice, and defraud the insurer, was filed in the district court. After numerous continuances, trial was had, and a jury returned a verdict of guilty May 19, 1933. August 7, following, a sentence of from two and one-half to five years in the penitentiary was imposed. On review by this court, the conviction was upheld in an opinion filed October 29, 1934. Rehearing was denied November 19, 1934. Militello v. People, 95 Colo. 519, 37 P. (2d) 527.

On September 17, 1932, before trial of the criminal charge, the present action was instituted in which Militello sued the insurance company for recovery on the policy. Answer was filed February 24, 1933. Supplemental answer alleged that plaintiff caused or allowed the premises to be saturated with gasoline and turpentine, and caused or allowed the purposely set explosion. Upon the trial to a jury, the record of the conviction in the criminal case, then pending on review on error, was admitted in evidence under an instruction to the jury that it was offered and admitted only for the purpose of impeaching the credibility of plaintiff, and was not to be considered by the jury as proving or tending to prove any fact in issue in the case other than such credibility. The jury's verdict, returned on September 22, 1934, was for Militello the plaintiff, in the full amount of the policy. Judgment on the verdict was entered October 30, 1934. January 8, 1935, the insurance company filed a motion in arrest of, and to vacate the judgment, and, as grounds therefor, stated that the judgment of conviction, record of which had been introduced in evidence in the case, had been affirmed by this court and became final on and after November 19, 1934, when petition for rehearing was denied; further that the judgment as affirmed was a final and irrevocable determination of the fact of the destruction of the property by plaintiff in fraud of the insurer which precluded recovery against the defendant insurance company, and that the judgment rendered against it thereby became an illegal judgment. These motions were overruled and the insurance company assigns error.

The principal errors upon which the company relies for a reversal are the denial of the motion for new trial, motion in arrest of judgment, and motion to vacate the judgment. The other assignment, relating to remarks of plaintiff's counsel in his closing argument to the jury, will not be discussed since our conclusion on the other assigned errors, necessitates a reversal of the judgment.

In apt time, after the judgment of plaintiff's conviction became a finality, by its affirmance in this court, the insurance company moved for the arrest, and vacation, of the judgment entered in the present action. We believe that when the fact of plaintiff's guilt of having caused the destruction of the building with intent to defraud the insurer was thus established beyond a reasonable doubt and unmistakably before the trial court as appeared from its own records and the motions presented, sound public policy required the vacation of the judgment, and the entering of an order granting a new trial, and the denial of the motion was error.

Counsel for plaintiff insists that the insurance company is now bound by its failure to plead the conviction of his client as a bar or in abatement and contenting itself with the introduction of the record of conviction in evidence for impeachment purposes only. He further contends that the conviction in the criminal case cannot be pleaded as a bar in this civil action. These contentions are not well founded. It must be remembered that at the time of the trial in this, the civil case, the judgment of conviction in the criminal case was still subject to a reversal and possible ultimate acquittal of Militello. In this uncertain state, it was wholly without value as a defense to be pleaded in this case, and if pleaded, a motion to strike would have been timely, and no doubt granted; therefore it necessarily follows that a failure to interpose this improper and useless pleading can in no way prejudice the pleader, who later, and at the first available opportunity, after the conviction ripened into an adjudicated fact, interposed same as an attack upon the judgment against the company. Its probable value at the time of the trial was such as was fixed within the limitations of the instructions of the trial court. Our statement, supra, that the conviction became an adjudicated fact has application only to the parties thereto; that is, the people and the defendant — now plaintiff — and not to, or as between the parties hereto. Otherwise there would be a mutuality of estoppel, and the matter adjudicated would be a sound basis for a plea in bar. The insurance company would not have been prejudiced had the criminal case resulted in an acquittal. Thus stands the great weight of authority.

On the question of the admissibility or inadmissibility of the evidence of a criminal conviction in a civil proceeding and the limitations, if any, to be placed thereon, this court has not committed itself, and we now are free to adopt the rule which seems most logical and in accord with public policy. There is precedent for both extremes; that is, that it is inadmissible for any purpose, and contra, that it is admissible and conclusive as to the fact proven. We embrace neither rule. Logic compels a relaxation of the long followed earlier rule of complete exclusion; but we are not ready to announce that all convictions are to be conclusive evidence for the purpose of establishing a material fact, even though such fact was the basis of the conviction. It would be more definitely a legislative function to declare such a public policy; however, an enlightened conscience does not permit us to cling to the archaic rule of exclusion for all purposes when such a fact has been solemnly and judicially determined. Greater weight is to be given to this conclusion when the fact of guilt is established beyond a reasonable doubt in a trial in which the accused is surrounded by all of the safeguards afforded by law. This is particularly true when the occasion as here, bears a close relation to an inter-party matter. The plaintiff, defendant in the criminal action, was convicted of defrauding the insurance company by the identical act resulting in the loss upon which he now predicates his claim for recovery against the same company. We are not in sympathy with any rule of law which would permit him to profit by his own wrong. The record of conviction in the criminal case was admissible in evidence in this case, and when so admitted carried proof of the conviction to be considered as prima facie evidence of the fact that plaintiff destroyed or caused to be destroyed the property for which he now seeks to recover judgment in the amount of the insurance thereon. It is such presumptive proof as to shift the burden to him to establish his innocence thereof. When the established fact of guilt was presented upon the first opportunity, as here, it was sufficient to vitiate the civil judgment otherwise established.

The judgment is reversed and the cause remanded for such further proceedings as may be had in harmony with the views herein expressed.

BURKE, C. J., and KNOUS, J., concur.

NORTH RIVER INS. CO. v. MILITELLO
104 Colo. 28, 88 P.2d 567 (1939)

BAKKE, Justice.

This is a suit on a fire insurance contract and was before us on a former occasion. North River Ins. Co. v. Militello, 100 Colo. 343, 67 P.2d 625. A retrial was had resulting in a judgment for plaintiff, which defendant seeks to have reversed. In view of the fact that the matter has been in litigation for over six years, we feel that it should now be decided promptly on the application for a supersedeas, since the legal principles involved — the law of the case having been established by our former opinion — are relatively simple.

As the former opinion indicates, Militello, defendant in error, plaintiff below, was convicted of arson (Militello v. People, 95 Colo. 519, 37 P.2d 527), for burning the very property on which he now seeks to recover insurance. In their brief in North River Ins. Co. v. Militello, supra, counsel for the insurance company advanced this proposition: "We submit, therefore, that this court should adopt either the rule of the case of Eagle, Star & British Dominions Ins. Co. v. Heller, 149 Va. 82, 140 S.E. 314 [57 A.L.R. 490] [that conviction of the policyholder of burning the insured property is a bar to recovery on the policy] or the rule of the case of Schindler v. Royal Ins. Co., 258 N.Y. 310, 179 N.E. 711 [80 A.L.R. 1142] [that such conviction is prima facie evidence of the facts involved, in a civil suit to recover on the policy]."

In response to this submitted alternative, we adopted the rule announced in the Schindler case, reversed the judgment, and remanded the cause "for such further proceedings as may be had in harmony with the views herein expressed." [100 Colo. 343, 67 P.2d 627.] The trial court carried out our instructions to the letter. In fact, counsel for the insurance company, "wrote their own ticket." All of their requested instructions were approved and given by the court without objection. They are liberally in the company's favor. No objection was made to any of the testimony of Militello in which he detailed his version of circumstances concerning the fire which destroyed the insured property, and denied starting it. Evidently the jury believed his story and gave him verdict accordingly.

We do not pause here to discuss the question of public policy. We considered that feature in our prior opinion, and it is fully discussed in the authorities above mentioned. We, however, make this observation: Counsel for the company on the former hearing quoted from "The Nature of the Judicial Process," a book written by the late Justice Cardozo, the following, found at page 43: "The social interest served by refusing to permit the criminal to profit by his crime is greater than that served by the preservation and enforcement of legal rights of ownership." The pronouncement does the author honor. It was written in 1921; yet in 1932, he joined with Judge Pound in rendering the opinion in the Schindler case. In his book he philosophized; in the Schindler case he spoke the law. This case is decided in accordance with his legal view.

Judgment affirmed.

KNOUS, OTTO BOCK, and BURKE, JJ., concur in the conclusion only, it being their view that the law in the case was settled by the opinion in North River Ins. Co. v. Militello, 100 Colo. 343, 67 P.2d 625.

FRANCIS E. BOUCK, J., dissents in part and specially concurs in part.

FRANCIS E. BOUCK, Justice (dissenting in part, but specially concurring).

In so far as the court's opinion herein bases the affirmance upon the ground that the opinion in North River Ins. Co. v. Militello, 100 Colo. 343, 67 P.2d 625, stated "the law of the case" which was then — and is now again — before us, I concur. I heartily approve the return of this court to the reasonable and wholesome principle of "the law of the case," which this court seemed deliberately to abandon in Black Diamond Co. v. Frank, 99 Colo. 528, 64 P.2d 797, as shown in the dissenting opinion at page 533 of 99 Colo., and page 799 of 64 P.2d, respectively.

However, the right of this court to reconsider in any future unrelated case the effect which the department opinion in the Militello case, supra, gave to the evidence of the criminal conviction, is, as I take it, fully reserved. Were the question an open one in the case at bar, I should under the disclosed circumstances hesitate to say that the defendant's criminal conviction of arson beyond a reasonable doubt was not as a matter of law a determination of the unlawful burning charged by the insurance company in the civil case. I am inclined to believe that the criminal conviction which was had according to the law of the land — and as between the defendant Militello and all the People of the State of Colorado — should be accepted as conclusive and decisive for all purposes, in the absence of a showing sufficient on recognized grounds to prove some illegality in the criminal verdict, a verdict which in the present instance was not so shown to have been illegal but was declared lawful by this court's affirmance in Militello v. People, 95 Colo. 519, 37 P.2d 527.

The matter of establishing the general rule seems important enough to demand consideration by the court en banc at the earliest opportunity, when the argument is not, as here, that the selection of a certain rule in the particular case is binding because a party saw fit to urge in its brief and argument that this court could properly choose either of two out of several alternative rules obtaining in other jurisdictions. My concurrence is limited accordingly, and I dissent as to other matters which need not be discussed.

WILCOX v. GREGORY
112 Ohio App. 516, 176 N.E.2d 523 (1960)

DOYLE, P. J.   Three assignments of error are presented in this appeal on questions of law from a judgment for the defendant, in an action for personal injuries, growing out of an automobile collision, tried before a jury in the Court of Common Pleas of Summit Country.

The claimed errors which are asserted to be prejudicial and sufficient to justify a reversal of the judgment are stated as follows:

"1.   The court erred in permitting the defendant to deny she pleaded guilty and to thereby deny the court record.

"2.   The court erred in charging the jury that if they believed her denial they should disregard the court records.

"3.   The court erred in charging the jury that the court records were required to be proven by the greater weight of the evidence."

The material facts of the grievance for which damages were sought are in the petition substantially as follows:

The plaintiff, Minnie L. Wilcox, operated her automobile in a northerly direction and in the easterly lane of High Street in the city of Wadsworth; the defendant operated her automobile behind the plaintiff, in the same direction and in the same traffic lane the defendant "failed to have her vehicle under control" and operated same so as to collide with the rear end of plaintiff's automobile, causing plaintiff to sustain serious injuries.

One of the specific allegations of negligence was "that the defendant failed to stop her automobile within the assured clear distance ahead." This allegation is of major importance in the case, because it claims a violation of a penal statute of the state, and a penal ordinance of the city of Wadsworth, which ordinance formed the predicate for a criminal prosecution of the defendant in the mayor's court of Wadsworth.

The defendant, Norma Gregory, in her answer, pleaded that she was not guilty of negligence, and specifically asserted "that any injuries or damages which the plaintiff might have suffered were directly or proximately the result of the negligence of the plaintiff herself, in that she stopped or decreased the speed of her automobile suddenly and unexpectedly without giving [defendant] any notice of her intention so to do; or that said negligence of the plaintiff directly and proximately contributed to her injuries and damages ***."

The reply of the plaintiff was in the form of a general denial of the claims of negligence against her.

It appears that, following the accident, the defendant, Norma Gregory, was charged by affidavit in the mayor's court of Wadsworth with operating "a motor vehicle contrary to ordinance 1761, Section 17, namely; did operate said vehicle at too great a speed so as to be able to stop within assured clear distance with conditions then existing." It is the claim of the appellant that the accused pleaded guilty to the charge, and, as a consequence thereof, she was entitled to have the jury charged as a matter of law that such fact was established, and that it was error "in permitting the defendant to deny *** the court record." (Assignment of error No. 1.)

If the record of a court shows without question that an accused pleaded guilty in a criminal prosecution, there may arise an exception to the general rule that a judgment in a criminal case cannot be received in a civil action, to establish the truth of the facts on which it was rendered. A record showing such plea may be received in evidence in a civil action against the guilty pleader growing out of the same offense. The record is admitted, not as a judgment establishing the fact, but as the deliberate declaration or admission against interest that the fact is so, or, "in other words, a solemn confession of the very matter charged in the civil action." 31 A.L.R., 278, annotation "V." See also: cases cited in 57 A.L.R., 504, 80 A.L.R., 1145, and 18 A.L.R.(2d), 1287.

In this state the general rule has been codified as follows:

Section 1.16, Revised Code:

"Anyone injured in person or property by a criminal act may recover full damages in a civil action, unless specifically excepted by law. *No record of a conviction, unless obtained by confession in open court, shall be used as evidence in a civil action brought for such purpose.*" (Italics ours.)

Case law is to the effect that, a plea of guilty by an alleged tort-feasor to a charge of traffic violation predicated upon a collision in which a person is injured, is admissible in an action brought against him by the party injured. *Freas v. Sullivan,* 130 Ohio St., 486, 200 N.E., 639.

See also: *Clinger v. Duncan,* 166 Ohio St., 216, at page 222, 141 N.E. (2d), 156; and *Clark v. Irvin,* 9 Ohio, 131.

Directing attention to the claims of error in the admission of oral testimony relative to the proceedings in the mayor's court, we recognize that in many situations a thing adjudged by a court of competent jurisdiction, under definite conditions, must be received in evidence as irrefragable truth; and in this case, if a substantially complete record of the mayor's court, as required in Section 1905.01, Revised Code, definitely showed a plea of guilty by the accused, we would hesitate to allow her to testify that such was not a fact, and, in doing so, challenge the verity of the record. However, under the state of the record kept by the mayor, we are of the opinion, and so hold, that oral testimony was admissible, tending to show that the accused had not pleaded guilty, but that she was found guilty by the court.

The language of the record is uncertain and ambiguous. On the front of the affidavit charging the offense appear the words "pleaded guilty." It does not appear who wrote the words. In the transcript of the criminal docket of the mayor's court appears a record of the various items of "costs" charged to the accused. Here we find: "Taking waivers of trial by jury" — 40 cents; "Hearing where evidence is introduced" — 2 dollars; etc. From this uncertain record, and no definite judgment entry indicating the proceedings or judgment, it was for the jury in the later civil action to determine whether the defendant in the criminal case, and who is also the defendant in this civil case, pleaded guilty to the criminal charge, or whether her version of the proceedings reflected the truth. She testified that, in response to the criminal charge, she went to the mayor's office and related to the mayor the facts of the accident, but has no recollection of entering a plea of any kind to the charge; that thereupon the mayor made known to her his disposition of the case — fine suspended and payment of costs.

It is our conclusion that the first claim of error is not sustained. By analogy, the case of *Woodruff v. Paschen,* 15 Ohio App., 276, affirmed in *Woodruff v. Paschen,* 105 Ohio St., 396, 137 N.E. 867, sustains our position.

In the second assignment of error it is stated that the court erred in charging the jury that "if they believed her denial they should disregard the court records."

We have heretofore stated that, because of the state of the record kept in the mayor's court, it was proper to admit oral testimony tending to prove that the defendant had not pleaded guilty to the criminal charge. It is obvious that if the jury believed the testimony of the defendant, and concluded that there was inadequate proof that she had pleaded guilty, and thereby made an admission against interest, then the court records were not material to any of the issues in the civil case and should have been disregarded by the jury. We find no error here.

The third assignment of error challenges the court's charge "that the court records were required to be proven by the greater weight of the evidence."

Pertinent to this claim, the court charged the jury as follows:

"The assured-clear-distance-ahead statute is a specific requirement and the violation thereof is negligence per se, or negligence as a matter of law.

"The statute is a safety regulation and imposes upon the operator of a motor vehicle at all times the unqualified obligation to be able to stop her car within the distance that discernible objects may be seen. The statute must be strictly construed and by its force the operator of a motor vehicle may therefore assume nothing that is not assured to her by the range of her vision. And I charge you in this instance that the plaintiff's automobile was a discernible object.

"If you find by the greater weight of the evidence that the defendant pleaded guilty to the charge of operating her automobile at a speed greater than would permit her to bring it to a stop within the assured clear distance ahead then you will consider that plea of the defendant as a declaration against interest in determining whether she is guilty of negligence in this respect; but if you conclude that such is not proved then you will not consider the fact that the records showed she pleaded guilty as going to the question of negligence." (Italics ours.)

We have heretofore stated in effect that admissions by a defendant, in a criminal case, by a plea of guilty, may be competent as judicial admissions against the accused in a civil action involving the same subject matter. Admissions of this character are not received in evidence, hovever, as admissions of negligence; and while they may be accepted as an admission of culpability of the criminal offense charged, and therefore an admission against interest in a civil action involving the same subject matter, the admission is not conclusive against a defendant in a civil action, and may be controverted. *Swigart v. Swigart,* 65 Ohio Law Abs., 582, 115 N.E. (2d), 871.

An adjudication of guilt by a court in a criminal action, pursuant to a plea of not guilty, of course is not admissible as an admission against interest in a subsequent civil action involving the same subject matter. If, therefore, there is a dispute in the record as to whether a plea of guilty was entered, or whether a finding of guilt was made by the court, proof by a preponderance of the evidence must satisfy a trier of the facts that a plea of guilty was entered before such evidence could be considered in the later suit involving the same subject. If this were not the rule, the trier of the facts could only guess or speculate whether an admission against interest existed.

We find no error in this claim.

Judgment affirmed.

STEVENS and HUNSICKER, JJ., concur.

QUESTIONS ON THE OHIO STATUTE

1. The statute quoted in the *Wilcox* case dates to the 19th Century. Why was the first sentence of this provision enacted?

2. How would the principal issue in the *Militello* case have been decided in Ohio? How would the principal issue in the *Militello* case have been decided in Argentina?

Section 5(a) of the Clayton Act, 15 U.S.C. § 15(a), provides, in part, as follows:

> A final judgment or decree . . . rendered in any civil or criminal proceeding brought by or in behalf of the United States under the antitrust laws to the effect that a defendant has violated said laws shall be prima facie evidence against such defendant in any action or proceeding brought by any other party against such defendant under said laws or by the United States . . ., is to all matters respecting which said judgment or decree would be an estoppel as between the parties thereto: *Provided,* That this section shall not apply to consent judgments or decrees entered before any testimony has been taken.

What is the purpose of this provision? Why was the proviso added? Should a guilty plea, or a plea of *nolo contendere* in a criminal antitrust prosecution be considered to be a consent judgment, for purposes of application of the proviso in a subsequent civil action based on the same alleged facts? See, *e.g.*, *Commonwealth Edison Co. v. Allis-Chalmers Mfg. Co.*, 323 F.2d 412 (7th Cir. 1963), *cert. denied,* 376 U.S. 939 (1964), which makes a distinction between pleas of guilty and *nolo contendere*. See also Note, *Nolo Pleas in Antitrust Cases,* 79 HARV. L. REV. 1475 (1966).

QUESTION ON THE EFFECT OF PROVISIONAL DISMISSAL OF CRIMINAL PROCEEDINGS

Suppose that the defendant has been charged with a violation of art. 172 of the Argentine Penal Code. He has been neither acquitted nor convicted; instead, his case has been provisionally dismissed at the stage of preliminary investigation, see p. 235, *supra.* This dismissal does not exclude the possibility of a future prosecution. After a specified time, such a dismissal becomes final; a final dismissal, like an acquittal, bars future prosecution. Before the provisional dismissal becomes final, the victim sues for (a) damages and (b) rescission of his contract with the defendant. What should the civil court do?

The following cases explore the problem, but you should try to work out your answer before you read them.

ENZIO FELIPE MONARI
Criminal and Correctional Chamber of the Capital
1950-IV J.A. 243 (1950)

1st Instance.—Buenos Aires, May 26, 1950, Year of the Liberator General San Martín.—Considering: [Monari, the criminal defendant, allegedly obtained some wood by theft or fraud from Vitali. Monari then sold the wood to Munari, a purchaser in good faith. Monari's prosecution for fraud, instigated by Vitali's complaint, has been provisionally dismissed. Vitali now seeks the aid of the criminal court in getting back the wood.] That in conformity with the provisions of arts. 2412 and 2767 of the Civil Code, the purchaser in good faith of a movable thing that was not stolen nor lost has the power to reject successfully any action of recovery that may be attempted with respect to the said movable thing.

That in the present case Roberto Munari is in said circumstances, having bought in good faith wood that, in addition, was neither stolen nor lost, but obtained by fraud.

In such circumstances, and the preliminary criminal proceedings against Monari, accused of fraud, having terminated with a provisional dismissal that restores things to the state in which they were found at the time of the complaint, it is proper to make definite the delivery of wood which was deposited [in court], to Roberto Munari. The acquisition of that wood by fraud motivated the institution of the present proceeding.—*Jorge Luis Gallegos.*— Before me: *Jorge Aquilar.*

2d Instance.—Buenos Aires, June 16, 1950, Year of the Liberator General San Martín. Considering: [Vitale Vitali appeals from the decision of the court of 1st Instance.] . . . It should be stated that there is no jurisdictional act declaring the existence of a crime, and consequently, it is not proper to consider the juridical assertions relating to civil obligations arising from the alleged facts; such consideration must take place in the appropriate civil court. It is proper here to restore things to the state in which they were found at the beginning of the investigation, as this court has repeatedly decided . . . .

Therefore, . . . the appealed decision is affirmed with costs.—*Jacinto A. Malbrán.*—*Mario A. Oderigo.*—*Oscar J. Cantadore van Straat.*

CHAUVIN v. CIA. GENERAL DE AUTOMOVILES
First and Second Civil Chambers of the Capital (Plenary Session)
3 J.A. 399 (1919)

2d Instance.—Buenos Aires, May 20, 1919.—Is the appealed decision void for having been given before the punishment of the author of the act in the criminal action?

Dr. Pico said:

I think that the procedure adopted by the tribunal of 1st Instance, suspending its decision until the definitive decision of the criminal court is made, keeps in mind the determining reason of art. 1101 of the Civil Code, which is to avoid the danger of having contradictory sentences and the resulting juridical scandal.

The civil decision remains, thus, in suspense as the law wishes, awaiting the decision of the criminal court, which takes precedence, and the authority of res judicata is maintained without retarding the procedure or giving sanction to nullities to the detriment of the parties.

The law does not say in which instance the [civil] action should be suspended; therefore it is fitting to decide that it should be suspended in that instance where the definitive decision is to be pronounced . . . and where contradiction may originate.

. . . The only objection that could be formulated against this procedure would be that the influence of the criminal decision upon the civil action would be adjudged only by the appellate tribunal. But since the latter is authorized to decide for itself on new facts arising after the termination of the period of proof in the 1st Instance, provided that they be pertinent to the case, and the criminal sentence is such a fact, the objection lacks substance.

For these brief considerations I give my vote in the negative.

Drs. Gigena, Helguera, Beltrán and Zapiola agreed in the foregoing vote.

Dr. Juárez Celman said:

I am in disagreement with the solution arrived at by the preceding judges, but I am sure that they would subscribe to the reasons upon which I shall base my opinion. [The doctor quotes art. 1101 of the Civil Code.]

This precept, obviously, is not fulfilled when the civil judge of 1st Instance makes a decision before the penalty or acquittal in the criminal case;
. . . .

* * *

I understand that by this system of accepting accomplished facts even though they may be void ..., one follows as a general rule the convenience of the parties, avoiding reversals in the procedure and prejudicial delays. But let us agree that the same argument can be put forth in regard to all [procedural] nullities, and perhaps one will find that such a plausible solution may not affect the principle of two instances, and a law imposing that solution may be prescribed. But meanwhile, it will be indispensable to follow the system of nullifying and ordering a new decision in the court of 1st Instance.

And if what the law proposes is to avoid the juridical scandal of two contradictory decisions on the same point, and the unedifying spectacle that would result for the parties, for the public and for the seriousness of justice, of two magistrates of different jurisdictions, face to face with equal authority, maintaining the pro and the contra, innocence or guilt, it must be agreed that such a disgrace and spectacle are generated with the same objective impact and, morally, with the same detriment to the principles by which it was hoped to inspire the stability of judicial decisions, when the decision is given by the judge of 1st Instance. . . .

These considerations and those which have served in general in former cases ... decide my vote in the affirmative.

Drs. de la Torre, Repetto, Pera and Giménez Zapiola adhered to the above vote.

Dr. Méndez said:

I am of the opinion that the provisional dismissal in the preliminary criminal instance [*sumario*] authorizes the pronouncement of a decision in the civil action, because it leaves the matter in the same situation in which it was found before the criminal action was put into motion.

But as I should not depart from the terms of the question that has led to the convocation of the full tribunal — since the majority of both chambers is in agreement that the civil action cannot be decided definitely so long as the criminal tribunal has not pronounced sentence, and the dissenters have spoken only in respect to the validity or nullity of the decision of the court of 1st Instance — I shall proceed from this concrete point to occupy myself with the exceptions left for discussion.

[Dr. Méndez agreed with Dr. Juárez Celman that it would be improper for the civil court of 1st Instance to decide a case arising out of an alleged criminal offense before the criminal action arising out of the same act had been decided. Thus, by a six to five vote, the question before the court of 2d Instance was decided affirmatively.]

CAMPOS DE PIANT v. TOSCANO
Civil Chamber of the Capital (Plenary Session)
14 J.A. 857 (1924)

[*2d Instance.*]—Buenos Aires, November 24, 1924.—1st. Is it proper to give a definite decision in the present action?

2d.   In case of an affirmative answer: Is the appealed decision in accordance with law?

Concerning the first question, Dr. Colmo said:

* * *

Here the full tribunal must decide concerning the first question, whether it is proper to give a definite decision, or, to repeat the expressions of the full court, "whether or not the provisional dismissal [in a criminal court] constitutes an obstacle to the giving of a decision in the civil action": . . . .

As I understand it, a definitive decision is proper, without any doubt.

Here, briefly, is the situation: the plaintiff, who was the victim of an automobile accident in which she suffered various injuries, claims indemnification from the owner of the vehicle. But as a result of the preliminary criminal proceeding against the driver . . . (in which there was no definite dismissal but only a provisional one), the defendant argues that the civil court cannot proceed.

* * *

[Dr. Colmo does not base his decision on any lack of identify of parties; he admits that for present purposes the owner and the driver of the vehicle may be regarded as sufficiently identified for the doctrine of res judicata to operate.]

My reasons for this decision would be two others, very different from one another.

The first is based on what follows: arts. 1101 and those following it legislate concerning civil "offenses" and not about quasi offenses (or, in the language of the Code, about "unlawful acts that are not offenses" . . .). There surely are various precepts applicable to quasi offenses, as set forth in art. 1108, but it is equally true that among those precepts, arts. 1101 and those following it do not figure.

From the above follows this conclusion: no prohibition or legal restriction exists regarding quasi offenses. Thus the courts may legally run the risk of giving two contradictory decisions about quasi offenses.

But that is such a harsh conclusion, it clashes so with the reality of things (which is fundamentally identical, in offenses and in quasi offenses), that one could observe contradictions to it in more than one meaning. Perhaps one might have recourse to analogy; one might argue that the possibility of that contradiction requires a preventive which should be created by the jurisprudence if it is not in the laws.

Following the above reasoning, I would prefer this other ground, as less debatable and more sure: a provisional dismissal [of the criminal case] is given (art. 435, C.Cr.Pr.) when there is no proof of the existence of the offense or of the identity of its author. Consequently, a provisional dismissal implies the legal inexistence of any offender, and if there is a suspect he is immediately set free, as happened to the driver in this case. That means that there is no preliminary decision about anyone expressly, and that if the action remains "open," it is so with respect to anyone, the former suspect or any other person who may turn out to be the author of the act (or accomplice or concealer, as may be applicable). In other words, there is no ... "pending" action against the suspect; he is as innocent, legally, as anyone. Later, in the face of new evidence, he might be formally charged if he turns out to be the author of a crime, but the same would happen to anyone who was the real author, since the proceeding remains open ... against whichever person may be the author of the offense, and not against this or that particular person.

* * *

More immediately: with this criterion of awaiting eventual developments, we should create an obstacle that does not exist in the laws. Actually, in any civil action for damages that could entail criminal responsibility (such as an automobile accident, the collapse of a building, etc.) a civil decision would be amiss, even though the respective criminal proceedings might not have been brought against anyone, because an absolving decision in the civil action could turn out to be contradictory to the criminal decision, begun after the civil action.

* * *

Further, it is helpful to keep in mind the lessons of our experience: the preliminary criminal proceeding that is provisionally dismissed contains a 100 percent probability of becoming definitely dismissed. In simple matters, such as the present case, in which there can have been only one person responsible, if it was not possible to gather adequate evidence in the freshness of the first moment, such evidence is even more difficult to obtain later.

* * *

For the rest, it is advisable to note two things:

The first would be this: what is actually harmful in a criminal proceeding is a condemnation, and not an acquittal. Criminal guilt is more intense and grave than civil guilt, and the latter is included in the former. It follows that the person found guilty in the criminal proceeding must be found responsible as well in the civil. The contrary is not necessarily true: acquittal in the criminal proceeding prejudges about the "existence of the principal act," when the decision says there is no act. Whenever that inexistence of the principal act is not found, the criminal acquittal is meaningless; there may have been no criminal intent, there may have been no criminal guilt; nonetheless, there may be civil responsibility since, as I have noted, mere negligence, simple imprudence and even purely vicarious fault can lead to it. Consequently, the provisional dismissal, which is, practically speaking, definite, and based upon the penal responsibility of the author of the act, does not induce any conclusion concerning the respective decision in the civil jurisdiction. The author of the act, having been acquitted criminally, may well be acquitted or condemned in the civil action, since the corresponding responsibilities are different . . . .

The second thing would be this: there is a plenary decision in which it was resolved, on May 20, 1919 [the *Chauvín* case], holding to be void a civil decision imposing liability, given in the face of a provisional dismissal in a preliminary criminal proceeding. But in this respect two things should be noted: 1) the decision was made with a bare majority; 2) although all the judges were in agreement regarding the substantive question (the provisional nature of the dismissal implied that the civil decision would be put off at least until the dismissal became definite), the present meeting of the full tribunal has responded to the need for prompt study of the problem of the influence of the provisional dismissal.

I conclude, then, summarizing my thesis: the preliminary criminal proceeding, which is provisionally dismissed, is a criminal action that at present, is not open against the defendant in the civil action. It is not "pending" against him in the words of art. 1101, and thus it is not a legal obstacle to giving a definite decision on the matter without delay in the civil action.

[The other judges agreed, although two of them noted in their opinions that they considered this decision to overrule the decision in the *Chauvín* case. Since the full court decided that it was proper to give a final decision in the civil action, one of the two chambers went on to decide the case, awarding damages to the plaintiff against the owner of the automobile in the amount of 3,000 pesos.]

PFLAUM v. CAFFARO
Second Civil Chamber of the Capital
64 J.A. 943, 13 La Ley 723 (1938)

1st Instance.—Buenos Aires, May 18, 1937.—Resulting: That Mauricio Pflaum complains against José Cáffaro for recovery of the sum of 7,372.40 pesos, for a civil offense.

[Cáffaro sold Pflaum some 500 gallons of varnish, which Cáffaro had no right to sell. When the authorities took the varnish from Pflaum's possession, he made a criminal complaint against Cáffaro, and against certain other business associates of Cáffaro, including one Spinetta Vidal. In that proceeding, Pflaum complained for the recovery of his damages: 7,000 pesos representing the purchase price that he paid for the varnish, plus 5,000 pesos in general damages (*daño moral*). Cáffaro was provisionally dismissed in the criminal proceeding, while Spinetta Vidal was convicted. Spinetta Vidal was ordered by the criminal court to compensate Pflaum in the amount of 9,000 pesos. The court of 1st Instance in the present civil action agreed that Cáffaro had committed a civil offense, but nonetheless decided that Pflaum was not entitled to any recovery from him. Only the portion of this opinion dealing with the relation between the criminal and civil actions is reprinted here.]

It is true that in the criminal action only Spinetta Vidal was found guilty . . . while the defendant in the present action was provisionally dismissed. But the criminal decision imposed upon Spinetta Vidal the obligation to pay the complainant the sum of 9,000 pesos in civil compensation, and this sum clearly includes the direct damage for which reparation is requested here.

And since art. 29, P.C., has derogated art. 1096, C.C. (as the Court has decided in [two cited cases], among others, the plaintiff cannot seek civil indemnification, independently of the result given on the matter in the criminal action, even though here he may be directing the action against a person who was convicted in the criminal action. There has been a final decision . . . which awards him indemnification for the same injury on which this complaint is based. His right with respect to the reparation of that injury is inevitably tied to the decision that adjudged the injury. It is in the fulfillment of that decision and not in these proceedings, that the extent of the civil indemnification should be established, as well as the plaintiff's right against Cáffaro, who was not convicted.

[The court stated that Pflaum was not entitled to a double recovery. The complaint was dismissed.]—*Tomás D. Casares.*—Before me: *Luis A. Sauze Juárez.*

2d Instance.—Buenos Aires, December 1, 1938.— . . .

* * *

3d. Now, then, the fact that the defendant may have been provisionally dismissed of the criminal accusation cannot be a legal obstacle to a claim against him for indemnification of the damages based on his civil responsibility. It cannot, because the dismissal is not the acquittal foreseen in art. 1103, C.C., and because that civil responsibility does exist, whether it is considered that there was civil fraud on his part, or whether his situation is contemplated from the point of view of nonfulfillment of the contract.

Within the first of the above suppositions [fraud], the conviction of Arnaldo Spinetta Vidal in the criminal action does not prevent the present defendant's being put in the position of a joint debtor, as long as the existence of a civil offense is affirmed, because art. 1081 of the Civil Code so provides, "even though it be a question of an act that might not be punished by criminal law." The responsibility of [Spinetta Vidal] would proceed from the criminal decision and the responsibility of [Cáffaro] from the civil decision; it is of small importance that in regard to this latter, penal guilt might not have been proved, by virtue of the legal provision quoted above.

An unlawful act performed knowingly and with intention to harm a person or the rights of another, constitutes a civil offense in the concept of art. 1072.

And these elements constituting responsibility *ex delictu* in the civil order, are present in this case, to my way of thinking.

* * *

It is accurate that in the criminal action for fraud the plaintiff claimed those damages ... and that only one of the accused, Arnaldo Spinetta Vidal, was ordered to pay damages in the sum of 9,000 pesos together with his imprisonment. But this is also a question of a joint obligation resulting from a civil offense, and solidarity has the function of a guarantee in debtor-creditor relations; and it is undoubtedly the right of the plaintiff to direct his complaint against any of the obligees, regardless of the jurisdiction in which they may have been adjudged responsible (arts. 1081, 669 and 705, C.C.)

[Furthermore, Spinetta Vidal was insolvent, having had civil insolvency proceedings commenced against him. Pflaum had not filed a claim in those proceedings.]

[In addition, the court found that Cáffaro was liable on his contract.] On these grounds, I vote in the negative on the question whether the decision of the court of 1st Instance was in accordance with law. The amount of indemnification having been fixed in the criminal court, it is proper to order the defendant to pay it, but limiting the quantity to what was asked in the complaint. With costs in both instances.

Drs. *Perazzo Naón* and *Quesada* adhered to the above vote.

[The defendant was ordered to pay the plaintiff 7,373.40 pesos, with costs of both instances.]

DOS SANTOS BOTTA v. DE SAN VITO
Civil Chamber of the Capital (Division D)
1961-I J.A. 425, 101 La Ley 145 (1960)

* * *

2d Instance.—Buenos Aires, November 11, 1960.—1st. Is the appealed decision void?

2d. In case of a negative decision on the first question: Is the appealed decision in accordance with the law?

1st question.—Dr. *Cichero* said:

At kilometer 330 of National Route Nº 2 (Buenos Aires to Mar del Plata) there was an accident between an "International" trailer truck owned by José Dos Santos Botta and driven by Humberto Ciarrocchi en route to the Capital, and a private Chevrolet automobile traveling in the opposite direction, driven by its owner Modesto De San Vito, accompanied by his wife and daughter. As a result of the collision one of the truck's gas tanks exploded, causing a fire in both vehicles, the unfortunate consequences of which were the death of San Vito and his daughter, and grave injuries and burns suffered by Sra. De San Vito, Ciarrocchi and a companion of the latter, in addition to the loss of the two vehicles and the trailer.

The complaint originating this action was raised by José Dos Santos Botta against the estate of Modesto De San Vito. In this complaint, Dos Santos Botta claims an indemnity payment of 160,000 pesos for the losses suffered, as well as interest and the costs of the action.

The decision of 1st Instance accepted the claim in part and ordered the defendant to pay the plaintiff 123,080 pesos with interest and costs. Both parties have appealed this decision and in addition, the defendant asks its nullification, which request I shall consider first in order to follow a logical sequence.

2d.   The defendant maintains that the decision of 1st Instance is nullified irremediably because it violates art. 1101, C.C. [which the judge quotes]. The defendant says that the judge of 1st Instance knew of the criminal action for homicide and injuries against Humberto Ciarrocchi, driver of the truck, in the tribunals of the city of Mar del Plata, despite which he gave a decision in this civil action, without previously finding out whether there had been a decision by the criminal court.

[The judge notes that the defendant did not pursue this argument in the court of 1st Instance, and suggests that ordinarily this would be a ground for refusing to consider the argument at the present time.]

3d.   However, art. 1101, C.C., contains a rule of public order ..., so that it can and must be applied by the civil judge on his own motion from the time that he knows of the existence of the criminal action. That knowledge is not doubtful in the present case, since the facts proved in the criminal action constitute part of the evidence that the judge of 1st Instance took into account in giving his decision. Consequently, and independently of the point raised by the defendant, it is proper to examine whether the appealed decision is void.

4th.   [The judge rejects the argument of the plaintiff that the criminal action, since it involved the owner of the truck instead of the driver, did not concern the same parties in the sense required by the doctrine of res judicata.]

5th.   In reply to the other argument upon which the plaintiff bases his opposition to the annulment of the decision, it should be pointed out that the prohibition contained in art. 1101 against giving a civil decision refers as much to the decision of 1st Instance as to that of 2d Instance, because both are equal in their substantive elements. . . .

Nonetheless, it can happen that even though a decision of 1st Instance is given in violation of the rule of art. 1101, its annulment may not be necessary if the harm produced by it is reparable through appeal. In this way, the determining purpose of art. 1101 is followed, suspending the definite decision of the appellate tribunal until the proper legal opportunity, with the advantage of avoiding setbacks in the procedure, a useless unfolding of jurisdictional activity, and harmful expenses and delays for the parties.

However, a plenary decision of the old Civil Chambers (March 20, 1919; 3 J.A. 399) [the *Chauvín* case, p. 273, *supra*], the grounds of which I do not share entirely, rejects that solution and decides that in all cases the decision must be annulled (see also 3 J.A. 531).

I shall not consider the reasons upon which that decision is based — the juridical scandal of contradictory decisions, the suppression of the principle of two instances — because I believe that the doctrine it contains is not applicable in the present case. In truth, . . . it has been shown that in the criminal action brought against Humberto Ciarrocchi for homicides and injuries . . . , a definite acquittal was given five months before the date of the decision of the court of 1st Instance in this civil action. That circumstance alone excludes the present case from the scope of art. 1101. It is not important that the judge of 1st Instance did not know of that criminal decision, since its mere existence removed the legal obstacle — a pending criminal proceeding — that was impeding the giving of a decision in the civil action.

These considerations decide my vote in the negative on the question propounded.

Drs. *Sánchez de Bustamante* and *Fleitas* adhered to the foregoing vote.

[The court decided the second question in the affirmative, and affirmed the decision of the court of 1st Instance.]

DEL GAIZO v. PELLEJERO
Civil Chamber of the Capital (Division B)
1962-V J.A. 443, 107 La Ley 392 (1962)

2d Instance.—Buenos Aires, April 9, 1962.—Is the appealed decision in accordance with law?

[This is an automobile accident case. The court of 1st Instance awarded damages to the plaintiff in the amount of 55,500 pesos. Both parties appealed the decision, and the court of 2d Instance reduced the amount to 42,500 pesos. The part of the opinion that concerns us deals with the subject of *daño moral* — translated by Joannini as "moral injury" — those damages which are not precisely calculable in money, and which are allowable (according to art.

1078, C.C.) only if the act should constitute an offense under criminal law. The problem in this case arises out of the fact that the defendant was released from custody after a final dismissal of his criminal case: the criminal court sentenced him to a fine of 1,000 pesos and one year of special disability (presumably the suspension of his driver's license), but he voluntarily paid his fine while his case was on appeal. Therefore, under art. 64 of the Penal Code, the prosecution had to be dismissed.]

Dr. *Fliess* said:

* * *

It is true, therefore, that there is no penal sentence, because the defendant did not want to take that risk, and had a legal means of avoiding it. But this does not prevent the civil court from following a doctrine already accepted by this chamber, classifying the act within the scope of criminal law, for the sole purpose of providing for the proper indemnification. In this case, that means the reparation of moral injury (art. 1078, C.C.).

It has been decided that the dismissal given by the penal court, based on prescription [*i.e.,* the running of the period of limitations], does not hinder the indemnification for moral injury in the civil action. . . . Similarly, this Civil Chamber (in its Division D and by vote of Dr. Cichero, whose reasoning I share, following Orgaz's systematic interpretation, which brings art. 1078 into logical congruence with the meaning of arts. 1096-1097 and 1101 to 1103, C.C.), recently maintained that "in all cases in which the penal action has ended without punishment and without acquittal — by prescription, amnesty, death, etc. — all danger of contradictory decisions disappears, and consequently, the civil judge fully recovers his freedom to consider whether or not the act that led to indemnification constitutes an offense in criminal law," including among those assumptions that of dismissal, owing to the extinction of the action through payment of the fine, which was precisely what was decided in this case (1957-IV J.A. 40, and Orgas, "El daño resarcible," 1952, No. 62, Chapt. 9, on "moral injury").

* * *

HOWK v. MINNICK
19 Ohio St. 462 (1870)

ERROR to the court of common pleas of Lorain country. Reserved in the district court.

On the 26th of November, 1866, Howk, plaintiff, filed in the court of common pleas his petition, stating: That, on or about the 20th day of March, 1854, he was the owner of certain United States and foreign gold and silver coin, of the value and amount of eight hundred and fifty dollars; that the same was in possession of an kept by the plaintiff in his dwelling-house at Wellington, Ohio; that the defendant, Minnick, in the night season, did unlawfully, feloniously, and with force and violence, against the will of the plaintiff, and without his knowledge, break and enter into said dwelling, and did then and there fraudulently take, steal, and carry away said coin, and convert the same to his own use, and, from that date to the present, fraudulently concealed such taking and concealing of the coin from the plaintiff; and that the defendant's connection with the taking and conversion of the coin was fraudulently concealed from the plaintiff's knowledge. That by reason of the premises the plaintiff has been damaged in, and there is due to the plaintiff from the defendant, the sum of one thousand and six hundred dollars, for which judgment is asked.

The defendant demurred to the petition on two grounds: 1st. It does not state facts sufficient to constitute a cause of action; 2d. It appears from the face of the petition that the cause of action is barred by the statute of limitations.

The demurrer was sustained, and the petition dismissed, and exception taken.

The plaintiff then filed his petition in error in the district court, wherein the case was reserved to this court for decision.

* * *

WHITE, J.   Two questions arise in this case.

The first is, whether the plaintiff's right of action is merged in the crime committed in the taking and conversion of his property; or rather, according to the more modern doctrine in England, is suspended until the determination of a criminal prosecution against the offender.

A great diversity of decision is found in regard to this doctrine in the different States. In some it is recognized in a modified form, while in others its existence is denied.

In the case of the *Boston and Worcester R. R. Co. v. Dana* (1 Gray, 83), it is held, by the supreme court of Massachusetts, that the doctrine of the English law, that for goods stolen no action lies against the felon before the institution of criminal proceedings against him, is not in force in that State. And in the lucid and elaborate opinion of Bigelow, J., the weight of American authority is stated to be in accordance with the conclusion arrived at in that case.

In this State we have no common-law offenses; and looking to the origin of the rule, and the reasons upon which it is founded, in connection with the policy of our system of criminal jurisprudence, we regard its adoption here as unnecessary for the purpose of public justice, and, in the absence of legislation to the contrary, as an unwarranted restriction upon the rights of the citizen.

The next question is, whether the fact that the money was taken under circumstances making the act larceny, and that the defendant concealed his guilt from the plaintiff, prevented the running of the statute of limitations.
* * *

[The court held that the "gist" of the action was not fraud, and that the statute had run, barring the plaintiff's claim.]
* * *

Judgment affirmed.

BRINKERHOFF, C. J., and SCOTT, WELCH, and DAY, JJ., concurred.

CATALA AND WEIR, DELICT AND TORTS:
A STUDY IN PARALLEL, Part I
37 TUL. L. REV.* 573, 582-89 (1963)

[The following is a statement by Dr. Catala.]

THE DISTINCTION BETWEEN CIVIL LIABILITY AND CRIMINAL LIABILITY

The study of primitive civilization[s] shows that they generally merged punishment and compensation. The first manifestations of civil liability take the form of private vengeance, in which are confounded the desire to punish and the desire to obtain compensation. Gradually, payment of a sum of money was substituted for pure vengeance. Each type of harm had its price, a price which had to be paid to the victim or to his heirs. In the beginning, therefore, a first advance consisted in replacing the law of retaliation, *lex talionis,* by an individual penalty which served both to punish and to indemnify.

It was in classical Roman law that a distinction grew up between private wrongs and public wrongs. Certain delicts or wrongs, such as disturbance of the peace at night, for instance, are harmful to the public but inflict no particular harm to any individual. More often, one and the same offense is contrary both to public order and to private interest: theft for instance, or the physical injuries that may result from assault with intent to cause bodily harm. In this last kind of situation Roman law eventually made a distinction between two different actions. A penal action was designed to punish the wrongdoer, a civil action was designed to compensate the victim. In this distinction between two remedies, concerning one set of facts, is to be found the origin of the modern distinction between civil liability and criminal liability.

In Roman law, however, these two standpoints remained more or less intermingled. Roman law always recognized a class of penal wrongs and a

---

class of civil wrongs. In this system, a particular act could be at the same time a penal wrong and a civil wrong, or simply one of these and not the other. However — and this is of fundamental importance — an act could be classified as a wrong, civil or penal, only if it corresponded to the legal definition of a particular wrong, civil or penal. Roman law, like English or American law, knew only particular, nominate wrongs. In this respect, it is perhaps easier to compare the common law with Roman law than with French law. It remains to be seen how there took place the evolution between Roman law and the Civil Code.

Among the civil wrongs known to Roman law was one, provided for in the *Lex Aquilia,* which was concerned in very general terms with harm unlawfully caused to another. The definition of harm in the *Lex Aquilia* lent itself to a wide interpretation. So, when it was found impossible to fit a particular case into one of the narrower categories, it became usual to apply the *Lex Aquilia.* Whereas the other civil wrongs remained restricted by by their legal definition, the Aquilian action showed a tendency to expand indefinitely. In the end this action came to absorb all new categories of liability. Thus was built up the idea that any fault which resulted in damage to another imposed an obligation on the party at fault to repair the damage.

In the older French law, this notion was developed, and in the course of this development the usefulness of having special categories of civil wrongs disappeared. The Canon law, a reflection of Christian morality, probably contributed to this evolution. In any event there came a time, well before the French Revolution, when it was accepted that anyone, by whose fault damage of any kind was caused to another, was obligated to compensate the victim of the damage.[39]

From that time onward, civil liability becomes sharply distinguished from criminal liability. Criminal liability is made up of a list of specific offenses: murder, assault, theft, defamation, and so on. And an act is not punishable unless expressly provided for by the criminal law, which is interpreted strictly. On the other hand, civil liability is not classified according to special wrongs. There is a definition in general terms of a civil wrong, that is to say there is a

---

[39] The development from the Roman to the French system is not easily discerned, but the distinction between compensation and punishment can be seen in the South (the part of the country dominated by Roman law) at any rate by the middle of the twelfth century.

The North was not won over to the idea until later; in the thirteenth century Beaumanoir barely understood the distinction. What is certain is that Domat (1625-95) recognizes the general clause: "All loss and damage which arises from the act of other persons, be it imprudence, carelessness, ignorance of what should have been known or other kindred faults, no matter how trivial, must be made good by the person whose imprudence or other fault gave rise to it. For even although he had no intention to do harm, it is still a wrong he has committed." 1 Domat, Loix Civiles 196 (1702). Compare Boyer, La Notion d'Equité et son Rôle dans la Jurisprudence du Parlement, Melanges Maury 264 (1960); Husson, Les Transformations de la Responsabilité (1947), 2 Marty & Raynaud § 369; 1 Mazeaud & Tunc § 33; Ranjard, La Responsabilité Civile dans Domat (1943); 2 Ripert & Boulanger § 890.

general principle of civil liability. Any act that comes within this general definition of what constitutes a civil wrong makes its author liable in damages.[40]

Such was the state of the law in the early nineteenth century when the [French] Civil Code and Penal Code were drafted. The distinction between the two kinds of liability is quite clear. A criminal offense is an act defined by law and contrary to the public good. A civil wrong is any act which causes harm to another. The same act can be both a crime and a civil wrong (murder, for instance). But not every criminal offense is also a civil wrong, for it may not necessarily cause harm to another person (vagrancy, for example, or being drunk and disorderly in public). Further, not every civil wrong is necessarily a criminal offense, because the harmful act does not always harmfully affect the public good (for example, a motor accident in which no one suffers physical injuries).

The penal offense gives rise to criminal proceedings, prosecuted by officials of the Public Prosecutor's department (*Ministere public*) in the criminal courts, according to the rules of criminal procedure. These proceedings envisage the punishment of the convicted person by penalties that affect him in his person or in his goods. The civil wrong gives rise to a civil action, instituted and pursued by the injured party (a private individual) according to the rules of civil procedure. The object of this action is to make good the damage suffered, and not to punish the guilty party; the plaintiff seeks a personal compensation, generally in the pecuniary form of damages. This action can in any event be brought by the injured party before the civil courts already mentioned. But when the facts have given rise to criminal proceedings, the injured party can join his civil action to the penal action. In such a case the injured party is said to constitute himself a civil party to the criminal proceedings, and

---

[40] There are considerable benefits (balanced by serious inconveniences, however — see 2 Carbonnier § 179) in defining civil liability by means of a *clausula generalis* such as Article 1382. By means of a simple unchanging formula it becomes possible to sanction a lot of very disparate faults, and thus to effect the necessary balance of interests between the freedom of the individual and the exigencies of social life. See 1 Mazeaud & Tunc § 417. Jurists have sometimes been alarmed at what one of them has called "the absorption of rules of law by the principle of civil liability." H. Mazeaud, L' *"absorption" des règles juridiques par le principe de responsabilité civile*, [1935] D. H. chron. 5. Compare 1 Mazeaud & Tunc § 15-2. They have distinguished three aspects of civil liability.

Delict as Sanction. This is its main function, and it is as definitive as were the specific delicts of the Roman law. We shall see later how Article 1382 can be used to repair not only damage caused by acts, that is, positive behavior, but also that caused by omissions.

Delict as Regulation. Delict, in this secondary function, can be used to restrict the exercise of individual rights within just limits. Thus the Court of Cassation has given judgment against a landowner for abusing his right of ownership.

Delict as Supplementation. This final function is the least explored. Before the law of 1912 permitted paternity suits by illegitimate children, the courts used Article 1382 to permit the mother, if seducted by fraud (and the phrase *seduction dolosive* was to become part of Article 340) to recover reparation from her seducer; included in the damage provable was the cost of raising the child. Compare, for paternity suits by adulterine children, which are still prohibited, Montpellier, June 2, 1932, [1932] S.II.48. Thus the significance of Article 1382, and of civil liability in general, becomes clearer. The *clausula generalis,* becomes a *clausula generativa,* pregnant with rights which the legislator had not explicitly recognized but to which the courts, in tune with the developing mores of society, may wish, and by this means are enabled to grant recognition.

both actions are tried by the same jurisdiction, namely the criminal jurisdiction.[41]

* * *

[The following are comments by Professor Weir, based on the English law of torts.]

If we refer, *more Anglico,* to procedure, we have no particular difficulty in distinguishing a crime from a tort. The same act can, of course, give rise to both proceedings, but we are never in any doubt which is which. If, however, we try to distinguish crime without reference to procedure, we immediately re-enter our "thicket of difficulties." "[I]t is, indeed, not possible to discover a legal definition of a crime which can be of value for English law. The reasons for this are to be found in the history of our common law."

That history shows neatly how the reward — the best incentive which young kingdoms can offer to encourage private prosecutions — shades into the compensation which they allow when the power is centralized. Thus the appeal, the vindictive private prosecution, may be seen as filling, until it closed,[45] the gap between the King's indictment and the writ of trespass sued out by the citizen. Trespass itself had the double flavor, and this fact, along with the extent of jurisdiction of the Star Chamber Court, is the primary cause of the difficulty of distinguishing the common law crime from the tort in terms of the act done.

The distinction made in the text — crime goes to punishment, tort to compensation — cannot hold for the common law, which awards punitive

---

[41] Article 2 of the Code of Criminal Procedure provides: "The civil action for reparation of damage caused by a felony, a misdemeanor or a statutory offense is open to all who have personally suffered damage directly caused by the offense." Article 3.1 provides: "The civil action may be brought at the same time and before the same tribunal as the public prosecution."

A person who has suffered any damage resulting directly from a criminal offense may rely on Article 1382 to claim damages from the criminal before the criminal court. Thus a person who, whether intentionally or not, wounds another with a knife will be prosecuted before the criminal judge for intentional or unintentional wounding, and the victim can, before the same judge, claim reparation of his damage.

Who may claim? The victim, of course, and those claiming through him, (subject to the remarks in a later instalment) on the right of relatives and heirs of a victim killed by the crime.

Against whom? In addition to the accused (*prévenu, accusé*) those civilly responsible for him (Article 1384.1, 4, 5, 6 — vicarious liability) and, within limits, the heirs, unless the offender died before the action was even instituted.

By what method? The victim may bring an action before either the civil courts or the criminal courts. But if he chooses the civil forum, he cannot quit it in favor of the criminal forum; the contrary is not true, as the criminal prosecution may be abandoned in favor of the civil suit. In any case, judgment for damages cannot be given until the criminal court has given its verdict — *le criminel tient le civil en état.*

Juristic as well as natural persons may be parties to the suit to protect their economic interests, but subtle distinctions are made when an association tries to bring a civil action before the criminal courts to protect a non-economic interest. See Bouzat, Traité de Droit Pénal § 871 (1951), *Action Civile* in Encyclopédie Dalloz, 1 Droit Civil; Vouin & Leaute, Droit Pénal et Criminologie 387 (1957).

Compare also Granier, *Quelques réflexions sur l'action civile,* [1957] J.C.P.I. 1386; *La partie civile au procès pénal,* 1 Revue de Sciences Criminelles (1958).

[45] 59 Geo. 3, c. 46, *overruling* Ashford v. Thornton, 1 B. & A. 405, 106 Eng. Rep. 149 (1818).

damages in tort suits.[47] Nor can the distinctions between the specificity of the conditions of criminal liability and the generality of the conditions of liability in tort help us. Crime and tort are equally specific in our system, and although the judges, more tender to liberty than the pocket, are often restrictive in dealing with crimes,[48] it is not beyond them either to invent new crimes[49] or deny new torts.[50]

On the procedural plane, at any rate, the distinction is complete; the common law does not know the *parti civile*. It is surprising then to find an exact parallel to *le criminel tient le civil en état*. It is the old rule that if a trespass was also a felony, no civil action would lie until after prosecution.[52] The aim of this was to protect the King's right to the property in the possession of the felon from the claims of his delictal creditors. But a more important consequence is that, even today, there is no principle that the victim of a crime may sue in tort.

For many years after the promulgation of the French Civil Code, the most striking example of this was criminal homicide, which was civilly neutral;[54] even today it has only those consequences which the legislator has specifically endorsed.[55] But there are other examples. If the victim of an assault consented to it, the assailant will go to jail, but will not pay damages. A person may be convicted of libel, but not civilly held, if either what he wrote was true or he published it only to the person defamed. An infant fraudulently obtaining credit may be criminally punished; the person defrauded has no action.[59]

Modern legislatures are constantly busy making acts of one sort or an-

---

[47]*E.g.*, Loudon v. Ryder, [1953] 2 Q.B. 202 (£1,000 compensatory and £3,000 punitive damages for assault).

[48]The crabbed common law view of *nullum crimen sine lege* appears to be nothing more than a facet of judicial dislike of legislative encroachments on the common law. Thus a shopkeeper who displayed in his window a flick-knife with a price tag was held not guilty of an offense under the Restriction of Offensive Weapons Act, 1959, 7 & 8 Eliz. 2, c. 37, § 1: "Any person who manufactures sells or hires or offers for sale or hire or lends or gives to any other person . . . a 'flick-knife' . . . shall be guilty of an offence." Fisher v. Bell [1961] 1 Q.B. 394 (Div. Ct.).

[49]*E.g.*, Shaw v. D.P.P., [1962] A.C. 220 (conspiracy to corrupt public morals); Rex v. Manley, [1933] 1 K.B. 529 (Public mischief). They can also resuscitate old ones. *E.g.*, Sykes v. D.P.P., [1962] A.C. 528 (Lord Denning): "If Staunford, Coke, Hale and Blackstone all say there is such an offence as misprision of felony, are we to say the contrary?" *Id.* at 559.

[50]*E.g.*, Hargreave v. Bretherton, [1959] 1 Q.B. 45 (no tort of perjury); Best v. Samuel Fox & Co., [1952] A.C. 716 (No tort of negligently injuring a wife's consortium).

[52]Smith v. Selwyn, [1914] 3 K.B. 98 (C.A.;) Markham v. Cob, Latch 144, 82 Eng. Rep. 316 (1625.) Indeed at one time it was held that if the act was a felony, it could not be a tort at all: "[T]he felony drowns the particular offence and private wrong offered to the master before and his action is thereby lost." Higgins v. Butcher, Yelv. 89, 80 Eng. Rep. 61 (1607) (Tanfield, J.)

[54]"In civil court the death of a human being cannot be complained of as an injury." Baker v. Bolton, 1 Camp. 493, 170 Eng. Rep. 1033 (1808). The rule was heavily criticized, and was modified by the Fatal Accidents Act, 1846, 9 & 10 Vict. c. 93, and subsequent legislation.

[55]Admiralty Comm'rs v. S.S. Amerika, [1917] A.C. 38; Young v. McCullium, 74 So.2d 339 (La. App. 1954).

[59]None in contract since it is utterly void, see Infants Contracts Act, 1874, 37 & 38 Vict. c. 62. § 1; none in tort, since it is too closely connected with the contract (sed quaere), R. Leslie Ltd. v. Sheill, [1914] 3 K.B. 607 (C.A.); none under the statute since it purports to give no civil action.

other punishable, often without *mens rea;* but the courts of England have shown "a general bias against the construction of penal statutes to create torts."[60] The victim of such a punishable act must show that the legislature specifically intended to give a civil action for damages.[61] Even where the statute is admitted to have given a civil action, the victim must bring himself within the class it intended to protect and show that the damage suffered is the very type of harm it intended to repair. The courts of the United States, with their doctrine of negligence per se, are rather more prepared to allow the victim of an act made punishable by statute to recover damages on proof of illegality and causation alone.

Finally, in one case success in the tort action is dependent on the criminal character of the act impugned. In the tort of public nuisance, the plaintiff must show that the Attorney-General could have obtained an injunction against the defendant; that done, he must go on to establish damage sustained by him over and above that suffered by the lieges at large.

Louisiana presents a classic confrontation between the common law of crimes and a law of delict originally civilian. The successive statutes speak for the development: in 1825 "personal actions arise from offenses, as when one has become liable to another for the injury he has inflicted on him by some crime or offense, such as theft or slander."[66] In 1870 the felony-trespass rule had to be specifically excluded: "In all criminal cases where injury to the person or property has been sustained, the party injured or damaged shall have his civil action for damages notwithstanding the conviction."[67]

Today all interconnection is cut: "[T]he person injured by the commission of a crime is no party to the criminal proceeding, and his rights are in no wise affected by such proceedings or by the result thereof,"[68] and "Nothing in this Code shall affect any civil remedy provided by the law pertaining to civil matters. . . ."[69]

[The other parts of this useful comparative series are in 38 TUL. L. REV. 221 (1964); 38 *id.* at 664 (1964); and 39 *id.* at 701 (1965). — Ed.]

---

[60] Salmond, Torts 490 (13th ed. 1961).

[61] The imposition of a criminal penalty may even be evidence that it was not the legislator's intention to give a civil remedy. Atkinson v. Newcastle & Gateshead Waterworks Co., 2 Ex.D. 441 (1877).

[66] La. Code of Prac. art. 31 (1825).

[67] La. R.S. § 985 (1870).

[68] La. R.S. 15:1 (1950).

[69] La. R.S. 14:6 (1950).

Chapter III

THE SOURCES OF COMMERCIAL LAW

The European civil law systems of private law had divided into two branches — commercial and "civil" (non-comercial) — well before the codification movement of the 19th Century embedded the distinction in legislative concrete, separately codifying civil and commercial law. At present, the great majority of European and Latin American private law systems are divided this way, although there is currently a counter-movement toward the unification of private law in single integrated codes, following the examples of Switzerland and Italy. The basic question examined in this chapter is the utility of a distinction that preserves separate rules of law and even a separate court system for the resolution of disputes found to be "commercial."

The following excerpts from the Commercial Code of Argentina are followed by several judicial decisions which draw and revise some of the boundaries of commercial law. Without looking at those cases, and using only the articles of the Code, which of these events and transactions would you classify as "commercial?"

1. A housewife buys a set of dishes from another housewife.

2. A housewife buys ten shares of company stock from another housewife, without using intermediaries.

3. A housewife buys ten shares of company stock through a stock exchange; the seller of the shares is another housewife.

4. A banker buys flowers from a flower merchant, for use in decorating his bank. (Would you reach a different conclusion if the banker bought the flowers to take home to his wife?)

5. A dealer in wines buys ten cases of wine from another dealer in wines.

6. A dealer in wines buy an automobile from another dealer in wines.

7. Two dealers in wines collide while driving their automobiles from a sales demonstration.

8. A building contractor builds a building on another's land.

9. A dealer in land subdivides a tract and sells ten lots to another dealer in land.

COMMERCIAL CODE OF ARGENTINA* (1889)
Preliminary Title

I.   The provisions of the Civil Code shall apply to cases which are not specifically governed by this Code.

II.   In matters in which private agreements may vary the general law, the nature of the acts authorizes the judge to inquire whether reference to custom is essential to the act in order to give contracts and acts their due effect according to the presumed intention of the parties.

III.   Judges are forbidden to issue general or governing resolutions, their duty being always to limit themselves to the particular case which they are trying.

IV.   It is competent solely to the Legislative Power to interpret the law in such a way as to bind everyone.

Such an interpretation shall take effect from the date of the interpreted law; but cannot apply to cases already finally concluded.

V.   Mercantile customs may supply rules for the determination of the meaning of the technical words or phrases of commerce and for the interpretation of mercantile acts and agreements.

Book I.   Of Commercial Persons
Title I.   Of Merchants
Chapter 1.   Of Merchants in General and Acts of Commerce

1.   The law declares to be merchants all individuals who, having legal capacity to contract, practice on their own account acts of commerce, making that their habitual profession.

2.   As a general rule, every person who makes a profession of buying or selling merchandise is termed a merchant. Particularly is he termed a merchant who buys and manufactures merchandise in order to sell it at wholesale or retail.

Booksellers, haberdashers and shopkeepers of every class who sell merchandise which they have not manufactured are also merchants.

3.   Retail merchants are those who habitually, as regards things which are measured, sell by meters or liters; as regards things which are weighed, by less than ten kilograms, and as regards things which are counted, by separate parcels.

4.   Those businessmen who are engaged in ventures abroad are merchants, as well as those who limit their trade to the interior of the State, and

---

* These articles were translated with the aid of Vol. I of THE COMMERCIAL LAWS OF THE WORLD (Scrutton and Bowstead ed. 1911-14), but numerous departures from that text have been made.

whether they are engaged in a single branch or in several branches of commerce at the same time.

5. All who according to the law possess the quality of merchants are subject to the commercial jurisdiction, regulations and legislation.

Acts of merchants are always presumed to be acts of commerce, in the absence of evidence to the contrary.

6. Those who perform casual acts of commerce are not considered merchants. Nevertheless, so far as concerns disputes which arise over such transactions, they are subject to the commercial laws and jurisdiction.

7. If an act is commercial as to only one of the parties, all the contractors are, by reason thereof, subject to the mercantile law, except for the provisions respecting the persons of merchants, and unless it appears from the provisions of the said law that it refers only to the contractor as to whom the act has a commercial character.

8. The law declares to be acts of commerce in general:

1. Every acquisition for valuable consideration of a movable or of a right over a movable, in order to profit by its alienation, whether in the same state in which it was acquired or after giving it another form of greater or less value;

2. The alienation to which the previous paragraph refers;

3. Every exchange, brokerage and auction transaction;

4. Every transaction in bills of exchange or local bills; checks and every other kind of paper whether endorsable or to bearer;

5. Undertakings for manufacturing, factoring, commercial agencies, depositories [bailments] and transportation of merchandise or persons by water or land;

6. Insurance, and limited companies, whatever may be their object;

7. Affreightments, construction, buying and selling of vessels, equipment, provisions and everything relating to maritime commerce;

8. Transactions of factors, bookkeepers and other merchants' employees, so far as concerns the business of the merchant to whom they are subordinate;

9. Agreements about salaries of subordinates and other employees of merchants;

10. Letters of credit, guarantees, pledges and other accessories of a commercial transaction;

11. Other acts specifically subjected to this Code.

* * *

Chapter 3. The Register of Merchants

25. In order to enjoy the protection which this Code gives to commerce and the persons of the merchants, the latter must be registered at the

Commercial Court of their address. If there is not a Commercial Court there, the register shall be kept at the corresponding Court of the Justice of the Peace.

26.   All merchants inscribed on the register enjoy the following advantages:

      1.   The credit given to their books in accordance with Art. 63;

      2.   The right of applying for composition with their creditors;

      3.   License to trade.

[Art. 26, Parts 4 and 5, repealed by Art. 207 of the Bankruptcy Law, formerly included discharge and the right to act as assignee in insolvency proceedings.]

      * * *

In order that the inscription may have legal effect it must be made at the commencement of the business, and when the merchant is not under the necessity of invoking the privileges mentioned.

27.   The inscription of the merchant must be made in the Register of Commerce by the applicant presenting a petition which contains:

      1.   His name, status and nationality, and if there is a partnership, the names of the partners and the partnership name adopted;

      2.   A statement of the nature of the trade or business;

      3.   The place or address of the establishment or office;

      4.   The name of the manager, factor or employee whom he places at the head of the establishment.

28.   Minors, children of the family and married women must add these descriptions of their civil capacity.

29.   Inscription in the Register will be ordered by the Commercial Court or Justice of the Peace without charge, whenever there is no reason to doubt that the applicant enjoys the credit and probity which ought to characterize a merchant of his class.

      The Justices of the Peace shall send each month a list of the persons registered to the Commercial Court, which shall cause them to be added to the Register.

30.   The Commercial Court shall refuse registration if it finds that the applicant has not legal capacity to practice commerce, saving a right of appeal to the superior court by a person who thinks himself aggrieved.

      If the refusal is made by a Justice of the Peace, the appeal shall be to the Commercial Court.

31.   Every alteration made by merchants in the particulars specified in Art. 27 shall be brought to the cognizance of the Court with the same solemnities and results.

32.   A person who is inscribed on the register is considered to possess the quality of merchant, with all the legal effects, from the day of inscription.

TITLE II. OBLIGATIONS COMMON TO ALL MERCHANTS
Chapter 1. General Provisions

33. Those who make commerce a profession, contract thereby the obligation to submit themselves to all acts and forms enacted by the mercantile law.

Among these acts are:

1. Inscription in a public register, both of the list of merchants and of the documents which require the same according to the law;

2. The duty of pursuing a uniform system of bookkeeping and of keeping the books necessary to that end;

3. The preservation of the correspondence which has relation to the merchant's business as well as of all books of account;

4. The duty to render accounts as required by the law.

* * *

TITLE IV. AUXILIARY COMMERCIAL AGENTS

87. The following are considered auxiliary commercial agents and, as such, subject to the commercial laws with respect to transactions which they carry out in that character:

1. Brokers;

2. Auctioneers;

3. Warehousemen and managers of depositories;

4. Managers and subordinate commercial employees;

5. Carters, carriers and transport-contractors.

* * *

BOOK II. OF COMMERCIAL CONTRACTS
TITLE I. OF COMMERCIAL CONTRACTS AND OBLIGATIONS IN GENERAL

Chapter 1. Of Contracts and Obligations in General

207. The civil law applies to commercial matters and business, so far as it is not altered by this Code.

208. Commercial contracts may be proved:

1. By public [notarial] instruments;

2. By notes made by brokers, and by certified extracts from their books;

3. By private documents, signed by the contracting parties, or by some witness at their request and in their name;

4. By written or telegraphic correspondence;

5. By merchants' books and by accepted invoices;

6. By admission of the party and by oath;

7. By witnesses.

Presumptions are also admissible according to the rules enacted in the present title.

209. Proof by witnesses is only admissible in contracts the value of which does not exceed two hundred silver pesos, except in the cases expressly mentioned in this Code.

In matters involving a larger amount, oral proof shall only be admitted after a foundation of written evidence.

Any document, whether public or private, which emanates from the opposite side, from its author or from a party interested in the defense or who would be interested if he were alive, is considered as a foundation of written evidence for this purpose.

* * *

217. The words of contracts and agreements must be understood in the sense which general use gives them, although the person bound thereby claims that he has understood them otherwise.

218. The following shall afford the bases of interpretation, when it is necessary to interpret the clauses of a contract:

1. When there is ambiguity in the words, the mutual intention of the parties should be sought rather than the literal meaning of the terms;

2. Equivocal or ambiguous clauses must be interpreted by means of clear and precise terms employed elsewhere in the same document, taking care to give them, not so much the meaning which generally suits them, as that which belongs to them from the effect of the general context;

3. Clauses which are susceptible of two meanings, from one of which would result the validity and from the other the nullity of the transaction, must be understood in the former sense. If both would equally give validity to the transaction, they must be taken in the sense which most agrees with the nature of contracts and the rules of equity;

4. The acts of the contracting parties subsequent to the contract, which have relation to the matter in dispute, will afford the best explanation of the intention of the parties at the time of making the contract;

5. Transactions of merchants are never presumed to be gratuitous;

6. The usage and practice generally observed in commerce in cases of like nature, and especially the custom of the place where the contract is to be performed, shall prevail over any contrary meaning which it is attempted to give to the words;

7. In doubtful cases which cannot be decided according to the foregoing established bases, ambiguous clauses must always be interpreted in favor of the obligor, that is to say, with a meaning which shall relieve him.

219. If in drawing up a contract any term is omitted which is necessary to its performance, and the interested parties are not agreed as to the true meaning of the bargain, it is presumed that they are subject to the usage and

practice in such cases among the merchants in the place of the performance of the contract.

* * *

TITLE IV. MERCANTILE CONTRACT OF SALE

450. A mercantile contract of sale is a contract by which one person, whether owner or possessor of the thing which is the subject matter of the agreement or not, binds himself to deliver it to or cause another person to acquire it in ownership, who on his part binds himself to pay the agreed price, and who purchases it in order to resell it or lease the use thereof.

451. A purchase of movables is considered mercantile only when it is made in order to resell them at wholesale or retail (whether in the same form as that in which they were bought or in a different form), or to lease their use, the term "movables" including bullion, State bonds, shares in companies and commercially negotiable instruments.

452. The following are not considered mercantile:

1. Purchases of immovable property and accessory movables. Nevertheless, purchases of things which are accessory to commerce, or which prepare or facilitate the same are commercial although they be accessory to real property;

2. Purchases of things intended for the consumption of the buyer, or of the person on whose order the acquisition is made;

3. Sales made by farmers and landowners of the produce of their harvests and herds;

4. Those made by owners and any other class of person, of produce and goods which they receive by way of rent, gift, salary, emolument or any other title whether by way of reward or gratuity;

5. The resale made by any person of the remains of the stores which he has acquired for his private consumption. Nevertheless, if the quantity which he sells is greater than that which he has consumed, it is presumed that he acted in the purchase with the intention of selling, and the purchase and sale are considered to be mercantile.

* * *

THE COMMERCIAL CODES: STRUCTURE AND CONTENTS

The four books of Argentina's original Commercial Code bore these titles:

> Of Commercial Persons
> Of Commercial Contracts

Of Rights and Obligations Resulting from Navigation
Of Bankruptcy

This four-part division came from the Spanish Commercial Code of 1829. Although Spain's Civil Code of 1889 came too late to influence legislation in America, its Commercial Code was highly influential. The Spanish Code was itself a modified — most would say improved — version of the French Commercial Code of 1807, and most of France's influence on the commercial legislation of the New World was indirect, through Spain.

The Argentine Commercial Code of 1889, still in force, is a revised version of an earlier code prepared by Dr. Vélez Sársfield (later the chief architect of the Civil Code) and a distinguished Uruguayan, Dr. Eduardo Acevedo, for adoption by the Province of Buenos Aires in 1859. Their original code was adopted for the whole Argentine nation in 1862, and then by Uruguay in 1866, only slightly modified. The Argentine Commercial Code thus antedates the Civil Code by some seven years. It is said that the Brazilian Commercial Code of 1850, the first in this hemisphere, was the model for Drs. Acevedo and Vélez Sársfield; one of the chief influences on the Brazilian Code was Spain's 1829 Code.

The Commercial Code of Argentina is typical of the commercial codes of Latin America in several ways. Its derivation is mixed; much of it comes from Spain, but the draftsmen borrowed freely from other models, particularly in Latin America. Its contents are not comprehensive as seen against the whole range of modern commerce, but are limited to the definition of merchant status, the creation of some special rules for merchants, and the establishment of rules of law for various specified types of commercial contracts, after the fashion of the "Obligations" portions typical of civil codes.

Nevertheless, civilian commercial codes do purport to govern all commercial activity. They are far more comprehensive in their coverage than is the Uniform Commercial Code, now well on the way to universal adoption in the United States. The nine articles of the UCC are:

1. General Provisions (construction, definitions, etc.)
2. Sales
3. Commercial Paper
4. Bank Deposits and Collections
5. Letters of Credit
6. Bulk Transfers
7. Warehouse Receipts, Bills of Lading and Other Documents of Title
8. Investment Securities
9. Secured Transactions; Sales of Accounts, Contract Rights
   and Chattel Paper

In the civilian sense, the UCC is not really a "code." See Schlesinger, *The Uniform Commercial Code in the Light of Comparative Law*, 1 INTER-AM.

L. REV. 11, especially at 22-25 (1959); other parts of Professor Schlesinger's valuable article are reprinted at the end of this chapter.

The commercial codes of Latin America have been heavily modified by succeeding legislation. In Argentina, the fourth book (bankruptcy) has been wholly repealed and the subject is covered by a separate bankruptcy law. In Mexico, some two-thirds of the articles of the Code have been changed. Regulatory legislation has tended to leave the civil codes relatively unscathed, but the commercial codes have been seriously affected. One prominent annotated version of the Argentine Commercial Code appears in four volumes, only two of which are devoted to the Code itself; the other two volumes include supplementary legislation, covering such subjects as aeronautics, bankruptcy, chain store regulation, patents, trade marks, and customs agency regulation.

ALFANO
Civil and Commercial Chambers of the Capital (Plenary Session)
32 J.A. 438 (1929)

[The commercial law of bankruptcy *(quiebra)* in Argentina is somewhat more favorable to the creditors of the bankrupt than is the civil law of insolvency *(concurso)*. In this case the bankrupt, Alfano, a building contractor, commenced civil insolvency proceedings. The assignee (for the benefit of Alfano's creditors) moved for a dismissal of the proceedings on the ground that the civil court did not have jurisdiction, since Alfano's business was commercial in nature, and thus subject to the bankruptcy provisions of the Commercial Code. It was argued that Alfano's business was commercial because he furnished the materials for the buildings that he constructed. He was thus considered by the assignee to be engaged in the sale of "goods." It was well established in the decisions of the courts of civil jurisdiction that the business of a building contractor was not commercial; on the other hand, the courts of commercial jurisdiction had concluded the opposite, after some vacillation. The leading case on the civil side was *La Cattiva Fernando,* 5 J.A. 25 (1914). In effect, the assignee in the present case was asking that the *La Cattiva Fernando* case be overruled. The judge of 1st Instance followed the precedent of the courts of civil jurisdiction, and denied the motion of the assignee. Because of the conflict between the two sides of the Court, both were convened to sit in plenary session as the court of 2d Instance.]

2d Instance. [p. 461]—Buenos Aires, December 27, 1929.—Are construction enterprises civil or commercial?

Concerning the question stated, Dr. Colmo said:

Each of these theses has been maintained in at least one decision by the respective judges of civil insolvency and commercial bankruptcy, with reasoning that merits due attention, the more so since it is a question of reviewing the plenary jurisprudence* established in 1914 by the civil chambers, and by other plenary jurisprudence of those chambers and of the commercial chamber. Criteria as well as times may have changed, and it is most proper to settle the orientation of the tribunals again.

The problem is not easy. I shall have to study it in respect to the principles written in the laws, in respect to the antecedents of those laws, and in respect to the juridical spirit of our epoch, by the light of which we interpret the positive texts.

Naturally, a building contractor, individual or associated [*sociedad:* partnership or corporation], is a person who hires work. The occupation is explicitly studied in the Civil Code, and omitted from the Commercial Code. Moreover, the Civil Code also considers the hypothesis that the builder may supply materials (art. 1629). In the face of this, the civil jurisdiction seems undoubtable.

But the following is argued on the basis of art. 8, par. 1, of the Commercial Code: the builder who supplies materials, as in this case, buys the necessary things for construction and re-sells them, transformed or changed, to the tenant or owner, making a profit in the process. We have here the typical characteristic of commercial conduct. For the same reason, the general provisions on the hiring of work in the Civil Code are annulled by the specific provisions of the Commercial Code.

I find that there is much to be said for such a point of view.

* * *

But even assuming that the builder provides the materials, this is far from the legal supposition of the Commercial Code: acquisition of a movable object in order to derive a profit from its transfer to another. The builder does not acquire materials in order to resell them. He acquires them in order to do his work. This acquisition is simply the means to an end, an accessory to the principal act. And we do not imagine that the means, the accessory act, should have to answer for the end, the principal act. The only certainty is that the owner is the one who pays for the materials finally, although the builder may have acquired them in his own name and paid for them previously from his own pocket. But this is reconciled as a kind of tacit authorization, by virtue of which the builder, since he knows materials and prices better, acts in his own name but in the interest of the owner, and in fact, he becomes an agent or intermediary.

It is argued that the builder charges more than he pays and that in this is the speculative, the profitable, commercial element. But that is pure supposition. The builder has no reason to turn to such an expedient. In the bill that he presents there is no price for the materials. The price he asks of the owner is for the work, sometimes in toto, sometimes in its fundamental parts

---

* *I.e.,* the case law established by the various chambers sitting in plenary session, or *en banc.*
— Ed.

(masonry, iron work, paint, etc.). Finally, the price includes the remuneration of the builder: a fictitious salary, a percentage above the value of the work (as happens with architects, etc.). . . .

* * *

[This opinion goes on in the same vein for many more paragraphs. The citations are all to textbooks on Argentine and European commercial law. The argument is almost entirely of the same deductive nature.]

Thus my vote: however much I may deplore the solution at which I arrive — since, among other things, the commercial rule would contain preventive or repressive virtues . . . that the civil rule would not contain so perfectly for situations of insolvency such as the present case — I have not been convinced of the commercial nature of a construction enterprise, and thus in my judgment it is proper to declare the same to be civil.

* * *

[Dr. Colmo's views did not prevail. Of the ten judges sitting in plenary session, eight voted against the jurisdiction of the civil court in the insolvency proceedings. Those who voted with the majority did so for two main reasons: some considered the case of a building contractor to be sufficiently analogous to that of a manufacturer so that the provisions of art. 8, par. 5 of the Commercial Code would govern. Others in the majority did not share this view; all of them, however, agreed that a building contractor who furnishes materials for the job is engaging in the acquisition of movable property for the purpose of making a profit through its transfer to another person. Such acts are declared to be acts of commerce in art. 8, par. 1 of the Commercial Code. The precedent of *La Cattiva Fernando* was rejected. The *Alfano* case thus became the new leading case.]

GRILLI
Second Civil Chamber of the Capital
44 J.A. 209 (1933)

1st Instance.—Buenos Aires, September 14, 1932.—Considering: That the result of the combined provisions of arts. 8 and 452 of the Commercial Code is, unquestionably, that a transaction concerning immovable property and its accessories is not an act of commerce nor is it considered mercantile (Malagarriga, vol. 1, p. 42, and vol. 2, p. 8; Segovia, vol. 1, p. 30, note 38; Siburu, vol. 2, p. 87; Obarrio, vol. 1, p. 43). This was the thesis adopted by the reform Commission for the Commercial Code, as may be seen in its report (Siburu, vol. 1, p. 230). And in view of the categorical terms of the report, although one may debate doctrinally the unfitness of such a system (see Segovia, vol. 1, p. 30, and Cermesoni, "Contratos comerciales," p. 47), it is proper for judges simply to apply the law without entering into a discussion of its usefulness (art. 59 of the Code of Procedure).

That even if the acquisition of an immovable had as its object the later construction of a building on it, and the realization of a profit from its sale, such an act would not be of a commercial nature for our legal system, because "buildings are only accessories of the ground and for that reason they become immovables" (note to art. 2313 of the Civil Code). Thus the transaction falls outside the provisions of the commercial law.

That for these considerations it is useless to analyze the evidence produced, which evidence tends to demonstrate the commercial quality of the alleged insolvent who performed such acts. This circumstance, it may be said in passing, has not been established.

For these considerations and in conformity with the opinion expressed by the Deputy Fiscal, the opposing argument advanced by the creditor Salvador Gallo is rejected, with costs.—*Ricardo F. Olmedo.*

2d Instance.—Buenos Aires, November 8, 1933.—By reason of its grounds, the appealed pronouncement is affirmed.—*Raymundo M. Salvat* [author of a leading treatise on civil law].—*César de Tezanos Pinto.*—*Juan Carlos Lagos.*

LASALLE
Second Civil Chamber of the Capital
1945-III J.A. 52, 38 La Ley 58 (1945)

1st Instance.—Buenos Aires, October 4, 1944. Considering: That the moving party, as a creditor of Lasalle, opposes the opening of insolvency proceedings, maintaining that Lasalle is a merchant because for some time he has been engaged in commercial activities and has made that his regular profession.

That from the facts in the record it is shown that Lasalle ... purchased and constructed buildings on properties valued at more than 5,000,000 pesos in the short space of little more than three years. He sold them for the most part immediately after the termination of the construction work, for the sum of approximately 3,000,000 pesos.

[Lasalle asks for the insolvency proceedings in order to discharge his obligations for materials, and so forth.]

That the jurisprudence of the tribunal in plenary session of December 27, 1929, recorded in the "Gaceta del Foro," vol. 84, p. 43 [the *Alfano* case], established that "Construction businesses, except when their participation is limited to the technical direction and supervision of the work, carry on commercial work and consequently are subject to the commercial jurisdiction."

That this jurisprudence is strictly applicable in the present case, inasmuch as the building [contractor] supplied the materials on his own account and directly executed the works. Because of this, in the judgment of the court, his activity must be understood as an act of commerce, because the transactions carried on by Lasalle could be accepted as being of a civil nature only in the hypothetical case that the person for whom he worked supplied the materials to him.

For these considerations, and because the case is found to be included in the provisions of art. 8, par. 1, Commercial Code, it is resolved to allow the opposition to the opening of the insolvency proceedings and consequently, there is no place for the petitioned civil insolvency; with costs . . . .—*José F. Oderigo.*—Before me: *Jorge P. Funes Lastra.*

Opinion of the Fiscal of the Chamber [to the court of 2d Instance].— Essentially, the act of buying lands in order to build on them and sell them does not constitute a commercial act; thus the commercial bankruptcy is not allowable and the civil insolvency proceeding is, as Your Honors decided in the opinion recorded in the "Gaceta del Foro," vol. 107, p. 161 [*Grilli,* 44 J.A. 209]. And in the judgment of this ministry, the incidental manifestations made by the obligor and obligee are not sufficient to be distinguished from that doctrine established by the tribunal in the previous decision.

Furthermore, there is an urgent necessity for the designation of an assignee in insolvency, given the situation created by the facts in the record, in order to safeguard the interests of the insolvent estate.

By virtue of the foregoing, and without prejudice to the timely renewal of the proceedings by new creditors or to the emergence of other elements in the proceedings that will bring out different aspects of the question, I am of the opinion that Your Honors should revoke the appealed decision.—*Manuel C. Olmos.*

2d Instance.—Buenos Aires, April 23, 1945.—By reason of its grounds, and because the doctrine established by this tribunal in the decision cited in the preceding opinion is not applicable to the case (since the two have different characteristics), and because the *Alfano* case is indeed applicable, the opinion of the *Fiscal* having been presented, the decision is affirmed, with costs.— *Raúl Perazzo Naón.*—*César de Tezanos Pinto.*—*Roberto E. Chute.*

Suppose that the parties to a building construction contract agree that in the event of a dispute, the civil courts shall have jurisdiction to decide any lawsuits between them. Is such a stipulation valid? In *Miceli v. Stacco,* 1952-III J.A. 121, 66 La Ley 249 (1952), the plaintiff landowner sued the defendants, his architect and building contractor, in a commercial court, seeking fulfillment of the contract and delivery of the completed building. A contractual stipulation of jurisdiction in the civil courts was pleaded by way of challenge to the court's jurisdiction. The challenge was rejected by the commercial courts at all stages of the proceeding, with prominent citations to the *Alfano* case.

Why should the parties not be permitted to specify by contract which court shall decide their disputes? Are the expert qualifications of the commercial judges relevant to your answer? Suppose that a question of commercial law arises collaterally in a civil court; should that court decide the question?

GIRALDI, COMERCIALIZACION DE LA COMPRAVENTA DE INMUEBLES 1961-II J.A.* 69 (1961)

[This is a comment on a decision by the Commercial Chamber of the Capital (Division B) in the case of *Sovieri v. Acerbo*, 1961-II J.A. 69 (1960). In that case, the plaintiff landowner had contracted to have a reinforced concrete apartment house built on his land. He also contracted with the three defendants to sell three of the completed apartments to them. His arrangement with the building contractor was that the concrete work would be paid from the proceeds of the sales of the three apartments. The defendants attacked the jurisdiction of the commercial court, arguing that the sale of the apartments was a civil transaction under art. 452(1) of the Commercial Code. Because of the close connection of those sale contracts with the construction contract, however, both the court of 1st Instance and the Chamber on appeal upheld the jurisdiction of the commercial court.]

The principle contained in the decision — recognizing the mercantile nature of a sale of immovable properties — establishes a notable exception to the general provisions of the Commercial Code, arts. 8, 451, and 452.

The Chamber decided a question of jurisdiction, affirming that the acquisition of three living units in an apartment house is a commercial act, inasmuch as the sale contracts — given the circumstances of the case — prove to be accessory to the hiring of work for the construction of the reinforced concrete building. The unquestionable mercantile character of the principal juridical relation implies the commercial nature of the accessory relations. *Jurisdiction* [according to the Chamber] *is determined by the nature of the act, not by accession to the* causa, *which appears to be the basis of the decision of the court of 1st Instance.* We are not presented, then, with a civil act, such as a mortgage [*hipoteca*], which acts as an accessory to a commercial act which establishes the commercial jurisdiction, but rather we have an act of commerce in itself.

The indicated difference is very serious, for a civil contract that could be extended into the commercial jurisdiction in exceptional circumstances is one

---

thing, and the precise essence — civil or commercial — of the contract in question is another. In the first case, the contract will continue to be governed by civil laws, even if they are applied by a judge of the other jurisdiction; in the second case, it will be governed by civil or commercial laws, according to what is decided about its nature.

In dealing with a contract of sale, the legal consequences of nonfulfillment of the obligations incurred by one of the parties may differ substantially according to whether civil or commercial laws are applied. This fact makes the elucidation of the point very important and gives relevance to the decision we are considering.

As has been said, transactions in immovables are not commercial in principle. Such is the rule of the Commercial Code in the cited articles, which are clear and express norms that do not allow argument in this respect.

Nonetheless, there is general agreement in considering as commercial certain special kinds of sales of immovables, such as the acquisition of a house in order to demolish it and sell the materials, or the purchase of a wood lot for the purpose of cutting down the trees and selling the wood, and so forth. In the same way, the purchase of a business inventory is a mercantile act, as is the transfer of the immovable property appurtenant to it.

The doctrine of the decision goes far beyond these cases. Here, the commercial nature of the sale of the apartments is a result of the application of the theory of "accessory acts of commerce," the existence of which in Argentine positive law is recognized by the Commercial Code, art. 8, par. 10.

Accessory commercial acts are "those which make possible, facilitate or assure a principal act of commerce, objective or subjective, from which act they therefore assume an absolute or presumed commercial nature, according to whether the principal act be objectively or subjectively commercial." [Quoting from Bolaffio's treatise on commercial law.] Thus there is an intimate connection between two acts, one of which depends necessarily upon the other. One makes the other possible, facilitates it, assures it, and therefore, cannot be separated from it. From the point of view of the classification of commercial acts, the accessory act *participates by logical necessity* in the juridical nature of the other act.

The Chamber understands the agreement about construction of the concrete building and the sale of three apartments to constitute one single transaction. This interdependence of the contracts impedes the Chamber from considering separately the conduct of the parties in the fulfillment of the reciprocal obligations. The *causa* of the dispute is singular even though composed of a leasing of commercial work and three civil sales accessory to it. By application of the principles expressed, the tribunal adjudges the sales to be commercial, notwithstanding that they concern immovables.

INMOBILIARIA MUÑOZ (S.A.) v. ITURRALDE COLOMBRES
Commercial Chamber of the Capital (Division B)
1961-IV J.A. 633, 102 La Ley 905 (1960)

1st Instance.—Buenos Aires, November 30, 1959.—Considering: 1st. The defendant [mortgagor] questioned the jurisdiction of the commercial court to hear this foreclosure action on the ground that ... the proceeds of the underlying loan were intended to pay the remainder of the cost of a building under construction, which is an eminently civil use for them. Furthermore, the defendant would not be a merchant, since he is involved customarily in the sale of immovables.

* * *

2d. a) As the defendant stated, the fact that one of the co-creditors is an anonymous society [comparable to a corporation] is in itself insufficient to establish the jurisdiction of the commercial court, and it is proper to consider instead the nature of the act or the contract (art. 8, par. 6, Commercial Code, and decision of the Civil and Commercial Chambers of the Capital in plenary session, published in "La Ley," vol. 8, p. 726 [1959-I J.A. 78]).

b) The mortgage in turn, being accessory, is of the same nature as the loan it guarantees. In order for the latter to be adjudged commercial, the thing mortgaged must be able to be considered commercial and apt for commercial use, and the debtor must share that commercial character (art. 558, Commercial Code; Fernández, "Código de comercio comentado," vol. 2, pp. 588-589).

c) The thing loaned — money — is undoubtedly of a commercial nature *par excellence.*

The purpose of the loan, on the other hand, cannot be considered commercial. Though it is true that Iturralde Colombres promised to use the loan to complete the building that he is constructing, for which he himself is providing materials, labor and technical direction, it is also true that the land and the building are his own property. In those conditions one does not conclude that an act exists such as those considered in art. 8, Commercial Code, since the activity of the defendant is not seen to be that of an intermediary regarding the services and materials that he provides. Note that they are intended for his personal use and even if he were to decide eventually to sell the immovable, this act would not be commercial either. In such conditions the loan is civil and it is unnecessary to clarify whether or not the defendant, an auctioneer, engages in commerce. Thus, the commercial court lacks jurisdiction, and a pronouncement about the other defense is not proper.

By virtue of these considerations, and having heard the *fiscal,* I decide: declaring the commercial court incompetent to consider this foreclosure and consequently rejecting it; costs to be imposed upon the plaintiff.—*Horacio Duncan Parodi.*

Opinion of the Fiscal of the Chamber.—The auxiliary business agents listed by art. 87 of the Commercial Code are subject, because of that legal precept, to the mercantile laws in respect to the functions they perform in that role. This doctrine is in harmony with the provisions of art. 8, *id.,* especially pars. 3, 5, 8 and 9, from which, according to Segovia . . ., "it follows . . . that the actions performed by brokers, auctioneers, warehouse owners, carters and their employees are subject to the commercial laws . . . ."

What is expressed above emphasizes once again the criticism by the quoted author in the same note, in respect to [a] the usefulness of the sweeping separation of the category of so-called auxiliary business agents established by the first article indicated, and [b] the interpretation properly given to that article in the sense that "according to the spirit of arts. 6 and 8, the factual element of an act of commerce must predominate over the personal . . . ." From this he concludes, finally, that the acts of some of these agents, such as auctioneers, warehouse owners and carters, "will carry the presumption of commercial character established by art. 5, par. 2 . . . ."

Upon this basis it is natural to conclude that auctioneers and other auxiliary business agents who perform commercial acts on their own account or in their own name, must be equated with the true merchants of art. 1 of the Commercial Code in matters touching on the application of commercial law and jurisdiction.

Consequently said persons, when they contract to borrow money as in this case, do so as merchants, and in this capacity they impress on the transaction a commercial seal, if the other circumstances required by art. 558 of the Commercial Code are present.

In the present case, the borrower . . . is, according to his own statement, an auctioneer and property owner . . . of an important organization dealing with all kinds of transactions relating to immovables. These transactions include, among others, brokerage, which he has made his regular profession, and which circumstance gives him the nature of a merchant . . ., since brokerage is always commercial, whatever may be the nature of the negotiations in which the broker is involved . . . .

Besides, the thing loaned — money — is of a characteristically mercantile nature, regardless of the purpose for which it may be intended.

Consequently, in view of the terms of art. 558 of the Commercial Code, and of the interpretation given to them by Your Honors previously . . ., the loan that gives rise to this action is commercial, and subject to the commercial law and jurisdiction.

Therefore, this office is of the opinion that it is proper to revoke the appealed decision insofar as it holds the commercial court to be incompetent in this action.—*Horacio Méndez Carreras.*

2d Instance.—Buenos Aires, September 14, 1960.—Considering: [Art. 558 of the Commercial Code provides: "A loan is subject to the commercial laws when the thing lent can be considered to be commercial in nature, or designed for commercial use, and when the contract is made between merchants, or when at least the debtor has that character."]

The debtor's having the profession of auctioneer is not disputed, . . . nor is it doubted that he acts as intermediary in the purchase and sale of immovables . . . .

But the commercial purpose of the money loaned was not proved, since the transaction seems to have been effected in order that the defendant might pay for the construction of the immovable owned by him . . . . This construction of the immovable in the circumstances described precludes any commercial character for the loan, in view of the doctrine of art. 8, pars. 1 and 5, and art. 452, par. 1 of the Commercial Code . . . .

On its merits, and the *Fiscal* of the chamber having been heard, the appealed decision is affirmed. Costs to be borne by those who have paid them in both instances in consideration of the peculiarities of the case . . . . —*Alejandro A. Vásquez.*—*Isaac Halperín.*—Dissenting: *Carlos J. Zavala Rodríguez* (Sec.: Federico González del Solar).

Dissent.—Considering: . . . .

* * *

That combination of circumstances indicates that the defendant took the loan for a commercial purpose (art. 558, Commercial Code), such as the application of it to that construction; for although it was carried out on an immovable that belonged to him, it was done for the purpose of speculating or making a profit from it. . . .

The exclusion of immovable property from commercial law (art. 8, par. 1, and art. 452, par. 1, Commercial Code) is not absolute and refers only to the transfer of it and the forms which this transfer must take, which are always governed by the Civil Code.

"But when a contract does not 'raise a question of immovable property,'" says Ripert, "there is no reason not to submit it to the general presumption of commercial character" . . . .

* * *

With precise reference to businesses devoted to speculation in immovables, Ripert says that French jurisprudence "prefers to consider the '*marchand de biens*' as a broker or as a business agent." Nevertheless, commercial practice does not commit this error, and the same denomination, "*marchand de biens,*" stamps the commercial juridical character of this speculation. . . .

* * *

RINALDI v. CORSETTI
Commercial Chamber of the Capital (Division C)
1961-I J.A. 490, 102 La Ley 487 (1960)

1st Instance.—Buenos Aires, June 15, 1959.—[Corsetti owned an urban lot. In 1954, he entered a building contract with Rinaldi, a contractor; from this point forward the stories of the parties diverge considerably. Rinaldi says that he hired a subcontractor, Cassano, to do the masonry work and some other tasks but that he (Rinaldi) and Cassano had difficulties, the nature of which is not specified in the complaint. Rinaldi says that Cassano offered Corsetti a lower price for the work and thereby persuaded the latter to stop making advance payments on the price of the work to Rinaldi. Rinaldi had to slow his pace of work for lack of money, and finally stopped it altogether. Cassano made a contract with Corsetti and continued working, thus depriving Rinaldi of the job. Rinaldi now sues Corsetti for lost profits of 100,000 pesos. For his part, Corsetti says that Cassano was jointly responsible with Rinaldi for the work and even signed an expanded contract subsequent to the first one. According to Corsetti, the falling out between Rinaldi and Cassano was caused by a disagreement over the proper use of some money paid by Corsetti on the contract; Cassano did not want to be liable for damages for not fulfilling the contract, and continued the work himself. Corsetti also says that he paid Cassano the total price and is not responsible for the disagreements between the two partners. Rinaldi claims that the money should have been paid to him, and not to any presumed partner. We take up the opinion of the court of 1st Instance at the point when it begins to state its findings of fact and conclusions of law. The omissions are references to the record.]

Considering: 1st. That on April 19, 1954, the plaintiff and defendant concluded the contract of construction . . . .

2d. That until November 6, 1954, . . . the parties to the said contract were, exclusively, the plaintiff and the defendant . . . .

3d. That the larger agreement . . . did not signify a rescission of the earlier contract . . . nor eliminate the plaintiff from the contractual relation. Neither did it give to Luis Cassano exclusively the direction and administration of the joint venture [*sociedad accidental*] between Cassano and the plaintiff (the existence of the joint venture is invoked by both parties . . .).

4th. That because of the principle of the relativity of contracts [the provisions of] contracts may not be opposed to third parties (art. 1195, C.C.). That, the plaintiff and the defendant being in agreement as to the existence of the joint venture Rinaldi-Cassano, this joint venture may be considered the successor — in respect to the defendant and with his agreement — of the original contracting party, Rinaldi.

5th. That, this being the case, it must be established whether the payment, which the defendant says he gave to only one of the two members of this joint venture, is valid and binds the other member of the same.

6th. That the plaintiff took a direct and personal part in the work until February 8, 1955 . . . .

7th. That up to that date the plaintiff had invested in the work the sum of 170,000 pesos . . . .

8th.   That until that day (February 8, 1955) the plaintiff had received on account of the work the sum of 118,000 pesos . . . .

9th.   That the work was completely ended . . . .

10.   That in the joint venture Rinaldi-Cassano, the plaintiff was the administrator, . . . [and that the other parties to the transaction recognized him as such].

11.   That his capacity as administrator (which has its explanation in the fact that the plaintiff, exclusively and in his own name alone, was the original contracting party with the defendant) was not limited nor restrained in the enlarged agreement . . . by which Cassano joined the contractual relation between the plaintiff and the defendant.

12.   That even if the plaintiff were not the administrator he had, in the joint venture Rinaldi-Cassano, the same rights and obligations as the other partner Cassano . . . .

13.   That, given the above, the defendant could not liquidate accounts and pay the balance to the joint venture Rinaldi-Cassano without the participation of one of those members (the plaintiff Rinaldi). And he could not exclude Rinaldi from such an important act as the payment of the price.

14.   That it is a generally accepted principle that a person who pays improperly must pay again (arts. 731, 733 ff., C.C.). The defendant knew of the questions between the members of the joint venture, and had been forbidden by Rinaldi to pay Cassano . . .; the prudent debtor in these circumstances should have made use of the solution provided by the law (art. 757, par. 4, C.C.), freeing himself from the obligation by making the payment to the court.

15.   Therefore, the right of the plaintiff is recognized to disavow, insofar as it affects him, the payment made by the defendant to Cassano, . . . without detriment to the rights that the defendant may have to recover the improper payment, if the recovery is allowable.

16.   From what is said above in paragraphs 7 and 8, there is a balance of 52,000 pesos payable to the plaintiff, to which sum should be added the profit that the plaintiff did not collect. For this purpose I accept the sum established by the only appraiser designated officially . . . . According to that expert . . . [the payment allowable under] this heading amounts to 10% of the total value of the work, or 38,000 pesos, since that total value was established by the parties . . . to be 380,000 pesos. Consequently, the complaint should be allowed, up to a total of 90,000 pesos, with interest since the notification of the claim, and the costs of suit.

Therefore, and in accordance with the provisions of arts. 1195, 1198, 731, 733 and following, C.C., I decide to allow the complaint in part, and order the defendant to pay to the plaintiff within 10 days the sum of 90,000 pesos, with interest since the notification of the action and costs of the suit.— *Eduardo N. Guzmán* (sec.: Carlos A. Ballbé).

2d Instance.—Buenos Aires, September 7, 1960.—Is the appealed sentence in conformance with law?

Dr. *Rossi* said:

With respect to the proceedings and the facts of this case, I return to the "resultandos" [*i.e.,* the statement of the positions asserted by the parties] of the judgment on appeal, which duly synthesizes them.

The judge of 1st Instance takes as established the existence of a joint venture between Rinaldi and Cassano, a conclusion to which both parties have consented, notwithstanding the equivocal attitude assumed by the plaintiff, who sometimes admitted . . . and at others denied . . . the existence of such a partnership.

With things thus established, it is necessary to ascertain — in accordance with the charges of the complaint — whether or not the payment made by Corsetti to Cassano releases the former with regard to the mentioned joint venture between Cassano and Rinaldi.

It is true, as the plaintiff maintains, that in joint ventures the juridical relation with third persons is established, in principle, between the latter and the managing partner (active joint venturer) who is acting in his own name. But it is also true that the managing partners can be several or all of the partners (art. 395, Commercial Code), and that when the managing partner makes known to third parties the names of the other partners — with their consent — all are jointly bound. The same situation occurs when contracts are made in common by all the partners (cf. Fernández, vol. 1, bk. 2, pp. 665, 669, 670 and 671). Such is, in my judgment, the situation found in the present case.

* * *

The consequence of all that has been shown, is that the juridical relationship upon which the plaintiff bases his claims must be considered as concluded in common by all the partners — Rinaldi and Cassano — with Corsetti, and thus we have the case of joint obligation to which I referred previously. At the worst, there would be the supposition (also referred to above) that the original managing partner (Rinaldi) made known to the third contracting party (Corsetti) the name of the other partner (Cassano), with the consent of the latter, who signed the document expanding the original contract.

* * *

A necessary consequence of all the foregoing is that Corsetti paid Cassano properly and is now released from obligation with respect to Rinaldi and the joint venture (cf. Fernández, loc. cit.). Furthermore, it should be kept in mind that the final terms of [the document that apparently accompanied the payment to Cassano] are sufficiently extensive and conclusive in this respect. The questions that could have arisen or that may exist between Rinaldi and Cassano with relation to the existence, dissolution or administration of the joint venture, are foreign to the defendant, and must be resolved between Rinaldi and Cassano, the more so since there has not been proved, as the plaintiff claimed, any collusion between Cassano and the defendant.

* * *

For the expressed reasons, I vote to revoke the decision and to reject the claim. With costs to be borne by the plaintiff (art. 221, Code of Procedure). If my vote were divided, the costs of this instance would also fall on the plaintiff.

For similar reasons, Dr. *Sussini* adheres to the foregoing vote.

On the grounds of the preceding opinion, the appealed decision is revoked and the claim rejected. With costs to be borne by the plaintiff. The costs of 2d Instance are also charged to the losing party.—*Abelardo F. Rossi.*—*Julio C. Sussini* (Sec.: Luis H. Díaz).

A QUESTION CONCERNING RINALDI v. CORSETTI

We have established that building contractors are engaged in commercial enterprises. Then what happened to the Commercial Code in this case?

MERCHANT STATUS v. COMMERCIAL ACTS

Problem 4 at the beginning of this chapter posed the question of a merchant's purchase of flowers to decorate his place of business. Is the sale civil or commercial in nature? In Argentina, such a case was decided in 1956 by the National Chamber of Appeals (Civil) of the Federal Capital (Division B). Both buyer and seller were merchants; the buyer frequently bought flowers from the seller. When the buyer died, his account showed a debit balance of almost 5,000 pesos. The flower merchant sued the buyer's heirs, who succeeded to his debts upon accepting heirship. The court of 1st Instance held for the plaintiff, over the objection of the heirs that the Civil Code's one-year period of prescription had run, terminating the flower merchant's rights. (The analogous limitations period established by the Commercial Code was five years.)

The court of 2d Instance revoked the judgment on appeal, and ordered that judgment be entered for the defendant heirs, on the ground that the transaction was a civil one, governed by the one-year period of prescription. The buyer, said the court, bought the flowers for his own consumption;

the express provisions of article 452, paragraph 2, exclude such sales from the definition of commercial sales. *Camuyrano v. Scannapieco*, 1957-I J.A. 337 (1956).

Does the result in this case suggest that a "subjective" definition of the commercial jurisdiction and the limits of commercial legislation would be preferable to the "objective" characterization of the Argentine Code? What do you suppose the expectation of the buyer would have been if he had been asked whether the Commercial Code governed his transaction? What would the seller's expectation have been?

Article 75 of the Commercial Code of Mexico contains a long list of commercial acts, which is supplemented by other legislation characterizing as commercial such activity as the mining and petroleum industries and even tourist enterprises. The "objective" theory is in full flower in Mexico: an act is said to be commercial by virtue of its own characteristics, and regardless of who performs it. Nonetheless, the list in article 75 begins with acquisitions and transfers for the purpose of gaining on the sale, hire, etc., of the thing acquired. Since the motive of the actor is crucial, may it not be important to know whether he is in the business of engaging in such transactions? Furthermore, the Mexican Code goes on to specify that the transactions of merchants are commercial. Yet Mexican commercial law scholars persist in saying that their law is not "subjective." In what sense is that statement accurate?

Whether the theory of the application of commercial law be described as "subjective" or "objective," it is possible for a transaction to be commercial for one of its parties and non-commercial for the other. Such "unilaterally commercial" acts in Argentina are expressly made commercial by article 7 of the Commercial Code. In Mexico, the question is not definitively settled, except with respect to the issue of judicial procedure. Article 1050 of the Commercial Code of Mexico provides that for this limited purpose, the character which the act has for the defendant determines whether the procedure for civil or for commercial acts will govern (there are no separate commercial courts in Mexico). With respect to the substantive law which is to be applied to such a mixed transaction, there is no statutory solution. One leading Mexican commercial law scholar takes the position that "the obligations of the party for whom the act is not commercial are ruled exclusively by the civil law." MANTILLA MOLINA, DERECHO MERCANTIL 75 (5th ed. 1961). Do you agree? Professor Warren's article, reprinted below, explores this issue in the context of retail sales to consumers.

WARREN, MEXICAN RETAIL INSTALMENT SALES LAW:
A COMPARATIVE STUDY
10 U.C.L.A. L. REV.* 15, 53-57 (1962)

The commercial law-civil law dichotomy prevailing in civil-law countries — always puzzling to common lawyers — is particularly perplexing in the area of retail sales. Like other civil law countries, Mexico has a special code governing "commercial acts."[139] Article 75 of the Commercial Code sets forth twenty-three specific categories of commercial acts, and concludes by admonishing that "all other acts which are of a similar nature to those mentioned in this Code" are also commercial acts. Under article 75 various factors may be relevant in determining whether an act is commercial. One factor may be the *purpose* of the act, *e.g.,* sales for the purpose of commercial speculation are included. The nature of the *parties* may be determinative, *e.g.,* all transactions involving banks are commercial. The kind of *property* may be variable, *e.g.,* sales of real property or stocks and bonds are commercial acts.[140]

The reason for having a special code to regulate commercial acts is to provide for fast, simple agreement-making in commercial transactions. Merchants are allowed to make virtually any agreement that they wish among themselves. The parties to a commercial act may agree upon the rules of procedure to govern their transaction, and, in default of such an agreement, the Commercial Code provides special rules of procedure.[141] The Commercial Code is a national statute, yielding a uniform law of commerce throughout the land, whereas each state has its own civil code.[142] Where the Commercial Code has no provision on point, the civil code is applicable.[143]

Which code regulates retail selling — commercial or civil? This problem, though of great importance, is not clearly answered in the codes. Article 75 designates as a commercial act: "All acquisitions, alienations and leasings, made with the *object of commercial speculation,* of necessaries, articles, movables, or merchandise, whether in their natural state or after having been manufactured or worked."[144] Under this provision it is clear that the retailer's act in selling goods to a consumer is a commercial act, but it would seem that the consumer's act in buying is a civil act, since he does not do so for the purpose of commercial speculation. Such a transaction is known as a "mixed act" to distinguish it from transactions wholly commercial or wholly civil.

---

[139] COMMERCIAL CODE art. 1: "The provisions of this Code are applicable only to commercial acts."
[140] COMMERCIAL CODE art. 75 concludes by stating: "In case of doubt, the commercial nature of an act shall be defined by judicial decision."
[141] COMMERCIAL CODE art. 1051.
[142] However, the similarity of the various state civil codes to the Federal District Civil Code yields a good bit of legal uniformity throughout Mexico.
[143] COMMERCIAL CODE art. 2.
[144] COMMERCIAL CODE art. 75 (I.) Emphasis added.

The Commercial Code makes only one reference to mixed acts — article 1050 — and the civil codes make no mention of them whatsoever. Article 1050 states:

> Whenever, in conformity with said Articles 4, 75 and 76, of the two parties who enter into a contract, one effects an act of commerce and the other an act purely civil, and such contract gives rise to litigation, it shall be prosecuted in conformity with the provisions of this Book, if the party who effected the commercial act is the defendant, in the other case the action shall be prosecuted in conformity with the rules of civil law.

Since the book referred to is book five of the Commercial Code which governs mercantile procedure, it seems that article 1050 only dictates the law which is to govern the procedure of the case and not the substance. Thus there is no clear indication in the codes as to what substantive law controls a mixed act such as a retail sale.

The importance of determining which code governs a retail sale becomes apparent when some of the differences between them are noted. Article 17 of the Civil Code sets forth the doctrine of *lesión*: [145]

> When any person, taking advantage of the supreme ignorance, notorious inexperience, or extreme poverty of another, obtains an excessive profit which is evidently disproportionate to the obligations assumed by him, the person damaged has the right to demand the rescission of the contract and, if this be impossible, an equitable reduction in his obligation.[146]

By contrast, article 385 of the Commercial Code states that there can be no rescission for *lesión*. Another significant distinction is found in the period of time within which a buyer has the right to complain of hidden defects in the article purchased. Under the Civil Code he has six months from the date of delivery;[147] however, the Commercial Code gives him but thirty days.[148]

Mexican scholars have given little consideration to the problem of which code governs a mixed act. Rodríguez y Rodríguez, noting the confusion inherent in the two codes overlapping on questions of mixed sales, concludes with

---

[145] ROBB, DICTIONARY OF LEGAL TERMS 77 (1955), defines *lesión* as "injury" or "damage"; an "injury arising from breach of an onerous contract, especially a sale."

[146] The injured party has one year in which to complain of *lesión* under CIVIL CODE art. 17. *Cf.* UNIFORM COMMERCIAL CODE § 2-302(1): "If the court as a matter of law finds the contract or any clause of the contract to have been unconscionable at the time it was made the court may refuse to enforce the contract, or it may enforce the remainder of the contract without the unconscionable clause, or it may so limit the application of any unconscionable clause as to avoid any unconscionable result." Although the right of rescission for *lesión* has long been a part of Mexican law, the action of the UCC in granting to an injured party the right to have an unconscionable provision of a contract avoided has been highly controversial. In the version of the UCC presented for passage to the California legislature in 1961, § 2-302 was omitted.

[147] CIVIL CODE art. 2149.

[148] COMMERCIAL CODE art. 383 gives a buyer five days to complain of patent defects of quality or quantity and thirty days to complain of inherent defects.

exasperation that one code or the other should in all cases wholly govern the substantive law of mixed sales.[149] His choice for the controlling statute is the Commercial Code, but he gives no reasons for his opinion and the brevity of his treatment of this point leads one to believe that he did not give the matter his usual careful consideration.

Application of the Commercial Code to provide the substantive law of mixed sales is difficult to defend either on a basis of statutory interpretation or policy orientation. If the Commercial Code were exclusively the governing statute both the rights of the retailer and the buyer would be governed by it. However, article 76 of that Code states: "Purchase of articles or merchandise which merchants effect for their own use or consumption or for that of their family do not constitute acts of commerce, nor resales by workmen, when a natural consequence of their work." Thus the rule espoused by Rodríguez y Rodríguez as modified by article 76 would attain this undesirable result: the rights of the private buyer purchasing for his own consumption would be governed by the more harsh strictures of the Commercial Code; on the other hand, the rights of a merchant, surely a more sophisticated buyer, would be controlled by the more lenient rules of the Civil Code so long as he was purchasing goods for his own consumption or that of his family.

Policy-wise, the contention that the Commercial Code should exclusively regulate mixed sales is indefensible. If a private person wished to sell his used refrigerator to a neighbor, the transaction would presumably be covered by the civil code since the seller was not a professional dealer who acquired and sold the article "with the object of commercial speculation."[150] If a large retail appliance store sold a refrigerator to a buyer, under Rodríguez y Rodríguez's theory, the Commercial Code would apply. The paradox is that a buyer purchasing from a nonprofessional seller would receive greater protection than one buying from a large professional seller. The thrust of the American retail instalment sales acts has been to protect the buyer in situations where there is apt to be a disparity in bargaining power or business experience between the seller and the buyer. For example, the California retail instalment sales act applies only when the seller is in the business of selling and when the buyer is a bona fide consumer.[151] The effect of applying the Commercial Code to retail sales would be to give the buyer less legal protection in situations where he most needs it, i.e., in cases where the greatest gap in bargaining power is likely to exist.

The more sound view is that since a retail buyer is committing a civil act when he purchases goods, his rights should be entirely governed by the code enacted to cover civil acts. He should not be shorn of the protection af-

---

[149] RODRÍGUEZ Y RODRÍGUEZ, CURSO DE DERECHO MERCANTIL 31 (2d ed. 1952).
[150] COMMERCIAL CODE art. 76(I).
[151] CAL. CIV. CODE § 1802.3. See [*Legislative Regulation of Retail Installment Financing,* 7 U.C.L.A. L. REV. 618, 631 (1960)].

forded him by the Civil Code because the seller's act was commercial in nature. Though not as helpful as they should be in this matter, the codes do provide some clues pointing toward this preferred interpretation. Article 20 of the Civil Code reads: "When there is a conflict of rights, in the absence of an express law applicable to the matter, the controversy shall be decided in favor of him who tries to avoid damage for himself, and not in favor of him who seeks to obtain profit." This provision favors sheltering the buyer under the protective coverage of the Civil Code in cases involving the *lesión* or warranty issues adverted to above. Moreover, the portion of the Commercial Code abrogating the right to rescission in *lesión* cases and reducing the period for claiming breach of warranty is entitled "Of Mercantile Sales . . . ."[152] Since the Mexican law generally classifies acts as those wholly commercial, wholly civil, and mixed, it could be contended that these provisions apply only to wholly commercial or mercantile acts, for it mentions only one of the three recognized categories. In lieu of specific application of the Commercial Code the various civil codes would control.

PROBLEM CASE

Eyherabide entered as a contestant on a toothpaste company's television quiz program, called "Odol Asks, for 200,000 Pesos." He was eliminated from the contest because one of his answers was rejected as incorrect. He disagreed with the program's "jury" and sued the sponsor on his contract. The defendant challenged the jurisdiction of the commercial court, and the complaint was rejected by the court of 1st Instance for want of jurisdiction. The *fiscal* of the chamber recommended reversal, arguing that the program was designed to sell Odol toothpaste, an essentially commercial objective; the contestant was the same as any other performer, or the composer of a commercial jingle. The conduct of the performer, then, was an accessory commercial act.

Do you agree that the transaction should be considered commercial? See Eyherabide v. Odol, S.A., 1961-V J.A. 43, 103 La Ley 341 (1961).

THE COMMERCIAL REGISTER

Suppose that you are about to transact business with someone who may or may not be a merchant. It is obvious that in many such cases it is important to know the commercial or non-commercial status of those with whom you

---

[152] The heading immediately preceding COMMERCIAL CODE art. 371 is: "Title Sixth. Of Mercantile Sales and Exchanges and the Transfer of Commercial Credits."

deal. Since there is no certain test for merchant status, it would be a great practical help to have an authoritative list of merchants. Such a list — the Commercial Register— is nearly universally found in the civil law jurisdictions, even in a country like Switzerland which does not separate commercial and civil law in distinct codes. The Latin American jurisdictions are no exception to this rule.

In Argentina, arts. 34-42 of the Commercial Code establish the Public Commercial Register, in which must be recorded the Register of Merchants (arts. 25-32, pp. 293-94, *supra*), as well as a great many documents such as marriage settlements of merchants, judgments of divorce (property settlements), public (notarial) documents of commercial partnerships or corporations, powers of attorney, and the like. In some countries, notably Germany, this Register is used as a control over the legality of documents that are filed for registration. Art. 34 of the Argentine Code notes that the secretary charged with keeping the Register "shall be responsible for the correctness and legality of its entries." While this provision was evidently intended to duplicate the German practice, the commercial courts have made it a dead letter, holding that the purpose of the Register was to give publicity to the matters entered in it, and that the legality of a contract, for example, could be challenged in the ordinary course of litigation arising out of the contract. While this conclusion has been criticized, *e.g.,* 1 ZAVALA RODRIGUEZ, CODIGO DE COMERCIO COMENTADO 84-85 (1959), it is hard to see how the courts could have decided otherwise. Would you favor turning our own registries of deeds into agencies for giving advisory opinions on all documents registered?

Commercial registers may be kept by the local commercial courts, or by justices of the peace, or, in a small country, there may be only one register. In Argentina, there are now many registers — one in each commercial court — with the result that local inquiries are often necessary. It has been proposed to establish a national Register of Merchants, but even more urgent is the establishment of registers that would cover whole provinces. The reciprocal exchange of such lists would satisfy much of the need for a national register.

QUESTIONS ON THE SEPARATION OF COMMERCIAL AND CIVIL LAW

The following historical materials should be read with these questions in mind:

1.   What purposes are served by the civilian division of private law into separate commercial and non-commercial bodies? Some light on this question may come from an examination of a few special rules governing merchants contained in our own Uniform Commercial Code:

(a)   Section 2-201(2) makes an exception to the usual Statute of Frauds rule which requires a signature of the memorandum by the party to be charged. A written confirmation of a transaction "between merchants" is effective to bind the recipient if he makes no objection within ten days.
(b)   Section 2-205 provides: "An offer by a merchant to buy or sell goods in a signed writing which gives assurance that it will be held open needs no consideration to be irrevocable for a reasonable time or during a stated time but in no event for a time exceeding three months; but such term on a form supplied by the offeree must be separately signed by the offeror."
(c)   Section 2-314(1) imposes a warranty of merchantable quality on a seller who is "a merchant with respect to goods of that kind or though not a merchant states generally that they are guaranteed." (Cf. Uniform Sales Act § 15(2).)

There are other provisions in the UCC which make special rules or exceptions for merchants. The problem of risk of loss is treated *infra* at pp. 331-61. What do these provisions have in common, and how does your conclusion bear on the question asked above?

2.   What conditions caused the division on the European continent? Is the absence of such a division in the common law system traceable to substantial differences in such conditions, or are there other historical explanations? If economic or other conditions once justified a separation in the civil law countries, are those conditions still present? In all such countries? In some?

3.   Would you favor or oppose the introduction of such a division into the common law system? Why?

4.   Has the Argentine legislation, as interpreted in the cases we have seen, made the distinction between commercial and non-commercial persons and transactions in a manner which is satisfactory, considering the purposes behind the separation of the two bodies of law?

5.   Is codification more appropriate for commercial law than for other branches of private law? Less appropriate? Why?

BARKER AND CORMACK, THE MERCANTILE ACT: A STUDY IN MEXICAN LEGAL APPROACH
6 SO. CALIF. L. REV.* 1, 3-6 (1932)

The strictly mercantile provisions of the Pandects [the Digest of Justinian] are meager, however — and this despite the commercial development which took place under the Roman Empire. Manuel Cervantes, a prominent Mexican jurist and text-writer of the present century, attributes this fact to the comprehensiveness and flexibility of the Roman civil law:

"Rome had a great industry and a great commerce — without doubt the most vast and the most active of her time; but, in spite of this, she never felt the need for dividing her private law into civil and mercantile ... for the very simple reason that as new juridic relations arose, they found a place easily in the domains of the civil law. So long as Rome lived, her law could evolve, could be transformed and moulded to the new conditions of actual life; could incorporate into itself the new institutions which sprang up as the result of commercial progress; and this vitality, this amplitude, this flexibility of the great body of the Roman civil law, made a succession of the mercantile law completely unnecessary."
* * *

"When commerce revived and acquired momentum in the medieval Italian republics, in the south of France, in Catalonia, in Germany, not only was she without adequate laws for her regulation, but she had to do battle against existing systems of law — the Roman, the German and the Canonical — which frequently opposed her purposes and shackled her aspirations. In effect, with Rome dead, Roman law could not be transformed, its evolution had ceased, it stood inert, petrified in the works of the jurisconsults, in the sentences of the judges, in the novels of the emperors; and in that condition, when the generations of the feudal times exhumed them, they could not then be utilized by commerce .... The Roman law was not only mute in the presence of the new and varied juridic relations created by the advance of navigation and of commerce, but often, not to say always, its rigid and inflexible texts were found to be in open opposition to the nature and tendencies of such relations."

THE MEDIEVAL GUILDS

It was at this period of history that the European guilds or corporations made their appearance. Cervantes' picturesque description continues:

"All men engaged in the same calling, in the same industry, in the same profession, grouped themselves into associations known as guilds, and each guild had its chief, its banner, its common treasury, its saint, and its own regulations. These regulations were at first merely usages, which rapidly became juridic customs, and in the end special laws of the community. The mercants also formed guilds, also joined together in large associations, and also aspired to have their own regulations and special laws, adequate to the exercise of the mercantile profession. And thus in fact it came about; but by reason of their wealth and power, they secured something more: the right to maintain an exclusive jurisdiction similar to the jurisdictions of the most privileged corporations, such as the church and the army. In a word, commerce obtained by these means not only a law of her own, distinct from the Roman, the local and the ecclesiastical, but at the same time the privilege of recourse to special judges (called consuls), appointed by the guild and vested with authority to hear and decide mercantile suits, to the exclusion of the municipal and feudal courts."
* * *

"This statutory legislation [of the Italian guilds] governed the mercantile activities of Italy from the twelfth century down to the beginning of the

> nineteenth century, and from this source are derived, in a direct manner, the contents of the [mercantile] codes, in their essence uniform, which are operative in the different parts of the world."

There is much divergence of opinion among jurists in writing of the law merchant of the Middle Ages, but they appear to agree on several points of interest to us here. The statutes of the guilds marked the first appearance in Europe of an autonomous mercantile jurisprudence and are the original source of the greater portion of the modern law of commerce. They owe little directly to the Corpus Juris of Justinian. Their provisions, at least prior to the Italian Renaissance, relate almost exclusively to maritime law, were based on the customs of merchants, without legal sanction of any constituted political authority and were in the main concrete, empirical and of summary administration, with a minimum of formal or dilatory proceedings. Their application was restricted to the merchants themselves and largely to members of the individual guild or corporation which administered them.

CODIFICATION OF THE MERCANTILE LAW

The first true codifications of the mercantile law, as such, are to be found in the two Colbert Ordinances of Louis XIV. The first, issued in 1673 and known as the Code Savary, treats of commerce on land; the second, issued in 1681, of maritime commerce. These codes are the principal source of the Napoleonic Commercial Code of 1807, and so of modern mercantile codes. Since the French Revolution, the law merchant, in the Latin- and English-speaking countries at least, has ceased to be a class legislation and now governs all commercial activities, largely regardless of the persons involved. From being subjective in character, it has become objective.

AZTIRIA, COMMERCIAL LAW AND PRIVATE LAW IN COUNTRIES HAVING A CONTINENTAL LEGAL SYSTEM
1 INTER-AM. L. REV.* 123, 125-29 (1959)

II. NATURE, FUNCTION, TECHNIQUES AND SPIRIT OF COMMERCIAL LAW

3. The study of the evolution of commercial law shows noticeable changes in its nature. It was typically professional in its origin under the guilds, local laws and customary laws of fairs and markets in medieval Europe; then it became the objective law of commercial transactions which came about because of the fear of maintaining the class feeling which was neces--

---

sarily given to it when restricted to merchants. That objective character, which begins to appear in the statutes of medieval guilds and is emphasized in the French Ordinance of 1673, is firmly embodied in the Code Napoleon of 1807 and extends its influence throughout the 19th century and even up to the present day in most of the Latin legal systems. The objective character is evidenced by an enumeration in the codes of commercial transactions as isolated activities, and in that manner determining the content of commercial law. This determination of its content at the same time enables one to identify the "merchant" by confirming the habitual repetition of those transactions in a professional manner. Among these transactions, however, some did not confer the status of merchant, even if the performance were habitual, as in the case of the issuance of checks.

Opposed to these general and traditional positions, we find the well-founded opinion of Ascarelli, shared by other writers, maintaining that commercial law constitutes a historical category. The position of commercial law, as it developed beside the civil or common law, offers a certain parallel to the formation of the *jus honorarium* alongside the classic Roman law, and the development of equity in relation to the common law. In each case, economic and social needs create a new body of law, a new legal order, vis-a-vis the general common law, which has become insufficient to satisfy these new needs. It is the law which adapts itself to the facts.

Commercial law, viewed historically, then appears as an exceptional body of law which little by little acquires a life of its own and attains an autonomous character until, with the passing of time, it becomes a branch of the law superseding in its field the former role of the civil law rules. We then find that commercial law, by degrees, takes over the field of economic relations displacing therefrom the civil law, until it even succeeds in strongly influencing the spirit of civil institutions. It is then that we witness the phenomenon known as "commercialization" of the civil law.

As a historical category, and at a certain stage in its development, commercial law is also linked to capitalism and necessarily is subjected to its influence while, at the same time, it furnishes capitalism with some of its great devices. Under this economic system the idea of risk and of the freedom of circulation flourish, breaking with the old principles of an economy characterized by the attachment to land and to a close, narrow, feudal regime. The formation of commercial law marks a new development in breaking those close circles of an economic and social order peculiar to that era and in creating a market economy and the possibility of domestic and international developments, aided by maritime communications. Thus, new techniques and institutions grow side by side, and the possibility of free initiative arises until, ultimately, mass economy arrives.

                    *   *   *

The role of commercial law, therefore, is that of leader in the field of private law. Its peculiar characteristic has been that of departing from the classic, from what is old or past, in order to create new techniques and offer its legal devices which are more easily adapted to the needs of economic life. In this process of adaptation, commercial law is a dynamic force, as opposed to the civil law which is slower, more static, more orthodox. Dynamism is the basic functional characteristic of commercial law.

5. Traditionally, and even more so throughout the great development of the civil law in the 19th century under the influence of that legal landmark, the French Civil Code, the "exegetic" method has dominated private law.

Commercial law, in its scientific evolution, was affected by exegetical principles, and it is still possible to note how law schools' curricula have remained close to statutory texts. However, this method is unable to fill the needs of a subject having characteristics such as those we have mentioned. This is particularly true since commercial law cannot be limited, as heretofore, to the bare provisions of the Codes of Commerce which at present are out of date in many respects and which, with reference to many institutions, have been amended repeatedly by numerous statutes, decrees and regulations, and only to a certain degree have been adapted to reality by court decisions, and have been left behind, as far as economic realities are concerned, by customs and usage.

This is why commercial law is something broader and more comprehensive than the codes of commerce. Therefore, the analysis of code provisions cannot have the same scope and meaning as commercial institutions. . . .

* * *

6. In its origin, commercial law is less formalistic than the civil law, at whose side it emerged. Usage and customs of medieval merchants progressively built new legal institutions the reiteration of which, observed by guilds, more and more attained a compulsory character. But, with the passing of time, this less formalistic system becomes a body of rules basically concerned with the safety of trade. Safety and stability of transactions become more important than the law itself. Thus, for instance, when a merchant signs a promissory note, what essentially matters is that the economic and legal device created by the document, the so-called negotiable instrument, attain a life of its own in order that it may circulate from person to person, and may be discounted at a bank. Commercial law chooses the safety, the validity of the promissory note, provided formal requirements are complied with, rejecting the principles of civil institutions which would eventually allow contests as to problems of consideration, or of lack of capacity, or of interruption of adverse possession, all of which would affect the circulation of the document.

* * *

Good faith, that volitional element which plays such an important role in the civil law for the purpose of mitigating the harshness of agreements and of curbing the exercise of rights, has much less influence in commercial law. Here, rather than considering the state of mind of the person executing the contract, the question is, as has been correctly observed, the objective regularity of a transaction. Generally speaking, what principally matters is to determine the declared will of the parties and, in doing so, according to the rule of interpretation contained in paragraph 6 of article 218 of the Argentine Commercial Code, "the custom and practices generally followed in commerce in cases of the same nature, and, especially, the custom of the place where the contract is to be performed, shall prevail over any attempt to assert an understanding to the contrary on the basis of the language."

---

1 HOLDSWORTH, A HISTORY OF ENGLISH LAW *
526-44, 568-73 (1922)

The Law Merchant of primitive times comprised both the maritime and the commercial law of modern codes. From the earliest period in their history an intimate relationship has subsisted between them. Both applied peculiarly to the merchants, who, whether alien or subject, formed in the Middle Ages a class very distinct from the rest of the community. Both laws grew up in a similar manner from the customary observances of a distinct class. Both laws were administered in either the same or in similar courts, which were distinct from the ordinary courts. Both laws differed from the common law. Both had in the Middle Ages an international character; and both continued to possess this international character right down to modern times.

* * *

It is probable that in Europe, in the troubled times of the ninth and tenth centuries, the merchants had always known a special market law. With the increase of commerce in the eleventh and twelfth centuries, and the rise of great commercial cities, the law of the merchants received a great impetus. Many of the commercial cities of Italy codified its rules; and so it became at once more definite and more elaborate. "As original authorities for the early history of the law merchant," says Mr. Mitchell, "the Italian commercial statutes are invaluable; they throw a flood of light on the origin and development of commercial rules and customs that then or afterwards found their way into the commercial laws of Europe." We shall see that the Italian jurists had produced in their Libri Feudorum something in the nature of a model code of feudal law. In the same way their collections of mercantile custom were the model to which the usages of the merchants of other states tended more or less to approximate. Usages differed from place to place. But it was generally recognized that the laws of markets and fairs and the law administered by the specially mercantile courts within the boroughs was a special law merchant, differing from the ordinary law.

Thus for mercantile as for maritime affairs various towns had their codes of customs by which mercantile transactions were governed. As we might expect, the towns which possessed laws dealing with maritime matters were the towns to which some sort of mercantile laws were a necessity. Oleron, Barcelona, and Wisby all possessed such bodies of law. In England similar bodies of law are contained in the White Book of London, the Red Book of Bristol, and the Domesday of Ipswich, and the Carta Mercatoria and the Statute of the Staple contain special codes of rules adapted to foreign merchants. Just as the various seaport towns imitated the customs of some one port, so the various towns modelled their charters and their laws upon certain of the more famous towns in England, such as London, Bristol, Oxford, or Winchester.

* * *

Such then was the Law Merchant. In the earlier part of the Middle Ages it was administered in local courts; but, in the middle of the fourteenth century, the rise of the court of Admiralty caused a cleavage between the maritime and the commercial branches of this law. In the sixteenth century the court of Admiralty showed signs of absorbing both these branches; but, in the latter part of the sixteenth and in the earlier part of the seventeenth centuries, this extension of Admiralty jurisdiction was prevented, and the cleavage between these two branches was widened, by the action of the common law courts. Their jealousy confined the court of Admiralty to maritime causes, and led them to appropriate to themselves jurisdiction over commercial causes. In the end they assimilated what they had succeeded in appropriating and constructed our modern system of commercial law. In consequence of their action our commercial law does not, like the systems of most continental states, form together with maritime law, a separate "code de commerce." It has become a branch of the common law, distinct from the maritime law administered in the court of Admiralty.

The peculiar history of the Law Merchant in England is thus due to the peculiar history of the courts which have administered it at different periods. It is clear from this summary that that history falls into three well defined periods: the period when the Law Merchant, maritime and commercial, was administered in local courts; the rise and development of the court of Admiralty and the settlement of its jurisdiction; the absorption of the commercial side of the Law Merchant into the common law.

The Period when the Law Merchant, Maritime and Commercial,
was Administered in Local Courts
* * *

The courts which administered the commercial law of the period necessarily presented features very similar to the courts which administered the maritime law. The Law Merchant applied both to the domestic trader and to the foreign merchant. Both formed in a sense a separate class. But, as we might expect, the separation is far more clearly marked in the latter than in the former case. These courts were either (i) the courts of Fairs and Boroughs, or (ii) the courts of the Staple.

(i) In the Anglo-Saxon period commerce had been practically confined to fairs held in "burhs" — strong places specially protected by the king's peace. In return for this protection the king took a toll. This right to take a toll was, like other governmental rights, granted out to his subjects. Thus the right to hold a fair and take its tolls became a franchise; and therefore, to allow another fair to be set up so near to an already existing fair that it abstracted its custom, was a nuisance to the franchise for which an action lay. As in the case of the other franchises, the right to hold a court was incident to it. This court comes to be known as the court of "piepowder." "The term 'piepowder' (*piepoudres, pede pulverosi*)," says Gross, "was not applied to this tribunal, as Sir Edward Coke and various other writers believed, because justice was administered as speedily as the dust could fall or be removed from the feet of the litigants, but because the court was frequented by chapmen with dusty feet, who wandered from mart to mart." The name was perhaps originally a nickname; but it became general, and was adopted in the official style of the court.

It is clear from the records of the courts of these fairs that they were of the same type as the courts of similar fairs which existed all over Europe. The court, if it belonged to a borough, was held by the mayor or bailiffs of the borough, if it belonged to a lord, by his steward; and the borough or other lord was responsible for the maintenance of order during the period of the fair. But though the court was held by the mayor, bailiffs, or steward, the judges of the court, in the thirteenth and fourteenth centuries, were the merchants who attended the fair. The court's jurisdiction extended to all cases except those concerning land, and except pleas of the crown. Thus it heard actions for breach of contract, and actions of trespass; and it dealt with various minor offences committed in the fair. It could exercise this jurisdiction irrespective of the amount at issue in the case, and it could hear cases which had arisen outside the limits of the fair. The procedure of the court was summary, and its session was continuous. These two characteristics are common to all the fair courts of Europe; and in England both the borough custumals and Bracton emphasize the need for this summary procedure in cases which concern merchants and mariners. We shall see that this summary procedure both in England and abroad took practical shape in many relaxations of the ordinary rules of procedure which would have hampered the development of commercial law.

The lords of these fairs were, as we have seen, sometimes individuals, sometimes corporate boroughs.

In cases where the lords of the fair were individuals the fairs were sometimes held by these lords in a borough; and in that case the jurisdiction of the ordinary courts was sometimes superseded during the time of the fair. . . .

In cases where the borough had the franchise of fair its piepowder court was often regarded merely "as a phase or special session" of the ordinary borough court. But sometimes the two courts were kept quite distinct. In other cases the piepowder court was kept separately during the time of the fair, and during the remainder of the year, the law merchant was administered in the ordinary borough court. It is obvious that whether or not a borough had the franchise of a fair it was in most cases a centre of trade. The law took account of this fact, and allowed that by custom a borough might have the right to hold a court of piepowder, just as if it possessed this franchise. And, whether or not it held such a court, the fact that it was a centre of trade often caused the customary law administered in its court to be better suited to the needs of commerce than the common law. At Winchelsea, Rye, and Fordwich, in the fifteenth century, the judges were directed to "have recourse to the laws of nature on which are founded and whence proceed all written laws." Such a direction clearly made for the reception and recognition of reasonable mercantile customs, and enabled such courts, when necessary, to administer the Law Merchant.

On the Continent the large towns enjoyed a great measure of independence; and this caused the mercantile courts and the law which they administered to play a very important part in the development of the Law Merchant. In England, on the other hand, there was already a common law, recourse to which was easy, and there was a legislature which had already begun to interfere with purely mercantile matters. And though in England the custom of the merchants was recognized as a law apart from the common law, the relation between these two laws was close. At an early period the Law Merchant, so far as it applied to domestic transactions, showed signs of becoming absorbed in a common law which had adopted certain of its rules. The Bristol treatise on the Law Merchant, which comes from the fourteenth century, testifies to this tendency. The writer regards the Law Merchant as a mere offshoot of the common law, and he can only point to three specific differences. Parties, he says, may always sue at common law, and this is the usual course — a fact borne out by the absence of similar treatises in the custumals of other boroughs dealing specially with the Law Merchant.

It is not therefore surprising to find that, in the latter half of the fifteenth century, the court of piepowder was declining in importance. In 1466 and 1467 the court of Common Pleas considered that the steward or other person who held the court, and not the suitors, was its judge — a view which tended to diminish its usefulness, as it deprived the merchants who attended it of much of their power to shape directly the law there administered. In 1477 a statute still further diminished the usefulness of the court, by restricting its jurisdiction to matters arising within the limits of the fair, and occurring during the time that the fair was held. We shall see that this statute, and the interpretation put upon it by the courts, combined with economic and social changes to bring about the total decay of the court in the sixteenth and seventeenth centuries.

(ii)   These courts of fairs and boroughs dealt mainly with domestic trade: the courts of the Staple dealt mainly with foreign trade. In order to understand the reason for the creation of these special courts it is necessary to say something of the manner in which the merchants were organized in the Middle Ages.

In the borough charters there is frequent mention of the Gild Merchant. This was an association of traders within the town, and, in some cases, of traders living outside its precincts, for the better management of trade. It sometimes arbitrated upon mercantile disputes. But as a rule it did not exercise a regular jurisdiction, its chief function being that of a trade union of a rigidly protective character. It was only those who belonged to the Gild Merchant who could trade freely within the town; and its conduct was sometimes so oppressive that trade was driven from the town. In fact all the various privileges, jurisdictional and administrative, which the towns possessed could be, and often were used in a manner adverse to the commercial interests of the country. The foreign merchant was hampered at every turn by the privileges of the chartered towns. They were averse to allowing him any privileges except those which they had specially bargained to give him. "The Great Charter provides that merchants may freely enter and dwell in and leave the realm; but the same Great Charter confirms all the ancient liberties and customs of London and the other boroughs, and thus takes away with one hand what it gives with the other. The burghers have a very strong opinion that their liberties and customs are infringed if a foreign merchant dwells within their walls for more than forty days, if he hires a house, if he fails to take up his abode with some responsible burgher, if he sells in secret, if he sells to foreigners, if he sells in detail." And it should be noted that all these restrictive rules were held to be valid by the common law.

The crown, on the other hand, was for many reasons interested in supporting the foreign merchant. It was able to take a broader view of the commercial interests of the country than any set of burghers; and its intelligence was quickened by the fact that it was easier to negotiate a supply from the alien merchant in return for protection, than to deal with a Parliament. For these reasons the needs of the crown gave to the alien merchant a defined position — in some respects superior to that of the native merchant — and the protection of a separate set of courts.

* * *

With a view to the better organization of foreign trade and the more convenient collection of the customs, certain towns, known as the Staple towns, were set apart. It was only in those towns that dealings could take place in the more important articles of commerce, such as wood, woolfells, leather, lead, and tin. Eleven such towns were named for England, one for Wales, and four for Ireland. In each of these towns special courts were provided for the merchants who resorted thither. A mayor and two constables were to be chosen annually to hold the court of the Staple; and the authorities of the town in which the Staple was held were ordered to be attendant upon them. They were to apply the Law Merchant, and not the common law. All manner of pleas concerning debt, covenant, and trespass fell within their jurisdiction. The jurisdiction of the king's courts was excluded except in cases touching freehold or felony; but the doings of the court were subject to the supervision of the Council. The mayor and constables had the assistance of two alien merchants, one of whom was chosen from the merchants who came from the north, the other from the merchants who came from the south. ...

All these courts — maritime and commercial — administered, and, by administering, helped to create the Law Merchant. It was a law which necessarily differed at many points from the ordinary law, for "no technical jurisprudence peculiar to any country would have been satisfactory to traders coming from many different countries." For the most part it was law laid down by the merchants in their courts; and, though particular rules may have differed slightly in different places, its character was essentially cosmopolitan. Of the contents of this customary law the common law courts as yet knew very little. It was admitted to be a law quite distinct from the common law. If a case occurred before them which turned upon a rule of this law merchants were summoned to inform the court. In fact, except in the cases in which English statutes made rules for merchants, or regulated mercantile customs, the common law courts had little chance of becoming acquainted with its important principles. We have seen that, during the fourteenth and fifteenth centuries, they were beginning to absorb jurisdiction over the smaller commercial transactions of internal trade; but the important principles of commercial law were applicable mainly to the larger transactions of foreign trade; and, as we have seen, the common law courts had at this period no jurisdiction over contracts made or torts committed abroad. One illustration of the ignorance of the common law courts of the commercial usages of the period, and of the rules of law which governed those usages, will sufficiently explain why the courts and law of the merchants were at this period wholly distinct from the common law courts and the common law. We know from the records of the fair courts that a writing obligatory payable to bearer was known among the merchants as early as the thirteenth century. We shall see that these writings are one of the germs from which sprang the negotiable instruments of our modern law. But the first reported case upon a negotiable instrument in the common law courts comes from the year 1603.

[The discussion of the Admiralty jurisdiction is omitted. — Ed.]
* * *

The Absorption of the Commercial Side of the
    Law Merchant into the Common Law

With the increase of commerce in the fourteenth and fifteenth centuries, a division and specialization of trades and industries began to take place. The large trader or the merchant became entirely distinct from the small trader or the craftsman. The old Gild Merchant, which embraced all the traders in a town, gave place to separate companies of merchants on the one side, and to separate craft gilds on the other.

* * *

Though the old organization of trade lingered on till the nineteenth century, the internal trade of the country had in the sixteenth century practically ceased to be ruled by a special law and by special courts. The companies of merchants and the craft gilds possessed no jurisdiction of their own. Some few courts of fairs survived. But the fairs and their courts were decadent by the end of the sixteenth century. There are few entries on their plea rolls; and the courts of common law rigidly confined their jurisdiction to what they considered to be its proper sphere. Thus, except in so far as statutes drew a distinction between traders and others, the traders' or the merchants' dealings were not treated differently from those of any other class in the community. They were governed by the common law and generally by the common law courts. The common law had borrowed certain rules from the Law Merchant. The rules that there is no warranty of title in a sale of goods, and that, under some circumstances, a sale in market overt by a non-owner will pass the property, probably come from this source. The merchant's view of the efficacy of the earnest money to bind the bargain was recognized by the Statute of Frauds. By the end of the sixteenth century the internal trade of the country was regulated by a common law thus modified and not by a separate Law Merchant.

The foreign trade of the country continued for a longer period to be governed by a separate Law Merchant. In France, Italy, and Germany juristic literature and mercantile practice had created a body of mercantile law. During the sixteenth and seventeenth centuries this mercantile law was being adapted to the use of Englishmen by writers like Malynes, Marius, Molloy, and Beawes. They all considered the merchant as a class apart and subject to a separate law. "It is a customary law," says Malynes, "approved by the authority of all kingdoms and commonwealths, and not a law established by the sovereignty of any prince;" and, "the said customary law of merchants hath a peculiar prerogative above all other customs, for that the same is observed in all places." "That commonwealth of merchants," says Davies, "hath always had a peculiar and proper law to rule and govern it; this law is called the Law Merchant whereof the laws of all nations do take special knowledge." Davies, however, recognized that it was only the foreign trade of the country that was now ruled by this special law. "Merchandises that cross the seas are goods of another nature, quality, and consideration than other goods and chattels, which are possessed within the realm, and do not cross the seas."

It is clear from these writers that specific differences between the Law Merchant and the common law could still be pointed out. There was no survivorship in the case of merchants who were joint tenants. Wager of law was unknown among them. Bills of exchange, policies of assurance, assignments of debts were all unknown to the common law.

But, by the end of the seventeenth century, this Law Merchant was being gradually absorbed into the general legal system of the country. As in the case of the internal trade, so in the case of the foreign trade, the older mercantile courts had ceased to exist. Jurisdiction was therefore assumed by the ordinary courts of law and equity.

* * *

The process was assisted, after the Revolution, by the greater freedom allowed to foreign trade. In the sixteenth and seventeenth centuries foreign trade was in the hands of companies incorporated by the crown with exclusive rights to trade. The validity of such grants was upheld, in 1684, in the *East India Company v. Sandys.* It is clear that such an organization of trade will tend to the settlement of disputes by the arbitration of the governing body of the company. But, in 1693, trade had been to a large extent freed by a resolution of Parliament, "that it is the right of all Englishmen to trade to the East Indies, or any part of the world, unless prohibited by Act of Parliament." It was a natural, though perhaps an indirect result, of the Great Rebellion and the Revolution that the ordinary courts should thus absorb jurisdiction over mercantile cases. The fact that the Law Merchant was not English law, but jus gentium, had been used to prove that the crown had such large powers over trade, that it could impose impositions, or create a monopoly. It was clear that the Law Merchant must be administered in the ordinary courts of law or equity if it was to be made to harmonize with the now established principles of English public law.

The complete incorporation of the Law Merchant with the common law was not effected till the time of Lord Mansfield. Up to his time mercantile business had been divided between the courts of law and equity. Little progress had been made in the task of creating a body of systematic principles. Lord Mansfield created such a body of principles; and this entitles him to the fame of being "the founder of the commercial law of this country." The Law Merchant has thus ceased to be a separate body of law administered by separate courts: "it is neither more nor less than the usages of merchants and traders . . . ratified by the decisions of courts of law, which, upon such usages being proved before them, have adopted them as settled law."

[See also volume 5 of HOLDSWORTH, at pp. 60-154. — Ed.]

PROBLEMS ON THE RISK OF LOSS

Using the following articles from the Civil and Commercial Codes of Argentina, together with the articles of the codes previously studied, decide these three problem cases:

1. Figueroa, an art dealer, agreed in writing to sell a Rivera painting

to García, another art dealer, for 250,000 pesos. Neither of them knew that the painting had been stolen from Figueroa's gallery the night before; it has not been recovered. García has not paid for the painting, but he will lose the profit from an expected resale for 300,000 pesos. Does he have a right to damages against Figueroa?

2.   Hernández, a dealer in hides, was going out of business. He had sold all but 200 hides of a certain standard quality, which were held to his order in a public warehouse. Ibáñez, another dealer, knew of these 200 hides; without referring to them specifically, he offered in writing to buy 200 hides of the same quality at a specified price, to be belivered on a specified date at Ibáñez' place of business. Hernández accepted in writing. Before the price had been paid, and before delivery had been made, the warehouse and its contents burned. May Hernández recover the price?

3.   Juárez, a lumber dealer, had contracted to sell to López, another dealer, some specially treated boards which were stored in a yard next to Juárez' place of business, and which were to be picked up by López at the yard. López had paid part of the price, but delivery was not yet scheduled, when the boards were destroyed by fire. Juárez had set a fire in a vacant lot next to the lumber yard, in order to burn off some weeds in preparation for storing more lumber there. An extraordinary and unforeseeable wind sprang up, and carried the fire to the lumber yard, where the damage was done. López now wants his partial payment back, and Juárez wants the rest of the price paid. Who owes whom? Would your answer be different if the parties were not lumber dealers but opera singers?

COMMERCIAL CODE OF ARGENTINA (1889)

* * *

460.   There being no stipulation to the contrary, the expenses of delivery of the thing sold, up to the time when it is placed in the hands of the buyer, weighed and measured, are to be borne by the seller.

The expenses of its receipt, as well as those of carriage or transport, are borne by the buyer.

461.   In the absence of an express stipulation, the delivery of the thing sold must be made in the place where the thing is at the time of the sale, and may be effected by way of actual or symbolic delivery, or by transfer of title documents or by the method in commercial use in the place where it is to be effected.

462.   In all cases in which the buyer, to whom goods have to be sent, does not bargain for a determined place or for a certain person who should receive them in his name, dispatch to his address is an effective delivery of the things sold.

There is excepted the case in which the unpaid seller sends the goods to his own consignee, for complete delivery only on receipt of the price or security.

463. The following are considered to be symbolic delivery, unless the contrary be proved in cases of error, fraud or deceit:

> 1. Delivery of the keys to the warehouse, shop or chest in which the merchandise or thing sold may be;
> 2. The fact of the buyer's placing his mark on the things bought in the presence of the seller or with his consent;
> 3. Delivery or receipt of the invoice without immediate opposition by the buyer;
> 4. The clause, "for account," placed in the bill of lading, not being objected to by the buyer within twenty-four hours, or by the second mail;
> 5. The declaration or entry in the book or office of the public counting-houses in favor of the buyer by consent of both parties.

464. When the contracting parties have not stipulated a time for the delivery of the goods sold and the payment of their price, the seller shall be obligated to hold the thing sold at the disposition of the buyer within twenty-four hours after the contract.

The buyer shall have the period of ten days to pay the price of the goods; but he cannot demand delivery without giving the seller the price at the time of delivery.

465. From the time when the seller places the thing at the disposal of the buyer, and the latter states his satisfaction with its quality, there is an obligation to pay the price immediately in cash or within the stipulated period, and the seller is constituted the depositary of the goods sold and is obligated to preserve them, under the laws relating to deposit.

466. As long as the goods sold are under the control of the seller, although it be by way of deposit, he has a right over them prior to any other creditor of the buyer, for the amount of the price and interest for the delay, as provided in art. 1500, par. 2 [dealing with bankruptcy, in the original code].

467. When the seller has not delivered the goods sold within the stipulated time, or within the time prescribed by Art. 464, the buyer may apply for rescission of the contract, or demand its performance along with damages resulting from the delay, or apply for authorization to buy in the market, for the account of the seller, an equal quantity of the same goods.

Nevertheless, when the failure to deliver the goods sold is caused by their having perished, or their having deteriorated because of unexpected accident, without fault [culpa] of the seller, all liability on his part ceases, and the contract is rescinded as a matter of law upon the return of the price to the buyer.

CIVIL CODE OF ARGENTINA
(enacted 1869) (Joannini translation 1917*)

OF OBLIGATIONS WITH RELATION TO THEIR OBJECT
TITLE VII.   OF OBLIGATIONS TO GIVE

CHAPTER I
Of Obligations to give Certain Things

574.   An obligation to give is one the object of which is the delivery of a thing, movable or immovable, for the purpose of constituting real rights therein, or of granting merely the use or tenancy thereof, or to return it to its owner.

575.   An obligation to give certain things includes all the accessories of such things, even though not mentioned in the instruments, or even though temporarily separated therefrom.

576.   The debtor of the obligation is liable to the creditor for damages due to a failure to take the proper steps to deliver the thing, at the place and time stipulated, or at the place and time fixed by the judge in the absence of an express stipulation.

577.   The creditor does not acquire any real rights in the thing before it is delivered.

578.   If the obligation to give a certain thing is to transfer real rights therein, and the thing is lot without the fault of the debtor, the obligation is dissolved as to both parties.

579.   If the thing is lost through the fault of the debtor, the latter is liable to the creditor for its equivalent and for damages.

580.   If the thing deteriorates without the fault of the debtor, the deterioration runs for his account, and the creditor may dissolve the obligation, or receive the thing in the condition in which it is, with a proportionate reduction in price, if any has been stipulated.

581.   If the thing deteriorates through the fault of the debtor, the creditor is entitled to demand an equivalent thing with compensation for damages, or to receive the thing in the state in which it is, with compensation for damages.

582.   If the thing has improved or increased, even though not owing to the expenditure of money thereon by the debtor, the latter may demand a higher price from the creditor, and if the creditor does not agree, the obligation shall be dissolved.

583.   All fruits, whether natural or civil, collected before the delivery

of the thing, belong to the debtor; but the fruits pendent at the time of the delivery belong to the creditor.

584. If the obligation is to give a certain thing for the purpose of restoring it to its owner, and the thing is lost without the fault of the debtor, the thing is lost to its owner, the righs of the latter to the day of the loss not being hereby affected, and the obligation shall be dissolved.

585. If the thing is lost through the fault of the debtor, the provisions of Art. 579 shall be observed.

586. It it deteriorates without the fault of the debtor, the owner thereof shall receive it in the condition in which it may be and the debtor shall not be liable for damages.

587. If it deteriorates through the fault of the debtor, the provisions of Art. 581 shall be observed.

* * *

PART SECOND. EXTINCTION OF OBLIGATIONS
TITLE XVI. OF PAYMENT

724. Obligations are extinguished:

> By payment.
> By novation.
> By compensation [comparable to common law set-off].
> By transaction [compromise].
> By confusion.
> By renunciation of the rights of the creditors.
> By remission of the debt.
> By inability to make payment.

725. Payment is the performance of the prestation which constitutes the object of the obligation, whether an obligation to do something or an obligation to give something is involved.

* * *

TITLE XXIII. OF IMPOSSIBILITY OF PAYMENT

888. An obligation is extinguished when the prestation [performance] which constitutes the subject thereof becomes physically or legally impossible without the fault of the debtor.

889. If the prestation becomes impossible through the fault of the debtor, or if the latter has assumed the liability for fortuitous events or *force majeure,* whether by virtue of a clause charging him with the risks which may arise thereunder, or by reason of having incurred delay, the original obligation, whether it be one to give or to do something, is converted into an obligation to pay damages.

890. When the prestation consists of the delivery of a certain thing, the obligation is extinguished by the loss thereof, and is converted into one to pay damages only in the cases of Art. 889.

891. The thing which was to have been given shall be considered as lost only when it has been totally destroyed, or taken out of commerce, or has disappeared in such a manner as to make its existence unknown.

892. When a debtor is liable for fortuitous events only when he incurs delay, he is relieved from the payment of damages, if the thing which he is unable to deliver as a consequence of a fortuitous event would have been similarly lost if it had been in the possession of the creditor.

893. When the object of the obligation is the delivery of a thing which, although not certain, is determined among a number of certain things of the same species, it is extinguished if all the things comprised therein are lost as a consequence of a fortuitous event of *force majeure*.

894. When the obligation consists of the delivery of uncertain things which are fungible, determined only by their species, the payment shall never be considered as impossible, and the obligation shall always be converted into an indemnity for damages.

895. In cases in which the obligation is extinguished on account of impossibility to make payment, it is extinguished not only as to the debtor, but also as to the creditor to whom the debtor must return whatever he received by reason of the extinguished obligation.

* * *

1172. Contracts the object of which is the delivery of things which are said to exist, when they do not as yet exist, or have ceased to exist, are void; and a person who has promised such things shall pay indemnity for any damage which he causes the other party.

* * *

TITLE III.   OF THE CONTRACT OF PURCHASE AND SALE

1323. There is a purchase and sale when one of the parties engages to transfer to another the ownership of a thing, and the latter engages to receive it and pay therefor a certain price in money.

* * *

CHAPTER I
Of the Thing Sold

1327. All things which can be the object of contracts may be sold, even though they be future things, provided their alienation is not prohibited.

1328. If the thing has ceased to exist at the time of the execution of the contract, the latter shall be null and void. If only a part of the thing has been destroyed, the purchaser may either dissolve the contract or bring an action to recover the part still existing, the price being reduced in the proportion of this part to the whole thing.

* * *

CHAPTER V
Of the Obligations of the Vendor

1408. The vendor cannot change the condition of the thing sold, and is obliged to preserve it as it was the day of the contract, until he delivers it to the purchaser.

1409. The vendor must deliver the thing sold, free from all other possession, and with all its accessories, on the date stipulated, and if no date has been stipulated, the day the purchaser demands it.

1410. The delivery must be made at the place agreed on, and if no place has been designated, at the place where the thing sold was located at the time of the contract.

1411. The vendor is also obliged to receive the price at the place agreed on, and in the absence of an agreement on the subject, at the place and time of the delivery of the thing, if the sale has not been made on credit.

1412. If the vendor fails to deliver the thing at the time fixed in the contract, the purchaser may demand the resolution of the sale, or the delivery of the thing.

1413. If the vendor is unable to deliver the thing, the purchaser may demand the immediate return of the price paid by him, without being obliged to wait for the inability of the vendor to cease.

1414. The vendor must warrant the thing sold, answering for eviction to the purchaser if defeated in court, in an action of revindication, or some other real action. He is also answerable for the redhibitory vices [material defects] of the thing sold.

1415. The vendor must defray the expenses of the delivery of the thing sold, in the absence of an agreement to the contrary.

1416. Until the vendor makes tradition of the thing sold, the risks of the thing, as well as its fruits and accessories, shall be governed by the provisions of the Title *Of Obligations to Give,* whether the thing sold be a certain or an uncertain thing.

* * *

1418. The vendor is not obliged to deliver the thing sold if the purchaser has not paid him the price.

1419. Nor is he obliged to deliver the thing, when he has given time for the payment, if after the sale the purchaser becomes insolvent, unless he furnish security for payment at the time agreed on.

1420. When the thing sold is a movable, and the vendor does not make tradition thereof, the purchaser, if he has already paid the price in whole

or in part, or has purchased on credit, has the right either to dissolve the contract, and demand the return of whatever he may have paid, with interest on
account of the delay and indemnity for damages; or to demand the delivery
of the thing and compensation for damages.

1421. When the thing is fungible, or consists of amounts which the
vendor has sold to another, he is entitled to demand a corresponding amount
of the same species and quality, and indemnity for damages.

* * *

AZTIRIA, COMMERCIAL LAW AND PRIVATE LAW IN COUNTRIES HAVING A CONTINENTAL LEGAL SYSTEM
1 INTER-AM. L. REV.* 123, 129-33 (1959)

III. THE RETURN TO THE UNIFICATION OF PRIVATE LAW

7. The point of maximum separation between commercial law and its
older brother, the civil law, was reached in the 19th century. The 20th century, on the contrary, shows a strong tendency toward unification. This tendency brings the Romanist systems in their present form closer to the common
law countries, inasmuch as they had for centuries considered private law as a
unit, without recognizing statutory distinctions regarding commercial matters
except by separately regulating from the viewpoint of either the applicable
law, or jurisdiction, some institutions which Romanist countries have generally
considered as part of the commercial law field.

We have seen the manner in which, within the private law, one of its
branches grows immeasurably, to the detriment of the other, absorbing it, invading it, limiting it. But, at the same time, its growth, and the results of this
phenomenon of "commercialization" of the civil field which has been mentioned, mean the self-destruction of the system, the disappearance of the autonomous regime of commercial law. This solves one of the fundamental problems implicit in the former division, that of determining the boundaries of
the commercial field, a problem which it is practically impossible to solve
satisfactorily. This is even more so when, for a long time, commercial law has
not been limited to merchants in the subjective or professional sense of the
term, but its application has been extended to activities between merchants or
artisans and those who are neither, and even to transactions in which merchants or artisans did not intervene. Thus, commercial law acquired an objective character, unknown to its medieval origin.

* * *

---

10. In the Argentine Republic, important legal and doctrinal antecedents are found revealing a clear tendency toward unification, the results of which will soon be evident.

It has been accurately pointed out that Argentine commercial law came into being under the banner of unification, after the political structure of the country was established. The first Code of Commerce succeeding the Spanish laws was enacted in 1859 for the Province of Buenos Aires, and was extended to the whole nation in 1862, and a few years thereafter was adopted by Uruguay. Since no new Civil Code existed, numerous rules on obligations and contracts were included in the Code of Commerce. This unitary system lasted until the enactment in 1869 of the Civil Code, thus creating a duality of rules which was partially eliminated by the commercial reforms of 1889.

Argentine doctrine, starting with Lisandro Segovia, leans toward unification. At the First Argentine Congress on Commercial Law, held in 1940, the following proposal by another champion of unification, Leopoldo Melo, was approved: "That it is from every viewpoint convenient that contractual relationships, both in civil and commercial matters, be governed by the same Code of Obligations, as in the case in Switzerland, and as has been approved in the 1927 draft prepared by the French and Italian Commissions."

Mauricio L. Yadarola contributed to this tendency at the same Congress, with an original idea, namely, his proposal for the drafting of a Code of Economic Relations, which seeks to unify economic legislation in the field of private law relationships, apart from the other civil institutions. His idea is broader, therefore, than the Swiss system, although it may be considered as showing the same tendency. Marcos Satanowsky, in his turn, in important writings, favored the unification of obligations and contracts under the Code of Commerce, in view of the fact that the most dynamic aspects of private law institutions belong to commercial law. Finally, one of the outstanding contemporary writers on the subject, Carlos C. Malagarriga, supports complete unification of private law. The Argentine Government has entrusted to him and to the present writer the preparation of a draft of a general law of business associations which has among its purposes legislative unification of the subject which is at present governed by both civil and commercial codes.

* * *

13. There remains for consideration, however, a basic question, namely, that of determining the legal status of the merchant. This status traditionally had been, as a result of the applicable legislative criteria, based upon the professional character of his activities which are a source of various rights and duties. The elimination of these bases for making this determination, and the disappearance of the lists of commercial transactions in the codes of commerce of the Continental type, make it necessary to find a distinguishing characteristic for determining the profession of merchant. I feel that the solution is to be found by substituting the entrepreneur concept for that of the traditional merchant. The entrepreneur is at present the characteristic professional figure

in the economic activities of our capitalist system. Already substantive laws, administrative regulations, labor laws, social security laws, labor contracts, etc., treat the entrepreneur in his special role covering various fields of activity. Thus, the entrepreneur, either as an individual, as in the case of the former merchant, or the collective entrepreneur, as in the case of business associations, would receive legal professional status by virtue of the manner in which its economic activity is carried on. This does not, of course, prevent recognition of certain differences on account of special types or sizes of enterprises which would call for less rigorous treatment. This is a return to the original approach of commercial law with regard to professional status, while giving that status a new definition. We thus solve the problems of legislative organization in the light of a reality which clearly reveals the predominance of commercial institutions, usages, and customs in the whole economic field. Lastly, we will arrive at a more technical and modern formula answering the need for legislation as to the professional activity of the merchant who is, today, the entrepreneur.

*   *   *

THE VENEZUELAN REFORM

In 1962 the Ministry of Justice of Venezuela presented to the Congress its proposal for a substantial reform of that country's commercial legislation. The basic proposal was to consign all of the Commercial Code's provisions on obligations and contracts to the Civil Code, making such modifications of both Codes as were necessary to unify the law. The Commercial Code was then to be restricted to three books, concerning (a) merchants and their activities in general, (b) commercial societies (partnerships and corporations), and (c) bankruptcy. Negotiable instruments, banking, insurance and navigation were left to special legislation outside the codes.

The great practical advance made by this reform is its abandonment of the concept of the isolated commercial act, subjecting non-merchants to the commercial law. Merchants continue to have special obligations such as inscription in the Commercial Register, but in general there is to be one law of contracts, etc. for merchants and non-merchants alike. See MINISTERIO DE JUSTICIA (Venezuela), REFORMA MERCANTIL: ANTE PROYECTOS (1962); Goldschmidt, *La Reforma de la Legislación Mercantil en Venezuela,* in NUEVOS ESTUDIOS DE DERECHO COMPARADO (1962).

A similar reform, preserving the separate identities of the Civil and Commercial Codes but unifying their substance, has been under study in France since the end of World War II. See Houin, *Reform of the French Civil Code and the Code of Commerce,* 4 AM. J. COMP. L. 485 (1955).

TARLING v. BAXTER
Court of King's Bench
6 B. & C. 361, 108 Eng. Rep. 484 (1827)

Assumpsit to recover back 145 £ paid by plaintiff to the defendant's use. The declaration contained counts for money had and received, and the other common counts. Plea, general issue, with a notice of set-off for goods sold and delivered and bargained and sold. At the trial before Abbott C.J., at the London sittings after Hilary term, 1826, a verdict was found for the plaintiff for 145 £, subject to the opinion of this Court on the following case.

On the 4th of January 1825, the plaintiff bought of the defendant a stack of hay belonging to the defendant, and then standing in a field belonging to the defendant's brother. The note signed by the defendant, and delivered to the plaintiff was in these words: "I have this day agreed to sell James Tarling a stack of hay, standing in Canonbury Field, Islington, at the sum of one hundred and forty-five pounds, the same to be paid on the 4th day of February next, and to be allowed to stand on the premises until the first day of May next." And the following note was signed by the plaintiff, and delivered to the defendant. "I have this day agreed to buy of Mr. John Baxter, a stack of hay, standing in Canonbury Field, Islington, at the sum of 145 £, the same to be paid on the 4th day of February next, and to be allowed to stand on the premises until the first day of May next, the same hay not to be cut until paid for. January 4th, 1825." At the meeting at which the notes were signed, but after the signature thereof, the defendant said to the plaintiff, "You will particularly oblige me by giving me a bill for the amount of the hay." The plaintiff rather objected. The defendant's brother, S. Baxter, on the 8th of the same month of January, took a bill of exchange for 145 £ to the plaintiff, drawn upon him by the defendant, dated the 4th of January 1825, payable one month after date, which the plaintiff accepted. The defendant afterwards indorsed it to George Baxter, and the plaintiff paid it to one Taylor, the holder, when it became due. The stack of hay remained on the same field entire until the 20th of January 1825, when it was accidentally wholly consumed by fire, without any fault or neglect of either party.

A few days after the fire, the plaintiff applied to the defendant to know what he meant to do when the bill became due; the defendant said, "I have paid it away, and you must take it up to be sure: I have nothing to do with it, why did you not remove the hay." The plaintiff said, "he could not, because there was a memorandum 'that it should not be removed until the bill was paid;' would you have suffered it to be removed?" and the defendant said, "Certainly not." The defendant's set-off was for the price of the hay agreed to be sold as aforesaid. The question for the opinion of the Court was, whether the plaintiff under the circumstances was entitled to recover the sum of 145 £ or any part thereof.

Chitty for the plaintiff. The loss in this case must fall upon the defendant. There is a difference between the two contracts; the one contains a stipulation not in the other, that the hay was not to be cut until paid for. Now if that be a material part of the contract, then there was no one sufficient contract in writing to satisfy the Statute of Frauds, but assuming that there was a complete contract of sale without the stipulation, and that the plaintiff thereby consented to waive a right which he otherwise would have had, still the property in the hay had not passed to the vendee, because this was a sale upon credit, and the vendee was not entitled to have possession of the goods until the credit expired; and if so, the property did not vest in him until the credit expired. . . .

Bayley J. It is quite clear that the loss must fall upon him in whom the property was vested at the time when it was destroyed by fire. And the question is, in whom the property in this hay was vested at that time? By the note of the contract delivered to the plaintiff, the defendant agreed to sell the plaintiff ["] a stack of hay standing in Canonbury Field at the sum of 145 £ the same to be paid for on the 4th day of February next, and to be allowed to stand on the premises until the first day of May next." Now this was a contract for an immediate, not a prospective sale. Then the question is, in whom did the property vest by virtue of this contract? The right of property and the right of possession are distinct from each other; the right of possession may be in one person, the right of property in another. A vendor may have a qualified right to retain the goods unless payment is duly made, and yet the property in these goods may be in the vendee. The fact in this case, that the hay was not to be paid for until a future period, and that it was not to be cut until it was paid for, makes no difference, provided it was the intention of the parties that the vendee should, by the contract, immediately acquire a right of property in the goods, and the vendor a right of property in the price. The rule of law is, that where there is an immediate sale, and nothing remains to be done by the vendor as between him and the vendee, the property in the thing sold vests in the vendee, and then all the consequences resulting from the vesting of the property follow, one of which is, that if it be destroyed, the loss falls upon the vendee. The note of the buyer imports also an immediate, perfect, absolute agreement of sale. It seems to me that the true construction of the contract is, that the parties intended an immediate sale, and if that be so, the property vested in the vendee, and the loss must fall upon him. The rule for entering a nonsuit must therefore be made absolute.

Holroyd J. I think that in this case there was an immediate sale of the hay, accompanied with a stipulation on the part of the vendee, that he would not cut it till a given period. Now, in the case of a sale of goods, if nothing remains to be done on the part of the seller, as between him and the buyer, before the thing purchased is to be delivered, the property in the goods immediately passes to the buyer, and that in the price to the seller; but if any act remains to be done on the part of the seller, then the property does not pass until that act has been done. I am of opinion, therefore, in this case, not only that the property immediately passed to the buyer by the contract, but that the seller thereby immediately acquired a right in the price stipulated to be paid for the goods, although that was not to be paid until a future day. The property having passed to the vendee, and having been accidentally destroyed before the day of payment, the loss must fall upon him.

Littledale J. The parties on the 4th of January stipulated for the sale and purchase of a stack of hay, to be paid for in a month. Thus the case would have stood, but for the note of the contract delivered to the buyer, and in that there was a stipulation, that the purchaser should not cut until the money was paid, but the property in the hay had already passed by the contract of sale to the purchaser, and the latter afterwards merely waived his right to the immediate possession. Then the property having passed to the buyer, the loss must fall upon him, and, consequently, this rule for entering a nonsuit must be made absolute.

Rule absolute.

TERRY v. WHEELER
Court of Appeals of New York
25 N.Y. 520 (1862)

APPEAL from the Supreme Court. Action by the assignee of Lewis Elmore, to recover the price paid for a quantity of lumber, purchased by Elmore of the defendant, at his lumber yard in Troy, which the defendant agreed, but failed, to deliver at the railroad in Troy. The defendant denied his liability, on the ground that the title to the property vested in Elmore at the time of the sale, and that the property was destroyed by fire immediately after the sale, without fault on his part. The cause was tried before the court, which found the following facts:

1. That on the 24th day of August, 1854, the defendant sold to Lewis Elmore, by a written bill of sale, a quantity of lumber of the character, at the price, and upon the terms set forth in the bill of sale, and that payment therefor was made as stated in said bill.

      * * *

2. That after such sale and payment, and after delivery of said bill of sale, and in the afternoon of the same day, the memorandum thereupon, as follows — "to be delivered to the cars free of charge" — was indorsed and signed by the clerk of the defendant. . . .

3. That the lumber so sold was, at the time of sale upon the defendant's yard, at the city of Troy, and had been inspected and measured; that the three first items named in the bill constituted one separate pile designated as the lumber sold to Elmore; and as to the remaining item, viz.: 600 pieces, these were to be taken from the top of another pile containing more than that

number, and a mark was made, showing how far the 600 pieces came on that pile.

* * *

5. That the lumber so sold was on the same day of the sale, and within a few hours thereafter, and before the removal of any part thereof, and without any fault or delay on the part of the defendant, accidentally consumed by fire.

* * *

And the court decided that, as the lumber sold was to be delivered by the defendant and was not delivered by him, he was liable to the plaintiff, and on that ground judgment was rendered in favor of the plaintiff for the amount claimed.

* * *

The Supreme Court at general term affirmed the judgment, and the defendant brought this appeal.

* * *

SELDEN, J. ...

* * *

But in the view which I take of the remaining question, it becomes immaterial whether there was a contract to deliver at the cars or not. The lumber had not been actually delivered, but remained in the possession of the vendor. In the absence of any express contract to deliver, there was an implied one to deliver at the yard of the vendor, when called for. In either case the lumber did not remain at the risk of the vendor, if the title did not remain in him. The risk attends upon the title, not upon the possession, where there is no special agreement upon the subject. (*Tarling* v. *Baxter*, 6 B. & C., 360; *Willis* v. *Willis*, 6 Dana. 49; *Hinde* v. *Whitehouse*, 7 East, 558; *Joyce* v. *Adams*, 4 Seld., 296; 2 Kent's Com., 492, 496; Noy's Maxims, 88.) I entertain no doubt that upon the facts found in this case, the title was in the vendee. The lumber was selected by both parties and designated as the lumber sold to Elmore, except the 600 pieces, which were selected by the parties, and the precise pieces sold designated with as much precision as if the purchaser had marked every piece with his name; that which was sold by measurement was inspected and measured, and the quantity ascertained; the price for the whole was agreed upon and paid, and a bill of parcels receipted and delivered to the purchaser. These facts, I think, vested the title in the purchaser, notwithstanding the agreement of the seller to deliver the lumber free of charge, at the cars. "The sale of a specific chattel passes the property therein to the vendee, without delivery." (Chitty on Contr., 8 Am. ed., p. 332.) "It is a general rule of the common law that a mere contract for the sale of goods, where nothing remains to be done by the seller *before* making delivery, transfers the right of property, although the price has not been paid, nor the thing sold delivered to the purchaser. (*Olyphant* v. *Baker*, 5 Denio, 382.) The authorities are numerous, where the expression is used that if anything remains to be done by the seller, the title does not pass; but the cases which are referred to to sustain that position, only go the length of showing that where something is to be done by the seller to ascertain the identity, quantity or quality of the article sold, or to put it in the condition which the terms of the contract require, the title does not pass. (2 Kent's Com., 496; *Hanson* v. *Myer,* 6 East, 614; *Simmons* v. *Swift,* 5 B. & C., 857; *Joyce* v. *Adams,* 4 Seld., 291; *Field* v. *Moore,* Labor's Sup., 418.) ... The questions which arise in such cases, as to sales, are questions of intention, such as arise in all other cases of the interpretation of contracts; and when the facts are ascertained, either by the written agreement of the parties or by the findings of a court, as they are here, they are questions of law. That the parties to the contract in this case intended to pass the title to the lumber immediately, appears very clear; nor do I suppose that any one would question it, were it not for the apparent hardship of the case to the purchaser. If the property, instead of being lumber, had been sheep or cows, capable of increase, (which follows the ownership,) and there had been a sudden and large increase to the flock, or drove, before they could be delivered at the point agreed upon, I think no one would have said that the defendant could have discharged his obligation to deliver, and yet retained the increase. Such, however, must be the conclusion, if the plaintiff's position is maintained. The judgment should be reversed and a new trial granted.

All the judges concurring.

Judgment reversed, and new trial ordered.

BIGLER v. HALL
Commission of Appeals of New York
54 N.Y. 167 (1873)

APPEAL from judgment of the General Term of the Supreme Court, in the sixth judicial district, entered upon an order directing judgment on a verdict in favor of the plaintiff, and denying a motion for a new trial.

This action was brought to recover damages for the nondelivery of all the logs specified in the following contract:

"DEPOSIT, N.Y., *April* 30, 1864.

"Contract between John Luscomb and Joseph M. Hall, of the first party, and Simon Bigler, of the second party.

"Said Luscomb and Hall do agree to deliver, in the Susquehanna river, at Binghamton, in rafts, from 150 to 200,000 feet of pine logs, above the Pratt & Tyler saw mill. Said lumber comprises a lot of logs, about 1,000 in number, six miles above Susquehanna Depot, now on the bank of the river, and about fifty more about one-half a mile farther up, and about 400 near Windsor, fifty of the poorest of these 400 may be thrown out and not rafted, more or less. They are all to be delivered as above. They are all to be measured in the log, by Mr. S. R. Carpenter. Said logs shall be rafted as soon as the middle of June, 1864, and delivered as soon as the water is high enough thereafter to run them. Said Bigler is to pay sixteen dollars per 1,000 feet, one-half at two months, and the balance at three months, in good bankable paper, to be dated when the account of measurement is handed in, $200 to be paid within six days of this date, by mail.

(Signed)

"J. M. HALL.

"JOHN LUSCOMB.

"SIMON BIGLER, *by James.*"

The logs were measured by Carpenter and paid for as agreed. A portion of the logs were lost by a freshet in the river, and on the trial the jury found a verdict for the plaintiff for the sum of $1,200, the price paid for the logs, which were not delivered.

The main question on the trial of the action was, whether the defendants were liable absolutely for the contract price of the lumber in the logs that were not delivered, or were only liable in case such logs were lost through their negligence. The ruling was that the defendants were liable absolutely.

* * *

LOTT, Ch. J. The defendants, by the express terms of the contract, for the breach of which this action was brought, did "agree to deliver, in the Susquehanna river at Binghamton, in rafts, from one hundred and fifty to two hundred thousand feet of pine logs, above the Pratt & Tyler saw-mill." . . . There is no ambiguity or uncertainty in any of its terms. It is a contract for the absolute delivery of the logs at a designated place and time, for a price to be ascertained in a specified manner.

Such being the construction of the contract, and the plaintiff having paid the defendants the whole amount for which he was liable, they were bound to deliver the logs according to its terms, and they were not discharged from the obligation by their inability to do it, in consequence of freshets which caused a loss of some of them. They did not make any provision against such a casualty or accident. It was one which they could have guarded against, and it is not unreasonable to assume that both parties contemplated the possibility of such a contingency in fixing the price to be paid by the plaintiff. Assuming, then, that the legal obligation of the defendants was as above stated, it is immaterial whether the logs were lost through their negligence or not. That question is not involved in the case.

It follows that the judge at the circuit properly ruled that the plaintiff was entitled to recover for what lumber he paid for and had not been delivered to him by the defendants according to their agreement, and as such payment was made at least two years before the day of trial, he, in charging the jury that the plaintiff was also entitled to interest on that sum for one year and ten months, charged more favorably to the defendants than the law required. The error, if any, was to the plaintiff's prejudice and their advantage. . . .

* * *

It may be proper to add, that it does not appear to have been made a question on the trial whether the contract was a contract of *sale,* but the points litigated seem to have been whether the defendants were absolutely liable for all of the logs that had not been delivered, on the construction of the agreement that he had bound himself, without any qualification of his obligation, to make *a delivery of all,* or whether they were only liable for such as had been lost or not delivered through their fault or negligence. I have consequently not considered it. It seems to me, however, immaterial. If it can be so construed, and if the logs mentioned in the contract became the property of the plaintiff as soon as they were measured and paid for by him, as the defendants claim on this appeal, it does not follow, as they say, that "from that time they were at his risk." The absolute and unqualified obligation of the defendants to *deliver* them at the place designated for that purpose still existed, and their failure to fulfill and discharge it, and their duty growing out of it, made them liable for the damages growing out of its breach.

In any aspect of the case the plaintiff was entitled to recover. It follows that the judgment appealed from is not erroneous, and it must, consequently, be affirmed, with costs.

REYNOLDS, C. (dissenting.)   The logs were designated or identified by their location at the time of the contract, and were to be delivered in the Susquehanna river at Binghamton in rafts. . . . A portion of the logs were never delivered having been carried away by an unprecedented freshet, it is claimed without any fault of the defendants, and the recovery was had for the supposed difference between the amount of lumber actually paid for and that actually delivered upon the ground that the logs and lumber were at the risk of the defendants until actually delivered, and if the title did not pass to the plaintiff when the lumber was measured and paid for[,] the recovery should be sustained. It appears to me that everything was done by way of identification, ascertainment of quantity and payment of price to make an executed contract of sale, and that the title passed to the plaintiff. Nothing remained but actual delivery, and that in very many cases, is not essential to the transfer of title to a purchaser. It would hardly be claimed that if a party went to a merchant and selected, purchased, and paid for a valuable article in his line of business, he did not acquire the title because it was left in the merchant's store to be sent to the residence of the purchaser. The case of *Terry* v. *Wheeler* (25 N.Y. 520), appears to be decisive of the one at bar. . . . The actual delivery of the logs as the contract provided was a very important element as it is in almost every contract of sale. Both parties appreciated its importance and were doubtless familiar with its perils. It cannot be supposed that the plaintiff intended to pay for more lumber than he received, or that the defendants took pay for more than they intended to deliver. But a contingency happened which neither party anticipated, and was not specially provided for. The defendants were bound to use their utmost efforts to deliver all the logs for which they had been paid; but they were not insurers. They offered to show that the logs were lost by no fault or negligence on their part, and they should have been allowed to do so, as I think upon that question alone depended their liability.

There should be a new trial.

All concur for affirmance except REYNOLDS, C., dissenting.

Judgment affirmed.

UNIFORM SALES ACT
(Adopted in New York 1911)

1. *Contracts to Sell and Sales.* (1) A contract to sell goods is a contract whereby the seller agrees to transfer the property in goods to the buyer for a consideration called the price.

(2) A sale of goods is an agreement whereby the seller transfers the property in goods to the buyer for a consideration called the price.

(3) A contract to sell or a sale may be absolute or conditional.

(4) There may be a contract to sell or a sale between one part owner and another.

* * *

7. *Destruction of Goods Sold.* (1) Where the parties purport to sell specific goods, and the goods without the knowledge of the seller have wholly perished at the time when the agreement is made the agreement is void.

(2) Where the parties purport to sell specific goods, and the goods without the knowledge of the seller have perished in part or have wholly or in a material part so deteriorated in quality as to be substantially changed in character, the buyer may at his option treat the sale —

(a) As avoided, or

(b) As transferring the property in all of the existing goods or in so much thereof as have not deteriorated, and as binding the buyer to pay the full agreed price if the sale was indivisible, or to pay the agreed price for the goods in which the property passes if the sale was divisible.

8. *Destruction of Goods Contracted to be Sold.* (1) Where there is a contract to sell specific goods, and subsequently, but before the risk passes to the buyer, without any fault on the part of the seller or the buyer, the goods wholly perish, the contract is thereby avoided.

(2) Where there is a contract to sell specific goods, and subsequently, but before the risk passes to the buyer, without any fault of the seller or the buyer, part of the goods perish or the whole or a material part of the goods so deteriorate in quality as to be substantially changed in character, the buyer may at his option treat the contract —

(a) As avoided, or

(b)   As binding the seller to transfer the property in all of the existing goods or in so much thereof as have not deteriorated, and as binding the buyer to pay the full agreed price if the contract was indivisible, or to pay the agreed price for so much of the goods as the seller, by the buyer's option, is bound to transfer if the contract was divisible.

* * *

17.   *No Property Passes Until Goods Are Ascertained.* Where there is a contract to sell unascertained goods no property in the goods is transferred to the buyer unless and until the goods are ascertained, but property in an undivided share of ascertained goods may be transferred as provided in section 6.

18.   *Property in Specific Goods Passes When Parties So Intend.* (1) Where there is a contract to sell specific or ascertained goods, the property in them is transferred to the buyer at such time as the parties to the contract intend it to be transferred.

(2)   For the purpose of ascertaining the intention of the parties, regard shall be had to the terms of the contract, the conduct of the parties, usages of trade and the circumstances of the case.

19.   *Rules for Ascertaining Intention.* Unless a different intention appears, the following are rules for ascertaining the intention of the parties as to the time at which the property in the goods is to pass to the buyer.

Rule 1.   Where there is an unconditional contract to sell specific goods, in a deliverable state, the property in the goods passes to the buyer when the contract is made, and it is immaterial whether the time of payment, or the time of delivery, or both, be postponed.

Rule 2.   Where there is a contract to sell specific goods and the seller is bound to do something to the goods, for the purpose of putting them into a deliverable state, the property does not pass until such thing be done.

Rule 3.   (1) When goods are delivered to the buyer "on sale or return," or on other terms indicating an intention to make a present sale, but to give the buyer an option to return the goods instead of paying the price, the property passes to the buyer on delivery, but he may revest the property in the seller by returning or tendering the goods within the time fixed in the contract, or, if no time has been fixed, within a reasonable time.

(2)   When goods are delivered to the buyer on approval or on trial or on satisfaction, or other similar terms, the property therein passes to the buyer —

(a)   When he signifies his approval or acceptance to the seller or does any other act adopting the transaction;

(b)   If he does not signify his approval or acceptance to the seller, but retains the goods without giving notice of rejection, then, if a time has been fixed for the return of the goods, on the expiration of such time, and, if no time has been fixed, on the expiration of a reasonable time. What is a reasonable time is a question of fact.

Rule 4.   (1) When there is a contract to sell unascertained or future goods by description, and goods of that description and in a deliverable state are unconditionally appropriated to the contract, either by the seller with the assent of the buyer, or by the buyer with the assent of the seller, the property in the goods thereupon passes to the buyer. Such assent may be expressed or implied, and may be given before or after the appropriation is made.

(2)   Where, in pursuance of a contract to sell, the seller delivers the goods to the buyer, or to a carrier or other bailee (whether named by the buyer or not) for the purpose of transmission to or holding for the buyer, he is presumed to have unconditionally appropriated the goods to the contract, except in the cases provided for in the next rule and in section 20. This presumption is applicable, although by the terms of the contract, the buyer is to pay the price before receiving delivery of the goods, and the goods are marked with the words "collect on delivery" or their equivalents.

Rule 5.   If the contract to sell requires the seller to deliver the goods to the buyer, or at a particular place, or to pay the freight or cost of transportation to the buyer, or to a particular place, the property does not pass until the goods have been delivered to the buyer or reached the place agreed upon.

* * *

22.   *Risk of Loss.* Unless otherwise agreed, the goods remain at the seller's risk until the property therein is transferred to the buyer, but when the property therein is transferred to the buyer the goods are at the buyer's risk whether delivery has been made or not, except that —

(a)   Where delivery of the goods has been made to the buyer or to a bailee for the buyer, in pursuance of the contract and the property in the goods has been retained by the seller merely to secure performance by the buyer of his obligations under the contract, the goods are at the buyer's risk from the time of such delivery.

(b)   Where delivery has been delayed through the fault of either the buyer or seller the goods are at the risk of the party in fault as regards any loss which might not have occurred but for such fault.

COCHRAN v. FRIEDMAN
Appellate Term, Supreme Court of New York
191 N.Y.S. 729 (1922)

GUY, J.   Action to recover for 136 boxes of apples which plaintiffs [Cochran] sold to defendants [Friedman] together with 609 like boxes of apples also sold to defendants after the 745 boxes had been unloaded on the Erie Railroad pier on June 4, 1920. The 609 boxes were removed and delivered by plaintiffs' truckman, who alone had the right to remove them from the pier, on June 4, 1920, and for the 609 boxes delivered plaintiffs were paid.

The 136 remaining boxes, not having been removed on June 4, 1920, were stolen from the pier during the night of June 4-5, and for their agreed price the action is brought, the parties stipulating the recovery shall be $442 or nothing.

Defense was a general denial.

Plaintiffs were consignees of the apples over the Erie Railroad. The proof establishes that upon arrival defendants bought from plaintiff the entire carload, consisting of 745 boxes; that plaintiffs refused to deliver except through their own truckman; that plaintiffs' truckman delivered 609 boxes as directed by defendants' buyer, but was unable to find room for the remaining 136 boxes in the storage warehouse where defendants directed them to be stored, so they were left on the pier by the truckman overnight and were stolen. The boxes remained in plaintiffs' constructive possession, through their truckman, until they were actually delivered. Plaintiffs, not defendants, are responsible for any losses that occurred before actual delivery. Brady v. Cassidy, 145 N.Y. 171, 176-180, 39 N.E. 814; Id., 104 N.Y. 147, 152, 156, 10 N.E. 131; Gross v. Ajello, 132 App. Div. 25, 28, 116 N.Y. Supp. 380; Personal Property Law (Consol. Laws, c. 41) § 100 [Uniform Sales Act § 19], rule 5.

Judgment reversed, with $30 costs, and complaint dismissed on the merits, with costs. All concur.

VOGT v. CHASE BROS. CO.
Court of Appeals of New York
235 N.Y. 206, 139 N.E. 242 (1923)

Action by John W. Vogt against the Chase Brothers Company. From a judgment of the Appellate Division of the Supreme Court (202 App. Div. 786, 194 N.Y. Supp. 986) affirming by a divided court a judgment of the Trial Term entered on the verdict of a jury for the plaintiff, defendant appeals. Judgments of the Appellate Division and of the Trial Term reversed, and complaint dismissed.

* * *

PER CURIAM. In October, 1919, the plaintiff made a contract to sell to the defendant at an agreed price a large quantity of apple trees, delivery to be made on board cars at Dansville. The defendant was to have the privilege at its option of requiring delivery in the fall or in the following spring. "Fall delivery to be paid December 1; storage and spring delivery June 1." The sale was limited to trees which conformed to stated requirements of size and quality.

After the trees were dug up, but before they were graded and sorted so as to be ready for the market, the plaintiff placed them in storage at Dansville in a warehouse suggested by the defendant. After they reached the warehouse, the work of grading and sorting was completed. During the winter the trees while yet in storage were damaged by the cold. The plaintiff has sued for the agreed price, asserting that the warehouse had been substituted for the railroad cars as the place of delivery. The defendant maintains that the trees while in storage, awaiting delivery in the spring, were still the property of the seller.

We think the evidence upholds the defendant's position and no other. The witnesses, who state the conversation leading up to the storage at the warehouse, differ in points of detail. By none of them is there said anything which requires the conclusion that there was a modification of the contract. What followed shows clearly that no modification was intended. The plaintiff, after utilizing the warehouse to put the trees in shape for delivery to the buyer, clearly recognized that he was under a continuing obligation to load them on the cars. The correspondence between the parties, read in the light of the contract with the option there conferred upon the buyer, permits no other inference. It follows that title did not pass, and that the risk of loss was with the seller. Personal Prop. Law § 100 [U.S.A. § 19], rule 5; Id., § 103 [U.S.A. § 22]; Consol. Laws, c. 41.

The judgment of the Appellate Division and that of the Trial Term should be reversed, and the complaint dismissed, with costs in all courts.

HOGAN, CARDOZO, POUND, and McLAUGHLIN, JJ., concur.

HISCOCK, C. J., and CRANE, J., dissent.

ANDREWS, J., absent.

Judgment accordingly.

LLEWELLYN, CASES AND MATERIALS ON THE LAW OF SALES* 561-66 (1930)

The law of Sales began, as its name implies, with property problems: present sale of existing, specified goods. "The property" in these goods passed on the sale from S to B. What is this property in, or title to goods? In the prevailing legal ideology it is a somewhat mystical something, located, as to any particular goods, in some definite person. From the fact that the person has the title various consequences are thought of as "flowing": his freedom to hold and use the goods; his rights that others shall do neither, nor interfere with his possession and use; his power to sell, and other persons' disability to sell and "give good title"; his power to recover the goods specifically from a bailee, even though the bailee be insolvent; his economic gain or loss if the market for the goods rises or falls, or the goods are worked up to advantage or are destroyed; the power of his creditors, and the disability of any other per-

---

*Reprinted from Cases and Materials on the Law of Sales, published by Callaghan & Company, 6141 North Cicero Avenue, Chicago, Illinois 60646.

son's creditors, to levy on the goods. All these things, and more, are conceived as "attributes of title"; not as its constituents, but as its consequences. Hence, when one of these matters is in issue, the quest is for the title. Who has it? Having located him and it, we have the wherewithal to solve the problem. And why trouble to define a concept so familiar, so established in every day experience, as "ownership," "title," "property in goods"?

If this were all, we should have little need for a law of Sales. And initially, this, or something closely like it, is about all. The picture is again that of the cash-and-carry market, with buyer and seller strangers and dealing at arm's length, as to a specific chattel physically before them. At the outset of the chaffering, title is in the seller; it remains there as the chaffering moves to its conclusion. If a bargain is struck (the phrase calls back the ancient formality of the handclasp before which mere words remained mere words) contract, payment, and delivery will be as close to simultaneous as man can make them. And B can then walk away with the chattel — it is his — title has leaped into him. No one saw it leap; but that occasions no confusion. Bargain, payment and delivery have occurred; the deal was single; and it is unambiguously closed.

But what if any of the matters which thus concur is postponed to a later date? (1) There has been a completed bargain, as to specific goods before the parties, but neither payment nor delivery. The goods then burn. Whose loss? If title was in B, it was not signalized by its common, every-day indication, possession. (2) There has been a completed bargain, as to specific goods before the parties, but S in bargaining misdescribed the goods, and B justifiably relied on the misdescription, it being a matter that inspection then and there could not determine. If the words of description were operative, has B title? What operated to vest it in him? If he has title, is it voidable, for fraud, or mistake, or breach of warranty? This will not fit the simple concept of a single, wholly completed deal. (3) What now, if the goods bargained for were not identified at the time of dicker — perhaps not in existence — but only described? A deal has been closed. But has title passed to B? Title to what? And when S later, in B's absence, sets apart, or makes, or buys, and marks the goods for B, what then? Suppose B has paid, and S after the marking goes insolvent. B claims the goods marked, in specie; S's trustee resists. Again the older simple mold refuses to fit. (4) Or, finally, after completed dicker as to present identified goods, B without paying walks off with the goods. Are they "his"? Was payment a condition to his getting "title"?

The difficulty is plain. "Title" cannot be seen; the only way to locate "it" is by reference to and inference from other facts. Possession and right to possession is one such fact; risk of loss is another; power to give good title to a third person is a third. In the simple case of every day commonsense, all these are found together. Indeed, each is commonly enough thought of off-hand as never found apart from title. From the presence of the attributes one can therefore — if one wishes — infer the mystic presence. *But in precisely those cases where a legal problem arises these attributes are split between the contending parties:* the "indicia" are ambiguous. Each contender is marked by one sign as "owner," by another sign as "not-owner." What to do? The confusion, if one searches for a solution merely by way of title, is obvious and inevitable. One might expect at this point some recognition of the fact that the ancient common-sense concept does not wholly fit the situation. One might expect that the litigated situation would be recognized as peculiar, as *abnormal,* and that men would set about developing concepts to fit and solve the peculiar problems of the peculiar situation: that *special concepts to cover the problems of buyer-seller disputes* would be built. In part, they have been. But slowly. The inertia of old ideas, reinforced by the common sense of every day life — ("Everybody knows what title is") — and especially the assumption in the early cases that *sale,* immediate outright sale of specific goods, was the normal course of events, kept people thinking and arguing in terms of "the title," of who as between B and S had "it" — of when and under what circumstances "it passed."

In the law of pledge the concept of "special property," as contrasted with "general property" was developed to care for a similar mixed situation; in the law of mortgages and trusts, the concepts of "security title" and "encumbrance," of "legal title subject to equities" and "equitable title" were developed for similar purposes. These split concepts were not wholly adequate, but they were an admirable beginning. Sales law has been curiously backward in building analogous concepts. They are, to be sure, definitely in process of emergence; a good number have already clearly emerged; but the vital thing to note is that the process is as groping and uncertain as it is stubborn; and that it is often obscured, still more often hindered or twisted, by the traditional language used in discussing the situations. This traditional language still presupposes that the determining problem in a sales case is the location of *"the"* title in either B or S; and that the decision will follow of necessity from that location. So the feeling and "the rule" that the price normally cannot be recovered unless "the title has passed" and that risk normally "follows title." *But it does not often happen that a decision on the location of title is really necessary to decide the issue in the case,* and the oftener the issue arises out of a contract for sale, the less often is the location of title really determinative.

* * *

. . . Lump-concept thinking moves in terms of *wide* premises. Decide that on specific facts "title" is in either B or S; and you can then proceed to draw a dozen conclusions, as to risk, price, rules of damages, levy by creditors, etc.; among the dozen will be one deciding the case in hand. And the ruling in one case as to "who had title" is authority for a "like" ruling in another case, although the narrow issues to be decided in the two cases are quite different; the emphasis in the deciding and in later use of the holding is on the lump-concept *as a lump.* . . .

The advantages of narrow-issue thinking and concepts are obvious. First, they make possible a neater description of what has happened. The meaning of a case is always clearer when one knows and states exactly what issue was decided, *as well as* what *ratio decidendi* was expressed; and ... the *ratio decidendi* will have clearer outline if the court has occupied itself with study of the narrow issues and differentiation of other narrow issues. Secondly, the policy aspects of the narow issues come in for observation and study, under narrow-issue thinking. ... The narrow issues that arise on questions "of title" are largely questions involving the allocation of a great number of distinct risks; risk of destruction; risk of disposing of the goods (can S have price, or only damages?); risk of being able to cover in the event of non-delivery (time and place of measure of damages); risk of S's insolvency (B opposing S's creditors); risk of S's or B's dishonesty or bad faith (attempted fraudulent resale to a third party). Each of these risk problems raises policy-questions all its own; different facts have different significance in regard to the different questions — as a matter of sense. Narrow-issue thinking, leads to weighing these differences as a matter of sense, in order to see whether similar differences should follow, in law. And it is safe to say that in matters involving title the trend of the last century and a quarter toward *differentiation* of narrower concepts and issues is as marked as is the trend toward coalescence of the varieties of seller's obligation. As marked, but not as consistently developed. Lump-thinking, even in a single court (as in the [Uniform Sales] Act,) will still be found running hand in hand with narrow-issue thinking.

QUESTION AND PROBLEMS

1. Did the concept of title, or property in the goods, importantly affect your solution of the problem cases on risk of loss, to be decided under Argentine law?

2. In Llewellyn's terms, does the Argentine Commercial Code emphasize lump-concept or narrow-issue thinking? Is the same true of the Civil Code of Argentina? Find some specific examples to support your conclusion.

3. Are there ever any advantages to the lump-concept approach? Consider the matter first from the point of view of a judge who must decide a case, and then from the point of view of a merchant planning his transactions.

4. Analyze and decide the problem cases stated at pp. 331-32, *supra*, under the provisions of the Uniform Sales Act reprinted above. Then consider the same problems under the provisions of the Uniform Commercial Code which follow.

UNIFORM COMMERCIAL CODE (1962 Official Text)

* * *

§ 1-102.—PURPOSES; RULES OF CONSTRUCTION.

(1)   This Act shall be liberally construed and applied to promote its underlying purposes and policies.

(2)   Underlying purposes and policies of this Act are

> (a)   to simplify, clarify and modernize the law governing commercial transactions;
> (b)   to permit the continued expansion of commercial practices through custom, usage and agreement of the parties;
> (c)   to make uniform the law among the various jurisdictions.

(3)   The effect of provisions of this Act may be varied by agreement, except as otherwise provided in this Act and except that the obligations of good faith, diligence, reasonableness and care prescribed by this Act may not be disclaimed by agreement but the parties may by agreement determine the standards by which the performance of such obligations is to be measured if such standards are not manifestly unreasonable.

(4)   The presence in certain provisions of this Act of the words "unless otherwise agreed" or words of similar import does not imply that the effect of other provisions may not be varied by agreement under subsection (3).

(5)   In this Act unless the context otherwise requires

> (a)   words in the singular number include the plural, and in the plural include the singular;
> (b)   words of the masculine gender include the feminine and neuter, and when the sense so indicates words of the neuter gender may refer to any gender.

§ 1-103.—SUPPLEMENTARY GENERAL PRINCIPLES OF LAW APPLICABLE.

Unless displaced by the particular provisions of this Act, the principles of law and equity, including the law merchant and the law relative to capacity to contract, principal and agent, estoppel, fraud, misrepresentation, duress, coercion, mistake, bankruptcy, or other validating or invalidating cause shall supplement its provisions.

* * *

§ 1-205.—COURSE OF DEALING AND USAGE OF TRADE.

(1)   A course of dealing is a sequence of previous conduct between the parties to a particular transaction which is in fact fairly to be regarded as

establishing a common basis of understanding for interpreting their expressions and other conduct.

(2) A usage of trade is any practice or method of dealing having such regularity of observance in a place, vocation or trade as to justify an expectation that it will be observed with respect to the transaction in question. The existence and scope of such a usage are to be proved as facts. If it is established that such a usage is embodied in a written trade code or similar writing the interpretation of the writing is for the court.

(3) A course of dealing between parties and any usage of trade in which they are engaged or of which they are or should be aware give particular meaning to and supplement or qualify terms of an agreement.

(4) The express terms of an agreement and an applicable course of dealing or usage of trade shall be construed wherever reasonable as consistent with each other; but when such construction is unreasonable express terms control both course of dealing and usage of trade and course of dealing controls usage of trade.

(5) An applicable usage of trade in the place where any part of performance is to occur shall be used in interpreting the agreement as to that part of the performance.

(6) Evidence of a relevant usage of trade offered by one party is not admissible unless and until he has given the other party such notice as the court finds sufficient to prevent unfair surprise to the latter.

* * *

§ 2-103.—DEFINITIONS AND INDEX OF DEFINITIONS.

(1) In this Article unless the context otherwise requires

(a) "Buyer" means a person who buys or contracts to buy goods.
(b) "Good faith" in the case of a merchant means honesty in fact and the observance of reasonable commercial standards of fair dealing in the trade.
(c) "Receipt" of goods means taking physical possession of them.
(d) "Seller" means a person who sells or contracts to sell goods.

* * *

§ 2-104.—DEFINITIONS. "MERCHANT"; "BETWEEN MERCHANTS"; "FINANCING AGENCY."

(1) "Merchant" means a person who deals in goods of the kind or otherwise by his occupation holds himself out as having knowledge or skill peculiar to the practices or goods involved in the transaction or to whom such knowledge or skill may be attributed by his employment of an agent or broker

or other intermediary who by his occupation holds himself out as having such knowledge or skill.

* * *

(3) "Between merchants" means in any transaction with respect to which both parties are chargeable with the knowledge or skill of merchants.

* * *

§ 2-301.—GENERAL OBLIGATIONS OF PARTIES.

The obligation of the seller is to transfer and deliver and that of the buyer is to accept and pay in accordance with the contract.

* * *

§ 2-303.—ALLOCATION OR DIVISION OF RISKS.

Where this Article allocates a risk or a burden as between the parties "unless otherwise agreed," the agreement may not only shift the allocation but may also divide the risk or burden.

* * *

§ 2-401.—PASSING OF TITLE; RESERVATION FOR SECURITY; LIMITED APPLICATION OF THIS SECTION.

Each provision of this Article with regard to the rights, obligations and remedies of the seller, the buyer, purchasers or other third parties applies irrespective of title to the goods except where the provision refers to such title. Insofar as situations are not covered by the other provisions of this Article and matters concerning title become material the following rules apply:

(1) Title to goods cannot pass under a contract for sale prior to their identification to the contract (Section 2-501), and unless otherwise explicitly agreed the buyer acquires by their identification a special property as limited by this Act. Any retention or reservation by the seller of the title (property) in goods shipped or delivered to the buyer is limited in effect to a reservation of a security interest. Subject to these provisions and to the provisions of the Article on Secured Transactions (Article 9), title to goods passes from the seller to the buyer in any manner and on any conditions explicitly agreed on by the parties.

(2) Unless otherwise explicitly agreed title passes to the buyer at the time and place at which the seller completes his performance with reference to the physical delivery of the goods, despite any reservation of a security interest and even though a document of title is to be delivered at a different time or place; and in particular and despite any reservation of a security interest by the bill of lading

(a)   if the contract requires or authorizes the seller to send the goods to the buyer but does not require him to deliver them at destination, title passes to the buyer at the time and place of shipment; but

(b)   if the contract requires delivery at destination, title passes on tender there.

(3)   Unless otherwise explicitly agreed where delivery is to be made without moving the goods,

(a)   if the seller is to deliver a document of title, title passes at the time when and the place where he delivers such documents; or

(b)   if the goods are at the time of contracting already identified and no documents are to be delivered, title passes at the time and place of contracting.

(4)   A rejection or other refusal by the buyer to receive or retain the goods, whether or not justified, or a justified revocation of acceptance revests title to the goods in the seller. Such revesting occurs by operation of law and is not a "sale."

* * *

§ 2-509.—RISK OF LOSS IN THE ABSENCE OF BREACH.

(1)   Where the contract requires or authorizes the seller to ship the goods by carrier

(a)   if it does not require him to deliver at a particular destination, the risk if loss passes to the buyer when the goods are duly delivered to the carrier even though the shipment is under reservation (Section 2-505); but

(b)   if it does require him to deliver them at a particular destination and the goods are there duly tendered while in the possession of the carrier, the risk of loss passes to the buyer when the goods are there duly so tendered as to enable the buyer to take delivery.

(2)   Where the goods are held by a bailee to be delivered without being moved, the risk of loss passes to the buyer

(a)   on his receipt of a negotiable instrument of title covering the goods; or

(b)   on acknowledgment by the bailee of the buyer's right to possession of the goods; or

(c)   after his receipt of a non-negotiable document of title or other written direction to deliver, as provided in subsection (4) (b) of Section 2-503.

(3)   In any case not within subsection (1) or (2), the risk of loss passes to the buyer on his receipt of the goods if the seller is a merchant; otherwise the risk passes to the buyer on tender of delivery.

(4) The provisions of this section are subject to contrary agreement of the parties and to the provisions of this Article on sale on approval (Section 2-327), and on effect of breach on risk of loss (Section 2-510).

§ 2-510.—EFFECT OF BREACH ON RISK OF LOSS.

(1) Where a tender or delivery of goods so fails to conform to the contract as to give a right of rejection the risk of their loss remains on the seller until cure or acceptance.

(2) Where the buyer rightfully revokes acceptance he may to the extent of any deficiency in his effective insurance coverage treat the risk of loss as having rested on the seller from the beginning.

(3) Where the buyer as to conforming goods already identified to the contract for sale repudiates or is otherwise in breach before risk of their loss has passed to him, the seller may to the extent of any deficiency in his effective insurance coverage treat the risk of loss as resting on the buyer for a commercially reasonable time.

* * *

§ 2-613.—CASUALTY TO UNIQUE GOODS.

Where the contract requires for its performance goods identified when the contract is made, and the goods suffer casualty without fault of either party before the risk of loss passes to the buyer, or in a proper case under a "no arrival, no sale" term (Section 2-324) then

> (a) if the loss is total the contract is avoided; and
> (b) if the loss is partial or the goods have so deteriorated as no longer to conform to the contract the buyer may nevertheless demand inspection and at his option either treat the contract as avoided or accept the goods with due allowance from the contract price for the deterioration or the deficiency in quantity but without further right against the seller.

* * *

§ 2-615.—EXCUSE BY FAILURE OF PRESUPPOSED CONDITIONS.

Except so far as a seller may have assumed a greater obligation and subject to the preceding section on substituted performance:

> (a) Delay in delivery or non-delivery in whole or in part by a seller who complies with paragraphs (b) and (c) is not a breach of his duty under a contract for sale if performance as agreed has been made impracticable by the occurrence of a contingency the non-occurrence of which

was a basic assumption on which the contract was made or by compliance in good faith with any applicable foreign or domestic governmental regulation or order whether or not it later proves to be invalid.

(b)   Where the causes mentioned in paragraph (a) affect only a part of the seller's capacity to perform, he must allocate production and deliveries among his customers but may at his option include regular customers not then under contract as well as his own requirements for further manufacture. He may so allocate in any manner which is fair and reasonable.

(c)   The seller must notify the buyer seasonally that there will be delay or non-delivery and, when allocation is required under paragraph (b), of the estimated quota thus made available for the buyer.

* * *

§ 2-709.—ACTION FOR THE PRICE.

(1)   When the buyer fails to pay the price as it becomes due the seller may recover, together with any incidental damages under the next section, the price

> (a)   of goods accepted or of conforming goods lost or damaged within a commercially reasonable time after risk of their loss has passed to the buyer; and
> (b)   of goods identified to the contract if the seller is unable after reasonable effort to resell them at a reasonable price or the circumstances reasonably indicate that such effort will be unavailing.

(2)   Where the seller sues for the price he must hold for the buyer any goods which have been identified to the contract and are still in his control except that if resale becomes possible he may resell them at any time prior to the collection of the judgment. The net proceeds of any such resale must be credited to the buyer and payment of the judgment entitles him to any goods not resold.

(3)   After the buyer has wrongfully rejected or revoked acceptance of the goods or has failed to make a payment due or has repudiated (Section 2-610), a seller who is held not entitled to the price under this section shall nevertheless be awarded damages for non-acceptance under the preceding section.

QUESTIONS ON THE UNIFORM COMMERCIAL CODE

1.   Taking the foregoing excerpts as typical, has the Uniform Commercial Code adopted Llewellyn's views on the desirability of narrow-issue thinking? Find some specific examples to support your conclusion.

2. Taking the foregoing excerpts as typical, does the UCC achieve the following basic purposes of codification:

> (a) Does it make commercial law more "knowable" than it would be in the absence of codification? Knowable by whom? Is the UCC a significant improvement in this respect over the Uniform Sales Act?
> (b) Will the UCC reduce commercial litigation by making the results of cases more predictable than they would be in the absence of codification? Is the UCC a significant improvement in this respect over the Uniform Sales Act?

3. Assuming near-universal adoption in the United States, will the UCC achieve interstate uniformity of commercial law? What are the minimum *legislative* requirements for achieving uniformity?

4. Does it strike you as anomalous that the civilians, who "invented" the notion of separate rules for merchants, have failed in their risk-of-loss rules to make the distinction made in UCC § 2-509(2) between merchants and others? From this apparent anomaly, what conclusions do you draw about civilian and common law analytical tendencies?

SCHLESINGER, THE UNIFORM COMMERCIAL CODE
IN THE LIGHT OF COMPARATIVE LAW
1 INTER-AM. L. REV.* 11, 40-51 (1959)

* * *

In the Anglo-American legal system, the law merchant was absorbed into the common law during the 17th and 18th centuries. As a result, the manifold difficulties arising from a dichotomy between "civil" and "commercial" law are practically unknown in the common law world. In legal writing, or for the purpose of curricular grouping of subjects, English and American scholars may find it convenient occasionally to use the term "commercial law." But it is not a term of art indicating a basic dichotomy between two sets of positive rules, the operation of one of which is predicated in the mercantile quality of the parties or their acts. To reintroduce the latter kind of dichotomy into the legal system of the United States, would have been a step backward, a step which the draftsmen of the Uniform Commercial Code wisely avoided. The Code, as distinguished from its European and Latin-Amer-

---

*Copyright ©, 1959 by the Inter-American Law Review, reprinted by permission.

In this article Professor Schlesinger made use of a Study which he had prepared for the Law Revision Commission of the State of New York. See N.Y. Leg. Doc. (1955) N° 65 (A), pp. 57-98. The views expressed in that Study and in this article are, however, exclusively those of Professor Schlesinger, and may not be attributed to the New York Law Revision Commission.

ican namesakes, does not create special rules for "merchants" or "mercantile acts." Only in a few provisions of the Sales Article do we find special rules for merchants. Apart from these few exceptions, the Code, in accordance with existing law, treats the merchant and the non-merchant alike, and subjects the occasional transaction of the farmer or the college professor, if it is of a type covered by the Code, to the same rules which govern the commercial deals of professional traders.[85]

An additional point must be considered in attempting to compare the Code with commercial codes of civil law countries. The latter codes almost invariably contain, as a feature of central importance, provisions concerning the *Commercial Register.* That institution somewhat mitigates the difficulties of demarcation between merchants and non-merchants; an individual, partnership or corporation listed in the Register may be deemed to be a merchant, at least for the benefit of other persons dealing with him who in good faith have relied on the entry in the Register. Commercial corporations often do not acquire juristic personality before being entered in the Register. Changes in the corporate charter or bylaws likewise may require such entry to become effective. Perhaps even more importantly, the Register informs the public as to what individuals have power to act for the registered firm, as owners, partners, officers or agents. Members of the public relying on such entry are protected in many civil law jurisdictions, the theory being that an entry in the Register, or sometimes even its silence, gives rise to a kind of estoppel. This is a matter of great convenience, because it obviates the trouble of inquiring into the powers actually given to officers and agents, and tremendously reduces the number of instances in which a commercial contract can be attacked by the principal on the ground of his agent's lack of authority. In the United States, the device of the Commercial Register is unknown to the law. Nor could it be created by a simple stroke of the pen, because it depends on institutions which do not presently exist here, and which would have to be built up by legislative fiat without the benefit of a living tradition. The Code, at any rate, makes no attempt to introduce the Commercial Register, which from a businessman's point of view may well be the most significant single feature of "commercial law" as understood by the civilians.

We conclude, then, that in coverage and basic organization the Code is radically different from the traditional commercial codes of the civil law orbit. In the interest of a world-wide uniformity, this may be regrettable. The fact, however, that European scholars and legislators themselves are turning away from their traditional dichotomy, weakens this uniformity argument. On balance, more would be lost than gained by wholesale imitation, as to coverage and over-all organization, of one of the civilian models of a commercial code.

---

[85] In many instances, of course, the Code holds the professional trader to a higher *standard;* but this is a far cry from creating a distinct law for merchants.

2. *The Code and the Modern "Unitary" Trend in Europe — Are the Problems the Same?*

a. *Coverage of the Code.* We may reject the dualistic approach of the civilians, who traditionally divide their private law into a "civil" and a "commercial" area. But the question remains whether the Uniform Commercial Code's own basic scheme, developed independently of continental learning, is clear and useful. Spokesmen for the sponsors have emphasized, as indeed the most cursory glance at the table of contents of the Code seems to indicate, that the attempted approach has been functional. The social function for which the Code apparently is intended to supply the legal framework, is the flow of goods from producer to ultimate consumer. This flow could not be maintained without financing, and thus the Code's coverage is extended so as to include financing and security devices. Carrying functional thinking a step further, however, one might observe that under present-day conditions the movement of goods requires insurance as much as financing. Yet, the subject of insurance law is left outside the Code, an exclusion not easily explicable on functional grounds. The draftsmen, for good practical reasons, did not ride the functional horse through thick and thin.

It is difficult to see, moreover, how the flow of goods can function without the help of brokers, sales agencies, commission agents, traveling salesmen and other agents and employees. A truly functional approach, therefore, would necessitate the inclusion of a considerable portion of the law of agency. In civil law countries, where the basic dichotomy between "civil" and "commercial" matters calls for an essentially functional distinction, the subject of "commercial" matters calls for an essentially functional distinction, the subject of "commercial" agency is treated in the commercial codes, along with "commercial" contracts, "commercial" partnerships and, in some instances, "commercial" corporations. It is, perhaps, this very functionalism of the civilian commercial codes (historically explicable, to be sure), which is responsible for their shortcomings. Had the draftsmen of the Uniform Commercial Code carried the functional approach to its logical conclusion, the resulting code probably would have suffered from similar weaknesses as did its European counterparts. The draftsmen, wisely, did not engage in such functional extremism.

Viewed analytically rather than functionally, the Code contains some but not all of the rules and principles of the law of contracts and of personal property which are pertinent to certain kinds of contracts and transfers. By and large, the Code states special rules applicable to special types of transactions; but occasionally, especially in articles 2 and 9, principles of considerable generality are stated or reflected in provisions of the Code. Questions which the Code does not answer, even though they pertain to a subject covered by the Code, must be answered on the basis of the general law of contracts and personal property — a body of law which, in the United States, is mostly uncodified and non-uniform.

* * *

A North-American observer, looking at the civilian developments briefly sketched above, and trying to relate them to the proposed Uniform Commercial Code, will seek an answer to the following question: If the civilians who have had centuries of experience under a system of separate, autonomous commercial law, now turn away from that system and seek to integrate their commercial law into their general private law, is it not a step backwards for us to go in the opposite direction, that is, to stimulate the growth of a distinct body of commercial law by the adoption of a separate commercial code, which by its very nature as a uniform code will serve to set our commercial law apart from the uncodified, non-uniform body of the general law?

In trying to find an answer to this question, we have to take account of the fact that a state legislature in the United States, which considers adoption of the Uniform Commercial Code, is dealing with practical problems very different from those encountered by reformers of commercial law in present-day Europe or Latin-America. In the countries of the civil law, the issue of codification *vel non* has long been settled. In those countries, virtually all legal rules and principles, at least in the area of private law, are embodied and systematized in the codes. Some code provisions, it is true, may be so general that they allow considerable scope for judicial lawmaking. Ultimately, however, most civilians regard it as clear at least in theory that the basis for decision in every case must be found in a provision, specific or general, of the code. The civilian reformer who seeks to abolish the separate commercial code and to reduce to a minimum the purely "commercial" titles and sections of a new integrated civil code or code of obligations, is tackling a problem of revision and reorganization of *existing codes.*

Lawyers in the United States, on the contrary, are now struggling with the fundamental issue: whether they should codify at all; or, to put it more precisely, whether they should codify the rules and principles of commercial law which until now have been either unwritten or contained in various disconnected statutes.

Another policy consideration which importantly bears on the desirability of the proposed Code, is that of uniformity. Again, this is not a live issue for the civilian legislator of today, because for him this question, too, has long been settled. In countries like France and Italy, which have a central form of government and vest almost all legislative pover in the national parliament, codification automatically means unification of the law. In countries having a federal system, such as Brazil, Germany or Switzerland, it would be possible, theoretically, to follow the example of the United States and to leave the bulk of substantive private law to the states. In by-gone days, this system actually prevailed in some federal countries of the civil law orbit. In time, however, the wave of the codification movement engulfed the federal as well as the centrally governed countries, with the result that today virtually all of these countries have federal codes covering the whole area of substantive private law. It follows that for most civilians the issues of codification *vel non* and of national uniformity *vel non* are of merely historical interest. On these questions, which are the over-riding policy issues in discussions of the proposed Uniform Commercial Code, lawyers and legislators in the United States cannot expect much help from present-day writings of civilian scholars.

The civilians' great debate, on the other hand, concerns the issue of unity of private law versus autonomy of commercial law, an issue which in the common law world was laid to rest more than a century ago when the law merchant was absorbed into the common law. The Code would not undo this process of absorption. On the whole, it does not purport to reestablish a separate set of rules for transactions of merchants, or for "mercantile transactions." Many of the arguments used in the debates among the civilians revolve around the issue of abolishing or at least minimizing the instances in which merchants' transactions are subject to rules differing from the general law. This, as has been shown, is an issue which in the common law world has been settled by the merger of law merchant and general law, and which the Code does not purport to revive, in spite of the possibly misleading emphasis which its title places on the "commercial" nature of its subject.

In most civil law countries, the issue is further complicated by the question whether or not separate commercial courts (or commercial "chambers" of civil courts) should be preserved. Again, this is an issue which does not trouble lawyers in common law countries. The jury system assures lay participation in the determination of many lawsuits, and common law judges, most of whom are veterans of the Bar, generally have more business experience than the career judges of civil law countries. Litigating businessmen who prefer to stay away from juries, from politically selected judges and from the unnecessary complexities of judicial procedure, may, moreover, submit their disputes to arbitration, which is favored by modern legislation in the United States, at least in the commercially important states. It is perhaps for these reasons that there is no agitation for the establishment of special commercial courts in the United States. At any rate, we have no such courts. The issues of defining the jurisdiction of these special tribunals and of properly differentiating their procedure from the more cumbersome practice of ordinary courts — important issues in the civil law world — do not exist here.

It follows that the problem facing legislators in the United States, i.e., the problem of assessing the desirability of the Uniform Commercial Code, and the civilians' problem of deciding whether the Code's namesakes in civil law countries should be continued as separate codes, are not comparable problems, and that the arguments used in the present great debate in Europe are largely irrelevant to the issue before us.

PART TWO

PART TWO

Chapter IV

LAND REFORM

A. Introduction

The demand for change in Latin America's land tenure system is only one phase of the social revolution which the region shares with other nations in the underdeveloped two-thirds of the world. See Szulc, The Winds of Revolution (1963); Heilbroner, The Great Ascent (1963). It is, however, a phase of the revolution which is closely bound to the legal and institutional structure of the developing societies, and thus a fit subject for law study. In this chapter, the focus is on issues of legislative policy; much of the material of the chapter is "non-legal," in that it relates to the factual background for legislation or administration. But it should be remembered that all law develops — in court decisions no less than through legislation — in response to the facts of social need as perceived by the lawmakers:

> In substance the growth of the law is legislative. . . . The very considerations which judges most rarely mention, and always with an apology, are the secret root from which the law draws all the juices of life. I mean, of course, considerations of what is expedient for the community concerned. Holmes, The Common Law 35 (1881).

At some stage in virtually all meaningful legal inquiry, a similar analysis of a legislative, policy-oriented nature must be made.

Much of the following discussion is cast in general terms such as rural society, Latin American agriculture, and so on. It must always be remembered that the region is diverse in its populations, its soils, its climates, its political and economic histories. One cannot legitimately equate the modern, large-scale commercial agriculture of northwestern Mexico or southern Brazil with the semi-feudal and stagnant agriculture of the Andes of Peru and Ecuador; and neither of these presents the same problems as the plantation economy of Central America. From time to time in these materials, the attempt is made to differentiate among the varying economic and social settings for purposes of legislative analysis. Where no such distinctions are explicitly made, however, it should not be thought that they can be ignored.

Land ownership in most of Latin America is highly concentrated. The statement is not new, but the following representative pre-reform figures make its full meaning clear. (In Peru, these data remain substantially accurate. In Venezuela, the reform movement that began in 1958 has modified the tenure structure significantly.)

Peru (1957):
Number of farms

		Farm area	
Total:	85,600	Total:	9,778,000 hectares*
Under 5 hectares:	50,910	Farms under 5 hectares:	83,000 hectares
	(59.5%)		(0.9% of total land area)
Over 1000 hectares:	1,404	Farms over 1000 hectares:	7,443,000 hectares
	(1.6%)		(76.2% of total land area)

Venezuela (1956):
Number of farms

		Farm area	
Total:	397,800	Total:	29,590,000 hectares
Under 5 hectares:	266,287	Farms under 5 hectares:	658,400 hectares
	(66.9%)		(22% of total land area)
Over 1000 hectares:	6,759	Farms over 1000 hectares:	22,038,000 hectares
	(1.7%)		(74.5% of total land area)

[Source: CARROLL (ed.), LA CREACION DE NUEVAS UNIDADES AGRICOLAS 32-33 (FAO, 1961;) see also U.C.L.A. LATIN AMERICAN CENTER, STATISTICAL ABSTRACT OF LATIN AMERICA (currently in its eighth edition).]

Although "the U.S. finds it extremely difficult to maintain a consistent and clearly defined position on reforms,"** land reform is coming to Latin America, and partly under the sponsorship of the United States. The Charter of Punta del Este, signed in August, 1961, commits this country "To encourage ... programs of integral agrarian reform, leading to the effective transformation, where required, of unjust structures and systems of land tenure and use; with a view to replacing latifundia [the large estates of the traditional landed oligarchy] and dwarf holdings by an equitable system of property ...." N.Y. Times, Aug. 17, 1961, p. 8, col. 3. The Alliance for Progress thus contemplates some of its progress in the area of land reform. The Alliance is sometimes criticized for being too frankly interventionist in character, and it is

---

* One hectare equals just under 2 ½ acres.
** Dorner and Thiesenhusen, *Relevant Research Programs to be Conducted in Developing Countries*, 46 J. FARM ECON. 1095 (1964).

sometimes criticized from another quarter for putting the "ins" in charge of a revolution aimed at converting them into "outs." (For the latter view, see FLORES, LAND REFORM AND THE ALLIANCE FOR PROGRESS 12 [1963].) Whatever its prospects, however, the Alliance does place the weight of official United States policy on the side of massive, fundamental and widespread reform.

It would be a mistake to think of land tenure structures primarily in physical terms. What is important is a series of relations among men, concerning land. The institutions of land tenure, like other legal institutions, can be analyzed in the abstract only at great risk of misunderstanding. Legal relations, especially those governing the allocation of basic economic resources, both shape and are shaped by a complex system of social organization.* While it is stretching the point to say that Latin American rural society is feudal, it is no exaggeration to say that very large numbers of men and women in the society live in conditions of serfdom. The English word "peonage" has a Spanish origin, and its connotation of bondage to service is prefectly apt to describe the state of much of the agricultural labor force in Latin America, especially in countries with large indigenous populations. The great mass of the Indian population of Latin America has lived in slavery or near slavery as far back as we can see or reconstruct. The Spanish Conquest did not originate the condition; it simply added some refinements designed to salve the Christian conscience. Professor Whetten summarizes the colonial experience below.

WHETTEN, RURAL MEXICO**
81-85, 91-94 (1948)

The *encomienda* was a device [established in 1576 by a Royal Charter of Philip II] for accomplishing the threefold purpose of (1) Christianizing the Indians, (2) bringing them into subjection to the Crown, and (3) rewarding the conquistadors for their exploits. It consisted of an allotment in trust of one or more villages to a given individual, and it carried with it the right to collect tribute from the inhabitants and to exact certain personal services from them, such as labor in the fields and in the household. The individual receiving such a grant was referred to as an *encomendero* and was obligated to Christianize the Indians falling under his jurisdiction and to protect their persons and property. At first, the *encomienda* was regarded as a temporary arrangement, subject to the pleasure of the king; but pressure from the recipients of such grants

---

* A recent and outstanding example of analysis of land and labor law in social context is Dawson, *Labor Legislation and Social Integration in Guatemala: 1871-1944*, 14 AM. J. COMP. L. 124 (1965).

** Reprinted from Rural Mexico by Nathan Whetten by permission of the University of Chicago Press. Copyright 1948 by The University of Chicago.

resulted in a series of decrees extending them from one generation to another for at least five generations.

* * *

Undoubtedly, some of the village lands were alienated during this period by means of direct purchase. We have mentioned the fact that *encomenderos* had the right to collect tribute and to exact services from the Indians entrusted to them as a part of the *encomienda*. Indians of the free villages, not falling under the *encomienda* system, were required to pay tribute directly to the Crown. This royal tribute, especially in years when harvests were poor, left the villagers almost constantly in need of money. Landowners took advantage of these needs by bargaining with the Indians for their lands. Although royal decrees had been issued to the effect that the Indians must not be cheated, these laws were easily circumvented, and some of the more valuable village lands were secured for a fraction of their value.

As a result of reports which reached Spain from time to time concerning the adverse effect that the *encomienda* system was having on the personal liberties and property rights of the Indians, a series of measures was dictated, with the object of restricting the control and influence of the *encomenderos*. These measures finally culminated in an edict, in 1720, abolishing the *encomienda* system entirely except for the one large grant in perpetuity to Cortes and his heirs; but the abolition came too late to be effective. By this time the *encomenderos* had such firm control on the lives and property of the Indians that the latter were virtually serfs. As indicated previously, most of the *encomenderos* had taken advantage of opportunities to acquire some degree of legal sanction to their intrusted holdings through the *composición** so that they no longer considered the *encomienda* as the legal source of authority for their landholdings. Furthermore, a system of small advanced payments to the Indians had developed which virtually bound them to the land through indebtedness that they were never able to liquidate.

* * *

The *encomienda* not only served as a means of destroying the autonomy of the landholding village but facilitated the formation of haciendas as well. It was not an entirely new device, since it had previously been used by Spain in the conquest of the Balearic and Canary Islands and in the reconquest of southern Spain from the Moors. It fitted neatly into the developments which had taken place among the aborigines, as described previously, and enabled the Spaniards to take the place of the conquered rulers with a minimum of disturbance to existing practices.

The *encomienda* grants varied greatly in size; some of them contained

---

* A settlement or confirmation of title in the "rightful" possessor of land. Lands not so confirmed, including most lands held by Indian villages, were subject to occupation as Crown lands, and subsequent confirmation to the occupant. — Ed.

numerous villages and thousands of Indians. To Cortes himself was allotted a vast concession consisting of 22 towns, including 23,000 vassals and a total population of about 115,000 inhabitants. The lands falling under his jurisdiction by means of this grant amounted to at least 25,000 square miles, located in the states of Morelos, Oaxaca, Puebla, Mexico, and Veracruz. This grant included some of the richest farming land in all Mexico. The royal grant specified that Cortes should have the vassals and the lands, including woods, pastures, and all water, both running and stagnant. Furthermore, he was to have complete civil and criminal jurisdiction over the inhabitants. All his possessions, including some that were acquired subsequent to the original grant, were converted into an entailed estate (mayorazgo) in 1535, so that they would pass undivided to his heirs. By the beginning of the nineteenth century these possessions were still largely intact and were reported to include 15 villas, 157 pueblos, 89 haciendas, 119 ranchos, 5 estancias, and a total population of 150,000 inhabitants. To one of Cortes' lieutenants were given towns, villages, and lands, which together constituted an area of over 10,000 square miles in what is now the state of Guanajuato. To Pedro de Alvarado was given the fertile alluvial farming district and town of Xochimilco, which contained at the time about 30,000 Indians. The conquistadors who had acquired less fame were given smaller concessions. Many had to be content with a few villages. Some received only one, and in a few cases a single town was divided between two conquistadors.

The encomiendas were confined for the most part to the more densely inhabited areas, since their chief value was to be found in the tribute to be collected and the labor that could be exacted from the Indians. The total number of villages granted in encomiendas or the exact amount of land involved is unknown, but McBride is of the opinion that a large proportion of the inhabited region of Mexico was held in encomienda before the end of the first half-century. He also presents data indicating that, by the year 1572, at least 507 encomiendas had been granted to private individuals and that these yielded an annual tribute amounting to 400,000 pesos. To these encomiendas, more than to any other single factor, may be attributed the origin of the hacienda. It was not originally intended that these grants should become permanent, but their duration was extended from time to time and the encomenderos gradually came to regard the land as their personal property and the inhabitants as their serfs. Many had taken advantage of the composiciones and other measures to secure confirmation of titles to their holdings, so that when the encomienda was finally abolished legally in 1720 it had already been largely transformed into the hacienda.*

---

* See also SIMPSON, THE ENCOMIENDA IN NEW SPAIN (1950). — Ed.

PEONIAS AND CABALLERIAS

Not all the conquistadors were given *encomiendas*. To some were given small outright grants of land, with no jurisdiction whatsoever over Indians. These grants were usually of two kinds: (1) the *peonía,* consisting of about 100-200 acres and including various types of lands considered necessary for the support of a single family; (2) the *caballería,* which was to consist of an area equal to five times that of the *peonía.* While these allotments were small in area, they frequently served as a nucleus around which to accumulate larger holdings. Many took advantage of the opportunity of doing this through the process of gradual annexation of adjoining lands and subsequent confirmation of titles. Information which would show the total land accumulations through these two types of grants is unavailable, but they are believed to be the source of a great many haciendas.

ENTAILED ESTATES

Another factor tending to perpetuate the large holding was the tendency for persons to seek titles of nobility, with which would go a *mayorazgo.* The *mayorazgo* must then remain undivided. How this tended to work out can best be described in the words of McBride:

> No sooner would a colonist acquire a fortune, whether from trade, mining, the tribute of Indian villages, or the product of his farms, than he would seek a title of nobility and with his title would go the estate, which must then remain undivided. Distinguished services to the crown were also rewarded by the bestowal of a title accompanied by the creation of a *mayorazgo,* and often with a large grant of land or of tribute villages. It was this custom of forming *mayorazgos,* a custom which prevailed until the era of independence, that was largely responsible for the preservation of large estates in Mexico. Aggregation was constantly going on; division of property was almost impossible. [Quoting from MCBRIDE, THE LAND SYSTEMS OF MEXICO 43 (1923).]

ECCLESIASTICAL PROPERTIES

One of the most important sources of the hacienda is to be found in the accumulation of vast landed estates in the hands of the church. The Spaniards were familiar with the church as a landholding institution in Spain, and measures were taken which were intended to prevent a similar occurrence in New Spain. A royal decree was issued in 1535 which forbade recipients of lands to sell them to church, monastery, or ecclesiastical persons under penalty of having them confiscated and given to others. It was specifically stated that not even a site for a monastery or other religious institution could be obtained without special permit from the king or viceroy. Yet these and other measures proved to be of little avail in preventing or curtailing the rapid accumulation of property by the clergy. These accumulations were facilitated by the tremendous political and secular power which the clergy rapidly acquired. An indication of the political influence which they achieved may be seen from the fact that, of sixty viceroys appointed in Mexico, eleven were bishops or archbishops. Furthermore, the clergy enjoyed the advantage of immunity conferred on them by the *fuero*. Through this measure they could claim the right to be tried only by ecclesiastical judges and could claim exemption from taxation.

The colonial era ended in the revolutions that brought independence to the countries of Latin America early in the 19th century. While support for some of the revolutions was sought from among the dispossessed, not one of the wars for independence produced any meaningful social reform. The great estates continued to flourish, and the church properties described above by Professor Whetten became enormous. During the reform movement led by Juárez in midcentury Mexico, an effort was made to break up the church holdings, much as had occurred in England during the reign of Henry VIII. But the application of this mortmain legislation resulted, ironically, in an increase in concentration of land holdings, not a decrease, as the following famous speech relates.

SPEECH OF LUIS CABRERA

before the Mexican Chamber of Deputies, December 3, 1912, in
SILVA HERZOG, 1 BREVE HISTORIA DE LA REVOLUCION MEXICANA
at 2 (1960); also in 2 LA CUESTION DE LA TIERRA at 267 (1961)

[The speaker is describing the three types of land held by the villages in Mexico during the colonial era]. The *casco*, which was the area alloted for truly urban living; the *ejido,* designated for the communal life of the village, and the *propios,* destined for the municipal life of the village.

We do not need to concern ourselves with the *casco*. The *ejidos* and the *propios* have been the origin of some very important economic phenomena in our country. Everyone who has read an abstract of title to lands in the colonial epoch can feel how the struggle between the haciendas and the villages dominates every page of the abstract of a hacienda or of a village. In the rural economic struggle that took place during the colonial epoch between the villages and the haciendas, the triumph went to the village because of its privileges, its organization, the effective cooperation which the indigenous population and the inhabitants of the villages had learned during centuries, and, above all, because of the enormous power put in the hands of the villages by possession of the *propios,* as elements of wealth for the struggle, and the *ejidos,* as sources of sustenance.

The *ejidos* assured the village its subsistence, the *propios* guaranteed power to the village authorities; the *ejidos* were the security of the families gathered around the church, and the *propios* were the economic power of the municipal authority of those villages, which were no more or less than great landowners in opposition to the haciendas. This was the secret of the preservation of the common people against the haciendas, despite the very great privileges in political matters which the Spanish landholders had in the colonial epoch.

The *propios* were abused, and they even came to constitute a veritable mortmain [inalienable estate in land], and when, by virtue of later laws, the freeing of dead-hand control over property was attempted, there was no hesitation in considering that the *propios* were a very dangerous form of mortmain, and that it was necessary to destroy them just as the mortmains of religious institutions and lay corporations were destroyed.

The situation of the villages with respect to the haciendas was manifestly privileged up to the mortmain laws of 1856.* These laws have already been perfectly well evaluated [by other writers] in their economic aspects, and you all know without my repeating it that while they were a necessity with respect to the *propios* of the villages, they were a very serious and great mistake when applied to the *ejidos.* The mortmain laws were applied to the *ejidos* in the form that you all know, in conformance with the circulars of October and December 1856, it being determined that, instead of being adjudicated to the tenants, the *ejidos* should be distributed, and from then on they were called lands for distribution, among the inhabitants of the villages. This was the beginning of the disappearance of the *ejidos,* and the origin of the absolute impoverishment of the villages. At present — I will not say because of usurpations, which there have been; I will not say because of thefts or complicities with the authorities, which there have been by the thousands — but because of the form given to the previously inalienable lands of the *ejidos,* it was natural, economically, that the latter should come into the hands of those who knew how to use them better. From the hands of the villagers favored in a distribution, sooner or later they would have to go to form a new estate or a new *latifundio* with the character of a hacienda, or to be added to the surrounding haciendas. You know the results; in certain zones of the Republic and principally in the zone of Central Mesa, all the *ejidos* are found to constitute an integral part of the neighboring estates. . . .

Thus, whether because of the mismanagement of small title holders, or because of abuses by the authorities, the truth is that the *ejidos* have passed almost completely from the hands of the villages into the hands of the *hacen-*

* See p. 453, *infra.*

dados; as a consequence of this, a great number of populations find themselves at present absolutely unable to satisfy even their most elemental necessities.
. . .

* * *

The mortmain laws of 1856, doing away with the *ejidos,* left nothing else as means of livelihood for the inhabitants of the villages (who previously were able to subsist throughout the year by means of the harvest and cultivation of the *ejidos*) than a condition of slavery, of serfdom to the estates. When you ask the reason for the rural slavery in the country, inquire immediately whether, within the estates from which the cries of slavery emerge, there is a population with *ejidos.* And if there is no population with *ejidos* surrounding it, . . . you will understand that the slavery of the haciendas exists in inverse ratio to the existence of *ejidos* in the villages.

Other devices for despoiling the villages of their land in Mexico were: (a) an 1894 law permitting any inhabitant to file a claim to land which had never been legally transferred by the government — which included most village lands, since under the 1856 reform laws villages were not eligible to hold land; (b) an 1888 law, later amended, the interpretation and application of which made it possible for politically influential persons to control the supply of water to village lands; and (c) the punishment of some villages on the ground that their people had participated in rebellion against the government. All these techniques are described in WHETTEN, RURAL MEXICO at 87-89 (1948).

A similar pattern of events is found in the history of other countries of Latin America. In the years following Independence (roughly from 1820 forward), political and economic thought in the region was dominated by classical 19th century liberalism, which was theoretically incompatible with paternalistic protection of the Indians. Bolívar himself wanted to break up the Andean villages' communal holdings; San Martín argued that no legal distinctions could be made among the citizens of Peru: all were to be called "Peruvians." The strong individualism of the property provisions of the Code Napoléon were reflected in the civil codes of the new nations. Throughout Latin America, the lands of the indigenous communities were absorbed by the haciendas and plantations. Theoretical devotion to liberal doctrine did not prevent the use of state coercion (*e.g.,* vagrancy laws) to obtain the labor force needed to operate the great estates.

Professor Tannenbaum's description of the classical hacienda, which follows, portrays one end of a continuum of large rural estates in Latin America. At the other end is the modern large-scale commercial farm, which pays cash wages and produces a cash crop for market. Most large rural properties in Latin America fall between the two; while the evils described by Professor Tannenbaum often are not fully present, they are present in some significant degree in a majority of the great estates throughout the region. The hacienda, partly because of its inability to adapt to changed circumstances, is a dying institution. The following description deserves careful attention, however, for it pictures the target of all modern fundamental land reforms in Latin America.

TANNENBAUM, TOWARD AN APPRECIATION OF LATIN AMERICA, in THE UNITED STATES AND LATIN AMERICA
(2d ed., Matthews)* at 5, 29-38 (1959)

The hacienda plays a special role in Latin America. It would be no exaggeration to say that the hacienda, or as it is known in Brazil, the *fazenda,* set the tone and determined the quality of Latin American culture during the nineteenth and early part of the twentieth century, until the first world war and in some instances (as in Ecuador, Chile and Peru, and in spite of appearances in Argentina and other areas) until the present. This is not an argument for unitary causation. There are also the Spanish tradition, the presence of the Indian and the negro, the broad influence of the Church and the impact of the larger world to consider. But we are dealing with an area where in most places over one half of the population is rural, and until very recently the rural proportion was much larger. We are also dealing with an area where the typical holding is in large units. The United Nations estimated in 1951 that 1½ per cent of the total land holdings in lots of over 15,000 acres are equal to half the agricultural land. Some of these are very extensive indeed. There were plantations in Mexico of a million acres, and there are similar units in Brazil and in other countries. And one family may have a number of agricultural units of large acreage scattered over the country.

It is not the size of the hacienda that is in question, but its organization. Before entering into a discussion of the hacienda as such, it is useful to note that at least in the Andean countries and in Central America and Mexico we are dealing with two distinctive agricultural systems: the hacienda and the village community. In Guatemala, for instance, the hacienda will have the valley, the slopes and rolling hills, the best agricultural lands, while the Indian villages will occupy the steep mountains, the inaccessible areas and the poor soil. This was true in Mexico; it is true in Ecuador and in Peru. In fact, the hacienda has the best agricultural lands, and the Indians or mestizo villages the poorest. The village may be communal, following an older Indian tradition, or it may have adopted every possible variation that lies between collective and individual ownership.

But the village is a community with its own local traditional government, and the closer one gets to an Indian community the truer this is, and this village government is participated in by the entire male population. It looks after the public works, the policing and the roads; it builds a school in common, if there is a school, and cares for the church. Each individual as he grows up has in turn to share in the various tasks that the community requires. In the case of Amatanango in the State of Chiapas, Mexico, as an example, each boy begins as a messenger for the town government, takes his turn in time as one of the policemen, and after satisfying all the required offices in the civil government and in the church, ends up as an *"anciano,"* one of the elders who govern the community as a council. The Indian and the mestizo village is a community, with its own collective personality. Each member has a recognized place of his own and a defined relation to all the others. He is a participant in government and church because he has regular functions to perform in both. This village may be next to a hacienda, and there are instances where the village somehow survived surrounded by a hacienda.

Generally speaking, however, the rural world divides sharply — the hacienda in the valley and the village on the steep mountain sides. Between these two agricultural organizations there has always been friction, the hacienda encroaching upon the village, absorbing its woods, pastures, water supply; and the village every now and then rising in rebellion, protesting, going to court. The story is an old one and goes back to the early days after the conquest when the Indians crowded the offices of the Spanish officials asking for protection against the hacendado who was encroaching upon their lands.

After independence, the Indians were less able to find protection against the neighboring hacienda. The history of rural land holdings since independence is one where in the name of liberalism, equality and individual rights the Indian was increasingly dispossessed of his lands in favor of the hacienda. The struggle against the Church by the new national governments tended to increase the size of the hacienda and the power and prestige of its owner. The little villages during the same period decreased in number, size and significance. Where they expanded — in relatively small number and isolated areas, as in Southern Chile, Southern Brazil, and some places in Argentina — they had little bearing on the general trend in rural organization. The private hacienda had carried everything before it.

The hacienda is not just an agricultural property owned by an individual. It is a society, under private auspices. The hacienda governs the life of those attached to it from the cradle to the grave, and greatly influences all of the rest of the country. It is economics, politics, education, social structure and industrial development. It is a curious fact in Latin American intellectual life that the hacienda, which is so all embracing in its influence is, except for an occasional novel, never written about or seriously studied. It is, or was, so taken for granted that the intellectuals who were mostly the children of a hacienda were not conscious of its existence — like the air we breathe. When the Latin American sociologist looked for something to write about he worried about the unemployed in London or about the new sugar or banana plantation in foreign hands. The hacienda, which was the basis of the politics of the country as a whole, he was hardly aware of.

The hacienda as a society may be described by saying that it was — and is — an economic and social system that seeks to achieve self-sufficiency or autarchy on a local scale. It seeks this not as a matter of malice, but in the logic of a given institution to expand so as to have within its own borders all that it needs, salt from the sea, *panela* (black sugar) from its own fields, corn, barley and wheat, coconuts, bananas, apples and pears. All of this depends upon where the hacienda is located. If it can run from the seacoast to the mountain top, from the river bottom where sugar cane will grow to the snow line, then it can raise all of the crops that will grow in all of the climates. Not all haciendas — not any perhaps — satisfy this ideal completely, but that is the bent of hacienda organization: buy nothing, raise and make everything within the limits of your own boundaries. The big house is built from the timbers on the place — and these may be, as I have seen them, of mahogany. The furniture is made at home; the cloth is woven on the place from the sheep; the llamas that graze in the hills, the oxen, the horses, are raised and broken on the place; the saddles, bridles, harnesses, are made from the hides of the slaughtered animals. The wooden plow, the wagon, the windmill for the grinding of the corn, or the watermill for the grinding of cane are all made on the place. The table may be loaded at a meal with every kind of meat, grain and fruit — and all of these, the table itself, the house, and the servants as well, will all have been raised, contrived, conserved, grown on the place, including the tablecloth that covers the table, the sandals of the servants, if they are not barefooted. And perhaps even the Indian musician who sits behind the screen and plays his old songs on the homemade instrument is also of the plantation. I am recalling this from personal experience on a plantation in the Province of Ayacucho in Peru.

The people on the plantation are born there. They cannot leave because they may be in debt, or because there is no place to go, for this is home and every other place is foreign. And here too their fathers and grandfathers were born and are buried. If the place changes hands, they change with it. In 1948 the leading newspaper in La Paz, Bolivia, carried an advertisement offering for sale on the main highway a half hour from the capital of the country a hacienda with five hundred acres of land, fifty sheep, much water and *twenty peons*. And similar advertisements have appeared even more recently in Ecuador and Chile. (This I have from others, one a native scholar, the other an American political scientist.) The point is that what we are dealing with is a closed economic, social, political and cultural institution.

Its administrative organization is an interesting adaptation to an aristocratic agricultural society of a non-commercial economy. For the hacienda is a way of life rather than a business. It is not an investment. It was inherited. It is operated with the expenditure of as little cash as possible. If the hacienda is large there may be a couple of hundred or more families residing within its borders. These are scattered in groups of five or ten families in different parts of the hacienda, depending on the kind of land, crops, forest. The laborer usually has a hut which he has built, and a given amount of land, which he works or shares. The hacienda provides the land, the work animals and the seed; and the peon turns over, carrying to the granary by the big house, the share of the crop belonging to the hacendado. The share is determined by the crop, and the tradition of the hacienda. In addition, the Indian also owes the landlord a given number of days' work each week throughout the year. This practice varies. It might be one day's work a week for each hectare of land, or so many days a week for living on the land. The families might also owe a certain amount of service in the big house. The point is that the hacienda has its labor supplied to it without the use of money. If there are two hundred families on the hacienda and if they each owed only one day's work a week for each of two hectares allotted to each family, it would have 400 work days each week.

The labor at its disposal without expenditure of any money for wages is used by the hacienda for working those lands which it tills on its own account. These lands might be in sugar cane, from which it can either with oxen or water power in a small homemade *trapiche,* squeeze out the juice and make *panela,* a dark unrefined sugar, and manufacture rum as well. Or its cash crop may be coffee or cacao, or other products which can be carried to the market on the backs of mules, or on the backs of men, over steep mountain and narrow gorges, to the nearest railroad station, or more recently to the nearest automobile road, or to the nearest town. The cash crop will have been raised, harvested and delivered part or all of the way to the nearest market without the expenditure of any money.

In a curious way, the hacienda is largely beyond the reach of the money economy. Internally it provides, so far as it can, for all of its needs as a going concern as well as a community without recourse to the market. The seed the hacienda supplies to the sharecroppers comes out of the store houses in which it was deposited in the fall; if the laboring population living on the hacienda runs short of food or other supplies they can be purchased in the store — *tienda de raya,* in Mexican parlance, or *company store* in our own economic history. The peon will pay no cash for his purchase for he has no money. It will be written down in a little book by a storekeeper, usually some distant relative or *compadre* of the hacendado. The debt can be liquidated by labor, but it rarely is and serves to tie the laboring population to the hacienda, as they cannot leave without first paying off their debt. This has long been so. It has roots in the colonial system. It persisted all through the nineteenth century, and is still in full vigor wherever the hacienda system survives. It is as hard to kill as was the company store, token coin, or script [sic], in the mining and lumbering camps in the United States. And token coin has its use on the hacienda, for the payment of wages, for the extra labor which may be needed beyond that owed by the peons or for tasks which for some reason lie outside the traditional work the peons accept as theirs. These token coins, sometimes bearing the name of the hacienda, or a piece of metal stamped with *vale un día de trabajo* (it is worth one day's work) can only be exchanged in the hacienda store.

As the hacienda satisfies its own and its community's needs with as little recourse to the market as possible, it buys little, and it sells little as well. The distances, the poor roads, the primitive means of communication, make the transport of goods from one part of the country to another difficult and expensive. The relatively small income from the hacienda is, so to speak, net profit — taxes on land have always been low, the cost of production is at a minimum in monetary terms.

The hacienda is, however, not merely an economic enterprise. It is also a social, political and cultural institution. Socially it is a closed community living within its borders. Part of the hacienda population will be located near the big house, where the store, the church, the school (if there is one), the repair shops, granaries, the blacksmith, carpenter, harness shop will also be. The grist mill and the *trapiche* (sugar mill) will also, in all likelihood, be near the big house if there is water close by. The stables for the favorite horses, cows and other animals raised for household use or consumption will also be close by. The laborers about the big house tend to all these different functions. This is usually the larger part of the hacienda community. The others are scattered in small groups in different parts of the domain, tending different duties and raising crops appropriate to the altitude, the climate, moisture and heat. Each little *rancho* hamlet is isolated and far away. It may be anything from one to ten or more miles from the next hamlet, depending upon the size of the hacienda. Their contacts with the outside world are few indeed, and the paths on the hacienda lead to the center where the big house is located, and only one rarely used path goes off to another hacienda, and to still another until the neighboring town is reached, which may be ten, twenty, thirty or more miles away.

Community activity takes place in front of the big house, on Sundays, when the peonage will have come to church, even if there is no priest in regular attendance. All burials, christenings, marriages, when they are solemnized, are social matters involving the church and as large a part of the hacienda community as is aware of the occasion. The important feast days are likely to be the saint's day of the owner, or of some other favorite member of the family. Then the entire community will turn the event into a holiday with decorations, music, dancing and drinking. A similar event is celebrating the patron saint of the church. There may be others, depending on the local Indian, mestizo or negro traditions. Beyond these festive occasions, the hacienda community has no public functions or responsibilities. It is not a political unit, an organized parish, a government, or a cooperative. If any vestige of the older Indian community survives on the hacienda, it is unrecognized by the hacendado and what functions it retains must of necessity lie outside of the hacienda as a going concern.

There may be and often is a bond between the peons and the hacendado which goes beyond the formal manager-laborer relation. The hacendado may have stood as godfather to may of the children born on the place. He may have a role not as employer primarily, but as the head of a family of which all the laborers consider themselves members. The hacienda laborers' community may have an integration resting on many years of cooperation, interdependence and mutual aid. The hacienda is an old institution. It has usually belonged to the same family over many generations, sometimes for centuries. Isolation from the larger world has tended to bring the hacendados within the same region close to each other. By intermarriage the owner of the hacienda tends to be related to most of the proprietors of the neighboring properties. Time, circumstance, and danger have brought the hacendados of the region close together, and their family connections will have knitted an extended family over a vast area where everyone knows and is related to everyone else.

One or another of these closely knitted families will have, through time, acquired an ascendancy over the others, a kind of traditional leadership in the region. And given the basis of fealty in the extended family and the godfather relation that always exists, you have the basis of political power and regional *caciquismo*. Because of the turbulence and instability that succeeded the independence, *caciquismo* served the important end of protecting its own. The interdependence of the regional hacienda owners became an essential means of self-protection and defense — either military or political. The rule that developed, logically required by the situation, was that the locality and its inhabitants followed their own leader against the national one. The leaders of the localities each had a following which belonged only to them, and the great leader was dependent upon the support of the little leaders each with his own following.

In that situation the power of the great leader tended to be unstable, temporary and subject to many hazards. He really lived on borrowed strength — while the power of the local *cacique* was very great and beyond the effective control of the central government, where the great leader was located. The hacienda thus became the basis of a system of local *caciquismo,* and the local *caciquismo* the major reason for political instability. It must be clear that with the weakening of the central power, the decline in the wealth, prestige and influence of the Church, the only power that remained was that of the locality — and the locality in Latin America has meant the haciendas in the locality. They were substantial; they had a strength which was genuine. The hacienda community's fealty gave the hacendado a power which was immediate and direct. And a group of hacendados, related and interdependent, controlled a region. The *cabildo* which they controlled was for a long time the only effective government.

Before closing this discussion of the hacienda, there are certain other elements which must be brought out. The hacienda both dominated the small neighboring city and prevented it from developing economically or politically. The complaint so often heard in the Latin American smaller town, that it has no "movement," that it is "dead," is true and no great mystery. The haciendas which surround this town for many miles about buy little. Their peons have no "movement," that it is "dead," is true and no great mystery. The haciendas sells relatively little, considering its size and the number of people living on it; and what it does sell is marketed, usually, on a wholesale basis, by some agent employed by the hacienda, or by a member of the family, and is sent on, if possible to a larger city at a distance, with the result that the smaller neighboring city is bypassed. Even the mule pack carrying the hacienda goods to the city or the nearest railroad belongs to the hacienda.

The better houses in the town usually belong to the neighboring haciendas, and are occupied by some members of the extended family, probably an old mother, or a brother who does not like to live on the hacienda, or who has some professional interest. The children of the hacendado will also be in this house during the school year. The servants in the house will come from the hacienda and will be a permanent part of the household, requiring no specific money wage. In the mountains of Peru, the house will also have the service of one or more *pongos* who come to work in turn for a week, and then go back to the hacienda. This is part of their payment for the few hectares of land they till on the hacienda. In addition the house will be supplied from the hacienda with a large part of its needs — wheat, barley, rice, corn, in the grain or as flour depending on whether the hacienda has a grist mill. It will also get what fruits are raised, and depending on the distance, may be supplied with butter, cheese and whatever else the distance and the climate will allow to be transported. So the big houses in the town are not important participants in the local market.

All of this and much more has kept the town commercially inactive. If the hacienda dominates the town economically, it does so politically as well. The great family will control every local office, from the colonel of the local militia to the rural police. The tax gatherer, the mayor, the judge, the postmaster will be related to or married into or be godfathers to, members of the family. And unless the president of the country feels strong enough to be indifferent to the interest and pride of the local leadership he will not impose "foreigners" on the locality.

If we now summarize the role of the hacienda in the development of Latin America we will see that it has been and has remained, where it still exists, an isolating and conservative influence. It lived by routine sharecropping methods which prevented the use of improved machinery, methods or seeds. It tied its labor force to the property and kept mobility down to a minimum. It was a dampening influence on commercial development by buying little in the open market and selling relatively little. Its huge areas and internal system of paths leading to the big house discouraged road building. It established and maintained — and still does — a system of dependence between the hacendado and his peons which perpetuated an authoritarian tradition of master and very humble servant (I saw in Bolivia the Indians on a plantation bend their knees and kiss ths hands of the hacendado) which leads directly into *caciquismo* and instability. It prevented the accumulation of capital, required no investment, called for no change, did nothing to prevent soil erosion or improve agricultural tecniques. The hacienda family controlled the local political scene and set the tone socially. As a dominant influence, the hacienda paid little taxes, and neglected to, or was unable to, put all of its resources to good use.

Perhaps most serious of all is that it fostered and maintained a social ideal in which the hacendado was the representative type — ideally a superior being possessed of broad acres and numerous servants, dominant, domineering, patronizing, and paternal, with nothing between himself and the peon on the plantation. All other elements in society (craftsmen, businessmen, entrepreneurs — in the parlance of the day, the middle class) were looked upon with disdain as a necessary affliction that had at best to be suffered. The hacendado was the master of all he surveyed, and the world looked good to him. It gave him economic stability, social prestige, political power, affluence and leisure. Those of his children who did not remain on the hacienda went off to the capital of the country, attended the university and became lawyers, doctors or literary men. Many of them combined literature with a profession. They might also meddle in politics, especially if the administration was one which their family — always the extended family, always the people who came from the same region, who followed the same local traditional leadership — had helped to bring to office.

Education fitted the ideal. Primary schooling for the mass of the people was a matter of indifference; higher education in the main led to a limited number of professions — medicine, law, and to a much lesser degree civil engineering. In the earlier days, the university also taught theology. The emphasis more recently fell upon philosophy and literature instead.

The hacienda system was thus a major influence in preventing either the democratic or economic development of Latin America. If Latin America has fallen behind the United States and Western Europe in industrial expansion, politically stable and democratic government and in the growth of an educational system adequate for the present time and present need, much of the fault lies with the hacienda system.

The hacienda system has in fact reached an impasse from which it cannot escape. The pressure for economic, political and social change is building up so rapidly that the system cannot avoid the challenge to its traditional ways, and it cannot meet it. *The hacienda has no built-in device that will allow for reform of the system,* that will enable it to transform itself so as to survive and propitiate the new ways that are undermining a traditional and age-old form of social organization. It has no way of meeting the challenge and yet cannot remain indifferent to television, atomic energy — and, if you like, psychoanalysis and Karl Marx as well.

In the two countries where the hacienda has been repudiated, Mexico and Bolivia, it was by revolution. The question of whether there is another way of dealing with impending change reamins to be seen. I say "impending," for it would require undue opaqueness to assume that the demands for industrialism and democracy can be met without seriously affecting the total role of the hacienda. What is happening in a small way in Peru is perhaps a suggestion that the government could if it had the energy, vision and political courage attempt a program of agrarian reform that would meet the modern challenge without a previous social convulsion. But who is there to say that the organized forces of government could move fast enough to satisfy the increasing pressure which the government would stimulate by its policies? I am not suggesting that cataclysm is inevitable. What is inevitable, if Latin America is to industrialize effectively and meet the demands for a higher standard of living and a more democratic society, is a wide agrarian reform which is not compatible with the survival of the hacienda system.

All of this discussion does not include the problem raised by the large commercial plantation in sugar, bananas and other crops raised for the international market. The fact that these large plantations may be foreign owned is only a minor complication to a difficult problem. What is involved in any attempt to apply agrarian reform policies to them is that they are efficiently operated, that they require a high degree of scientific and technical skill, that they have a foreign market which they control; or that they have to meet the the world price at which the commodity is selling; that they yield a cash income per acre higher than any other crop that could be grown. These are questions of such magnitude, especially where the government gets a large part of its income from the export of a single commodity, that any policy that would price the commodity out of the market, reduce the required investment, and cut down efficiency would not necessarily improve the economic conditions either of the peasantry or of the government. The fact that the properties have to be paid for merely increases the difficulties. But it must be clear that in their modern form these enterprises are relatively new, that they are to a considerable extent foreign owned and foreign managed, and that they are so large that they tend to dwarf all other domestic enterprise.

This raises political questions that may in fact be insoluble. This is a hard thing to recognize and to accept. But politically a certain institution may prove intolerable even if economically it can be shown to be highly beneficial. The large modern plantation is probably more like a factory than a farm, and if it were possible for modern management, the workers and the government to believe that they are involved in an industrial rather than an agricultural enterprise, then issues other than land reform would control whatever controversy might arise and require attention.

The modern sugar and banana plantations are, however, not the major issue in any discussion of the hacienda. These enterprises, except in isolated areas like Cuba, are only a small part of the total agricultural plant. The hacienda is another matter; it has set the tone for a whole society — and while it differs greatly between Argentina and Peru, for instance, it has been the controlling influence in shaping the cultural development of the area and has influenced the educational system in many ways.

FORD, MAN AND LAND IN PERU* 57-67 (1955)

The coastal valleys of Peru have experienced the greatest economic changes in recent times, the obvious reason being their easy accessibility and rich soils. The peculiar physical geopraphy of the coastal strip, though, limits the amount of cultivated land to only slightly more than a million acres. There is more farm land than this in the small and industrial state of Connecticut; there is over one hundred times as much in the state of Texas. Yet the coastal acreage of Peru is highly productive and of great importance to the national economy. About 120,000 acres of land are planted in sugar cane, and about 321,000 acres in cotton. Rice, which has become an increasingly important coastal crop, is cultivated on about 140,000 coastal acres. These three are generally considered the principal commercial crops, although rice is not exported to any appreciable extent. The rest of the coastal area is devoted to pastures and various food crops, especially maize. Because the land-use is an important factor in the interpretation of land distribution, crop production areas provide logical subdivisions for analyzing the coastal holdings.

Sugar cane production, for example, presents technical problems that rice and cotton do not, in that fairly large units of cultivation are required for profitable operations. At the present time sugar cane is commercially raised in only seven valleys of the coast, mostly in the northern and central regions. Since before the turn of the century the almost constant trend has been to consolidate the separate sugar haciendas into few and larger units. One index to this trend is the number of operating sugar mills, which was reduced from thirty-three in 1922 to fifteen in 1950, even though the area cultivated in cane decleased only about 2 per cent in the same period. Another measure of the consolidation trend is the increase in average size of sugar plantations and the concurrent reduction in number. In the sugar-producing Chicama valley of the department of La Libertad, for instance, there were in 1950 four large enterprises, each of which represented the consolidation of numerous small farms and haciendas. The hacienda *Cartavio,* owner by W. R. Grace and Company, was cultivating some 10,000 acres of cane and represented the absorption of more than twenty smaller farm units. The holdings of the Empresa Agrícola Chicama, Ltd., owned by the firm of Gildemeister and Company brought under common ownership more than sixty independent haciendas. This enterprise annually cultivates around 37,000 acres of cane and 12,000 of other food crops. The total area held by the Chicama corporation is in excess of 220 square miles, but this includes thousands of acres of uncultivated and uncultivable lands. The holdings of the other two major haciendas of the Chicama valley are less extensive, but they also have been developed through the consolidation process. In another valley, the Nepeña, in the department of Ancash, 95 per cent of the 60,000 acres of cultivated land has been acquired by the Negociación Azucarera Nepeña, controlled by the commercial firm of A. y F. Wiese, S.A. All these large sugar estates demonstrate the expanding development of corporate farming on the coast. The importance of their enterprise is seen from the fact that in 1947 the value of exported sugar and sugar products constituted approximately 30 per cent of the total value of national exports.

The commercial orientation of the sugar estates has naturally led them to apply such techniques as they have felt would increase production, and in no few instances their application has generated hostility. Modern farm equipment has increased the size of optimum efficiency land units, and the expansion of corporate landholdings has been bitterly resented in some quarters. Even with mechanization manpower requirements for such commercial enterprises are great, and complex systems of social organization of the workers have been developed by the various companies . . . .
            * * *

Another general observation that might be made of the sugar industry in Peru is that it presents the same question that has confronted every country where capitalistic expansion has taken place, namely, whether the most economically efficient operations are necessarily the most desirable from a social viewpoint. It seems unlikely that there will be agreement on the answer so long as there remain basic differences in the value premises upon which the arguments are based. The yet unsolved problem of monopolistic developments in the United States would indicate that no generally acceptable answer to the question of "bigness" has been provided in the most advanced capitalistic economy in the world. There seems little doubt that the issue will be debated for many years to come, and to an increasing extent in Peru.

Turning to the cultivation of rice and cotton, one finds a different situation. Both crops can be profitably produced on small or large tracts, although certain economic advantages may be gained by increasing the unit area of production.

Cotton is the greatest export crop of Peru, and is cultivated in all parts of twenty-seven of the coastal valleys . . . .
            * * *

In the sierra the relationships between land use and size of holdings can be traced only along the most general and obvious lines. Ranching enterprises, for example, of necessity require larger holdings than are necessary for crop cultivation. Particularly in the high sierra, where natural pasture is scanty and cultivation virtually impossible, each animal requires a number of hectares of grazing land. What appear to be tremendous holdings in terms of area, therefore, may in actuality represent extremely modest ranches in terms of the actual stock they can carry.

* * *

The data on general land distribution in the sierra are even less adequate than those available for the coast, and more difficult to interpret. There are, for example, more than five times as many sierra farms larger than 500 hectares as there are coastal farms in this size category, but many of these extensive sierra farms contain vast expanses of uncultivable land. It would be a difficult task to ascertain how many of these large holdings in the sierra are relatively unproductive because of topography, soil, and climate, and how many are potentially productive but inefficiently operated. The latter type conforms more closely to the traditional concept of a latifundium, and it is apparent that some such do exist in the Peruvian highlands. As in the colonial period, cultivation is done by Indian laborers who eke out a bare subsistence while the landlords (often absentee) receive small profits, which are possible only because of the low operating cost.

In many of the Indian communities the other size extreme of land holdings is to be found. Frequently the population has increased several fold while the lands of the community have either remained the same size or even diminished. The result has been continuous subdivision of family plots until the individual units are almost microscopic. It is not rare to find an individual's share of the more fertile community lands measured in terms of one or two furrows. One case is cited in the SCIPA publication *La Situación Alimenticia en el Perú,* in which no fewer than two hundred persons cultivated strips of a three-hectare plot that had been irrigated. In the same sierra province there were six villages populated by 3,100 farmers and their families. No farmer owned more than one hectare of farm land.

The coexistence of extremely large and extremely small holdings such as occurs in Peru is not unusual. If the agricultural population is large, land limited, and a considerable portion of the land held in large blocks, the probability is high that the remainder of the land will be greatly subdivided. In Peru this process of subdivision is furthered by the custom of bequeathing equal land shares to heirs. As plots become too small to yield a livelihood, the owners are forced either to work as laborers on near-by large holdings or to migrate. The strong desire of many of the Indians to cultivate their own holdings leads to their choice of the former alternative. In this manner, the large haciendas are assured a constant, if not efficient, labor supply which is cheap enough to make operations profitable, thus serving to perpetuate the system.

* * *

... Using the most conservative figures again, we find that the two largest groups of units, making up 9.9 per cent of the numerical total, contain over thirty-seven times as much land as the smallest group, into which 64.6 per cent of the total number of units fall. The pattern of distribution resembles very closely that of the coast, but it does not have the same meaning. The concentration of ownership on the coast represents the expansiveness of capitalistic enterprise; that of the sierra represents the survival of the colonial latifundium. Until the fundamental differences in these two types of "bigness" are understood rational approaches to the solving of the social and economic problems associated with each will be virtually impossible.

For those who remain identifiable as members of the indigenous populations — about half the population of Bolivia; about 40% of Ecuador; about 46% of Peru; about one-fourth of Mexico — there has been little social or economic progress since pre-Conquest days. In some respects there has even been decline:

> As a rule the living standard of the aboriginal populations in independent countries is extremely low, and in the great majority of cases is considerably lower than that of the most needy layers of the non-indigenous population. The aboriginal groups in many regions stagnate in conditions of economic destitution and pronounced cultural and technical backwardness, which severely limit their production and consumption capacity. This is due to the primitive conditions in which they are obliged to earn their living, to the lack of educational stimuli and opportunities and to the almost complete absence, in some areas, of welfare services and measures for social and labor protection.
>
> Although these conditions vary from country to country, or from region to region within the same country, owing to differing ethnic, climatic or environmental factors, it is nevertheless true that, with few exceptions, they remain considerably below the most elementary education and health requirements. In the case of food, there is generally speaking a notable lack of proteins, minerals and vitamins, and an excess of carbohydrates, resulting in a variety of deficiency diseases, particularly in children. This condition of undernourishment is artificially palliated in some areas of Latin America by the excessive use of alcohol and coca. The aboriginal dwelling is almost always damp, insufficiently ventilated, overcrowded and devoid of the most rudimentary sanitary facilities, all of which factors strongly favour the spread of respiratory and digestive diseases, malaria, etc. Clothing is usually inadequate both for protection against the severity of the climate and from the point of view of personal hygiene. This latter factor, combined with unhealthy housing, encourages the spread of skin and parasitic diseases.

Contact with non-indigenous groups frequently results in the spread of infectious and contagious diseases, particularly tuberculosis and syphilis, among the aboriginal peoples.

Scientific medical care, both preventive and curative, is inadequate in the majority of the areas inhabited by aborigines. For professional and economic reasons a very high percentage of doctors, pharmacists, nurses and social workers is concentrated in the capital cities and other urban centres, at great distances from areas with a large indigenous population. The situation is aggravated by the survival among aborigines of empirical practices of mythical or religious origin, in matters of food, illness, childbearing, weaning, etc., and by the illiteracy of an extremely high proportion of the aboriginal population, which in some areas is due not only to the great lack of educational facilities, but also to the aboriginal's hostile and suspicious attitude towards anything he regards as connected with European civilization. INTERNATIONAL LABOUR OFFICE, INDIGENOUS PEOPLES 89-90 (Studies and Reports, n.s., Nº 35, 1953).

In part, the land tenure problem is a problem of racial subordination. But Uruguay has no Indians; in Argentina, the ratio of indigenous persons to the whole population is roughly equivalent to that in the United States; Brazil has more than a million Indians, but they form less than 3% of the national population, and many of them are isolated from the rest of society, in both a physical and a social sense. Yet the adjustment of man-land relationships remains important in all these countries, crucial to both political stability and social-economic development.

ROSTOW, THE STAGES OF ECONOMIC GROWTH* 21-24 (1960)

TWO SECTORAL PROBLEMS

The rise of the investment-rate, as well as reflecting these more profound societal changes, is also the consequence of developments in particular sectors of the economy, where the transformation of the economy actually takes place. The analysis of economic growth can, then, proceed only a short and highly abstracted way without disaggregation.

To illustrate the need to pierce the veil of aggregative analysis in the transitional period we shall look briefly now at two particular problems shared, in one way or another, by all societies which have learned to grow: the problem of increased productivity in agriculture and the extractive industries; and the problem of social overhead capital.

AGRICULTURE AND THE EXTRACTIVE INDUSTRIES

Although a good deal of the early growth process hinges on the food-supply, the first of these two sectoral problems is properly to be defined as

---

that of agriculture and the extractive industries. The general requirement of the transition is to apply quick-yielding changes in productivity to the most accessible and naturally productive resources. Generally, this means higher productivity in food-production. But it may also mean wool, cotton, or silk — as in nineteenth century New Zealand, the American South, and Japan. And in Sweden it meant timber; in Malaya, rubber; in the Middle East, oil; and in certain American regions, Australia, and Alaska, gold helped to do the trick.

The point is that it takes more than industry to industrialize. Industry itself takes time to develop momentum and competitive competence. In the meanwhile there is certain to be a big social overhead capital bill to meet; and there is almost certain to be a radically increased population to feed. In a generalized sense modernization takes a lot of working capital; and a good part of this working capital must come from rapid increases in output achieved by higher productivity in agriculture and the extractive industries.

More specifically the attempt simultaneously to expand fixed capital — of long gestation period — and to feed an expanding population requires both increased food output at home and/or increased imports from abroad. Capital imports can help, of course, but in the end loans must be serviced; and the servicing of loans requires enlarged exports.

It is, therefore, an essential condition for a successful transition that investment be increased and — even more important — that the hitherto unexploited back-log of innovations be brought to bear on a society's land and other natural resources, where quick increases in output are possible.

Having made the general case in terms of requirements for working capital, look for a moment more closely at the question of agriculture and the food supply. There are, in fact, three distinct major roles agriculture must play in the transitional process between a traditional society and a successful take-off.

First, agriculture must supply more food. Food is needed to meet the likely rise in population, without yielding either starvation or a depletion of foreign exchange available for purposes essential to growth. But increased supplies and increased transfers of food out of rural areas are needed for another reason; to feed the urban populations which are certain to grow at a disproportionately high rate during the transition. And, in most cases, increased agricultural supplies are needed as well to help meet the foreign exchange bill for capital development: either positively by earning foreign exchange, as in the United States, Russia, Canada, and several other nations which generated and maintained agricultural surpluses while their populations were growing (and their urban populations growing faster than the population as a whole); or negatively, to minimize the foreign exchange bill for food — like a whole series of nations from Britain in the 1790's to Israel in the 1950's.

The central fact is that, in the transitional period, industry is not likely to have established a sufficiently large and productive base to earn enough foreign exchange to meet the increments in the nation's food bill via increased imports. Population increases, urbanization, and increased foreign exchange requirements for fixed and working capital are all thus likely to conspire to exert a peculiar pressure on the agricultural sector in the transitional process. Put another way, the rate of increase in output in agriculture may set the limit within which the transition to modernization proceeds.

But this is not all. Agriculture may enter the picture in a related but quite distinctive way, from the side of demand as well as supply. Let us assume that the governmental sector in this transitional economy is not so large that its expanded demand can support the rapid growth of industry. Let us assume that some of the potential leading sectors are in consumers' goods — as, indeed, has often been the case: not only cotton textiles — as in England and New England — but a wide range of import substitutes, as in a number of Latin American cases. In addition, the modern sector can — and often should — be built in part on items of capital for agriculture: farm machinery, chemical fertilizers, diesel pumps etc. In short, an environment of rising real incomes in agriculture, rooted in increased productivity, may be an important stimulus to new modern industrial sectors essential to the take-off.

The income side of the productivity revolution in agriculture may be important even in those cases where the transition to industrialization is not based on consumers' goods industries; for it is from rising rural incomes that increased taxes of one sort or another can be drawn — necessary to finance the government's functions in the transition — without imposing either starvation on the peasants or inflation on the urban population.

And there is a third distinctive role for agriculture in the transitional period which goes beyond its functions in supplying resources, effective demand or tax revenues: agriculture must yield up a substantial part of its surplus income to the modern sector. At the core of the *Wealth of Nations* — lost among propositions about pins and free trade — is Adam Smith's perception that surplus income derived from ownership of land must, somehow, be transferred out of the hands of those who would sterilize it in prodigal living into the hands of the productive men who will invest it in the modern sector and then regularly plough back their profits as output and productivity rise.

In their nineteenth-century land-reform schemes this is precisely what Japan, Russia, and many other nations have done during the transition in an effort to increase the supply of capital available for social overhead and other essential modernizing processes.

Professor Rostow's first point — that one requisite for development is that agriculture produce more food — is nowhere more true than in Latin America. The population of Latin America is rising at a rate which is not exceeded anywhere else in the world. In 1962 it was estimated variously from 206 million to 209 million; in 1980, it is expected to exceed 330 million; by the end of the century, there will almost surely be half a billion Latin Americans, all needing food. In fact, per capita food consumption has declined from pre-World War II levels. The Alliance for Progress set a minimum goal of a 2½% increase in living standards each year for ten years. That goal, added to a 2.9% rate of population growth, means that to meet the Alliance's minimum expectations, each year food production will have to increase at least 5.4%. It will have to increase more if, as is to be expected, an increase in real income for the lowest economic groups will mean a disproportionate increase in demand for food consumption.

Where does land reform fit into this depressing picture? There is no easy answer. In Bolivia, the immediate result of the distribution of land was a food shortage in the cities. The transfer of land in tiny parcels largely converted Bolivian agriculture to a subsistence economy. See Patch, *Bolivia: U.S. Assistance in a Revolutionary Setting,* in SOCIAL CHANGE IN LATIN AMERICA TODAY at 108, 130 (1960). Not all of this urban shortage of food can be blamed on declining food production; part of the reason for it was that food consumption among the rural population increased radically. As yet there is no reliable statistical survey of the relation between a distribution of land and agricultural production, although some writers insist that the Mexican experience permits an inference that production has increased because of the land reform. See, *e.g.,* FLORES, TRATADO DE ECONOMIA AGRICOLA, ch. XVIII-XIX (1961).

Proponents of land reform argue that the present land tenure structure does not make efficient use of agricultural land. Much of the land in the typical hacienda is left idle, for as Tannenbaum explains, the hacienda is not run primarily to make a profit. "The hacienda is not a business," said Andrés Molina Enríquez, one of the fathers of Mexico's land reform. Proponents of reform say that after a land reform, cultivation will be more intensive because each farmer will be producing for his own subsistence and in addition for his own profit. (At present, the typical *campesino* on a hacienda in Latin America works for 100-150 days each year.) Furthermore, a land distribution might reduce some of the rigidity which attends hacienda-dominated agriculture.

The quoted excerpt from Rostow's book also makes the point that agriculture has a key role to play in forming the capital which ist he basis for development. Will land reform aid or hinder capital formation? Answers must vary, depending on the way the question is posed. Over the short run, for example, tax receipts from agriculture may drop; if the government is trying to amass capital itself through taxation, then to this extent capital formation will be hindered. If agricultural production is ultimately increased, however, then over the long run tax receipts will also increase. (To go back to the short run: A shift from export crops to crops for local consumption may reduce the country's foreign exchange, just when it is most needed to buy plant and equipment abroad. Very heavy governmental expenditures are needed at the outset for "social overhead capital" — roads, irrigation projects, etc. — just when tax receipts may decline; furthermore, if the expropriated owners are paid in bonds instead of cash, the bond issue may weaken the government's borrowing power, so that both tax revenues and borrowing ability may fall off at the same time.)

For some time, productivity is unlikely to increase very much. But the prospects for capital formation over the long run are fairly bright. See Raup, *The Contribution of Land Reforms to Agricultural Development,* 12 ECONOMIC DEVELOPMENT AND CULTURAL CHANGE 1 (1963). Agricultural profits will first be drained off in consumption, since many of the newly-endowed farmers will for the first time be feeding their families adequately. After a satisfactory level of consumption has been reached, initial investment by these farmers, encouraged by their new security of tenure, will be in their own farms; only after the at-home investment needs are satisfied can the farmer be expected to save in a bank, or otherwise make his income available for capital expenditure. If the government places capital formation high on its list of needs in agriculture, then it may have to tax the farmer to make sure that enough is saved, not consumed. The political climate which follows land reform is not likely to encourage very heavy taxation of the distributed land.

Still, on-the-farm investments *are* investments; if they are prudently made, agricultural production should increase. And even increased consumption of some kinds may be thought of as an investment in the human resources used in agriculture; poor nutrition is often called a major obstacle to increased productivity. Fundamentally, the relation between land reform and capital formation depends on the increase or decrease in agricultural production. See Dorner, *Land Tenure, Income Distribution and Productivity Interactions,* 40 LAND ECONOMICS 247 (1964). If production declines and stays down, land reform will hinder development. If production eventually climbs, then the reform program may or may not be helpful to the general development of the country, depending on available alternative courses of action which might achieve the same results at a lower economic cost, or in a shorter period of time. Professor Hirschman argues that agriculture has little "forward linkage" effect — little generating power for development at points forward in time from the basic productive process (*e.g.,* processing, transportation, marketing,) but that some industries may have considerable "backward linkage" effect to stimulate agriculture. Thus the building of a sugar refinery may stimulate sugar production in a way which is economically superior (*i.e.,* achieves more development at less cost in resources or time) to the more sluggish stimulation of sugar refining by increased sugar cane production. And a growing urban (industrial) population needs food, and provides a similar "backward linkage" stimulus to agricultural production. HIRSCHMAN, THE STRATEGY OF ECONOMIC DEVELOPMENT 109-13 (1958).

Proponents of land reform as an impetus to development finally rest their case on the Keynesian doctrine that the magnitude of a society's income is a function of its distribution. That is, that a more even distribution of income will itself contribute to development. A sophisticated and sympathetic analysis of this position is made in Carroll, *Reflexiones Sobre la Distribución del Ingreso y la Inversión Agrícola,* 1 TEMAS DEL BID 19 (1964.) That the present income distribution in Latin America's agricultural sector is highly uneven will hardly be denied. Translated to the context of land reform, the argument is essentially this: a redistribution will put new purchasing power into the hands of those who work the land, enabling them to buy consumer goods and, eventually, such light capital goods as farm machinery. Paradoxically, an increase in such spending seems likely even though the total farm production and income may drop at first. A large portion of farm profits are now siphoned off from the domestic economy into foreign banks or foreign-bought luxury. When that drain is stopped, local industry and business can look for an increased volume of activity growing out of rural areas. One side effect will be the decentralization of the economy — the formation of new towns around the secondary industry which will absorb the farmers' new cash incomes. A major Latin American economic and social problem (and a political problem as well) is the antagonism between the all-rural provinces and the highly concentrated capital cities, and this decentralization of distribution and light manufacturing may help to relieve some of the antagonism.

Another possible effect of the redistribution of agricultural income is that it may help to protect a country's economy from the bumps and shocks of world commodity prices. The theory is that a more even distribution of income will restructure the market for the country's products, creating a new internal market for food and other products, and permitting the diversification of an economy previously dependent on one or a few commodities such as sugar, coffee, bananas, etc. In other words, not only will previously unproductive agriculture be encouraged to produce for the market in areas in which the market has previously been a negligible factor — the hacienda — but also previously productive agriculture — the plantation — will be freed from its ties to a few export crops; so the argument goes.

HAZLITT, SOCIALISTIC "REFORMS" *
Newsweek, November 20, 1961

I recently received a letter from a prominent Mexican. "The propaganda in Latin America in favor of socialistic measures," he wrote, "goes on and on. The astounding part is that those who make it are not Russians but Americans.

Last week it was the turn of your Under Secretary of State, Chester Bowles. In a speech delivered on Oct. 19 before the Mexican-North American Cultural Institute, besides agrarian reform and 'a more just distribution of wealth which *already* exists' [underlined in the official text], he came out in favor of high progressive income taxes and exchange controls. . . .

"What can we do to awaken the American people and to make them realize that their present leaders are delivering them into the hands of their enemies? Except for the French aristocracy in the eighteenth century, I do not believe history offers a comparable example of a social class collaborating in its own disappearance and destruction. If the United States preaches socialism, there is very little that we [Mexicans] can do here. All your millions will not only be wasted; they will speed the present trend to socialism and the ultimate take-over by Communists."

Urging "Revolution"

Thinking that perhaps my Mexican correspondent was unduly alarmed, I sent for the full text of the Bowles speech. In addition to the remarks he quoted I found:

Allusion to the United States as a "privileged society" and part of "the well-fed and comfortable minority of mankind." Constant advocacy of a *"continuing* revolution," "revolutionary change," "the right of revolution." True, these references were sometimes preceded by the adjective "peaceful." But Latin Americans are not apt to interpret "revolution" in this purely metaphorical way.

Bowles advocated high corporation taxes and a steeply progressive income tax: "Such tax systems are needed to soak up idle profits." He held up the U.S. practice as a shining example: "The corporation tax on annual business earnings above $25,000 is now set at 52 per cent. On top of that is a tax on *personal* income [his italics] that rises rapidly as incomes rise to a top level of 90 per cent." Bowles backed this up with a direct quotation from the Punta del Este Declaration which calls for "tax laws which demand more from those who have most, punishing tax evasion severely, and *redistributing the national income in order to benefit those who are most in need."* (My italics.)

Expropriating Land

Bowles demanded "land reform," and supported this by a direct quotation from the Punta del Este Declaration condemning "unjust structures and systems of land tenure and use." How this is likely to be interpreted in Latin America was illustrated by President Goulart of Brazil, as reported in The New York Times of Nov. 5: "He urged constitutional changes to permit agrarian and other reforms. At present the Constitution forbids any take-over of lands without compensation." In other words, he wants to seize lands without compensation.

"I do not see," added Bowles, "why my government or any other capital contributor should be asked for loans or grants to replace runaway indigenous capital that could be kept at home by" exchange controls and similar "curbs." The private capital that has "run away" from Latin America has done so in fear of further galloping inflation or of direct confiscation. Bowles urges that it not be allowed to escape.

Of course the "reforms" recommended by Bowles would frighten off domestic saving and investment, disrupt and demoralize production, move toward socialism, totalitarianism, or chaos — and of course enormously increase the foreign aid burden that the American taxpayer will be asked to assume.

The real reforms are the precise opposite. What the retarded countries need most is political stability, internal peace and order, security of life and property, due process of law, economy, balanced budgets, a halt to inflation, and the maintenance of free markets. The policies that would do most to attract private investment from abroad are precisely those that would encourage saving and investment at home.

The opponents of fundamental land reform in Latin America are not all landowners who stand to lose. Nor are they indifferent to the region's need to develop. Some of the opponents rest their opposition on the principle of the inviolability of private property. But others are willing to meet the economic arguments of advocates of reform head-on. Development, they argue, requires capital. Movements to redistribute income drive capital away, or at best make investors reluctant to enter. The dip in North American investment in Latin America in the years just following the nationalization of foreign investments in Cuba can be cited in support of this argument. Furthermore, argue the opponents, agricultural production can best be increased by the application of modern technology to larger units of production under rather centralized management; after a distribution of land, neither centralized management nor the use of modern methods seem very likely. Economists are divided over the question whether there are economies of scale in agriculture — that is, whether there is such a thing as an optimum size for a farming enterprise. They differ also over the value of mechanization in the short run. It is clear that there must be very great increases in *per-hectare* productivity; it is not so clear, in view of the high rate of urban unemployment in Latin America, that an increase in agricultural productivity *per worker* is presently a serious concern. Mechanization by and large does not greatly increase per-hectare productivity; rather it permits the replacement of labor. At the same time, all agree that the use of modern technology with respect to the kind of seed planted, the kind of fertilizer used, the conservation of the soil, and the like, is essential. The disagreement relates to the capacity of the *campesino* to adapt his farming to the new technology without the direction of the *patrón,* and to adapt to the radical social change which is implicit in forced economic development, with traditional controls removed.

In the end, land reform advocates hope for an increase in the economic responsibility of the farm population; men who have money to spend, it is argued, will also have new incentives to save it — to care for their families, to educate them. It is only when a man can see that there is a chance to get ahead that he is interested in trying. The argument is that the increased upward mobility which a land reform program will help to create will provide new incentive for education to take advantage of new opportunities. Rural education, it need hardly be added, is an indispensable ingredient of any land reform venture.

In addition to the sources already cited, discussions of the relation between land reform and development may be found in: JACOBY, INTER-RELATIONSHIP BETWEEN AGRARIAN REFORM AND AGRICULTURAL DEVELOPMENT (FAO Agricultural Studies N° 26, 1953;) CONFERENCE ON AGRICULTURAL TAXATION AND ECONOMIC DEVELOPMENT (Wald and Froomkin ed., Harvard Law School, 1954) (especially articles by Papanek and Raup, pp. 189, 245); URQUIDI, VIABILIDAD ECONOMICA DE AMERICA LATINA (1962); LACOSTE, LES PAYS SOUS-DEVELOPPES (1959), translated as LOS PAISES SUBDESARROLLADOS (1962); Carroll, *The Land Reform Issue in Latin America,* in LATIN AMERICAN ISSUES AND COMMENTS at 161 (Hirschman ed. 1961); LAND TENURE (Parsons, Penn and Raup ed., 1956); DELGADO (ed.), REFORMAS AGRARIAS EN LA AMERICA LATINA (1965); the series of individual country studies by the Inter-American Committee for Agricultural Development; and the valuable publications of the Land Tenure Center of the University of Wisconsin. For study of land reform in Latin American beyond this course, the indispensable bibliography is CARROLL, LAND TENURE AND LAND REFORM IN LATIN AMERICA: A SELECTED ANNOTATED BIBLIOGRAPHY (2d rev. ed. 1965, Inter-American Development Bank.) For historical sketches of the world's principal reforms, see TUMA, TWENTY-SIX CENTURIES OF AGRARIAN REFORM (1965).

The foregoing discussion of arguable economic advantages and disadvantages of a land reform gives more space to the claimed advantages, not for purposes of indoctrination but simply in recognition that land reform is coming in some countries of Latin America, and has already arrived in others. In order to understand the legislation which has gone before and that which is yet to be enacted, it is necessary to understand the motives which have inspired the legislators. No doubt it is incorrect to speak of the objective of a complex social event like a land reform; the point is well made in BARRACLOUGH, LO QUE IMPLICA UNA REFORMA AGRARIA (mimeo 1963). The same writer does, however, identify some of the motives of land *reformers.*

There is no doubt that the primary short-range motives of reformers over the years have been political — to get and keep power. There may also be personal motives of varying degrees of worthiness. But beyond such motives, others can often be discerned. Fundamentally, the goal has been to create a greater equality among the members of a society. Whether land be thought of only in economic terms, or whether it be thought of as the base for political liberty or for effective citizenship, the distribution of rights in land is only instrumental, aimed at a greater social equality. Talk about distribution of land rights in a vacuum is common, but it is sterile.

One land reformer who has had some recent success is the former President of Venezuela, Rómulo Betancourt. An idea of his goals for the Venezuelan reform may be obtained from the following passages from an election campaign speech, given on November 21, 1958, at the Central University in Caracas, just sixteen days before his election.

BETANCOURT, LA REFORMA AGRARIA
in Posicion y Doctrina* at 121 (1959)

* * *

The Venezuelan agrarian problem is as old as our nation. Agricultural production began in Venezuela, as in almost all the countries of Latin America, under the sign of the *latifundio*. The Spanish kings granted lands to the colonists "as far as one can see." Thus the indigenous persons were despoiled of their property. Furthermore, in Venezuela there existed no tradition of agricultural production at a certain level of development, as had existed in countries where the indigenous populations had evolved and progressed before the Discovery and the Conquest. The Venezuelan Indians lived within the *encomienda* and the mine, without the subconscious spur of memory of a pre-Spanish epoch in which they collectively worked the land, which in Mexicans and Peruvians was the ferment of rebellion.

In the rambling course [*discurrir*] of the colonial era, there operated a process of evolution, in our country as in others of Latin America, that culminated in the movement of independence of 1810. In Venezuela this movement was directed, not by the bourgeoisie as was the great French Revolution (because this class did not exist in our Country), but rather by the most radical and jacobin wing of the landholding class.

Here perhaps is the explanation of a phenomenon which has been incomprehensible to the superficial historical critic. While in France the public resolutely followed an iconoclastic bourgeoisie which was breaking down the

---

feudal system of ownership and was irreverently opposed to all dogmas, in Venezuela the popular groups never stopped believing in the promises which the national landholding class made to them.

* * *

[Here is described the history of post-Revolution attempts at agrarian reform, all of which failed.]

[After the Federal War of the late 1860s] the Liberal Oligarchy succeeded the Conservative Oligarchy, and the system of land tenure remained unmodified until the advent of the obstinate and prolonged dictatorship of Juan Vicente Gómez, in the course of which the process of land concentration was accelerated.

Gómez was an almost pathological land-grabber [literally, *terrófago*: land-eater]. He, his family and friends, monopolized almost all the workable lands of the country. Simultaneously with this monopolizing of lands resulted two phenomena: a progressive decline of agricultural production of exportable fruits, coffee, and cacao, and the flourishing, around 1920, of petroleum production. Two parallel phenomena: While the country's agricultural and fishing production fell vertically, petroleum production ascended geometrically until the arrival in 1928 of the first boom, the first "leap," during which the country became one of the great petroleum producers of the world.

One could not have an exact idea of the structure of the Venezuelan countryside because, in those years of the Gómez dictatorship, none of the rudiments of modern research was used; statistics were not compiled. It was in 1937 that the first agricultural census of the country was made, dramatically revealing the situation of the Venezuelan countryside.

It is well known that only one-third of the national territory is inhabited. That is the area of socially useful territory. The rest is hinterland, to be colonized in the future. Well then, according to the census of 1937, 85% of the workable land of the country was dedicated — perhaps more accurately one could say that it was abandoned — to the production of cattle, which, more than the raising of cattle, was the hunting of cattle — to open plains. The other three million hectares (of which barely 700,000 were cultivated) were the Agricultural Zone; that is to say, only 1% of the workable land of the country was cultivated, and that was under the ownership of a few people. Of 500,000 owners, only 2,500 (or rather 5% of the rural population) possessed 79% of the agricultural lands. Of the half million small farmers, only 10% worked on their own land, and the rest worked under the semi-feudal methods of *medianería* [rental equals one-half the crop], of sharecropping and of rental. These data were confirmed by the much more reliable agricultural censuses of 1941 and 1950, and, finally, in the very precise and illuminating investigation completed in 1956 by a technical mission of the FAO, a specialized organization of the United Nations, together with our Ministry of Agriculture and Husbandry.

The conclusions of this latest investigation are very precise, and they dis-

play in a dramatic form the agrarian panorama of Venezuela. It was found*
that in the country there were some 400,000 agricultural entities in exploitation with an area of 3,000,000 hectares, over a total exploitable surface of
30,000,000 hectares. Of the estates in production, 80% had an area of barely
3 hectares, which made them definitely anti-economic and unproductive. These
minifundios [very small holdings] occupied one million of the 30 million
hectares which, as we have said, are considered the socially useful, workable
area of the country. The active rural population was about 800,000 persons,
of which barely 100,000 were landowners, and many of them were owners of
haciendas which were unproductive. Of the nearly 3,000,000 cultivated hectares, only 700,000 were cultivated by modern methods of industrialization
and mechanization. In the remaining 2,3000,000 hectares, the prevailing
systems were those which are so extensive in the countryside of our nation:
sharecropping, rental tenancy, and *medianería*.

The economic and social consequences of this anachronistic and unjust
system of tenancy and exploitation of the land are expressed in impressive
figures. Conclusive information to this effect was produced in a study carried
out by the Department of Sociology of this University in association with the
FAO, and published in a work signed by the North American, Professor
George Hill. The study included a sample of 304 *campesino* families scattered
in the various regions of the nation and it was concluded that 14% of these
families lived exclusively in a subsistence economy, in conditions as primitive
as those of the Caribes or Jirajaras whom Christopher Columbus encountered
when, on his third voyage, he discovered the eastern coast of Tierra Firme, as
our country was called in the poetic geography of that time. Of the families
in the sample, 46.4% had an income of barely a hundred Bolivars** per year
and 1,250,000 *campesinos,* one-quarter of the inhabitants of the nation, had
a per capita income of barely eleven Bolivars a month.

The social and cultural effects of the under-productivity of the immense
majority of rural Venezuelans is well known. The majority of our rural mass
lives in *ranchos* [shacks]. There are more than 700,000 living in *ranchos* in
our country, and as was pointed out in a Pan American Health Congress by a
delegation of doctors specializing in tropical diseases, presided over by the
modest and wise Dr. Félix Pifano, the *rancho,* rather than being the protector
of the human species, conspires against it. Even laymen know that the earthen
floor is the source from which innumerable intestinal diseases penetrate the
organism. . . .

The economic ill-being of our rural mass, together with the lack of concern for popular education on the part of autocratic or dictatorial governments,
is one of the fundamental causes of this painful balance of ignorance and

---

* See chart, p. 370, *supra.* — Ed.
** The Bolivar has been quoted in the 1960s at about \$.22 (U.S.); at the times referred to in
this speech, the Bolivar was worth more. — Ed.

backwardness in our country. The immense, the determinate majority of these 2½ millions of illiterate Venezuelans, is located in the countryside. It is precisely in the most rural States that the greatest index of illiteracy is estimated. It is 74% in Trujillo, for example, and in Estado Portuguesa it reaches a figure as high as 85%; and this situation of extreme misery, this condition of "subhuman life," (to repeat a phrase of the Archbishop of Caracas and Venezuela in his famous pastoral letter of May 1, 1957) is one of the causes of the scanty industrial development of our country. We have about 7,000,000 inhabitants but it would not be exaggerated to say that we barely number 2,000,000 consumers. In Venezuela there is not really, as is often affirmed, overproduction of textiles and overproduction of shoes. In Venezuela what there is is underconsumption of primary products and of manufactured products, because a great mass of the population is a marginal sector, which barely produces and which consumes very little.

For all these reasons the realization of an Agrarian Reform in our country cannot be postponed; in this sense, there is a new state of national conscience, one very definite expression of which is the composition of the Commission designated by the Ministry of Agriculture and Husbandry to study the Agrarian Reform. On it are represented the industrial sectors; the Church, by the Archbishop; the laboring sectors; the technical sectors; and, of course, representatives of all the political parties active in the country. This means that the Agrarian Reform is no longer today, as it was in 1936, a heterodox watchword embellished by a certain suspicious Bolshevik shade, but a national necessity on whose realization all sectors of our community are agreed.

This problem of the Agrarian Reform — and now I am going to give no technical opinion, but some of my experiences as a political leader — cannot be conceived simply as the mere partition of lands among the *campesinos*. That would be like throwing a blunt instrument at a *piñata* of lands,* so that each *campesino* might own a piece of soil and be fascinated by it as the child is fascinated by the caramel or the toy which has fallen in his hands when the clay vessel has been broken, dropping its fragile gifts.

The agrarian reform must be focused, and on this technicians and statisticians agree, as a joint and complex action. The distribution of lands is not enough if it is not supplemented by timely and cheap credit for the *campesinos;* the replacement of antiquated methods of production (which in Venezuela are the Roman plow, the *chicura,* the machete weeder, and, what is worse, fire) by the tractor, by the mechanical sower and by the mechanical reaper; and the timely assistance and orientation of the *campesinos* by a legion of agronomists, of veterinarians, and experts in agricultural production; and, complementing this series of measures, social action: the fight against the *rancho,* the fight against disease. In the language of modern military strategy, the Agrarian Reform must come about with a sense of global war, of total war.

---

* The *piñata* is a dangling container of goodies which children break during the holiday season by striking it with a stick while blindfolded. — Ed.

Some of this we tried to do, in an incipient form and during the limited period of time when the honor and responsibility of directing the destinies of this country fell to us. We encountered, on coming to the government in 1945, a secular agrarian problem, as old as Venezuela itself, and by way of solutions, only an Agrarian Law which had not begun to be executed. Our action consisted in beginning to locate *campesinos,* and in order to impede dislocation a decree was ordered by which, during a fixed period, dislocations [ejectments] could not be ordered. In view of the countryside's need for credit, the capital and disposable capital of the Agricultural Bank were increased substantially, and its credit action was decentralized by agencies and sub-agencies throughout the country. In the triennium 1945-1948 the capital and reserves of the Agricultural Bank ... and the index of credit activity reached high levels. Also the Venezuelan Corporation of Development [*Fomento*] was created, charged with granting credits to the large enterprises which were to industrialize the country. At that time there was initiated a policy of development of sugar production which has permitted Venezuela to pass from the situation of 1946, in which we imported 40,000 tons of sugar from Cuba and from Brazil, to today's situation, in which at least potentially, our country is ready to export sugar. CEPAL, the Economic Commission for Latin America of the United Nations, undoubtedly the highest regional authority on economic and fiscal matters, in a monograph published in 1951 on Venezuela, confirmed this concept. Agricultural credit was insignificant until 1964, when the Venezuelan Corporation of Development was founded and when the Agricultural Bank intensified its action.

We encountered the problem of an extraordinarily limited number of agricultural technicians. By means of fiscal measures, ... the number of students of Agronomy and Veterinary Medicine could be increased from 1,200-odd in 1945, to 5,000 in 1948.

One of the important questions, related to the system of land tenure in our country, is the vagueness of the borders of the haciendas, and the illegal incorporation of *ejidos* [common land] and of national property into private estates on numerous occasions. It was necessary to begin a survey and one was begun. And in only four States of the Republic there were recovered for the nation some 700,000 hectares.

The question of rural roads also had to be faced; such roads are very important in our country because they put the agricultural producer into contact with the centers of consumption; 5,000 kilometers of rural roads were opened in those years.

Our national experience and that of other countries came together in a Law of Agrarian Reform signed by [President] Rómulo Gallegos on the 18th of October of 1948. Complemented and improved by the conclusions arrived at by the present Agrarian Reform Commission, this law would perhaps serve as a good model for the necessary agrarian legislation which the Constitutional Congress should adopt.

It was a realistic law, which viewed the different features of the Venezuelan agrarian problem, recognizing the different local characteristics of the regions in this vast country. It was a pragmatic law, not guided by pre-fixed or dogmatic criteria, but providing various solutions to the complex agrarian system of our country. Thus, it established as a fundamental goal the creation of a governing organism for the whole process of Agrarian Reform, the National Agrarian Institute. Furthermore, the Institute was endowed with economic resources. Its initial capital was fixed at one hundred million Bolivars, which was later to be substantially increased since it was also provided that every year there would be an apportionment for this purpose of from two to fourteen per cent of the General Budget of Expenses of the Nation. The fulfillment of this provision would * have made available to the National Agrarian Institute very appreciable sums of money, with which to face the agrarian problem. A wide variety of methods for grantint lands was established, ranging from the system of granting mere usufruct of the land to the system of individual ownership, including the system of cooperatives. This Agrarian Reform Law took into account that it would not be mechanically possible for cooperative systems of production to be imposed, despite their well known advantages, because in Venezuela the immense majority of *campesinos* are *conuqueros* ** and this system is not just an anti-economic form of production but also an exacerbated sysmbol of individualism. In Venezuela we do not have any kind of underlying tradition in the countryside, oriented toward group labor. In Russia the *artel* axisted before the revolution of 1918; in Bolivia the *aillu* existed before the revolution of 1951; in the Nordic countries — Norway, Sweden, etc. — cooperativism has existed for decades. In Venezuela our producer is essentially individualistic. In some regions there is supposed to be an incipient system of group labor, called the *cayapa* or hand-to-hand labor, but in reality the Agrarian tradition in our country is of an exacerbated individualism. Only through an educative process will town dwellers and *campesinos* be convinced of the advantages of cooperative labor. The most important thing may be to establish a system of cooperative service, similar to that which exists in the United States, in which the farmer owns his land and its product, but uses cooperatively with other members of the community such things as tractors, transport vehicles, silos, etc.

The Agrarian Law of 1948 provided that land holdings of moderate size were inexpropriable, when they were in fact dedicated to agriculture: 150 hectares of first class (irrigated) land, and 300 hectares of land of the second class. Lands dedicated to cattle raising were made inexpropriable up to 5,000 hectares of first class land and 25,000 hectares of second class land.

The Law established a priority scale of expropriation, beginning with idle,

---

* The government of President Gallegos was overthrown by a military coup in 1948, and the Agrarian Reform Law of that year was never operative. — Ed.

** From *conuco*, which describes a small parcel of agricultural land, often of insufficient size to support a family. — Ed.

uncultivated lands, lands belonging to those persons who, to use a creole expression, "neither wash nor loan the basin." [*Ni lavan ni prestan la batea* — a *batea* is a trough for bathing hands or feet.] Then came lands worked for absentees, by intermediary agents, and so on. And these expropriable lands would be paid for at their fair price, because the goal is not to punish the landowner personally, but to end an anti-economic, unjust system of tenancy and exploitation (or rather, non-exploitation of the land, because the majority of these great *latifundios* are in ruin).

A system of payment was established, partly in money and the rest in bonds guaranteed by a solvent State, a State without external debt — or at least which then did not have any — but, in any case, by a State relatively rich, whose bonds are always quoted at the peak of their face value. Another very important point recognized by this Agrarian Reform Law was the relation of irrigation to the land. It was established in one article that system of irrigation were considered public utilities, and that their management should be regulated by provisions of aspecial law. This is a problem of extraordinary importance, because Agrarian Reform in Venezuela must be bound to a large and ambitious irrigation policy. In this vast geographic space which is our country we have scarcely some two hundred or three hundred thousand hectares of permanent irrigation. The rest are lands submitted to the capricious choices of nature, lands which are inundated during intense winters or toasted brown during prolonged droughts. If there is anything which we must bring about in Venezuela, it is a policy of irrigation similar to that followed in Mexico, in the United States (Texas), and in some countries of the Middle East, among them Egypt: A program which permits us to irrigate at least a million hectares in the near future.

The advantages of irrigated lands are obvious: even persons least versed in problems of the countryside know them. In irrigated lands up to three harvests a year may be obtained. The income of irrigated lands may be compared to that of urban businesses. In [one part of] Estado Aragua, for example, where since 1947 scarcely three thousand of the six thousand irrigated hectares have been exploited, in only one year of use 40% of the total investment was recovered, including all that had been invested in constructing the irrigation works. But here there is a very important aspect: scarcely half of the lands were in cultivation. This is unacceptable. Irrigated lands must be cultivated in their totality, and in this respect the State must take the lead, when a work of irrigation is completed, in obtaining for the nation the greater part of the lands which come to be irrigated, to use them for purposes of agrarian reform and for substantial increases in agricultural production, in which we have such an acknowledged deficit. We did something of this kind in the effort at El Cenizo, which was interrupted after the overthrow of President Gallegos. There are [in El Cenizo] 100,000 hectares of very rich level lands, because through the decades the vegetable humus which descends from the Andean mountains has been accumulatin on them. Well then, those 100,000 hectares were in the hands of the Venezuelan Corporation of Development, because a part of them was rented for terms of ninety-odd years to Municipal Councils, others were purchased, and perhaps one or two haciendas were expropriated and paid for at their fair price.

The program of Agrarian Reform must be linked to a program of irrigation. Works designed to irrigate some 500,000 hectares are now being studied by the Department of Irrigation of the Ministry of Public Works. It is to be desired that the next Government, whoever it may be who presides, pledge that during the five-year period (1959-64) at least those 500,000 hectares may be irrigated, using the better part of them in a modern and just Agrarian Reform and in due course, achieving a substantial increase in the national agricultural production.

I am going to conclude, now that perhaps I have taken more than due time, stating that Agrarian Reform in Venezuela, besides being a necessity of social justice which may not be put off, is an imperative of economic liberation. Venezuela cannot continue importing from the exterior black beans, rice, a million eggs per day, even importing meat, because of an acknowledged deficit in our production of cattle, pigs and sheep. We have been using the dollars which petroleum produces for us — a transitory wealth, because it is a wealth derived from a product typically unrenewable — not to lay the solid bases and foundations of the national economy, but to import from the outside that which we can and must produce perfectly well in our country. So that the Agrarian Reform is not only an immediately necessary response to the claim of justice made by the rural majority of our country, but also an indispensable means to economic independence. (Prolonged ovation.)

Early in President Betancourt's administration, Venezuela adopted comprehensive land reform legislation. That law is reprinted here in its entirety. At this stage, you should not try to master the law's details; rather, you should seek an understanding of the broad outline of the law's provisions, and their relation to President Betancourt's program. We shall return to the details in the succeeding sections of this chapter.

VENEZUELA, AGRARIAN REFORM LAW (1960)
(*Gaceta Oficial* N° 611 Extraordinario, 19 March 1960, p. 1)
(FAO translation)

INTRODUCTORY TITLE
PRINCIPLES OF THE AGRARIAN REFORM

1. The purpose of this Act is to transform the agrarian structure of the country and to incorporate its rural population into the economic, social and

political development of the Nation, by replacing the latifundia system with an equitable system of land ownership, tenure and operation based on the fair distribution of the land, satisfactory organization of credit, and full assistance to agricultural producers, in order that the land may constitute, for the man who works it, a basis for his economic stability, a foundation for his advancing social welfare and a guarantee of his freedom and dignity.

2.   In view of these purposes, this Act:

(a)   Guarantees and regulates the right of private land ownership, in accordance with the principle that such ownership should fulfill a social function, and in accordance with other provisions laid down in the Constitution and in law.

(b)   Guarantees the right of any individual or group, capable of farm work and lacking land or possessing insufficient land, to be provided with economically profitable land, preferably in the places of their work or residence, or, when circumstances so require, in duly selected regions within the limits and under the provisions laid down in this Act.

(c)   Guarantees to farmers the right to remain on the land they cultivate, under the terms and conditions prescribed by this Act.

(d)   Guarantees and recognizes to the indigenous population, which de facto maintains tribal or clan status, without diminishing their rights as Venezuelan citizens, as provided in the preceding paragraphs, the right to enjoy the land, forests and waters which they occupy or own in those places in which they habitually reside, without prejudice to their incorporation into national life in accordance with this or other enactments.

(e)   Fosters and protects in particular the development of small and medium rural property and of agricultural cooperatives in such a manner as to render them stable and efficient.

For that purpose, the right to small family property is hereby established in accordance with the provisions of this Act governing allocations free of charge.

3.   The obligations arising out of the principle that land ownership should fulfill a social function devolve both upon private persons and upon the State.

4.   For the purposes of the provisions of Article 2, paragraph b), the State shall gradually incorporate into the economic development of the country those zones or regions which are under-exploited or not suitable for technical and rational exploitation due to lack of means of communication or irrigation, drainage or other similar works.

For that purpose, it shall put forward integrated development plans of economic or hydrographic regions, provided that in every case hydraulic improvement and agricultural development work shall be executed with a view to integrated development and shall be in accordance with agrarian reform plans.

5.   The State shall establish and develop the public services necessary

and sufficient for the transformation of the rural class and for aiding the agricultural producers bound by the responsibilities arising from the social function of property to comply with the obligations imposed upon them by this Act.

6. The General Budget Act shall contain appropriate provisions for financing the Agrarian Reform and the agricultural plans arising therefrom.

7. The State shall be required to lay down the bases and conditions necessary for raising the status of hired agricultural labor through satisfactory regulation of such labor and of its juridical status in keeping with the changes which will arise out of the Agrarian Reform.

8. Under conditions established or to be established, foreign nationals shall enjoy equality of rights with Venezuelan citizens and shall be subject to the same obligations in respect of the matters coming under this Act.

9. Persons entitled to request allocations of land may report the existence of lands which do not fulfill their social function.

Such reports shall be filed with the competent local office which shall, within thirty days, inititate the appropriate investigation and inform the person having filed the report.

If the report proves to be justified, the lands shall be subject to acquisition or expropriation, in accordance with the provisions of this Act.

TITLE I

AGRICULTURAL PROPERTY

CHAPTER I

LANDS OF PUBLIC AGENCIES

10. Lands of the public agencies shall be set aside for the purposes of the Agrarian Reform; in this respect, and without prejudice to the provisions of other special legislation, there shall be considered as such:

> (a) Public land;
> (b) Rural properties forming part of State lands (*dominio privado*);
> (c) Rural properties belonging to the autonomous national agencies;
> (d) Rural property having become property of the Nation as a result or consequence of illicit profiteering against the State.

11. Lands belonging to the States and municipalities and to the public agencies thereof shall also be set aside for the Agrarian Reform. Accordingly, the Government shall enter into the agreements necessary therefor.

12. With the exception of the areas reserved for urban and industrial expansion, those specifically excepted in Article 14, and those intended for the common use of inhabitants of towns, all other communal lands shall be set aside for the Agrarian Reform; for this purpose, the Government shall enter into such agreements with the municipalities as it deems appropriate.

13. For the purposes of the provisions of Articles 11 and 12, the formalities prescribed by the Basic Act on National Property in respect of alienation of property shall not be applicable.

14. The areas of rural properties forming the subject of this Chapter and occupied by petroleum or mineral exploitations, and those reserved or destined by the public administration for the establishment of public services or other works, may be set aside for the purposes of the Agrarian Reform when the National Agrarian Institute considers that agricultural activities may be carried out thereon without interfering with the operation of the said activities, and the Government shall so provide.

For such purpose, the Government shall prescribe regulations governing the necessary expropriations for the use of the said areas in accordance with the plans of the Agrarian Reform.

15. The lands set aside for the Agrarian Reform under the provisions of this Chapter shall not be alienated, encumbered, or leased unless the Government finds that they are required for other purposes of public or social policy and so authorizes.

16. In view of the provisions of Article 10 of this Act, the competent authorities shall not approve further requests for leases of public land. Without prejudice to the provisions of Article 69, and provided that no allocation procedure forms an obstacle thereto, any person who duly proves to the National Agrarian Institute that he has occupied public land without let or hindrance for more than one year prior to the promulgation of this Act shall be entitled to be awarded, to the extent and within the limits laid down in Article 29, that part of such land which he is actually cultivating in conformity with the principle of the social function and under the conditions laid down in this Act.

Similarly, the occupation of areas greater than those specified in the Public and Common Land Act shall not give rise to the privileges granted by the said Act to the occupier of such land in respect of the lease or purchase thereof.

17. After agreement with the municipalities, and provided that no interference with the establishment of Agrarian Centers is caused thereby, the National Agrarian Institute shall grant, to those persons who on the date of publication of this Act are cultivating land leased from municipalities in accordance with the principles of the social function, ownership of areas not exceeding the limits laid down in Article 29 of this Act, without prejudice to the provisions of Article 12; in such cases, the plus-value and real improvements shall be paid according to fair expert valuation.

18. Properties belonging to or administered by the State and set aside in conformity with the provisions of this Chapter shall be transferred without charge to the National Agrarian Institute by the Government, which is hereby

expressly authorized to take such action; the authorization of the National Congress or other government agency shall not be required to carry out the said conveyance.

After the appropriate agreements have been made, economically exploitable rural properties of the other public bodies and establishments shall be likewise transferred.

CHAPTER II
PRIVATELY-OWNED LAND
SECTION I
SOCIAL FUNCTION OF PROPERTY

19. For the purposes of the Agrarian Reform, private ownership of land fulfills its social function when it combines all the following essential elements:

> (a) The efficient exploitation and profitable use of the land in such a manner as to bring usefully into play the productive factors thereof, according to the zone in which it is located and its special characteristics.
> (b) Personal operation and management of, and financial responsibility for, the agricultural enterprise by the landowner, except in special cases of indirect exploitation for good reasons.
> (c) Compliance with the provisions governing conservation of renewable natural resources.
> (d) Respect of legal provisions governing paid labor, other labor relations questions, and other farm contracts, under the conditions laid down in this Act.
> (e) Registration of the rural property in the Office of the National Register of Land and Waters in accordance with appropriate legal provisions.

20. In particular, it shall be considered contrary to the principle of the social function of property and incompatible with the national welfare and economic development for uncultivated or unprofitable properties to exist and to be maintained, especially in economic development regions. Indirect systems of land exploitation, such as those carried out through leasing, the various types of sharecropping, day labor and squatting, shall also be considered contrary to the principle of the social function of property;

Provided, that the State shall in particular impose upon uncultivated or unprofitable properties a graduated tax scale to be prescribed in the appropriate enactments, without prejudice to expropriation in cases provided for under this Act.

21. When a private fragmentation program is planned for a property inhabited or worked by farmers entitled to receive land allocations, fragmentation shall be authorized by the National Agrarian Institute only if due care

has been taken to safeguard the interest of such farmers as beneficiaries of the Agrarian Reform.

22. Failure by private landowners to comply with any of the obligations arising out of the social function of property shall constitute sufficient cause for the assignment of the land to the Agrarian Reform and, consequently, such land shall not be immune from expropriation on the grounds laid down in Article 26 of this Act.

23. The State shall provide incentives to those persons who utilize land in accordance with its social function and who thus contribute to the economic development of the country.

SECTION II
ACQUISITION OF LAND

24. Land acquired by the Institute to be used for the Agrarian Reform shall be economically exploitable. Acquisition for valuable consideration may take place only after a prior favorable technical report indicating that the provisions of this Article are satisfied; the said report shall be included in the file of documents in the appropriate Public Registry Office.

25. In evaluating rural properties to be acquired in whole or in part for valuable consideration for the purposes of the Agrarian Reform, the following factors shall be taken into consideration:

(a) The average production over the six years immediately preceding the date of acquisition or of the request for expropriation.

(b) The declared or assessed official value for tax purposes under enactments relating thereto.

(c) The acquisition price of the property in the last conveyances of ownership carried out during the ten-year period prior to the date of valuation, and the acquisition prices of similar properties in the same region or zone in the five-year period immediately preceding the date of the expropriation request or purchase proposal:

Provided, that although in evaluating properties the abovementioned factors shall primarily be taken into account, any other factors which may be useful in fixing a just price, and all those mentioned in the Act relating to Expropriation in the Public or Social Interest, shall also be taken into consideration;

Provided, further, that the valuation shall include, in addition to the value of the land, the value of the buildings, installations, chattels, equipment and improvements existing thereon;

Provided, finally, that the determination of value shall take into account only the actual fair value of the property, to the exclusion of any consideration of possible damages or disadvantage or of the sentimental value of the property.

SECTION III
EXPROPRIATION

26. Rural properties which fulfill their social function in accordance with the provisions of Article 19 shall be immune from expropriation for the purposes of the Agrarian Reform, except as specifically provided otherwise by this Act.

27. Expropriation shall be resorted to when, at the site of allocation or at neighboring sites, there exists no public land or other rural properties mentioned in Title I, Chapter I, of this Act, or if such land or properties are inadequate or unsuitable, and if the National Agrarian Institute has been unable by any other means to acquire other land equally exploitable from an economic point of view.

Such expropriation shall be applied primarily to such land as fails to fulfill its social function, in the following order of priorities:

> 1) Uncultivated properties, and, in particular, those of the greatest area; properties exploited indirectly through tenants, sharecroppers, settlers and occupiers; and properties not under cultivation during the five years immediately prior to the initiation of expropriation proceedings.
> 2) Properties on which private land fragmentation programs have not been brought to completion, provided that if the National Agrarian Institute requests expropriation thereof after the said programs have been initiated, the rights of beneficiaries of such fragmentation already in occupation shall be safeguarded.
> 3) Crop lands being used for range livestock grazing.

Expropriation of other land shall be resorted to when the above possibilities have been exhausted and there is no other means of solving an agrarian problem of evident gravity; in such cases, the provisions of Article 33 of this Act shall apply.

28. The national parks and forests, forest reserves, protective zones, natural and artistic monuments and wild-life sanctuaries shall be immune from assignment for the purposes of the Agrarian Reform.

29. Land or properties the area of which is not in excess of 150 hectares of the first category, or the equivalent thereof in land of other categories, in accordance with criteria to be laid down in Regulations, shall also be immune from expropriation.

The equivalents referred to in this Article shall be included between 150 and 5000 hectares.

In extreme flood or drought zones, individual maxima shall be fixed in each case by the National Agrarian Institute.

30. Owners of properties under expropriation shall be entitled to reserve for themselves thereon the area defined in Article 29 as immune from expropriation.

Land annexed to the principal reserve and required for proper operation of the property (*e.g.,* pastures, land occupied by buildings, and land covered with high trees and acting as protective zones for water conservation or as wind-breaks), shall not be considered as forming part of the reserved areas referred to in this Article, and shall be the object of an additional reserve, not to exceed 15% of the area of the principal reserve.

The Court may, at the request of the National Agrarian Institute, grant reductions in reserves up to 50% of the area immune from expropriation, on the grounds that the land is situated in a zone of high population density or that it is adjacent to a zone within the purview of the provisions of Article 183. In the case of lands lying near population centers of less than 3000 inhabitants, the reserve may be reduced to one third when such action is necessary to satisfy land allocation requirements. In no case may a reserve be granted in such part of a property as is being cultivated indirectly through a tenancy, sharecropping, *fundación* or other similar system.

31.   Any person owning or acquiring more than one rural property which is expropriated shall be entitled to reserve for himself an area, not exceeding the limits laid down in Article 29, on one such property only.

32.   In the cases mentioned in Articles 29 and 30, immunity from expropriation shall lapse in respect of properties and reserves made up of uncultivated or fallow land which has not been cultivated within three years, or on which an efficient stock-grazing enterprise has not been installed within five years from the date on which the land was allocated or the reserve was established, or if during the said period such land has been operated indirectly.

For the purposes of this Act, efficiently operated stock-grazing enterprises shall be those enterprises on which cultivated pastures predominate and on which exist such improvements as fences, stables, or watering troughs, or on which the practice of burning over pastures has been eliminated, so that a maximum herd of stock may be maintained on a minimum land area without adverse biological effect upon the soil or the stock.

33.   When it becomes necessary to organize land in a given place, and when the existence thereat of one or more properties forms a technical or economic obstacle to proper execution of the scheme, the total or partial expropriation of such properties shall be authorized even when they fall within any of the classifications specified in Articles 26 and 29 of this Chapter. In order to take such action, the Institute shall be required to prove, during the appropriate judicial proceedings, that the conditions laid down in this Article exist. In such cases, cash payment shall be made for existing useful improvements, livestock, mortgages or preferential debts incurred and used for development and improvement purposes. The balance shall be paid in Class "C" bonds in accordance with the provisions of Article 174 of this Act.

Small or medium landowners whose properties have been totally expropriated under this Article shall be entitled, after the said land has been organized, to obtain, against payment, ownership of a parcel of the said land of a size equal to the largest area allocated.

Total expropriation shall take place where partial expropriation would destroy the economic unity of the property or would render it useless or unfit for the purpose for which it was destined.

34.   When the properties are made up of lands of various qualities, the area immune from expropriation shall be determined by taking as one hectare of first-category land the appropriate equivalents to be prescribed by Regulation.

35.   Prior to proceeding to the expropriation of a property the National Agrarian Institute shall directly propose an amicable arrangement with the owner. If such amicable arrangement is not reached within a period which may not exceed 90 days, the Institute shall request expropriation; no prior declaration of public interest shall be required, expropriation of land or properties for the purposes of this Act being of such nature.

36.   In expropriating properties for the purposes of the Agrarian Reform, the provisions of the Act relating to Expropriation in the Public or Social Interest shall be complied with, except as otherwise provided by this Act, and especially as follows:

> 1)   The request for expropriation, submitted to the Court having jurisdiction over the locality where the property is situated, shall be accompanied by a certificate issued by the competent Public Registry Office relating to tax assessments on the property during the ten preceding years, a report on the general characteristics of the property, and the classification of the property, prepared by the National Agrarian Institute in accordance with Article 29, for the purposes of the reserve mentioned in Article 38.
> To this end, the competent Public Registry Office shall be required to furnish such certificates and reports within three working days after the date of request therefor.
> At the session at which the expropriation request is received, or at the following session, the Court shall take cognizance thereof and shall summon the interested parties to reply thereto.
> 2)   Appeals or other recourses against decisions of the trial judge shall lie in second instance before the Federal Court, against the decision of which no appeal whatsoever shall lie.
> 3)   The expropriation request and summons for hearing shall be published twice, at intervals of not more than six days and not less than three days between the first and second publications, by notices affixed in the most public places and published in a daily newspaper of the Capital of the Republic.
> 4)   Within five sessions after the date of the final publication, the persons summoned shall appear before the Court, personally or through an attorney, to file replies to the expropriation request. At the session following the expiration of the said period, an attorney shall be named for persons having failed to appear, and he shall be deemed to have been summoned.

If the attorney thus named fails to appear to be sworn at the first session after his appointment, such appointment shall be taken as having been refused. In such cases, the Court shall proceed to appoint a new attorney in the session immediately following.

5)   If the appeal is on formal grounds only, a decision shall be rendered on such grounds at the fifth session following the filing of replies, after oral statements from all parties have been heard. In other cases, without a decree or order of the Court being necessary, a period of 15 working days after the full hearing shall be allowed, to permit the parties to collect and submit the necessary evidence; in no case may a *término de distancia** be granted for the collection of evidence.

6)   At the expiration of the period allowed for taking evidence, a hearing shall be called within the two following sessions, at which time the parties shall file their written pleadings; the following session shall be fixed for hearing oral arguments on the points raised therein, provided that no party or the attorney thereof shall be authorized to speak more than once or for more than 30 minutes. After termination of the hearing, the Court shall announce its decision within the five following sessions. The Court may, once only, call a new hearing for further information. Such new hearing shall be held within the five following sessions, and the decision shall be announced within the three sessions following the expiration of the said period.

7)   At the session following the filing of replies, the parties shall be present at a time to be fixed by the Court in order to reach an agreement on the price of the property under expropriation. If no such agreement is reached, the Court shall set a time at the following session for the appointment of experts to make a valuation; proceedings in respect thereof, when an appeal has been filed, shall be entered on a separate docket and shall be carried forward independently of the principal action. When the experts designated by the parties to the same case have twice in succession declined to act, the Court shall appoint experts.

37.   When, under the provisions of this Act, expropriation of a property is required for an immediate allocation of land, the prior occupation of the lands and properties in question may be carried out under the conditions laid down in Articles 51 an 52 of the Act in force relating to Expropriation in the Public or Social Interest, taking into account, in respect of the payment of the amount at which the property is evaluated, the provisions of Article 33 of this Act.

38.   The owner shall be required to decide upon the location of the land he desires to reserve under the provisions of Articles 29, 30 and 31 prior to the day fixed for the swearing-in of the experts. If he fails to do so at the proper time, the Court shall indicate the location of the reserve prior to execution of the valuation, within a period of ten calendar days after administration of the oath; prior to and during such period, the Court may order the execution of any acts it finds necessary. If, after the interested party has chosen a

---

* Trans. Note: Under Venezuelan law, a delay granted when distances remote from the seat of the Court are involved.

location, a conflict arises with the agrarian authorities concerning the unsuitability of such location in view of execution of the agrarian scheme, the Court shall decide the question in accordance with the procedure laid down in Article 386 of the Code of Civil Procedure.

39. When it is necessary for the purposes of the Agrarian Reform to assign common land *(tierras baldías)* occupied by third parties carrying out agricultural activities thereon, and the National Agrarian Institute has not reached agreement with the occupiers, the expropriation of the works and improvements shall be requested, and a right shall be recognized to the occupier to retain part of his exploitation, such part being fixed in accordance with the project establishment plans, unless he prefers to be relocated on another parcel assigned him by the National Agrarian Institute. If in the expropriation proceedings the occupier claims ownership of the property and produces proof thereof, the provisions of Article 37 shall apply.

40. If an occupier of public land has failed to establish thereon a useful agricultural enterprise, the National Agrarian Institute shall request of the ordinary Court having jurisdiction in expropriation matters judicial authorization to occupy such land, and shall pay the occupier for the works and improvements he has installed thereon at a fair rate established by experts. In case the occupier claims ownership of the land but fails to present title thereto, the National Agrarian Institute shall request the same measure, and may recognize the occupier as a beneficiary of an allocation under this Act. If, during either expropriation proceedings or final occupation proceedings the occupier has claimed ownership of the land, he shall be entitled to request that the Government make an adjustment or settlement of the matter, unless the Government considers that resort should be had to an administrative claims procedure; such procedures hall be initiated within one year after occupation by the National Agrarian Institute has been authorized.

CHAPTER III
WATERS

41. For the purposes of the Agrarian Reform, the use, possession and employment of waters shall be subject to the limitations, regulations and restrictions laid down in this Act and in the Acts and Regulations relating to waters and irrigation, drainage and land improvement works, and governing the use of zones benefited thereby.

42. Public waters, and private waters in excess of amount required for rational exploitation of the lands of which they form an integral part, shall be placed at the disposal of the Agrarian Reform.

43. The allocation of water, within the meaning of this Chapter, may have as its purpose the irrigation of fields and pastures, domestic uses, and sufficient services and installations for the development of land allocations and

the operation of industries based upon agriculture, stock-raising and other connected activities.

44.   Immunity from allocation shall apply to:

1)   Waters required for the supply of population centers and other public services.
2)   Waters used in irrigation works constructed by private persons, waters used in rationally-exploited properties and sufficient waters for the proper exploitation of land reserves established under this Act.
3)   Waters used for industrial purposes.
4)   Waters used for small and medium agricultural enterprises, experimental stations and model farms.
5)   Other waters which the Government finds are fulfilling other functions necessary to the service of the community.

45.   Simultaneously with the General Register of Land and Waters established under Chapter IV of this Title, municipalities and parishes shall, in accordance with regulations thereon, take a census of the persons and enterprises using public waters; users shall be required to funish information concerning such use.

46.   As census-taking operations provided for in the preceding Article are completed in each zone, region or river-basin of the country, the Government shall proceed to regulate the use of the waters thereof in accordance with law.

When the diversion and use thereof are defective or irrational, the Government shall order the agricultural or industrial enterprise concerned to remedy the deficiencies observed; if the said enterprise fails to comply with the order, the Government may declare the temporary or final suspension of the right thereof to divert and use public waters on its land or in its industries. Other cases, as provided in the Waters and Irrigation Acts and in other legal provisions of the Agrarian Reform, shall also give rise to such suspension.

47.   The Government shall also be empowered to modify public water use rights, whatever be the title from which they are derived, in the following cases:

(a)   If the waters are required for domestic use or for public services;
(b)   When the execution of the Agrarian Reform so requires, under the conditions laid down in this Act;
(c)   In regulating the use of a stream, reservoir or collective utilization;
(d)   When the output of the source of supply diminishes;

Provided, that compensation shall be payable only in cases of evident and proved damage suffered by the user concerned.

48.   The Government shall, when it finds such action necessary for the purposes of this Act, regulate the use of privately-owned lands which are to constitute protective zones at the headwaters and along the banks of sources of waters and streams feeding the rivers.

49.   The Government may declare that schemes of private persons destined to provide an improved and more rational use of waters are in the public interest, and may authorize the execution of such schemes, provided that they do not conflict with hydraulic installation, overall development or land allocation schemes under study by the competent public agencies.

In the execution and utilization of such works, first preference shall be given to the present users and second preference to the initiator of the project; in each case, satisfactory guarantees shall be procured concerning the capacity of the latter, the benefit to and improved utilization of the waters by the users thereof, and the benefit to the widest possible sector of the local community.

50.   The State shall cooperate with owners of neighboring properties within the purview of Articles 19 and 29 of this Act who voluntarily set up users' associations for the collection and use in common of public waters derived from a same source or contiguous sources. Works to be constructed and the regulation of the use thereof shall be in accordance with legal requirements;

Provided, that if no agreement between the parties is reached, the users' association may also be set up by the Government on its own initiative, in order to obtain better use of waters.

The compulsory constitution of such an association may also be requested by the minimum number of owners concerned as provided for in the applicable legislation.

51.   After compliance with legal requirements, such users' associations shall enjoy juridical personality, in order to be in a position to obtain concessions for the use of public waters, to construct irrigation works and generating plants, to procure funds necessary for the construction of projected works and to acquire property required for their purposes.

The rights granted such associations nowithstanding, the Government shall retain the capacity to provide for the protection and rational use of the waters and of land benefited thereby.

CHAPTER IV
GENERAL REGISTER OF LAND AND WATERS

52.   The State shall make an inventory of all land and waters, both private and property of the Nation, States, municipalities, and autonomous institutions or public establishments; for this purpose it shall proceed immediately to drawing up the proper Land Register.

53.   Landowners shall record their properties in the appropriate Registry Offices, by presenting their titles of ownership, duly registered within the period and in the form prescribed by this Act.

54.   Among the purposes of the Land Register shall be to examine titles and cadastral maps, to carry out the necessary verifications of the areas and

boundaries of rural properties, and to bring to notice existing uncultivated or unprofitably-used land.

The Office of the National Land Register shall be required to inform the Government of cases in which titles fail to constitute due proof of ownedship of property, for the purpose of taking the consequent legal action.

55.   Under conditions laid down in Regulations, the State shall cooperate with landowners, for land registration purposes, in the technical work of delimitation, preparation of topographical charts of properties, and the division of land held in co-ownership, in order that such operations may not give rise to excessive costs.

56.   The Land Register shall be established progressively, initially in those zones or States in which the Government finds that property disputes exist or are most acute, or in which the conservation of renewable natural resources is urgent, without prejudice to the continuation of work already begun.

The preparation of the Land Register shall in no case constitute a prior condition for the execution of the Agrarian Reform in any zone or region.

TITLE II
ALLOCATION OF LAND
CHAPTER I
GENERAL PROVISIONS

57.   Allocations, either collective or individual, shall include land suitable for cultivation and required by the applicants, and such technical assistance and credit as may be required. In general, housing shall be provided, either by founding a population center or by improving such a center already existing, taking into account its future expansion, the installations intended for the common benefit of allottees, the community pastureland and the forests and waters required for the normal and projected requirements of the group, as well as the additional public works and services referred to in Article 79.

58.   Beneficiaries of collective allocations in every case, and of individual allocations when they so demand expressly, shall be organized, with the cooperation of the National Agrarian Institute, into Agrarian Centers administered by an Administrative Committee nominated by the members of the Center and advised, where necessary, by a Technical Director appointed by the National Agrarian Institute.

59.   Administrative Committees shall be elected annually by Assemblies of Allottees. When more than one list of candidates is nominated, seats shall be filled on a proportional representation basis, as shall be determined by Regulations under this Act.

60.   The collective or administrative allocations referred to in this Chapter shall be carried out as dictated by the urgency of their execution,

the ordinary, extraordinary and administrative financial resources available to the Agencies of the Agrarian Reform, and the assistance of the other official bodies referred to in this Act. Such grants shall have priority in the rural regions of greatest population pressure. In every case the National Agrarian Institute shall proceed as rapidly as possible.

61. Parcels shall in all cases be granted in freehold, with or without payment, under the conditions and within the limits laid down in this Act. The foregoing shall be without prejudice to the provisions of Article 74.

62. Individual or collective allocations, within or outside Agrarian Centers, shall be made free of charge when the economic position of the beneficiary warrants an allocation in order to incorporate him into the economically productive life of the Nation.

63. Parcels allocated free of charge shall be of the area prescribed by this Act or by Regulations hereunder as the indispensable minimum required for satisfying the necessities of the beneficiary and of his family, and capable of being operated by the said group without need for the permanent assistance of paid labor. In assigning such parcels, account shall be taken of:

(a) The number of persons dependent upon the beneficiary and composing his family, and the requirements thereof for a livelihood;
(b) The economic and agricultural characteristics of the land.

64. Beneficiaries of free parcels may subsequently request authorization to purchase additional land areas, provided that such additions do not exceed the legal limit, and that the conditions laid down in Article 77 of this Act have been met. The National Agrarian Institute shall decide whether the reasons given in the request justify a further allocation. In each case it shall communicate its decision to the petitioner within a period of no more than 60 days.

65. The basic value of the parcels or additional areas allocated for valuable consideration shall be the proportional part of the cost of acquisition of the land per hectare and of the works and improvements carried out on the parcel, plus the cost of first-year production financing which the National Agrarian Institute shall furnish the beneficiary.

In no case shall the beneficiaries be held responsible for payment of works for the common benefit intended for the public services of the Agrarian Centers, such as highways, rural roads and other general services, or for interest on the debt arising out of allocation for valuable consideration;

Provided, that in view of the social function of land ownership, for which the farmer is primarily responsible, when parcels to be granted for valuable consideration prove to be excessively costly by reason of their being located in regions where land values are very high, the sale price thereof shall be fixed by a study carried out by the National Agrarian Institute covering the economic and agricultural aspects of such land.

Provided, further, that the beneficiary shall be granted a 5% reduction in the price fixed for his parcel in respect of each ascendant and of each descendant under 15 years of age living under the same roof and depending directly upon him. The same reduction shall apply in respect of the spouse or of the woman permanently living with the allottee as his wife.

66. The annual amortization payment shall be determined by dividing the price of the parcel by the number of years fixed for complete payment thereof, which shall not be less than 20 nor more than 30 years. The first such payment shall be made at the time fixed by the National Agrarian Institute according to the nature of the crop, but not prior to the third year after the beneficiary has received temporary title.

In no case may the National Agrarian Institute require that the annual amortization payment be superior to 5% of the gross price of the yield of the parcel;

Provided, that if the beneficiary complies with the obligations arising out of the allocation during half the original payment period, and obtains, in the opinion of the National Agrarian Institute, an above-average productivity level, he shall be entitled to be exonerated from payment of the outstanding portion of the debt.

67. To be allocated a parcel, and without prejudice to the provisions of Article 62, the applicant must fulfill the following conditions:

> 1) Undertake to work the parcel personally or with his legitimate or natural descendants or with his ascendants and collaterals to the second degree by blood or to the second degree by marriage, respectively, living with him;
> 2) Lack land or possess land insufficient for furnishing the yield referred to in Article 76;
> 3) Be over 18 years of age.

68. Among the applicants fulfilling the requirements laid down in Article 67, an order of priority shall be established as follows:

> (a) Day laborers, tenants, sharecroppers, settlers and occupiers cultivating the land subject to allocation, and laborers thereon;
> (b) Heads of families who are farmers, according to the number of legitimate or natural children living with or dependent on them;
> (c) Persons having completed their military service or in the last six months of such service;
> (d) Farmers;
> (e) Persons having completed courses of study in Schools of Agriculture or of Veterinary Studies, Rural Training Schools, Model Farm Schools and other similar institutions;
> (f) Foreign nationals, whether residing in the country or immigrants, who are farmers.

Persons over 18 years of age shall be considered as being legally of age for the purposes of allocation and administration of parcels and for obtaining credits;

Provided, that special priority shall be granted to day laborers, tenants, share-croppers, settlers, occupiers and farm laborers who have been evicted from lands to be allocated.

69. When the Ministry of Agriculture finds that problems of conservation of renewable natural resources exist in regions which have been or are declared to be protective or reserved regions, the transfer of the populations occupying such regions shall be declared obligatory and urgent. In such cases, the National Agrarian Institute shall be required to relocate the said populations in suitable places, preferably in the same regions, establishing Agrarian Centers and paying the appropriate compensation.

70. If no land of public or private agencies which may be set aside for the Agrarian Reform exists in the region where the applicant individual or group is located, the National Agrarian Institute shall make an allocation in the nearest region or regions.

71. In cases where the land area is insufficient, as defined in Article 76, to provide for the installation thereon of all applicants entitled to allocations under Article 67, the following priority system shall apply:

> *(a)* Applicants having been cultivating the said lands for the greatest number of years;
> *(b)* Other factors being equal, heads of families according to the number of their dependents;
> *(c)* Other factors being equal, applicants who have demonstrated the greatest efficiency and work capacity.

The other applicants who meet the conditions laid down in Article 67 shall be installed by the National Agrarian Institute in the region closest to their present location, under the priority system laid down in Article 68.

72. Beneficiaries shall be exempt from all taxes arising out of the acquisition of parcels and other operations carried out in that connection.

73. In case of the decease of a beneficiary, whether or not he has paid for his parcel, if his heirs fail to agree in the administration and operation of the property or decide on the partition thereof, the National Agrarian Institute, after having heard the recommendation of the Administrative Committee, may annul the allocation and re-allocate the parcel, priority being granted to a member of the family, provided that he meets the conditions laid down in Articles 62 or 67 and the other provisions of this Act. In such cases, the Institute shall pay to the order of the deceased's estate the cost of the parcel and of the improvements made thereto, less the outstanding balance of the debt owed by the previous allottee to the agencies of the Agrarian Reform.

74. The beneficiaries of this Act may convey their rights to land derived from allocations, even where the total price thereof has not been paid, provided that such conveyance shall be subject to the written authorization of

the National Agrarian Institute and in favor of persons meeting the requirements of Article 67; the parcel shall, however, first be offered for sale to the National Agrarian Institute and the latter shall have replied, provided that such reply shall be made within not more than 60 days after the offer was made. If proof of fulfillment of the foregoing conditions is not duly furnished to the Land Registry Sub-office, the Registrar shall refrain from registering the document.

The deed of transfer shall stipulate that the purchaser assumes the obligations devolving upon the vendor arising out of the allocation.

In order to obtain agricultural credit, the beneficiary may give a mortgage on chattels or industrial equipment. The beneficiary may not grant the parcel under lease or under any other type of contract implying indirect cultivation of the land, except in duly proved cases of *force majeure* and with the authorization of the Institute after favorable recommendation of the Administrative Committee.

75. If a favorable decision on allocation is reached, the allottee shall be issued the appropriate title deed, in which shall be included the description of the parcel, the conditions of allocation, the boundaries and other information required by the Public Land Registry Act, and the restrictions referred to in Articles 83 and 84 of this Act. The said deed shall be entered in the Agrarian Register which shall be maintained for that purpose by the National Agrarian Institute, and in the appropriate Land Registry Sub-Office.

76. The form and area of the parcels shall depend upon the topographical and agrological characteristics of the land to be distributed, in such a manner that the beneficiary may carry out the greater part of the farm labor by his own means and with the aid of his family, and in order that the productive capacity of the parcel may suffice for his increasing economic progress, the efficient operation of the enterprise and an increase in national production.

Two or more beneficiaries may organize themselves on a joint or cooperative basis for the operation of their parcels when they deem such action desirable, without prejudice to the applicable provisions of the Cooperative Societies Act.

77. No beneficiary may possess more than one parcel. However, he may request and obtain an additional area of land if the following conditions are met:

(a) He has a large family dependent on him;
(b) The original parcel is insufficient for providing the economic output required for maintaining his family;
(c) He shows that he has been properly operating the parcel he possesses.

78. In a manner to be laid down in Regulations, the National Agrarian Institute shall provide incentives for allottees who encourage the cultural and technical education of the family group, who obtain superior output on their

parcels and who take pains to conserve renewable natural resources. Such incentives shall take the form of reductions in the outstanding balance due in the case of parcels allotted for valuable consideration, and of bonuses in the case of parcels allotted free of charge.

79. The Institute or the competent Ministries shall proceed to supplement land allocations by the construction of road, irrigation and drainage works indispensable to the success of the Agrarian Centers, and of allottee housing, buildings and other community services.

The National Agrarian Institute shall, further, install or encourage the establishment of processing and industrial plants, equipment, mechanical services, warehouses and whatever may be necessary for the proper operation of the Agrarian Centers.

80. In each Agrarian Center there shall be created centers of agricultural education and training, and rural schools for the formation of qualified farm workers; such centers and schools shall plan their programs on the basis of the technical and social objectives of the Agrarian Reform.

81. In order to supplement farm revenues, the organization of parcels as mixed undertakings shall be encouraged, and for that purpose the National Agrarian Institute shall grant to beneficiaries, as an aid to installation, means to acquire adequate quantities of livestock, barnyard fowl and any other kind of animals which promote the well-being of the rural family. Where necessary, there shall similarly be established common pastures for grazing of livestock of such beneficiaries.

82. Agrarian Centers may contain nationals and foreigners, provided that in no case may the latter be in excess of 30% of the beneficiaries of the Center or be installed in conditions superior to those of the nationals.

83. The title deed referred to in Article 75 shall include a stipulation that the National Agrarian Institute may, by a decision approved by the Directorate thereof, after study and for stated cause, revoke or annul the allotment, for the following reasons:

1) Use of the parcel for purposes other than those of the Agrarian Reform;

2) Unjustified abandonment of the parcel or of the family. In the latter case, the Institute shall allot the parcel to the wife, or, in the absence thereof, to the concubine, or, in the absence thereof, to the child who in the opinion of the Institute is the best qualified, provided that he meets the conditions laid down in Article 67;

3) Negligence or manifest unfitness of the beneficiary to operate the parcel or to maintain the buildings, improvements or equipment entrusted to him or belonging to the organization;

4) Upon proof of indirect operation of the parcel, except as authorized by this Act;

5) Failure without good reason to comply with payment obligations to the National Agrarian Institute, either directly, with the Agricultural

Bank, or through Farm Loan Cooperatives or Unions;

6) Repeated violation of legal provisions concerning the conservation of natural resources.

In cases 1, 3, 4, 5, and 6, a previous warning must have been ignored and a favorable opinion, stating the reasons justifying the said penalty, shall have been obtained from the Administrative Committee.

84. In case of revocation or annulment of allocations or grants, the fair value of existing useful improvements made by the beneficiary, as determined by experts, shall be paid to the said beneficiary. Up to the time of payment of such indemnity, compensation may be effected by deduction of sums due by the beneficiary in the form of loans or credits.

In such cases the beneficiary shall also receive reimbursement of amortization payments made; in the cases provided for in Article 83, such reimbursement shall be subject to a reduction of 10%.

85. The crops, seeds, livestock, chattels and equipment necessary for the cultivation and operation of parcels shall be immune from seizure or foreclosure arising out of obligations to physical or juridical persons, except in the case of credits previously authorized by the National Agrarian Institute.

86. In order to grant preference to independent producers lacking land, and in conformity with the applicable provisions of this Act, the National Agrarian Institute may make special allocations in undeveloped regions, not having the nature of Agrarian Centers, to sufficiently fit and qualified persons, within the limits laid down in Article 29 of this Act.

An absolute requirement for such allocations shall be the prior submission to the National Agrarian Institute of a draft development scheme and a report on the funds available therefor.

Such allocations may be supplemented by technical assistance and grants of credit.

The National Agrarian Institute shall apply this provision, insofar as it applies to the area allocated, for allocations to individual applicants inhabiting the regions mentioned in the first paragraph of this Article.

No such allocation may give rise to delay in development of an Agrarian Center, or impair the rights conferred by Article 68 upon day laborers, tenants, sharecroppers, settlers and occupiers.

87. Landowners may provide land without charge and establish such land as family estates in favor of tenants, sharecroppers, day laborers, occupiers or laborers working on their properties, in accordance with the provisions of this Chapter, without prejudice to the right of such beneficiaries to request and obtain from the National Agrarian Institute the appropriate allocation in accordance with this Act.

Such lands shall be required to be unencumbered and of an area sufficient for the purposes prescribed in Article 76.

Allocation plans shall be submitted to the National Agrarian Institute for prior approval, with a detailed statement of all information required for reaching a decision thereon.

88. When for good reasons it becomes necessary to provide for the transfer of a population group to another more suitable place, if no appropriate land exists in the region, such transfer shall be subject to the prior consent of the local authorities of the group, except as provided in Article 69.

89. The National Agrarian Institute, in cooperation with the Ministry of Justice, shall ensure that relocations of native tribes or clans, when necessary, are carried out in conformity with the applicable provisions of this Act.

90. The water allocations referred to in Article 57 shall be limited exclusively to the excess water not used by landowners and users of the region in irrigating their land; such waters may, however, be regulated with a view to their rational use, and, if resort has been had to expropriation, regulations may be issued governing the volume in excess of that necessary for the irrigation of the reserve immune from expropriation.

When the expropriated property has its own waters or water use rights which are sufficient for the adequate irrigation of the expropriated areas and the reserve, they shall be divided proportionally among the said areas and reserve. When the waters are insufficient for the irrigation of both the expropriated areas and the reserve, preference for rational use thereof shall be granted to the expropriated area, unless the reserve is already under cultivation; in the latter case, the excess shall be allocated to the expropriated area. However, in order to ensure the best use of waters, the system of irrigation by rotation shall be employed.

The National Agrarian Institute may also make use of non-utilizable water surpluses on partially expropriated or neighboring properties for land allocations.

Reserves and expropriated areas shall remain reciprocally subject to easements of passage, support of aqueducts, or others necessary for the operation of the expropriated area or of the establishments created in the zone.

91. Already-existing hydraulic works destined to serve the operation of properties under expropriation or for the normal use of residents thereon shall be used in common and in proportion to the rights of owners of reserves and expropriated areas. Maintenance and improvement costs of such works shall be divided in the same proportion.

92. When it is economically suitable to make use of hydraulic facilities already existing in the region, either in view of their capacity or because they require only expansion or improvement, the landowner shall be required to create the necessary easements thereon; he shall be paid an appropriate indemnity, and the National Agrarian Institute shall be required to carry out the necessary work at its own expense.

CHAPTER II
ALLOCATION PROCEDURES

93. Any individual or rural population group exercising the right granted under Article 2, paragraph *b)*, shall present a land allocation request to the local Allocations Branch of the National Agrarian Institute.

When the request is for allocation of land not fulfilling its social function, the petitioner shall so state.

94. Members of population groups shall elect from among their number temporary committees, composed of not less than five members, to represent them during the processing of the allocation request. Elections to the said committees shall be held under the procedure laid down in Article 59.

95. Every request shall include the name, age, sex, place of birth, occupation and number of persons constituting the legitimate or natural family of the individual or of each member of the group. In addition, when possible, the request shall include approximate data concerning the land of the region, specifying whether State, public, municipal or private, the area and quality thereof, watercourses, present and possible types of culture, average production, information on rainfall, means of communication, distance from markets and, in general, all information of such a nature as to permit proper consideration of the case.

96. After receipt of the request and verification of the qualifications of the requesting individual or group, the Allocation Delegate shall proceed to process the request by verifying the information submitted by the interested parties, causing to be noted whatever observations or modifications appear appropriate, and collecting missing data, making use therein of his own knowledge or the advice of special commissions composed of qualified persons appointed for the purpose. Within not more than 90 days after receipt of the request, he shall forward it, thus processed, to the Allocations Department of the National Agrarian Institute.

97. The National Agrarian Institute shall proceed to consider such requests in the order of their receipt and, in the case of favorable decisions, shall grant the allocation within a period of not more than 30 days, placing the interested parties in possession of the land by delivery of the appropriate title deed.

98. In determining the form and area of parcels, the provisions of Article 76 shall be taken into account; however, the final boundaries shall be established only on the appropriate title deed referred to in Article 75, the necessary boundary adjustments having been made during the year on the basis of experience and as a result of systematic and continuing studies to be made by the National Agrarian Institute.

99. When the population group is in possession of the land, the temporary committee shall call a General Assembly, which shall require the pres-

ence of at least two thirds of the allottees, to proceed to the establishment of the Agrarian Center and, in conformity with Article 59, to the election of the Administrative Committee. If two thirds of the allottees fail to be present at the said first meeting, the temporary committee shall call another meeting, at which the presence of an absolutely majority shall suffice; if the said quorum is not attained, a third assembly shall be called, which shall be held whatever be the number of the members present, and which shall proceed to the establishment of the Center and the election of the Administrative Committee.

100. The Administrative Committee of the Center shall serve as the agency of liaison with the National Agrarian Institute, and shall:

> (a) Draw up draft statutes and submit them to the Assembly for consideration and approval;
> (b) Draw up and approve production and credit plans, in consultation with the Technical Director and the beneficiaries, and ensure the proper marketing of the products and the provisioning of the Agrarian Center;
> (c) Cooperate with the National Agrarian Institute in view of the proper development of technical, health, educational and social assistance programs, and call upon the Institute to implement such programs;
> (d) Take all measures in its power to promote the economic, social and civic progress of the group;

Provided, that in accordance with production programs prepared on a nation-wide basis, the National Agrarian Institute may modify the plans provided for in paragraph *b)* of this Article; it shall, however, be required in such cases to state the reasons for the modification or rejection thereof.

101. In order to make as rapidly and effectively as possible the allocations referred to in Article 2, paragraph *b),* of this Act, in cases of properties on which completed works and established services already exist, allocation shall be required to take place within not more than six months after date of receipt of the request therefor.

CHAPTER III
FAMILY ESTATES

102. Lands allocated under this Act, or parts therof, may be declared constituted as family estates by the National Agrarian Institute on the request of the interested party, who shall for the purpose comply with the formalities of registration therefor in the appropriate offices of the Rural Property Register, Public Register and Family Estates Register, as provided in Articles 75 and 171. Such estates shall be inalienable and indivisible and shall be immune from seizure or any other judicial measure whether provisional or final, and from any encumbrance whatsoever, except in cases of community use, social or public interest, voluntary formation of agricultural cooperatives approved

by the National Agrarian Institute, or revocation or annulment of the allocation of the parcel and other exceptions provided for in this Act.

The interested parties may dissolve family estate status established voluntarily, provided that five years have elapsed since the registration thereof, by duly justifying the said dissolution to the Institute and complying with the formalities established in the first paragraph of this Article.

103. A family estate as constituted shall consist of an economic unit, formed by an area of land having the characteristics and fulfilling the conditions laid down in Article 76, and the permanent improvements installed thereon.

104. The exploitation of the family estate shall be carried out directly and personally by the owner and the members of his family, except when impossible for reasons of age, illness and legal absence or prohibition; in the latter cases, indirect exploitation shall be permitted as long as the causes therefor continue to subsist, subject to the prior authorization of the National Agrarian Institute upon request of the interested party, submitted directly or through the competent Delegate.

Paid labor by third parties shall be permitted only for not more than 30% of the days of the year, except in the exceptional circumstances referred to in this Act.

105. The National Agrarian Institute shall foster, among owners of family estates, the constitution of associations for mutual assistance, cooperation, administrative representation and others useful or necessary for the production and distribution of products, procurement and use of credit and farm machinery, and any other works or enterprises of mutual benefit.

106. Small independent landowners whose properties are free of all encumbrances and have the characteristics laid down in Article 76 may also take advantage of the constitution of family estates; for the purpose they shall apply to the National Agrarian Institute, requesting the appropriate declaration of constitution and, if such declaration is granted, proceeding to comply with the other legal requirements.

If the land belonging to the applicant does not have the characteristics referred to in Article 76, the Institute shall proceed to allocate to him sufficient supplementary land if it is available at that place; otherwise, it shall proceed to relocate him to permit of constitution of a family estate.

If the properties are encumbered, the National Agrarian Institute shall order the necessary measures for freeing them therefrom.

Obligations of the beneficiary to the Institute arising from supplementary allocations or extinction of encumbrances referred to in this Article shall wherever applicable be subject to the provisions of this Act governing allocations of land.

107. Small rural landowners having family estates may constitute with their lands agricultural cooperatives or associations enjoying juridical personality; in such cases, after registration of the act of constitution in the appro-

priate registers, the benefits of family estates shall be extended to such cooperatives or associations.

108. The protection granted by this Act to family estates shall be inoperative in respect of the National Agrarian Institute and of the public farm credit agencies as long as the owners benefited have not completely satisfied their obligations thereto.

TITLE III
FARM CREDIT

109. For the purposes of the Agrarian Reform, a farm credit service shall be organized by the State in such manner as to ensure preferential treatment to satisfy the credit requirements of small and medium rural producers and of agricultural cooperatives.

110. For grants of credits to farmers other than those referred to in Article 109, the State shall promote the creation of such agencies as it deems necessary, without prejudice to the use of those already existing for similar purposes.

111. Granting and administration of credits contemplated in this Act shall be governed by the principles and standards of controlled credit to be established by appropriate Regulations. Pending establishment of the organization necessary for full supervision, there shall be applied a system which shall permit of the gradual introduction of controlled credit.

112. The farm credit service shall be guided by the following principles:

(a) Small and medium farmers, whether or not beneficiaries of allocations under this Act, shall be considered to be entitled to such credit;

(b) Credit grants shall be individual or collective; collective credits shall be defined as those granted to cooperatives or to farm credit unions authorized in accordance with Article 113 of this Chapter;

(c) Credits shall be granted at such times and for such periods as are in keeping with the productive capacity of the farm and the useful life of the investment, in order that the specific purpose of such credits may be fulfilled. Such credits shall not bear interest of more than 3% per year, in the case of small producers;

(d) Credits shall be employed for the following purposes:

1) Working capital intended to cover living costs of the farm family, the acquisition of small livestock and barnyard fowl, seeds, fertilizers, insecticides, fungicides, land preparation, sowing, cultivation, harvesting, insurance and minor repairs;

2) Supplementary credit to cover urgent and immediate costs of family life, to be considered in relation to the applicant's need and ability to repay;

3) Equipment credits, destined for the acquisition of machinery, tools, farming instruments and animals for draft, fattening, production or breeding;

4) Credits for processing, conservation and industrialization of the yield, and for operations destined to improve yield quality.

5) Rehabilitation credits, to be granted to persons who for reasons beyond their control or due to *force majeure* have failed to pay their debts;

6) Credits for permanent improvements, such as the construction of housing, silos, outbuildings, roads, drainage, irrigation, conservation of resources, reforestation, fruit and other permanent plantations, construction of fences, waterholes, wells, and seeding of artificial pastures;

7) Any other type of credit needed for agricultural production;

Provided, that the terms and conditions of such credits shall be laid down in Regulations, taking into account the abovementioned characteristics.

113. The said credits may be granted individually if requested by one person acting on his own behalf and responsibility, or collectively if requested by a farm credit union or by a cooperative, without prejudice to the provisions of the Cooperative Societies Act.

Five or more small or medium farmers or stock-breeders may organize a farm credit union or cooperative, which shall request whatever credits it deems necessary under conditions provided by this Act.

Small and medium fishermen may also benefit, individually or collectively, from the credit services referred to in this Chapter.

114. Such credits shall be secured by mortgages on chattels or industrial equipment, drawn up in favor of the institution granting the said credit, and preferably in respect of the following property:

1) Plantations and cultures;
2) Yield of all kinds, whether or not harvested;
3) Animals of all species, their young, and animal products;
4) Wood and other forest products;
5) Vehicles, machinery and other farm equipment;
6) Processed products;
7) Industrial machinery;
8) Packaging materials.

115. In accordance with the provisions of Article 194, requests for farm credits referred to in the preceding Articles, whether individual or collective, shall be submitted to the specially-designated local agencies of the Agricultural Bank. Decisions shall be taken on such requests within a period of not more than 25 working days if the bank agency granting the credit is located at the place of domicile of the applicant, or 45 days if it is located in the District or State capital having jurisdiction, or 90 days if it is located in the Capital of the Republic;

Provided, that the officials directly responsible for deciding on credit requests who fail to decide thereon within the time-limits prescribed by this Article shall be punished by a reprimand and, if the offense is repeated, by dismissal if they are personally responsible for such failure.

116.   Both individual and collective credit requests originating with beneficiaries of Agrarian Centers shall require the authorization of the competent Administrative Committees, with the approval of the Technical Director. Good reasons shall be given for refusal to authorize such credit requests, and the interested party shall have a right to appeal against the decision before the local delegate of the National Agrarian Institute.

117.   In order to expedite the credit operations referred to in this Act and to facilitate savings, the Agricultural Bank shall establish a system of current accounts in its agencies for the beneficiaries of the Agrarian Centers, the farm credit unions, the cooperatives formed by beneficiaries, and the other beneficiaries under this Act.

118.   Within the framework of general development plans, the Agricultural Bank shall draw up its annual credit programs and shall fully acquaint interested parties therewith.

TITLE IV
CONSERVATION AND DEVELOPMENT OF RENEWABLE NATURAL RESOURCES
CHAPTER I
ZONING

119.   The Government, through the Ministry of Agriculture, shall draw up the agrological and ecological maps of the country, which shall serve as the basis for the classification of lands according to their productive capacity.

120.   The Government shall take the necessary measures for guiding and encouraging types of operation most suitable for each region, in accordance with the classification mentioned in the preceding Article and with other social and economic factors.

121.   When one or more farmers in a given region are obliged to change their type of operation as a result of regulations governing the use of renewable natural resources, or of the zoning system established, the State shall accord them whatever technical assistance and credit they may require for their proper readaptation.

CHAPTER II
CONSERVATION AND DEVELOPMENT

122.   One of the fundamental objectives of the Agrarian Reform being the conservation and development of renewable natural resources, the State shall take whatever action is required to ensure that the use of such resources is pursued in rational and dynamic manner.

123.   The utilization of renewable natural resources, in any zone of

agricultural development, shall be subject to a rational management plan prepared and put into force by the technical services of the Ministry of Agriculture.

In order to ensure strict compliance with the plan, the said Ministry and the other agricultural authorities shall provide the beneficiaries and other farmers with the training necessary therefor, based principally upon practical demonstrations, and shall furnish them, through agricultural extension programs, the necessary technical assistance.

124. The State shall ensure that the agricultural, stock-raising or mixed exploitation development plans are executed in conformity with regulations governing conservation.

The National Agrarian Institute shall require that beneficiaries of allocations comply with all provisions relating to the conservation and development of renewable natural resources, and shall assist them therein.

CHAPTER III
RESEARCH AND EXTENSION WORK

125. The State shall prepare and carry out scientific research necessary for agricultural development, and in particular for full knowledge of renewable natural resources.

126. The research referred to in the preceding Article shall be coordinated and guided in view of the solution of the problems facing the agricultural development of the country. For that purpose, the State shall establish appropriate research centers, endowing them with the necessary facilities and adequate personnel, who shall be guaranteed stability and continuity of employment.

127. The extension programs to be carried out by the State shall be subject to agricultural development planning, in accordance with the characteristics of each region, and shall be coordinated with the other related public services.

TITLE V
ORGANIZATION OF THE MARKET IN
AGRICULTURAL PRODUCTS AND SUPPLIES

128. The State shall be required, on behalf of the producers and consumers of the country, to promote, operate and control the services destined to facilitate and regulate storage, conservation, transport and distribution of agricultural and fisheries products in and to local and foreign markets, and the acquisition and distribution of supplies to rural producers, without prejudice to cooperation which private enterprise may furnish in such activities in accordance with regulations and limits prescribed by law.

129. The State shall create the specialized central agency responsible

for the activities mentioned in the preceding Article; pending the establishment thereof, it shall provide for the Agricultural Bank to render such services in cooperation with the other official agencies and with cooperatives of small and medium producers performing similar functions.

130. The Agricultural Bank shall accept on deposit, as a gage, or to be applied against amortization of and interest on their debts to the said Institution, from small and medium producers who so desire, such agricultural products derived from their farms as are included in the list of products and prices referred to in the following Article.

131. The Government shall guarantee minimum prices for agricultural and fisheries products, in accordance with the type and quality thereof. The list of such products and of minimum prices shall be drawn up by the Ministry of Agriculture during the first quarter of each year.

Products minimum prices of which are guaranteed shall be purchased directly from producers, or from their associations and cooperatives, through the Agricultural Bank or the agency the creation of which is provided for in this Title.

132. In view of the provisions of Article 128, the Government may, in conformity with the provisions of law or regulations, participate in determining the most appropriate sites for the location of silos, warehouses, slaughterhouses, refrigerating plants and other similar installations. It may also supervise the operation thereof and fix the prices payable for such services, whether rendered by public agencies or by private persons.

TITLE VI
RURAL HOUSING

133. The transformation and improvement of rural housing being an objective of the Agrarian Reform, the State or private bodies created for that purpose shall act in accordance with planning standards whose fundamental principle shall be to avoid the dispersion of the rural population and to ensure the concentration of such population in centers in order to make the best use of public services, without prejudice to the provisions of Article 2, paragraph *(a)*, of this Act.

Rural housing policy shall be coordinated through the competent national agency.

134. The National Agrarian Institute shall foster the construction, expansion and improvement of housing for small and medium rural producers, and to that end shall make or facilitate the appropriate agreements with the national agency responsible for rural housing and with private bodies carrying out rural housing construction work.

135. Employers on large farms shall be required to provide housing for their permanent workers under terms and conditions to be prescribed in Regulations under this Act. In order to fulfill this obligation the State may

assist employers by providing technical assistance, credit or any other form of aid it deems desirable.

136.   In the construction of rural housing, the National Agrarian Institute shall ensure that materials of the region and the labor of the beneficiaries themselves are used to the greatest extent possible.

The State shall grant assistance to rural allottees in the form of credit for construction or for the purchase of indispensable furnishings.

Rural housing allottees may take advantage of the family estate system established in Title II, Chapter III, of this Act.

In no case may they alienate or encumber such housing without the prior consent of the competent bodies, which shall have a right of preemption.

TITLE VII
AGRICULTURAL COOPERATIVES

137.   The State shall in every way foster the establishment of agricultural cooperatives for credit, production, acquisition and use of equipment, marketing, consumption, and other similar purposes, and shall through the use of every type of aid and incentive protect the activity and development of such organizations.

138.   The State shall promote the creation of study courses on the cooperative system within agricultural organizations and schools and other similar establishments; it shall organize training programs and sponsor pilot projects.

139.   The State shall foster the creation of Rucal Cooperative Banks for aiding in the proper diffusion of agricultural credit and savings among small and medium farmers, and for the establishment of rural industries and handicrafts.

TITLE VIII
AGRICULTURAL CONTRACTS
CHAPTER I
GENERAL PROVISIONS

140.   Agricultural contracts, as governed by this Act, shall, without prejudice to the provisions of special enactments and regulations, be the following:

> (a)   All contracts under which the agricultural operation of a rural property is carried out, and all transactions in respect of such operations by any person other than the owner or usufructuary of the property;
> (b)   Contracts of sale of products of the land, between farmers and industrial enterprises using such products as raw materials;
> (c)   Any other type of relation in respect of labor or the performance of services within the agricultural enterprise, not governed by the Labor Act and regulations thereunder.

141. When disputes and differences between the parties to agricultural contracts and arising therefrom prejudice or threaten to prejudice collective interests of major importance, the Government, acting through its competent agencies, may intervene as arbitrator or conciliator for the solution threof.

If the Government decides to exercise this authority, under the afore-mentioned terms and conditions, the parties to the dispute or difference shall be required to submit to conciliation or arbitration and to accept the decision or finding made.

CHAPTER II
TENANCY CONTRACTS

142. Every contract concerning land tenancy, either under lease or of any other nature, shall be governed by the provisions of this Act and of Regulations hereunder.

As from the date of effect of this Act, the conclusion of leases or contracts of any other nature involving the indirect exploitation of lands, or the prolongation of such contracts, in respect of areas equal to or less than the minimum necessary for the sustenance of the family, shall be prohibited; in respect of already-existing contracts of such nature, the National Agrarian Institute shall proceed to allocations as rapidly as possible;

Provided, that every lease signed while this Act is in effect shall be considered to contain a purchase option clause in favor of the tenant, under terms and conditions to be laid down in Regulations.

143. Provisions of leases of rural properties containing the following obligations are hereby declared to be null and void:

(a) To receive supplies from the owner or lessor;
(b) To sell the yield to the landowner or to a specified person;
(c) To process the yield with machinery belonging to the lessor or to persons specified by him;
(d) To renounce the rights and benefits granted tenants by this Act;
(e) To procure machinery or other equipment, clothing or foodstuffs from a specified factory, commercial house or store;
(f) To sow specified plants which serve to benefit the property, if the owner or lessor is not required to pay fair compensation therefor;
(g) To pay the rent in cash or in labor;
(h) To renounce rights to compensation for damage caused by animals of the lessor to crops of the tenant;
(i) Any other clause intended to require the tenant to trade with the owner.

144. In no case may advance payments of rent be required.

In the case of leases tenants under which are classified as small or medium producers, failure to pay the rent shall not be grounds for requesting eviction or cancellation of the contract, when such failure is due to the proved loss of one half or more or the crop or livestock, provided that such loss is due to one of the causes stipulated in Article 1624, paragraph 1, of the Civil Code or to any other cause beyond the control of the tenant, and provided further that the said tenant carries out no other economic activity and has no other source of income separate and distinct from the exploitation of the leased property and sufficient for payment of the rent.

145. Rents under leases of land to small and medium producers shall be regulated in accordance with the special characteristics of the region and of the property concerned. After regulations for a given zone have been issued, excessive rents collected therein shall be applied against future rent payments, or shall be reimbursed at the request of the interested party without prejudice to any fine which the National Agrarian Institute may decide to impose according to the circumstances of each case.

146. Upon expiration of the contract, the lessor shall be required to compensate the tenant for improvements of any kind made by the latter on the property with his consent, except that, in respect of the consent of the lessor, the provisions of the following Article shall also apply.

147. The tenant may make on the leased property such improvements as are required for the proper operation thereof; he may construct a house when no house existing on the property is so fitted and installed for convenience and hygiene as to render it habitable.

Upon expiration of the contract, the lessor shall be required to compensate the tenant for such improvements, even when he has not granted his consent for the execution thereof, paying him the value of the useful expenditures incurred in improving the property or the plus-value conferred upon the property, whichever is the smaller.

In every case the tenant shall be required to reach agreement with the lessor-owner concerning the site on which such house is to be constructed.

148. Any person who, while this Act is in force, operates a rural property as an agricultural, stock-raising or mixed enterprise in virtue of a fixed- or indefinite-term contract shall be protected by this Act, and may not be evicted without the authorization of the National Agrarian Institute, which shall decide whether to grant the authorization requested or to proceed to the allocation of the land under this Act.

Such immunity from eviction shall also apply to small and medium producers occupying land of third parties for more than one year who maintain a herd of livestock for breeding purposes as their principal economic activity or who cultivate crops, provided in both cases that they perform actual work.

In procuring the authorization referred to in this Article, and without prejudice to the right granted the National Agrarian Institute to proceed to allocation of the land, the following procedure shall be followed:

The person concerned shall submit to the President of the National Agrarian Institute, or to the latter's branch office in the competent jurisdiction, a request stating the reasons therefor and attaching such evidence as he deems desirable. Upon receipt of the request a period of 20 consecutive working days shall commence, during which the office shall notify the opposing party who may, if he sees fit, submit his reasons and arguments against the request; during the said period the office shall further make all investigations deemed necessary for the proper consideration of and decision on the case, including whatever measures may, in accordance with equity, bring about agreement between the parties. Upon expiration of the said period, the office shall within three working days render its decision, against which appeal shall lie within three working days to the Ministry of Agriculture. The Ministry shall decide upon the case within 15 working days following receipt of the file, and may prior thereto issue any order it deems necessary to obtain other information required for reaching its decision.

149. The following shall be considered acts of indirect eviction:

(a) Refusal to authorize a chattel mortgage required by credit agencies as a condition for granting credit to tenants or occupiers;

(b) Obstruction of the normal use of water by tenants or occupiers, or prevention of access thereby to water sources from which they normally draw a supply for their personal needs and for the requirements of their draft and breeding animals;

(c) Reduction, or authorization of reduction, in the area which tenants or occupiers have been utilizing in their agricultural work;

(d) Allowing livestock and other animals to stray outside pastures and enclosures, in such a manner as to intrude upon and damage the crops of tenants or occupiers, except where straying occurs in open country or within already-existing pasturages;

(e) Interference, by means of fences or any other method, with the right of passage by tenants or occupiers over rural roads, wagon trails and paths;

(f) Requiring occupiers, after the crop has been harvested, to plant seed free of charge or against payment of a price well known to be less than fair;

(g) Any other like act tending to perturb the existing working conditions of tenants and occupiers.

CHAPTER III
FARM-INDUSTRY CONTRACTS

150. In conformity with the provisions of Article 140, farm-industry contracts shall be governed by this Act and by the special Regulations to be issued applicable thereto.

151. Official agencies shall give full protection and shall accord preferences for the granting of credit to those industries, established or to be established, which utilize raw materials produced primarily by small and medium farmers independent of the industrial enterprise, and especially if the latter provides them with credit and technical assistance.

152. Pending the establishment of classification standards for farm products, farmers selling their products to industrial enterprises shall be entitled

to verify, either personally or through officials of the Ministry of Agriculture or their own organizations, any preliminary technical test to which the enterprise submits such products in order to establish the price to be paid on delivery thereof.

In certain cases, and especially when the parties fail to agree, the State may issue regulations governing minimum prices of such products and the time and method of payment therefor.

153. This Act shall govern farm-industry contracts already in force, insofar as no retroactive application hereof is implied.

TITLE IX
AGENCIES OF THE AGRARIAN REFORM
CHAPTER I
THE NATIONAL AGRARIAN INSTITUTE

154. In order to implement all the provisions of this Act and in conformity with the regulations laid down herein, the National Agrarian Institute shall operate as an autonomous body, attached to the Ministry of Agriculture, enjoying autonomous juridical personality, authorized to own property, and separate from and independent of the National Treasury; it shall enjoy all the privileges and prerogatives conferred upon the latter body by the provisions of the Basic Act on National Finances and other relevant legislation.

155. The property of the National Agrarian Institute shall consist of:

1) Property owned by it at the present time;

2) Property of public agencies which, for the purposes of the Agrarian Reform, are conveyed to it in conformity with the provisions of the Introductory Title or of Article 18;

3) The annual contributions made by the Government to the National Agrarian Institute in accordance with Article 6;

4) Land or other property acquired or set aside for the purposes of the Agrarian Reform;

5) The proceeds derived from Agrarian Debt bonds and any other issue of negotiable instruments whatsoever;

6) Bequests and gifts in its favor;

7) The proceeds of the sale of parcels or other property and payments in amortization of permanent improvements made for and payable by beneficiaries under this Act, as provided herein;

8) Income derived from services performed or operations carried out by the said Institute;

9) Other income which may be credited to the Capital Account.

156. The seat of the Institute shall be in the Capital of the Republic; it shall establish branches and sub-offices wherever required. Branches shall include representation of the farmers, in such form and by such method of appointment as shall be prescribed in the appropriate Regulations.

157. A Directorate shall be responsible for the direction and administration of the Institute. The Institute shall be organized into whatever Departments or Divisions are deemed necessary.

SECTION I
DIRECTORATE

158. The Directorate shall consist of a President and four Directors, two of whom shall represent the farmers' organizations and another of whom shall be a professional agronomist. All members of the Directorate shall be appointed by the Government.

For each of the Directors there shall be designated an alternate, who shall be appointed by the Government at the same time as the Director.

159. The members of the Directorate and their alternates shall be Venezuelan citizens and of age; they may not possess rural properties of areas in excess of the maximum limits defined by this Act as immune from expropriation.

No person shall be appointed who is related, to the fourth degree by blood or to the second degree by marriage, both inclusive, to the President of the Republic, the Minister of Agriculture or another member of the Directorate. The Directors shall be required to devote their full time to the Institute, and may not hold any other public office except as authorized by the National Constitution or as members of committees of a technical nature.

160. The Directorate shall meet at least once a week, or whenever summoned by the President, or when two or more of its members so request.

A valid meeting of the Directorate shall require the presence of three of the members thereof, one of whom shall be the President or the person acting in his stead. Decisions shall be reached by simple majority, provided that when only three Directors are present a unanimous vote shall be required.

The Directorate shall designate one of its members to act for the President during the temporary absence of the latter.

161. The Directorate shall have the widest policy-making and administrative powers for managing the operations which constitute the object of the Institute, and, in particular, shall:

1) Draw up plans for the execution of the Agrarian Reform and the budget of the Institute, which in each case shall be submitted, through the Ministry of Agriculture, for the consideration and approval of the Government;

2) Consider and decide upon land allocations, establishment of Agrarian Centers, alienation or encumbering of property belonging to the Institute, by any means in conformity with this Act, and authorization of private rural fragmentation schemes when appropriate in accordance with this Act;

3) Promote the return of land, forests and waters to the native tribes

and clans and proceed, together with the Ministry of Justice and other official agencies competent in the matter, tc the allocation of land to the Indians;

4) Decide on the acquisition, alienation or expropriation of properties;

5) After authorization by the Government, order the issuance of Agrarian Debt bonds and other State-guaranteed instruments and securities, and enter into the necessary agreements with the competent agencies for the financing of the Agrarian Reform;

6) Draw up internal Regulations required by the Institute, submitting them for the consideration and approval of the Government;

7) Create such Divisions, Departments, Delegations and Services as are required by the Institute, and establish the responsibilities and remuneration of the personnel of the National Agrarian Institute;

8) Promote the establishment of agricultural insurance;

9) Adopt adequate means for the direction of and technical assistance to the agricultural operations of the beneficiaries of the Agrarian Reform;

10) Request the Government to recover State lands held by third parties;

11) Foster, by every means, the improvement of rural housing, and for that purpose enter into the necessary agreements with the competent agencies;

12) Provide for the cultural improvement and technical training of the rural population;

13) Organize, promote and render service in agricultural mechanization;

14) Draw up credit plans for the beneficiaries of the Agrarian Reform, in accordance with the provisions of Article 112, and enter into the necessary agreements with the official agencies operating in this field;

15) Encourage the rural cooperative movement and establish cooperative industries for the processing of agricultural products;

16) Regulate rents of leased land, and supervise the contracts referred to in Article 142 *et seq.;*

17) Ensure the progress and increase in the dignity of rural labor and recommend the incorporation into enactments and regulations of methods for improving the condition of the said workers;

18) Appoint attorneys to represent the rural population on agrarian questions before the courts and official agencies and corporations, or in dealings with private persons, where necessary;

19) Insure the fulfillment of the social function of land ownership and take the necessary measures for that purpose;

20) Instruct the officials of the National Agrarian Institute to report to the competent authorities any violation of legal provisions which is prejudicial to the rural population;

21) Prevent the direct or indirect eviction of farmers from land they have been occupying, in conformity with the provisions of this Act;

22) Consider and decide on all questions not the specific responsibility of another agency of the Institute or of other agencies established by this Act or by other enactments and regulations.

162. In the month of November of each year the Directorate shall meet with the Ministers of Finance, Development, Public Works, Education, Agriculture, Health and Welfare, Labor, and Justice; the Director of the National Coordination and Planning Agency; the Presidents of the Central Bank

and of the Venezuelan Development Corporation; the Managing Directors of the Agricultural Bank and of the Labor Bank; the Director of the National Nutrition Institute; and the representatives of any other agency or institution necessary, in order to prepare and coordinate the budgetary items to be incorporated into the respective draft budgets with a view to cooperating in implementing the annual Agrarian Reform program; another meeting shall be held to finalize the proposed General Budget.

163. The Directorate may assign to any of its members responsibility for supervising and advising one or more branches of the Institute; such member shall report periodically to the Directorate thereon.

164. No valid contract of any kind whatever may be concluded with the Institute by the President of the Republic or his Secretary; the Cabinet Ministers; the Senators and Deputies of the National Congress; the Governors of the Federal District and Territories and of the States, and their respective Secretaries General; the Directors of the autonomous institutions; the Legal Advisor of the Presidency of the Republic; the members of the Directorate; and the employees of the Institute, of the Ministry of Agriculture and of the Agricultural Bank, either personally or through a third party, while they exercise their functions or for a period of three months following their transfer or separation therefrom; however, when the said officials possess suitable land which technical studies show to be required for the purposes of the Agrarian Reform, they may exceptionally, subject to prior approval by the National Comptroller, enter into contracts of sale of such land to the Institute, without prejudice to the expropriability of such land in conformity with this Act.

SECTION II
PRESIDENT OF THE DIRECTORATE

165. The President shall:

1) Preside over the meetings of the Directorate;
2) Act on behalf of the Institute in approving and signing every type of act and document which has been approved by the Directorate in the execution of its duties and responsibilities;
3) Represent the Institute before the political, judicial and administrative authorities;
4) Direct the offices and branches of the Institute;
5) Execute the decisions of the Directorate;
6) Appoint and remove the personnel of the Institute, reporting to the Directorate thereon;
7) Perform such other duties as are prescribed by law and regulations;

Provided, that subject to the approval of the Directorate the President may delegate, by officially certified act, part of the duties specified in paragraphs 2 and 3 of this Article to other members of the Directorate, senior officials of the Institute or agents thereof, as shall be established in the said act.

CHAPTER II
NATIONAL OFFICE OF THE REGISTER OF LAND AND WATERS

166.   Land registry functions shall be the responsibility of the National Office of the Register of Land and Waters, which shall operate as an agency of the Ministry of Agriculture, in close cooperation with the Institute and the Directorate of National Cartography of the Ministry of Public Works, both of which shall fulfill specific duties in the preparation of the Register. Officials representing the two abovementioned agencies shall participate on a permanent basis in the organization, execution and control of the work of the said Office.

167.   The Register shall be drawn up by municipality, and shall cover in particular the examination and delimitation of:

1)   Public lands;
2)   Common lands;
3)   Other land belonging to public bodies;
4)   Land having belonged to extinct native communities and land possessed or occupied by native tribes or clans;
5)   Privately-owned land;
6)   Public and private waters;
7)   Land classified according to its suitability in accordance with the provisions of this Act.

168.   Geodesic and topographical surveys made in connection with the Register shall be properly based upon the reference points fixed by the Directorate of National Cartography and shall be carried out in accordance with the technical standards adopted by the said Directorate insofar as applicable.

169.   The Government shall prescribe the work to be carried out immediately in order to implement such first stages of the registry as are considered most necessary to contribute to the execution of agrarian plans, to recover public and State land unlawfully possessed by third parties, and to facilitate registration of land by the owners thereof in the Register of Rural Property.

170.   All public authorities and officials, owners of rural property and other citizens shall be required to cooperate actively in the preparation of the Register. Failure to comply with this requirement shall give rise to the immediate dismissal of the former and the imposition upon the latter of a fine of from 1000 to 10,000 bolivars, according to the gravity of the offense.

171.   There shall be established a Register of Rural Property within the National Office of the Register of Land and Waters, in which landowners shall register their rural properties by presenting the titles in proof of their rights. The purpose and effect of the said Register shall not replace or affect the provisions of the Public Registry Act.

Landowners shall so register their properties within one year after the date of commencement of operation of the Registry Office in their regions.

The mere presentation of titles by owners, and their claim to rights submitted in the registration request shall not have the effect of affirming the juridical position thereof with respect to other owners or the State; actions and claims filed by other owners or by the State in respect thereof shall be receivable.

TITLE X
MEANS OF EXECUTION
CHAPTER I
AGRARIAN DEBT

172. In order to contribute to the financing of the Agrarian Reform under this Act, the constitution of an internal public debt, to be known as the Agrarian Debt, payable by the National Agrarian Institute and guaranteed by the State, is hereby authorized.

173. In accordance with the provisions of the preceding Article, the Directorate of the Institute, subject to compliance with the rules laid down in the Public Credit Act, shall be authorized to issue Agrarian Debt bonds, for the following purposes:

    (a) Payment of the cost of property expropriated under this Act;
    (b) Payment of the cost of property acquired by amicable agreement and intended for the Agrarian Reform;
    (c) Financing of other investments necessary to the Institute.

174. The bonds referred to in the preceding Article shall be of three classes:

    1: Class "A," maturing 20 years from date of issue, bearing interest at 3% per annum, the coupons of which shall be acceptable upon maturity for payment of national taxes. These bonds shall be nontransferable, but shall be accepted as security for loans made to expropriated owners by official financial institutions for agricultural or industrial purposes, or in reimbursement of credits obtained by such owners from the said institutions, prior to the publication of this Act, for agricultural purposes. Bonds of this class, the acceptance of which shall be compulsory, shall be applied against payment of the expropriation price of uncultivated properties or properties operated indirectly, as provided in Article 27, paragraph 1, and Article 179, paragraph 1, of this Act. Issues of bonds in this class shall be made in amounts not exceeding 100,000,000 bolivars each.

    2: Class "B," maturing 15 years from date of issue and bearing interest at 4% per annum. Bonds of this class, the acceptance of which shall be compulsory, shall be applied against payment of the price of expropriated properties other than those mentioned in the preceding paragraph, and of those acquired by negotiation or amicable agreement between the Institute and the owners. Issues of bonds in this class shall be made in amounts not exceeding 100,000,000 bolivars each. The other conditions laid down in respect of Class "A" bonds shall also apply to bonds of this class.

3: Class "C," maturing 10 years from date of issue, bearing annual interest at a rate to be fixed in accordance with the conditions of the bond market, and exempt from income tax. Issues shall be placed directly on the market through the Central Bank. These bonds shall be applied to the financing of other investments of the Agrarian Reform and to payment of the price of properties which, although fulfilling their social function, it has become necessary to acquire or expropriate under Article 33 of this Act, without prejudice to the provisions of the said Article relating to payment in cash for existing useful improvements, livestock and mortgages or privileged debts of the expropriated property, incurred and used for the development and improvement thereof.

175. Each bond shall be provided with a sheet of 20, 15 or 10 coupons respectively according to its period of maturity, and against presentation of which annual interest shall be paid.

176. The interest on and principal of the Agrarian Debt shall be paid by the National Agrarian Institute.

177. When the National Treasury is in a favorable position, the Government may decree the total or partial redemption of bonds prior to the maturity dates prescribed in Article 174, preference being always given to bonds bearing the highest interest and the earliest dates.

178. In accordance with the provisions of Article 174 relating to classes of bonds, payment of the price of properties acquired or expropriated for the purposes of this Act shall be made by the National Agrarian Institute, without prejudice to the provisions of Article 33, and in conformity with the following scale:

1) Properties the expropriated portions of which do not exceed a value of 100,000 bolivars: in cash;
2) Properties the expropriated portions of which are valued in excess of 100,000 and not exceeding 250,000 bolivars: 40% in cash and 60% in bonds;
3) Properties the expropriated portions of which are valued in excess of 250,000 and not exceeding 500,000 bolivars: 30% in cash and 70% in bonds;
4) Properties the expropriated portions of which are valued in excess of 500,000 and not exceeding 1,000,000 bolivars: 20% in cash and 80% in bonds;
5) Properties the expropriated portions of which are valued in excess of 1,000,000 bolivars: 10% in cash and 90% in bonds;

Provided, that in all cases where the expropriated portions are valued in excess of 100,000 bolivars, the sum paid in cash shall not be less than this figure.

179. If privileged debts or mortgages encumber properties expropriated for the purposes of the Agrarian Reform, these rights are over-reached to the expropriation price under the same conditions applicable to the owner, who

shall be required, however, to pay creditors the sums due under such obligations while he remains in material possession or enjoyment of the property; the necessary precautions shall be taken therein to protect creditors' rights, and the whole shall be without prejudice to the provisions of Article 33 of this Act;

Provided, that when properties referred to in Article 32 are expropriated, the owner shall receive payment therefor in Class "A" bonds, as provided in Article 174, and a fine not to exceed 75% of the said price may be imposed upon him.

CHAPTER II
IRRIGATION, DRAINAGE AND OTHER HYDRAULIC WORKS

180. An Irrigation Institute may be created for the purpose of coordinating, planning, constructing and operating irrigation, drainage, purification and other hydraulic works carried out with public funds. In every case, such works shall be carried out in harmony with the plans of the Agrarian Reform.

181. Lands benefited by irrigation works constructed by the State or other public bodies shall be destined for the purposes of the Agrarian Reform and agricultural development. The distribution thereof shall be properly adjusted to the primary object of fostering family parcels and agricultural cooperatives, in order to make efficient use of the resources developed by such works in keeping with the interests of national production.

All necessary land shall be reserved for the installation of experimental farms, industrial plants, warehouses, schools, offices, population centers and other community works.

182. When the Government orders the planned development of the resources of a river basin or portion thereof, such area shall be declared a total development region.

183. In the same decree which orders acquisition of the zone or zones to be benefited by the execution of basic works for the establishment or expansion of irrigation systems, hydroelectric plants, and other hydraulic works and uses of waters by agrarian organizations, and of the zone or zones complementary to those thus acquired or which are to be affected by the execution of such works, the Government may declare such public waters as are required for use in the said works to be a Hydraulic Reserve, due regard being paid to the provisions of Article 186.

184. In land on which water sources exist, or which are bounded or crossed by watercourses included in the Hydraulic Reserve, prior Government authorization shall be required for all captation, diversion, current alteration, flow modification or other similar works, and for works of such nature as to alter the use being made of such land on the date of the declaration establishing the said Hydraulic Reserve.

185. After publication of the Decree relating to the construction of

any hydraulic work, as provided in Article 183, the acquisition of land included in the zones indicated therein shall be effected by amicable agreement with the owners thereof.

If no agreement is reached, recourse shall be had to expropriation in the public interest, under the special regulations in respect thereof laid down in this Act.

186. The useful and actually irrigated areas of properties located in such zones, which are to be improved by irrigation works and which previously enjoyed rights and concessions or which diverted public or private waters, shall be set aside, due account being taken of the totality of the legal rights and concessions existing and of the lowest summer water level of the watercourse. Owners of such properties may, after complying with the appropriate obligations and making the appropriate payments, obtain for their land the improvements to be derived from such works, and shall be subject to the regulations to be laid down for each irrigation work. However, where already-existing hydraulic works interfere with the operation of the new system, they may be acquired or expropriated. The above principles shall also apply in the proportion of one to three in the case of unirrigated land which is fulfilling its social function.

187. In addition to landowners, those persons who have been cultivating or exploiting land as tenants, occupiers or sharecroppers shall be entitled to family parcels in allocations of land benefited by irrigation works constructed by the Government.

188. The price of the parcel awarded to the owner and cost of improvements made thereon shall be deducted from the price payable to him for his property.

189. Save in exceptional cases, the use free of charge of waters derived from State-owned artificial works shall not be authorized. The Government shall be responsible for establishing the proportions and conditions under which owners of reserves and beneficiaries of land allocations may enjoy the benefits thereof.

TITLE XI
TRANSITIONAL PROVISIONS

190. Rural properties which, prior to the date of publication of this Act, have been the object of State action in virtue of procedures established under the Illicit Profits of Public Officials and Employees Act, shall be set aside for the Agrarian Reform.

191. In requesting permission to clear and burn over land for agricultural purposes, occupiers concerned may petition the competent authorities of the Ministry of Agriculture, without the prior authorization of the owner or his representative, and the said authorities may grant such permission unless the owner, who shall be informed of the request, can offer substantial grounds

for objection thereto. Where objection is made, the competent official of the Ministry of Agriculture shall decide the case. Objections shall be filed within ten days of notification. At the expiration of the said time-limit, the competent official shall act immediately on the request for permission.

192.   Any natural or juridical person having a scheme for the development of totally uncultivated land located in zones of low population density, who proves that he disposes of the financial and technical means to implement the scheme and that it will so transform the property as to bring it to fulfill its social function, shall present the said scheme to the National Agrarian Institute which shall decide, within the following six months, whether or not the said scheme would interfere with its own development plans. Where no interference would arise, and where there are no technical objections, the National Agrarian Institute shall grant its authorization, fixing annual development targets. During execution of the scheme, and provided that the said targets are met, the property concerned shall be immune from expropriation, without prejudice to the provisions of Article 33.

193.   The Ministry of Agriculture may grant temporary immunity from expropriation to fattening, repasturing or acclimatization centers previously approved by the said Ministry, but may suspend such protection when the said centers fail to comply with the requirements established thereby; the whole shall be without prejudice to the provisions of Article 33.

194.   The Government, for the purposes of the Agrarian Reform and in accordance with the provisions of Article 34 of the Agricultural Bank Act, shall render the said Institution responsible for processing and granting credits to beneficiaries under this Act and for performing other allied operations until such time as the Institution responsible for such activities has been created.

195.   Until an Agricultural Credit Act has been passed, credit grants shall be governed by the applicable provisions and regulations of the Agricultural Bank Act and of the Basic Statute of the Venezuelan Development Corporation, as provided in this Act.

In case of conflict between various provisions, the provision most directly favorable to the beneficiaries of this Act shall prevail.

196.   Credits granted to small or medium rural producers by other official credit agencies shall be centralized in the Agricultural Bank, in order to unify the said service for the benefit of recipients of such loans.

197.   Pending the creation and organization of the Irrigation Institute, an Irrigation Works Coordinating Committee shall operate, which shall be composed of one member of the Directorate of the National Agrarian Institute, and the Director of Hydraulic Works of the Ministry of Public Works. The said Committee shall serve as liaison between the abovementioned agencies concerned with the works provided for in this Chapter; the execution and operation of such works shall be the responsibility of the last-named of the said agencies, in which shall immediately be centralized the services specialized in irrigation questions presently operating within other official agencies.

State and Municipal Governments may construct hydraulic works subject to plans formulated by the Ministry of Public Works.

198. Pending publication of the Regulations provided for in Article 204 concerning classification of land, the following scale of values shall apply:

Land	Points	Hectares
First Category	90-100	150
Second Category	80-89	151-200
Third Category	70-79	201-300
Fourth Category	60-69	301-500
Fifth Category	50-59	501-1000
Sixth Category	40-49	1001-2500
Seventh Category	less than 40	2501-5000

In arriving at the number of points, the following criteria shall be applied:

1) Population density; distance from marketing centers and transportation time: 40 points;

2) Meteorological conditions and existence of surface water utilizable for irrigation: 20 points;

3) Agrological capacity (topography, physical, chemical, and biological condition of the soil): 40 points.

In accordance with the International Classification, the agrological capacity shall be determined by the following conditions:

A) Suitable for culture:
   (a) Without requiring special conservation measures: 40 points;
   (b) Requiring moderate conservation measures: 35 points;
   (c) Requiring intensive conservation measures: 25 points.
B) Suitable for partial or limited culture:
   (a) With limited use and intensive methods: 15 points.
C) Unsuitable for culture but adequate for permanent vegetation:
   (a) Without restriction or use of special methods: 10 points;
   (b) With moderate restrictions: 5 points;
   (c) With severe restrictions: 0 points.

However, the National Agrarian Institute shall be authorized to decide any extreme cases which may arise.

199. The provisions of the first paragraph of Article 142 notwithstanding, present tenants or occupiers of areas equal to or less than the minimum indispensable for the sustenance of their families may conclude new contracts or extend already-existing contracts until two years from the date of promulgation of this Act.

TITLE XII
FINAL PROVISIONS

200. All matters relating to the accomplishment of the purposes and objectives of this Act are hereby declared to be in the public interest; the rights granted hereunder to beneficiaries of the Agrarian Reform shall not be subject to renunciation.

201. Any decision made by the Directorate of the National Agrarian Institute in application of Articles 28; 69; 83, paragraph 6; 119 to 127, both inclusive; 161, paragraph 19; 192 or 193 of this Act shall be subject to appeal to the Ministry of Agriculture within five days following the date of notification of the said decision to the person concerned, plus travel time where appropriate.

Immediately after the appeal has been heard, the Directorate shall deliver the file to the Ministry of Agriculture, which shall decide thereon within a period of 30 days after receipt thereof.

202. Fragmentation and any other schemes in direct relation to the Agrarian Reform, whether put forward by the Nation, the States, the municipalities or by individuals, may be carried out only after prior authorization of the Institute in each case, and in accordance with the general provisions of this Act applicable thereto.

203. Owners of rural properties shall, within six months of the date of publication of this Act, forward to the Institute a list of the tenants and occupiers present on their properties, indicating the class of culture or type of operation carried on by each, the approximate areas they occupy, period of time installed on the property, rent paid and any other pertinent data;

Provided, that the Institute shall proceed to any investigations it may deem necessary to determine the exact situation of such tenants and occupiers and may, for this purpose, call for the cooperation of national, state and municipal officials and public employees or private persons, who shall be required to furnish such assistance.

204. The Government shall issue the appropriate regulations in view of an equitable technical classification of land, for the purposes of this Act.

205. The National Agrarian Institute shall be exempt from all taxes or contributions in respect of utilities and operations, and shall enjoy postal and telegraphic franking privileges.

206. The Ministry of Agriculture and the National Comptroller shall inspect the operations and financial position of the National Agrarian Institute as often as they deem necessary, and at least twice yearly.

For the purpose of this Article, the National Comptroller shall appoint a Deputy Comptroller in the main offices of the Institute.

207. The members of the Directorate of the Institute shall be considered public officials. The general services staff of the Institute shall receive the remuneration provided for in the Labor Act, except the utilities allowance.

Provided, that the Institute shall, during the month of December of each year, grant its officials and general services staff a special remuneration, which shall not be less than that granted by the Government to public employees.

208. The general and special provisions of this Act shall be applied in preference to the provisions of any national legislative provision which may be in conflict therewith.

209. The Agrarian Statute promulgated on 28 June 1949 is hereby repealed.

B. Acquisition of Land

1. Restitution and Related Theories

Given the history of land-grabbing which resulted in the loss of village lands to the haciendas, it is not surprising that one of the earliest calls for land reform took the form of a demand for restitution. The land had been aggregated illegally, it was said, and should be restored to its true owners. Similar arguments have been heard in all the countries in which there is a large indigenous population, since in every such case it can be said that the land belonged to the people who held it before the Conquest. (The Indians of Latin America, unlike their North American counterparts, tended to be settled rather than migratory, farmers rather than hunters.) Land reform thus began in Mexico on the basis of a "title" theory.

Pleas for the restoration of land to the villages were heard from early colonial times forward. The Laws of the Indies themselves were partly addressed to the problem, although they were never really enforced in the villages' favor. Father Hidalgo, the first leader in Mexico's war for independence, called the countryside to arms in distinctly agrarian terms: "Will you make the effort to recover from the hated Spaniards the lands stolen from your forefathers three hundred years ago?" (quoted in GREUNING, MEXICO AND ITS HERITAGE 30 (1928).) But the *hacendados* soon captured the revolution. In the mid-19th century, some influential Mexican leaders sought to restore the rights of the villages. Here are the words of a member of the legislative committee which drafted the document which became the Constitution of 1857:

> And, limiting ourselves to the object which we have proposed, shall it be necessary in an assembly of public deputies, in a congress of representatives of this poor and enslaved people, to demonstrate the bad arrangement of territorial property in the Republic, and the infinite abuses to which it has given place? ... With good reason the public now feels that constitutions are born and die, that governments succeed each other, that codes are enlarged and made intricate, that pronouncements and plans come and go, and that after so many mutations and upheavals, so much

inquietude and so many sacrifices, nothing positive has been done for the people, nothing advantageous for these unhappy classes, from which always emerge those who shed their blood in civil wars, those who give their quota for the armies, who populate the jails and labor in public works, and for which were made, finally, all the evils of society, and none of its goods.

The miserable servants of the countryside, especially those of indigenous race, are sold and traded for their whole life, because the master regulates their salary, gives them the food and the clothing which he wishes to give, and at the price which is convenient for him, under the treat of putting them in jail, punishing them, tormenting them and dishonoring them, whenever they do not submit to the decrees and orders of the landowner. It should be understood that we are speaking in general terms, and that while we recognize many and very honorable exceptions, while we know that there exist respectable and even generous proprietors, which in their haciendas are nothing more than beneficent fathers and even charitable brothers of their servants, who help them in their misery, alleviate their suffering and cure their diseases; there are others, and they are more numerous, who commit a thousand arbitrarinesses and tyrannies, who make themselves deaf to the cries of the poor, who have not one sentiment of humanity, nor recognize any law beyond money, or any morals beyond avarice. Of some it can be said what an illustrious representative of the French people said on picturing the frightful disorder of feudalism: "Taxes under every form, corporal services of every kind, were not enough to placate the voracity of that host of little tyrants. The thought of a man and his dignity, the chastity of virgins, the fidelity of wives, all was conquered, usurped and attacked, and nothing more was then seen but men degraded by their tyranny or their servitude."

He who may believe that we are exaggerating can read the important articles which our worthy companion Sr. Díaz Parriga published a few days ago in the "Monitor Republicano," which have been published in the press of Aguascalientes, San Luis Potosí and other States, and above all he can visit the districts of Cuernavaca and others to the South of this capital, the banks of Rioverde in the State of San Luis, all the region of the Juasteca, and without going very far, see what is going on in the very Valley of Mexico. But what part of the Republic could he not choose to convince himself of what we are saying, without lamenting an abuse, without feeling an injustice, without being pained by the fate of the unfortunate workers of the countryside? In what tribunal of the country would he not see a people or an entire republic of indigenous citizens, litigating over lands, complaining of despoilments and usurpations, praying for their restitution of forests and waters? Where would one not see congregations of villagers or *rancheros,* small populations which do not extend themselves, which do not grow, which barely live, growing smaller every day, surrounded as they are by the ring of iron which the landlords have placed around them, without permitting them the use of their natural fruits, or imposing on them very grave and exorbitant requirements? ... Special vote (report) of Ponciano Arriaga, June 23, 1856, in TENA RAMIREZ, LEYES FUNDAMENTALES DE MEXICO, 1808-1957 at 573, 577-79 (1957).

The Constitution itself said nothing about restitution of village lands, nor did Juárez Laws of Reform (1856) touch on the question (they were principally directed against the power of the clergy). Much less did Maximilian's imperial government (1862-67) show an interest in the claims of the villages. After Juárez' army had forced the French troops to withdraw, and after Maximilian had been shot, the Reform had a few more years left. But Juárez died in 1872, having done little for the villages' cause, and the Reform itself died in 1876 when Porfirio Díaz entered the capital with his army and arranged to be elected President. As noted earlier, the legislation of the Reform was applied during Díaz' long rule (1876-1910) to the villages' corporate holdings, and with a vengeance.

The revolution of 1910, which Mexicans now call the Revolution, began not as an agrarian revolt but as a political one, against the prolongation of the Díaz regime. Díaz had previously given an interview to a New York journalist, in which he stated that he would not be a candidate for re-election. When he announced that after all he would run again, a mild sort of revolution was on, under the odd leadership of Francisco I. Madero, himself a landowner of some wealth and position. Madero announced as a candidate; when Díaz "won," the real revolution started. Madero's Plan of San Luis Potosí set the guidelines for the new government, and included a word concerning the restitution of village lands.

PLAN OF SAN LUIS POTOSI

* * *

3d.— ...

* * *

In abuse of the law of vacant lands, numerous small property owners, in their majority indigenous, have been despoiled of their lands, either by rulings of the Ministry of Development, or by decisions of the Tribunals of the Republic. It being a matter of complete justice to restore to the former possessors the lands of which they were despoiled in such an immoral manner, or to their heirs, let them be restored to their original owners, *to whom shall also be paid an indemnity for prejudices suffered.* Only in the case in which the lands may have passed to third persons, before the promulgation of this plan, the old owners shall receive indemnity from those in whose benefit the despoilment is proved.

* * *

Effective Suffrage. No Reelection.
San Luis Potosí, October 5, 1910.
[Signed] FRANCISCO I. MADERO
[TENA RAMIREZ, LEYES FUNDAMENTALES DE MEXICO, 1808-1957, at 732, 736, 739 (1957). (Emphasis added.)].

A year later, with the revolution apparently over and the government in Madero's hands, land reform became the central political issue. Emiliano Zapata, the great Indian leader of the State of Morelos, attacked Madero for his failure to carry out the promised land reform. Zapata issued his own plan, the Plan of Ayala.

PLAN OF AYALA

* * *

4th.—The Revolutionary Junta of the State of Morelos makes known to the Nation, formally declaring:

That it makes its own the Plan of San Luis Potosí with the additions which are expressed below for the benefit of the oppressed peoples, and that it will make itself the defender of the principles which it defends until it conquers or dies.

* * *

6th.—As an additional part of the Plan which we invoke, we make clear: that as to the lands, forests and waters which have been usurped by the *hacendados, científicos* [a kind of palace guard of technocrats around the dictator Díaz] or bosses in the shadow of tyranny and venal justice, there shall enter into possession of these lands from now on those villages or citizens who may have their respective titles to these properties, of which they have been despoiled by the bad faith of our oppressors, maintaining resolutely, with arms in hand, that possession, and usurpers who may consider themselves to have a right to the lands shall allege such right before special tribunals which may be established upon the triumph of the Revolution.

7th.—By virtue of the fact that the immense majority of the Mexican villages and citizens are not owners of more than the ground which they tread, suffering the horrors of misery without being able to improve their social condition in any respect nor to dedicate themselves to industry or to agriculture because the lands, forests and waters are monopolized in a few hands, for this reason there shall be expropriated by means of previous indemnity, one-third of these monopolies, from their powerful owners, to the end that the villages and citizens of Mexico may obtain *ejidos,* villages, legal estates for villages or fields to be sowed or worked, and so that the lack of prosperity and well-being of Mexicans may be remedied thoroughly and for everyone.

8th.—The *hacendados, científicos* or bosses who may oppose the present plan directly or indirectly shall have their goods nationalized, and the two-thirds which correspond to them shall be destined for war indemnities, pensions for the widows and orphans of the victims who die in the struggle for this Plan.

9th.—In order to settle the proceedings with respect to the property above mentioned, the laws of mortmain and nationalization shall be applied as they may be convenient, so that by precept and example these laws put in force by the immortal Juárez may serve for ecclesiastical property, which laws gave warning to the despots and conservatives who in every era have attempted to impose on us the ignominious yoke of oppression and backwardness.

* * *

Justice and Law.

Ayala, Nov. 28, 1911. [Signed by Zapata as general in chief, and by six other generals, twenty-seven colonels, four captains and others.] TENA RAMIREZ, LEYES FUNDAMENTALES DE MEXICO, 1808-1957, at 740, 741-43 (1957); also in SILVA HERZOG, BREVE HISTORIA DE LA REVOLUCION MEXICANA, vol. I, p. 240, 242-45 (2d ed. 1962).

Over the next few years, generals and politicians deposed one another with a frequency unusual even in Latin America, until General Venustiano Carranza asserted his authority as First Chief of the Constitutionalist Army. (It was called "constitutionalist" because it supported the "constitutional" President, Madero, who had been elected in a special election in 1911 after the resignation and exile of Díaz. When Díaz resigned, no one suggested that he be replaced by his vice-president, General Ramón Corral, "who was detested for his barbarity in selling Yaqui Indians from Sonora into slavery on the henequen plantations of Yucatán." HERRING, A HISTORY OF LATIN AMERICA 352 (2d ed. 1961).) Carranza, under fire from Zapata in the south and Pancho Villa in the north, issued a decree which became the basis for all of Mexico's modern agrarian legislation. The decree was in large part the product of the same Luis Cabrera whose description of the despoiling of the villages had moved the Chamber of Deputies in 1912. (See p. 375, *supra*.)

AGRARIAN LAW OF JANUARY 6, 1915

VENUSTIANO CARRANZA, First Chief of the Constitutionalist Army, Agent of the Executive Power of the Mexican Republic, and Chief of the Revolution, in use of the powers with which he finds himself invested, and CONSIDERING:

That one of the most general causes of the ill-being and discontent of the agricultural populations of this country has been the despoiling of the lands of communal property or allotment lands which had been conceded by the Colonial Government, as a means of assuring the existence of the indigenous class, and which under the pretext of complying with the law of June

25, 1856, and other dispositions which ordered the fractioning and reduction to private property of those lands, among the inhabitants of the villages to which they belonged, came to rest in the power of a few speculators;

That at the same time there are found a multitude of other towns of different parts of the Republic, and that so-called congregations, communities or settlements, had their origin in some family or families which possessed in common more or less great extensions of lands, which continued to be kept undivided for various generations, or rather originated in a certain number of inhabitants who came together in appropriate places to acquire and exploit commonly waters, lands and forests, following the ancient and general custom of the indigenous villages;

That the despoilment of the said lands was done, not only by means of alienations carried into effect by the political authorities in open contravention of the mentioned laws, but also by means of concessions, compositions or sales agreed upon with the Ministries of Development and Finance, or under the pretext of surveys and demarcations, to favor those who made denunciations of surplus lands and to the so-called border-marking companies; but in any case there were invaded lands which during long years belonged to the villages and in which the latter had their subsistence base;

That as may be inferred from existing litigation, the rights of the villages and communities have always been flouted, the villages lacking — in conformance with Article 27 of the Federal Constitution — the capacity to acquire and possess real property, they were also caused to lack juridical personality to defend their rights and, on the other hand, it became entirely illusory to provide for the protection which the law of vacant lands then existent attempted to grant them (by empowering the syndicates of the City Councils of the Municipalities to reclaim and defend communal property as to questions in which those properties might be confused with vacant lands), since by general rule, the syndicates never bothered to fulfill this mission, as much because they lacked interest to stimulate them to work, as because the political chiefs and State governors were almost always interested in seeing that the spoliation of the lands in question be consummated;

That once the indigenous villages were deprived of lands, waters and forests which the colonial government conceded to them, as well as the congregations and communities deprived of their undivided lands, and once the rural property of the rest of the country was concentrated in a few hands, there has remained for the great mass of the population in the countryside no other recourse for obtaining the necessities of life, than to hire out at a low price their labor to powerful landowners, which in turn brings as an inevitable result the state of misery, abjection and effective slavery in which this enormous quantity of workers has lived and still lives;

That in view of the foregoing, the necessity is obvious of returning to the villages the lands of which they have been despoiled, as an act of elemental justice and as the only effective manner of assuring peace and promoting the well-being and improvement of our poor classes, without hindering the interests created in favor of persons who presently possess the lands in question, because not only have those interests no legal foundation, from the moment in which they were established in express violation of the mortmain laws which ordered only the distribution of the communal property among the residents themselves, and not their alienation in favor of strangers, neither have these rights become sanctioned or legitimate through a long possession, as much because the aforementioned laws did not establish prescriptive rights with respect to these goods, as because the villages to whom they belong could not defend themselves for lack of juridical personality necessary to take part in a law suit;

That it is probable that in some cases the restitution in question cannot be realized, either because the alienation of the lands which belonged to the villages may have been made in accordance with the law, or because the villages may have lost the titles or because those which they have may be deficient, or because it may be impossible to identify the lands or fix their precise area, or, finally, for any other cause; but since the reason which prevents the restitution, however just and legitimate it may be supposed, does not solve the difficult situation which so many villages find themselves in, nor much less justify that this painful situation continue existing, it is necessary to remove the difficulty in another manner which may be reconcilable with the interests of all;

That the manner of supplying the necessity which has just been pointed out can be none other than to authorize the superior military authorities which operate in each place, so that, effectuating the expropriations which may be indispensable, they may give lands which are sufficient to the villages which lack them, realizing in this manner one of the great principles inscribed in the program of the Revolution, and establishing one of the primary bases on which the reorganization of the country must be supported;

That establishing the manner by which many villages may recover the lands of which they were despoiled, or may acquire those which they need for their well-being and development, there is no intention to revive the old indigenous communities, or to creater other similar ones, but only to give that land to the miserable rural population which today lacks it, so that it may be able to develop fully its right to life and to free itself from the economic servitude to which it is reduced; it is to be noted that ownership of lands does not belong to the village in common, but that it must be divided in full ownership, although with the necessary limitations to avoid avid speculators, particularly foreigners, being able to speculate in this property easily as almost invariably happened with the division legally made of the *ejidos* and legal estates of the villages because of the revolution of Ayutla [Juarez' revolution].

Therefore,

I have considered it proper to issue the following DECREE:

Article 1st. The following are declared void:

[This article is virtually identical to paragraph VIII of Article 27 of the 1917 Constitution. See *infra* at p. 463.]

Article 2d. The division or allotment of land which may have been made legitimately among the inhabitants of a village, settlement, congregation or community, and in which there may have been some defect [such as mistake, fraud, etc.] may be nullified only upon the petition of two-thirds of the inhabitants or their representatives.

Article 3d. [This is almost exactly the same as paragraph X of Article 27 of the 1917 Constitution, except that there is no lower limit on the size of individual parcels.]

* * *

[Articles 5 through 9 establish the machinery for obtaining grants of land, or restitution of lands. The scheme is much the same as that outlined in Article 27 of the 1917 Constitution, in paragraphs XI through XIII.]

Article 10th. Interested persons who believe themselves to be prejudiced by the decision of the Agent of the Executive Power of the Nation may resort to the tribunals to assert their rights, within the period of one year, counting from the date of said decisions, but after this time no claim shall be admitted.

In cases in which claims are entered against restitutions and in which the interested party may obtain a judicial decision declaring that the restitution made to a village is not proper, the judgment should give only a right to obtain the corresponding indemnity from the Government.

In the same period of one year the owners of the expropriated lands may resort [to the tribunals] claiming the indemnities which should be paid to them.

* * *

Transitory. This law shall begin to take effect from the date of its publication. So long as the present civil war shall not have concluded, the military authorities shall cause the present law to be published and proclaimed in each of the village squares or places which shall be occupied.

Constitution and Reforms. Given in Veracruz, January 6, 1915.

The First Chief of the Constitutionalist Army, Agent of the Executive Power of the Republic and Chief of the Revolution, *Venustiano Carranza.*

To the C. Engineer *Pastor Rouaix,* Managing Subsecretary of the Office of Development, Colonization and Industry. Present.

The 1915 law thus emphasized restitution, although it also provided more generally for distribution of lands to villages which lacked them. The same scheme was adopted — almost copied — by the framers of the 1917 Constitution.

MEXICO, CONSTITUTION OF 1917, as amended
(Pan American Union translation)

ARTICLE 27. Ownership of the lands and waters within the boundaries of the national territory is vested originally in the Nation, which has had, and has, the right to transmit title thereof to private persons, thereby constituting private property.

Private property shall not be expropriated except for reasons of public use and subject to payment of indemnity.

The Nation shall at all times have the right to impose on private property such limitations as the public interest may demand, as well as the right to regulate the utilization of natural resources which are susceptible of appropriation, in order to conserve them and to ensure a more equitable distribution of public wealth. With this end in view, necessary measures shall be taken to divide up large landed estates; to develop small landed holdings in operation; to create new agricultural centers, with necessary lands and waters; to encourage agriculture in general and to prevent the destruction of natural resources, and to protect property from damage to the detriment of society. Centers of population which at present either have no lands or water or which do not possess them in sufficient quantities for the needs of their inhabitants, shall be entitled to grants thereof, which shall be taken from adjacent properties, the rights of small landed holdings in operation being respected at all times.

In the Nation is vested the direct ownership of all minerals or substances which, in veins, ledges, masses, or ore-pockets, form deposits of a nature distinct from that of the earth itself, such as the minerals from which industrial metals and metalloids are extracted; deposits of precious stones, rock-salt and the deposits of salt formed by sea water; products derived from the decomposition of rocks, when subterranean works are required for their extraction; mineral or organic deposits of materials susceptible of utilization as fertilizers; solid mineral fuels, petroleum, and all solid, liquid, or gaseous hydrocarbons.

In the Nation is likewise vested the ownership of the waters of the territorial seas, within the limits fixed by international law; those of lagoons and estuaries permanently or intermittently connected with the sea; those of interior lakes which are directly connected with streams having a constant flow, those of rivers and their direct or indirect tributaries from the point in their source where the first permanent, intermittent, or torrential waters begin, to their mouth in the sea, or a lake, lagoon, or estuary forming a part of the public domain; those of constant or intermittent streams and their direct or indirect tributaries, whenever the bed of the stream, throughout the whole or a part of its length, serves as a boundary of the national territory or of two federal divisions, or if it flows from one federal division to another or crosses the boundary line of the Republic; those of lakes, lagoons, or estuaries whose basins, zones, or shores are crossed by the boundary lines of two or more divisions or by the boundary line of the Republic and a neighboring country or when the shoreline serves as the boundary between two federal divisions or of the Republic and a neighboring country; those of springs that issue from beaches, maritime areas, the beds, basins, or shores of lakes, lagoons, or estuaries in the national domain; and waters extracted from mines. Underground waters may be brought to the surface by artificial works and utilized by the surface owner, but if the public interest so requires or use by others is affected, the Federal Executive may regulate its extraction and utilization, and even establish prohibited areas, the same as may be done with other waters in the public domain. Any other waters not included in the foregoing enumerations shall be considered an integral part of the private property through which they flow or in which they are deposited, but if they are located in two or more properties, their utilization shall be deemed a matter of public use, and shall be subject to laws enacted by the States.

In those cases to which the two preceding paragraphs refer, ownership by the Nation is inalienable and imprescriptible, and concessions may only be granted by the Federal Government to private individuals or to civil or commercial companies organized in accordance with Mexican laws, on condition that regular works are established for the exploitation of the resources concerned and that all requisites prescribed by law are complied with. Concessions for petroleum and solid, liquid, or gaseous hydrocarbons shall not be issued, and the respective regulatory law shall specify the manner in which the Nation shall bring about the exploitation of those products.

Legal capacity to acquire ownership of lands and waters of the Nation shall be governed by the following provisions:

I.   Only Mexicans by birth or naturalization and Mexican companies have the right to acquire ownership of lands, waters, and their appurtenances, or to obtain concessions for working mines or for the utilization of waters or mineral fuels in the Republic of Mexico. The Nation may grant the same right to foreigners, provided they agree before the Ministry of Foreign Relations to consider themselves as Mexicans in respect to such property, and bind themselves not to invoke the protection of their governments in matters relating thereto; under penalty, in case of noncompliance with this agreement, of forfeiture of the property acquired to the Nation. Under no circumstances may foreigners acquire direct ownership of lands or waters within a zone of one hundred kilometers along the frontiers and of fifty kilometers along the shores of the country.

The State, in accordance with internal public interests and with principles of reciprocity, may in the discretion of the Secretariat of Foreign Affairs authorize Foreign States to acquire, at the permanent sites of the Federal Powers, private ownership of real property necessary for the services of their Embassies or Legations.

II.   Religious institutions known as churches, regardless of creed, may in no case acquire, hold, or administer real property or hold mortgages thereon; such property held at present either directly or through an intermediary shall revert to the Nation, any person whosoever being authorized to denounce any property so held. Presumptive evidence shall be sufficient to declare the denunciation well-founded. Places of public worship are the property of the Nation, as represented by the Federal Government, which shall determine which of them may continue to be devoted to their present purposes. Bishoprics, rectories, seminaries, asylums, and schools belonging to religious orders, convents, or any other buildings built or intended for the administration, propagation, or teaching of a religious creed shall at once become the property of the Nation by inherent right, to be used exclusively for the public services of the Federal or State Governments, within their respective jurisdictions. All places of public worship hereafter erected shall be the property of the Nation.

III. Public or private charitable institutions for the rendering of assistance to the needy, for scientific research, the diffusion of knowledge, mutual aid to members, or for any other lawful purpose, may not acquire more real property than actually needed for their purpose and immediately and directly devoted thereto; but they may acquire, hold, or administer mortgages on real property provided the term thereof does not exceed ten years. Under no circumstances may institutions of this kind be under the patronage, direction, administration, charge, or supervision of religious orders or institutions, or of ministers of any religious sect or of their followers, even though the former or the latter may not be in active service.

IV. Commercial stock companies may not acquire, hold, or administer rural properties. Companies of this kind that are organized to operate any manufacturing, mining, or petroleum industry or for any other purpose that is not agricultural, may acquire, hold, or administer lands only if an area that is strictly necessary for their buildings or services, and this area shall be fixed in each particular case by the Federal or State Executive.

V. Banks duly authorized to operate in accordance with the laws on credit institutions may hold mortgages on urban and rural property in conformity with the provisions of such laws but they may not own or administer more real property than is actually necessary for their direct purpose.

VI. With the exception of the corporate entities referred to in clauses III, IV, V hereof, and the centers of population which by law or in fact possess a communal status or centers that have received grants or restitutions or have been organized as centers of agricultural population, no other civil corporate entity may hold or administer real property or hold mortgages thereon, with the sole exception of the buildings intended immediately and directly for the purposes of the institution. The States, the Federal District, and the Territories, and all Municipalities in the Republic, shall have full legal capacity to acquire and hold all the real property needed to render public services.

The federal and state laws, within their respective jurisdictions, shall determine in what cases the occupation of private property shall be considered to be of public utility; and in accordance with such laws, the administrative authorities shall issue the respective declaration. The amount fixed as compensation for the expropriated property shall be based on the value recorded in assessment or tax offices for tax purposes, whether this value had been declared by the owner or tacitly accepted by him by having paid taxes on that basis. The increased or decreased value of such private property due to improvements or depreciation which occurred after such assessment is the only portion of the value that shall be subject to the decision of experts and judicial proceedings. This same procedure shall be followed in the case of property whose value is not recorded in the tax offices.

The exercise of actions pertaining to the Nation by virtue of the provisions of this article shall be made effective by judicial procedure, but during these proceedings and by order of the proper courts, which must render a decision within a maximum of one month, the administrative authorities shall proceed without delay to occupy, administer, auction, or sell the lands and waters in question and all their appurtenances, and in no case may the acts of such authorities be set aside until a final decision has been rendered.

VII. The centers of population which, by law or in fact, possess a communal status shall have legal capacity to enjoy common possession of the lands, forests, and waters belonging to them or which have been or may be restored to them.

All questions, regardless of their origin, concerning the boundaries of communal lands, which are now pending or that may arise hereafter between two or more centers of population, are matters of federal jurisdiction. The Federal Executive shall take cognizance of such controversies and propose a solution to the interested parties. If the latter agree thereto, the proposal of the Executive shall take full effect as a final decision and shall be irrevocable; should they not be in conformity, the party or parties may appeal to the Supreme Court of Justice of the Nation, without prejudice to immediate enforcement of the presidential proposal.

The law shall specify the brief procedure to which the settling of such controversies shall conform.

VIII. The following are declared null and void:

a) All transfers of the lands, waters, and forests of villages, *rancherías,* groups, or communities made by local officials (*jefes políticos*), state governors, or other local authorities in violation of the provisions of the Law of June 25, 1856, and other related laws and rulings.

b) All concessions, deals or sales of lands, waters, and forests made by the Secretariat of Development, the Secretariat of Finance, or any other federal authority from December 1, 1876 to date, which encroach upon or illegally occupy communal lands (*ejidos*), lands allotted in common, or lands of any other kind belonging to villages, *rancherías,* groups or communities, and centers of population.

c)   All survey or demarcation-of-boundary proceedings, transfers, alienations, or auction sales effected during the period of time referred to in the
preceding sub-clause, by companies, judges, or other federal or state authorities
entailing encroachments on or illegal occupation of the lands, waters, or forests of communal holdings (*ejidos*), lands held in common, or other holdings
belonging to centers of population.

The sole exception to the aforesaid nullification shall be the lands to
which title has been granted in allotments made in conformity with the Law
of June 25, 1856, held by persons in their own name for more than ten years
and having an area of not more than fifty hectares.

IX.   Divisions or allotments of land among the inhabitants of a given
center of population which, although apparently legitimate are not so, due to
a mistake or defect, may be annulled at the request of three fourths of the
residents holding one fourth so divided, or one fourth of such residents holding three fourths of the lands.

X.   Centers of population which lack communal lands (*ejidos*) or
which are unable to have them restored to them due to lack of titles, impossibility of identification, or because they had been legally transferred, shall be
granted sufficient lands and waters to constitute them, in accordance with the
needs of the population; but in no case shall they fail to be granted the area
needed, and for this purpose the land needed shall be expropriated, at the
expense of the Federal Government, to be taken from lands adjoining the
villages in question.

The area or individual unit of the grant shall hereafter be not less than
ten hectares of moist or irrigated land, or in default of such land its equivalent
in other types of land in accordance with the third paragraph of section XV
of this article.

XI.   For the purpose of carrying out the provisions of this article and
of regulating laws that may be enacted, the following are established:

a)   A direct agency of the Federal Executive entrusted with the application and enforcement of the agrarian laws;

b)   An advisory board composed of five persons to be appointed by the
President of the Republic and who shall perform the functions specified in the
organic laws;

c)   A mixed commission composed of an equal number of representatives of the Federal Government, the local governments, and a representative
of the peasants to be appointed in the manner set forth in the respective regulating law, to function in each State, Territory, and the Federal District, with
the powers and duties set forth in the organic and regulatory laws;

d)   Private executive committees for each of the centers of population
that are concerned with agrarian cases;

e)   A communal office (*comisariado ejidal*) for each of the centers of population that possess communal lands (*ejidos*). [Until 1934, the distribution of land was left to the laws of the several States; each State had its own substantive agrarian reform law as well as its own procedure. The present national scheme was adopted in a 1934 amendment, and in the first Agrarian Code. — Ed.]

XII. Petitions for a restitution or grant of lands or waters shall be submitted directly to the state and territorial governors.

The governors shall refer the petitions to the mixed commissions, which shall study the cases during a fixed period of time and render a report; the State governor shall approve or modify the report of the mixed commission and issue orders that immediate possession be given to areas which they deem proper. The case shall then be turned over to the Federal Executive for decision.

Whenever the governor fails to comply with the provisions of the preceding paragraph, within the peremptory period of time fixed by law, the report of the mixed commission shall be deemed rejected and the case shall be referred immediately to the Federal Executive.

Inversely, whenever a mixed commission fails to render a report during the peremptory time limit, the Governor shall be empowered to grant possession of the area of land he deems appropriate.

XIII. The agency of the Executive and the Agrarian Advisory Board shall report on the approval, rectification, or modification of the reports submitted by the mixed commissions, containing the changes made therein by the local governments, and so notify the President of the Republic, who as the supreme agrarian authority will render a decision.

XIV. Landowners affected by decisions granting or restoring communal lands and waters to villages, or who may be affected by future decisions, shall have no ordinary legal right or recourse and cannot institute *amparo* proceedings.

Persons affected by such decisions shall have solely the right to apply to the Federal Government for payment of the corresponding indemnity. This right must be exercised by the interested parties within one year counting from the date of publication of the respective resolution in the *Diario Oficial*. After this period has elapsed no claim is admissible.

Owners or occupants of agricultural or stockraising properties in operation who have been issued or to whom there may be issued in the future certificates of non-affectability may institute *amparo* proceedings against any illegal deprivation or agrarian claims on their lands or water. [This last paragraph of Par. XIV was added by a 1947 amendment. — Ed.]

XV. The mixed commissions, the local governments and any other authorities charged with agrarian proceedings cannot in any case affect small agricultural or livestock properties in operation and they shall incur liability for violations of the Constitution if they make grants which affect them. [The rest of Par. XV was added by the 1947 amendment. — Ed.]

Small agricultural property is that which does not exceed one hundred hectares of first-class moist or irrigated land or its equivalent in other classes of land, under cultivation.

To determine this equivalence one hectare of irrigated land shall be computed as two hectares of seasonal land; as four of good quality pasturage (*agostadero*) and as eight of *monte* (scrub land) or arid pasturage.

Also to be considered as small holdings are areas not exceeding two hundred hectares of seasonal lands or pasturage susceptible of cultivation; or one hundred fifty hectares of land used for cotton growing if irrigated from fluvial canals or by pumping; or three hundred, under cultivation, when used for growing bananas, sugar cane, coffee, henequen, rubber, coconuts, grapes, olives, quinine, vanilla, cacao, or fruit trees.

Small holdings for stockraising are lands not exceeding the area necessary to maintain up to five hundred head of cattle (*ganado mayor*) or their equivalent in smaller animals (*ganado menor* — sheep, goats, pigs) under provisions of law, in accordance with the forage capacity of the lands.

Whenever, due to irrigation or drainage works or any other works executed by the owners or occupants of a small holding to whom a certificate of non-affectability has been issued, the quality of the land is improved for agricultural or stockraising operations, such holding shall not be subject to agrarian appropriation even if, by virtue of the improvements made, the maximums indicated in this section are lowered, provided that the requirements fixed by law are met.

XVI.   Lands which are subject to individual adjudication must be partitioned precisely at the time the presidential order is executed, according to regulatory laws.

XVII.   The Federal Congress and the State Legislature, within their respective jurisdictions, shall enact laws to fix the maximum area of rural property, and to carry out the subdivision of the excess lands, in accordance with the following bases:

a)   In each State, Territory, or Federal District, there shall be fixed a maximum area of land of which a single individual or legally constituted society may be the owner.

b)   The excess over the fixed area shall be subdivided by the owner within the time fixed by the local law, and these parcels shall be offered for sale under terms approved by the governments, in accordance with the aforementioned laws.

c)   If the owner should oppose the subdivision, it shall be carried out by the local government, by expropriation.

d)   The value of the parcels shall be paid by annual installments which will amortize principal and interest, at an interest rate not exceeding 3% per annum.

e)   Owners shall be required to receive bonds of the local Agrarian Debt to guarantee payment for the property expropriated. For this purpose, the Federal Congress shall enact a law empowering the States to create their Agrarian Debt.

f)   No subdivision can be sanctioned which fails to satisfy the agrarian needs of neighboring settlements (*poblados inmediatos*). Whenever subdivision projects are to be executed, the agrarian claims must be settled within a fixed period.

g)   Local laws shall organize the family patrimony, determining what property shall constitute it, on the basis that it shall be inalienable and shall not be subject to attachment or encumbrance of any kind.

XVIII.   All contracts and concessions made by former Governments since the year 1876, which have resulted in the monopolization of lands, waters, and natural resources of the Nation, by a single person or company, are declared subject to revision, and the Executive of the Union is empowered to declare them void whenever they involve serious prejudice to the public interest.

Although it was Carranza who had called the 1916 constitutional convention, under his administration land reform principally took the form of wholesale transfers of land from the old *hacendados* to revolutionary generals and political chiefs. Yet another revolt formed, this time under Alvaro Obregón, the northern general and champion of social reform. In 1920, having been deserted by his army, Carranza put his family, some friends, and large quantities of gold from the national treasury on a train for Veracruz. He was betrayed by an associate and assassinated. The fighting ended, and Obregón was elected President; the 1917 Constitution remained in force as it remains today.

Even so, the restitution of village lands proceeded slowly. "As long as this was the principal basis for distributing land, very little was restored. During the entire period from 1916 to 1944, only 6 per cent of the total land distributed was by the method of restitution." WHETTEN, RURAL MEXICO 129 (1948). (40 per cent of that 6 per cent had been distributed by 1927.) It is not hard to see why a title theory of land reform was insufficient to get much land distributed. Simpson recounts one typical case in the following extract from his outstanding work on the Mexican land reform.

SIMPSON, THE EJIDO: MEXICO'S WAY OUT* 465-66 (1937)

Among the very first of the agrarian communities to take advantage of Carranza's famous decree was Zacapan. On August 17, 1915, a petition was addressed by the citizens of Zacapan to the governor of the state which held: (a) that from time immemorial the village had been in pacific and uninterrupted possession of its land; (b) but that for over forty years the owners of the hacienda of Manantiales had been persecuting the village "even to the extent of starting armed combats" and that, during the Díaz regime, supported by the "dictatorial government of the time," the hacienda succeeded in absorbing most of the village land; (c) that the old Quiroga swamp was the property of Zacapan and neighboring villages and when the swamp was drained by Lorenzo Garza and his associates Zacapan was thus further despoiled; and (d) that, therefore, the village, encouraged by the promises of the revolution, hereby petitioned the government to restore to it the lands unlawfully taken away.

Unfortunately, when the time came for Zacapan to present its titles and other documents proving its ownership to the property claimed, the most that the village could do was to produce a map whereon were marked the lands which "according to the memory of the oldest inhabitant" had once belonged to the community. The *hacendados,* on the other hand, were able to bring forward all sorts of *testimonios, contratos, escrituras* and other legal documents to show their right to the land in dispute. Although some of the agrarian authorities believed there were grounds for "reasonable presumption that in truth the lands of the village had been invaded" by the *hacendados,* in the absence of documentary proof, there was nothing to do but declare Zacapan's petition for restitution *no procedente* [not allowable].

The village finally did get its land. In 1922, 450 hectares from three haciendas were granted in provisional possession; the final decree in 1924 increased the grant to 632 hectares for the 316 heads of families. SIMPSON, *supra,* at 466-67. The case illustrates the progress of the Mexican land reform — early reliance on the restitution theory, followed by its gradual abandonment in favor of more far-reaching measures, which turned out to be almost equally confiscatory. Even so, the Mexican law still provides for restitution as one manner of distributing land to the villages.

MEXICO: AGRARIAN CODE OF 1943
SECOND BOOK
Redistribution of Agrarian Property

FIRST TITLE
Restitution of Lands ond Waters

FIRST CHAPTER
General Provisions

46.—Centers of population which may have been deprived of their lands, forests or waters, by any of the acts to which Article 27 of the Constitution refers, shall have the right to have them restored to them, when it is proved:

> I.—That they are the owners of the lands, forests or waters whose restitution they ask;
> II.—That they were despoiled by any of the following acts:
> a).—Alienations made by Political Chiefs [mayors], State Governors or any other local authority, in contravention of the provisions of the Law of June 25, 1856, and other related laws and provisions.
> b).—Concessions, settlements or sales made by the Ministries of Development or Finance or any other federal authority, from the 1st day of December, 1876 to January 6, 1915, by which the property which is the object of the restitution may have been invaded or illegally occupied.
> c).—Works of survey or border marking, *composiciones,* alienations or auctions carried on during the period of time to which the preceding paragraph refers, by companies, Judges or other authorities of the States or of the Federation, by which the property whose restitution is petitioned may have been invaded or illegally occupied.

47.—[Deals with the disposition of excess waters, beyond the needs of the villages to which land is restored.]

SECOND CHAPTER
Property Inaffectable by Restitution

48.—Upon the granting of restitution of lands, forests or waters, there shall be respected only the following:

> I.—Lands and waters, title to which was obtained in the distributions made in conformance with the Act of June 25, 1856;
> II.—Up to 50 hectares of lands, with their respective waters when they may be irrigated, provided that they have been possessed in the name of the owner under his title for more than 10 years prior to the date of initial modification of the proceeding to the owner or possessor under the terms of the Law in force on the date of the petition;
> III.—Waters necessary for domestic use of the villages which are using

them at the time the respective resolution [of restitution] is given;
IV.—Lands and waters which may have been the object of a previous
grant to a nucleus or new center of agricultural population; and
V.—Waters devoted to the service of the public interest.

49.—Persons who fit the case foreseen by paragraph II of the foregoing
article shall have the right to locate the 50 hectares in the place which they
may designate, upon the formation of the respective plan-project.

The Bolivian land reform decree of 1953 provides:

> 42.   Lands wrongfully taken from Indian communities since 1 January
> 1900 shall be returned to them, where they can prove their right, in ac-
> cordance with special regulations.
> 43.   Rural property on which the right of restitution is claimed by one
> or more communities shall be appropriated temporarily . . . until the ap-
> plication of restitution is decided upon by the respective authorities.

Landowners whose land is claimed under these provisions may reserve "an area
of land equal to that established for the medium property" (variable according
to the region). No compensation is to be paid in cases of restitution. The lands
are to be cultivated by the community, not divided into individual parcels; the
law thus reaffirms the Indian tradition of collective ownership. However, if
any parcels are, at the time of the distribution, possessed and worked individually, then the persons in possession become individual owners. Articles 44-47.
In speaking of the restitution provisions of the 1953 law, one writer says,
"This article, in practice, recognized the *de facto* occupations of land which
had already been carried out by the *campesinos*." Patch, *Bolivia: U.S. Assistance in a Revolutionary Setting* in SOCIAL CHANGE IN LATIN AMERICA
TODAY at 108, 127 (1960).

A different kind of confiscation principle, also based on the theory of
restitution, is to be found in the legislation of several Latin American countries which have recently overthrown dictatorships. Laws of "illicit enrichment" have been enacted in countries such as Argentina (aimed at Perón),
Venezuela (Pérez Jiménez), Cuba (Batista), and the Dominican Republic
(Trujillo). Such a law typically confiscates the property of the dictator and
his family and of various persons associated with him who may have obtained
their property by means later found to be foul. Personal property is confiscated
as well as land. In principle, there is nothing wrong with recapturing for the
public what may have been looted during a period of political absolutism. The
crucial question concerns the type of procedure used to make the determination. It is one thing for a relatively unbiased board of judges to make such a
decision after a hearing, at which the accused may present evidence. It is an-

other for groups of militia to range the cities and countryside, informally confiscating property. See CUBA AND THE RULE OF LAW (Int'l Comm'n of Jurists 1962). Cuban legislation also provides for confiscation of all property of persons guilty of counter-revolutionary offenses, including many economic regulation offenses of a minor nature.

---

2. "The Social Function of Ownership"

When the Colombian dictator Gustavo Rojas Pinilla was deposed in 1957, a plebiscite was held to determine whether the public approved the retention of the constitutional reforms of 1936. The resulting affirmative vote adopted as Article 30 of the new Constitution these provisions, which had been established in the 1936 Constitution:

> Private ownership is guaranteed along with other rights acquired by rightful title, in accord with civil laws, by natural or juridical persons, which rights shall not be ignored or injured by later laws. When, because of the application of a law enacted for reasons of public utility or social interest, the rights of individuals come into conflict with the necessity recognized by the law itself, the private interest shall give way to the public or social interest.
> Ownership is a social function which implies obligations.
> For reasons of public utility or social interest, as defined by the legislative power, there may be expropriation, by means of judicial decision and prior compensation.
> Nevertheless, the legislative power, for reasons of equity, shall have the power to determine those cases in which there shall be no compensation, by means of the favorable vote of an absolute majority ██████ of the members of both Houses.

Before 1964, about the only judicial gloss to be added to the words about "social function" was that the obligation in question was to use one's property "in such a form as not to prejudice the community." Supreme Court of Justice, Gaceta Judicial, vol. XV, pp.349-400 (1943), quoted in MORALES BENITEZ, REFORMA AGRARIA — COLOMBIA CAMPESINA at 242-43 (1962). This language is like a public-oriented version of the famous common law maxim: *sic utere tuo ut alienum non laedas,* "use your own property in such a manner as not to injure that of another," and is equally unhelpful as a guide to decision. The language does, however, represent a shift of emphasis and mood: "What we have wanted to do is, then, to loosen the fetters which the Constitution of 1886 placed on the legislator with respect to private ownership . . .," said Darío Echandía, the Minister of Education and one of the leading advocates of the 1936 reform. (Quoted in MORALES BENITEZ, *supra,* at 243.)

In 1936, the Colombian Congress adopted Law 200, an important piece of legislation aimed at the elimination of private ownership of *uncultivated* land. But for a variety of reasons, political and administrative, little came of the law. Finally in late 1961, after very great difficulties, and at least in part in response to the prodding of officials of the Alliance for Progress, the Colombian Congress adopted a comprehensive land reform law. See HIRSCHMAN, JOURNEYS TOWARD PROGRESS, Ch. II (1963). The 1961 law reaffirms Law 200 of 1936, and gives its administration over to the newly-created Colombian Land Reform Institute (INCORA). The same Institute is given responsibility for administering a program of settlement of state owned land, and also charged with the acquisition of private land for reform purposes. The key provisions relating to the affectability of privately owned land for expropriation are reproduced below. What meaning does this legislation give to the expression "social function of ownership"? Is this meaning constitutional? In 1964, Colombia's Supreme Court of Justice upheld the law. For excerpts from that decision, see p. 557, *infra.* For further discussion of the content of the "social function" concept, see Karst, *Latin-American Land Reform: The Uses of Confiscation,* 63 MICH. L. REV. 327, 346-68 (1964).

COLOMBIA: Act N° 135 on Social Land Reform, December 13, 1961, Diario Oficial N° 30691, Dec. 20, 1961, p. 801 (FAO translation)

* * *

54.   The Colombian Land Reform Institute is hereby authorized to acquire privately-owned land in pursuance of the aims set forth in paragraphs 1, 2 and 4 of Article 1 of this Act, with a view to combatting soil erosion, carrying out reafforestation, facilitating irrigation and marsh reclamation work and improving transit and transport facilities in rural areas.

If the owners of land which it is deemed necessary to acquire fail to sell or transfer their land voluntarily, the Institute may compulsorily acquire such land in accordance with the provisions of the succeeding Articles. The acquisition of such land is hereby declared to be of social interest and public utility in accordance with Article 30 of the Constitution.

55.   Except as otherwise specified in Article 58 of this Act, the Institute shall, in making dispositions of land, give preference to easily accessible common land which shall be granted to the peasants in the area. The land must, however, be entirely suitable for the establishment of settlement areas in accordance with Articles 43 *et seq.* of this Act.

If privately-owned land has to be acquired for the purposes of making such dispositions, this shall be done in accordance with the following order of priority:

> 1. Uncultivated land not covered by the rules on the termination of rights of ownership;
> 2. Inadequately-worked land;
> 3. Agricultural land which is totally or very largely farmed by tenant farmers or share-croppers, when in the case of sharecropping the owner does not himself manage the farm and is not, under the sharecropping agreement, responsible for any part of the expenses or operation of the farm. This shall not apply to farms owned by minors or persons without full legal capacity;
> 4. Properly farmed land not covered by sub-paragraph 2 above but whose owners are prepared to alienate it voluntarily in accordance with the terms of this Act.

56. For the purposes of sub-paragraph 1 of the preceding Article, uncultivated land shall be considered that which while being economically usable is visibly not used for organized crop-farming or stock-breeding. Account shall not be taken for this purpose of land covered with natural forest required for water conservation and the needs of the holding nor of forest plantations of useful timber varieties. In classifying an area of land as being inadequately farmed, the Institute shall take the following factors into consideration: situation in relation to large urban centers; relief; quality of the soil; possibility of irrigation and reclamation; possibility of continuous and regular use; type and intensity of farming; capital and labour employed on the farm; commercial value and yield of the property and population density in the rural area where the property is situated.

57. In matters pertaining to the acquisition of privately-owned land, the Institute shall furthermore observe the following rules:

> 1. It shall give priority to those areas where concentration of land holdings is particularly high or where there is total or partial unemployment affecting a large rural population. It shall also give priority to other areas, including those suffering from active erosion, inequitable labour relationships or noticeably lower levels of living amongst the rural population than in other areas of the country.
> 2. The Institute shall acquire only such land as is suitable for small-scale crop-farming or stock-breeding. Land shall be considered suitable in this respect if it is irrigable or if without irrigation it normally has sufficient rainfall to grow crops or pasture to serve as a basis for the regular upkeep and profitable working of "family farms."

The Institute may, however, acquire adjacent areas which do not have such characteristics to use them as communal pasture land where this seems suitable.

The acquisition of land in respect of which irrigation works, flood defence works and land or marsh reclamation works may make for economic exploitation or a substantial change in farming methods, shall be governed by the provisions of Articles 68 *et seq.* of this Act.

58.   Well-farmed land may only be expropriated when it is proposed to put an area of small-holdings (*minifundios*) together with contiguous or nearby properties as part of land consolidation operations; well-farmed land may also be expropriated to enable small tenant farmers or share-croppers to acquire or extend the plots on which they have been working or to transfer to other land in the same area if such a course seems the most suitable; well-farmed land may also be expropriated when its acquisition is necessary to establish thereon small landowners, tenant farmers or share-croppers who are the occupiers of land that is no longer to be farmed; lastly, well-farmed land may be expropriated as provided in paragraph 3 of Article 55, or to facilitate the piping of water, the execution of land reclamation works and the provision of transit facilities in rural areas.

Each owner subject to expropriation shall, however, be entitled to retain an area of one hundred hectares. This right shall also apply to the owners of inadequately farmed land which the Institute has decided to expropriate under this Article.

Proviso.   Small tenant farmers or share-croppers shall be considered to be those who occupy in that capacity areas not larger than that which they can themselves farm with the aid of their families. Such areas should not be covered with permanent plantations or if they are so covered, the plantations should be the property of the tenant farmers, share-croppers or settlers concerned and not of the landowner.

59.   Except as otherwise specified in the foregoing Article, owners of inadequately farmed land shall, in the event of expropriation proceedings being instituted against them, be entitled to retain an area of up to two hundred (200) hectares, not more than one hundred (100) of which may be suitable for crop farming.

In computing the above-mentioned area, account shall not be taken of land that is too steep to be cultivated, of natural forests required for water conservation and the needs of the holding nor of enclosed areas, lakes, and areas covered with roads and buildings. Nor shall account be taken of areas normally subject to periodic flooding and which for that reason can be used only during a part of the year. Artificial forest plantations of useful timber varieties shall also not be counted.

It is one thing identify the land which is to be taken for an agrarian reform; it is quite another to carry out the expropriation. In Colombia, the administrative proceedings for executing the takings authorized by the foregoing legislation can be complicated in the extreme. One example saw a two-year delay between the Institute's initial determination to acquire the land

and the court's disposition of the case on review of the Institute's ultimate decision to expropriate. In that case, the court decided that the Institute had not complied with the formalities established by law; thus, the entire proceedings (determination to acquire, negotiations for purchase, and ultimately the decision to expropriate) had to be commenced anew. The defect in the Institute's action was that it had failed to affix a copy of the notice of intention to expropriate to the principal house located on the land — although personal notice had been given to the landowner, and although the proper papers had been recorded in the local registry. The case is discussed, and the slowness of the Colombian procedure trenchantly criticized, in THOME, LIMITACIONES DE LA LEGISLACION COLOMBIANA PARA EXPROPRIAR O COMPRAR FINCAS CON DESTINO A PARCELACION (Centro Interamericano de Reforma Agraria, mimeo, 1965).

In Bolivia, the revolution of 1952 did not begin as an agrarian revolution, but soon was required to take on an agrarian cast. The following account of the circumstances which brought about the Bolivian land reform is in turn followed by extracts from the 1953 land reform decree. How does the Bolivian decree compare to the law of Colombia in its references to the social function of ownership and its standards for affectability of private land?

PATCH, BOLIVIA: U.S. ASSISTANCE IN A REVOLUTIONARY SETTING in SOCIAL CHANGE IN LATIN AMERICA TODAY* at 108, 122-26 (1960)

In the early months after the revolution the national government in La Paz paid little attention to the rising tide of peasant unrest. It announced that the innocuous reforms decreed ten years before by the Villarroel government, which had placed certain restrictions on the exploitation of *pegujaleros* by latifundium owners, were again to be put into effect. The landowners were not much concerned over this mild gesture, and for a time the traditional landlord-peasant pattern seemed likely to remain unchanged by this as by so many previous revolts.

Then, on November 9, 1952, the syndicate of Ucureña demanded the return of eleven parcels of land to *pegujaleros* who had been driven from one of the latifundia a few years before. The landowner refused. Thereupon, the syndicate called for a general uprising of the *campesinos* in the provinces of Cliza, Punata, and Tarata. It threatened to pillage the town of Cliza and burn the houses of the nearby landowners. This threat of direct action, reported to

---

* Published for the Council on Foreign Relations by Harper and Row; reprinted by permission.

Cochabamba, the departmental capital, found the governor and his officials, with their limited forces, understandably reluctant to interfere. Only prompt action by the sub-prefect of Cliza finally succeeded in pacifying the *campesinos* and in preventing a general assault upon the latifundia and the smaller towns. The *campesinos* had now come to realize their strength, and acts of violence became more frequent.

The uprising of the *campesinos* could not but arouse the national government to the necessity for drastic action. If far-reaching concessions could no longer control but only channel the emergence of the *campesinos,* they would at least demonstrate that the sympathies of the government were on the side of the now irresistible movement. Fortunately, the *campesinos* also had a direct channel to the national leaders of the MNR [the government party] in La Paz. The minister of *campesino* affiars, Ñuflo Chávez, was acutely aware of of the government's dependence on the good will of the village population, and was in close contact with José Rojas and other *campesino* leaders. Ñuflo Chávez became an early and insistent advocate of an extreme type of agrarian reform. His concept, if carried out, would have divided all the land in areas of predominantly Indian population into *minifundios* (small parcels). A reform of this type would have converted the country's entire system of agriculture to subsistence farming, leaving little or no marketable surplus to feed the cities. Had the *campesinos* been left to their own devices this would assuredly have been the final upshot.

As it was, the syndicates rapidly took over the most accessible latifundia or *haciendas,* divided up the land among their members, and expropriated the vehicles, machinery, and houses of the former *patrones.* For example, at Ucureña the *casa hacienda,* or manor house, of one *patrón* was seized by the syndicate, which renamed it the "General Barracks" or village headquarters of Ucureña. Other houses were converted to serve as hospitals, schools or syndicate headquarters. By this time those landowners who had so far remained in the rural areas finally realized the full sweep of the revolution and fled for safety to the cities, especially to Cochabamba and La Paz. Since then most of them have not been able so much as to go near their former *haciendas.* Large areas of Bolivia have remained inaccessible for this class of *blancos,* often called *"la rosca,"* a bitter term applied to persons popularly believed to have used their wealth and power to exploit the Indians.

The Government and Agrarian Reform

The *campesino* uprising with its demand for agrarian reform posed several difficult questions to the MNR. As a political party, the MNR had risen to power as a congeries of groups each of which had its own purposes, and their amalgamation was not accompanied by a genuine unity of views or goals. The original inspirers of the MNR, leaders such as Victor Paz Estenssoro and Wálter Guevara Arze, minister of foreign affairs until February 1956, were supporters of moderate, evolutionary "socialism." As such, they attempted to keep the use of force to a minimum. Hernán Siles, then vice-president and president of the republic from 1956 to 1960, also belonged to the moderates.

In the 1940's the moderate intellectuals had been joined by a group which called itself the Vanguardia of the MNR. The Vanguardia in turn was, in its origins, close to the RADEPA, an organization of younger army officers, veterans of the Chaco war, who had turned against the higher officers, holding them responsible for Bolivia's defeat.[8] However vague the political platform of the Vanguardia, its leaders were more conservative in social outlook than the Paz Estenssoro group, and also more willing to resort to force.

The Universities had been another source of recruits and ideas for the MNR. While some professors and students were close to the moderate views of the MNR, many other students, no longer attracted to the older MNR intellectuals, had formed their own groups. The Avanzadas Universitarias (Avant-Garde University Students), as they were called, were young enough to be strongly influenced by the Marxist thinking that had flourished at the universities in the 1930's and 1940's. These groups were far to the left of the rightist Vanguardia wing of the MNR, whose adherents were barely lukewarm toward agrarian reform. Other influential leaders within the MNR took strong postions for or against the peasants' demands. Among them, the very influential Juan Lechín was an advocate of extreme land reform.

As the pressure of the *campesinos* and their syndicates was rising explosively, President Paz Estenssoro decided to put the government and the MNR at the head of the movement. On January 20, 1953, he proclaimed Supreme Decree N° 3301, creating an agrarian reform commission to study the "agrarian-*campesino* problem" and suggest the best ways in which the reform could be carried out. The commission, headed by Vice-President Siles, was given 120 days in which to prepare a report and draft a decree dealing with all interrelated aspects of the reform. These included property and tenure patterns of agricultural and grazing lands; "an adequate redistribution of this land, in order to raise the standard of living of the *campesinos*, intensify agricultural and livestock production, and develop the national economy"; procedures for liquidating the latifundia and supressing "semifeudal" exploitive practices in rural areas; the effect of these reforms on agricultural production, work patterns, and the payment and protection of the *campesinos; campesino* housing; technical assistance and credit for agricultural producers; conservation of natural resources. While Paz Estenssoro assigned responsibility for carrying out the decree jointly to the ministers of *campesino* affairs, agriculture, and finance, the primary responsibility, significantly enough, was assigned to the minister of *campesino* affairs, Ñuflo Chávez, an intimate of the Indian leader, José Rojas, rather than to the minister of agriculture, Germán Vera Tapia, one of the stronger leaders of the MNR's Vanguardia wing.

---

[8]RADEPA stands for Razón de Patria.

Within the stipulated period of four months the commission completed a series of reports and prepared a draft decree which Paz Estenssoro enacted into law by Supreme Decree N° 3464. On August 2, 1953, the decree was signed with much pomp and ceremony by the president and the entire cabinet bafore a huge convocation of *campesinos* held in the village of Ucureña.

BOLIVIA: Legislative Decree N° 03464 relative to
Agrarian Reform, August 2, 1953 (FAO translation)

1. The soil, the sub-soil and the waters of the territory of the Republic shall belong by original right to the Bolivian Nation.

2. The State shall recognise and guarantee private agrarian property where it serves a purpose benefiting the national community: it shall plan, regulate, supervise and organise the exercise thereof and shall promote the equitable distribution of the land in order to ensure the economic and cultural liberty and welfare of the Bolivian population.

3. Considered as public property over and above the assets recognised as such under legislation in force, are roads, even if built by private initiative, lakes, lagoons, rivers and all physical forces capable of economic exploitation.

4. Considered as State domains shall be uncultivated lands reverting thereto owing to lapse of concession or for some other reason, vacant lands outside the urban radius of population centres, lands belonging to the organs and self-administering bodies of the States, forest lands under Government control and all property considered to be of such character under legislation in force.

5. Private agrarian property is that which is acknowledged and granted to natural or juridical persons in order that they shall exercise their right in accordance with the civil laws and the conditions of this Legislative Decree. The State recognises only those forms of private agrarian property enumerated in the following Articles.

6. The farm-house plot has the function of a rural residence, inadequate to satisfy the needs of a family.

7. The small property is that worked by the peasant and his family personally, the produce of which enables them reasonably to satisfy their needs. The personal labour of the peasant does not exclude the collaboration of possible assistants for certain tasks.

8. The medium property is that having an area larger than the small property as defined above, which while lacking the characteristics of the capitalist agricultural undertaking, is operated with the assistance of paid workers or with the aid of technical and mechanical equipment, the bulk of its produce being intended for the market.

9. The Indian community property is that acknowledged as such under

legislation in force, on behalf of certain social groups of Indians.

10. The co-operative agrarian property is:

a) That property granted to farmers forming a co-operative association for the purpose of acquiring the land, putting it in order, cultivating it and settling thereon;

b) The lands of small and medium property owners, contributed for the establishment of the registered capital of the co-operative;

c) Lands of peasants who have received grants of land belonging to former latifundia and who have formed a co-operative society for their cultivation;

d) Lands belonging to agricultural co-operative societies under any other title not included in the foregoing paragraphs.

11. The agricultural undertaking shall be characterised by the investment of supplementary capital on a large scale, a system of paid labour and the use of up-to-date technical methods, exception being made as regards the latter in the case of areas with an uneven terrain. The determination of these factors in detail shall be governed by special regulations.

12. The State does not recognise the latifundium which is a rural property of large area varying according to its geographical situation, either undeveloped or substantially under-developed, by the diffuse field-cropping system with the use of obsolete implements and methods resulting in the waste of human effort, or by the imposition of lease rent; it is also characterised as regards the use of the land in the inter-Andean zone by the grant of parcels, small plots (*pegujales*), allotments (*sayañas*), part holdings and other equivalent forms, so that its profitability owing to the disequilibrium [among] the factors of production, is fundamentally dependent upon the extra yield which is contributed by the peasants in their capacity of servants or tenant-farmers and which is taken by the landowner as rent in the form of service, thus constituting a system of feudal oppression reflected in agricultural backwardness and a low standard of living and culture of the peasant population.

* * *

29. This Legislative Decree establishes the bases for the achievement of economic and political democracy in the rural area by the designation and grant of lands affected thereby as established under its provisions.

30. The latifundium shall be abolished. The possession of large corporative agrarian property or of other forms of large-scale concentration of land by private persons and by bodies which, by their legal structure, hinder its equitable distribution among the rural population, shall not be permitted.

31. Industrial capital investment in rural areas, for example in grain and sugar mills, cold storage plants and other forms of enterprise for manufacturing production shall be considered as beneficial wherever such enterprise exists side by side with medium and small properties and purchases their products at a fair price without arrogating to itself large areas of land. Large-scale

capital investment which acquires extensive areas of land for itself shall be considered harmful, because besides retaining the source of wealth, it monopolizes the market and eliminates the independent farmer by unfair competition.

32. The small property is not affected by this Legislative Decree within the limit established in Article 15.

33. The medium holding is not affected. It may, however, in exceptional cases, be affected in respect of those areas owned by farmers (allotments, small plots, etc.) the possession of which is assumed by the workers, without prejudice to the grant of land in other zones, to the extent of the minimum area of the small property. Where these areas, which are inalienable, become vacant by the departure of those workers to whom land has been granted, they shall be consolidated on behalf of the medium property holder to the extent of the maximum area of the medium property, subject to the requirement that compensation shall be made for the improvements carried out by the worker.

34. Landed property defined as a latifundium in accordance with Article 12 shall be affected by this Legislative Decree to the extent of its entire area.

35. For the purposes of the preceding Article, property whereon the owner has invested capital in modern agricultural methods and machinery and which is worked by him personally or by his closest relatives shall not be considered as a latifundium. In those regions where the topography of the cultivable land hinders the use of machinery, only the personal labour of the owner or of his closest relatives shall be stipulated.

This type of property as well as those properties having the characteristics referred to in Article 8 shall be reduced to the dimensions of the medium property with all the rights and duties devolving upon the owner of medium property.

36. The agricultural undertaking [which] on the date of proclamation of this Legislative Decree employs the mixed system of colonization and wage-payment shall not be affected if it has been ascertained that an amount of supplementary capital has been invested which is at least double that of the land capital and that up-to-date cultivation techniques have been employed thereon.

———

Late in December, 1960, the State of São Paulo, Brazil, adopted an Agrarian Reform Law, providing for the expropriation of poorly exploited rural land, after due notice and opportunity for landowners to bring the exploitation of their land up to the standards provided by the law and by its supplementary regulations. The expropriated land was to be sold in small parcels, with 15-year financing. The new law also established a system of progressive land taxation, in which the tax rate was increased with the size of the holding. An escape was provided for landowners who complied with a number of requirements: rational cultivation, soil conservation measures, the provision of housing for their workers, and the avoidance of indirect exploitation of the land through tenants. The application of the São Paulo law was effectively prevented when the Federal Congress enacted a law transferring the power to assess and collect taxes from the states to the municipalities, which have been traditionally under the control of the large landowners and those associated in interest with them. In late 1964, however, the Brazilian Congress enacted a comprehensive land reform law (the Land Statute of 1964), which included a complex system of progressive taxation of rural land (arts. 47-52). The basic tax is 2/10 of 1% of the value of the land, excluding improvements. That tax, however, is multiplied by a series of factors, as follows:

> (a) depending on the size of the land in relation to an administratively determined minimum size, up to a factor of 4.5;
> (b) depending on the land's location, up to a factor of 1.6;
> (c) depending on the type of management (personal management v. sharecropping, etc.,) up to a factor of 1.6 or down to a factor of .3;
> (d) (after the necessary soil, etc., surveys are made) depending on the relation of the land's productivity to the minimum yields established by regulation, up to a factor of 1.6 or down to a factor of .4.

Finally, the owner may get a reduction of up to 50% of his total tax by carrying out a program of amplification of land used, if his plan is approved by the Brazilian Institute of Agrarian Reform. Obviously, the operation of this progressive tax scheme requires a sophisticated body of administrators, whose existence in today's Brazil is doubtful.

Cuba's Agrarian Reform Act also contains provisions that make concessions to economic efficiency, and which resemble the provisions in other legislation concerning the social function of ownership. It should be noted that the land for the Cuban land reform has come only in part from the application of this Act. From May, 1959, to May, 1961, some 330,766 *caballerías* had been affected for the reform; one *caballería* equals about 30½ acres. Of this figure, reported by INRA, the land reform agency of the Cuban government, only some 27% was affected under the Agrarian Reform Act. The rest came from the application of various confiscation laws — some 28% from a law directed expressly against United States interests, by way of "retaliation" for the abandonment by this country of the preferential quota for Cuban sugar — and from voluntary sales (13%) and donations to INRA (7%). The figures appear in Chonchol, *Análisis Crítico de la Reforma Agraria Cubana*, EL TRIMESTRE ECONOMICO, vol. XXX(1), N° 117, p. 69, 97 (1963). The writer suggests that when all the data are in concerning confiscation, recuperation of property under the laws of illicit enrichment and the like, even the figure of 27% from the Agrarian Reform Act will have to be reduced.

CUBA: Agrarian Reform Act, 17 May 1959, Gaceta Oficial (Edición Extraordinaria Especial) N° 7, 3 June 1959, p. 1 (FAO translation)

1. Latifundia shall be abolished. The maximum area of land that may be possessed by a natural or juridical person shall be thirty *caballerías*. Lands owned by any natural or legal person in excess of that limit shall be expropriated for distribution among landless peasants and agricultural workers.

2. The following lands shall be exempt from the provisions of the preceding Article:

> a) Sugar cane plantation areas, the yield of which is not less than the national average plus 50%;
> b) Livestock breeding areas on which the number of livestock kept per *caballería* is at least that fixed by the National Agrarian Reform Institute having regard to the breed of livestock, the period of their development, percentage of births, diet, percentage of yield in the case of livestock intended for meat, or for milk production, according to the class of livestock of the class concerned. The productive possibilities of the area concerned, ascertained by physical-chemical analysis of the soils, and their humidity and rainfall shall be taken into account;
> c) Rice plantation areas normally yielding not less than 50% above that which in the judgment of the National Agrarian Reform Institute is the average national production for the variety concerned;
> d) Areas with one or more crops or used for agriculture and livestock breeding with or without industrial activity and for whose efficient exploitation and rational economic yield it is necessary to maintain an area of land in excess of that established as the maximum limit under Article 1 of this Act.

Notwithstanding the foregoing provisions a natural or juridical person may in no case possess lands exceeding one hundred *caballerías* in area. In cases where a natural or juridical person possesses lands exceeding one hundred *caballerías* in area which are given over to the production of two or more crops of the kind enumerated in paragraphs a), b), and c) of this Article, the benefit of the exception established up to the maximum limit of one hundred *caballerías* shall be conferred in such manner as the National Agrarian Reform Institute shall determine, the remaining area being subject to assignment for the purposes of this Act.

In the cases of the crops referred to in paragraphs a) and c), the yields in question shall be assessed on the basis of the last gathered harvest. The benefits of exceptions shall be maintained insofar as production levels are maintained.

In the case of the exception referred to in item d) the National Agrarian Reform Institute shall determine the area in excess of the maximum limit of 100 *caballerías* assignable for the purpose of this Act, while ensuring that the economic unit of production and in cases of several different crops, the correlation between those crops and between the crops and livestock breeding activities are maintained.

3. Lands belonging to the State, the Provinces and Municipalities shall also be subject to distribution.

Further light is cast on the meaning of the social function of ownership by the following excerpts from the record in a Venezuelan case in which the court was required to apply the provisions of Article 19 of the Agrarian Reform Law. Articles 19, 20 and 26 are reproduced here for convenience (see also Articles 27 *et seq.*, p. 413, *supra*):

19. For the purposes of the Agrarian Reform, private ownership of land fulfills its social function when it combines all the following essential elements:

> (a) The efficient exploitation and profitable use of the land in such a manner as to bring usefully into play the productive factors thereof, according to the zone in which it is located and its special characteristics.
> (b) Personal operation and management of, and financial responsibility for, the agricultural enterprise by the landowner, except in special cases of indirect exploitation for good reasons.
> (c) Compliance with the provisions governing conservation of renewable natural resources.
> (d) Respect of legal provisions governing paid labor, other labor relations questions, and other farm contracts, under the conditions laid down in this Act.
> (e) Registration of the rural property in the Office of the National Register of Land and Waters in accordance with appropriate legal provisions.

20. In particular, it shall be considered contrary to the principle of the social function of property and incompatible with the national welfare and economic development for uncultivated or unprofitable properties to exist and to be maintained, especially in economic development regions. Indirect systems of land exploitation, such as those carried out through leasing, the various types of sharecropping, day labor and squatting, shall also be considered contrary to the principle of the social function of property;

Provided, that the State shall in particular impose upon uncultivated or unprofitable properties a graduated tax scale to be prescribed in the appropriate enactments, without prejudice to expropriation in cases provided for under this Act.

* * *

26. Rural properties which fulfill their social function in accordance with the provisions of Article 19 shall be immune from expropriation for the purposes of the Agrarian Reform, except as specifically provided otherwise by this Act.

NATIONAL AGRARIAN INSTITUTE v. MUÑOZ

Court of First Instance, Civil and Commercial
District of Paz Castillo
State of Miranda, Venezuela (1961)

[The record in this case has been published under the title of "Alegación y Prueba de la Función Social" (1962).]

Petition for Expropriation

Citizen Judge of the First Instance, Civil and Commercial, of the State of Miranda. His office. I, Leopoldo Márquez Añez, Attorney, resident of Caracas, identified by Identity Card Nº 528,560, proceeding in my status as attorney for the National Agrarian Institute, . . . a representation proved by a power of attorney which is attached and marked "A," . . . before your competent jurisdiction appear with the purpose of petitioning for the expropriation of the estates denominated "El Rosario" and "El Carmen" (or "La Haciendita"), both located in the municipality Reyes Cueta, District of Paz Castillo of the State of Miranda and included respectively within the following boundaries: [here follows a very long description of the properties by metes and bounds]. The ownership of the said estates belongs to citizen Juan José Muñoz, in accordance with the document recorded in the sub-registry office of the District of Paz Castillo of the State of Miranda [stating the books in which the estates are registered]. This expropriation is petitioned in conformity with the provisions contained in the Third Section, Second Chapter, of the Agrarian Reform Law and based on the following reasons: *FIRST:* The derivation of this petition is based on Article 27 of the Agrarian Reform Law, in that the insufficiency or the inappropriate condition of publicly owned lands, described in the First Chapter of the cited Law, impedes the realization of grants without cost to the grantees of estates owned by the government, equally affected by the reform. In addition there is operating as a sufficient reason for the expropriation the first paragraph of the same Article 27, which declares uncultivated lands to be expressly subject to expropriation. *SECOND:* The absence in this case of grounds for inexpropriability which might impede the affecting of the property in accordance with Article 26 of the same Law. *THIRD:* In execution of the provisions of Article 35, my client has taken steps to secure from the owner the amicable acquisition of the described estates, the steps taken resulting negatively. There are anexed to this petition, in fulfillment of the conditions outlined in Article 36, the following collected items: a) Certified Copy of the resolution of expropriation adopted by the Directory of the Institute in session held the 13th day of April, 1961; b) certification of encumbrances executed by the competent Registry; and c) a report containing the general characteristics of the estates and their classification for purposes of the reservation of property for use of the owner. Based on the foregoing I request the admission of this petition, and that it be definitely declared proper. Los Teques, the 23rd day of the month of May, 1961. (Signed) Leopoldo Márquez Añez.

Answer

Citizen Judge of First Instance, Civil and Commercial. I, Antonio José Puppio, attorney, resident of Caracas and here as a transient, acting in representation of Citizen Juan José Muñoz, farmer and cattle raiser, adult, resident in the jurisdiction of the municipality Reyes Cueta, District of Paz Castillo of the State of Miranda, a representation which I exercise according to the Power which I attach marked "A," before you respectively appear and expound on the opportunity of answering the petition for expropriation formulated by the National Agrarian Institute before this Tribunal, and respecting the estates owned by my client, denominated "El Rosario" and "El Carmen" (or "La Haciendita"), both located in the jurisdiction of the municipality Reyes Cueta, District of Paz Castillo of the State of Miranda, and whose boundaries and other descriptions are stated in the said petition for expropriation: Chapter I. My client is the owner of the named estates whose expropriation has been petitioned for by the National Agrarian Institute, ... Chapter II. It is true that a mortgage on the hacienda "El Carmen" (or "La Haciendita"), whose boundaries have been outlined in the petition for expropriation, did exist in favor of Sebastián Suárez, deceased, but the said mortgage was cancelled by means of payments which were made in various installments as the attached exhibits ... show .... [The owner admits also that there is a mortgage on the other estate in favor of the Agricultural Bank amounting to some 38,000 Bolivars. From the time of this decision to the present time, one Bolivar has equalled approximately $ .22 in United States money.] Chapter III. My client formally rejects the "Technical Report and Evaluation of the Estates of 'El Carmen' and 'El Rosario' " attached to the petition, and signed on September 28, 1960, by the agronomist, Juan Bta. Castillo and the agricultural expert Samuel Peralta, as well as its conclusions and amount. From this time forward my client states that the said Report and Valuation cannot be opposed to him and therefore can produce no legal effects against his rights and interest, and therefore, my client does not accept it, refuses to recognize it and rejects it, in particular with respect to the price, to the property [included] and the area of the estates, and the conditions of the same. Chapter IV. My client formally opposes the petition ... insofar as it refers to the estate "El Carmen" (or "La Haciendita"), since, in respect to it, the said Institute took no steps, direct or indirect, before proceeding to petition for expropriation, to arrange an amicable settlement with my client, as Article 35 of the Agrarian Reform Law requires. Neither has the petitioner taken steps to secure said settlement after the petition. The representative of the National Agrarian Institute orally negotiated with my client for the acquisition by means of a friendly settlement, of the estate "El Rosario," with the qualification that said negotiations were limited to asking him how much he wanted for said estate and without making him any offer in the respect and demonstrating little interest or seriousness in the matter, by reason of which my client is obliged to deny the affirmation contained in the petition, ... Chapter V. My client also formally opposes the petition ... because in conformity with Article 26 of the Agrarian Reform Law, the lands of my client to which the petition refers ... are inexpropriable for the purposes of the Agrarian Reform, since they fulfill their social function in conformity with Article 19 of the same. In effect, "El Rosario" and "El Carmen" (or "La Haciendita") are agricultural and cattle raising estates. Their exploitation has been efficient and their income has always been very good. In "El Carmen" and in "El Rosario" cultivated pastures predominate, and my client has built stables, watering places (36) and lakes (6); on the estates there are maintained the greatest possible number of head of cattle — approximately 800 — in the least possible area, and without either the land or the animals suffering. There has been an average birth of 25 calves per month; because they are duly attended, almost all survive. The burning of the fields has been abolished, and both estates are totally and completely fenced in an adequate form. In "El Carmen" and "El Rosario" there are produced more than 250 liters of milk daily for sale by others, with the qualification that the calves are not deprived of their food. My client attends to and carries on personally the working and direction of his two estates, and he has the financial responsibility for the agricultural enterprise as well as the cattle raising enterprise which he directs in "El Carmen" and "El Rosario." In addition, my client has always complied with the existing provisions for conservation of woods and waters and renewable natural resources, and has fulfilled all the provisions of the Law which regulates rural labor relations.... . [The client is also taking steps to register his property in the correct Registry Office.] For the reasons expressed, my client is also obliged to reject categorically the affirmation contained in the petition according to which in the present case there are no "grounds for inexpropriability which might impede the affecting [of the property] in accordance with Article 26" of the Agrarian Reform Law. And he also denies and categorically rejects the affirmation of the petitioner according to which the aforementioned estates of my client are expropriable for the reason that they are uncultivated lands. Chapter VI. For the reasons expressed in the two foregoing Chapters, my client expressly requests the Citizen Judge that, on deciding the substance of this action, as a previous question, he declares: a) that the National Agrarian Institute did not fulfill the requirement demanded by Article 35 of the Agrarian Reform Law with respect to the estate "El Carmen," since it took no steps to arrange an amicable settlement with my client for the acquisition of the same; and b) that both the estate "El Rosario" and "El Carmen" whose expropriation has been petitioned by the Institute, are inexpropriable according to Article 26 of the Agrarian Reform Law because they fulfill their social function. And that in conformity with the same Article, only "by exception" should the total or partial expropriation of said estates be allowed, and always on the conditions and by means of the fulfillment and proof in the respective action, of the requirements set out in said provision [Article 33], whose application has not been invoked. .... *And in case that it be decided that the estates are expropriable, by exceptional means, according to the said Article 33 of the Agrarian Reform Law, my client requests that it be declared and ordered that the corresponding payment should be made and the form established by that provision.* [Emphasis in original.] Chapter VII. On the supposition that the Tribunal may declare that the expropriation requested is proper — either by the ordinary or exceptional means — I state that my client has decided to exercise and does exercise the right to reserve for himself in the estate "El Carmen" the respective area fixed as inexpropriable, all in conformity with Articles 29 and 30 of the Agrarian Reform Law. As the estate "El Carmen" is constituted by lands which in their conjunction — it is said — have been classified as of the fourth class, the reservation should amount to 500 hectares, which in this case are constituted by all the level lands of the estate "El Carmen," including the area where my client has constructed his living house and other buildings, and to which there should be added the lands which (in accordance with the second part of Article 30 of the Agrarian Reform Law) are the object of an additional reservation, which my client also requests, and which are indispensable to him for the due exploitation of the estate since they are destined for the pasturing of animals and for buildings, and they are covered with high woods which serve as protection zones for the conservation of waters and as wind breaks. At the opportune time my client will present further allegations in the respect. Chapter VIII. .... [There is no petition for expropriation of livestock. This constitutes a partial expropriation, in violation of the Law of Expropriation for Reasons of Public or Social Utility.] Chapter IX. Article 23 of the Agrarian Reform Law provides that "the State shall provide incentives for those persons who utilize land in accordance with its social function and thus contribute to the economic development of the country." The petition for expropriation presents a tremendous irony and a painful drama for my client, Citizen Judge. During 29 years he has worked the lands whose expropriation have been petitioned for, without any more help than his own efforts and with his product has maintained his family — 16 live children and four grand-children — and has contributed to the economic development of the region and of the Country. And today he finds himself compensated with a petition for expropriation. Will that be, Citizen Judge, the incentive created by the State and to which the cited legal provision refers? If the other invoked provisions did not aid him, that expressed in this Chapter would be sufficient to justify the opposition that my client formulates to the petition for expropriation. Chapter X. I ratify the opposition formulated in the foregoing Chapters to the petition for expropriation which has commenced this action, and for the expressed reasons I request that said petition be declared inadmissible and without place, at least that it be declared admissible only by virtue of the exception established in Article 33 of the Agrarian Reform Law, and that the payment be ordered corresponding to all the property which should be expropriated, as alleged, in order that in the established form the cited Article 33 of the mentioned Law be effectuated. My client reserves the right to exercise the legal actions which may be appropriate. *Es justicia.* Los Teques, Jan. 14, 1961. (Signed) Dr. Antonio José Puppio.

[The next document in the record is a statement by the Secretary of the Court that the attorneys for the plaintiff and defendant appeared at a hearing on June 14, 1961, and that the answer was accepted by the Court. The Court declared open the period of proof provided by Article 36, Paragraph 5 of the Agrarian Reform Law.]

Offers of proof

[Counsel for both sides then requested that certain witnesses be called and asked certain specified questions. The attorney for the Institute requested that Dr. Merchán, an attorney, Dr. Villalba Villalba, an agronomist, and an agricultural expert named Baggio Baggio be called. They were to be asked these questions:]

A) The witness Doctor Antonio Merchán: 1st. If he knows by sight, dealings and communication the citizen Juan José Muñoz, defendant in the present action; 2nd. If in his capacity as a member of the Directorate of the National Agrarian Institute he carried on conversations with the mentioned citizen, directed to the amicable acquisition of the estates "El Carmen" and "El Rosario," in fulfillment of the requirements of Article 35 of the Agrarian Reform Law; 3d. If with such a purpose he ordered Doctor Jesús Villalba Villalba, the Chief of the Division of Lands of the National Agrarian Institute, to make a formal offer of purchase to the defendant in accordance with the amount of the valuation which is shown in the file of this case, and that the amicable acquisition was impossible because the owner demanded the quantity of 20 million Bolivars for both estates. B) The witness Doctor Jesús Villalba Villalba: 1st. If he knows by sight, dealings and communication the citizen

Juan José Muñoz, defendant in the present action; 2nd. If in his capacity as Chief of the Division of Lands of the National Agrarian Institute and in execution of instructions of Doctor Antonio Merchán, Member of the Directorate, offered to the defendant for the two estates "El Carmen" and "El Rosario," the quantities which respectively represent the valuation of each estate and which are shown in the file; 3d. That the amicable acquisition was impossible because the owner asked for the quantity of 20 million Bolivars for both estates; 4th. That in the mentioned capacity as Chief of the Division of Lands of the National Agrarian Institute he knows and there is clear to him the agricultural capacity of the estates whose expropriation is requested and that, consequently, the lands being devoted to cattle raising exploitation, proper advantage has not been taken of them in accordance with the zone in which they are found, which is essentially agricultural. C) The witness Giuseppe Baggio Baggio: 1st. If he knows the estates "El Rosario" and "El Carmen," whose expropriation is petitioned; 2nd. If through such knowledge it is apparent to him that on those estates a cattle-raising enterprise is being carried on; 3d. If he knows their agricultural capacity; 4th. If, in consequence, the exploitation which is carried on there is in conformance with such capacity. . . . [Counsel for the Institute requests the admission of testimony along the foregoing lines.]

[Counsel for the defendant submits a copy of the request his client made for the registration of his ownership in the proper Registry Office. He also submits various communications from government officials relating to the manner of exploitation of his land. In addition he asks that five named men be called as witnesses to answer the following questions:] 1st. If they know my client and if they have no impediment preventing them from testifying as witnesses in the present action. 2nd. If it is true and clear to them that for 29 years my client has been promoting and developing agricultural and cattle-raising enterprises on the estates which he owns called "El Carmen" and "El Rosario." 3d. If it is true and clear to them that on the named estates there abound and predominate cultivated pastures; there exist more than 800 head of beef cattle which are adequately attended without harming the land; there exist six lakes and more than 30 watering places; the estates are completely fenced and there exist ditches and canals for irrigation; they are not uncultivated; and the fields are attended and sowed using machines and not burning. 4th. If it is true and clear to them that in the average month 25 to 30 calves are born, and all live, since mortality is practically nil because they are duly attended; and that in addition to the milk with which said calves are fed there are produced on the estates "El Carmen" and "El Rosario" from 200 to 250 liters of milk per day which are sold to outsiders. 5th. If it is true and clear to them that Mr. Muñoz personally directs his enterprises and works on them with his children; pays with his own money the wages of his workers and other expenses which the exploitation of the same may cost, that he sells trees only when competent authorities authorize it; that he replants trees in order to care for the woods and waters; and that he fulfills the obligations which the Labor Law imposes on him and other laws which regulate labor activities. . . . [The attorney for the defendant requests the admission of testimony along these lines, and also asks that the deposition of the President of the National Agrarian Institute be taken in Caracas, for the purpose of denying certain testimony to be expected from other officials of the Institute. He also asks that testimony be taken from four other men who are familiar with the operations of Mr. Muñoz, for the purpose of showing that Mr. Muñoz operates his lands directly and not through intermediaries, and that he takes personal direction of the management and financing of his operation, including taking the risks of loss. Finally, he requests that the Judge make a visual inspection of the two estates in order to verify that they are completely fenced and cultivated, that they include lakes and watering places as stated in his answer, that tractors and other machinery are used in the cultivation of that portion of the estates which is cultivated, etc.]

Completion of proof
    [The Judge did visit the estates as requested by the defendant and made some neutral findings, avoiding conclusions concerning the degree of intensiveness with which the land was used or cultivated. The visit was carried out on July 6, 1961. On the same day, the testimony of the defendant's witnesses was taken, put in written form, and added to the record. It appears that the Judge was personally present during the taking of the testimony of each witness. All the witnesses for the defendant testified to the same effect, answering affirmatively to the leading questions set out above. A typical set of answers came from the witness Medardo Villegas, as follows:]
    On the same date appeared in the Office of this Tribunal, by means of previous citation, the citizen Medardo Villegas; he gave the oath required by law, stated that he was named as noted above, that he was 50 years of age, a bachelor, by profession farmer, resident of this Municipality, bearer of Identity Card N° 2578509 and without any legal impediments to testify. Apprised of the purpose of his citation and having been read the offer of proof by the defendant, to the First question, he said: "Yes, I know Mr. Juan José Muñoz and I have no impediment to testify." To the Second, he said: "Yes, it is true and clear to me because I have worked for 29 years with him." To the Third, he said: "Yes, it is true in all the parts of the question, and it is clear to me because I have seen all this in the 29 years that I have worked for Mr. Muñoz." To the Fourth he said: "Yes, it is true and clear to me in all respects and every part of the question put to me, because since I work with Mr. Juan José Muñoz I know of all this, as to the average of 200 to 250 liters of milk daily; it varies." To the Fifth and last, he said: "This is true, because, as I said before, I worked for Mr. Muñoz for 29 years on the said estates." — He finished, he was read [an account of what he had stated] and in conformance he signed, the witness not doing it himself because he did not know how to write, but in its place he stamped his fingerprints. . . .

[The plaintiff's witnesses had been interviewed on July 4, 1961, but their testimony appears following that of the defendant's witnesses in the record. Counsel for the defendant objected to permitting the officials of the Institute to testify, on the ground that they were interested in the litigation. The Judge did not rule on the objection at this time. He permitted the testimony to be taken. The Judge ultimately overruled the objection in his final decision of the case. The three witnesses for the plaintiff all testified affirmatively to the questions listed in the offer of proof. Counsel for the defendant was permitted to formulate questions, which were put to the plaintiff's witnesses by the Secretary of the Court. All of these questions related to the possible interest of the witnesses in the outcome of the case, and were designed to show partiality. The witnesses denied any interest in the case other than an interest in seeing that the law be complied with.]

[The two best witnesses for the defendant appeared on July 7, 1961. They were both merchants, and both had worked for Mr. Muñoz previously. Luis Gabriel Rodríguez testified that he had worked for Mr. Muñoz from 1952 to 1960. He testified that Mr. Muñoz had exploited the estates directly and had complied with the obligations which various laws imposed on him. He also testified that Mr. Muñoz had personally run the financial risks of the operation, and that he had obtained a good return for his efforts, achieving an increase of about 500 head of livestock during the eight-year period described. He also testified that Mr. Muñoz ran a sugar mill, grew some sugar cane, and generally dedicated himself to the raising of livestock, both cattle and hogs. Heraclio Antonio Silva Valladares testified that he had worked for Mr. Muñoz from 1957 to 1960, and he verified the testimony of Mr. Rodríguez. Counsel for the Institute asked that certain questions be put to this witness, which questions and their answers are reproduced here:] First: Let the witness state whether the success and the income obtained by the owner refers exclusively to the livestock raising, or in addition to agricultural exploitation. Answer: "The success obtained during the time when I worked on the estate refers to both branches, to livestock and to agriculture. Another: Let the witness state whether there is presently maintained an exploitation on a large scale in relation to the area of the estates. Answer: [Question withdrawn by counsel.] Another: Let the witness state, up to the year 1960 and during the period in which he served the owner on the estates "El Carmen" and "El Rosario," what kind of cultivation was carried on and over what area. Answer: Sugar cane in a large area of land which I cannot describe precisely, and minor cultivation such as sweet potatoes, [and various other indigenous vegetables] and another large area of land which I cannot describe precisely. Another: Let the witness state whether with relation to the livestock exploitation now existing, what percentage approximately of the estates is occupied by agricultural exploitations. Answer: I cannot answer this question exactly; I quit working on the estate in 1960 and from that time forward I do not know in what condition the estates are, with relation to cattle raising and agriculture. When I worked on said estates there was 30% devoted to agriculture and 70% to livestock. Another: Let the witness state whether the system of exploitation of those minor crops was by means of *conuco* [literally, a small plot of land; here used to refer to a form of tenant farming]. Answer: Cultivation was carried on in the form of *conuco* and in the form of *arado* [literally, plow; refers to another form of tenant farming]. Another: Let the witness state whether in the years during which he worked on the estates he received "utilities" [that is, services or other benefits in addition to a salary], considering the extraordinary income of the exploitation. Answer: The utilities were paid annually to all the employees in accordance with the production and income of the estates and in accordance with our salary. I am certain that I received utilities. Another: Let the witness state the salary obtained during the last year and the approximate amount of the utilities received. Answer: I received a salary of 300 Bolivars per month, and during this year they gave me a utility or bonus of 1,500 Bolivars. [Signed by the Judge, the witness, the Secretary, and the attorneys for both parties.]

Written arguments of counsel

[At the close of the period for submitting proof, each counsel submitted a written argument summarizing the evidence and drawing conclusions favorable to his side. The arguments dealt not only with the question of the social function of ownership, but with the other issues as well. Only the portions dealing with the social function of ownership are reproduced here.]

[Argument for the National Agrarian Institute:]

II.   As was observed before, the allegation and proof of the ground of inexpropriability established in Article 19 of the Agrarian Reform Law corresponds to the defendant owner who in this case so understands the article and consequently has offered various proofs directed to such an end. For particular consideration in these arguments are the testimony and the visual inspection, opportunely offered and taken. A) *Testimonial proof.* Apart from the fact that only doubtfully can the proof of witnesses be considered proper for the demonstration of the requisites demanded in Article 19 of the Law, there should be particularly observed the negative result of the responses of the offered witnesses. In effect, the citizens who gave their declarations before the Judge of the District of Paz Castillo of the State of Miranda limited themselves in the most important particulars of the interrogatories (that is, numbers 2, 3, and 5), without exception, to grounding their affirmations on the fact that they had some 29 (and others 24) years of experience working with the owner of the estates "El Carmen" and "El Rosario"; and in similar terms those who gave their declarations before the Judge of the Municipality Chacao, District of Sucre of this State were also distinguished by their laconic and vague manner of expressing themselves. Especially the witness Heraclio Silva

Valladares, cross-examined by the attorney for the plaintiff, shows an absolute failure to understand the exploitation of the estates, even to the point of referring to a system of *conucos,* whose significance is well understood to be contrary to rational systems of agricultural exploitation; this apart from declaring as a monthly salary the quantity of 300 Bolivars and 1,500 Bolivars by way of utilities, almost 40% of the total of annual salaries, when it is well known that the participation of the worker by way of utilities does not exceed the salary or wage of two months. In the record there is no offer of proof which concretely accredits the owner with the fulfillment of the legal requirements with respect to rural wage labor. B) *Visual inspection.* This means of proof of superior fitness and certainty to demostrate the social function of the land, has had for the offering party [the defendant] a constant negative result. It could not be shown that these estates are cultivated, since the report of the inspection says [that the area and quality of cultivation will be left to the expert reports in the case]; and 2d) neither was it demonstrated that among the pastures which exist the cultivated ones predominate, since such an estimate was naturally referred to the proper expert report. ...

[Argument of the defendant:]

Chapter II. My client also opposes the expropriation of his estates "El Carmen" and "El Rosario" because in conformity with Article 26 of the Agrarian Reform Law, *they are inexpropriable* because they fulfill their social function in conformity with Article 19 of the same. The expropriation agency has based its action on the strange affirmation, among others, that the said estates *are uncultivated lands,* and therefore expropriable. No proof has been offered in the record which demonstrates such an assertion. On the other hand, from the procedural record the alleged ground of inexpropriability has been demonstrated evidently, since the result of the visual inspection made by this Judge as well as the declarations of the witnesses [seven men named] and also, the documents attached to the offer of proof, evidence that said estates have been exploited in an efficient form; that my client has personally worked and directed the enterprise, and has kept it under his financial responsibility; that my client has fulfilled and complied with the legal norms that regulate rural labor relations and has complied with the existing rules concerning the conservation of renewable natural resources; that the estates whose expropriation has been requested have been inscribed in the proper Registry Office; and that cultivated pastures predominate on them, they are completely fenced, and there exist lakes, stables, and watering places, and the cultivation is brought to effect by means of adequate machines and tools. The productivity of the estates and the existence on them of herds of livestock [beef cattle, horses, and hogs] also are demonstrated. Thus not only "El Carmen" but also "El Rosario" fulfill their social function and therefore are inexpropriable. Therefore it is evident, that in case expropriability should be decreed, it can be done only by means of the exceptional manner provided in Article 33 of the Agrarian Reform Law, and, in such a case, their price must be paid in the form and on the conditions provided in said provision. [Signed on July 17, 1961.]

Decision

[The Judge held for the Institute on all questions except the issue of partial expropriation. The Court ordered the estates expropriated, but referred the valuation question back to the expert appraisers, so that they might include the value of the cattle, etc. in the amount to be paid to Mr. Muñoz. Only that portion of the opinion dealing with the question of the social function of ownership is reproduced here.]

Now then, in the technical report and valuation of the estates "El Carmen" and "El Rosario" subscribed by the agronomist Juan Bautista Castillo and Manuel Peralta, and dated in Guarenas the 28th of September, 1960, and although said report has been rejected formally in Chapter III of the Answer of the defendant . . . the following appears: "The natural vegetation of the region is generally of a shrubby character, of dry zones, except the banks of ravines and little streams where the vegetation is wooded. There predominate [various varieties of trees from which charcoal may be made]. Of the 2,200 hectares at which we estimate the area, the most irregular parts and the most level parts also are covered with this natural vegetation, there being realized on part of them a relatively slight pasture. The area under such conditions we estimate at 1,500 hectares of which some 500 are used for pasture. Of the remaining area, 700 hectares are cultivated as pastures and with sugar cane in very bad conditions. The estate "El Carmen" has a mill which is not in use. It is estimated that Mr. Muñoz presently has some 300 cattle of various ages and 25 pigs. He produces daily some 250 liters of milk. From the foregoing it can be clearly established that only on a very low scale do these estates fulfill the social function to which Article 19 of the Agrarian Reform Law refers. A few cattle, with some watering holes, without selection of livestock, without installations, with a few workers poorly paid, represent a very low investment of capital in a zone where the natural and social conditions deserve intensive exploitations, agricultural as well as of livestock." In the same report, with relation to the agricultural capacity of the estate, it is said: ". . . Capacity for use I.—Lands apt for agricultural use, with current conservation practices — 200 hectares. Capacity for use II.—Lands apt for agricultural use with simple conservation practices — 200 hectares. Capacity for use III.—Lands apt for agricultural use, intensive conservation practices — 160 hectares. Capacity for use IV.—Lands apt for occasional agricultural use and principally for permanent vegetation (pastures, woods) — 230 hectares. Capacity for use VI.—Use of permanent vegetation (pastures) with moderate restrictions — 110 hectares. Capacity for use VII.—Use of permanent vegetation (pastures, woods) with severe restrictions — 200 hectares. Total of hectares

— 1,200 [sic]. [Similar figures for "El Carmen" total 1,000 hectares. The report goes on to place the land of these two estates in the fourth category of lands as described in Article 198 of the Agrarian Reform Law. It concludes that the ownership of this land is fulfilling barely 10% of its social function, considering the natural conditions of the land. The opinion in this case does not make clear the source of the figure of 10%, but it would seem that the report said that only some 10% of the land was being used at a level commensurate with its capacity to absorb investment, cultivation, etc.] *The Tribunal gives full probative value to the foregoing report, since it constitutes a document of vital importance for the characterization of the lands as fulfilling or not the social function in conformity with Article 19 of the Agrarian Reform Law.* [Emphasis in original.] . . . Now then, as to the witnesses presented by the defense, apart from the fact that they appeared making declarations over various highly technical aspects, their statements are too insufficient. [Here the Court reviews the testimony of those witnesses who simply answered affirmatively to the various leading questions about the manner of cultivation of the two estates.] *There are undoubtedly notions which, by reason of their evidently scientific flavor, somewhat escape the purposes of testimonial proof. It is clear that a witness, unless he be a technician in the subect, cannot appear declaring that an estate does or does not have cultivated pastures, that its owner has developed and forwarded agricultural and cattle raising enterprises, that the lands are not uncultivated, etc., because to the contrary the expert testimony has denied these arguments, and it would be made very easy to impugn a technical report with testimonial proof, most often of easy elaboration and of foreseeable practical effects.* [The Court then notes that the witnesses Rodríguez and Silva Valladares were unable to state how much area was being used for crops, how much "utility" the estates were producing, etc., and that they did point out the indirect form of exploitation of the lands by means of *conuco* and *arado*. The Court concludes that the defendant's evidence is insufficient to overcome the technical report, and that there is no ground for the defendant's claim that his lands are not expropriable. The opinion is signed by the Judge and the Secretary, and dated November 7, 1961.]

Consider these questions about the *Muñoz* case:

1. What were the grounds for the decision that Mr. Muñoz' ownership had not fulfilled its social function?
2. Upon what evidence did the court base each ground?
3. Has the court established any standard for proof in such cases? To what extent does the court's position leave the question of social function to administrative discretion? What can a landowner do to resist an expropriation action?

4. What was the landowner's objective in resisting expropriation? Did he really expect to prevent the taking of his land?

Before examining some North American constitutional standards for "affectability" of property in expropriation proceedings, it may be helpful to consider some broad questions aimed at making clear where expropriation stands in a system which protects rights of property. It is seldom helpful to ask questions like "What is property?" in a vacuum; but such questions can be useful if they are asked with concrete issues in mind, for the purpose of analyzing specific problems. With that caution, the following excerpted readings are offered: a classic of utilitarianism, an early 20th century socialist work, and a criticism which seems directed at them both. Morris Cohen's book review of the volume which contains these readings is followed by one of his own efforts at generalization. (An additional reading which may be helpful is F. S. Cohen, *Dialogue on Private Property*, 9 RUTGERS L. REV. 357 (1954).) Can you relate these general statements to land reform legislation based on assumptions about the social function of ownership?

BENTHAM, THEORY OF LEGISLATION 109-13, 119-21
(Hildreth ed. 1871, translated from 1830 French ed. of Dumont)

OF SECURITY

We come now to the principal object of law, — the care of security. That inestimable good, the distinctive index of civilization, is entirely the work of law. Without law there is no security; and, consequently, no abundance, and not even a certainty of subsistence; and the only equality which can exist in such a state of things is an equality of misery.

* * *

Law alone has done that which all the natural sentiments united have not the power to do. Law alone is able to create a fixed and durable possession which merits the name of property. Law alone can accustom men to bow their heads under the yoke of foresight, hard at first to bear, but afterwards light and agreeable. Nothing but law can encourage men to labours superfluous for the present, and which can be enjoyed only in the future. Economy has as many enemies as there are dissipators — men who wish to enjoy without giving themselves the trouble of producting. Labor is too painful for idleness; it is too slow for impatience. Fraud and injustice secretly conspire to appropriate its fruits. Insolence and audacity think to ravish them by open force.

Thus security is assailed on every side — ever threatened, never tranquil, it exists in the midst of alarms. The legislator needs a vigilance always sustained, a power always in action, to defend it against this crowd of indefatigable enemies.

Law does not say to man, *Labor, and I will reward you;* but it says *Labor, and I will assure to you the enjoyment of the fruits of your labor — that natural and sufficient recompense which without me you cannot preserve; I will insure it by arresting the hand which may seek to ravish if from you.* If industry creates, it is law which preserves; if at the first moment we owe all to labor, at the second moment, and at every other, we are indebted for everything to law.

* * *

OF PROPERTY

The better to understand the advantages of law, let us endeavor to form a clear idea of *property.* We shall see that there is no such thing as natural property, and that it is entirely the work of law.

Property is nothing but a basis of expectation; the expectation of deriving certain advantages from a thing which we are said to possess, in consequence of the relation in which we stand towards it.

There is no image, no painting, no visible trait, which can express the relation that constitutes property. It is not material, it is metaphysical; it is a mere conception of the mind.

To have a thing in our hands, to keep it, to make it, to sell it, to work it up into something else; to use it — none of the physical circumstances, nor all united, convey the idea of property. A piece of stuff which is actually in the Indies may belong to me, while the dress I wear may not. The aliment which is incorporated into my very body may belong to another, to whom I am bound to account for it.

The idea of property consists in an established expectation; in the persuasion of being able to draw such or such an advantage from the thing possessed, according to the nature of the case. Now this expectation, this persuasion, can only be the work of law. I cannot count upon the enjoyment of that which I regard as mine, except through the promise of the law which guarantees it to me. It is law alone which permits me to forget my natural weakness. It is only through the protection of law that I am able to inclose a filed, and to give myself up to its cultivation with the sure though distant hope of harvest.

But it may be asked, What is it that serves as a basis to law, upon which to begin operations, when it adopts objects which, under the name of property, it promises to protect? Have not men, in the primitive state, a *natural* expectation of enjoying certain things, — an expectation drawn from sources anterior to law?

Yes. There have been from the beginning, and there always will be, circumstances in which a man may secure himself, by his own means, in the enjoyment of certain things. But the catalogue of these cases is very limited. The savage who has killed a deer may hope to keep it for himself, so long as his cave is undiscovered; so long as he watches to defend it, and is stronger than his rivals; but that is all. How miserable and precarious is such a possession! If we suppose the least agreement among savages to respect the acquisitions of each other, we see the introduction of a principle to which no name can be given but that of law. A feeble and momentary expectation may result from time to time from circumstances purely physical; but a strong and permanent expectation can result only from law. That which, in the natural state, was an almost invisible thread, in the social state becomes a cable.

Property and law are born together, and die together. Before laws were made there was no property; take away laws, and property ceases.

As regards property, security consists in receiving no check, no shock, no derangement to the expectation founded on the laws, of enjoying such and such a portion of good. The legislator owes the greatest respect to this expectation which he has himself produced. When he does not contradict it, he does what is essential to the happiness of society; when he disturbs it, he always produces a proportionate sum of evil.

                    * * *

Opposition Between Security and Equality

In consulting the grand principle of security, what ought the legislator to decree respecting the mass of property already existing?

He ought to maintain the distribution as it is actually established. It is this which, under the name of *justice,* is regarded as his first duty. This is a general and simple rule, which applies itself to all states; and which adapts itself to all places, even those of the most opposite character. There is nothing more different than the state of property in America, in England, in Hungary, and in Russia. Generally, in the first of these countries, the cultivator is a proprietor; in the second, a tenant; in the third, attached to the glebe; in the fourth, a slave. However, the supreme principle of security commands the preservation of all these distributions, though their nature is so different, and though they do not produce the same sum of happiness. How make another distribution without taking away from each that which he has? And how despoil any without attacking the security of all? When your new repartition is disarranged — that is to say, the day after its establishment — how avoid making a second? Why not correct it in the same way? And in the meantime, what becomes of security? Where is happiness? Where is industry?

When security and equality are in conflict, it will not do to hesitate a moment. Equality must yield. The first is the foundation of life; subsistence, abundance, happiness, everything depends upon it. Equality produces only a certain portion of good. Besides, whatever we may do, it will never be perfect;

it may exist a day; but the revolutions of the morrow will overturn it. The establishment of perfect equality is a chimera; all we can do is to diminish inequality.

If violent causes, such as a revolution of government, a division, or a conquest, should bring about an overturn of property, it would be a great calamity; but it would be transitory; it would diminish; it would repair itself in time. Industry is a vigorous plant which resists many amputations, and through which a nutritious sap begins to circulate with the first rays of returning summer. But if property should be overturned with the direct intention of establishing an equality of possessions, the evil would be irreparable. No more security, no more industry, no more abundance! Society would return to the savage state whenece it emerged.

If equality ought to prevail to-day it ought to prevail always. Yet it cannot be preserved except by renewing the violence by which it was established. It will need an army of inquisitors and executioners as deaf to favor as to pity; insensible to the seductions of pleasure; inaccessible to personal interest; endowed with all the virtues though in a service which destroys them all. The leveling apparatus ought to go incessantly backward and forward, cutting off all that rises above the line prescribed. A ceaseless vigilance would be necessary to give to those who had dissipated their portion, and to take from those who by labor had augmented theirs. In such an order of things there would be only one wise course for the governed, — that of prodigality; there would be but one foolish course, — that of industry. This pretended remedy, seemingly so pleasant, would be a mortal poison, a burning cautery, which would consume till it destroyed the last fiber of life. The hostile sword in its greatest furies is a thousand times less dreadful. It inflicts but partial evils, which time effaces and industry repairs.

DUGUIT, LES TRANSFORMATIONS GENERALES DU DROIT PRIVE
(Register transl.), in THE PROGRESS OF CONTINENTAL
LAW IN THE 19TH CENTURY* 130-136 (1918)

Property under the Individualistic System.—How have the codes founded on the individualistic principle developed this social instrumentality? Very simply. In the first place, those who drafted the codes were not concerned with inquiring into the legality of property rights then in fact existing, nor with determining on what they were founded. They accepted existing facts and declared them inviolable. Furthermore, being profoundly individualistic, they had in mind only the application of wealth to individual ends, for this is the very fulfillment, the very cornerstone, as it were, of individual autonomy. They did not, and have not since, been able to understand anything but a *protection* thrown about the individualistic use of property. They believed that the only way of protecting such a use was to endow the holder with a subjective right, absolute in duration and in effect. The right attached to the thing appropriated, and the duty corresponding to this right rested on all persons other than the owner of the thing. In a word, they adopted the rigid legal construction of the Roman "dominium."

The declarations of principles which created this system are well known. Article 17 of the "Declaration of the Rights of Man" of 1789 begins: "Property being a sacred and inviolable right," etc. Article 17 of the Argentine Constitution declares that: "property is inviolable . . . ."

Consequences Rejected To-day.—The consequences of the conception of property as a right are well known; it will be well, however, to recall the principal ones.

In the first place, the owner, having the right to use, benefit by, and to dispose of the thing which is the object of his ownership, has, for like reasons, the right *not to use it,* not to derive benefit from, and not to dispose of it, consequently to leave his lands uncultivated, his city lots unimproved, his houses untenanted and unrepaired, his capital consisting of personal property unproductive.

The right of property is *absolute.* It is absolute even as against public authority, which can, indeed, place upon it certain restrictions of a police nature, but cannot lay hands upon it, save after paying a just indemnity. It is absolute in so far as it affects individuals and, in the words of Baudry-Lacantinerie, the owner "may lawfully perform upon the object of his ownership acts even though he have no demonstrable interest in performing them," and if in so doing he injures another party, "he is not liable, because he is but acting with his right."[1]

The right of ownership is also absolute *in duration.* Upon this attribute is based the right of transmitting property by will, because the owner or titleholder of an absolute right has logically the power of disposing of his property both during his life and also for a time after his death.

It is easy to show that as a matter of fact none of these consequences represents the truth; at least in certain countries, notably in France. To be less categorical, I will say that the entire individualistic system of property law is disappearing. This assertion is not unfounded; it is based upon a direct obser-

---

[1] Baudry-Lacantinerie, "Droit civil" (10th ed., 1908,) Vol. I, N° 1296, p. 726. I should, however, add that this statement is not found in the 11th ed. published in collaboration with Cheneaux (1912,) N° 1296, p. 738. But Cheneaux declares that the owner "enjoys the object as he pleases and, if he desires, in an abusive manner." Baudry's collaborators have been far less categorical regarding property as an absolute right. Chauveau, "Des biens," N° 215, writes: "In spite of its absolute character, ownership must still be circumscribed within reasonable limits." Barde, "Des obligations," Vol. IV, N° 2855, p. 342, says: "The truth is that there is no absolute right and that ownership itself is not an absolute right but subject to limitations."

vation of facts, for both in statutory and in case-law there is appearing a body of principles directly opposed to the consequences of the individualistic system. It this not proof that the legal system from which those consequences spring is breaking down and disappearing?

The general causes of this disappearance are again those that we have studied above, which are determining the direction of the general transformation of individualistic institutions.

First, property, as a subjective right, is a purely *metaphysical* conception, in radical opposition to modern positivism. To say that the possessor of capital has a right over it, is equivalent to saying that he has a power, of itself superior to, and prescribable upon, the will of other individuals. The "dominium" of the individual is no more intelligible as a right than the "imperium" of the Government as the seat of force.

Furthermore, the individualistic system of property is breaking down because it tends to protect *individual uses alone,* which are considered as sufficient in themselves. The system reflected perfectly the individualistic conception of the society of the period. It found a perfect medium of expression in Article 2 of the "Declaration of Rights of Man" of 1789: "The aim of every political association is the preservation of the natural and imprescriptible rights of man. These rights are: liberty, property, security, and resistance to oppression." If the application of wealth to private uses was protected, it was solely out of consideration of the individual; it was solely the utility to the individual that was kept in view. To-day there is a very clear sense abroad that the individual is not the end but the means; that the individual is only a wheel of a huge mechanism, the body social; and that his only reason to exist is the part which he performs in the labor of society. The individualistic system is seen, therefore, to be in open opposition to the temper of the modern conscience.

* * *

Every individual is under an obligation to perform a certain function in the community, determined directly by the station which he occupies in it. The possessor of wealth, by reason simply of his possession, is enabled thereby to accomplish a certain work where others can not. He alone can increase the general stock of wealth by putting his capital to use. For social reasons he is under a duty, therefore, to perform this work and society will protect his acts only if he accomplishes it and in the measure in which he accomplishes it. Property is no longer a subjective right of the owner; it is the social function of the possessor of wealth.

* * *

I am anxious to avoid being misunderstood in this matter. I do not say, and I have never said or written, that private ownership as an economic institution is disappearing or should *disappear.* I maintain merely that the *legal notion* upon which protection of property is founded is *being modiffied.* Individual ownership, nevertheless, continues to be protected against all attacks, even those of the State. I will go even further and say that it is more strongly protected under the new than under the old conception.

I accept also as a fact the possession of capitalistic wealth by a limited number of individuals. There is no need to criticise or justify the fact; it would, indeed, be labor lost, for the reason that it is a fact. Nor shall I inquire whether (as certain schools of thought assert) there is an irreconcilable conflict between those who possess wealth and those who do not, between capital and labor, and whether in this conflict capital is to be despoiled and annihilated. I cannot refrain, however, from voicing the opinion that these schools take an altogether erroneous view. The structure of modern society is not so simple. In France, in particular, many persons are both capitalists and laborers. It is a crime to preach the struggle of classes; I believe that we are moving, not toward the destruction of one class by another, but towards a society where there will be a coordination and a hierarchy of classes.

The Obligation to Cultivate Land.—The conception of property as a function, and the idea of society extending its protection to the application of wealth to certain uses, provide a very simple and clear explanation of the laws and decisions which are repugnant to the conception of property as a right.

An objection has been repeatedly raised to this explanation. Opponents have argued: "We understand your view; we even admit that society is moving toward a system of law in which the right of property will rest upon the duty of the owner to fulfill a certain function. But we have not yet reached that state; and the proof is that no statute yet imposes upon an owner the obligation to cultivate his field, repair his house, or utilize his capital. And yet that is the necessary and logical consequence of the conception of property as a function."

The objection does not embarrass me. From the fact that the law does not yet directly force the owner to cultivate his land or repair his houses or utilize his capital, it cannot be concluded that the idea of social function has not yet supplanted the idea of a subjective right of property. Such a law has indeed not made its appearance, because the need for it has not yet been felt. In France, for example, the amount of land left uncultivated by the owner or the number of houses which are unproductive is insignificant in comparison to the total capital in real estate which is being worked. But the fact that the question of such a law has been raised is itself evidence of the transformation that has taken place. Fifty years ago such a question was in no man's mind; to-day, it is everywhere agitated. And if, in a country like France, the time should come when the non-cultivation of the land became a serious problem, no one would then deny, certainly, the justification of intervention by legislation.

TAWNEY, THE ACQUISITIVE SOCIETY* 52-54 (1920)

The application of the principle that society should be organized upon the basis of functions, is not recondite, but simple and direct. It offers in the first place, a standard for discriminating between those types of private property which are legitimate and those which are not. During the last century and a half, political thought has oscillated between two conceptions of property, both of which, in their different ways, are extravagant. On the one hand, the practical foundation of social organization has been the doctrine that the particular forms of private property which exist at any moment are a thing sacred and inviolable, that anything may properly become the object of property rights, and that, when it does, the title to it is absolute and unconditioned. The modern industrial system took shape in an age when this theory of property was triumphant. The American Constitution and the French Declaration of the Rights of Man both treated property as one of the fundamental rights for the protection of which Governments exist.

On the other hand, the attack has been almost as undiscriminating as the defense. "Private property" has been the central position against which the social movement of the last hundred years has directed its forces. The criticism of it has ranged from an imaginative communism in the most elementary and personal of necessaries, to prosaic and partially realized proposals to transfer certain kinds of property from private to public ownership, or to limit their exploitation by restrictions imposed by the State. But, however varying in emphasis and in method, the general note of what may conveniently be called the Socialist criticism of property is what the word Socialism itself implies. Its essence is the statement that the economic evils of society are primarily due to the unregulated operation, under modern conditions of industrial organization, of the institution of private property.

The divergence of opinion is natural, since in most discussions of property the opposing theorists have usually been discussing different things. Property is the most ambiguous of categories. It covers a multitude of rights which have nothing in common except that they are exercised by persons and enforced by the State. Apart from these formal characteristics, they vary indefinitely in economic character, in social effect, and in moral justification. They may be conditional like the grant of patent rights, or absolute like the ownership of ground rents, terminable like copyright, or permanent like a freehold, as comprehensive as sovereignty or as restricted as an easement, as intimate and personal as the ownership of clothes and books, or as remote and intangible as shares in a gold mine or rubber plantation. It is idle, therefore, to present a case for or against private property without specifying the particular forms of property to which reference is made. The journalist who says that "private property is the foundation of civilization" agrees with Proudhon, who

* From THE ACQUISITIVE SOCIETY, by R. H. Tawney, copyright, 1920, by Harcourt, Brace & World, Inc.; renewed, 1948, by R. H. Tawney. Reprinted by permission of the publishers.

said it was theft, in this respect at least that, without further definition, the words of both are meaningless. Arguments which support or demolish certain kinds of property may have no application to others; considerations which are conclusive in one stage of economic organization may be almost irrelevant in the next. The course of wisdom is neither to attack private property in general nor to defend it in general; for things are not similar in quality, merely because they are identical in name. It is to discriminate between the various concrete embodiments of what, in itself, is, after, all, little more than an abstraction.

M. R. COHEN, BOOK REVIEW OF THE RATIONAL BASIS OF LEGAL INSTITUTIONS, 33 YALE L.J. 892 (1924)

Almost all the selections on property — which fill nearly half of the volume — illustrate what philosophers call the fallacy of vicious abstraction. Property is discussed as if it were just one simple thing existing by itself. In view of the fact that almost everyone believes both (1) in some amount of government or limitation on the right of individuals to do as they please, and (2) in some sphere of individual freedom to dispose of things in accordance with our pleasure, the significant question is not whether you are for or against private property, but rather where you will draw the line between public and private things and affairs. May there be private property in human beings (slavery), in public office, in the immoral use of things (intoxicants, etc.)? How far may a state expropriate an industry by entering into competition with it, or how far may it use the power of taxation to discourage undesirable enterprises? Questions of this sort are really more significant as to the meaning of private property than abstract arguments such as the one that private property is a guarantee of the desire for possession. For obviously the institution of private property is also a thwarting of this desire on the part of all who are not legal possessors. Indeed modern ownership of capital really amounts to a right to tax those who wish to use certain tools. This tax may be for the good of all in the long run, but the argument that such a system sets examples of thrift sounds too ironic.

M. R. COHEN, PROPERTY AND SOVEREIGNTY, 13 CORN. L.Q.* 8 (1927)

Anyone who frees himself from the crudest materialism readily recognizes that as a legal term "property" denotes not material things but certain rights. In the world of nature apart from more or less organized society, there are things but clearly no property rights.

Futher reflection shows that a property right is not to be identified with the fact of physical possession. Whatever technical definition of property we may prefer, we must recognize that a property right is a relation not between an owner and a thing, but between the owner and other individuals in reference to things. A right is always against one or more individuals. This becomes unmistakably clear if we take specifically modern forms of property such as franchises, patents, good will, etc., which constitute such a large part of the capitalized assets of our industrial and commercial enterprises.

The classical view of property as a right over things resolves it into component rights such as the *jus utendi, jus disponendi,* etc. But the essence of private property is always the right to exclude others. The law does not guarantee me the physical or social ability of actually using what it calls mine. By public regulations it may indirectly aid me by removing certain general hindrances to the enjoyment of property. But the law of property helps me directly only to exclude others from using the things which it assigns to me. If then somebody else wants to use the food, the house, the land, or the plough that the law calls mine, he has to get my consent. To the extent that these things are necessary to the life of my neighbour, the law thus confers on me a power, limited but real, to make him do what I want. If Laban has the sole disposal of his daughters and his cattle, Jacob must serve him if he desires to possess them. In a regime where land is the principal source of obtaining a livelihood, he who has the legal right over the land receives homage and service from those who wish to live on it.

The character of property as sovereign power compelling service and obedience may be obscured for us in a commercial economy by the fiction of the so-called labour contract as a free bargain and by the frequency with which service is rendered indirectly through a money payment. But not only is there actually little freedom to bargain on the part of the steelworker or miner who needs a job, but in some cases the medieval subject had as much power to bargain when he accepted the sovereignty of his lord. Today I do not directly serve my landlord if I wish to live in the city with a roof over my head, but I must work for others to pay him rent with which he obtains the personal services of others. The money needed for purchasing things must for the vast majority be acquired by hard labour and disagreeable service to those to whom the law has accorded dominion over the things necessary for subsistence.

To a philosopher this is of course not at all an argument against private property. It may well be that compulsion in the economic as well as the political realm is necessary for civilized life. But we must not overlook the actual fact that dominion over things is also *imperium* over our fellow human beings.

The extent of the power over the life of others which the legal order confers on those called owners is not fully appreciated by those who think of the law as merely protecting men in their possession. Property law does more. It determines what men shall acquire. Thus, protecting the property rights of a landlord means giving him the right to collect rent, protecting the property of a railroad or a public-service corporation means giving it the right to make certain charges. Hence the ownership of land and machinery, with the rights of drawing rent, interest, etc., determines the future distribution of the goods that will come into being — determines what share of such goods various individuals shall acquire. The average life of goods that are either consumable or used for production of other goods is very short. Hence a law that merely protected men in their possession and did not also regulate the acquisition of new goods would be of little use.

From this point of view it can readily be seen that when a court rules that a gas company is entitled to a return of 6 percent on its investment, it is not merely protecting property already possessed, it is also determining that a portion of the future social product shall under certain conditions go to that company. Thus not only medieval landlords but the owners of all revenue-producing property are in fact granted by the law certain powers to tax the future social product. When to this power of taxation there is added the power to command the services of large numbers who are not economically independent, we have the essence of what historically has constituted political sovereignty.

* * *

I have already mentioned that the recognition of private property as a form of sovereignty is not itself an argument against it. Some form of government we must always have. For the most part men prefer to obey and let others take the trouble to think out rules, regulations and orders. That is why we are always setting up authorities; and when we cannot find any we write to the newspaper as the final arbiter. But although government is a necessity, not all forms of it are of equal value. At any rate it is necessary to apply to the law of property all those considerations of social ethics and enlightened public policy which ought to be brought to the discussion of any just from of government.

OHIO CONSTITUTION of 1851, Article I, Section 19

Private property shall ever be held inviolate but subservient to the public welfare. . . .

COLORADO CONSTITUTION of 1876, Article II, Section 14

Private property shall not be taken for private use unless by consent of the owner, except for private ways of necessity, and except for reservoirs, drains, flumes or ditches on or across the lands of others, for agricultural, mining, milling, domestic or sanitary purposes.

2 ELY, PROPERTY AND CONTRACT IN THEIR RELATIONS TO THE DISTRIBUTION OF WEALTH * 490-98 (1914)

The chief limitation of eminent domain as it exists in the United States is found in the concept "public" in public purpose; and when obstacles to a sufficiently wide scope of eminent domain are encountered, these may be traced back to a narrow view of public purpose.

Generally expropriation has been confined to real estate, but property in railways, water, dikes, mines, would come under this term in our own and other countries. When we come, however, to the transfer of property during a transition from one economic period to another, we find that expropriation has had a wider range and that rights have been expropriated in one way or another. For example, when we passed over from feudalism to modern industrialism, a great many rights were done away with, either with or without compensation. That was true in regard to serfdom. The old rights of the lords, the serf owners, were abolished in Russia with some compensation. It is generally held that the compensation was not a full one. The same is true with regard to slavery. This shows that in expropriation we have to go beyond real estate in order to accomplish economic purposes. Moreover, we cannot, as Stahl does, limit expropriation to public necessity as distinguished from public utility. What do we mean by necessity, and what do we mean by utility? We have simply different degrees of utility. Perhaps it can scarcely be said that there is any absolute necessity that any right of expropriation should be exercised. We could have lived without railways, but we could not have had them without exercising the right of expropriation. And as we could have lived without railways, how can we say that it was absolutely a case of necessity? We have only varying degrees of utility. . . .

It is time now for a definition of expropriation, and the author quotes Wagner's definition with the statement he makes, and also a statement of Professor von Ihering concerning expropriation. Wagner's definition is, — *"The right of expropriation is the right of the state to seize a specific object of property without the consent of the owner in order to employ it in a manner demanded by the public interest; or to limit the property right of the proprietor in order to place a servitude (easement) upon it; or to take the use of it in the public interest."* His statement in this connection is that "the proper economic and socio-political conception of expropriation regards it as the legal institution by means of which, when free contract fails, changes are compulsorily brought about in the division and ownership of specific pieces of capital and land among the various economic units *(Verteilung der individuellen Kapitalien und Grundstücke)* —, especially between compulsory public economies on the one hand and private economies on the other, and then among these last named with respect to one another, in order that there may be such a division and ownership of land and capital as the development of national life requires."

* * *

Changes are brought about in the division and ownership of property among the various economic units, that is, among various persons. The units in economic society are natural and artificial persons, individuals, cities, etc., and this conception regards expropriation as a legal institution for use especially when it is desirable to bring about changes between compulsory public economies (political units, nations, state, city, etc.), on the one hand and private economies on the other. We must make this distinction, and we must also admit that sometimes it is necessary to exercise this right of eminent domain or expropriation in order to bring about a different distribution among various private persons. That was the case in the abolition of feudalism. There was then a different distribution of the rights of property effected among private units. So we do not have to deal simply with changes between political units on one hand and private units on the other, but with changes among the private units themselves. The purpose is that there may be such a division and ownership of land and capital as is required by the development of national life. The idea is growth, natural evolution, and these changes cannot be brought about in all cases by voluntary methods; consequently compulsion has resulted and is the lesser of two evils. Otherwise we would have the whole suffering for the sake of the few and we cannot consider that to be just. . . .

Expropriation is out of harmony with the absolute idea of property. Expropriation makes the interest of the individual conform to the social interest, to the growth and evolution of the ethical ends of society. It is, to use Wagner's expressive phase, a "postulate of the social coexistence of individuals." We cannot then establish any definite limit, but every age has its own needs of expropriation brought about by changes in the organisation of the national economy and by changes desired in individual productive processes.[15]

---

[15] P. 497. J. B. Clark, "Capital and its Earnings," *Publications of the American Economic Association,* Vol. III, N° 2, p. 67. "Eminent domain, by changing one capital in form, may preserve or increase a hundred others in substance. It is in the interest of value, the fruit of personal sacrifice, that the course is taken. If land, then, is anywhere dangerously monopolized, take it, pay for it, and use it as you will. Expediency here has much to say, but not equity. You will have guarded the essential wealth that, by your invitation and in your interest, has vested itself in this form. The evidence of *a priori* law, and the practical signs of the times, indicate that measures not a few for the diffusion of land ownership are in store for us in future eras. What our government has already done it may do hereafter, though in the face of greater obstalcles. It may divide lands and put owners and cultivators upon them, even though it cannot continue always to present a farm to every man who asks for it. The land reform of the future will curtail great holdings and multiply small ones, while protecting to the uttermost the value that is anywhere invested."

It still holds true that the chief use and requirement of expropriation is in land sales because it is in these chiefly but not exclusively that we need to exercise compulsion. We have already pointed out the needs which arose from the change from feudalism into modern industrialism. The Reformation also had its needs, when there was a change from one religious order to another. When the idea concerning the ownership of property by religious bodies changed we had again need of exproprition. And in the case of the land of the Friars in the Philippines, if the owners had been unwilling to sell for a reasonable compensation, expropriation might have been desirable. The passage from slavery to freedom has frequently involved expropriation, and it is in that way alone that the change can be brought about in such a manner as to secure the greatest gain with the least harm. Otherwise we would have social convulsion as in the United States, and we have not reached the end of the evils of the change without recompense from slavery to freedom.

CLARK v. NASH
198 U. S. 361 (1905)

THIS action was brought by the defendant in error Nash, to condemn a right of way, so called, by enlarging a ditch for the conveying of water across the land of plaintiffs in error, for the purpose of bringing water from Fort Canyon Creek, in the county and State of Utah, which is a stream of water flowing from the mountains near to the land of the defendant in error, and thus to irrigate his land.

The plaintiffs in error demurred to the complaint upon the ground that the same did not state facts sufficient to constitute a cause of action against them. The demurrer was overruled, and the defendants then waived all time in which to answer the complaint and elected to stand on the demurrer. Thereafter there was a default entered against the defendants, and each of them, for failing to answer, and the case was under the practice in Utah then tried and evidence heard on the complaint of the plaintiff, showing the material factors as stated in the complaint. . . .

[The defendants owned land lying between plaintiff's land and some mountains. A stream flowed through the defendants' lands; defendants had dug a ditch for irrigation purposes, which ran to within 100 feet of plaintiff's land. Plaintiff's land was arid, and useless for agriculture without irrigation; with irrigation, it would produce grain, vegetables, fruits and hay. Plaintiff asked permission to widen the ditch on defendants' land, and to extend it to his own for use in irrigation (offering to pay any resulting damages, and to help maintain the ditch); he owned a part of the waters of the creek, so that the only question was his right to construct a ditch on defendants' land. A Utah statute permitted condemnation by an individual for the purpose of ob-

taining water for his land. The plaintiff paid $40.00 into court as damages for
the enlargement and extension of the ditch, and the trial court entered judgment condemning a right of way through the land of the defendants.]

Judgment having been entered upon these findings, the defendants appealed to the Supreme Court of the State, where, after argument, the judgment was affirmed. 27 Utah, 158.

     * * *

MR. JUSTICE PECKHAM, after making the foregoing statement, delivered
the opinion of the court.

The plaintiffs in error contend that the proposed use of the enlarged
ditch across their land for the purpose of conveying water to the land of the
defendant in error alone is not a public use, and that, therefore, the defendant
in error has no constitutional or other right to condemn the land, or any portion of it, belonging to the plaintiffs in error, for that purpose. They argue
that, although the use of water in the State of Utah for the purpose of mining
or irrigation or manufacturing may be a public use where the right to use it
is common to the public, yet that no individual has the right to condemn land
for the purpose of conveying water in ditches across his neighbor's land, for
the purpose of irrigating his own land alone, even where there is, as in this
case, a state statute permitting it.

In some States, probably in most of them, the proposition contended for
by the plaintiffs in error would be sound. But whether a statute of a State permitting condemnation by an individual for the purpose of obtaining water for
his land or for mining should be held to be a condemnation for a public use,
and, therefore, a valid enactment, may depend upon a number of considerations relating to the situation of the State and its possibilities for land cultivation, or the successful prosecution of its mining or other industries. Where the
use is asserted to be public, and the right of the individual to condemn land
for the purpose of exercising such use is founded upon or is the result of some
peculiar condition of the soil or climate, or other peculiarity of the State, where
the right of condemnation is asserted under a state statute, we are always,
where it can fairly be done, strongly inclined to hold with the state courts,
when they uphold a state statute providing for such condemnation. The validity of such statutes may sometimes depend upon many different facts, the existence of which would make a public use, even by an individual, where, in
the absence of such facts, the use would clearly be private. Those facts must
be general, notorious and acknowledged in the State, and the state courts may
be assumed to be exceptionally familiar with them. They are not the subject
of judicial investigation as to their existence, but the local courts know and
appreciate them. They understand the situation which led to the demand for
the enactment of the statute, and they also appreciate the results upon the
growth and prosperity of the State, which in all probability would flow from
a denial of its validity. These are matters which might properly be held to
have a material bearing upon the question whether the individual use pro-

posed might not in fact be a public one. It is not alone the fact that the land is arid and that it will bear crops if irrigated, or that the water is necessary for the purpose of working a mine, that is material; other facts might exist which are also material, such as the particular manner in which the irrigation is carried on or proposed, or how the mining is to be done in a particular place where water is needed for that purpose. The general situation and amount of the arid land, or of the mines themselves, might also be material, and what proportion of the water each owner should be entitled to; also the extent of the population living in the surrounding country, and whether each owner of land or mines could be, in fact, furnished with the necessary water in any other way than by the condemnation in his own behalf, and not by a company, for his use and that of others.

These, and many other facts not necessary to be set forth in detail, but which can easily be imagined, might reasonably be regarded as material upon the question of public use, and whether the use by an individual could be so regarded. With all of these the local courts must be presumed to be more or less familiar. This court has stated that what is a public use may frequently and largely depend upon the facts surrounding the subject, and we have said that the people of a State, as also its courts, must in the nature of things be more familiar with such facts and with the necessity and occasion for the irrigation of the lands, than can any one be who is a stranger to the soil of the State, and that such knowledge and familiarity must have their due weight with the state courts. *Fallbrook Irrigation District v. Bradley,* 164 U.S. 112, 159. It is true that in the *Fallbrook case* the question was whether the use of the water was a public use when a corporation sought to take land by condemnation under a state statute, for the purpose of making reservoirs and digging ditches to supply land owners with the water the company proposed to obtain and save for such purpose. This court held that such use was public. The case did not directly involve the right of a single individual to condemn land under a statute providing for that condemnation.

We are, however, as we have said, disposed to agree with the Utah court with regard to the validity of the state statute, which provides, under the circumstances stated in the act for the condemnation of the land of one individual for the purpose of allowing another individual to obtain water from a stream in which he has an interest, to irrigate his land, which otherwise would remain absolutely valueless.

But we do not desire to be understood by this decision as approving of the broad proposition that private property may be taken in all cases where the taking may promote the public interest and tend to develop the natural resources of the State. We simply say that in this particular case, and upon the facts stated in the findings of the court, and having reference to the conditions already stated, we are of opinion that the use is a public one, although the taking of the right of way is for the purpose simply of thereby obtaining the water for an individual, where it is absolutely necessary to enable him to make any use whatever of his land, and which will be valuable and fertile only if water can be obtained. Other land owners adjoining the defendant in error, if any there are, might share in the use of the water by themselves taking the same proceedings to obtain it, and we do not think it necessary, in order to hold the use to be a public one, that all should join in the same proceeding or that a company should be formed to obtain the water which the individual land owner might then obtain his portion of from the company by paying the agreed price, or the price fixed by law.

The rights of a riparian owner in and to the use of the water flowing by his land are not the same in the arid and mountainous States of the West that they are in the States of the East. These rights have been altered by many of the Western States, by their constitutions and laws, because of the totally different circumstances in which their inhabitants are placed, from those that exist in the States of the East, and such alterations have been made for the very purpose of thereby contributing to the growth and prosperity of those States arising from mining and the cultivation of an otherwise valueless soil, by means of irrigation. This court must recognize the difference of climate and soil, which render necessary these different laws in the States so situated.

We are of opinion, having reference to the above peculiarities which exist in the State of Utah, that the statute permitting the defendant in error, upon the facts appearing in this record, to enlarge the ditch and obtain water for his own land, was within the legislative power of the State, and the judgment of the state court affirming the validity of the statute is therefore

Affirmed.

MR. JUSTICE HARLAN and MR. JUSTICE BREWER dissented.

STRICKLEY v. HIGHLAND BOY GOLD MINING CO.
200 U.S. 527 (1906)

MR. JUSTICE HOLMES delivered the opinion of the court.

This is a proceeding begun by the defendant in error, a mining corporation, to condemn a right of way for an aerial bucket line across a placer mining claim of the plaintiffs in error. The mining corporation owns mines high up in Bingham Canyon, in West Mountain Mining District, Salt Lake County, Utah, and is using the line or way to carry ores, etc., for itself and others from the mines, in suspended buckets, down to the railway station, two miles distant and twelve hundred feet below. Before building the way it made diligent inquiry but could not discover the owner of the placer claim in question, Strickley standing by without objecting or making known his rights while the company put up its structure. The trial court found the facts and made an order of condemnation. This order recites that the mining company has paid into court the value of the right of way, as found, and costs, describes the right of way by metes and bounds and specifies that the same is to be used for the erection of certain towers to support the cables of the line, with a right to drive along the way when necessary for repairs, the mining company to move the towers as often as reasonably required by the owners of the claim for using and working the said claim. The foregoing final order was affirmed by the Supreme Court of the State. 78 Pac. Rep. 296. The case then was brought here.

The plaintiffs in error set up in their answer to the condemnation proceedings that the right of way demanded is solely for private use, and that the taking of their land for that purpose is contrary to the Fourteenth Amendment of the Constitution of the United States. The mining company on the other hand relies upon the statutes of Utah, which provide that "the right of eminent domain may be exercised in behalf of the following public uses: ... (6) Roads, railroads, tramways, tunnels, ditches, flumes, pipes and dumping places to facilitate the milling, smelting or other reduction of ores, or the working of mines." In view of the decision of the state court we assume that the condemnation was authorized by the state laws, subject only to the question whether those laws as construed are consistent with the Fourteenth Amendment. Some objections to this view were mentioned, but they are not open. If the statutes are constitutional as construed, we follow the construction of the state court. On the other hand there is no ground for the suggestion that the claim by the plaintiffs in error of their rights under the Fourteenth Amendment does not appear sufficiently on the record. The suggestion was not pressed.

The single question, then, is the constitutionality of the Utah statute, and the particular facts of the case are material only as showing the length to which the statute is held to go. There is nothing to add with regard to them, unless it be the finding that the taking of the strip across the placer claim is necessary for the aerial line and is consistent with the use of all of the claim by the plaintiffs in error for mining, except to the extent of the temporary interference over a limited space by four towers, each about seven and a half feet square and removable as stated above.

The question thus narrowed is pretty nearly answered by the recent decision in *Clark v. Nash,* 198 U.S. 361. That case established the constitutionality of the Utah statute, so far as it permitted the condemnation of land for the irrigation of other land belonging to a private person, in pursuance of the declared policy of the State. In discussing what constitutes a public use it recognized the inadequacy of use by the general public as a universal test. While emphasizing the great caution necessary to be shown, it proved that there might be exceptional times and places in which the very foundations of public welfare could not be laid without requiring concessions from individuals to each other upon due compensation which under other circumstances would be left wholly to voluntary consent. In such unusual cases there is nothing in the Fourteenth Amendment which prevents a State from requiring such concessions. If the state constitution restricts the legislature within narrower bounds that is a local affair, and must be left where the state court leaves it in a case like the one at bar.

In the opinion of the legislature and the Supreme Court of Utah the public welfare of that State demands that aerial lines between the mines upon its mountain sides and the railways in the valleys below should not be made impossible by the refusal of a private owner to sell the right to cross his land. The Constitution of the United States does not require us to say that they are wrong. If, as seems to be assumed in the brief for the defendant in error, the finding that the plaintiff is a carrier for itself and others means that the line is dedicated to carrying for whatever portion of the public may desire to use it, the foundation of the argument on the other side disappears.

Judgment affirmed.

STATE v. CLAUSEN
Supreme Court of Washington
110 Wash. 525, 188 Pac. 538 (1920)

PARKER, J.   This is an original mandamus proceeding in this court, wherein the relators seek a writ of mandate to compel the state auditor to issue a warrant against the state reclamation revolving fund to the relator George J. Hurley, in payment for 160 acres of land purchased from him by the state reclamation board under the land settlemement act, Laws of 1919 c. 188, p. 583. The auditor has refused to issue the warrant as demanded of him, basing his refusal upon the sole ground that the land settlement act is unconstitutional.

[The Act provided for the colonization of "undeveloped" land. The state reclamation board was to purchase land from willing sellers; to subdivide the land purchased, setting aside land for roads and other public purposes; and to sell or lease the subdivided tracts to prospective settlers — notably war veterans and industrial workers "desiring a rural life," who did not hold other agricultural land of substantial value. To finance the board's purchases, money was appropriated from a fund which had been raised by the state's general property tax.]

   . . . In view of [a severability provision], we need only concern ourselves in this case with the question of the constitutionality of the act in so far as it authorizes the expenditure of public funds raised by taxation in the purchase by the reclamation board of land to be subdivided, improved, and disposed of as provided by the terms of the act, since we do not understand the contention here made in support of the auditor's refusal to issue the warrant as demanded of him, to be rested upon any other grounds of unconstitutionality than that the act, in so far as it authorizes the expenditure of public funds raised by taxation, is in excess of legislative constitutional power; in that it is, in effect, an exercise of the power to tax and to expend public funds so raised, for a purpose not public, but private — that is, for a purpose not governmental in the sense that such purpose is not a legitimate function of government.

We must, of course, proceed with our inquiry, having in view the elementary principle that a tax can be lawfully levied, and the public funds so raised lawfully expended, only for a public purpose. . . .

* * *

Our problem, then, is reduced to this: Is the raising of funds by taxation and the expenditure thereof for the purchase of land to the end that it be subdivided, improved, and disposed of as by the terms of this act provided, the exercise of the power of taxation and the expenditure of public funds, for a public purpose? It may well be doubted that there has ever come to the American courts any more vexatious question than that of determining whether or not a particular purpose for which public funds were sought to be raised by taxation and expended is a public purpose, when the particular purpose in question lay within that twilight zone wherein the minds may reasonably differ as to such purpose being a public one; the bounds of which zone are ever changing with the passing of time, and within which new problems of public welfare always first appear. That such a question when arising in the courts has proven so vexatious is, we apprehend, because of its inherent nature; in that, in its last analysis it is not one of exclusive legal logic, but is one more or less of policy and wisdom, properly determinable in the light of public welfare, present and future, in a broad sense, and hence is not a pure judicial law question, except in those cases clearly outside of the twilight zone we have alluded to.

Some 50 years ago it became a much debated question in this country as to whether or not the levying of a tax and the expenditure of public funds raised thereby for the purpose of construction or to aid in the construction of a railroad in a state or a community of the people so taxed was the exercise of the taxing power and the expenditure of public money for a public purpose. Different state courts, the judges of which were counted of eminent legal learning, even in a time of great judges and great lawyers, entertained opposing views upon this question. Touching the real nature of the question, and recognizing that it lies very close to that line of uncertain location dividing judicial from legislative functions, in a decision holding that such purpose was public or rather that the court could not say that it was not public when the Legislature authorizing the levy of the tax for the purposes had, in effect, determined that it was public, Justice Ladd, speaking for the New Hampshire court, in Perry v. Keene, 56 N.H. 514, 531, said:

"Where is the line that divides the province of the court from that of the Legislature in a matter of this sort? The court is to expound and administer the laws, and there the judicial function and duty ends. How much of the question, whether a given object is public, lies within the province of the law,

and how much in the domain of political science and statesmanship? When
the judge has declared all the law that enters into the problem how much is
still left to the determination of the legislator? Admitting, as has indeed been
more than intimated in this state (Concord Railroad v. Greeley, 17 N.H. 57),
that it is for the court finally to determine whether the use is public, what is
the criterion? What are the rules which the law furnishes to the court wherewith to elucidate a true answer to the inquiry? In what respect does the question as presented to the court differ from the same question as presented to the
Legislature? If the court stop when they reach the borders of legislative
ground, how far can they proceed?

"If the Legislature should take the property of A., or the property of all
taxpayers in the town of A., and hand it over, without consideration, without
pretense of any public obligation or duty, to B., to be used by him in buying
a farm, or building a house, or setting himself up in business, the case would
be so clear that the common sense of every one would at once say the limits
of legislative power had been overstepped by a taking of private property, and
devoting it to a private use. That is the broad ground upon which such cases
as Allen v. Jay, 60 Me. 124 [11 Am. Rep. 185], Lowell v. Boston, 111 Mass.
454 [15 Am. Rep. 39], and Citizens' Loan Association v. Topeka, Sup. Ct.
U.S., not yet reported [20 Wall. 655, 22 L. Ed. 455], were decided. And yet,
what rule of law do the courts find to aid them in thus revising the judgment
of the Legislature? Is it not clear that the question they pass upon is the same
question as that decided by the Legislature, and that they must determine it in
the same way the Legislature have done, simply by the exercise of reason and
judgment? What is it that settles the character of a given purpose, in respect
of its being public or otherwise? It has been said that for the Legislature to
declare a use public does not make it so (17 N.H. 57); and the same may
certainly be said with equal truth of a like declaration by the court. A judicial
christening can no more affect the nature of the thing itself, than a legislative
christening. Judging a priori, and without some knowledge of the wants of
mankind when organized in communities and states, I do not quite understand
how it could be predicated of any use, that it is 'per se' public, as is said by
Dixon, C. J., in Whiting v. Sheboygan Railway Co., 9 Am. Law Reg. (N.S.)
161. Of light, air, water, etc., the common bounties of providence, it might,
indeed be said beforehand that they are in a very broad sense public; but it is
not of such uses that we are speaking. Without knowledge of human nature,
knowledge derived from experience and observation of what may be needful
for the comfort, well-being, and prosperity of the people of a state advanced
in civilization — and knowledge, gained in the same way, as to what necessary
conditions of their welfare will be supplied by private enterprise, and what
will go unsupplied without interference by the state — I do not see how any
use could be said to be per se public, or how either a Legislature, or a court,
could form a judgment that would not be founded almost wholly upon theory
and conjecture. No one doubts that the building and maintaining of our com-

mon highways is a public purpose. Why? Certainly for no other reason than that they furnish facilities for travel, the transmission of intelligence, and the transportation of goods.

"But why should the state take this matter under its fostering care, imposing upon the people a very great yearly burden in the shape of taxes for their support, any more than many others that might be mentioned, of equal and perhaps greater importance to its citizens? Is it of greater concern to the citizen that he should have a road to travel on, when he desires to visit his neighbor in the next town, or transport the products of his farm or of his factory to market and bring back the commodities for which they may be exchanged, than that he should have a mill to grind his corn — a tanner, a shoemaker, and a tailor to manufacture his raw material into clothing, wherewith his body may be covered? Doubtless highways are a great public benefit. Without them I suppose the whole state would soon return to its primal condition of a howling wilderness, fit only for the habitation of wild beasts and savages. How would it be if there were no mills for the manufacture of lumber, no joiners or masons to build houses, no manufacturers of cloth, no merchants or tradesmen to assist in the exchange of commodities? These suppositions may appear somewhat fanciful, but they illustrate the inquiry: Why is the building of roads to be regarded as a public service, while many other things equally necessary for the upholding of life, the security of property, the preservation of learning, morality, and religion, are by common consent regarded as private, and so left to the private enterprise of the citizens? The answer to this question, surely, is not to be found in any abstract principle of law. It is essentially a conclusion of fact and public policy, the result of an inquiry into the individual necessities of every member of the community (which in the aggregate show the character and urgency of the public need), and the likelihood that those necessities will be supplied without interference from the state. Obviously it bears a much closer resemblance to the deduction of a political, than the application of a legal principle by a judge. * * *

"Enough has been said to show the delicate nature of the task imposed upon the court when they are called upon to revise the judgment of the Legislature in a matter of this description. It is especially delicate for two reasons: First, because the discretion of the Legislature, with respect to the whole subject of levying taxes, is so very large, and their power so exclusive, that it is not always easy to say when the limits of that discretion and power have been passed; and, second, because the rule to be applied is furnished, not so much by the law, as by those general considerations of public policy and political economy to which allusion has been made. I do not deny the power and duty of the court, when private rights of property are in question, to settle those rights according to a just interpretation of the Constitution; and the discharge of that duty may involve a revision of the judgment of the Legislature upon a question which, like this, partakes more or less of a political character. But before the court can reverse the judgment of the Legislature and the executive, and declare a statute levying or authorizing a tax to be inoperative and void, a very clear case must be shown.

"After the Legislature and the executive have both decided that the purpose for which a tax is laid is public, nothing short of a moral certainty that a mistake has been made can, in my judgment, warrant the court in overruling that decision, especially when nothing better can be set up in its place than the naked opinion of the court as to the character of the use proposed."

* * *

We feel certain that these considerations, general as they are, lead irresistibly to the conclusion that the question of public purpose involved in this case, because of its inherent nature, because of the opportunity for difference of opinion as to whether or not the purpose is public in the sense of it being a legitimate function of government, and because of the question of public policy necessarily involved in it, is one which we are not permitted to render a different decision upon than that rendered by the Legislature. Is there not abundant room for arguing that the development of our unoccupied lands suitable for agriculture, by a land policy which would encourage the settlement thereon of home owning farmers, will materially contribute to the welfare of our people as a whole? Can it not be argued with a fair show of reason that, not only will such a policy ultimately lead to the enhancement of the material wealth of the state, but that it will also make for better citizenship, better notions of necessity for law and order, and a sounder and saner patriotism? In the light of the debatable character of these questions, we are quite convinced that it is not within the province of the judicial branch of our state government to answer them in the negative. . . .

* * *

The contention that the law violates the fourteenth amendment of the federal Constitution, we think, is answered by what we have already said. We must concede that the question of whether or not the tax is levied for a public use is a federal as well as a state question. To take property by taxation for other than a public purpose is as much a violation of the due process of law guaranty of the fourteenth amendment to the federal Constitution as of any similar provision of the state Constitution. This is made plain by the decision of the Supreme Court of the United States in Olcott v. Fond du Lac, 83 U.S. (16 Wall.) 678.

We are quite convinced that we are not privileged to now decide that this tax and the expenditure of public funds raised thereby is for other than a public purpose, the Legislature having decided that it is for a public purpose, which decision not being manifestly wrong [sic]. The writ will issue as prayed for.

TOLMAN, BRIDGES, MITCHELL, MAIN, and FULLERTON, JJ., concur.

MACKINTOSH, J. As I gather the gist of my Brother PARKER'S opinion, it is that the court will not declare unconstitutional an act which calls for the collection of taxes to be used in the purchase and improvement of lands to be sold to private individuals, for the reason that the Legislature has decided that such taxation is for a public purpose. Courts have found this an easy way to justify the laying of taxes to be utilized in ways that appeal to them as beneficial or agreeable to their ideas of proper commercial or economic development. The purpose of the act may be highly commendable and, did it not call for the payment from the pockets of the taxpayer of money in the possession of which he is supposed to be protected by constitutional limitation, as a land development plan, it would merit the approval of those interested; but to call it a "public purpose" is to stretch to the breaking point all fundamental ideas of what is meant by that term.

In Lowell v. Boston, 111 Mass. 454, 15 Am. Rep. 39, an act was declared unconstitutional which authorized Boston to bond itself for $20,000,000, to be loaned to the owners of land, the buildings upon which had been destroyed by fire, for the purpose of rebuilding the city. Repayment was secured by mortgages. The court said:

"The power of the government, thus constituted, to affect the individual in his private rights of property, whether by enacting contributions to the general means, or by sequestration of specific property, is confined, by obvious implication as well as by express terms, to purposes and objects alone which the government was established to promote, to wit, public uses and the public service. This power, when exercised in one form, is taxation; in the other, is designated as the right of eminent domain. The two are diverse in respect of the occasion and mode of exercise, but identical in their source, to wit, the necessities of organized society; and in the end by which alone the exercise of either can be justified, to wit, some public service or use. It is due to their identity in these respects that the two powers, otherwise so unlike, are associated together in the same article. So far as it concerns the question what constitutes public use or service that will justify the exercise of these sovereign powers over private rights of property, which is the main question now to be solved, this identity renders it unnecessary to distinguish between the two forms of exercise, as the same tests must apply to and control in each. An appropriation of money raised by taxation, or of property taken by right of eminent domain, by way of gift to an individual for his own private uses exclusively, would clearly be an excess of legislative power."

In another portion of the same opinion it is said:

"The power to levy taxes is founded on the right, duty, and responsibility to maintain and administer all the governmental functions of the state, and to provide for the public welfare. To justify any exercise of the power requires that the expenditure which it is intended to meet shall be for some public service or some object which concerns the public welfare. The promotion of the interests of individuals, either in respect of property or business, although it may result incidentally in the advancement of the public welfare, is, in its essential character, a private and not a public object. However certain and great the resulting good to the general public, it does not, by reason of its comparative importance, cease to be incidental. The incidental advantage to the public, or to the state, which results from the promotion of private interests, and the prosperity of private enterprises or business, does not justify their aid by the use of public money raised by taxation, or for which taxation may become necessary. It is the essential character of the direct object of the expenditure which must determine its validity, as justifying a tax, and not the magnitude of the interests to be affected, nor the degree to which the general advantage of the community, and thus the public welfare, may be ultimately benefited by their promotion. The principle of this distinction is fundamental. It underlies all government that is based upon reason rather than upon force. It is expressed in various forms in the Constitution of Massachusetts."

* * *

It is needless to prolong a discussion already too ambagious. On principle and under the authorities I cannot agree that a public purpose is being served by this attractive bit of paternalistic legislation, and therefore dissent.

MOUNT, J., concurs in the dissent.

HOLCOMB, C.J. (concurring). The purpose of the reclamation act, as set forth therein, is the settlement of undeveloped lands. The settlement and development of unimproved lands for agricultural purposes is certainly a public benefit. It means a direct increase in production of foodstuffs and an indirect increase in industry within the state. That the state generally will receive a benefit, it seems to me, there can be little doubt.

The fact that benefits will inure to certain classes of citizens within the state does not lessen the public benefit that will result from the operation of the statute. The benefit received by a class of citizens does not destroy the primary purpose the Legislature had in enacting the statute to increase the agricultural products of the state and make productive lands heretofore unproductive.

Distinction can be made between the present case and Lowell v. Boston, 111 Mass. 454, 15 Am. Rep. 39, quoted from in the dissenting opinion filed herein. There the purpose of the statute was to raise funds to be loaned to owners of land, the buildings upon which had been destroyed. The purpose in that case was to rebuild a devastated portion of a city. It was peculiarly a private benefit, although to a large number of inhabitants. It is not difficult to understand that the benefits to be derived from the expenditure of money in that case could hardly be conceived as belonging to the public generally.

While there might be a remote public benefit, there hardly could be such a direct and general one as under the statute here in question.

For the above reasons, I concur with the majority.

In 1900, Congress enacted a joint resolution forbidding any corporation to own or control more than 500 acres of land in Puerto Rico. No sanction was specified, and many instances were recorded of corporate land ownership on the Island in excess of 500 acres. In 1935, the Puerto Rico territorial legislature authorized the Attorney General of Puerto Rico to bring a *quo warranto* proceeding in the territorial Supreme Court, to require any corporation owning excess land to divest itself of such land. In *Puerto Rico v. Rubert Hermanos, Inc.*, 309 U.S. 543 (1940), the United States Supreme Court upheld the application of the 1935 territorial legislation to the defendant company, rejecting the defense that the Congress had "occupied the field," pre-empting the territorial legislature.

For a discussion of the political context of efforts to enforce the 500-acre law, see MATHEWS, PUERTO RICAN POLITICS AND THE NEW DEAL (1960). See also Rosenn, *Puerto Rican Land Reform: The History of an Instructive Experiment*, 73 YALE L.J. 334 (1963).

PEOPLE OF PUERTO RICO v. EASTERN SUGAR ASSOCIATES
United States Circuit Court of Appeals, First Circuit
156 F.2d 316, cert. denied,
329 U.S. 772 (1946)

Before MAGRUDER, MAHONEY, and WOODBURY, Circuit Judges.

WOODBURY, Circuit Judge.

This appeal is from an order of the District Court of the United States for Puerto Rico dismissing a petition to condemn approximately 3,100 acres of land situated on the Island of Vieques owned by the appellee, Eastern Sugar Associates, subject to a mortgage held by the appellee, National City Bank of New York, on the ground that the petition fails "to state a public use or purpose for which private property may be acquired by eminent domain."

By Act N° 26 approved April 12, 1941, (Laws of Puerto Rico 1941, p. 388 et seq.) called the "Land Law of Puerto Rico," the insular Legislature launched a far-reaching program of agrarian reform. This law is long and rather complicated. At the moment it will suffice to say that after a lengthy "Statement of Motives" the Act creates a board in the "nature of a governmental agency or instrumentality of the People of Puerto Rico" in the Department of Agriculture and Commerce, to be called the "Land Authority of Puerto Rico," "for the purpose of carrying out the agricultural policy of The People of Puerto Rico as determined by this Act, and to take the necessary action to put an end to the existing corporative latifundia in this Island, block its reappearance in the future, insure to individuals the conservation of their land, assist in the creation of new landowners, facilitate the utilization of land for the best public benefit under efficient and economic production plans; provide the means for the agregados[1] and slum dwellers to acquire parcels of land on which to build their homes, and to take all action leading to the most scientific, economic and efficient enjoyment of land by the people of Puerto Rico." The the Act goes on to make detailed provisions with respect to the organization, powers, and duties of the Land Authority, and to authorize it both to expropriate lands held in violation of the so called 500 acre provision of the Organic Act (39 Stat. 964, 48 U.S.C.A. § 752) and also to request the Insular Government to acquire on its behalf by eminent domain "title to any real property or estate thereon (sic) which might be necessary or advisable for the purposes of the Authority." The act fully establishes the procedure to be followed in condemnation proceedings and provides, apparently adequately, for payment of "just compensation" for property so taken.

As this Land Law stood, after amendment, at the time the present condemnation proceedings were instituted, the Land Authority was authorized to dispose of lands which it acquired for three purposes: (1) in small parcels to individual agregados for the erection of their dwellings, (2) in somewhat larger parcels to individual farmers for subsistence farms, and (3) in large parcels by lease to expert farmers, agronomists, or other qualified persons with experience in agricultural management, for the operation of "proportional-profit" farms as described in detail in §§ 64-73 of the Act.

Following enactment of the Land Law, the Insular Legislature by Act N° 90, approved May 11, 1944, popularly called the "Vieques Act," made specific provisions for the relief of economic distress which it said existed on the small outlying islands of Vieques and Culebra, both municipalities of Puerto Rico. In its "Statement of Motives" this statute refers to the condemnation of some 20,000 acres of land on Vieques by the United States for Naval purposes (see Baetjer et al. v. United States, 1 Cir., 143 F.2d 391), which it said paralyzed the sugar industry on that island and caused acute economic distress to its inhabitants which could only be relieved by a renewal of that industry there, and the establishment thereon of a distillery, and then it provides:

"Section 1.—The Land Authority is directed and empowered to acquire, through purchase or condemnation proceedings, or in any other form or by

---

[1] An agregado, frequently referred to in Puerto Rico as a "squatter," is defined in § 78 of the Act as "any family head residing in the rural zone, whose home is erected on lands belonging to another person or to a private or public entity, and whose only means of livelihood is his labor for a wage."

any other means compatible with the laws of Puerto Rico, the lands belonging to the Eastern Sugar Associates in the Island of Vieques, as well as any other lands in the Island of Vieques, Puerto Rico, that may be necessary, in the judgment of the Land Authority of Puerto Rico, to carry out the provisions of this Act.

"Section 2.—As soon as the Land Authority acquires these lands from the Eastern Sugar Associates, it shall establish the consequent organization of the same and shall devote them principally to the planting of sugar cane and of any other products that may be necessary to develop in Vieques the sugar industry and the liquor industry."

With this brief outline of the most pertinent statutory provisions, we turn to the proceedings in the case at bar.

In accordance with the provisions of Act N⁰ 26 of 1941, (The Land Law) the Governor of Puerto Rico on March 20, 1945, "representing The People of Puerto Rico, in the name and on order of the Land Authority," filed a petition in the District Court of the Judicial District of Humacao (an Insular Court) for the condemnation of the lands on the Island of Vieques here in litigation. In this petition it is alleged:

"3. The Land Authority desires to condemn the said lands to carry out all of the objects or purposes of the Land Law of Puerto Rico in force, that is to say:

"(a) Distribution and transfer of lands to an number of "squatters' ('agregados') at the rate of one parcel of not less than one fourth of a cuerda[2] nor more than three cuerdas per family, in which said 'squatters' may erect their dwellings, in harmony with the provisions of Title Fifth of the said Land Law.

"(b) Distribution and operation of lands in individual farms whose area shall fluctuate between five (5) and twenty-five (25) cuerdas, in harmony with the provisions of Title 25 and following of the said Land Law.

"(c) Establishment of farms of proportional benefit whose area shall fluctuate between one hundred (100) and five hundred (500) acres to be dedicated principally to the planting and cultivation of sugar cane in harmony with the provisions of Title Fifth of the said Land Law and Law numbered 90 approved May 11, 1944."

Then the petition goes on to characterize the above purposes as "of public utility" and to aver that the acquisition of the property "is also a public necessity"; that $270,326.33 "is the just and reasonable compensation which the plaintiff should pay for the acquisition of the said properties, with all their plantations, improvements, uses, servitudes and appurtenances, as well as the buildings thereon and that the above sum has been deposited in the office of the Secretary of the Court for the use of the persons entitled thereto.

---

[2] A cuerda is .9712 of an acre.

[The petition for condemnation was granted by the insular District Court, whereupon Eastern Sugar Associates successfully sought to remove the case to the United States District Court for Puerto Rico. After removal, Eastern Sugar Associates moved to dismiss, principally on the ground that, in the words of Judge Woodbury, "the taking was not for a public use and purpose and thus violated rights guaranteed by the Fifth and Fourteenth Amendments to the Constitution of the United States and § 2 of the Organic Act of Puerto Rico, ..." The U.S. District Court dismissed the petition for condemnation, setting aside the order of the insular District Court].

* * *

. . . The basic question presented is whether on the pleadings it can be said that the appellees' land is sought to be taken for a public use. And this requires consideration of the nature as public or private of four possible uses to which the land here involved may, if acquired, be put, to wit, the three specific uses enumerated in the Land Law and in addition the more general use permitted by the Vieques Act. . . . [If] any one of those uses, each considered, however, as part of a broad, integrated program of agrarian reform as will be pointed out hereafter, is not public, the petition was properly dismissed.

* * *

But the power of the Insular Legislature in the respect is not unlimited. In § 2 of the Organic Act, as already appears, Congress saw fit to allow the Insular Government to take or damage private property only for public use, and then only upon payment of just compensation, and furthermore in the same section it provided that "no law shall be enacted in Porto Rico which shall deprive any person of life, liberty, or property without due process of law." . . .

* * *

. . . It is therefore clear that the ultimate test imposed by § 2 of the Organic Act, as well as by the Fourteenth Amendment, is a due process test and thus it is immaterial whether the limiting criteria are stated in terms of "due process of law" or in terms of "public use." In sum, the limitations imposed upon the Insular Government by § 2 of the Puerto Rican Organic Act are substantially the same as the limitations imposed upon the state governments by the Fourteenth Amendment, and therefore, as the powers held by the Insular Government are analogous to the powers held by the governments of the individual states, the Insular Government's power of eminent domain is entitled to the same scope that has been given to the power of eminent domain possessed by the state governments.

This brings us to the concrete question of the nature of the uses to which the Insular Government proposes to put the appellees' lands. But at the threshold of our consideration of this question, we come face to face with the question upon which the Supreme Court was apparently divided in United States ex rel. Tennessee Valley Authority v. Welch et al., 66 S. Ct. 715, that is, the question whether a legislative decision that a taking is for a public use is subject to judicial review. However, we do not feel that we have to attempt to answer this question, because even if it is one within our competence, we think the taking here attempted does not violate "due process."

The four contemplated uses for the land enumerated above are closely inter-related. Each use plays a part in a comprehensive program of social and economic reform. Thus we see no basis for analyzing each proposed use separately. Instead we think the entire legislation should be regarded "as a single integrated effort," United States ex rel. Tennessee Valley Authority v. Welch, 66 S. Ct. 718, to improve conditions on the island, and so viewed we think enactment of the statutes within the power of the Insular Legislature.

   *   *   *

The argument is made that due process is denied because the purpose for taking the appellees' land is only to sell or lease it to others for them to use personally instead of for use by the general public. This argument has been advanced several times in the Supreme Court of the United States in cases of this sort and every time it has been rejected. In Fallbrook Irrigation District v. Bradley, 164 U.S. 112, 162, 17 S. Ct. 56, 64, 41 L. Ed. 369, decided in 1896, the Supreme Court considered the argument fully and in the light of that consideration announced that "It is not necessary, in order that the use should be public, that every resident in the district should have the right to the use of the water." It was considered, and rejected again in Clark v. Nash, 1905, 198 U.S. 361, 367, 25 S. Ct. 676, 49 L. Ed. 1085, 4 Ann. Cas. 1171 et seq., and in Strickley v. Highland Boy Mining Co., 1906, 200 U.S. 527, 531, 26 S. Ct. 301, 50 L. Ed. 581, 4 Ann. Cas. 1174; and in 1916 in Mt. Vernon Cotton Co. v. Alabama Power Co., 240 U.S. 30, 32, 36 S. Ct. 234, 236, 60 L. Ed. 507, Mr. Justice Holmes speaking for a unanimous court said: "The inadequacy of use by the general public as a universal test is established." Then later in 1923 in Rindge Co. v. Los Angeles, supra, page 707 of 262 U.S., 43 S. Ct. 692, 67 L. Ed. 1186, the Supreme Court said: "It is not essential that the entire community, nor even any considerable portion, should directly enjoy or participate in any improvement in order to constitute a public use."

It does not follow from this, however, that a taking of property from one, for the purpose of transferring it to another, without anything more, conforms to due process of law. Some public benefit or advantage must accrue from the transfer and mere financial gain to the taker is not enough, since the Supreme Court has intimated that the power of eminent domain cannot be used by the taking authority in aid of "an outside land speculation." Brown v. United States, 263 U.S. 78, 84, 44 S. Ct. 92, 94, 68 L. Ed. 171. But the local Legislatures nevertheless have wide scope in deciding what takings are for a public use. This is definitely established by the cases arising under the Fourteenth Amendment already cited and by many more. In the first place a state's power of eminent domain does not necessarily have to be rested upon the ground that the taking is considered necessary for the public health, but may be exercised if the taking "be essential or material for the prosperity of the community." Fallbrook Irrigation District case, 164 U.S. page 163, 17 S. Ct. 65, 41 L. Ed. 369. And in the second place a local Legislature, because of its intimate knowledge of local conditions, has great latitude in determining what uses of land are conducive to community prosperity. The wide scope allowed a state Legislature in this respect is emphasized in Clark v. Nash, supra, and in Cincinnati v. Vester, 281 U.S. 439, 446, 50 S. Ct. 360, 362, 74 L. Ed. 950, decided in 1930, the Supreme Court, citing many cases, said that although the question of what is a public use is a judicial one "In deciding such a question, the Court has appropriate regard to the diversity of local conditions and considers with great respect legislative declarations and in particular the judgments of state courts as to the uses considered to be public in the light of local exigencies." In fact, in Old Dominion Co. v. United States, 269 U.S. 55, 66, 46 S. Ct. 39, 40, 70 L. Ed. 162, cited with approval in United States, ex rel. Tennessee Valley Authority v. Welch, supra, the Supreme Court said that a legislative decision that a given use is public "is entitled to deference until it is shown to involve an impossibility."

In view of these principles we cannot strike down the legislative program for the Island of Vieques as in violation of the appellees' right to due process of law. That program in part, may be radical in that if carried out it will put the Insular Government in business in direct competition with the appellee Eastern Sugar Associates. This may be, as the appellees contend, "state socialism." But concrete cases are not to be decided by calling names. Our function is to pass upon the statutes before us without regard to our views of the wisdom of the political theory underlying them; (McLean v. Arkansas, 211 U.S. 539, 547, 29 S. Ct. 206, 53 L. Ed. 315) it is our duty to determine whether their enactment rested upon an arbitrary belief of the existence of the evils they were intended to remedy, and whether the means chosen are reasonably calculated to cure the evils reasonably believed by the Legislature to exist. Tanner v. Little, 240 U.S. 369, 385, 36 S. Ct. 379, 60 L. Ed. 691. And thus, although we cannot substitute our estimate of the extent of the evils aimed at for that of the Insular Legislature, we are required to make some inquiry into the facts with reference to which the Legislature acted.

... It seems to us that the reasonableness of the Insular Legislature's belief in the existence of the evils it attempted to cure is amply attested by social and economic conditions in Puerto Rico generally, and on the Island of Vieques in particular, so well known that we, at least as a court having appellate powers over the Supreme Court of Puerto Rico and hence as a sort of insular court, may notice them judicially.

Puerto Rico, including its adjacent islands, is small in area and densely populated, and that congested population is largely dependent upon the land for its livelihood. Puerto Rico v. Rubert Hermanos, Inc., 309 U.S. 543, 548, 60 S. Ct. 699, 84 L. Ed. 916. But it is not directly dependent upon the land because the basic agricultural crop is sugar cane. Indeed it is no secret that sugar dominates the whole insular economy. And the exigencies of sugar cane growing and grinding, which must be done promptly after the cane is cut, are such that rural landholdings have tended to become large and the majority of the workers thereon employable for only a few weeks during the year. Then, in addition to the foregoing, the economy of the Island of Vieques has been disrupted by the withdrawal of a substantial part of its best agricultural land for naval purposes, see Baetjer et al. v. United States, 1 Cir., 143 F.2d 391, thereby rendering it commercially expedient to transport the relatively small amount of cane still grown on that island to Puerto Rico proper for grinding instead of grinding it locally as had been done in the past. Were it necessary we might even go further and point to the plight of Puerto Rico during the late war brought to our attention in Buscaglia v. District Court of San Juan, 1 Cir., 145 F.2d. 274. But enough has been said to indicate both that the Puerto Rican Legislature's belief in the existence of a serious economic and social problem was not arbitrary, and that the program to provide not only homesteads and proportional profit farms for agregados and subsistence farms for more skilled farmers, on the Island of Puerto Rico proper, but, in addition to the foregoing, to provide for the renewal of sugar cane grinding and the development of the liquor industry on the Island of Vieques, embodied means reasonably calculated to deal with these problems.

One further point remains to be briefly considered. The appellees contend that the Land Authority which the People of Puerto Rico seek to vest with title to the 3,100 odd acres of land here in question lacks legal capacity to take title because of the five hundred acre provision of the Organic Act, referred to at the outset of this opinion. Their argument in a nutshell is that the Land Authority, although denominated "a governmental agency or instrumentality" in fact has all the essential attributes of a corporation and hence should be regarded as such, and as within the scope of the provision. We do not agree.

Even assuming, although we do not by any means decide, first, that the Land Authority is in fact a corporation, and second, that it is one "authorized to engage in agriculture," it does not seem to us to be the kind of a corporation intended to be included within the scope of the five hundred acre provision. Instead we are of the view from the wording of the provision that it was not intended to apply to governmental corporations created by the Insular Legislature to carry on a public function, but was intended to be limited in its application to private business corporations chartered by the insular government to engage in agriculture for profit, and clearly the Land Authority, whatever it may be, is not such an organization.

The order of the District Court is set aside and the case remanded to that Court for further proceedings not inconsistent with this opinion.

The *Eastern Sugar Associates* case was cited, and its results distinguished, by the United States District Court in the case of *Schneider v. District of Columbia*, 117 F. Supp. 705 (D.D.C. 1953). In the *Schneider* case, the owners of urban real property sought to enjoin the condemnation of their land and buildings, which condemnation was to be part of a general plan for the development of Southwest Washington, D.C. The court adopted the plaintiffs' argument that while a taking of slum property in order to do away with slums would be a taking for public use, a taking of property which was not a slum for the purpose of developing a better balanced community was not. The court did not hold the Redevelopment Act invalid; rather, it construed the Act to authorize only the taking of slum property. In distinguishing the *Eastern Sugar Associates* case, the court pointed to "the public necessity for solution of the general and acute [economic] conditions" in Puerto Rico.

On appeal, the Supreme Court reversed, holding the Redevelopment Act applicable to non-slum property, including the plaintiffs', and holding the Act as so interpreted to be constitutional. *Berman v. Parker, 348 U.S. 26 (1954).* Mr. Justice Douglas, speaking for the Court, went to some length to show the breadth of "what traditionally has been known as the police power," *i.e.*, police power objectives. Finding that the atractiveness and balance of a community were within the scope of proper governmental objectives, Justice Douglas found no obstacle in the "public use" doctrine:

> Once the object is within the authority of Congress, the right to realize it through the exercise of eminent domain is clear. For the power of eminent domain is merely the means to the end. See *Luxton* v. *North River Bridge Co.,* 153 U.S. 525, 529-530; *United States v. Gettysburg Electric R. Co.,* 160 U.S. 668, 679. Once the object is within the authority of Congress, the means by which it should be attained is also for Congress to determine. Here one of the means chosen is the use of private enterprise for redevelopment of the area. Appellants argue that this makes the project a taking from one businessman for the benefit of another businessman. But the means of executing the project are for Congress and Congress alone to determine, once the public purpose has been established. See *Luxton* v. *North River Bridge Co., supra; cf. Highland* v. *Russell Car Co.,* 279 U.S. 253. The public end may be as well or better served through an agency of private enterprise than through a department of government — or so the Congress might conclude. We cannot say that public ownership is the sole method of promoting the public purposes of community redevelopment projects. What we have said also disposes of any contention concerning the fact that certain property owners in the area may be permitted to repurchase their properties for redevelopment in harmony with the over-all plan. That, too, is a legitimate means which Congress and its agencies may adopt, if they chose. [348 U.S. at 33-34.]

What is left of the public use requirement, after this language is made the doctrine of the Court? To what extent does the doctrine of the *Berman* case, coupled with the language of legislation such as the Redevelopment Act ("blight," "sound development"), confide the question of public use to administrative discretion?

Is the question before a United States court in a public use case the same as the question before the Venezuelan court in the *Muñoz* case? Can you think of more perfect analogies in our law? Is there any reason why a court in the United States might be less concerned to protect against unjustifiable takings of property than its Latin American counterpart might be?

3. Affectability on the Basis of the Needs of the Reform

The theories thus far considered for taking property in a land reform have related to the manner in which the owner acquired his land, and the manner in which he has used it. There is in each theory an element of fault or illegitimacy on the landowner's side, which may bring the theory into line with traditional ideas about the protections that should be given property interests. But land reforms normally take place in revolutionary settings, and political necessities have frequently caused revolutionary governments to give in to demands for land distribution for its own sake. The theories of economic development noted earlier made little distinction among the various legal rationalizations for redistributing wealth and income; it is the redistribution that counts. So it was that Peru's 1964 land reform law included as one ground of affectability: "Concentration of land in such a manner as to constitute an obstacle to the diffusion of small and medium rural ownership, and which causes extreme or unjust dependence of the rural population on the owner." (Art. 13 (b).)

Althought the restitution theory of expropriation may have been conceived in part as a solution to the invasions or occupations by *campesinos* in Mexico and Bolivia, it became clear that any serious attempt to trace titles would be hopelessly inefficient to achieve the reforms required by political leaders for political reasons. In Mexico, the result was the early adoption of the principle that the villages deserved lands whether or not they could prove title to any lands in particular. Article 3d of the 1915 Decree of General Carranza and paragraph X of Article 27 of the 1917 Constitution provide the basis for a system of grants to the villages of land expropriated by the government for the purpose. The system, by which affectability is largely a geographical question, is now governed by the Agrarian Code.

MEXICO: AGRARIAN CODE OF 1943

* * *

Affectable property

57.   All estates whose borders are touched by a radius of 7 kilometers from the most densely populated part of the petitioning nucleus of population shall be affectable for granting to *ejidos* [village land holding units], under the terms of this Code.

58.   Properties of the Federation, of the States or of Municipalities shall be affected in preference to private properties in order to make grants to or enlarge *ejidos* or to create new centers of agricultural population.

* * *

The colonization of private properties is prohibited.

Nuclei of indigenous population shall have preference to be granted the lands and waters that they possess.

59.   The grant [of land to the *ejido*] should preferably be made in affectable lands of the best quality and closest to the petitioning nucleus.

The Mexican land reform has been carried our largely on the basis of this expropriation-and-grant system. Although little was done by way of formal distribution of land during the revolution, by 1920 the land reform began to take shape under Obregón. The number of hectares distributed increased steadily, until 1929, when over a million and a half hectares were distributed. Then there was a noticeable cooling of attitude toward land reform on the part of the Mexican government, which reflected the new attitude of Calles, an ex-president (1924-28) who still selected presidents and made their major decisions. Many thought that the Mexican land reform had run its course. Nonetheless, in 1934, the first Agrarian Code was adopted, under the leadership of President Rodríguez, who was willing to challenge Calles on the issue.

> When Lázaro Cárdenas was elected president in 1934 it was generally assumed that he would follow the dictates of Calles and that the agrarian program would gradually be liquidated. Such ideas were soon dispelled. Cárdenas spent a good share of his time travelling among the villagers, frequently by mule-back, studying their problems at firsthand and listening to their grievances. On the basis of information thus obtained, he resolved to carry out the Agrarian Reform Laws with utmost dispatch, and he streamlined the governmental machinery for doing so. In order to remove possible obstacles to his program, he deported the former *Jefe Máximo* [Calles] to the United States.
>
> During the Cárdenas regime (1935-40) more land was distributed than in all previous administrations put together. In not a single year of the

six-year term did the area distributed fall below 1,700,000 hectares, while in 1937 it reached a total of over 5,000,000 hectares.

Prior to Cárdenas, many politicians had thought of the ejido program as a more or less temporary measure, designed to prepare the Indians for becoming private property holders. They thought of the ejido mostly in terms of subsistence agriculture that would serve to supplement the wages of agricultural workers. They tended to shy away from the expropriation of haciendas that had developed a highly commercialized agriculture through the use of modern machinery and efficient methods and techniques of production. Cárdenas, on the contrary, was convinced that the ejido must become a fundamental part of the national economy, and he proceeded to expropriate and redistribute some of the most highly developed farming areas in Mexico. WHETTEN, RURAL MEXICO 127-28 (1948).*

Toward the end of the Cárdenas administration, the amount of land distributed tapered off, largely because the new system had to have time to absorb so much new land. But succeeding regimes have continued to make land distributions in substantial amounts, as the following table shows:

President	Years	Hectares Distributed
Carranza	1915-20	224,393
Huerta	1920-21	157,532
Obregón	1921-25	1,677,067
Calles	1925-29	3,195,028
Portes Gil	1929-30	2,065,847
Ortiz Rubio**	1930-33	1,203,737
Rodríguez	1933-35	2,094,637
Cárdenas	1935-41	20,072,957
Avila Camacho	1941-47	5,327,942
Alemán	1947-53	4,057,993
Ruiz Cortines	1953-59	3,664,379

(Figures from FLORES, TRATADO DE ECONOMIA AGRICOLA 311, 314 (1961). There is no source for this information that is completely exact. These calendar-year figures do not correspond precisely to the presidential terms; each term now begins late in the election year. E.g., President Alemán's term ran from late 1946 to late 1952.)

President López Mateos' administration (1958-64) exceeded the number of hectares distributed by the Cárdenas administration, but much of the land recently distributed has been of marginal quality. At present, over half of the

---

* Reprinted from Rural Mexico by Nathan Whetten by permission of The University of Chicago Press. Copyright 1948 by The University of Chicago.

** After Calles, the presidential term was changed from four to six years; Ortiz Rubio and Rodríguez were filling unexpired terms.

agricultural land of Mexico has been distributed to the villages. There are still some large estates: hundreds over 50,000 hectares in size, and thousands over 1,000 hectares. Some of these estates belong to politically influential persons; others are outside the seven-kilometer radius of affectability around each village; by far the greatest number, however, are inaffectable because they are part of the "small property." Unless drastic changes are made in standards of inaffectability, Mexico has nearly run out of land to distribute.*

From the beginning, it was contemplated that small farmers' land would not be touched in the reform. Just what *was* a small farm was left to be determined according to local conditions; the size would vary, depending on what was needed in the region to support a family agricultural unit. Then in late 1946, at the beginning of President Alemán's term, some important changes were made in the law. Article 27 of the Constitution was amended, adding to paragraphs XIV and XV the provisions that defined the small property and gave judicial remedies to its owners against encroachments made on behalf of the land reform. The key to these provisions, which are reflected in amendments to the Agrarian Code and in a long regulation issued in 1948, is the procedure for obtaining certificates of inaffectability. Every owner of 100 hectares may be issued such a certificate; by a judicious distribution of land among the members of a family, including babies and grandmothers, aunts and grand-nephews, a sizeable estate may be covered by many certificates of inaffectability and yet operated as a unit. The 100-hectare figure applies only to the best land; in cases of less desirable land, the inaffectable area may range much higher per person. See generally MENDIETA Y NUÑEZ, EL PROBLEMA AGRARIO DE MEXICO, ch. XXVII, XXVIII (9th ed. 1966); BURGOA, EL AMPARO EN MATERIA AGRARIA 79-110 (1964).

Since the days of Alemán, distributions of land have been largely limited to regions in which agriculture is difficult — desert or jungle land, for example. The emphasis has been directed toward the building of dams, roads, and other social overhead capital items. Meanwhile, Mexico's rural population is mounting at an alarming rate, and there is renewed pressure on the land. In the dry Laguna region, there have been invasions of land, often by persons who have already received some land in the reform — but land without water, or land of uneconomically small dimensions. Troops have been called out to remove the invading *campesinos,* but the invaders regularly reappear. The invasions are by no means limited to the Laguna region. In an open letter to the President of the Republic, the Regional Livestock Association of the State of Chihuahua protested against invasions of its property, and printed these extracts from an instruction leaflet which had been circulated among the invaders:

---

*For a general history of the Mexican land reform, see SILVA HERZOG, EL AGRARISMO MEXICANO Y LA REFORMA AGRARIA (2d ed. 1964).

This occupation of *latifundios* is of a peaceful character; but we shall not for any reason accept ejection from the lands we occupy, and we shall apply the tactic of passive resistance in our effort to stay on the land.

If the army troops or police should force our companions to leave the *latifundio*, they should enter again as soon as possible.

* * *

When the Authorities seek the leaders or responsible parties for the movement, our men should say that there are no leaders, that all in common accord have determined to occupy the lands and that no one in particular is to blame. Advertisement, Excelsior, Mexico City, June 2, 1963, p. 17-A.

The land reform legislation of other countries also provides for the exemption of small parcels from expropriation or for the allowance of a reserve for an expropriated owner. Thus in Bolivia (p. 480, *supra*) the small and medium properties are not affected (art. 32, 33); in Colombia (p. 474, *supra*), each expropriated owner has the right to reserve 100 hectares (art. 58); and in Venezuela (art. 29), each owner is allowed 150 hectares.

What is the effect of the following provision of the Venezuelan law on the 150-hectare reserve? In view of this provision, what answer can be given to the question: Which lands are affectable in the land reform?

33. When it becomes necessary to organize land in a given place, and when the existence thereat of one or more properties forms a technical or economic obstacle to proper execution of the scheme, the total or partial expropriation of such properties shall be authorized even when they fall within any of the classifications specified in Articles 26 and 29 of this Chapter. In order to take such action, the Institute shall be required to prove, during the appropriate judicial proceedings, that the conditions laid down in this Article exist. In such cases, cash payment shall be made for existing useful improvements, livestock, mortgages or preferential debts incurred and used for development and improvement purposes. The balance shall be paid in class "C" bonds in accordance with the provisions of Article 174 of this Act.

Small or medium landowners whose properties have been totally expropriated under this Article shall be entitled, after the said land has been organized, to obtain, against payment, ownership of a parcel of the said land of a size equal to the largest area allocated.

Total expropriation shall take place where partial expropriation would destroy the economic unity of the property or would render it useless or unfit for the purpose for which it was destined.

How does the Venezuelan law differ from the Mexican law which permits expropriation of any land — whether or not it fulfills its social function — provided that a village lacks land, etc. Which of the two laws gives more protection to the landowner? What kinds of protection?

C. Compensation and Confiscation

1. The Rationale of Confiscation: To Compensate or Not?

HOLMES, INTRODUCTION TO RATIONAL BASIS OF
LEGAL INSTITUTIONS, xxxi-xxxii (Wigmore and Kocourek ed. 1923)

... I will go no farther than to repeat that most even of the enlightened reformers that I hear or read seem to me not to have considered with accuracy the means at our disposal and to become rhetorical just where I want figures. The notion that we can secure an economic paradise by changes in property alone seems to me twaddle. ... I can understand a man's saying in any case, I want this or that and I am willing to pay the price, if he realizes what the price is. What I most fear is saying the same thing when those who say it do not know and have made no serious effort to find out what it will cost, as I think we in this country are rather inclined to do.

The passion for equality is now in fashion and Mr. Lester Ward has told us of the value of discontent. Without considering how far motives commonly classed as ignoble have covered themselves with a high sounding name, or how far discontent means inadequacy of temperament or will, the first step toward improvement is to look the facts in the face.

An article that has had much vogue in underdeveloped countries is Bronfenbrenner, *The Appeal of Confiscation in Economic Development,* 3 ECONOMIC DEVELOPMENT AND CULTURAL CHANGE 201-13 (1955). The title alone has been a popular citation, despite the author's reminder that he was not advocating confiscation, but warning us to expect it and defend against it. See 11 *id.* at 367 (1963). Bronfenbrenner's thesis is that confiscation is an attractive device for a government which wants to achieve rapid development "without sacrifice of the scale of living of the mass of the population ... by shifting income to developmental investment from capitalists' consumption, from transfer abroad, and from unproductive 'investment' like luxury housing." He uses economic models to illustrate that confiscation gives the government control over the investment of the income from the confiscated property, and that even a highly inefficient investment for developmental purposes can produce substantial changes in per capita income growth over a generation. Even his figures for forced-draft industrialization on the Stalin model are gloomy, however, in relation to the expectations which have been awakened in the minds of many in the underdeveloped world. When it is added that he has used a very conservative net population growth figure (1.5% per year), the picture becomes even more discouraging; Latin America is expected to grow at a net rate of around 3% over the next generation. Even confiscation, given Bronfenbrenner's calculations and a 3% yearly population growth rate, will not be enough.

Still, the economic appeal of confiscation has not gone unnoticed by the leadership of the world's revolutionary and developing nations. In particular, the land reforms that have taken place in Mexico, Bolivia and Cuba have all been largely confiscatory in nature. The only major land reform in all Latin America in which a serious effort has been made to compensate the expropriated owners has been in Venezuela, and the presence of high income from oil makes that country a special case. Consider the plight of the government of an underdeveloped country. The country's disposable resources are, by definition, highly limited. There is a need for enormous immediate investment in all sorts of capital items. Shall the government use its scarce resources to build roads, dams, irrigation canals, power plants and the like, or shall it pay the expropriated owners? Rationalizations for confiscation need not be very powerful to gain acceptance in such a climate. Just as Emerson and others once argued that it was the slaves — not their owners — who should be compensated upon the abolition of slavery, so some Latin American writers have agreed with Madero's Plan of San Luis Potosí, p. 454, *supra*, that it is the dispossessed villages and *campesinos* who deserve compensation, and not the expropriated landowners:

> In the case of restitution there is, logically, no indemnification. Land stolen from the original owners is restored to them. The fact that [the ones who stole it] are not forced to pay for the use they have made of the land speaks highly for Mexican revolutionary moderation. BOSQUES, THE NATIONAL REVOLUTIONARY PARTY OF MEXICO AND THE SIX-YEAR PLAN 20 (1937), quoted in SENIOR, LAND REFORM AND DEMOCRACY at 220 n.46 (1958).

The history of efforts made before and during the Civil War to free the slaves offers an instructive North American parallel.[*] Before the slave-owners' interests were confiscated by the Emancipation Proclamation, a great variety of schemes were devised for achieving the result gradually, or by means of partial or complete compensation:

1. A Virginia judge proposed in 1796 that every female slave born after the adoption of his plan be free, and "transmit" freedom to all her descendants, but be required to work until she should reach the age of 28. See COLEMAN, VIRGINIA SILHOUETTES, appendix, 54-56 (1934). A similar plan had been adopted by Pennsylvania. See COBB, AN INQUIRY INTO THE LAW OF NEGRO SLAVERY clxxi-clxxii (1858).

2. Various other Northern states adopted legislation setting free all Negroes born after specified dates without adding any period of obligatory service. See COBB, *supra*.

---

[*] Legislation strikingly similar to these proposals served to achieve the gradual emancipation of slaves in Brazil.

3. An English doctor offered a plan for "self-emancipation," in which each slave would be paid for all work which he should do beyond certain assigned tasks; his earnings would be placed in a savings bank to gather interest until they reached a certain amount; at that time, some branch of government, or some private aid society, would contribute an additional amount, and upon payment of the money so saved and contributed to the owner, the slave would be free. See HALL, THE TWO-FOLD SLAVERY OF THE UNITED STATES (1854).

4. In 1825, a resolution was offered to the United States Senate for appropriating the proceeds of the sales of some public lands to pay for a voluntary (on the owners' part) emancipation of slaves. See CHILD, AMERICANS CALLED AFRICANS 102 (1836).

5. It was frequently proposed that Congress expropriate the owners' rights in slaves, paying compensation. E.g., OWEN, THE WRONG OF SLAVERY, THE RIGHT OF EMANCIPATION 150-55 (1864) (basing the constitutional power of Congress on the war powers).

Lincoln himself first preferred a solution less drastic than confiscation. See SELBY, ABRAHAM LINCOLN: THE EVOLUTION OF HIS EMANCIPATION POLICY (1906). He even submitted this resolution to Congress:

> Resolved, That the United States ought to co-operate with any State which may adopt gradual abolishment of slavery; giving to such State pecuniary aid, to be used by such State in its discretion, to compensate for the inconveniences, public and private, produced by such change of system.

After bitter debate, both Houses passed the resolution in April, 1862. See WILSON, HISTORY OF ANTISLAVERY MEASURES OF THE THIRTY-SEVENTH AND THIRTY-EIGHTH UNITED-STATES CONGRESSES, 1861-64, ch. IV (1864). The resolution appears in 12 STAT. 617 (1862). When slavery was abolished in the District of Columbia, 12 STAT. 376 (1862); 12 STAT. 538 (1862), compensation was provided for. This legislation was enacted in April and July, 1862. By September of the same year, Lincoln became convinced of the necessity for a general emancipation. Since he regarded the question as beyond the ordinary legislative power of the Congress, he was persuaded to issue an executive order as a war measure. (In the meantime, General Hunter had proclaimed freedom for all slaves in Georgia, Florida and South Carolina, which order was revoked by the President in May, 1862 on the ground that such a decision had to come from the Commander-in-Chief and not from an officer in the field. See 12 STAT. 1264-65 (1862).) Even in the Emancipation Proclamation itself, Lincoln noted that he intended to recommend new legislation "tendering pecuniary aid to the free acceptance or rejection of all slave states, so called, the people whereof may not then be in rebellion against the United States, and which states may then have voluntarily adopted, or thereafter may voluntarily adopt, immediate or gradual abolishment of slavery. . . ." 12 STAT. 1267 (1862). When the Proclamation became effective on January 1, 1863,

Lincoln's new proclamation referred to emancipation as "as act of justice, warranted by the Constitution upon military necessity." 12 STAT. 1268, 1269 (1863). At that, the Proclamation applied only to the states in rebellion and not to the border states. Arguments over the legality of the Emancipation Proclamation raged until the adoption of the Thirteenth Amendment. The slaveowners were never compensated.

Other measures taken during the Civil War find echoes in the revolutionary land reforms of modern Latin America. It will be recalled that the theory of restitution obviates the need for agonizing over the question of compensation; the idea is that lands are returned to their rightful owners. It is only a slight extension of this theory to confiscate the land of opponents of a revolution as enemy property. Zapata proposed to take one-third of the lands of the *haciendas* in Mexico, paying compensation for them. But if the owners did not cooperate, he proposed to take all their lands, paying nothing; enemies of the revolution were not to have their property respected. It will be recalled that the Cuban government has found similar theories useful in marshalling land for the land reform. See p. 470, *supra.*

During our Civil War, both sides enacted general legislation confiscating property owned by their opponents. The American Revolution had already produced its share of confiscations; laws confiscating or placing special taxes on property owned by Tories were enacted by every one of the thirteen colonies. See VAN TYNE, THE LOYALISTS IN THE AMERICAN REVOLUTION 275-81, 335-41 (1929) ("To prevent 'dangerous monopolies of land,' the estates were to be divided and sold in small tracts. Finally, none but persons who had taken the test oath were permitted to buy." P. 279). Since the Union armies eventually penetrated deep into the South, the question naturally arose what to do with all the property which was coming into the government's hands, not only through confiscation but also as a result of delinquencies in the "direct tax," a form of indirect confiscation. The chairman of the Committee on Public Lands of the House of Representatives wrote to William Whiting, Solicitor of the War Department, asking his advice. Whiting's reply, written in February, 1864, and reprinted below, proposed what we should now call a land reform.

WHITING, LETTER TO HOUSE COMMITTEE ON PUBLIC LANDS (1864)

Large Estates must be divided.
The Reasons for so doing.

Whether this measure [the constitutional amendment abolishing slavery] be adopted sooner or later, it is necessary that the large landed estates in the South, which shall become the property of the United States, should be broken up into farms of moderate size, and be distributed among those having claims to the protection of government. Large estates in land are essential to the perpetuation of slaveholding aristocracy, and of slavery itself. They furnish the means of reducing and of retaining a numerous but degraded population under the control of a small number of capitalists. Proprietorship of the soil renders all tenants subservient to the will and subject to the control of the owner. Estates of inordinate size retard and exclude internal improvements. It is also well known among agriculturists that very large farms are wasteful and comparatively unproductive. Subdivision increases productiveness. *Villages* are scarcely possible when many large estates are contiguous. Without villages, the country lags in its progress. The proprietor of large plantations, peopled by slaves and by poor whites more degraded than slaves, becomes a *feudal lord,* while his subjects are deprived of feudal rights; and such a petty sovereignty does not educate the master to become a patriotic and peaceful citizen of a republican form of government. Lands descending in the same family for several generations perpetuate a *quasi* feudal aristocracy, wherever the lords of the land inherit the subjects from whose toil it derives its value. The history of the states of South America, and especially of Mexico, where some of the proprietors own lands greater in extent than two or three of the smaller States in our Union, might well demonstrate the impossibility of preserving a permanent republican government over the proud, independent, selfish, turbulent, vindictive, and revolutionary spirits engendered by the inordinate accumulation of real estate in the hands of an oligarchy, even without the aggravating evils of slavery.

Speculators.

The destruction of slavery in the Southern States will not remove these evils, so unavoidable, yet so deplorable. Negroes and poor whites hired to labor on large plantations will suffer as severely from their employers as from slaveholding masters. Following the army, like crows after the battles, speculators are going south to purchase farms in the new Eldorado. They will have, to some extent, the control of negroes found there, even though they may hire laborers. They will prove a curse to the country and a curse to the negroes. Men of grasping avarice, who have no interest in protecting the life or health of their employés, will be far more unrelenting than slave-owners who have an interest in preserving what they claim as property. Experience in Tennessee and other States has already demonstrated that the negroes suffer more under lessees, who are determined to get rich in a hurry by raising cotton, than they formerly suffered from their selfish masters. It is shocking to learn that Union men, as speculators, are allowed to drive their laborers to unwonted activity in the field, and yet to withhold from them fair wages. To deprive this hard-hearted class of men of the temptation of buying great estates for the purpose of levying black mail upon the first earnings of freedmen, it is only necessary to require the lands to be leased or sold in small sections, and to actual settlers.

Other Reasons why the Land should be subdivided into small Sections.

There is but one way of recalling the common people of the South, who are non-slaveholders, to a hearty and honest support of the Union; and that is, by making the population of all parts of the country homogeneous. Small farms, free labor, diversity of occupations, general education, northern institutions, republican and not aristocratic ideas of the respectability of honest industry, the substitution of cheerful and hopeful productive labor in place of listless southern indolence, the thrift of profitable energy instead of the wasteful extravagance of unpaid toil, the exchange of the slave-driver's lash for the spur of self-interest, and of the slave-pen for the school-house, will produce, in a few years, a revolution more wonderful than all the hard-fought battles of this civil war.

* * *

Small Farms are Pledges of the Perpetuity of the Union.

If the southern lands which shall belong to the United States be divided into small farms, and owned by a large number of proprietors, every one of them will hold his homestead under title from the United States. Each proprietor will thus become bound to maintain the government. His homestead will be pledged by bond and mortgage to perpetuate the Union. Every farm will be Union stock. It will be a guarantee of the credit and good faith of the country. It will secure in the South all the benefits of the *credit mobilier,* or of the circulation of governmental currency. The larger the number of persons owning the same amount of land, the stronger is the government in the number of its indorsers. Such, then, are some of the reasons why the lands of the United States in the rebellious districts should be subdivided into small homesteads.

What may be done with Homesteads.

These lands, thus subdivided, are wanted for four important objects.

1. For bounties to soldiers who have been in active service, and to the widows or heirs of those who have perished therein.

2. For homesteads for persons, of whatever color, who, while the war continues, or after it is over, may be found resident thereon.

3. For homesteads for those who shall emigrate southward.

4. Those lands, not wanted for bounties or for homesteads, or the proceeds thereof, should be pledged for and applied to the extinction of the war debt.

Property abandoned by or taken from those who instigated the war should be appropriated to pay its expenses.

* * *

A Principle of Political Economy.

To abolish slavery and cut up the lands of those slaveholders who will not accept the amnesty, and to distribute them as above suggested, would benefit the South even more than the North. For in a few years, the productiveness of the lands would be enormously increased by reason of improvements in agriculture, and by the conversion of eight millions of southern white men into *producers,* who are now *only consumers* of the products of the labor of four millions of slaves. To add such a vast source of wealth as this, will do more to develop and increase our wealth and our resources than the discovery of hundreds of mines of silver or of gold. This result of converting consumers into producers, interested in the perpetuity of our government, elevated in civilization, and with feelings so changed as to make them loyal citizens, is to be accomplished only by introducing among them northern improvements, northern institutions, and northern men to put them in practice. This end can be accomplished only by so managing the lands of the South as to render these great movements practicable.

Seizure of Lands. Bureau of Industry.
Land Office System.

The first step in this direction is to seize the lands, and to acquire title as rapidly as possible.

The second step is, to place them in charge of proper persons, under the authority of the United States. (This is to be provided for by the bill for an Emancipation Bureau.)

The third step is to have the land system extended over these districts.

For without this precaution, there will be disputes as to proprietorship; disputes as to boundary; disputes as to titles of traitors and their agents; claims for indemnity; disputes as to the application of the Amnesty Proclamation; and an interminable train of difficulties.

The Land System.

By applying to the southern plantations the land system, the titles can be given and guaranteed directly by the United States. These titles will be reliable, and held sacred. The security of title will enhance the value of the lands for lease or for sale; and the government can, through its land officer, keep a correct account of all that is done with its property, and account for the proceeds thereof, and keep a register of loyal and disloyal men. If general laws are made, regulating the use or appropriation of such lands, these laws can be best carried into effect by the Land Office, and its surveys will be *conclusive,* both as to location of lots, and its grants or warrants may be made conclusive as to validity of title. By regulations of the Land Office, speculators can be kept off, settlers, soldiers, and emigrants can be protected most effectually. Considering all these things, it seems advisable that the land system of the United States should be extended to all such estates as vest in the United States as rapidly as possible. The disposition of these lands may be placed in the control of the chief of the Emancipation or Industrial Bureau. And it is desirable that lands of great value should not be sold, as they now are, for nominal prices, but that Congress should so legislate that these estates may be held for the benefit of the United States, or for such uses as they may be applied to hereafter by law.*

I am, Sir, very respectfully,
WILLIAM WHITING
Solicitor of the War Department.

This letter is contained in WHITING, WAR POWERS UNDER THE CONSTITUTION 469-78 (43d ed. 1871). Whiting's recommendations were not carried out with respect to many of the confiscated lands, because in May, 1865 President Johnson declared an amnesty which extended to all rights, including property rights, of persons who participated in the rebellion, with the large exception of specified officials of the Confederacy (including army officers), certain deserters from the Union army, etc. 13 STAT. 758 (1865). Nonetheless, substantial tracts of land remained in the hands of the government, chiefly as a result of "direct tax" delinquencies and tax sales. Many of Whiting's recommendations were carried out on these lands, through the operation of the Freedman's Bureau Act, 14 STAT. 173 (1866), which authorized the sale of land at low cost and in small parcels to former slaves, which land was to be inalienable for six years.

Despite the obvious attractions of confiscation, with the exception of Cuba the tendency among the countries of Latin America which have experienced land reform has not been to confiscate openly. Without exception, the legislation provides for payment for expropriated land. This is not to say that the reforms have not been confiscatory; it is to say, however, that the forms of compensation have been retained, and that confiscation has been somewhat disguised, although not very subtly. The principal techniques for disguising non-payment have been the use of deferred payment schemes — agrarian

---

* How far the policy recommended in this letter has been approved by Congress may be seen by examination of the Freedmen's Bureau Act of July 16, 1866, Chap. 200. [Footnote in Whiting's book. — Ed.]

bonds — and the valuation of property at less than market values. The next two sections explore these techniques.

---

2. Deferred Compensation

3 NICHOLS, EMINENT DOMAIN § 8.2
(3d ed., Sackman, 1950)

While the constitutions of the states do not ordinarily prescribe the medium by which compensation shall be paid, that the compensation must be in money is a qualification that has been read into the phrase now under consideration by all the courts in which the question has arisen.

Statutes providing that the person whose land is taken shall accept stock or bonds, or municipal warrants which the holder could enforce only by a suit at law, if not paid, have been unhesitatingly held invalid. . . .

UNITED STATES v. 1,000 ACRES OF LAND, etc.
162 F. Supp. 219 (E.D. La. 1958)

WRIGHT, J. . . .

. . . At the outset, the landowners challenge the constitutionality of Section 6 of the Rivers and Harbors Act in that that section of the Act requires that special and direct benefits to the remainder of a lot, parcel or tract, arising from the Government improvement for which the land is taken, shall be considered "by way of reducing the amount of compensation or damages" awarded. They argue that while special benefits may reduce the amount of severance damage, they cannot in any way affect the amount of compensation for the part actually taken. In this argument, the landowners have some support from the cases interpreting condemnation laws of various states. But the Supreme Court of the United States has held many times, and with reference to this particular statute, that special benefits may be set off not only against severance damage but against the value of the part taken as well.

Admitting that these cases may be persuasive on the point, the landowners then argue that here, as to some lots, parcels or tracts, special benefits set off against the value of the part taken, as well as against severance damage, resulted in no award in money to the landowners. Certainly, they say, since they get no money at all for the part taken, they have been denied just compensation therefor. But the Fifth Amendment does not require payment in money. The constitutional command is "just compensation." And the Supreme Court has held that special benefits to the remainder of a lot, parcel or tract is just compensation for the part taken. Merely because the value of the special benefits is the same as, or greater than, the sum of the value of the part taken and severance damages to the remainder, thereby requiring no payment in money to the landowner, that does not mean, logically and mathematically it cannot mean, that just compensation has not been awarded to the landowner for the part taken. Money is but a medium of exchange. When just compensation is obtained through direct benefits to the remainder, use of the medium becomes unnecessary. The quotations, urged by landowners, from certain cases which indicate that just compensation means money are aberrations which become clear when the full text of the opinions are read.

TOVAR CONCHA, LA TESIS CONSERVADORA SOBRE PROPIEDAD, in TIERRA: 10 ENSAYOS SOBRE LA REFORMA AGRARIA EN COLOMBIA* at 235, 242-43 (1962)

[These are remarks of a Senator, a member of the Conservative Party, before a Senate committee considering the bill which became the Colombian land reform law of 1961.]

We defend the thesis that compensation must be made prior to taking because the Constitution says so. And we defend the thesis that compensation must be paid in money, because the Constitution so gives us to understand. The constitutional principle may be good or bad, but it is a constitution. If it is bad, we expect that an appropriate amendment will be presented, and at that time we shall consider the problem. But for the moment what we desire is that the Constitution be respected.

Payment is proposed for the expropriated lands by means of bonds. That is to say that the requirement of "prior compensation" will be fulfilled in bonds. Is that constitutional? I do not believe so.

If compensation corresponds to "damages"; or if it corresponds to a *conditio juris,* the payment must be in money. And that is so because of what money is; because of its juridical nature.

If the Constitution of 1936 had contemplated non-monetary forms of compensation, it would have said so. The Senate should not forget that the Spanish Constitution of 1932, which had such an influence on ours of 1936, foresaw that situation when it said that the statute law would establish the forms of compensation. Is there something similar in our own Article 30? No. Consequently it must be accepted that compensation must be in money.

Nevertheless, that is not the fundamental point in the Conservative position. Let us forget the problem of compensation for a moment, and ask ourselves if above all, an economic process benefitting the community will be achieved through the process of expropriation. Or, in technical terms, if in the agrarian reform which is proposed there is or is not one chapter of a determined economic policy. [The Senator goes on to argue that the policy expressed in the proposed agrarian reform statute represents a mixture of liberal and social reforms, which he regards as incompatible with each other. He argues that this logical inconsistency makes a coherent economic policy impossible.]

LLERAS RESTREPO, ESTRUCTURA DE LA REFORMA AGRARIA, in TIERRA: 10 ENSAYOS SOBRE LA REFORMA AGRARIA EN COLOMBIA* at 11, 63-64 (1962)

[This is a very brief excerpt from a long report which was the principal official statment of position concerning the same bill, made by a Senator and member of the Liberal Party who was the single most influential individual in the enactment of the law, and who was elected President of Colombia in 1966.]

Persons who are still not completely familiar with the constitutional reform of 1936, supported in referendum by the Colombian people in the plebiscite of 1957, continue to argue that there can be no expropriation without full and previous compensation in cash. But such a pretension has no support in the text of the Charter.

[The Senator quotes article 30 of the Constitution, which concludes: "Nevertheless, the legislative power, for reasons of equity, shall have the power to determine those cases in which there shall be no compensation, by means of the favorable vote of an absolute majority ▮▮▮▮ of the members of both Houses."]

Thus it is obvious that the legislature is also sovereign to determine when reasons of equity are present. Now then, if the statute law can say that in one case there is no need for compensation, with much greater reason it can say that compensation be only partial, that it be paid in instruments [bonds] of the State or that it be paid in instalments. The greater includes the lesser power, according to a well known juridical axiom. And it should be remembered that in the course of the debates over the constitutional reform of 1936 precisely this point was raised, and not only Dr. Darío Echandía, co-author of the reform, but also the parliamentary representatives were in accord as to the indicated interpretation, and they left it so expressly.

There is not, then, any difficulty of a constitutional origin preventing the articles of the agrarian project from being converted into law.

LOPEZ MICHELSEN, HACIA UNA VERDADERA REFORMA QUE COMPLETE LA "REVOLUCION EN MARCHA," in Tierra: 10 Ensayos Sobre la Reforma Agraria en Colombia* at 85, 93-94 (1962)

[This is a statement by the legislative chief of the Revolutionary Liberal Movement, in floor debate.]

In accordance with Article 30 of the Constitution, which pertains to the Reform of 1936, there exist two classes of expropriations: one for reasons of *public utility* and *social interest,* another for reasons of *equity.* With respect to expropriation for reasons of public utility and social interest, defined by the Legislature, expropriation is authorized, provided there be judicial decision and prior compensation. . . .

Then I affirm the following: When compensation is not prior, when it is made in five instalments, or when it is made in bonds, the statute law should be based, not on the article requiring prior compensation, but on the article which requires reasons of equity, because, in accordance with the judical principle that the greater includes the lesser power, and based on the power to expropriate the land without any compensation, it is obvious that expropriation with partial compensation or with compensation in instalments can be made, based on this article.

[Mr. López is concerned that an expropriation based on the theory of public utility might be subject to judicial review, and might be held unconstitutional in the event that compensation should not be paid prior to the taking of the property.]

This possibility of expropriation for reasons of equity is particularly delicate, considered in the light of foreign investments, of the Alliance for Progress, and of the "due process of law." . . . It is particularly delicate, because, as I say, and as [Senator Carlos Lleras Restrepo] says in his study of this agrarian reform project, equity is a concept which is not subject to review by the Supreme Court of Justice. All Colombian laws may be challenged before the Court on the ground of unconstitutionality, that is to say, making a comparison between the statute law and the Constitution. But when questions of equity are put in the hands of the Legislature, no one can complain before the Court against a law, arguing that it is inequitable and that the Court should decide whether there is equity or not, because the Court only decides on questions of

Law. Equity is discretionary with the Legislature, which is the branch with power to decide (and so the text states) when there is equity. Then, if an expropriation with bonds is presented, as this agrarian reform project suggests, the compensation is neither prior nor complete, because bonds are not the same as cash payment, and the expropriation must be based on the article concerning equity, since the greater includes the lesser power.

Doctor Carlos Lleras understands it thus, and in his exposition of purposes of the law he makes the same argument. But the truth is that in the very context of the law the invocation of equity is not defined, and above all there was no reference to the quorum required in cases of equity, which is that of a two-thirds majority. Whenever the equity argument is to be used, it is necessary to determine equity in each case and also to adopt the law with the ▮▮▮ majority required in cases of equity. This would be the "due process of law" of which Senator [Hubert] Humphrey speaks, with respect to land ownership, in Colombia.

GOMEZ HURTADO, EL AUTENTICO CONTENIDO DE UNA
REFORMA AGRARIA, in TIERRA: 10 ENSAYOS SOBRE LA
REFORMA AGRARIA EN COLOMBIA* at 169, 192-94 (1962)

In the first place we have the so-called uncultivated lands. The determination that the land is "uncultivated" is made through a system that gives our colleagues the opportunity to make an analysis of the rectitude and efficiency of the systems which the project proposes. But once it is established that the lands are uncultivated, they are paid for in bonds of class B with 2% interest, over 25 years. I believe that, to begin, it is necessary to establish the current rate of interest. The country's rate of interest today is 10% in banks; in non-bank transactions it is 12%. In a magazine commonly distributed here, the "National Statistical Bulletin," we see how the mortgages given in Bogotá have even reached the usurious levels of interest of 18 and 24 per cent. But let us limit ourselves to the bank interest rate of 10% or the non-bank rate of 12%. ... Then, how much is a bond worth which produces 2%? That is elementary. It is a matter of applying a simple rule of short division. Then we find that if the current interest is 12%, the bond is worth 16.66% of face value; if the interest is 10, the bond is worth only 20%. That is to say, if a property owner to whom bonds with a nominal value of 100 pesos are given is going to sell them as a function of their income-producing capacity, he will sell them for 20 pesos. If we consider the current interest to be 12%, he will have to sell them for 16.66 pesos.

There is, then, a confiscation of 80% in the first case, or 83½% in the second case. Why is there a confiscation? Because the bond has no market. It is very difficult to get anyone to buy a bond of 2% at 25 years. Because the bond has nothing except a possibility of being recieved at par by the Institute: for the payment of 15% of the principal [in payment for parcels] in some cases of colonization. . . . Then the person who receives those bonds, which for him have an income-producing capacity of scarcely 20%, has to suffer the consequences of devaluation. Instruments of fixed interest, as is well known, have no corrective power in the face of devaluation of the currency. Here I have figures from the Bank of the Republic, which show that the currency in the last eight years has lost 50% of its purchasing power. That means that in 25 years the bonds with which these uncultivated lands will be paid will value zero, and since they have had an income-producing capacity of 2% the confiscation has been practically 96.96% of the commercial value.

[For a description of the political maneuvering required to enact the Colombian law, see HIRSCHMAN, JOURNEYS TOWARD PROGRESS, ch. II (1963).]

COLOMBIA: Act N° 135 of Social Agrarian Reform, December 13, 1961, *Diario Oficial* N° 30961, Dec. 20, 1961, p. 801
(FAO translation)

* * *

62. Land acquired by the Institute as a result of voluntary sale or expropriation shall be paid in the following manner:

1. For uncultivated land, in class B Agrarian bonds issued in pursuance of this Act.
2. . For improperly farmed land, in cash. An amount equivalent to 20% of the price shall be paid on the date of the transaction without, however, exceeding a maximum of one hundred thousand (100,000) Colombian pesos. The remainder shall be payable in eight successive annual instalments of an equal value, the first of which shall fall due one year after the date of the transaction.
Land farmed by small-scale tenant farmers or share-croppers shall be paid for in the same manner when in the case of share-croppers the owner does not participate in the management of the farm and does not assume responsibility for any part of the costs or operation involved. The farms referred to in paragraph 3 of Article 55 shall also be paid for in the same manner.
3. For land not accounted for under the two preceding paragraphs, in cash. An amount equivalent to 20 per cent of the price shall be paid on the date of the transaction without, however, exceeding a maximum of three hundred thousand (300,000) Colombian pesos. The remainder shall be payable in five successive annual instalments of an equal value, the first of which shall fall due one year after the date of the transaction.

The amount of the payment to be made by the Institute at the time of completion of the transaction shall, in accordance with paragraphs 2 and 3 above, amount to up to seventy-five thousand (75,000) and one hundred and fifty thousand (150,000) Colombian pesos respectively, if the 20 per cent referred to therein does not reach either of such figures as the case may be.

The Institute shall pay interest at the rate of 4 per cent *per annum* on the amounts outstanding to its charge under paragraph 2 above and at the rate of 6 per cent *per annum* on amounts outstanding under paragraph 3 of this Article. Such interest shall be paid at the expiry of each six-monthly period. The Institute's liabilities whether in respect of capital or of interest shall be guaranteed by the State and may at the request of a creditor be divided into two or more promissory notes which shall not be negotiable in accordance with Act N° 46 of 1923 and shall not be issued for sums of less than fifty thousand (50,000) Colombian pesos. They may, however, be transferred and ceded as guarantee in accordance with the provisions of Title XXV, Book IV of the Civil Code.

The owners of land referred to in paragraphs 2 and 3 above shall be entitled to full payment by the Institute at the time of the conclusion of the transaction and to payment of any part outstanding to their credit thereafter in Class A Agrarian Bonds at face value. Any person to whom such credit rights have been transferred shall automatically thereby acquire this entitlement.

* * *

74. The Government is hereby authorized to issue Agrarian Bonds in the quantity and manner and of the type specified in this and the succeeding Articles.

An issue shall be made to the value of one thousand million (1,000 million) Colombian pesos of Class A Bonds and of up to two hundred million (200 million) Colombian pesos of Class B Bonds.

Class A Bonds shall be issued in successive annual series of two hundred million (200 million) Colombian pesos each and the first issue shall be made within sixty (60) days from the date on which the Land Reform Institute starts operation. The second issue shall be ordered by the Government in accordance with requests to the effect by the Managing Board of the Institute and after approval by the Ministry of Agriculture and shall go forward in successive series of no less than five million (5 million) Colombian pesos each.

Once the Bonds in each series have been issued, the Government shall deposit them in the *Banco de la República* making them payable to the order of the Institute, and from that moment forward they shall be deemed part of the Institute's property.

75. Agrarian Bonds shall be of the following types:

Class A carrying 7 per cent interest *per annum* to be amortized over fifteen years.

Class B carrying 2 per cent interest *per annum* to be amortized over twenty-five years.

Interest shall be payable at the conclusion of each quarterly period; the Bonds shall be amortized by the accumulative fund system of gradual amortization in sixty and one hundred quarters respectively depending on the class to which they belong, and with effect from the first three months following their issue through the drawing of lots at face value. Both the capital and the interest shall be free of all national, departmental and municipal tax other than income tax and other taxes assimilated thereto.

76. The Government shall enter into a contract with the *Banco de la República* for the latter to act as trustee in all matters pertaining to the issue, servicing and amortization of the Agrarian Bonds. To be valid this contract shall require only the approval of the President of the Republic with the assent of the Council of Ministers.

The provisions of this Act relevant to Agrarian Bonds shall be considered part of the trusteeship contract and shall rate as obligations of the Government in respect thereof.

Proviso. The Government shall not charge to the minimum contribution laid down in Paragraph 1 of Article 14 any amounts which it has to spend in servicing the Agrarian Bonds.

77. The Institute shall issue class A Agrarian Bonds only when the owners of land which it acquires in pursuance of this Act request payment for their land in such Bonds or use them to pay off the credits made by the Institute as a result of the acquisition.

The Institute shall, however, use the funds it receives from the State in interest and amortization on the Bonds to meet any cash payments to which the acquisition of land gives rise, and it may also use funds to prepare land for cultivation through irrigation works, the regulation of water courses and land reclamation works in accordance with Article 68 *et seq.* of this Act.

The Institute may also use class A Agrarian Bonds as guarantee for any credit transactions which it carries out under the foregoing paragraph. It may also use any sums it is due to receive from the State on account of the Bonds for the same purpose.

78. Class A Agrarian Bonds shall be received by the Institute at face value as the price of land which it sells in organized settlements areas. Class A Agrarian Bonds may also be used for paying: the capital part of the periodic payments which persons acquiring land in land partition or consolidation areas must make to the Institute; the outstanding amounts which the purchasers of land referred to in the third and fourth paragraphs of Article 70 must pay and the tax on the increased value of land referred to in paragraph 4 of Article 68.

Class B Agrarian Bonds shall also be received by the Institute at par for the payments referred to in the final part of the third paragraph of Article 70 if the owner was paid for the land with class B Agrarian Bonds and in the proportion corresponding thereto.

Persons acquiring land in partition or consolidation areas shall also be entitled to make payment in class B Agrarian Bonds at par up to an amount equivalent to 15 per cent on capital of the instalment payments which they must make to the Institute.

So as to facilitate payment by persons receiving plots in partitioned land of the amount corresponding to the principal of their debts, the Institute shall organize a revolving fund which it shall use for the purchase of bonds on the open market and it shall then sell such bonds to its debtors for the average purchase price in the amounts and proportions which they need to make their payments.

Any bonds which the Institute receives in payment for the lands it sells may be used by it again for the purchase of other land.

79. The transfer and granting of funds and Agrarian Bonds as provided for in Article 16 of this Act may also be made by the Institute on behalf of other public law institutions or official agencies to which it delegates its responsibilities.

In the event of responsibility for the acquisition and partition of privately-owned land and for carrying out land consolidation work being delegated, the agencies exercising the responsibility shall act as agents of the Institute and hence shall give undertakings on its behalf in respect of obligations deriving from the acquisition of land to the same extent as is laid down for the Institute itself.

VENEZUELA, CONSTITUTION OF 1961, Article 101

Only for reasons of public utility or social interest, by means of judicial decision and payment of just compensation, shall the expropriation of any class of property be declared. In the expropriation of land [immovables] for purposes of agrarian reform or of extension or improvement of towns, and in cases determined by law for grave reasons of national interest, the deferment of payment may be established for a determined time, or its partial cancellation may be established by means of the issue of bonds of obligatory acceptance, with sufficient guarantee.

[See articles 172-79 of the Agrarian Reform Law of Venezuela, pp. 445-47, *supra*, for the provisions establishing the methods of deferred payment to be used in various classes of expropriation.]

Early in 1963, article 10 of the Chilean Constitution was amended to permit the expropriation of land which is "abandoned" or "manifestly badly exploited" upon immediate payment of 10% of the compensation, with payment of the balance in 15 annual instalments. The balance was to draw interest, and to be adjusted annually for the purpose of maintaining its real value during periods of inflation. Under the amendment, if the government wished to expropriate land on any other basis, *e.g.,* excessive size, it had to make immediate compensation in full. Because even this amendment was too restrictive, the administration of President Frei (elected in 1964) has sought the adoption of a further amendment to article 10, which is reprinted below.* The administration's projected land reform law, based on this proposed constitutional amendment, authorizes compensation according to the following scheme: Lands expropriated because of their "excessive size" are paid for in cash in the amount of 10% of the compensation, and in 25-year bonds for the remainder. Owners of "badly exploited" lands that are expropriated receive 5% in cash and the remainder in 25-year bonds; owners of "abandoned" lands that are expropriated receive 1% in cash, and the rest in the same bonds. The bonds are redeemed in yearly instalments. Their value, in the case of expropriation for "excessive size," is adjusted upward annually by a percentage which corresponds to 80% of the increase in the cost of living index for the first 200 "basic hectares" ** taken, 60% for the next 100 basic hectares, and 40% for the next 100 basic hectares; bonds which correspond to lands taken after the first 400 basic hectares are to be readjusted at a 20% rate. Each of these adjustment percentages is halved in cases of expropriation for bad exploitation or abandonment, so that the rates run from 40% down to 10%. While tax appraisals are to be used for purposes of evaluating expropriated land, those valuations are now at market-value levels. Improvements are to be paid for in cash, immediately.

PROPOSED 1966 AMENDMENT TO CONSTITUTION OF CHILE

Article Second.—N° 10 of art. 19 is replaced by the following:

The right of property in its various forms.

The statute law will establish the means of acquiring property, of using, enjoying and disposing of it, and the limitations and obligations that allow the assurance of its social function and that make it accessible to all. The social function of property includes whatever is required by the general interests of the State, public utility and health, the best exploitation of productive sources and energies in the service of the community and the elevation of living conditions of the general public. Whenever community interest requires, the law may reserve to the State exclusive domain over certain kinds of property.

---

* As this book goes to press, adoption of the amendment is characterized as "imminent" by experienced observers in Chile.

** A basic hectare is one hectare of irrigated land in a specified valley near Santiago or its equivalent, which may be nearly 300 hectares of the worst land or half an acre of the best.

No one can be deprived of his property except by virtue of a general or special law that authorizes the expropriation in order that the property fulfill the social function specified by the legislator. The expropriated owner shall always have a right to indemnification. The statute law shall determine the rules for fixing indemnification, as well as the tribunal that shall hear claims concerning the amount, the form of discharging this obligation, the portion that must be paid immediately, the period and conditions on which the balance is to be paid, if there be one, and the suitable times and manner in which the expropriating agency shall take material possession of the expropriated property.

The State shall aim at the appropriate distribution of ownership and at the establishment of family property.

BOLIVIA: Legislative Decree Nº 03464 relative to Agrarian Reform, 2 August 1953 (FAO translation)

PAYMENT FOR EXPROPRIATIONS AND REDEMPTION OF THE AGRARIAN DEBT

156.   Lands affected by this Legislative Decree in accordance with Article 34 shall be paid for at the current registered valued to the extent corresponding to the part concerned, with Agrarian Reform Bonds which shall earn a non-capitalizable interest of 2 per cent per annum, over a term of 25 years.

157.   As regards the redemption of the bonds preference shall be given to the Bolivian Bank of Agriculture and to small creditors over large creditors, and payment shall be guaranteed by mortgages on the lands granted to the peasants, with their crops, livestock and industrial installations and, subsidiarily, by a State guarantee.

158.   Such bonds shall have redemptive power to cancel mortgage debts contracted with the Bolivian Bank of Agriculture on properties affected by this Legislative Decree, for payment of arrears of taxes on the expropriated property and for the acquisition of State lands in colonizable zones, within the limits prescribed for the various types of property.

159.   The conditions, the redemptive power and the terms of issue and of transmission of such bonds to the creditors shall be governed by special regulations.

160.   Peasants who have been granted lands shall pay the amount of the registered value of such lands within the term of 25 years taking effect from the date of possession.

The National Agrarian Reform Service shall specify procedures to be followed in determining the shares to be paid by the peasants for their parcels.

[The foregoing provisions of the Bolivian law have never been carried out. The bonds have not even been printed. An economist who was advising the Bolivian government on public finance once suggested that the bonds be issued, just for the purpose of creating a security which might be traded in Bolivia, which has no securities market. The suggestion met with some initial favor, but was abandoned as politically dangerous. These mortgage bonds are naturally connected in the minds of the *campesinos* with the requirement of Article 10 that they pay for the land distributed to them; issue of the bonds might be interpreted as an indication of the government's intent to enforce Article 160, and there is no such present intention.]

SIMPSON, THE EJIDO: MEXICO'S WAY OUT* 219-28 (1937)

In the matter of agrarian bonds and indemnification in expropriations for ejidos, as in the case of all other aspects of the agrarian reform, there has been a very considerable amount of patching up and making over the laws. . . .
* * *

The government is authorized to issue Agrarian Public Debt, twenty-year 5 per cent bearer bonds to the extent of 50 million pesos in series as and when required. Amortization is by annual drawing when the market quotation of the bonds is equal to or greater than par at the time of the drawing (January of each year). Whenever the market value is less than par, bonds are retired by purchase in the open market.[12]

In case of nonpayment of interest (due at the end of each calendar year), or of the nonpayment of bonds favored in a drawing, both bonds and interest coupons may be used at their face value to pay "any federal taxes not especially pledged." Agrarian bonds are receivable at any time, whether drawn or not, at par in payment for public lands; for the payment of rentals or the purchase price of lands granted to villages and subdivided among their inhabitants; for guarantee deposits in any case where bonds of the public debt are permitted in place of cash, and for the payment of certain taxes. Also, agrarian bonds may be offered as collateral in the National Bank of Agricultural Credit up to 66 per cent of their commercial value.

---

* Copyright © , The University of North Carolina Press, reprinted by permission.

[12]This "foxy" measure, not introduced in the law until December 29, 1928, is to be credited to the Portes Gil administration. It means in practice that agrarian bonds are always retired by purchase in the open market, since they have never been quoted at anywhere near par, much less at more than par. [In 1938, holders of agrarian bonds were authorized to exchange them for ordinary government bonds of 40 year maturity. In 1951, during the Alemán administration, the law was amended to provide that small property owners whose land was taken in violation of their rights under certificates of inaffectability, and who had secured favorable administrative decisions on their claims against the government, were required to accept the same type of 40 year bonds in settlement. — Ed.]

Any person whose land has been expropriated for the purpose of ejido dotations may solicit indemnification from the Ministry of Agriculture within one year after official notification of such expropriation. The basis of indemnity in all cases is the assessed tax value of the land in question plus 10 per cent and allowances for the value of any improvements made after the date of assessment. Those dissatisfied with the evaluation placed on their lands have the right to request a review of their case before the District Courts.

Finally, it should be recalled in connection with this summary of the laws governing compensation in agrarian expropriation cases, that the decree of December 23, 1931, which reformed the original agrarian decree of January 1915 and denied the right of landowners to be granted *amparos* in agrarian cases involving the dotation of lands to villages, expressly states that the only legal recourse open to landowners affected by such dotations is to petition the government for indemnification and that solely in the manner set forth in the agrarian debt laws.*

* * *

... About the only conclusion that can be drawn on the basis of any calculation possible at present is that the agrarian debt, whether by that term is meant the potential debt for land already expropriated or what might with some awkwardness be called the potentially potential debt for the possibly 12.7 million hectares of crop land and anywhere from 25 to 40 million hectares of other types of land yet to be expropriated, is very large. Indeed, so large is the debt compared with Mexico's fiscal resources that one may say without fear of contradiction that it will never be acknowledged in an amount even approximating its entirety and that part which is acknowledged will not be paid at more than a fraction of its face value.

Some support for the foregoing statement may be found in the fact that of the total of approximately 9.7 million pesos of bonds amortized, less than 16 per cent have been retired at their face value, either in cash or in payments for certain classes of taxes, national lands, and so forth. The remaining 84 per cent has been amortized by purchases in the open market at prices far below the face value of the bonds. (The quotation on agrarian bonds at the present time — June 1934 — is around twelve centavos.) The failure of the government in recent years to pay interest regularly on the bonds outstanding has, of course, greatly facilitated the business of buying the bonds in the open market.

In the final analysis, the attitude the government will take with reference to its liabilities assumed and yet to be assumed under the laws governing indemnification in agrarian expropriation cases will be determined by the position eventually adopted toward the whole problem of the ejido. Attention has already been drawn to the fact that some of the older and more conservative of the revolutionary leaders have advocated, as part of their general policy of

---

* After 1931, the government stopped issuing agrarian bonds. See MADDOX, LAND REFORM IN MEXICO (American Universities Field Staff, 1959). — Ed.

bringing the distribution of ejido lands to a speedy close, that in the near future the agrarian bond mill should be stopped and that the government should
undertake to pay in cash for any further expropriations necessary to complete
the program of giving land to villages. . . .

* * *

. . . When the new Agrarian Code was enacted in March, 1934, nothing
at all was said about payment in cash for initial ejido grants and even the provision regarding payment for *ampliaciones* was quietly omitted. If the younger
group of *agraristas* now actively pushing the distribution of ejido lands "to the
last man and the last village" has its way, the payment for expropriated lands
in bonds will continue to be the order of the day. When these bonds will be
redeemed, if ever, is another matter. It has already been suggested by one of
the prominent leaders in the revolutionary group that the government will
probably have to extend the date of maturity for agrarian bonds anywhere
from twenty to sixty years. It may even come to pass that, while the laws are
kept on the books as a gesture of international good-will and while bonds will
continue to be handed out to those with an appetite for unravelling red tape,
the bonds will never be redeemed and the problem of compensation for lands
expropriated for ejidos will be solved by the simple process of allowing it to
sink deeper and deeper in the morass of bureaucratic inaction until finally it
disappears altogether.

* * *

In justiying its position with reference to the right to interpret the phrase
mediante indemnización as permitting the state to indemnify owners of expropriated properties by the method of deferred payment (that is, in bonds) instead of in cash at the time of the making of such expropriations, the government has pointed first to the new conceptions of property established in Article 27 of the constitution and, second, to the doctrine of social necessity. As
long as the protection and preservation of private property was conceived as
the be-all and end-all of society, it was natural to consider that the right of
expropriation was a right to be exercised with the utmost caution. Article 27,
however, "in keeping with modern theories," is based on the assumption that
"individual private property is social in nature for it is society which creates the
right of private property and not private property which creates society." Under this conception expropriation becomes a right which the state exercises
with as much freedom as social needs may demand. The point of departure,
the entity to be protected, is society and not the individual. Whereas it is desirable whenever possible that, in expropriating private property, payment should
be made previous to or at the time of the act, the state is by no means bound
to follow this procedure. It may — and that is clearly the implication of the
word *mediante* in Article 27 — if social necessity so dictates and if the financial resources of the nation so determine, defer payment.

In answer to the third charge of the *hacendados* to the effect that the
bonds offered in payment for land taken for ejidos were without value, the

government has held that, whereas it is true that these agrarian bonds cannot be sold in the open market for their face value, it cannot be claimed for this reason that the bonds were worthless. They may be used to pay certain taxes and in a variety of other ways in government transactions. Moreover, on the bonds which have been issued, interest payments have been kept up with at least a fair degree of regularity. Nor must it be forgotten that the government, although under no obligation to do so, has repeatedly extended the period within which petitions for bonds could be made by landowners whose properties have been affected under the ejido laws. The fact that the landowners have, for the most part, refused to avail themselves of this privilege and have consistently declared on all and sundry occasions that the bonds are worthless, is precisely one of the principal reasons why the bonds do not, and cannot, increase in value.

FLORES, TRATADO DE ECONOMIA AGRICOLA *
335-36, 344-45 (1961)

Only 170 [Mexican] national claimants were indemnified; they had presented 381 claims for the expropriation of an area of 222,797 hectares, which equals .55% of the total of 40 million hectares distributed up to [1959]. The compensation amounted to 24,426,800 pesos, which were paid in bonds of the public agrarian debt. [At present one peso equals $.08 in United States money. The inflation in Mexico has been somewhat more rapid than that experienced in the United States, so that earlier equivalences to the dollar were higher. — Ed].

The redemption of those bonds was achieved by purchases in the market, at quotations which fluctuated between 5% and 16% of their nominal value; or by accepting them, also with a penalty, in payment of certain taxes; or by exchanging them, in certain cases, for ordinary bonds of the internal public debt of 40 years.

In addition, an unspecified number of influential large owners was indemnified with bonds of the public internal debt; or compensated either in rural or urban lands or in cash; or even in all three of these forms. The area of lands obtained in this manner (as well as the amount of the compensations) is unknown, but it can be conjectured that, as in the foregoing case, it represents an insignificant fraction of the total redistributed lands. The rest of the lands given to *ejidatarios* [beneficiaries] were expropriated without compensation.

* * *

Based on the Law of January 6, 1915, and on Article 27 of the Constitution, around two million hectares (1,936,729), property of North American citizens, were affected, to which the owners attributed in their claims a total value of $56 million. With respect to lands owned by other foreigners, the government indemnified their owners by means of private agreement. An indeterminate number of foreign properties were acquired and continue to be acquired by means of mutually satisfactory agreements of sale.

The Mexican Government paid $12.5 million [U.S.], between 1938 and 1955, for lands expropriated from North American citizens in the period 1927-40, which was the critical stage of the Revolution. Although the United States insisted vigorously on the traditional principle of "adequate, prompt payment in cash," finally, as we have seen, the indemnification was agreed upon on a compromise basis, taking into account Mexico's possibilities for payment.

In such a way the third original goal of the agrarian reform was fulfilled, thus preventing the interference of foreign powers from making impossible the immediate application of laws designed to renew the economic structure of the country.

Once more the principle of International Law was confirmed that establishes, without departing completely from traditional norms, that the duty to compensate can be delayed and subordinated to the possibility of payment. This compromise appears to be just in the face of the double necessity of offering a reasonable degree of protection to the property of foreigners and of encouraging the State to maintain the reform even when the payment of compensation turns out to be greater than the State's immediate financial possibilities.

With respect to common, current and isolated expropriations, the rule of prompt and full indemnification is valid; but, on the other hand, with respect to the agrarian reform, given the importance of its objectives and its collective and impersonal character, indemnification must be adjusted to the possibility of payment by the debtor State, not only with respect to the value of the expropriated property but also with respect to the time required for payment.

CASE OF CONSTITUTIONALITY OF LAW N° 135 *
Supreme Court of Justice of Colombia (Plenary Session 1964)
VII Derecho Colombiano N° 37, p. 3 (1965)

[Under Colombia's procedure for testing abstract questions of the constitutionality of legislation (see Grant, *Judicial Control of Legislation,* 3 AM. J. COMP. L. 186 (1954), a citizen challenged the 1961 Law of Social Agrar-

* For comment on this decision, see Karst, *The Colombian Land Reform: "The Contribution of an Independent Judiciary,"* 14 AM. J. COMP. L. 118 (1965).

558 CHAPTER IV. LAND REFORM

ian Reform. He urged that various provisions of the Law violated the principle of separation of powers, and he made a number of other arguments based on the constitutional aspects of administrative law doctrine. The Court's discussion of those issues — all decided in favor of the Law's validity — is omitted here. The plaintiff also argued that the deferment of payment of compensation for expropriated land (articles 62 and 74 of the Law) violated article 30 of the Constitution. He contended first that the compensation was not "previous," and secondly that the last paragraph of article 30, p. 471, *supra*, was not applicable, since (a) the Congress, in considering the Law to provide compensation, had not relied on this paragraph; (b) the paragraph did not apply to takings for "reasons of public utility or social interest"; (c) takings for "reasons of equity" required case-by-case consideration by the legislature, and could not be authorized generally by statute; and (d) there had been no two-thirds vote (no "absolute majority") for the Law. The Court was able to avoid this latter four-part argument by holding that the payment provided by the Law was "previous." Only the portions of the opinion dealing with the plaintiff's contentions under article 30 are reprinted here.]

The Court considers:

The political constitutions of Colombia withtout exception have established the principle of the superiority of public over private interest. It follows that they authorize the expropriation of private property for reasons of public utility, with the correlative indemnification to the owner.

The constitutions of 1811, 1812, 1821, 1832 and 1842 did not specify that the indemnification must be *previous*,* but those of 1830, 1853, 1858, 1863 and 1886 and the Legislative Acts Nos. 3 of 1910 and 1 of 1936 did indeed so require.

Article 10 of [the 1936 Constitution — the present article 30] introduced to the constitution of 1886 a reform of the highest importance: *the social function of ownership*, in the common good. This source of the owner's obligations results from the process of the socialization of law begun in the middle of the 19th century and vigorously pursued after the First World War.

Between the individualist conception of property — result of a Revolution directed at redeeming the "sacred, inalienable, and imprescriptible" rights of man — and the collectivistic conception which negates private ownership, the "social function of ownership" is seen as an intermediate system. But in this system at the same time that one current abolishes property as a right, radically transforming it into a *function,* which is the responsibility of the owner (who is like a state functionary), another current maintains property to be a subjective right of the owner, but attributes to it an essential function imposed by the interests of the community.

The function has not been substituted for property rights merely because

---

* All the italicization in this opinion is in the original. — Ed.

article 30 of the Constitution says that "ownership is a social function". . . .
The first part of the same article 30 guarantees "private ownership," acquired
with a proper title in accordance with the laws. This interpretation, besides,
is the only one that is consistent with the individualistic structure of our democratic organization, and such has also been the uniform jurisprudence and
doctrine of the country. . . .

Thus, to the classical characteristics of ownership — to be perpetual,
exclusive, complete, etc. — is added that of having a social function. But while
the former characteristics were set forth in former times, the latter is barely
beginning its process of conformation, after having been established in Constitutions after the last world wars, especially in America.

Neither the Constitution nor the law defines the social function. *Function*
is a specific activity directed at an end, within the organism which it serves.
In other words, this new characteristic of ownership affects the exercise of the
owners' right. Since the right is composed of the elements *usus, fructus and
abusus* [Latin in the original], in any given moment the function . . . can
affect one or all of them. And if this functionalism has an object, that of being
social, it is obvious that the function established in article 30 of the Supreme
Law has no other purpose than the common good, based inevitably upon the
prevalence of social interests over private ones, in all instances and circumstances.

The constitutional text provides help in defining the function. It says of
the function that it "implies obligations," which can be none other than the
responsibility of the owner . . . toward the community. What are these obligations? We know from the language of the precept only that they are a product of the new function, and that this function is revealed publicly and collectively through their performance. But, being a generic characteristic of ownership, the function cannot be manifested except through burdens which must
be specified by the legislative branch, as the Court (Sala de Negocios Gene-
rales) has said in a decision of March 24, 1943 (vol. LV, pp. 1966 and 1997.
399. 2a.) and in the cassation decision of August 31, 1954 (vol. LXXVIII,
p. 2145. 432. 2a.). The Framers of the amendment themselves applied the
new principle in the last part of article 30, in authorizing expropriation without compensation, and shortly after the constitutional reform took effect, Law
200 of 1936 imposed upon landowners the obligation of working their lands
economically, under the threat of losing them.

The Court began the process of interpretation of the constitutional reform
in the following terms, according to the decision of the Plenary Session on
March 10, 1938:

> "The Framers of the 1936 amendment made the fundamental right of
> ownership relative, accentuating its subordination to the interests of the
> community, and also accentuating limitations on the free choice of the
> owner.

"The Framers founded individual ownership on the social function that involves obligations, in accordance with the views of modern social function theorists who reject the fixed and ever identical form attributed to that institution by the [classical] economic schools, recognizing that, since ownership has taken very different forms throughout history and is susceptible to very great modifications, it is fully guaranteed through [the present article 30] only to the degree that it responds to the collective necessities of economic life." (Vol. XLVI, p. 1934, 193.)

The social function, according to this doctrine, accentuated the subordination of ownership to community interests, to the point that the guarantee given in the Constitution in favor of property rights is conditioned to the extent to which the rights correspond to the needs of the community. It is precisely this which must be determined in this part of the present decision: whether the law can introduce [new forms of payment of indemnification in cases of expropriation].

Article 62 of the Law contains the formula by which the State should attend to the compensation payment corresponding to the expropriation of land. The motives of public utility and social interest that justify it are stated in the Law. [The opinion quotes art. 54 and summarizes art. 62, pp. 472, 547-48, *supra*.]

The plaintiff challenges article 62, not because it orders payment for uncultivated land in bonds, but because it authorizes instalment payments for the balances to be paid on [improperly farmed or other land]. The Procurador General agrees, but he adds that it is contrary to the text of the Constitution to make payment in bonds on the basis of their face value.

Article 30 of the Constitution does not specify that the indemnification must be made *in cash* or *immediately*. The text does provide that payment be *previous,* and so it must be determined whether by being in bonds (lands of group a)), or part in money and the balance *in instalments* (lands of groups b) and c)) *it is no longer previous.*

Previous indemnification is, primarily, the definition and recognition of the right of the owner before the expropriation, so that, on the one hand, there will not be arbitrary expropriations and on the other, the owner will be able to count on receiving commercial goods or paper, alienable and certain, equivalent to the damage caused.

A) In regard to uncultivated lands.—Class B bonds are commercial goods, have the backing of the State, earn interest, are negotiable, are amortized quarterly by means of drawing lots, and besides, can be given to the Institute in payment for lands, according to article 78 of the Law.

* * *

In this case the Law substitutes for an unproductive property, the ownership of bonds, guaranteed by the State, which earn interest and represent the commercial valuation of the land (art. 61, par. 5, Law 135). The interest is in any case greater than the income from uncultivated land. The constitutional precept does not guarantee private ownership to the extreme of protecting persons who do not work their estates; thus the reversion of titles to the state is permitted as a sanction applied to owners who allow their lands to go unexploited for the periods established in article 6 of Law 200 of 1936 and article 10 of Law 100 of 1944. Thus, with regard to uncultivated lands, for which those periods have not yet terminated, the compensation prescribed by articles 62 and 74 of the Law amounts to generous treatment to those who maintain their land outside the performance of the social function, in expectation of an increase in value owing to some outside force. ... The depreciation that the bonds might suffer in the market does not affect their intrinsic worth as an indication of compensation, because this risk is a phenomenon from which no securities, governmental or commercial — indeed, no goods of any kind — can escape.

   B)   In regard to lands of groups b) and c).—With respect to lands that are adequately or inadequately exploited, or whose exploitation is carried out by small sharecroppers or tenants without the direct participation of the owner, it is true that the compensation is not made *entirely in money and immediately,* but the balance is paid in goods that are equivalent to money, since the balances are *credits* guaranteed by the State and which produce, respectively, interest of 4% and 6% annually, paid twice a year. Furthermore, upon being reduced to *private documents,* at the option of the expropriated party or creditor, these obligations can be transferred or mortgaged in accordance with the Civil Code; or if they prefer, the owners receive Class A bonds, guaranteed by the State, bonds that earn 7% interest annually, are negotiable, are amortized through quarterly drawings at their nominal value and may be used to pay the Institute for lands, in the cases under the conditions specified by articles 70 and 78 of the Law.

   Credits with or without documents, or bonds.—These constitute the performance of the obligation of the State, previously satisfied, because from the beginning they are added to the patrimony of the expropriated party, thus accomplishing previous compensation. The Constitution, in order to make expropriation an easier and more adequate instrument for the common good, does not require payment in money, but simply indemnification. ...

   * * *

   [The Procurador General argues that] payment in bonds conforms to the constitutional precepts, "so long as the bonds represent irrevocable and certain titles, of a fixed monetary value, liquid, commercially acceptable and transferable, with an adequate periodical income, ... and that they serve to indemnify the value of the expropriated property." But, [he argues,] it is not so when the Institute pays with bonds, computing them *at their nominal value,* be it a case of expropriation of lands of group a), or of those included in groups b) and c). The censure of the Public Ministry does not refer, therefore, to payment in bonds, which it accepts as being in harmony with the statute, but rather to such payment based on the nominal value of the bonds. But the

Procurador General fails to note that in cases involving lands in groups b) and c), the payment in bonds depends on the will of the owner or expropriated party or of his successors. And as for lands of group a), we deal with uncultivated, abandoned lands, almost subject to an uncompensated reversion of title to the State.

It is superfluous to add that the concept of *indemnification* for expropriation cannot be confused with the concept of *price* paid in a sale. The latter is a bilateral agreement under private law, the result of freedom of contract, in which the buyer's obligation must be fulfilled in money. Expropriation is not a contract; it is not a sale, not even a forced one, such as those which take place at public auctions in certain cases; it is of an essentially different order, of public law, dedicated to the good of the community. For these higher motives, the Administration takes private property, and as this method engenders *damage* and not a *price,* it is rectified through an *indemnification.* . . .

The foregoing should influence the interpretation of article 30 of the Constitution, in order not to impose the geometric rigor of a contract upon the process of expropriation, but rather to promote the spirit of equity and justice that governs the institutions of Public Law, tested by the subject matter of this action of unconstitutionality, through the social orientation of Private Law.

And it is fitting to repeat that from among the criteria for evaluation of land that have been accepted in the countries that have faced land problems, Law 135 has followed the criterion of market value as determined by experts (art. 61, par. 5), ...

      * * *

[The decision was concurred in by all but three of the twenty members of the Court. One dissenter's objections were limited to the separation of powers issues; the other two dissented on the previous compensation issue. — Ed.]

Article 31 of the Cuban Agrarian Reform Act provides for compensation in agrarian bonds for expropriated owners. Nevertheless, it is the policy of the government of Cuba to confiscate the property of both the government and the citizens of the United States. See p. 481, *supra.* The action of the Cuban government has been attacked as a violation of public international law. "The duty of a government to compensate in case of nationalization is almost universally recognized." Domke, *Foreign Nationalizations,* 55 AM. J. INT'L L. 585, 603 (1961). The further duty to compensate fairly and promptly is a corollary to that rule; to the extent that an owner is not compensated fairly and promptly, he goes uncompensated for a portion of the property taken. One recent expression of the rule in the context of public international law is to be found in the Draft Convention on the International Responsibility of

States for Injures to Aliens, a model multination treaty, prepared by two North American scholars at the request of the International Law Commission. This draft holds a taking to be wrongful "if it is not accompanied by prompt payment of compensation," on terms at least as favorable as those given to nationals of the expropriating state, in an amount equal to the fair market value of the property taken. Sohn and Baxter, *Responsibility of States for Injuries to the Economic Interests of Aliens*, 55 AM. J. INT'L L. 545, 553 (1961).

But the same Draft Convention recognizes an inescapable fact of modern political life: the expropriating state is typically underdeveloped, in desperate need of capital, and quite unable to make compensation immediately. Thus it is that Article 10, Section 4 of the Draft Convention states that a taking for purposes of general economic and social reform is not wrongful if compensation is paid "over a reasonable number of years," provided that "a reasonable part of the compensation due is paid promptly," and a reasonable rate of interest is paid on the balance. The traditional standard of "prompt, adequate and effective" compensation was invented by investor nations, and is not supported by the governments of modern "developing" countries. It is ably criticized in Dawson and Weston, *"Prompt, Adequate and Effective": A Universal Standard of Compensation?*, 30 FORDHAM L. REV. 727 (1962). See also Karst, *Land Reform in International Law*, in ESSAYS ON EXPROPRIATION (to be published by Ohio State University Press in 1967).

Remedies for United States owners of expropriated property in Cuba are getting more scarce as time passes. First of all, one must find some property of the Cuban government to attach. Then, assuming that a Cuban airliner, or gunboat, or whatever, can be found, one must convince the Department of State that it should not make a "suggestion of immunity" to the court. Such a suggestion, in effect, clothes the foreign sovereign with an immunity similar to that which it would have in its own courts. Since the airline-hijacking incidents of 1961, the Department of State has not been very encouraging to United States litigants who wish to seize property of the Cuban government.

Even if the foreign sovereign is not immune from suit, the usual rule of international law is that the validity of acts of foreign governments cannot be challenged in the courts. Even if, say, the sugar expropriated by Cuba might be traced to a buyer amenable to suit in our courts, the act of state doctrine* would protect the buyer against the owner's claim:

> The effect of the act of state doctrine is to extend the sovereign immunity rule to actions between private litigants unless the State Department indicates to the court in which an action is commenced that it has no objection to the case being adjudicated. Allison, *Cuba's Seizure of American Business*, 47 A.B.A.J. 48, 187 at 188 (1961).

---

* See Banco Nacional de Cuba v. Sabbatino, 376 U.S. 398 (1964;) Metzger, *Act-of-State Doctrine Redefined: The Sabbatino Case*, 1964 SUP. CT. REV. 223.

Diplomatic settlement of claims of United States nationals appears to be the most promising of a generally unpromising set of remedies for confiscated owners. For the future, a number of suggestions have been made for the protection of foreign investments against risks of confiscation, war and the like. In some cases the United States will provide a limited guarantee against some such risks, upon the payment of a fee. See Surrey and Hill, *Investment Transactions Between Private Individuals Across National Frontiers,* 22 OHIO ST. L.J. 520, 532-34 (1961); Note, *Avoiding Expropriation Loss,* 79 HARV. L. REV. 1666 (1966).

---

3. Valuation of Expropriated Property

COLOMBIA: Act N° 135 of Social Agrarian Reform, December 13, 1961, *Diario Oficial* N° 30961, Dec. 20, 1961, p. 801 (FAO translation)

61.   When the Institute after survey of a particular area considers the acquisition of certain lands to be necessary to fulfill the social and public utility purposes set forth in Article 54, it shall proceed in the following manner:
1.   It shall issue a summons to the owner or his agent in person or if this proves impossible through the procedure laid down in the relevant regulatory decree, to attend in person or send a representative so that a thorough survey may be made of the land concerned, including if necessary the taking of measurements.

Landowners must allow the aforesaid survey to be made and in the event of their opposing or hindering it, the Institute may use compulsion, imposing successive fines of up to five thousand (5,000) Colombian pesos.
2.   Once the Institute and the owner of the portion of the farm which is to be compulsorily acquired have reached an agreement and have classified the land in accordance with Articles 55 and 58, the Institute shall have an estimate made by the experts of the body of valuers which the Augustín Codazzi Geographical Institute shall form for this purpose; on the basis of the estimate the Institute shall proceed with negotiations to determine the purchase price to be paid in accordance with Article 62 of this Act.
3.   If no agreement is reached regarding the price and classification of the land or if the owner refuses to sell voluntarily, the Institute shall issue a resolution laying down the classification of the land, specifying the technical and economic considerations on which it is based; the Institute shall then order expropriation proceedings to be taken. This action shall be notified in person to the owner or to his agent or legal representative.

If such notification cannot be given in person, it shall be made by using the procedure set forth in the decree issuing regulations under this. Act. The order made by the Institute shall be placed before the appropriate Administrative Disputes Court (*Tribunal de lo Contencioso Administrativo*) for decision as regards the classification of the land and its expropriability, if the owner of the land so requests within the five days following the notification. The Court, following the procedure laid down in the regulatory decree and after hearing the opinion of three experts appointed one by each of the parties plus one appointed by the Augustín Codazzi Geographical Institute, shall approve or alter the classification of the land and determine its expropriability.

4. Once the expropriation order has been issued, it shall be placed before the appropriate Circuit Judge (*Juez del Circuito*). Notwithstanding the provisions of the first paragraph of Article 67, the Institute may enter a request to take immediate possession of the land whose expropriation it has ordered, depositing with the *Banco de la República* the equivalent of the value of the expropriated land in Class B Agrarian Bonds in the case of uncultivated land, or the cash amount that must be paid as a first instalment in the case of other types of land. For this purpose alone the value of the land shall be considered as that established in the estimate made by the Augustín Codazzi Geographical Institute; the estimate shall be attached to the request for expropriation.

It shall be understood that the Institute shall pay interest at the rate established in this Act on the unpaid value in accordance with the expropriation order from the date on which it enters into possession of the land.

5. Valuation for the expropriation proceedings shall be carried out by three experts appointed as follows: one, by the Colombian Land Reform Insitute, another by the owner of the land and the third by the Augustín Codazzi Geographical Institute. If any objection is raised by any of the parties to the experts' finding and if the Judge upholds any such objection, three other experts shall be appointed in the prescribed manner, their finding being final.

In any matters not expressly laid down in this Act, the experts shall act in accordance with the relevant rules of the Code of Civil Procedure.

LOPEZ MICHELSEN, HACIA UNA VERDADERA REFORMA QUE COMPLETE LA "REVOLUCION EN MARCHA," in TIERRA: 10 ENSAYOS SOBRE LA REFORMA AGRARIA EN COLOMBIA* at 85, 96-99 (1961)

... What is the spirit of the Agrarian Reform? First to try to buy in every case within a principle of bargaining. In his statement, Doctor Arias says that there will be expropriation only exceptionally, that this law contains barely a potential authorization to expropriate, but that in the majority of the cases, the land will be purchased ....

But even in cases of expropriation one must return to the commercial criterion resulting from the law of supply and demand, to market prices, because the law says that the proceedings will be carried on by means of an evaluation in which the expropriated owner names one expert, the Agrarian Reform Institute names another and the Augustín Codazzi Institute a third. I have said previously that the result was going to be perhaps even higher prices than those which would be arrived at through direct negotiation. It was only a hypothesis; I said: the expert, as happens in every case in which he represents the owner, will put the value in the clouds; the expert of the Agrarian Reform Institute will make a relatively low valuation and the Augustín Codazzi Institute will step in to make an intermediate estimate, so that the land will be acquired at prices exactly equal to those of the market. Well then, I was mistaken. It turns out the Augustín Codazzi Institute values property higher than the commercial prices. [The speaker mentions some high valuations which the Augustín Codazzi Institute has recently made.] And I ask myself: what is going to happen to the agrarian reform on the day when instead of having the Agustín Codazzi Institute play the part of the balancer, the owner becomes the balancer, since the Agustín Codazzi Institute markes the highest valuation, the owner the medium valuation and the Agrarian Reform Institute the lowest valuation. . . .

I have read various Agrarian Reforms. . . . In accordance with the criterion of what an Agrarian Reform is, there always exist in the context of the Laws a series of provisions conditioning the form of valuations in order to avoid speculation factors. Our distinguished friend the Minister of Agriculture in his erudite study, shows how the value of land in Colombia bears no relation to its productivity, in the greater number of cases. Land is like a money box; land is sought for purposes of maintaining valuation; . . . and ultimately land, according to the Tax Reform of last year, has been placed in conditions such that it may be declared at two, three or four times more than its real value during this year for the purpose of avoiding future taxable gains. So the price of land in Colombia is not as it might be in the United States, an economic relation between what it can produce for whoever might acquire it and what it might be worth in commerce. Thus we see the paradox that the best land in the United States, in the State of Illinois, is worth $400 to $500, or rather 4,500 pesos, at the exchange of nine pesos to the dollar [the value of the peso in 1966 is about half that quoted here — Ed.], while in Colombia we see similar lands at 10,000, 15,000 and 20,000 pesos, according to the Agustín Codazzi Institute itself. [The speaker quotes Article 25 of the Venezuelan Agrarian Reform Law, and also a similar provision in a draft land reform law prepared for Peru with the assistance of members of the faculty of Cornell University.]

. . . I should like to go further, to mention the classes given in American universities concerning Agrarian Reform. Here I have some lectures of Professor Rothenstein Rodan, a professor of Massachussetts Institute of Technology .... [His students] are taught with respect to Agrarian Reform, that compensation should never be greater than 60% or 70% of the product [presumably the capitalized product — Ed.] of the expropriated estates. Where would expropriation in Colombia be if the criterion were the acquisition of properties for 60% or 70% of their product, at the time of the acquisition on the part of the State? . . .

* * *

I should like the defenders of the project, when they answer these objections, to show me the case of some other country where the announcement of an agrarian reform has produced so much enthusiasm, so much demand and so much prosperity for the landowners.

MORALES BENITEZ, REFORMA AGRARIA — COLOMBIA CAMPESINA* 269-70 (1962)

With respect to valuations, there is Article 3 of Law 20 of 1959. Said provision was adopted in order to forward a policy of colonization. It is proper to reproduce it, as well as Article 2, since they show very great similarities in their statements of this problem of land. The text of the two articles is as follows:

[Article 2 outlines the purposes of the 1959 Statute, which are similar to those of the Agrarian Reform Law of 1961.]

"Article 3. The distributions of land to which this law refers are declared to be of public utility and social interest.

"By executive resolution of the Ministry of Agriculture shall be determined . . . the lands that may be expropriated [for the purposes stated in Article 2], by means of judicial proceeding and appropriate compensation. The value of this compensation shall not exceed 30% above the registered value [for land tax purposes] on December 31 of the year prior to the initiation of the expropriation action."

It should not be forgotten, also, that the Government has been proposing this Agrarian Reform to the country for several months. Therefore, it may be presumed that the owners have used the opportunity given them by Law 81 of 1960 and its regulatory Decree to place a commercial value on their lands, if they consider the tax registry values to be out of adjustment. This Law, which refers to taxes, has tried to avoid burdening owners heavily — with respect to capital gains — if their estates have not been correctly valued in the tax registry, in case they should later sell their lands. It was a good occasion avoiding any misadjustment of the price. . . .

One need not be a very acute interpreter to notice the similarity that exists between the ends and purposes announced in the two transcribed articles of the Law of 1959 and the object of the projected Social Agrarian Reform, which is announced in six points in the first article.

FR. GONZALO ARROYO, S.J., LETTER TO OTTO MORALES BENITEZ of Oct. 29, 1962, in MORALES BENITEZ, REFORMA AGRARIA — COLOMBIA CAMPESINA* at 275 (1962)

Unless enormous sums of money are available, which I do not believe to be the case in Colombia, an agrarian reform that compensates the old owners for the commercial value of lands will be very *limited* and *partial* in practice. A true solution to the problem of the *campesino* will not be obtained. The reason is that a true redistribution of incomes in favor of the *campesino* class is needed, so that the latter can be incorporated into the productive process. . . . In addition, on behalf of the thesis of tax registry value the fact may be advanced that the value of land is inflated above its real productivity, owing to the concentration of lands in a few hands. Still a third argument might be added: If landowners have paid taxes to the State in accordance with the tax registry value, they should also be compensated in accordance with this same value and not with the commercial price of the land.

The ambiguities in the Colombian Law concerning valuation were clarified seven months after the Law's enactment by an administrative regulation (Decreto N° 1904, 1962, art. 1), limiting the appraisers to values not exceeding 130% of the assessed tax valuation for the previous year, following the precedent recommended by Dr. Morales Benítez. Professor Hirschman called this regulation "perhaps the strongest [provision] of the whole body of new legislation . . . ." JOURNEYS TOWARD PROGRESS 152 (1963).

In 1963, however, after the change in administrations (from Liberal to Conservative), the rule was changed to permit an owner to make a new estimate for land valuation purposes, which valuation also serves for determining the land's value in cases of expropriation. Excessive valuations for tax purposes do not bind the acquiring agency. Decreto N° 2895, Nov. 26, 1963; Decreto N° 181, Feb. 1, 1964.

SIMPSON, THE EJIDO: MEXICO'S WAY OUT*
225-26 (1937)

The vast majority of the landowners affected by the agrarian laws have undoubtedly felt that they have been very badly treated. They have held, quite naturally, that the whole system of compensation for expropriated lands is grossly unjust on the grounds: (a) that, in view of the chaotic and often confiscatory system of taxation, it has been the traditional and accepted practice in many states in Mexico to declare rural properties at something less than their real value and that, hence, indemnification on the basis of 110 per cent of the tax valuation is unfair; . . . .

In reply to the charges and complaints of the landlords, the revolutionary government has said in effect that so far as the basis used in the evaluation of expropriated properties is concerned, if the *hacendados* have found this unfair, they have no one to blame but themselves. What could be more just than to take the hacendados' own statements, sworn before the tax authorities, of the value of their properties? Is the government in any way responsible for the fact that the landlords chose to undervalue their properties in order to defraud the government of taxes? Moreover, the landlords have been given repeated opportunities to rectify the valuation they have placed on their lands. Nevertheless, they have refused to take advantage of the government's efforts to make it possible for them to declare their properties at their true worth.

Can the government be blamed for this?[29] Finally, the government has pointed out that it is an acknowledged fact that the pre-revolutionary market values of farm properties were greatly exaggerated and dependent upon artificial tariff barriers and the exploitation of the peon. Since the revolution these values have been deflated and the post-revolutionary market values are probably not far from the fiscal values which the *hacendados* saw fit to place on their properties during their heyday.

---

[29] "The Mexican Commissioners further stated that since 1914 the Government had given the owners various opportunities to rectify the fiscal value [of their property.] On the 19th of September of that year a law was passed to determine the value of real property in the Republic, and provided that said assessment would serve as a basis to establish the value in case of expropriation. Later the Constitution of 1917 established the same basis. The owners, however, did not correct their declarations at the time, nor have they up to the present time; as in spite of the fact that a regulation of the decree of October 11, 1922, was issued the 30th of May of the present year [1923], its object being also to determine the value of real property in the country, the owners continued to resist complying with the legislation in that regard.

"Under these circumstances, the Mexican Government believes that the owners have had the opportunity of placing themselves in a position not to suffer damage, and if any of them have not wished to take advantage of this opportunity granted them by the law, it is their own fault." Proceedings of the United States-Mexican Commision, p. 34.

VENEZUELA: Agrarian Reform Act, March 5, 1960,
Gaceta Oficial N° 611 Extraordinario, March 19, 1960,
p. 1 (FAO translation)

25. In evaluating rural properties to be acquired in whole or in part for valuable consideration for the purposes of the Agrarian Reform, the following factors shall be taken into consideration:

(a) The average production over the six years immediately preceding the date of acquisition or of the request for expropriation.
(b) The declared or assessed official value for tax purposes under enactments relating thereto.
(c) The acquisition price of the property in the last conveyances of ownership carried out during the ten-year period prior to the date of valuation, and the acquisition prices of similar properties in the same region or zone in the five-year period immediately preceding the date of the expropriation request or purchase proposal;

Provided, that although in evaluating properties the above-mentioned factors shall primarily be taken into account, any other factors which may be useful in fixing a just price, and all those mentioned in the Act relating to Expropiation in the Public or Social Interest, shall also be taken into consideration;

Provided, further, that the valuation shall include, in addition to the value of the land, the value of the buildings, installations, chattels, equipment and improvements existing thereon;

Provided, finally, that the determination of value shall take into account only the actual fair value of the property, to the exclusion of any consideration of possible damages or disadvantage or of the sentimental value of the property.

The Colombian Law, p. 564, *supra,* establishes the agencies to evaluate expropriated land, although it does not provide them with any guides to decision. With respect to valuation as well as other issues, *who* decides may turn out to be as important as the substantive standards for decision provided by law. In the United States, valuation in eminent domain cases is normally a jury question — and always subject to judicial review. The jury is not a federal constitutional requirement; see Blair, *Federal Condemnation Proceedings and the Seventh Amendment,* 41 HARV. L. REV. 29 (1927). Of course juries are not used for this purpose in Latin America.

In Venezuela, the judicial review afforded on the issue of valuation appears to be somewhat more real than it is on the issue of affectability. The courts may appoint their own experts to advise on the question. If the National Agrarian Institute wishes to take possession before the expropriation action is completed, it must deposit in court not the sum which corresponds to its own valuation, but that which the court determines as the probable compensation.

MEXICO: AGRARIAN CODE OF 1943

* * *

70.—Encumbrances on property affected by the Agrarian Reform shall be extinguished proportionally to the part which is affected. The creditors shall retain their personal action against the affected owners; but they cannot exercise it except in the following manner:

I.—The area left to the debtor, once the expropriation has been accomplished, shall be subjected only to a proportional part of the debt, taking as a base for determining the latter, the value which the whole estate had on the date when the encumbrance was established.

II.—The rest of the personal action derived from the debt may be exercised only with respect to the indemnification proceeds corresponding to the affected part of the encumbered property, exclusive of other property of the debtor, unless he, upon establishing the encumbrance, contracted to the contrary, expressly renouncing the benefits of this article.

4. Some Concluding Questions About Confiscation

a. Granted the nearly universal confiscatory nature of the reforms which we have considered, why is it that such pains have been taken to disguise the fact? See Karst, *Latin-American Land Reform: The Uses of Confiscation*, 63 MICH. L. REV. 321, 369-72 (1964).

b. The principal early Civil Code in the Soviet Union (Civil Code of the R.S.F.S.R. of 1922)* provided for compensation at market value for property expropriated. 2 GSOVSKI, SOVIET CIVIL LAW 79 (1949). The market-price principle has been displaced generally by fixed prices — government controlled prices. *Id.* at 80. Buildings are expropriated at prices fixed by appraisals for tax or insurance purposes. *Id.* at 81. Why does a communist government adopt the principle of compensation? Is there any practical distinction between the wholesale takings of property associated with a social revolution and takings thereafter by the revolutionary government in power which would justify the decision to compensate for takings only in the latter case?

---

* The Civil Code was revised in 1964.

D. Land Distribution: Problems of Structure and Operation

1. Individual v. Collective Ownership

The "new agrarian structure" which emerges from a land reform may simply be the substitution of many little estates for a few great ones. For several reasons, the leaders who have carried out land reforms in Latin America have been reluctant to cut the beneficiaries entirely free. From the very beginning in Mexico, there has been tension between the proponents of individual ownership and management and the proponents of various forms of cooperative or collective systems. Basically, the latter position rests on certain assumptions about rural society in Latin America — in particular, about the need for a kind of paternal guidance and control of the *campesino*.

Paternalism in the law of Latin America is not a product of our century. The pre-Conquest governments left little that was important to the decision of individuals. The Spanish colonial government not only kept the indigenous population in a state of near-slavery; it created and perpetuated a highly authoritarian government over everyone. The Church made its contribution in the form of the Inquisition, which was extended to America. In the years of struggle which followed Independence, the new nations maintained security by concentrating power in single individuals, the so-called "integrating dictators," such as Rosas in Argentina. The adoption of the Code Napoléon, with its highly individualized outlook on ownership and contract, was more ironic than it was productive of change in such a social-political context. Written permissions, official registrations, legal disabilities abound in the law of Latin America, apparently reflecting a serious doubt on the part of the law-making classes concerning the capacity of very large numbers of people to look out for their own affairs. Some such limitations are surely politically inspired; it is still dangerous for most central governments to give up power. But even if the political situation were to change radically — not merely with the substitution of one strongman system for another, but fundamentally, with widespread diffusion of power — it would probably be wrong to expect the disappearance of the legal paternalism just described.

The issue of paternalism is at the heart of questions concerning the form and content of the rights to be distributed in a land reform. It must be faced in deciding whether to distribute individual parcels or shares in a cooperative organization; whether to permit free transferability of the interest which the beneficiary receives or to impose restrictions on alienation, etc. In deciding these questions, legislative planners must make the best possible accomodation of competing considerations such as: the level of agricultural production; political demands for "land," which may mean title, or something like it, to one who has no training in the sophistications of intangible property; the adjustment of agriculture to the rest of the economy. The institutions which emerge from this process are not textbook models, but the resultant of the forces which pushed various politicians to act. The materials in this section should be read partly as an exercise in historical reconstruction.

WHETTEN, RURAL MEXICO* 182-84, 202-04 (1948)

DEFINITION OF THE EJIDO

The term "ejido" (pronounced ā-heé-do), as now used in Mexico, refers to an agrarian community which has received and continues to hold land in accordance with the agrarian laws growing out of the Revolution of 1910. The lands may have been received as an outright grant from the government or as a restitution of lands that were previously possessed by the community and adjudged by the government to have been illegally appropriated by other individuals or groups; or the community may merely have received confirmation by the government of titles to land long in its possession. Ordinarily, the ejido consists of at least twenty individuals, usually heads of families (though not always), who were eligible to receive land in accordance with the rules of the Agrarian Code, together with the members of their immediate families.

The term "ejidatario" refers to an indivudual who has participated as a beneficiary in a grant of land in accordance with the agrarian laws. The totality of ejidatarios participating in a given grant, together with their families and the lands which they received, constitute an ejido. Thus the term "ejido" refers to a community, while "ejidatario" refers to a specific individual.

The total population of an ejido might vary from less than one hundred inhabitants to several thousand. In the smaller villages where ejidos have been established or in newly settled villages resulting directly from the formation of an ejido, the ejido and the village with its surrounding lands are almost coextensive, though not entirely so. There are almost always a few families in the village, however small, who are ineligible to benefit from the agrarian laws. These may be small shopkeepers or other persons whose traditional occupation is not farming. Their interests might be closely bound up with the ejido, but they would not be considered members of it. Other residents of the village who do not belong to the ejido are those families who were already in possession of small private holdings of their own and for this reason did not qualify to receive land under the agrarian laws. In the larger villages and towns there might be two or more ejidos in the same village; or the ejido population might constitute only a fraction of the total population of the town.

The lands of any given ejido do not always form a contiguous block. They are often interspersed with the remnants of the pre-existing hacienda from

---

* Reprinted from Rural Mexico by Nathan Whetten by permission of the University of Chicago Press. Copyright 1948 by The University of Chicago.

which the ejido lands were taken. Ordinarily, when lands were expropriated, the hacendado was permitted to select the land he wished to retain, and he often chose irregularly shaped areas in order to include what he regarded as the most desirable for his purpose.

* * *

TYPES OF FARM ORGANIZATION

There are two principal types of farm organization among the ejidos. These are what might be termed "individual" and "collective." These two types as differentiated here apply only to the crop lands, since, according to the Agrarian Code, all pasture lands, woodlands, and other noncrop lands in all ejidos are held and used in common and can never be divided among the individual ejidatarios unless opened up for cultivation. In this sense all ejidos use at least part of their lands in common. However, with reference to the crop land only, ordinarily a given ejido may be classified into one of the two types.

The Agrarian Code stipulates that the president of the Republic shall determine the type of farm organization in the ejidos in accordance with the following principles (Art. 200):

I. Lands which constitute economic units requiring the joint efforts of all the ejidatarios for their cultivation should be worked on a collective basis.

II. Ejidos whose crops are intended for industrial uses and which constitute agricultural zones whose products are homogeneous within an industry shall also be worked on a collective basis. In this case the crops which should be grown shall be specified.

Collective organization may also be adopted in other ejidos whenever technical and economic studies show that in this way better living conditions can be obtained for the peasants, and its establishment is feasible.

In all other cases the ejidatarios of a given ejido have been more or less free to choose the type of farm organization they wanted to follow, although their decisions have no doubt been strongly influenced, in some instances, by the persuasions of the officials of the Ejido Bank, who could withhold credit unless the type of organization appeared feasible to them.

THE INDIVIDUAL EJIDO

An overwhelmingly large proportion of the ejidos are of the individual type. This means that each ejidatario is allotted a plot of farm land (*parcela*) which he tills in his own way with the help of his family. These plots of crop land on the average for the entire country consist of 4.4 hectares. . . . The collective ejidos are found mostly in the northern areas and in the Gulf states. Only 3.6 per cent in the central region are operating collectively, and only 5.9 per cent in the south Pacific. The officials of the [Ejido Bank] are firmly convinced that almost all the ejidos which operate collectively are co-operating with the bank. If this is true, it would mean that, of the 14,683 ejidos appearing in the census of 1940, only about 5 per cent are operating collectively while 95 per cent operate on an individual basis.

SIMPSON, THE EJIDO: MEXICO'S WAY OUT* 318-34 (1937)

CIRCULAR 51 — SIMPLE COLLECTIVISM

For almost eight years after the promulgation of the basic agrarian decree of January 1915 no especial attention was given to the matter of ejido social and political organization. When specific questions arose the National Agrarian Commission dealt with them in circulars sent to the State Agrarian Commissions or to the municipal and state political authorities as the case demanded. It was not until October 11, 1922, however, that the Commission in its Circular N° 51, attempted to set forth a really comprehensive plan for the ordering of the political, social, and economic life of the ejidos.

Circular 51 opens with a statement of what in the opinion of the National Agrarian Commission were basic principles: (a) The distribution of land to villages is only the first step in the work of the National Agrarian Commission. The Commission must also assume the responsibility for "regulating the development of the ejidos and directing their progress." It is its duty to work out a program of ejido exploitation "in accordance with the level of social development and the state of agricultural evolution" of the villages and to nominate the authorities who will be charged with putting this program into action. (b) "Just as the development of the technical instruments of modern industry brought to an end small industry and produced capitalism, so also, the evolution of agricultural technology tends to abolish small scale agriculture, for there is an unsurmountable incompatibility between small scale agriculture and mechanization. . . ." (c) It follows, therefore, that if Mexican rural life is to derive the greatest possible benefit from modern methods of machine production, the ejido villages must be organized along strictly cooperative and communal lines. Moreover, "organization of the type in question . . . must not be left to the initiative of the peasants, impoverished by prolonged exploitation," but the National Agrarian Commission itself "must undertake to control the functioning and even to impose the installation" of cooperatives. By proceeding in this fashion the Commission will not only be adjusting its action to the "current of human progress . . . which dictates that social action shall take precedence over the egoism of personal convenience and that public rights shall be enriched each day at the expense of private rights," but will also be achieving the desideratum "of putting an end to the divorce existing between the . . . productive forces which tend to be collective and the totally antiquated regime of individual private property."

As the first step in the collectivization of the ejidos Circular 51 provides that each ejido shall elect a governing board of three individuals to be known as the Ejido Administrative Committee. This Committee is to receive the village lands from the Ejido Executive Committee[2] and thereafter is empowered "to dictate the regulations necessary for the best cultivation of the ejido lands and for the appropriate division of the various types of agricultural labor." The freedom of action of the Administrative Committee is restricted first by the requirement that it must "freely receive and present to the community any petitions or suggestions made by the members thereof" and that "no Committee is permitted to resolve questions of general interest unless the majority of the . . . [ejidatarios] manifest their conformity in a public assembly legally convoked and constituted." In the second place, the Circular provides that the Committees will be directly subject to the National Agrarian Commission; that they must agree to follow the suggestions made by the Commission's Agricultural Instructors; and, finally, that the Delegates and the Agricultural Inspectors appointed by the Commission are to be considered members of the Committees with the right of suspending any action they may see fit until the case can be reviewed by the National Agrarian Commission. Still another safeguard against the concentration of too much power in the hands of the Committee is the provision that if at any time as many as 20 per cent of the ejidatarios in a given community are dissatisfied with the behavior of the Committee, they can petition the Delegate of the National Agrarian Commission to call a new election.

When a village receives its ejido lands either in provisional or definitive possession it becomes the duty of the Administrative Committee to divide the lands into the following classes: (a) an urban zone or *fundo legal*; (b) agricultural lands proper — actual and immediately potential (*de pronto cultivo*); (c) forest, pasture, and brush lands; and (d) a section of not less than five hectares of cultivable land for each school in the community. The agricultural lands are to be cultivated in common and for this purpose the Committee is to apportion the work and assign to each of the ejidatarios his particular task. The forest, brush, and pasture lands are to be reserved for the use of the whole community under the direction of the Committee. The products of all sorts derived from ejido lands exploited communally are to be distributed as follows: 85 per cent is to be divided among the ejidatarios in the manner which they themselves shall determine; 10 per cent is to be placed in a fund for coöperative development to be used to purchase agricultural machinery, work animals, and so forth; and 5 per cent is to be reserved for the payment of taxes and for urban and other improvements.

A most important section of the Circular states: "The cultivable lands

---

[2] It will be recalled that it is the function of the Ejido Executive Committees to represent the communities during the period in which petitions for lands are pending before the State and National Agrarian Commissions.

... [as well as] the forest, brush and pasture lands in no case shall be subject to lease, mortgages, antichresis, embargo or sale."

The last four articles of Circular 51 state the principles on the basis of which the National Agrarian Commission through its Department of Ejido Development is to organize the ejido cooperatives. These principles are: (a) "distribution of profits in proportion to work contributed"; (b) "equal rights for members ... following the formula: 'one member one vote' "; and (c) the right of one-fifth of the members of the society to exercise at any time the privileges of initiative, referendum and recall.

Coöperatives are to be governed by the Ejido Administrative Committee enlarged by the addition of three members. The National Agrarian Commission through its Department of Ejido Development is to assume responsibility for organizing coöperatives in each of the ejido villages and supervising their operations "until they are able to prosper without official aid," and for the establishing of regional unions of coöperatives which, in turn, are to be brought together in a single national association.

With the promulgation of Circular 51 the ejido villages were launched upon a career of what, for lack of a better term, may be called simple collectivism. Ejido lands were to be held and worked in common — all for one and one for all, and no questions raised concerning mine and thine. Ejido villages, like their prototypes of Colonial days, were to be the wards of the nation. State and municipal authorities might levy taxes, but there, for all practical purposes, their rights over the ejido lands ended. Economic and social control of ejidos was to be vested immediately in Ejido Administrative Committees. But the powers of these Committees were to be strictly limited by the guarantees of initiative, referendum and recall on the one hand, and the direct intervention and supervision of the National Agrarian Commission on the other.

Thus the program in theory. Thus the vision of simple collectivism. For three years the National Agrarian Commission struggled to translate theory into action; vision into reality. Then, in 1925, nine months after Calles took office as president, came the day of accounting. Circular 51 was tried, judged and sentenced to that large and overflowing ash-can especially reserved in Mexico for *proyectos* of social reform. Why? What was the trouble? Was there somthing wrong with the program of the common chicken in the communal pot?

THE LAW OF EJIDO PATRIMONY — (FAIRLY) RUGGED INDIVIDUALISM

According to the sponsors of the law which took the place of Circular 51, there were wrongs aplenty and enough trouble to threaten the whole agrarian reform with wrack and ruin and the country with starvation to boot. In a speech before the Chamber of Deputies on September 12, 1925, the Minister of Agriculture, Luis L. León, summarized the charges against the program then in effect as follows: (a) In point of fact, there was hardly an ejido in the country in which the lands were worked communally in the manner required by Circular 51. The regular procedure, as everyone knew, was for a village just as soon as it got its lands to allot them in severalty. Thus the regulations of the National Agrarian Commission were being openly flouted and the ejidatarios by this very action had clearly demonstrated their lack of faith in the communal method. (b) It was a generally acknowledged fact that production on the lands distributed under the agrarian laws had fallen below that which had been hoped for. (c) There was a pervading sense of insecurity among the ejidatarios. This was partly to be explained by the constant threats of the *hacendados* and the malicious rumors that the government was abandoning the agrarian reform, but the main reason for the peasants' uneasiness and discontent was to be found in the character of the control exercised over the ejidos by the local Administrative Committees. These Committees had come to be dominated by the most ambitious and, often most unscrupulous individuals who did not hesitate to pursue their personal gain to the sacrifice of the collective welfare. In many communities no sooner did the ejidatarios get their crops planted on their little parcels than the local politicians would decide to have a reallotment. In a word, the peasants had been rescued from the tyranny of the *hacendados* only to become the victims of the *caciquismo* (bossism) of the Ejido Administrative Committees.

* * *

SUMMARY OF THE LAW OF EJIDO PATRIMONY
[Enacted in 1925 — essentially the same as the present governmental structure of the ejido. — Ed.]

* * *

1. *Village Agrarian Authorities.* Under the Law of Ejido Patrimony (Agrarian Code), the Ejido Administrative Committee is abolished and in its place are two new local agrarian authorities: the Ejido Commissariat (*Comisariado Ejidal*) and the Board of Vigilance (*Consejo de Vigilancia*). The Ejido Commissariat, the principal governing authority in the village, is composed of three members in good standing in the community duly elected by a majority vote. The term of service is for two years,* unless (as the law ominously provides) the members are previously removed for due cause. The functions of the Commissariat are to represent the village before the administrative and judicial authorities; to administer and to seek to improve the ejido lands in general and to be directly responsible for the exploitation of the common properties (pastures, forests, and so forth, and the water rights which, as will be noted shortly, are not subject to division); to call meetings of the ejidatarios; and to carry out the instructions of the community and those dictated by the Agrarian Department and the National Bank of Agricultural Credit or their representatives.

---

* The term is now three years. — Ed.

As its name suggests, the principal function of the Board of Vigilance is to see that the Ejido Commissariat behaves property. To this end it is empowered to revise the accounts of the Commissariat, to order the calling of meetings of the Ejido Assembly when in its judgment this is necessary or when 20 per cent of the ejidatarios so request and to report to the Agrarian Department any irregularities in the financial or other operations of the Commissariat. The Board of Vigilance, like the Commissariat, is composed of three members elected to hold office for two years [now three years — Ed.].

2. *National Agrarian Authorities.* Authority over and responsibility for the organization and supervision of ejido communities is vested in the first instance in the Agrarian Department. . . .

* * *

3. *The Division of Ejido Lands.* At the time of the execution of the presidential decree granting or restoring ejido lands to a village, these lands must be immediately divided up in the manner prescribed by (the present) law.

In dividing up the village lands the following areas are not subject to parcelization: (a) an "urban zone" including a special lot set aside for the rural school and its experimental field; (b) pasture and timber lands; and (c) special areas (*cajas, bolsas y lotes bordeados*) which constitute "a natural, physically nondivisible unit and require for [proper] cultivation the collective intervention of all the ejidatarios."

All the rest of the land (that is, the crop land, actual and potential) granted to the village must be apportioned among the individual ejidatarios and the law sets forth in some detail the manner in which this is to be done with a view to insuring justice and fair dealing to all concerned. In no case may any individual be given a tract of land smaller than the area defined in the presidential resolution making the grant, or, in default of such definition, of the area stated in the agrarian laws in force at the time the grant is made.

If any of the land subject to division is left over after each ejidatario receives his tract, a "reserve zone" is formed from which the sons of ejidatarios upon coming of age, or people from neighboring villages having insufficient lands, may receive parcels.

In those cases, on the other hand, where it is found that there is not enough land to give each head of a family his proper share, the law provides that an effort shall be made to work out a plan whereby with the financial help of the federal government, the states, the Bank of Agricultural Credit and of the ejidatarios themselves new lands shall be made available for cultivation by clearing some of the ejido pasture and timber lands, building irrigation works, and so forth. However, if this is not feasible, the Agrarian Department shall declare a "deficit of parcels" and shall institute proceedings for an additional expropriation and dotation from surrounding private properties.

4. *Definition of Property Rights.* In defining the nature of the property rights vested in the villages receiving lands under the ejido laws, the Law

of Ejido Patrimony (Agrarian Code) restates and reaffirms the principles laid down in the decree of January 1915 and in Article 27 of the constitution in the following words: "The agrarian rights which shall be acquired by centers of population shall be imprescriptible and inalienable and therefore cannot in any case or in any form be ceded, conveyed, hypothecated or made the subject of lien in whole or in part."

Exceptions to the foregoing statement are: (a) the renting of pasture rights, the granting of concessions for the exploitation of timber lands and the sale of irrigation waters when these acts are approved by the Ejido Commissariat and the Agrarian Department as contributing to the best utilization of the pasture and timber lands and other products held in common by the villages; (b) the surrendering of properties of whatever kind when it is necessary to expropriate these properties for the pupose of creating urban zones, constructing means of communication, building irrigation works of public interest, or exploiting natural resources belonging to the nation. No such expropriation of the type in question may be made except by specific presidential resolution and after previous compensation for the economic value of the properties affected either in lands of equal quality or in cash, in the order named.

Property rights in the separate ejido parcels of crop land vested in the individual ejidatarios are also imprescriptible and hence cannot be alienated[16] or made the subject of lien. Neither may the beneficiareis of ejido parcels rent them or work them on shares or "make any other contract which implies the indirect exploitation of the land."

An ejidatario may be deprived of his ejido parcel either temporarily or permanently under certain conditions. Temporarily: if he leaves the community for more than six months without permission of the Commissariat, or if he cultivates his parcel in a manner prejudicial to the interests of the community. Permanently: if he attempts to sell, mortgage, lease, rent, or in any other form or fashion alienate his property; for failure to cultivate his land for a period of two consecutive agricultural years; if he does not contribute promptly to the funds for the payment of taxes or for any other purpose related to the ejido and approved by the Assembly; or, because of "mental derangement, alcoholic degeneration or imprisonment for a period greater than two years providing that there are no members of his household (*familiares*) to take charge of his parcel." Women who possess parcels by reason of being heads of families may be deprived of them if they change their civil status "providing that in their new situation the family [still] enjoys the use of a parcel."[17]

---

[16] However, ejidatarios living in separate communities may make exchanges of their parcels upon receiving the approval of the ejido Assemblies and the Agrarian Department.

[17] Although they do not accurately describe the relationship of the ejidatario to his parcel, as a matter of convenience and to avoid awkward legal circumlocutions, the terms "proprietor," "possessor," "owner," etc., are used in this and other paragraphs in referring to ejido parcels. *Usufructuary* is probably a better indication of the real nature of the property rights involved.

Each case of deprivation must be considered on its merits and no individual can be deprived of his land by the Ejido Assembly without fully justified cause and until the case has been reviewed and a definitive judgment handed down by the Agrarian Department. Parcels declared "free" in the manner just indicated automatically return to the community and their disposition is determined by the Assembly with the approval of the Agrarian Department.

Ejido parcels may be bequeathed and inherited, and for this purpose each proprietor of a parcel is required to required to register a list of succession indicating the person who shall become the head of the family in the event of his death.[18] The list of succession may not include individuals who already have parcels or those who reside in other ejido communities. If there be no one who fulfills the requirements for inheritance, the property reverts to the community and becomes subject to a new adjudication.

The undivided ejido lands — pasture, timber lands and the special areas referred to above — are reserved for the common use of all the ejidatarios. This use may take the form of privileges granted to individual ejidatarios (to cut timber, pasture, cattle, and so forth); or of communal exploitation; or of commercial and industrial exploitation by concession to ejidatarios or outsiders. In the latter cases the proceeds in kind or in money must be placed in the ejido common fund (see below). Rights to irrigation waters are vested in the community in its corporate capacity and the use of these waters is subject to the regulation by the Commissariat in accordance with the rules of the Agrarian Department and the Ministry of Agriculture.

5. *Taxes.* The municipal, state, and federal governments are prohibited from imposing more than one predial tax on ejido properties. Taxes shall be imposed upon the fiscal value of the properties, but in no case may they exceed 5 per cent of the annual production of the ejido. Fiscal responsibility for the individual parcels rests on the individuals concerned but fiscal coaction can be brought to bear only upon the crops in cases of delinquency. For the corporate ejido lands the fiscal responsibility is joint and common.

6. *The Common Fund.* Each ejido community must establish a fund (*fondo común*) to be constituted from special quotas determined by the Assembly and paid by each ejidatario and from the products derived from the exploitation of the common lands. This fund is to be used for the purchase of machinery, work animals, and equipment for general improvements such as irrigation works, and for certain other purposes.

* * *

---

[18] It is not without significance that the Law of Ejido Patrimony was originally called the Law of *Family* Patrimony. It was clearly the intention of those who framed the law to make the family unit the depository of ejido parcel property rights and not the individual ejidatario. Also, the law extends somewhat the ordinary concept of family and provides that in the case of the death of the beneficiary of an ejido parcel "the rights to the same shall pass to the person or persons whom he maintained, even though they were not his relatives (*parientes*) provided that they had lived with him as members of its family."

At bottom — curious as it may sound to those who have been fed on stories of "red Mexico" — the Law of Ejido Patrimony represented a flight from communism. In the eyes of the group which came into power with Calles, the conception of the ejido and the program for its organization contained in Circular 51 *was* communism and, moreover, communism imported directly from Moscow. Now, in the judgment of these gentlemen, communism was not for Mexico. Or, at any rate, not agrarian communism. They had no idea (as had the authors of Circular 51) of "putting an end to the divorce existing between the productive forces which tend to be collective and the totally antiquated regime of individual private property." On the contrary, they believed that the ultimate goal of the reform was private property — private property more justly distributed, private property controlled in the interest of the public, but private property nonetheless. The ejido was not to be an end in itself and certainly not a communistic end. Rather the ejido was looked upon simply as one of several possible methods of redistributing land, a stepping-stone to individualistic ownership and modified laissez-faire. Holding these views it was but natural that the Calles group should have found good and sufficient reasons — in "human nature," in "economic realities," and in "common sense" — for discarding the program of Circular 51. The Law of Ejido Patrimony, from the point of view of its sponsors, was a reasonable and necessary step in the development of the agrarian reform. For its opponents, the law was a specious attempt to mix oil with water, a desertion and a betrayal of the ideals of the revolution.*

BOLIVIA: Legislative Decree N° 03464 relative to Agrarian Reform, 2 August 1953 (FAO translation)

* * *

Preference in Right of Grant of Ownership

77. All Bolivians over 18 years of age, irrespective of sex, who are engaged, or wish to engage, in agricultural pursuits, shall be granted ownership of lands, where available, in accordance with Government projects and provided that within the term of two years they introduce agricultural activities.

78. Peasants who have been subject to a feudal work and exploitation system, in their capacity of servants, dependents, labourers, tenant-farmers, *agregados,* outside workers etc., and who are over 18 years, of age, married males over 14 years of age and widows with children who are minors shall, upon the proclamation of this Decree, be declared the owners of the parcels

---

* The most thorough recent analysis of the ejido system is ECKSTEIN, EL EJIDO COLECTIVO EN MEXICO (1966.) This work, a Harvard doctoral dissertation in Economics, was written in English but has been published only in Spanish translation. — Ed.

at present in their possession and cultivated by them, until the National Agrarian Reform Service shall grant them all that they are reasonably entitled to in accordance with the definitions of the small property or shall compensate them in the form of collective cultivation of lands enabling them to meet their family needs.

79. The preceding Article shall be subject to restrictions in respect of the provisions relative to the exceptions prescribed for the small property.

80. Aliens shall have the same rights as those referred to in Article 77, provided that they comply with the provisions relative to immigration and colonization.

81. The preferential right of any person to the grant of lands in a certain area is conditional upon his having permanent residence in the place concerned and upon his being a farmer. The degree of preference shall be defined in accordance with the provisions established for each type of zone and property.

82. On the lands of a latifundium cultivated under the colonization system, the tenant farmers and agricultural workers of such latifundium having completed a period of residence of two years or more, calculated retrospectively as from the date of proclamation of this Legislative Decree, shall have a preferential right to a grant.

When the initial grant is made, an area of not less than ten per cent of the total of the individual allotments shall be reserved for collective cultivation by the community.

An area equivalent to or larger than that received by each tenant farmer shall be made available for the school field.

83. In cases referred to in Article 82 the following procedure shall be followed in determining the right to assignable areas:

> a) If sufficient land is available, a grant shall be made to each family at the rate of one grant unit. Where there remains cultivable land in excess, it shall be considered as vacant land to be granted to peasants of medium and small properties who are without land and who live in the same district or in the neighbourhood up to a distance of six kilometres from the latifundium concerned. If residual land still remains after the grants referred to in the preceding Article have been made, the community may extend the area of lands for collective cultivation.
>
> b) If the lands are not sufficient to afford a grant unit to each family, the assignable areas shall be reduced to the necessary extent so as to satisfy the claims of all those who, by law, have a preferential right to such land. Peasants who receive insufficient grants of land shall have the right to new grants in other available areas.

84. Peasants of medium properties shall have the preferential right to the grant of excess lands from neighbouring latifundia within the radius prescirbed by this Legislative Decree.

85. Tenant farmers who had their own land on a property shall receive

a grant only in the proportion necessary to supplement the area to which tenants on the same property are entitled.

* * *

89.   Graduates of Faculties of Agronomy and of Agricultural Colleges shall enjoy the preference extended to peasants on medium properties, in colonizable areas and in the vacant lands formed from the latifundia situated in the rural district nearest to their residence.

90.   The concession of excess lands expropriated from the sub-zone of the Yungas of La Paz and Cachabamba is restricted to the preferential grants of small properties primarily to invalids and relatives of those who fell in the National Revolution, to all Bolivians of the middle class, employees and professional persons, railwaymen, transport and building workers and to all workmen in factories and mines who desire to settle thereon.

91.   Independently of the allotments of land to which this Chapter refers, every agricultural labourer of the Highland and Valley regions shall receive 50 hectares in the eastern region, subject to his making application to such effect and subject to his undertaking to start work within the term of two years.

The National Service for Agrarian Reform shall issue regulations governing the system and procedure relative to such grants.

The Unit of Grant

92.   In those regions where adequate land affected by this Legislative Decree exists, allocation to each family shall be made at the rate of a unit of grant having an area equivalent to that of the small property. In regions where there is not sufficient land, the area assignable to each family shall be reduced accordingly, so as to satisfy the claims of all persons having a right to land.

93.   In those regions where reductions in the units of grant are necessary, they shall be made by the National Service for Agrarian Reform.

94.   The Co-operatives of Smallholders shall have preferential right to the grant of lands in those colonization regions nearest to them which have access to the main highways of communication.

PATCH, BOLIVIA: U.S. ASSISTANCE IN A REVOLUTIONARY SETTING
in SOCIAL CHANGE IN LATIN AMERICA TODAY*
at 108, 128 (1960)

It was these provisions of the decree that opened the way for multiplying the small subsistence plots or *minifundios*. As the framers of the decree

---

* Published for the Council on Foreign Relations by Harper and Row; reprinted by permission.

foresaw clearly, in those densely populated areas which stood in greatest need of land redistribution, there was simply not enough land to give each family an allotment even approaching the prescribed "small holding." By reducing the defined minimum holding in order to satisfy all *campesinos* legally entitled to receive land, the decree made a gesture toward appeasing the greatest possible number of *campesinos*. But it thereby made the sub-subsistence *minifundio* the dominant pattern in the more densely populated regions. Agricultural production and marketing have not recovered from this drastic change. That is the root of many of Bolivia's economic straits today.

CHONCHOL, ANALISIS CRITICO DE LA REFORMA AGRARIA CUBANA in EL TRIMESTRE ECONOMICO,[*] vol. XXX (1), N° 117, p. 69, 117-26 (1963)

[This long and very informative article describes the Cuban land reform in detail. The author makes a number of interesting points, including the following: From June of 1959 to the end of 1960, the government created around 800 agricultural cooperatives of all kinds. These were cooperatives in name only, since they had neither "a defined organization, a statute, a determined number of members, nor cooperative leaders." Toward the end of 1960, however, the government created over 600 sugarcane cooperatives, covering nearly half of the sugar producing land in the country, and including virtually all the best land devoted to such uses. These cooperatives, of vital importance because of the dominance of sugar in the Cuban economy, were regulated by a "General Regulation of Sugarcane Cooperatives" issued by the Agrarian Reform Institute (INRA) in May of 1960. The Regulation provided, among other things, that the members of each cooperative would receive an advance on their share of the earnings in the form of wages, and that 80% of the net income of each cooperative would be set aside for the building of houses and other buildings during the first five years of the cooperative's existence. A member could withdraw voluntarily, or exchange his rights, but he could not sell his rights in the cooperative. Presumably this meant that a withdrawal involved relinquishing one's rights. The administrator of each cooperative was to be designated by INRA, at least "until the cooperatives may be perfectly organized and their members may have acquired the experience necessary for their administration." INRA has not yet relinquished this power. The sugarcane cooperatives generally have 200 to 300 workers each, and from 1,000 to 1,500 hectares of land. What was involved was a change from large-scale capitalist enterprise to large-scale cooperative enterprise, so that the principal change has been a change of management. The shortage of trained manage-

---

* Copyright ©, Fondo de Cultura Económica, reprinted by permission.

ment personnel has been one of the most serious problems of the sugar cooperatives.

[The author also describes the formation in 1961 of the National Association of Small Famers (ANAP). This association grew out of various associations devoted to particular crops such as rice, tobacco, coffee, potatoes, etc. "The general regulation of ANAP, as distinguished from that of the Sugarcane Cooperatives issued in 1960, contains considerations not only of economic organization, but also of clear political content. In effect, ANAP is defined as an organism in support of the Revolution and aimed at organizing, unifying and orienting the small farmers in the application of the agrarian program of the Revolution." Membership in ANAP is virtually obligatory for any small farmer who needs credit, since credit is channeled through ANAP. Nevertheless, some 43% of the farm land of Cuba remains outside the "socialist sector" (Sugarcane Cooperatives, People's Farms and ANAP). The author apparently believes that it is the ultimate purpose of the government to use ANAP as a means for organizing small producers into some form of collective production, but that the government is reluctant to press this plan at the present time, for fear of losing the political support of the small farmers. The author goes on to describe and evaluate the People's Farms as follows:]

The People's Farm is a state farm which is considered property of the Nation, such as the large nationalized industrial enterprises. Its basic structural characteristics were defined, at the beginning of 1961, by the president of INRA, Commander Fidel Castro, with the following words, which had to appear in large letters at the principal entrance of every farm:

"This Farm belongs to the People; on it indispensable food for our population is produced, many workers decently obtain their sustenance; families also enjoy the right to housing, education, medical assistance, a social circle, electricity and water, without charge. The income which is obtained from it is invested in this very center or in the establishment of other similar ones throughout the country."

* * *

The People's Farms were organized in the first months of 1961, taking as their fundamental base the old livestock and rice latifundios, in addition to other kinds of farms intervened by INRA. ["Intervention" is the government's assumption of management control. — Ed.] All these farms, when they were geographically close, were regrouped in much larger new units called People's Farms.

* * *

For each Farm there was designated an administrator and an accountant. ... In general, the level of preparation of the administrators initially designated was that of practical peasants who previously were administrators of traditional farms, small producers, agricultural workers and, in certain cases, agricultural teachers or agronomists. Of course in all these appointments a decisive factor was the political confidence which the various authorities of

INRA had in the persons designated, an aspect which often brought about the appointment as farm administrators of people little prepared for the task.

* * *

On May 17, 1961, two years after the promulgation of the Agrarian Reform Act and less than five months after the organization of the People's Farms was initiated, there were in all Cuba 266 such farms which occupied a total area of 2,433,449 hectares. [This is approximately the same area as that covered by farms of members of ANAP. — Ed.] The average area of these farms was greater than 9,000 hectares, although this average does not reflect the complete reality with respect to size, since although it is hard to find farms of less than 4,000 hectares, there are many which have more than 15, 20 or 25 thousand hectares.

* * *

With respect to the workers on the farms, in a census carried out in May of 1961, it was determined that altogether there were 96,498 workers on these farms in all Cuba, of whom 27,321 were permanent and 69,177 transient.

If this figure is compared with the total area occupied by the farms, one immediately notices the low occupational level of the People's Farms in relation, for example, to that of the Sugarcane Cooperatives. In effect, in the latter there were at this same period a ratio of 6.6 hectares per cooperative member and 4.8 hectares per worker, considering both permanent cooperative members and transient laborers. In spite of the fact that this occupational level of the best lands in Cuba shows that still they are far from realizing the degree of intensification possible, it is still immensely superior to that of the People's Farms: 89.1 hectares per permanent worker and 25.2 hectares per worker generally, including the transients and permanent workers together.

* * *

... The People's Farms that have been organized in Cuba constitute a production structure which, without doubt, presents some advantages although, to our way of thinking, the disadvantages involved in their organization are greater than the advantages. ...

The principal advantage of the People's Farms is that, because they are State exploitations, integrally financed by the State with their salaried workers receiving the same wage and other benefits regardless of the production level and income of the farm, it is possible, without great opposition from the workers, to raise crops in which the country is interested, though they may not be commercially remunerative. These crops may be important to assure certain supplies or to permit the long-range functioning of large factories that may be under-utilized ..., for the purpose of making available certain fundamental elements for making concentrated food for livestock (corn), etc.

* * *

A second advantage of the People's Farms is that one already mentioned, concerning the possibility of having centers of production in the hands of the

State designed fundamentally to develop certain norms which permit the regulation of the market supply. . . .

Other advantages also exist in the mentioned formula, such as that invoked by the President of INRA, that the People's Farm gives equal economic and social conditions to all workers, whatever the natural conditions of the respective agricultural enterprises. Without doubt, from a certain point of view it could be argued that equality of conditions signifies a lack of incentive to progress, but there cannot be any doubt that a living minimum wage for all the workers of the country, although the conditions in which some work may be less favorable than those of others, is one of the fundamental requisites of social justice and respect for the individual person.

It is also true, on the other hand, that equality of opportunities and the correction of natural disadvantages might be achieved through means of which the Cuban Agrarian Reform seems not to have thought. [For example, variable taxation.]

But with these advantages in mind, let us see what are the disadvantages presented by the formula of the People's Farm in the concrete reality of today's Cuba.*

In the first place, it is an expensive formula. As the People's Farms have been conceived, they require large investments which weigh heavily on the State's budget. This is perhaps one of the reasons why there has been no attempt at this stage to transform all the collective agriculture of the country, including the Sugarcane Cooperatives, into People's Farms.

* * *

A second disadvantage, which tends to aggravate the danger just pointed out, is the too-great size of all the farms. . . .

This excessive size presents . . . the possibility of a deficient distribution of investments. . . .

Another inconvenience of this excessive size for each farm is the practical impossibility of carrying out an efficient administration and control. Theoretically the large agricultural enterprise should have the same economic advantages as the large industrial enterprise: maximum specialization of different groups of workers, chain operations, mass production, reduction of general administrative expenses, economic yield at a low unit cost of the product obtained, etc. In practice, nevertheless, the process of agricultural production is much more complex, variable and insecure, owing especially to the operation of a series of unforeseeable natural factors which are often difficult to control.

* * *

[In addition, the central government is unwilling to assign sufficient personnel to operate these farms, even where trained personnel may be available — which they normally are not.]

---

* The author's study concluded in 1961. — Ed.

Insufficiency of administrative personnel and excessive centralism (since every People's Farm must deal directly in all its actions with the General Administration of People's Farms in Havana) create very serious problems, especially of delays in the delivery of funds, which sometimes retard payments to the workers or the carrying out of certain indispensable labors.

There are other inconvenient aspects of the excessive size of the People's Farms such as the high cost of transport and distribution within each farm, the impossibility of an efficient control of animals, etc., but it is not worth the trouble to enter into an analysis of these aspects.

It should also be pointed out, finally, that this excessive size has not only economic consequences, but also unfavorable social consequences. The principal social disadvantage is that only with great difficulty can the salaried workers obtain some concept of their participation in the farm other than as mere salaried workers. Indeed, on a State farm, they have more guarantees than before, but psychologically they continue to be salaried workers without active participation in the enterprise.

What has been said makes us think that the myth of the People's Farm — that by virtue of its being a great enterprise of the State in a socialist economy it "is a superior formula of production" — will be seen to be very seriously denied in the concrete reality of the Cuban situation.

An imaginative suggestion for phased transfer of corporate (cooperative) shares from the government to certain beneficiaries of a land reform is contained in Dorner and Collarte, *Land Reform in Chile: Proposal for an Institutional Innovation*, 19 INTER-AM. ECON. AFFAIRS 3 (1965).

---

2. Transferability of Beneficiaries' Interests

MEXICO: AGRARIAN CODE OF 1943

* * *

158. The rights of the ejidatario over his parcel, over the unit of grant, and generally over the property of the ejido to which he belongs shall be immune from execution, inalienable, and not subject to encumbrances for any reason; acts which may be carried out in contravention of this precept are legally inexistent.

159. The individual rights of the ejidatario over the normal unit of grant or the parcel, as well as rights over the property of the ejido, cannot be the object of contracts of sharecropping or rental, or any other contracts which may imply indirect exploitation or the employment of wage labor, except in the following cases: [women with families, minors, and other incapacitated

persons may make such contracts, under the supervision of the Board of Vigilance].

* * *

162. The ejidatario has the power to designate an heir who may succeed him in his agrarian rights from among the persons who may be economically dependent on him, whether or not they are relatives. . . .

163 and 164. [If the ejidatario makes no such designation, his lawful or free-union wife shall take his rights; if there be no wife, then his children take; failing children, other persons dependent on the ejidatario take his rights, with preference to the oldest among them. Anyone who already has one parcel cannot inherit another. If there be no designated heir and no one entitled to take the rights under art. 163, then the ejido may, by two-thirds vote, grant the parcel to another person, following the order of preference which is established in art. 153 of the Code.]

* * *

169. The ejidatario shall lose his rights over the parcel and generally those which he has as member of a nucleus of ejido population, except for the house plot granted to him in the urban zone, only and exclusively if during two or more consecutive years he fails to work his parcel personally, or to carry out the work that falls to him in case his ejido is exploited collectively.

The transferability of an ejido parcel is a current question of great interest in Mexico. It is widely asserted that violations of the foregoing provisions of the Agrarian Code are constant and widespread:

> It has been estimated that in the State of Morelos 60% of the ejido parcels are rented out. The Yaqui Indians rent their communal lands, obtained by way of restitution. Fernández y Fernández, *Propiedad Privada Versus Ejidos* (1954) in HISTORIA DEL EJIDO ACTUAL at 19, 23 (Palomo Valencia ed. 1959.)

The same phenomenon, although on a smaller scale, is reported in Bolivia and in Venezuela, where there are restrictions on transferability which are less strict than those in the Mexican Law. The reasons for these unauthorized transfers are not hard to find. A beneficiary may not want to be a farmer, or may prefer to work in a factory, and yet may not have anyone else in the family to run his parcel for him. Or, a parcel may be so tiny as not to provide enough income to support a family. The beneficiary may be willing to rent his parcel to a so-called "speculator" — one who rents several parcels and hires various beneficiaries to work for him as *peones* or day laborers. The beneficiary may even be able to earn more as a laborer than he could earn exploiting his own parcel.

Thus there are modern proposals, echoing the Reform of Juárez, that the ejido parcels be granted in full ownership, with the right to transfer them freely. Similar proposals have been made, and followed, from time to time in the case of Indian community lands in the United States. One unhappy result, occasionally seen in the United States, may be that land buyers will buy up the newly-transferable parcels at relatively cheap prices, taking advantage of the beneficiaries' sudden needs for cash (for an illness, a wedding, etc.) with the result that the land becomes concentrated again. At the very best, ejido parcels may be allowed to be concentrated to the point that an owner might feed his family from the produce of his land. Economically speaking, it is hard to see what would be wrong with that result. But even consolidating the ejido parcels into minimum-size units would almost certainly have the effect of freeing large numbers of people to leave the villages for the cities, which are already crowded with the unemployed — and frequently unemployable — rural dispossessed. Even Mexico, for all its economic growth, is not immune to the grave political consequences that are a risk of any serious effort to rationalize or restructure the ejido. As a consequence, successive Mexican governments have done nothing along these lines, although there continues to be much talk of freeing the *ejidatario* from his condition as "glebe serf," "bound to the land."

---

3. Payment by Beneficiaries; Other Obligations

SIMPSON, THE EJIDO: MEXICO'S WAY OUT* 218-19 (1937)

The first thought of the revolutionary leaders, or at least of those associated with the Carranza regime, was that the villages themselves should pay for the land they received. The original agrarian decree of January 1915, to be sure, stated that lands for dotation to villages should be "expropriated for the account of the National Government," and that "interested parties who believed themselves injured" could present demands for compensation to the courts. Article 27 of the 1917 constitution assumed with equal definiteness the Nation's responsibility for the payment of properties expropriated for the purpose of ejido grants. But nothing was said in either the decree of 1915 or in Article 27 about the manner in which payments were to be made or whether the government was to assume final as well as initial responsibility for such payments. From other sources, however, it is clear that it was the original intention for the government, in the case of properties expropriated for ejido grants, to undertake only the functions of a financial intermediary.

The principal evidence in support of the foregoing assertion is to be found, first, in the already mentioned Circular N° 34 of the National Agrarian Commission (issued on January 31, 1919) requiring the inhabitants of villages petitioning for lands to agree in writing "to pay the Nation the value of the lands which they were going to receive by dotation, in accordance with the indemnity which the Nation must pay to the proprietors of the land expropriated"; and, second, in the original enabling act of January 10, 1920, that authorized the creation of the Public Agrarian Debt. This decree (which is still in force) states in Article 6 that for the payment of the bonds and coupons attached thereto, issued to indemnify owners of properties expropriated for ejidos, the government will apply all the revenues coming into the Treasury from the sale of ejido lands to the residents of the respective localities. The plain implication of Article 6 is that is was intended that the villages receiving ejido lands would, sooner or later, reimburse the government for the outlays for land made on their behalf.

When Obregón came into power one of his earliest political moves was to have the National Agrarian Commission rescind Circular N° 34. Although no change has ever been made in the sections of the decree of January 10, 1920, quoted above, generally speaking since Obregón's action removing Circular 34 from the books, there has been no further recognition of even the possibility of villages paying for ejidos.

The Mexican experience of non-payment by land reform beneficiaries has been followed almost everywhere, with the exception of various schemes of colonization in countries which have not seen fundamental land reforms, such as Argentina and Uruguay. Are there any arguments in favor of requiring some eventual payment from the beneficiaries, even though they may not be able to pay anything at the time their parcels are distributed to them? Is there any reason why a *campesino* might want to make at least a token payment?

There are, in any case, other kinds of obligations which may be imposed on beneficiaries, relating to the manner in which they exploit their parcels. Some such obligations are suggested by the Venezuelan law: Article 67 requires the beneficiary to undertake to work his parcel personally or with his family; other articles contemplate both the providing of technical services and some form of supervision over the way the beneficiary cultivates his land. (Articles 78, 80, 122-24.)

The lawyer's interest in such efforts centers on the creation of institutions to make them work. Suppose that a beneficiary burns the weeds on his parcel instead of using the approved methods of cleaning? What kinds of sanctions can be imposed on him? Money fines? Reprimands? Forfeiture of his rights to the parcel? None of these seems satisfactory. It may be more practical to offer rewards for proper behavior than to impose sanctions for violations.

All of these supervisory efforts depend on the creation and maintenance of an effective corps of agricultural extension agents, something which does not now exist in adequate numbers in any country in Latin America. The following excerpt from a speech by the Venezuelan Minister of Agriculture to the Congress (December, 1961) is typical in its discouraging description of the state of agricultural extension.

GIMENEZ LANDINEZ, EVALUACION DE LA REFORMA AGRARIA ANTE EL CONGRESO NACIONAL 25-26 (1962)

Another failure is the lack of technical assistance. This is a problem which belongs to the Ministry of Agriculture. There are two forms of carrying out this technical assistance in the Agrarian Reform: one, which the Law itself foresaw, is that there be a Technical Director in every settlement, but according to our data, out of 371 settlements only 47 have Technical Directors, and I assure you that while we are going to search for those technicians, we do not now have them.

The other is the agricultural extension proper, which is also under the jurisdiction of MAC [the Ministry of Agriculture]. Of 40 extension agencies in 1948, the dictatorship [of Pérez Jiménez], which was not interested in these aspects of benefit to the *campesino,* eliminated all but 20, which were in disarray and practically with no function or often in the service of the powerful landowners. From 1958 to the present we have made an effort; at the beginning of the constitutional period [1961] there were 43 agencies and at this moment we have 136 agricultural extension agencies. But undoubtedly even these are not sufficient if we note that an agricultural agent in the Venezuelan countryside cannot attend to more than 400 families, and even that is a lot. So we have to begin to create the necessary instruments for extension, or rather, for this informal education which is given to the *campesino* on the land so that he may learn new methods that are indispensable for a greater income and productivity. . . .

Would I dare to say that the 136 agricultural extension agencies are functioning well? It would be to lie before the Congress. I can say only that we have created the 136 agencies, but that an extension agent, this agricultural apostle, this technician . . . who knows how to get close to the *campesino* and to know his troubles, is not something which can be manufactured in the Universities nor in the practical Schools of Agriculture. He is a product only of the countryside itself, contract with the *campesino* and his own social sensibility, and that we cannot manufacture; in spite of these 136 agencies, I know that more than one of you will tell me of agents who do not effectively get close to the *campesino.*

The extension scheme which now seems most favored is tied to the system of agricultural credit. "Supervised credit" refers to a loan in which the lender takes some responsibility for overseeing the application of the loaned funds. When an agricultural bank grants credit under such a system, it offers its own program of technical assistance to the borrower. The next section thus deals not only with traditional credit problems, but also with some of the extension service problems, which are necessarily associated with supervised credit for land reform beneficiaries.

4. Agricultural Credit

WHETTEN, RURAL MEXICO *204-07 (1948)

From the standpoint of financing the agricultural activities of these individually operated ejidos, there are a great many difficulties which present themselves. These stem from a variety of factors, among which are (1) the small size of the plots, (2) the relatively poor quality of the land, (3) the culturally retarded status of the ejidatarios. The size of the holding is, in general, too small to be operated economically. With only 4.4 hectares of farm land, on the average, and much of this either too dry or too mountainous for efficient cultivation, there is little specialization of crops, little use of farm machinery and lack of full employment on the part of the entrepreneur and his family. The general tendency in such cases is for the ejidatario to raise only subsistence crops, usually corn, whether the land is suited for this or not, in the fear of going hungry if the fails to grow what he eats. Ordinarily, his methods of production are backward, and, without a great deal of supervision, he is likely to produce little beyond his subsistence needs. Even with a great deal of supervision, it is questionable whether the return he could realize on his surplus products would be sufficient to compensate a credit agency for providing the necessary supervision. This is the problem with which the [Ejido Bank] is confronted. In order to get a clear conception of the difficulties involved, we shall examine them with reference to the procedure of the bank.

First, in order for the society to recieve credit from the bank, a plan of operations for the year must be prepared and approved. Ideally, these would be worked out, first, by each ejidatario for his own plot, then co-ordinated with those of the other members of his credit society, so as to present the bank with a composite plan in requesting specified funds for the society as a whole.

Since membership in the societies carries joint liability, it is quite impor-

---

* Reprinted from Rural Mexico by Nathan Whetten by permission of The University of Chicago Press. Copyright 1948 by The University of Chicago.

tant that each one know what the others request, so that this may be approved, modified, or rejected by the group in accordance with their knowledge of his needs, capacities, and resources. Actually, it does not work out that way. Many of the ejidatarios lack the experience and the cultural development for working out any such plan. When they meet to discuss the plan in a general assembly, jealousy and rivalry arise, with the result that, regardless of needs or arbility to repay, the local officials are reluctant to assign less funds to one individual than to another for fear of unpleasant repercussions. This usually means that the local representative of the bank must consider each case individually, approve each plan separately, and make allotments of credit accordingly. This is almost an impossible task to perform adequately, since there are, on the average, 27 societies per zone and 67 ejidatarios in a society. This would give the local bank representative an average of about 1,809 ejidatarios to look after individually and many of these would be widely scattered.

A second major problem is concerned with the actual dispensing of funds after the plans of operation have been approved and the credit allotted. Again the ideal method would be for the bank to deal only with the member-delegate of a given society and let him distribute the funds among the members; but the bank has found that in most cases the member-delegate is not prepared to shoulder such responsibility. Sad experience has resulted from giving cash to the ejidatarios, since, like children, they often spend it for frivolities rather than for production purposes. For this reason the bank urges its local representatives to ascertain the needs of the ejidatarios and to grant loans to them in the form of supplies and equipment, such as seed, plows, and oxen, instead of giving them the cash. This procedure is very time consuming and costly, however, since the needs of each one must be considered and acted upon separately.

A third problem lies in the gowing and marketing of the crop. Ordinarily, the plots are too small to warrant the purchase or use of modern farm machinery, and most of the ejidatarios probably are not even aware that such machinery exists. They use the same primitive methods that have been in use for centuries. In a few instances societies have purchased machinery jointly for the use of their members, but such cases are exceptional. In the last few years the bank has alleviated the machinery problem somewhat by establishing an agency known as the Department of Agricultural Services. About 16,000,000 pesos were invested in farm machinery from the United States which was placed in conveniently located "machinery centers." The machinery is owned by the bank. Work requiring the use of machinery is then performed at the request of the ejidatarios who pay the bill on a cost basis. . . .

Little uniformity exists in the products from the individual ejidos. Ordinarily, each ejidatario uses his own judgment as to when and what to plant and how to tend the crop. There are no uniform grades for products of a given area, and this makes for difficulty in marketing. The lack of warehouses is also a hindrance to any attempt at marketing the crops co-operatively or holding them for favorable prices. As a rule, the ejidatario lives at, or near, subsistence level, and he is eager to get a return for his crop as quickly as possible. He does not think through the economics of marketing but often bargains away whatever crop he thinks he will be able to spare long before it is ready for harvesting. The *acaparadores* ("monopolizers") have been a plague in rural Mexico for generations, and they are still going strong.

The Ejido Bank is struggling with the problem of convincing the ejidatario that his interests are being jeopardized by such practices and is trying to displace the *acaparador* by more efficient marketing procedures; but when each ejidatario is concerned only with his own little plot and bargains individually, he plays into the hands of the *acaparadores*.

A fourth problem, and one of the most serious, concerns the collecting of debts on loans. Theoretically, all members are supposed to bring their payments to the member-delegate and let him make the society's payments to the bank in a lump sum. It does not work out that way, however. Ejidatarios simply do not bring in their payments. In some cases, as indicated above, the ejidatario has already promised his crop, gets what little money is due him as soon as the crop is harvested, and spends it without considering the debt he owes. Other ejidatarios, sometimes through carelessness in tending their crops, sometimes through factors beyond their control, do not receive enough from their harvests to subsist upon and pay debts in addition. Still others are influenced by propaganda against the Ejido Bank, which not infrequently sweeps through the ejidos, to the effect that ejidatarios need not repay any debts to the bank, since these are government funds and should be given to them as a part of the fruits of the Revolution, just as was done in the case of the land. In one state which the author recently visited, the governor was elected to office on the platform that he would see to it that the ejidatarios would not need to repay their loans. Thus the bank often finds itself under the necessity of trying to collect from each ejidatario individuallly, necessitating numerous calls, thus greatly augmenting administrative expenses. In many areas these expenses have become so high that operations have had to be suspended entirely.

The problems described above have tended to limit the operations which the bank feels it can safely undertake with the ejidos operating on an individual basis. This is emphasized by statistics showing that the three agencies of Torreón, Ciudad Obregón and Los Mochis, in which practically all the ejidos were operating on a collective basis, received 65.4 per cent of all funds loaned by the bank in 1943. These three agencies included only 11.5 percent of all ejidatarios-operating with the bank.

SIMPSON, THE EJIDO: MEXICO'S WAY OUT* 377-79 (1937)

The Special Nature of the Ejido Credit Problem

Even if Mexico at the beginning of the agrarian reform had possessed a system of agricultural credit and even if this system had been adapted to the needs of small farmers, it is doubtful that it could have been made to serve the ends of the ejidatarios. For so special are the legal, economic and social problems presented by this class of farmers created by the revolution that, for all practical purposes, they lie outside the field of any customary type of either private or public banking enterprise. The problem of providing ejidatarios with funds to work their newly acquired lands and market their products has been, and is, a problem of creating an entirely new type of credit structure.

In the first place it must be recalled that both as a matter of fact and as a matter of law the vast majority of the ejidatarios have very little, if any, private capital. As a matter of fact, because by definition those who receive ejidos are drawn from the vast body of "the miserable and the disinherited"; as a matter of law, because no person who possesses "commercial or industrial capital of more than 2,500 pesos," or land "equal to or greater in extension than a [ejido] parcel" may benefit under the ejido laws.

Second, ejido parcels are "imprescriptible and inalienable . . . and therefore in no case and in no form whatsoever may they be ceded, conveyed, rented, hypothecated, or made subject to lien in whole or in part." Moreover, ejido lands may not be the object of seizure as the result of a suit, law, decree, order or otherwise by any authority private or official, whether Federal, State or Municipal. All of which means that practically the only security an individual ejidatario can offer a loan is his crop; and even with respect to this crop there are certain restrictions which render this security of doubtful value to an ordinary bank.

Finally, to the legal and economic peculiarities of the problem of providing credit for the ejidatario there must be added certain complicating factors of a social and political nature. It must be constantly held in mind that the great mass of Mexico's rural population has for centuries been living outside of and divorced from the institutions and procedures of modern economic life, and is, for the most part, profoundly ignorant of financial and credit

---

[12] Most of the lower strata of the farmers have, of course, had some experience with the widespread system of crop-advances by which the *hacendados* have traditionally provided their renters, tenants, resident laborers and sometimes even neighboring "independent" small farmers with seeds, plows, work animals and small amounts of cash. Familiarity with this personalistic and usurious system, however, can hardly be regarded as knowledge of credit operations. Indeed, the system may be said to foster attitudes — servile dependence and lack of responsibility and initiative — just the opposite of those demanded for the successful working of modern methods of financing agricultural operations. For example, consider the following report (not at all uncommon) with reference to an ejido with the charming name of Agua de la Mula in the state of Coahuila:

"A number of the ejidatarios still lament the disappearance of the 'boss' who used to lend

operations of any type.[12] The problem of credit for the ejidatario in its simplest form, therefore, is one of education. They must be taught the meaning of loans, notes, bonds, checks, shares, warehouse receipts, interest rates — in a word, they must be taught first that there *is* such a thing as agricultural credit, and, second, how this mysterious thing works.

But there is also another type of training the lack of which makes it difficult to introduce obviously indicated types of credit organization. The legal set-up of the ejido being what it is, it would seem that some form of coöperative society with collective responsibility would be the most satisfactory means for financing agricultural operations. Any attempt, however, to proceed along these lines meets the obstacle of what the prominent agrarian leader, Luis León, has described as the "lack of spiritual preparation." "The Mexican peasants," writes León, "are still too individualistic. ... As the result of their experience as an exploited class they feel a profound lack of confidence in any undertaking in which they cannot see complete compensation for their work clearly guaranteed. ... They have no interest in collective work unless they are sure of its advantages." From this point of view, then, agricultural credit for the ejidatario becomes a question of education of a somewhat more complicated type — education, that is, in coöperative enterprise, mutual confidence, and in the meaning of moral responsibility in business transactions.

SUPERVISED CREDIT PROGRAMS

In Mexico and in other countries (notably Chile and Venezuela), money supplied by the Alliance for Progress has recently been deposited with lending agencies for the purpose of establishing programs of supervised credit. Essentially, these programs combine credit with extension services in the hope of securing a better rate of repayment, thus reducing the drain on the countries' resources which is implicit in the old system of subsidies disguised as credit.

The Venezuelan program operates as follows: The *campesino* — often, but not necessarily, a beneficiary of the land reform — prepares a plan for the improvement or cultivation of his parcel, with the aid of an extension agent assigned to his village or district. The request for a loan is submitted to a local committee, composed of village leaders, the extension agent, etc. This committee must approve the request, and is to consider primarily the personal characteristics of the borrower — his good faith and the likelihood of his doing his best to fulfill his contract. The technical aspect of his proposal is

---

them seed, implements, oxen and corn for their plaintings. Now they have no one to whom they can turn for help. The majority of the ejidatarios are quarreling with the former President of the Executive Committee ... over loans for seed and implements." *Las misiones culturales*, 1932-1933, p. 46.

confided largely to the extension agent, and to the credit committee in the local office of the Agricultural Bank, which has the main responsibility for deciding on requests for credit. Loans are granted for periods of from six to eighteen months, and at interest rates, depending on the size of the loan (the greater the loan, the higher the interest), of from three to six per cent. Security may be given in the form of a mortgage of the borrower's interest in his land, or of his equipment, or probably most frequently, a pledge of the next crop. The supervision of the borrower's operation takes the form of regular visits by the extension agent, who checks to see that the plan which he has helped to formulate is being carried out. Sanctions for failure to carry out the plan are limited to the usual lender's remedies — termination of the loan, recourse to the security, etc. BANCO AGRICOLA Y PECUARIO (Venezuela), MANUAL DE CREDITO SUPERVISADO (AID) (1962).

Another scheme is being tried in Mexico, also with the aid of money from the Alliance. The Bank of Mexico has established a fund designed to guarantee up to 90% of loans made by private banks to farmers. There is no political pressure on the private banks to permit borrowers to escape their obligations to repay; on the contrary it is hoped by the scheme's proponents that the private lenders will exercise some degree of supervision over the loaned funds. It remains to be seen whether the private banks — which traditionally have limited themselves to loans to large-scale farmers, or at least farmers who can mortgage their land — will be willing to make loans to smaller farmers if they are backed by the guarantee. The program's critics on the political left are already claiming that it is designed to give still another advantage to the "small property owners" — or, as they see it, to rich farmers.

E. Notes on Other Reforms

1. Colonization

Another way to avoid the pain occasioned by widespread expropriation of property is to colonize lands which are unoccupied. Where the State itself is a big landowner, as President Betancourt noted in his speech on Venezuelan land reform, colonization may be a politically attractive alternative. Furthermore, if there are constitutional or other requirements of immediate and full compensation for expropriated property, a colonization program avoids the necessity for some cash outlays by hard-pressed governments. A number of countries in Latin America have already inaugurated such programs — particularly the larger countries: Argentina, Bolivia, Brazil, Chile, Colombia, Mexico, Venezuela; the list is not exhaustive.

It should not be assumed that the absence of land *acquisition* costs makes colonization inexpensive. A Colombian observer says:

Land redistribution requires capital investments of some size. The poor farmer has to be given long terms in which to redeem his lands; probably he will be able to do nothing more than meet the interest payments during the first few years until he has his little enterprise well under way. He must also be given the means for constructing his home, and he must be provided with working tools.

Colonization requires even greater investments. In some of the valleys, such as the Cauca, the population has increased considerably during the last thirty years, and mechanized agriculture had developed on these lands of excellent quality, which lands formerly were used for grazing in the most primitive way. But we still have very extensive valleys with good soil for agriculture, low population density, and immense zones of virgin forest, largely the property of the state.

We feel the strong necessity of occupying these valleys, not only to make a greater number of Colombians landholders but also to increase production and lower prices, of mechanizing agriculture wherever possible, and of reducing the agriculture, carried on on the mountainous slopes in order to reduce erosion. We cannot do this without opening communication routes, building schools, improving sanitation, without, in many cases, engaging in irrigation, and without being able to fall back on even the most elementary amenities of life. The tropics [are] an unbridled enemy of man, and the fight for a living in the tropics is a hard one. Bernal, *Land Tenure Problems of Colombia*, in LAND TENURE at 289, 292 (Parsons, Penn and Raup ed. 1956.)

An additional difficulty is that it is often hard to attract colonists to leave their native areas to establish colonies. In a time of increasing urbanization (more than a quarter of Latin America's population lives in cities of 1,000,000 or more) there may exist the paradox of land hunger in some parts of the country and a scarcity of agricultural population in others. See Browning, *Recent Trends in Latin America Urbanization*, 316 ANNALS iii (1958). Then why not take the obvious step, and transport some of the landless rural population to the new areas of colonization? To some extent, such a program is being carried out in the countries listed above. But there may be complications based on a form of human inertia which causes many people — especially those of little education and understanding of the world outside their immediate community — to balk at transplantation. The Indians of Bolivia's *altiplano*, for example (the high plateau bordering Peru and Chile) at first resisted the government's efforts to move them from their rather unproductive lands into the *Oriente*, the fertile and largely unoccupied lowlands that border on Brazil and Paraguay. Partly because of their low resistance to lowland diseases, experienced during the Chaco War of the 1930s, they did not want to move from the highlands into a steamy, tropical climate, although the land was fertile and given to them for nothing. Recent indications are that the government is finding more success in getting people to move, in part because of heavy investment in social overhead capital items. Inexpensive colonization seems not to work.

The experience of Brazil with colonization of the Northeast is also in-structive. In 1953 the government was faced with widespread migration of workers out of the colonized area to the industrialized South; "emergency colo-nization stations" were established to assist the colonists and protect agricul-tural workers, giving them shelter when they needed it, offering vocational training, etc. Order N° 387, *Diario Oficial* I, N° 80, 8 April 1953, p. 6160, translated and reprinted in FOOD AND AGRICULTURAL LEGISLATION, V. 2/53.3 (U.N., F.A.O. 1953). See generally INTERNATIONAL LABOUR OF-FICE, WHY LABOR LEAVES THE LAND 146-56 (Studies and Reports, n.s., N° 59, 1960).

Some of the countries of Latin America have included colonization pro-grams in their general land reform legislation; in such a scheme, the state own-ed or unoccupied lands are simply one more source of lands for distribution. Argentina and Chile state in their legislation a policy of initial recourse to state owned land and voluntary sales by landowners to the government, before resort to expropriation.

The parallel of all this legislation to the homestead laws of the United States and the colonization of our West is close. In fact, some of the Latin American legislation shows signs of preparation with the North American model in view. Thus: colonists may be required to make certain improvements, on penalty of forfeiting their right to colonized lands; colonists may be re-quired to remain on the colonized land for a specified period of time; the amounts of land granted may be increased if the land is not irrigated, or is otherwise limited in its desirability as farm land; there may be special pater-nalistic rules for Indians who become colonists (as, restrictions on their power to alienate). The homestead laws are contained in 43 U.S.C. § 161 *et seq.* (1958).

---

2. Tenancy Regulation

Articles 140-49 of the Venezuelan Law, pp. 436-39, *supra,* regulate land-lord tenant relations. Similar legislation has been adopted in a number of Latin American countries, sometimes as an adjunct to fundamental land reforms, but often as a substitute for redistribution of land. Examples of the latter type may be found in Argentina and Uruguay.

The Venezuelan law is typical in its coverage. These laws normally are aimed at providing: greater security of tenure for the tenant farmer; greater independence from the landowner with respect to such matters as the purchase of supplies and the marketing of the product; fair rents; and, occasionally, an option to purchase the rented parcel.

---

3. Consolidation of Uneconomically Small Parcels

CARROLL, THE LAND REFORM ISSUE IN LATIN AMERICA
in LATIN AMERICAN ISSUES: ESSAYS AND COMMENTS*
at 161, 165-67 (Hirschman ed. 1961)

Now let us look at the other end of the scale. The great majority of the farms are small, often so small that at the present levels of technology these *minifundios* cannot give the farm family an acceptable minimum level of living. In Guatemala 97 per cent of all farms are in units of less than 20 hectares. The corresponding figure for both Peru and Ecuador is 90 per cent, for the Dominican Republic it is 95 per cent, for Venezuela 88 per cent and for the private sector of the Mexican farm economy 88 per cent. In Colombia some 325,000 farms average ½ hectare, and a further half a million farms average 2½ hectares.

The gravity of the *minifundio* situation is increased by fragmentation, by illegal occupancy (squatting) and by shifting cultivation. In many areas (especially in the Andean mountains) these small holdings have become subdivided as a result of population pressure into tiny plots, often only a few feet wide. Métraux reports, for example, that in the Conima region on the eastern shore of Lake Titicaca there is not a single holding that is not broken up into fifteen or twenty plots. Many of the smallest units are operated by squatters on either public or private land who hold no title and whose farming operations both from the point of view of security and use of resources are extremely unsatisfactory. Finally, there is the problem of migrant or shifting small-scale agriculture, practiced in vast areas of usually forested land in the tropical belt, mostly accompanied by burning and other wasteful methods. The vast majority of *minifundios* represent a hand-to-mouth type of farming and are outside the market economy.

The origin of the *minifundios* also goes back to colonial times, when land grants were "bestowed on the lower order, the conquering armies or upon civilians of humble rank." Some of the more recent ones are homesteads conferred upon or sold to colonists who settled in frontier regions. Some are the result of simple occupancy, which may or may not have been confirmed legally. The extraordinarily rapid growth of population in recent decades has aggravated the *minifundio* problem both through further subdivision by inheritance and through spontaneous migration into new areas. The owners or occupants of small plots of land are beset by many problems. Many are at the margin of the market economy and represent neither a producing force of farm commodities nor an effective demand for industrial products. They generally lack not only land but other inputs necessary to raise productivity. Their plots are frequently exhausted and eroding. Institutional services, schools,

---

roads, hospitals, are conspicuously lacking in *minifundio* areas. The peasants are at the mercy of unscrupulous tradesmen, money lenders, lawyers and petty officials.

It should be emphasized that the *minifundio-latifundio* patterns are not independent, but are often closely interrelated. Large estates are surrounded by many small *ranchos, chacras, huertas, hijuelas* or *sitios,* drawing seasonal labor from them and in many ways contributing to the maintenance of the system. The *latifundios* exercise an influence far beyond their own boundaries, and they are frequently a limiting force on regional development. More importantly, perhaps, the system acts as a barrier to social mobility, participating citizenship and the emergence of a broad base for upgrading the quality of human effort, which is a pre-requisite for dynamic development.

The third paragraph of Article 27 of the Mexican Constitution of 1917 authorizes the National Government "to develop small landed holdings in operation. ..." The same Article, however, exempts the small property (*pequeña propiedad*) from agrarian proceedings; thus estates under certain sizes (depending on the quality of the land) are not "affectable" and may not be taken for the creation or augmentation of ejidos.

The existence of a large number of uneconomically small farms seemed to call for an early legislative remedy, but it was not until 1945 that action was taken. In that year, the Congress enacted the "Regulatory Law of the Third Paragraph of Article 27 ...," providing for the regrouping of certain small parcels. The first article of the Act states that it is designed to protect snall property against uneconomic fragmentation. The terms of the Act make it clear that some small property owners are to be protected by consolidation whether they like it or not.

Consolidation was to take place in two classes of circumstances:

> (1) When at least 30% of the area in question was made up of small properties, the exploitation of which was uneconomic owing to their size, and upon the petition of 40% of the owners of the area, owing 60% of the land (by area,) or, alternatively, on petition of 60% of the owners, owing 40% of the land, or, finally by decision of the Federal Government, upon proposal by the Secretary of Agriculture and the government of the State in which the area was located.
>
> (2) When agricultural conditions, or natural boundaries, were changed appreciably by irrigation or other public works, making necessary a redistribution of land in order to assure economic size for properties, access ways, etc., by decision of the Federal Government upon the proposal of the agency which was responsible for the public work in question.

The 1945 law took as its guide the provisions of the Agrarian Code, which define the minimum limits for small property by reference to the amount of labor needed to cultivate it: The minimum parcel is that which, in view of the prevailing local technology, requires at least 240 man-days per year for its cultivation, provided that the parcel's cultivation will suffice to sustain an average peasant family.

The Act provided for the establishment of Consolidation Councils, made up of governmental and small property representatives, to carry out the re-grouping of small property pursuant to the petition presented by 40% (or 60%) of the owners. The Act cautioned the Councils to take care that each owner receive in exchange for property that he relinquished, other property of equal quality and value. It will be seen that the Act contemplated the situation in which one owner owns several small, non-contiguous plots, the cultivation of which may be necessarily inefficient when performed by his family. But what of the many owners of single parcels of agricultural property below the economic minimum size?

The answer is that the Act left them alone, even though these parcels are obviously uneconomic. Article 27 of the Constitution makes "inaffectable" parcels under 100 hectares in size (with provision for upward adjustment of the maximum in cases of land which is less desirable in quality), and the official position of all administrations since the Revolution has been protective of small property. Such owners may be encouraged to sell to adjoining owners, but they are not to be forced to sell out.

Is that policy wise? What are the considerations which lie behind it? How does the case of the owner of a single tiny parcel differ from that of the owner of two tiny parcels? Is a forced exchange essentially different from a forced sale? If some future legislation should require forced sales by owners of single small properties, would Article 27 of the Constitution be violated?

The 1945 Act did not limit its reach to a regrouping of property once and for all. The draftsmen knew that the effects of any consolidation might be dissipated by future divisions of the consolidated property, either by sale or by inheritance. The solution was to forbid such future fractionalizing. Thus Article 16 of the 1945 Act provided:

"Except in the cases foreseen in Articles 4 and 5 [establishing exemptions for suburban lots, for parks, and for other lands inappropriate for consolidation], the sale of agricultural lands shall be prohibited when the result of the transaction is that the property of the seller or the buyer is left with an area smaller than the limit established in Article 3 [the 240 man-day provision mentioned above], except when the area which is to be sold may be the only property of the seller."

Article 17 establishes a similar prohibition with respect to inheritances, which is in substance a prohibition against partition into parcels below the minimum set in Article 3. (Co-owners or heirs who give up rights to possession are to be indemnified, and given government loans of money to buy other small property in replacement.)

The most remarkable thing about this legislation is that it has never been applied. The Act is still "in force" — if the expression is not meaningless under the circumstances — but the machinery for its administration was never created. Thus Mexico has provided Latin America with a model law, in the purest sense of the term.

Several similar consolidation projects have been carried out in Chile, with a high degree of success, measured by gains in agricultural production and income for the areas affected. The programs have been criticized as expensive, but the criticism must be measured against future gains of the kind mentioned.

---

4. Land Taxation

CARROLL, THE LAND REFORM ISSUE IN LATIN AMERICA
in LATIN AMERICAN ISSUES: ESSAYS AND COMENTS*
at 161, 192-93 (Hirschman ed. 1961)

The experience with land taxation in Latin America is not encouraging. Colombia is the best example. As in other Latin American countries, land taxes in Colombia are extremely light and in many ways favor the large operators who have non-agricultural investments. The standard rate is 0.4 per cent.

Although the International Bank for Reconstruction and Development is generally reluctant to touch the controversial problems of land tenure, one of the principal recommendations of its missions to Colombia in 1950 and 1956 was the imposition of a graduated land tax based on potential land use. The first of these missions recommended (in what became known as the Currie Report) a graduated land tax which called for a rate of 0.4 per cent for well-utilized lands and higher rates for poorly used lands. The 1956 mission suggested assessing agricultural land based on optimum rather than current use and subjecting owners of speculative holdings to an income tax based on a presumed net return of between 3 and 5 per cent of the value of land and capital assets.

In 1957 governmental Decree 290 made a variant of these ideas into law, providing an elaborate system of tax incentives and deterrents designed to improve land use practices. The key provision required owners and tenants with more than fifty hectares to cultivate part of their land at least once a year. The cultivation requirements varied with the type of land, according to a classification to be made by the Geographic Institute. Non-compliance was to be punished by a progressive land tax based on cadastral value. There was

---

no attempt in this decree to expropriate unused or underused private land whose owners did not comply with the cultivation quotas. The key to this whole procedure was the rapid completion of the land classification. A special ownership and use survey based on a questionnaire was also necessary to put the law into effect.

As of this writing [1961], the penalties prescribed by Decree 290 for inadequate land utilization have not been applied. True, the Geographic Institute classified almost a million hectares, mostly in areas already fairly well developed. The low cultivation quotas pose no serious problem for farmers in these areas, and even where additional classifications have been available the provisions of Decree 290 have been inoperative. A land ownership and land use questionnaire was sent out in early 1958 but answers were incomplete and of questionable validity; in any event, the results have never been tabulated. This left the government without any basic data for the effective administration of the law, and no further attempts have been made to enforce it. However, this has not discouraged Colombian policy-makers from their determination to design some kind of land tax proposal. During the last two years a number of projects incorporating a graduated land tax have been elaborated and presented to the legislature. The over-all land reform bill prepared at the end of 1960 also involves tax incentives and penalties, although it relies upon other means to reform the agrarian structure. The Colombian experience shows that little can be achieved through a land tax if there is no effective enforcement machinery.

The abortive plan to tax agricultural land progressively in the State of São Paulo, Brazil, and the new Brazilian national progressive tax law have been mentioned earlier. See p. 480, *supra*. The progressive tax system proposed in Article 20 of the Venezuelan law, p. 411, *supra*, has not yet been enacted into law. By means of an effective system of taxation, much of the economic purpose of a land reform might be achieved. But tax systems in Latin America are subject to serious weaknesses in administration which, up to the present time, have prevented them from being effective. The Alliance for Progress calls for tax reforms as well as land reforms, but the kinds of drastic reform visualized by the creators of the Alliance have not yet been forthcoming in any country. The most optimistic tax reformers hope only for improvements in administration in the near future. Recent Mexican experience suggests that corruption on the part of tax officials can be reduced to a low level. But efficiency in tax administration requires trained administrators, and there is no shortage more critical in Latin America than the shortage of personnel to run the middle and lower levels of public administration.

Chapter V

JUDICIAL PROTECTION AGAINST
ARBITRARY OFFICIAL ACTION

A. Introduction

Any contribution by Latin America's judiciary to the protection of individuals against governmental abuse must be made in the face of formidable obstacles. The tradition of the *caudillo*, the strong personal leader, is just one phase of a broader and very old tradition of authoritarianism. Salvador de Madariaga, an outstanding contemporary Spanish historian and social critic, says that the Spaniard's outlook oscillates between the two extremes of man and the universe — that his patriotism is not so much *group* consciousness as a tendency on the one hand for the individual to absorb the nation, and on the other for the individual to reach beyond his nation to the whole world:

> It is easy to see how these psychological premises lead to the two constant features of Spanish political life which may be symbolized in the words: *dictatorship* and *separatism*. The individual, moved by stronger vertical than horizontal impulses, i.e., by natural forces expressed directly in him rather than by forces transmitted by tradition or absorbed from the environment, tends to assert his personality and (like a bottle already full of its own contents) to refuse other influences. This leads to dictatorship, observable not merely in the public man, statesman, general, cardinal, or king at the head (or on the way thereto) of every village, city, region, business firm, or even family in the country.
> The dictator is most averse to separatism in others, since it limits the area of his own dictatorship; but he is a separatist himself, for he separates himself from others in what concerns the usual collective functions of study, discussion, give-and-take, and agreement. The strong individual, vertical pattern of the Spaniard and the weakness of his horizontal tendencies, those of course which weave men together in a social tissue, explain the separatism of Spaniards and the ease with which, at the slightest shock, regions, cities, political parties, classes, services of the state, are torn asunder and fall away from each other. DE MADARIAGA, SPAIN: A MODERN HISTORY 22-23 (1958).*

Cortés and those who followed him had little difficulty in enslaving the

---

* See also Morse, *Toward a Theory of Spanish American Government*, 15 J. OF THE HISTORY OF IDEAS 71 (1954), reprinted in HAMILL (ed.), DICTATORSHIP IN SPANISH AMERICA at 52 (1965).

indigenous population, for slavery or something close to slavery had been their condition before he came. The Conquest itself perpetuated a typically Iberian mixture of paternalism and repression. While the Puritans came to Massachusetts to build a permanent society, most Spaniards came to Mexico and Peru to make a fortune and then return to Spain. As a consequence, Latin American society was essentially "extractive" from the beginning. The *repartimientos* and *encomiendas* assigned Indians to their new masters, not only to make them Christians but also to work them in the mines.

The feudal structure of colonial Latin America rested in part on a military base, and not simply because military power was needed to keep the indigenous peoples in line; after all, the men who were assigned lands and mines were the soldiers, the *conquistadores*. Cortés himself became the Marqués del Valle de Oaxaca. Even after Independence, military power remained the most important base for political power.

> The collapse of Spanish authority in Latin America ushered in an era of predatory militarism. The leaders of the revolutionary armies who secured independence and claimed the credit for creating and consolidating the new republics emerged as the new rulers. Within each nation undisciplined, ambitious local chieftains vied for supreme power. Politics became the plaything of the military. For more than a generation, nation after nation was subjected to the whims of army-officer politicians who ruled by the sword, perverted justice, and pillaged the treasury. Through the first half of the nineteenth century these *caudillos* and their followers lived, with all too few exceptions, as parasites upon the society they were supposed to protect. LIEUWEN, ARMS AND POLITICS IN LATIN AMERICA 17 (rev. ed. 1961).

Ironically, the emergence of local *caudillos* may be traced to a desire for security, at a time when the central governments were too weak to provide it. Once in power, the local chiefs had to acquire wealth in quantities sufficient for the purchase of political loyalty. The power of the state in turn was and still is a source of wealth, particularly from foreign businesses which have often been willing to pay for concessions. See Kling, *Towards a Theory of Power and Political Instability in Latin America*, 9 WESTERN POL. Q. 21 (1956). This circular reinforcement of wealth and political power is surely not peculiar to Latin America, but it has been especially visible there.

The power of the local chiefs has gradually given way to national political power, and the tradition of the *caudillo* itself often has been the instrument of material change. National *caudillos*, by military force or by assimilation of local leadership into their political organizations, emerged during the 19th century, at the same time advancing the centralization of power through improving communication between national capitals and provincial centers. See Chevalier, *The Roots of Personalismo*, in HAMILL (ed.), DICTATORSHIP IN SPANISH AMERICA at 35 (1965).

Under such circumstances, no one could expect the development of effective protections of the individual against government, nor even the development of an independent judiciary. In modern Latin America, nowhere save Haiti are conditions so extreme as those described by Lieuwen in the first half century of independence. Yet the tradition remains. The paternalism which first governed the Indians has been extended to touch the illiterate, then to those who benefit from government programs ranging from ordinary welfare to land reform, and to the population at large. Requirements of written permissions and official registrations are present in dazzling profusion. When it is added that governments throughout the region are under overwhelming pressure to force-develop their countries' economies, guidance from the top sometimes becomes an irresistible political necessity, although other political realities may compel an attempt to conceal the centralization of control. Such attention to appearances is of less concern in countries relatively untouched by social revolution, where the government "knows best."

A Latin American judge, challenged to justify the failure of the judiciary to taken an active role in limiting administrative action, would no doubt answer that the judge in the typical administrative law case is protecting the whole citizenry (represented by a bureau) as against one individual who seeks something for himself. It would be easy to surrender to pessimism, concluding that there is nothing the courts can or will do to create constitutional or other limits on governmental power. One hopeful reply might be that even a strong government may wish to support the legitimacy of its actions by submitting them to the scrutiny of judges who have the power to negate them.* Another historical answer is perhaps more persuasive: This chapter explores two developments, one in Mexico and one in Argentina, which have contributed in important ways to an emerging constitutionalism. The theme is supplied by Professor Hart's reply (p. 612, *infra*) to Judge Hand's famous disclaimer of judicial competence. The chapter closes with a brief investigation of the judiciary in action in times of stress, dealing with assertions of de facto governmental power and with declarations of states of seige.

HAND, THE CONTRIBUTION OF AN
INDEPENDENT JUDICIARY TO CIVILIZATION
in The Spirit of Liberty**
at 172, 177-82 (Dilliard ed. 1952)

But American constitutions always go further. Not only do they distrib-

---

* See BLACK, THE PEOPLE AND THE COURT, ch. II (1960). For a relatively optimistic view of the role of the modern military, see JOHNSON, THE MILITARY AND SOCIETY IN LATIN AMERICA (1964).

** Reprinted with permission of the publisher from THE SPIRIT OF LIBERTY by Learned Hand. Published, 1952 by Alfred A. Knopf, Inc.

ute the powers of government, but they assume to lay down general principles to insure the just exercise of those powers. ... Here history is only a feeble light, for these rubrics were meant to answer future problems unimagined and unimaginable. Nothing which by the utmost liberality can be called interpretation describes the process by which they must be applied. Indeed if law be a command for specific conduct, they are not law at all; they are cautionary warnings against the intemperance of faction and the first approaches of despotism. The answers to the questions which they raise demand the appraisal and balancing of human values which there are no scales to weigh. Who can say whether the contributions of one group may not justify allowing it a preference? How far should the capable, the shrewd or the strong be allowed to exploit their powers? When does utterance go beyond persuasion and become only incitement? How far are children wards of the state so as to justify its intervention in their nurture? What limits should be imposed upon the right to inherit? Where does religious freedom end and moral obliquity begin? As to such questions one can sometimes say what effect a proposal will have in fact, just as one can foretell how much money a tax will raise and who will pay it. But when that is done, one has come only to the kernel of the matter, which is the choice between what will be gained and what will be lost. The difficulty here does not come from ignorance, but from the absence of any standard, for values are incommensurable. It is true that theoretically, and sometimes practically, cases can arise where courts might properly intervene, not indeed because the legislature has appraised the values wrongly, for it is hard to see how that can be if it has honestly tried to appraise them at all; but because that is exactly what it has failed to do, because its action has been nothing but the patent exploitation of one group whose interests it has altogether disregarded. But the dangers are always very great. What seems to the losers mere spoliation usually appears to the gainers less than a reasonable relief from manifest injustice. Moreover, even were there a hedonistic rod by which to measure loss or gain, how could we know that the judges had it; or — what is more important — would enough people think they had, to be satisfied that they should use it? So long as law remains a profession (and certainly there is no indication that its complexities are decreasing) judges must be drawn from a professional class with the special interests and the special hierarchy of values which that implies. And even if they were as detached as Rhadamanthus himself, it would not serve unless people believed that they were. But to believe that another is truly a Daniel come to judgment demands almost the detachment of a Daniel; and whatever may be properly said for the judges, among whom there are indeed those as detached as it is given men to be, nobody will assert that detachment is a disposition widespread in any society.

It is not true, as you may be disposed at first blush to reply, that all this can be said with equal force of any other decision of a court. Constitutions are deliberately made difficult of amendment; mistaken readings of them cannot be readily corrected. Moreover, if they could be, constitutions must not degenerate into vade mecums or codes; when they begin to do so, it is a sign of a community unsure of itself and seeking protection against its own misgivings. And that is especially true of such parts of a constitution as I am talking about; these particularly must be left imprecise. If a court be really candid, it can only say: "We find that this measure will have this result; it will injure this group in such and such ways, and benefit that group in these other ways. We declare it invalid, because after every conceivable allowance for differences of outlook, we cannot see how a fair person can honestly believe that the benefits balance the losses." Practically, it is very seldom possible to be sure of such a conclusion; practically, it is very seldom possible to say that a legislature has abdicated by surrendering to one faction; the relevant factors are too many and too incomparable.

Nor need it surprise us that these stately admonitions refuse to subject themselves to analysis. They are the precipitates of "old, unhappy, far-off things, and battles long ago," originally cast as universals to enlarge the scope of the victory, to give it authority, to reassure the very victors themselves that they have been champions in something more momentous than a passing struggle. Thrown large upon the screen of the future as eternal verities, they are emptied of the vital occasions which gave them birth, and become moral adjurations, the more imperious because inscrutable, but with only that content which each generation must pour into them anew in the light of its own experience. If an independent judiciary seeks to fill them from its own bosom, in the end it will cease to be independent. And its independence will be well lost, for that bosom is not ample enough for the hopes and fears of all sorts and conditions of men, nor will its answers be theirs; it must be content to stand aside from these fateful battles. There are two ways in which the judges may forfeit their independence, if they do not abstain. If they are intransigent but honest, they will be curbed; but a worse fate will befall them if they learn to trim their sails to the prevailing winds. A society whose judges have taught it to expect complaisance will exact complaisance; and complaisance under the pretense of interpretation is rottenness. If judges are to kill this thing they love, let them do it, not like cowards with a kiss, but like brave men with a sword.

And so, to sum up, I believe that for by far the greater part of their work it is a condition upon the success of our system that the judges should be independent; and I do not believe that their independence should be impaired because of their constitutional functions. But the price of this immunity, I insist, is that they should not have the last word in those basic conflicts of "right and wrong — between whose endless jar justice resides." You may ask what then will become of the fundamental principles of equity and fair play which our constitutions enshrine; and whether I seriously belive that unsupported they will serve merely as counsels of moderation. I do not think that

anyone can say what will be left of those principles; I do not know whether
they will serve only as counsels; but this much I think I do know — that a
society so riven that the spirit of moderation is gone, no court can save; that
a society where that spirit flourishes, no court need save; that in a society
which evades its responsibility by thrusting upon the courts the nurture of
that spirit, that spirit in the end will perish. What is the spirit of moderation?
It is the temper which does not press a partisan advantage to its bitter end,
which can understand and will respect the other side, which feels a unity between all citizens — real and not the factitious product of propaganda —
which recognizes their common fate and their common aspirations — in a
word, which has faith in the sacredness of the individual. If you ask me how
such a temper and such a faith are bred and fostered, I cannot answer. ...
But I am satisfied that they must have the vigor within themselves to with-
stand the winds and weather of an indifferent and ruthless world; and that
it is idle to seek shelter for them in a courtroom. Men must take that temper
and that faith with them into the field, into the market-place, into the factory,
into the councilroom, into their homes; they cannot be imposed; they must
be lived.

HART, COMMENT in GOVERNMENT UNDER LAW at 139, 140-41
(Sutherland ed. 1956)

My other footnote is prompted by a quotation which Judge Wyzanski
makes, without protest, from Judge Learned Hand. "A society so riven that
the spirit of moderation is gone, no court *can* save; ... a society where that
spirit flourishes no court *need* save." I cannot help believing that Judge Hand,
when he wrote that, had his attention fixed on the turning of a phrase. But
if the statement is projected into a serious discussion of constitutional government, something more needs to be said. It needs to be said that the statement
is an example — a particularly clear example — of the fallacy of the undis-
tributed middle.

What the sentence assumes is that there are two kinds of societies — one
kind, over here, in which the spirit of moderation flourishes, and another kind,
over here which is riven by dissension. Neither kind, Judge Hand says, can be
helped very much by the courts. But, of course, that isn't what societies are
like. In particular, it isn't what American society is like. A society is a something in process — in process of becoming. It has always within it, as ours
does, seeds of dissension. And it has also within it forces making for moderation and mutual accommodation. The question — the relevant question — is
whether the courts have a significant contribution to make in pushing American society in the direction of moderation — not by themselves; of course

they can't save us by themselves; but in combination with other institutions. Once the question is put that way, the answer, it seems to me, has to be yes.

FOURNIER, COMMENT in GOVERNMENT UNDER LAW* at 83
(Sutherland ed. 1956)

I think it is quite important to bring here the point of view of the civil law countries on this problem of government under Law. ... [The author is a prominent Costa Rican lawyer and diplomat. — Ed.]

It is then important to see how a Latin American country has approached that same problem, because even though in regard to private law and administrative law our countries have all their historical roots in France and Spain, in regard to constitutional law we and you have a common parenthood. Our constitutions are daughters at the same time of the French tradition and the United States tradition. For that reason it may interest you to see how a civil law country, whose original governmental ideas were somewhat different, has tried to apply the doctrines of Chief Justice Marshall.

Chronologically, the first guarantee that we tried to build, in order to save the people from the government, from a government which perhaps might become too strong, was a habeas corpus writ. In a way this device has some origins in the Middle Ages in Spain where the kingdom of Aragon used to have a similar thing. But we have had it in our countries — at least in my own — since our first Constitution of 1825.

In that same Constitution, we have also, chronologically speaking, the second guarantee that we tried to build to save the people from a too-strong government. And it was in a way a first and tentative application of the doctrines of Chief Justice Marshall. It was a declaration of the Constitution at that time saying that any law enacted against the Constitution was unjust. It did not say exactly that it was void. It was not until 1844 that the Constitution provided that any law against the Constitution was void. Still for many years the Constitution did not say which body of the government or the state was to have the authority to say when a law was unconstitutional — when a law was against the Constitution. However, the Supreme Court of my country, since the last century, has taken to itself that authority, without any written authority in the Constitution. And it applied the same doctrines of Chief Justice Marshall and declared many laws all through our history unconstitutional, without having any express authority in the constitutional text. It was not until our present Constitution of 1949 that we had an express authorization to the Supreme Court to declare it so.

The third guarantee by which we have tried to build a system of government under law is what we call the "amparo" writ, which may be translated as the protection writ, which is a sort of habeas corpus applied to all other civil rights which are not related to the personal liberties. That is to say, inviolability of the domicile, or correspondence, or freedom of speech. Any time that you have a threat from government against any of those freedoms you can go by means of a summary proceeding before the Supreme Court and ask for protection. That measure was also established in the recent Constitution of 1949.

And finally the fourth guarantee that we have is the "contentious-administrative" procedure or action. Since the Republic has existed, it has been possible in our country, and I understand in all Latin American countries, to sue the government for damages, regarding an action of the administration which is considered unjust or illegal. But until recently there was, in my country, not exactly a prohibition against suing the government in order to obtain a declaration that an action of the administration was void, but no procedure provided to do it. Now, according to the present Constitution, it is possible, not only to sue the government for pecuniary damages, but also to sue the government in order to obtain from the courts a declaration that a certain administrative act is void and should be set aside.

B. The Mexican Amparo

GUAL VIDAL, MEXICAN AMPARO PROCEEDINGS
in A.B.A. SECTION OF INT'L AND COMP. LAW SELECTED PAPERS AND REPORTS at 82 (1941)

This is a constitutional suit of a summary nature [in the federal courts], the object of which is to protect, in a special case and at the request of an injured party, private persons whose individual rights as established in the Constitution have been violated through laws or acts of the authorities, or when the laws or acts of the Federal authorities injure the sovereignty of the States. . . .

* * *

The fundamental object of the *amparo* is the protection of individual rights as defined in Articles 1-29 of the Constitution. [*Amparo* is the Spanish word for protection. — Ed.]

* * *

The Supreme Court rules that the *amparo* may not only be brought for direct violations of the first 29 articles of the Constitution, but also, if there is injury to persons through violation of some other constitutional article, this article may be related with the guarantee of Article 14. [This article began as a guarantee of procedural fairness, but its broad guarantee of legality in judicial proceedings effectively constitutes the federal Supreme Court as the court of last resort on *all* questions of law. See note, p. 627, *infra.* — Ed.] So, in the subject of taxes, even though the obligation of Mexicans to contribute for the public expenditure in the proportional and fair manner provided for by law is contained in Article 31, it has been regarded that its violation constitutes likewise a violation of the guarantee of Article 14.

The fact that individual persons must be involved prevents the authorities from bringing an *amparo* in the case of invasion of jurisdiction. However, they may resort to that action when the defense of the public domain is involved, where, in pursuance of a traditional theory of Mexican Public Administrative Law, the State is not doing acts of authority proper. Article 9 of the new *Amparo* Law incorporates this principle.*

MEXICO, CONSTITUTION OF 1917
(Pan American Union translation)

* * *

ARTICLE 103.   The Federal courts shall decide all controversies that arise:

I.   Out of laws or acts of the authorities that violate individual guarantees.

II.   Because of laws or acts of the federal authority restricting or encroaching on the sovereignty of the States.

III.   Because of laws or acts of State authorities that invade the sphere of federal authority.

* * *

ARTICLE 107.   All controversies mentioned in article 103 shall be subject to the legal forms and procedure prescribed by law, on the following bases:

I.   A trial in amparo shall always be held at the instance of the injured party.

II.   The judgment shall always be such that it affects only private individuals, being limited to affording them redress and protection in the special case to which the complaint refers, without making any general declaration as to the law or act on which the complaint is based.

A defect in the complaint may be corrected, whenever the act complained of is based on laws declared unconstitutional by previous decisions of the Supreme Court of Justice.

---

* A very instructive analysis of the Mexican amparo is Fix Zamudio, *Estudio Sobre la Jurisdicción Constitucional Mexicana,* in CAPPELLETTI, LA JURISDICCION CONSTITUCIONAL DE LA LIBERTAD at 129 (Fix Zamudio transl., 1961). — Ed.

A defect in the complaint may also be corrected in criminal matters and in behalf of workers in labor disputes, when it is found that there has been a manifest violation of the law against the injured party who is left without defense, and in criminal matters, likewise, when the trial has been based on a law not precisely applicable to the case.

III. In judicial civil, criminal, or labor matters a writ of amparo shall be granted only:

a) Against final judgments or awards against which no ordinary recourse is available by virtue of which these judgments can be modified or amended, whether the violation of the law is committed in the judgments or awards, or whether, if committed during the course of the trial, the violation prejudices the petitioner's defense to the extent of affecting the judgment; provided that in civil or criminal judicial matters opportune objection and protest were made against it because of refusal to rectify the wrong and that if (the violation) was committed in first instance, it was urged in second instance as a grievance.

b) Against acts at the trial, the execution of which would be irreparable out of court, or at the conclusion of the trial once all available recourses have been exhausted.

c) Against acts that affect persons who are strangers to the trial.

IV. In administrative matters, amparo may be invoked against decisions which cause an injury that cannot be remedied through any legal recourse, trial, or defense. It shall not be necessary to exhaust these remedies when the law that established them, in authorizing the suspension of the contested act, demands greater requirements than the Regulatory Law for Trials in Amparo requires as a condition for ordering such suspension.

V. Except as provided in the following section, a writ of amparo against final decisions or awards, for violations committed therein shall be applied for directly to the Supreme Court of Justice, which shall render its decision without other evidence than the original complaint, a certified copy of the claims of the aggrieved party, which shall be added to those made by the third party affected, the latter's complaint submitted either by the Attorney General of the Republic or his designated agent, and that of the responsible authority.

VI. A writ of amparo against final decisions or awards shall be applied for directly to the Full Circuit Court (Tribunal Colegiado de Circuito) within whose jurisdiction is the domicile of the authority who pronounced the decision or award, whenever the complaint is based on substantial violations committed during the course of the trial or on civil or criminal judgments against which there is no recourse of appeal, regardless of what such alleged violations may be.

Whenever a writ of amparo is sought against final civil or criminal judgments or awards relating to labor matters, based on alleged substantial violations committed during the course of the trial or violations contained in the judgment or award, it must be invoked jointly for all such allegations, submitting the writ to the appropriate Full Circuit Court, which shall render a decision solely with respect to the substantial violations during the trial, and if the judgment is unfavorable to the aggrieved party, shall remit the case to the Supreme Court of Justice to decide on the violations committed in the judgment or award.

As to the application and procedure in amparo cases before the Full Circuit Court, the provisions of the preceding section shall be observed. When this procedure has been completed, a judgment shall be rendered according to the procedure prescribed by law.

VII. When a writ of amparo is sought against acts at the trial, outside the trial or after its conclusion, or if persons foreign to the case are affected, against laws or against acts of administrative authorities, application shall be made to the District Judge in whose jurisdiction is located the place in which the act in question was performed or was to be performed, and the procedure shall be limited to the report from the authority in question, to a hearing to which a single summons will include the order for submission of the report and for evidence to be presented by the interested parties and their allegations, the judgment to be rendered at this same hearing.

VIII. Judgments in amparo rendered by District Judges are subject to review. The Supreme Court of Justice will review such judgments in the following cases:

a) When a law is impugned as unconstitutional or if any of the cases included in sections II and III of article 103 are concerned.

b) Whenever the responsible authority against whom amparo is granted is a federal administrative authority.

c) Whenever, in criminal cases, merely the violation of article 22 of this constitution is alleged.

In all other cases the review will be made by a Full Circuit Court and their decisions may not be appealed.

IX. Decisions in direct amparo rendered by a Full Circuit Court may not be appealed unless the decision involves the unconstitutionality of a law or establishes a direct interpretation of a provision of the Constitution, in which case it may be appealed to the Supreme Court of Justice, limited exclusively to the decision of actual constitutional questions.

A decision of a Full Circuit Court may not be appealed if it is based on a precedent established by the Supreme Court of Justice as to the constitutionality of a law or the direct interpretation of a provision of the Constitution.

X. Contested acts may be subject to suspension in those cases and under conditions and guarantees specified by law, with respect to which account shall be taken of the nature of the alleged violation, the difficulty of remedying the damages that might be incurred by the aggrieved party by its performance, and damages that the suspension might cause to third parties and the public interest.

A suspension must be granted with respect to final judgments in criminal matters at the time notice is given of the application for a writ of amparo, and in civil matters when bond is posted by the complainant to cover liability for damages occasioned by the suspension, but this is waived if the other party gives bond (contrafianza) to ensure restoration of things as they were if amparo is granted and to pay resulting damages.

XI.   The suspension shall be requested from the responsible authority, in the case of direct amparo before the Supreme Court of Justice or the Full Circuit Court, in which case the aggrieved party shall notify the responsible authority, within the period fixed by law and under affirmation to tell the truth, of the claim for amparo, accompanied by two copies, one for use in the case and the other to be transmitted to the opposing party. In other cases, decisions as to suspension shall be made by the District Courts.

XII.   Violation of the guarantees set forth in article 16, in criminal matters, and articles 19 and 20 may be taken before the court above the one where it was committed, or before the appropriate District Judge, and in either case the decision shall be rendered in accordance with the terms prescribed in section VIII.

If the District Judge resides in the same place as the responsible authority, the law shall specify the judge before whom the writ of amparo is to be presented, and that judge may provisionally suspend the act in question, in those cases and under the terms established in the same law.

XIII.   The law shall specify the terms and cases in which the precedents of the courts of the Federal Judicial Power are binding, as well as the requirements for their modification.

If the Full Circuit Courts sustain contradictory opinions in amparo cases within their jurisdiction, the Ministers of the Supreme Court of Justice, the Attorney General of the Republic, or those Courts, may denounce the contradiction before the appropriate Panel, to decide which opinion shall prevail.

When the Panels of the Supreme Court of Justice sustain contradictory opinions in cases of amparo within their jurisdiction, any one Panel or the Attorney General of the Republic may denounce the contradiction before the Supreme Court of Justice, which, sitting as a full Court, shall decide which opinion shall prevail. Both in this instance and in the case provided for in the preceding paragraph, the decision rendered shall be solely for the effect of fixing the precedent and shall not affect the concrete juridical situation deriving from contradictory judgments in the cases in which they were rendered.

XIV.   When the contested act originated with civil or administrative authorities, and provided that the constitutionality of a law is not involved, proceedings will be discontinued by inactivity of the aggrieved party in those cases and according to terms indicated in the law regulating this article.

XV.   The Attorney General of the Republic or an Agent of the Federal Public Ministry appointed for the purpose, shall be a party in all suits in amparo, but they may abstain from intervening in such cases, if the matter in question lacks public interest, in their opinion.

XVI.   If after amparo is granted, the responsible official persists in repetition of the contested act or attempts to evade the decision of the federal authority, he shall be immediately removed from office and taken before the appropriate District Judge.

XVII.   The responsible authority will be taken before the appropriate authority whenever he fails to suspend the act when bound to do so, and when he posts bond that is invalid or insufficient, and in such cases the responsible authority and bondsman are jointly and severally liable.

XVIII.   Bailiffs and jailers who do not receive an authorized copy of the order of imprisonment of an arrested person within the seventy-two hours prescribed by article 19, counted from the day the party was at the disposal of the judge, must notify the judge of this fact at the end of such period, and if the order is not received within three hours, the prisoner shall be released.

Anyone violating the article cited in this provision will be immediately turned over to a competent authority.

Likewise, anyone who, after an arrest, does not take the arrested person before a judge within twenty-four hours, shall himself be turned over to such authority or his agent.

If the detention takes place outside the locality in which the judge resides, sufficient time is to be added to the above period to cover the distance involved.

NOTES AND QUESTIONS ON THE MEXICAN AMPARO

Mexican writers are fond of tracing the amparo to very old roots. In Rome, for example, there was a proceeding called "De homine libero exhibendo," which was much like the Anglo-American habeas corpus. And in Aragón, the late middle ages saw the recognition of a similar proceeding in the *Privilegio General* of Pedro III, a document comparable in its scope to Magna Carta. The modern amparo, however, is only about a century old. Ironically, it was first proposed by a close political associate of one man in Mexican history who closely fits the classic model of the military *caudillo*, General Santa Anna.

The very turbulent middle years of the 19th century saw a large number of proposed reforms to the Mexican Constitution. One by-product of all this drafting of projects was that it gave an exceptional opportunity for a succession of would-be founding fathers to experiment with devices for protecting against unconstitutional governmental activity. One central doctrinal dispute of that time concerned the role of the judges in protecting the Constitution. Should they limit themselves to protecting individuals in proceedings narrowly conceived for such protection, or should they assume a broader political role, issuing general declarations of unconstitutionality with all the authority of a legislative repeal?

The Constitution of 1857 grew out of the *Reforma* of Benito Juárez, whose forces had dislodged Santa Anna from power for the last time only two years before. This was a "liberal" constitution, not only in that it was dictated by the Liberal Party, but also because it reflected the dominant individualism of the century. Its articles 101 and 102 remain, almost verbatim, in the present Mexican Constitution as articles 103 and 107 (paragraphs I and II), printed just above. It will be seen that the 1857 Constitution resolved the issue of the judges' role by emphasizing the strictly judicial aspect of the protection of individuals, and minimizing the legislative aspect of construing the Constitution.

The following extract from the Law of Amparo — the statute which fills in the details left open by the Constitution — thus emphasizes limitations on judicial enforcement of the Constitution. Can you identify requirements which are parallel to our own doctrinal limitations of:

—standing to litigate?
—ripeness for review?
—mootness?
—exhaustion of administrative remedies?
—adequacy of remedy at law?
—irreparable injury?
—political questions?

To what extent are limitations of this nature simply logical consequences of the doctrine of separation of powers? To what extent are they based on considerations of convenience in judicial administration? In the United States, such limitations on the judiciary are often said to protect it from damaging conflicts with the political branches of government. Are such limitations equally useful in the Mexican political context?

MEXICO, LAW OF AMPARO
(Organic Law of Article 103 and 107 of the Federal Constitution)

[The first law of this kind was enacted in 1861; the present law dates from 1935, and was enacted during the administration of President Cárdenas; the most recent amendments were enacted in 1957.]

* * *

4.   The amparo proceeding can be instituted only by the party prejudiced by the act or the law which is challenged, the party being empowered

to institute it by himself, by his representatives, by his defense counsel if it is a question of an act that relates to a criminal case, or by means of any relative or stranger in the cases in which this law expressly permits; and the proceeding can be pursued only by the aggrieved person, by his legal representative or by his defense counsel.

5. The following are parties in the amparo proceeding:

I. The aggrieved person or persons;

II. The responsible authority or authorities;

III. The prejudiced third person or persons, who are empowered to intervene in this capacity:

a) The party opposing the aggrieved person when the challenged act emanates from a legal proceeding or controversy which is not of a penal character, or any of the parties to the same legal proceeding when the amparo is instituted by a stranger to the procedure;

b) The victim or persons who, in conformance with the law, have a right to reparation of damages or to demand civil liability arising out of the commission of a wrong, in amparo proceedings instituted against judicial acts of a criminal nature, provided that the latter affect said reparation or liability;

c) The person or persons who have taken steps in their own behalf regarding the act against which amparo is requested, whenever it is a question of orders given by authorities other than the judicial authority or the labor authorities.

IV. The Federal Public Ministry [like the U.S. Department of Justice], who may refrain from intervening when, in its judgment, the case in question lacks public interest.

* * *

17. When it is a question of acts involving danger of deprivation of life, attacks on personal liberty outside judicial proceedings, deportation or exile, or one of the acts prohibited by Article 22 of the Federal Constitution, and the person injured finds it impossible to institute the amparo, any other person may do so in his name, even a minor or a married woman. In this case the judge shall order any measures necessary to secure the appearance of the person aggrieved and whatever the circumstances, shall require him to ratify the complaint for amparo within the period of three days; if the interested person ratifies the complaint, the proceeding shall continue; if he does not ratify it, the complaint shall be deemed as not presented, any orders which may have been given being null.

* * *

21. The term for filing the complaint for amparo shall be 15 days. Said term shall be counted from the day following the one on which the complainant was notified of the resolution or decision that he challenges; that following the day on which he learned of them or of their execution; or that following the day on which he appeared to know of the same.

22. There are excepted from the provisions of the preceding article:

I.   Cases in which the mere issuance of a law allows it to be challenged by way of amparo, in which case the term for filing the demand shall be 30 days, to be counted from the time the same law takes effect. . . .

II.   Acts that constitute danger of deprivation of life, attacks on personal liberty, deportation, exile, any of the acts prohibited by Article 22 of the Constitution, or forcible induction into the national army or navy.

* * *

In these cases, the demand for amparo may be interposed at any time;

III.   When it is a question of final judgments given in civil suits to which the aggrieved person has not been legally summoned, said person shall have the term of 90 days for the filing of the demand if he resides outside the locality where the proceedings are held but within the Republic, and 180 days if he resides outside the Republic; counting in either case from the day following that on which he learns of the judgment; but if the interested person should return to the place where said proceeding takes place, he shall be subject to the preceding article.

Those parties who have agents to represent them at the place of the judicial proceeding shall not be considered absent for the purposes of this article; nor shall those who have designated an address for receiving notifications, or those who have manifested in any way that they have knowledge of the proceeding that motivated the challenged act.

* * *

35.   In amparo proceedings no [more special pleas of particular pronouncement] shall be instituted other than those expressly established by this law.

Other incidents which arise, if by nature they are preliminary and special, shall be decided completely and without any formal pleadings. Apart from these cases such incidents shall be decided together with the amparo in the final judgment, excepting what this law provides concerning the incident of suspension [see arts. 122 *et seq.* — Ed.].

* * *

73.   The amparo proceeding is not allowable:

I.   Against acts of the Supreme Court of Justice;

II.   Against decisions given in proceedings of amparo or in execution of the same;

III.   Against laws or acts which are the basis of another amparo proceeding which is pending decision, either in the first or only instance, or in review instituted by the same complainant, against the same authorities and for the same challenged act, although the constitutional violations may be different;

IV.   Against laws or acts which have been the basis of a final decree in another amparo proceeding as outlined in the preceding sub-paragraph;

V.   Against acts which do not affect the legal interests of the complainant;

VI.   Against laws which, by their promulgation alone, do not cause injury to the complainant, but rather require the subsequent act of an authority to put them into operation;

VII.   Against the decisions or declarations of [various electoral officials];
VIII.   Against resolutions or declarations of the Federal Congress or of the Houses which constitute it, the Legislatures of the States or of their respective Permanent Committees or Deputations, in the election, suspension or removal of officials in the cases in which the respective Constitutions confer on them the power of sovereign or discretionary decision;
IX.   Against acts consummated in an irreparable manner;
X.   Against acts emanating from a judicial proceeding, when by virtue of a change of juridical situation in the same, the violations claimed in the new amparo proceeding should be considered to be irreparably consummated, because of inability to decide the claimed violations in said proceeding, without affecting the new juridical situation;
XI.   Against acts consented to expressly or by manifestations of will which imply that consent;
XII.   Against acts tacitly consented to, that is those against which the amparo proceeding is not instituted within the periods established by articles 21 and 22. . . .
A law shall not be considered to be tacitly consented to, in spite of the fact that being impugnable in amparo proceedings from the moment of its promulgation, in the terms of sub-paragraph VI of this article, it has not been challenged, but only in case there has neither been interposed an amparo proceeding against the first act of the law's application in relation to the complainant;
XIII.   Against judicial decisions with respect to which the law concedes some recourse or means of defense, within the proceedings for their modification, revocation, or nullification, even when the party aggrieved has not taken timely advantage of the recourse, except that which sub-paragraph IX of Article 107 of the Constitution provides for third parties who are foreign to the proceedings.
There are excepted from the preceding provision cases in which the challenged act involves a danger of deprivation of life, deportation or exile, or any of the acts prohibited by Article 22 of the Constitution.
XIV.   When some legal recourse or defense proposed by the complainant which might have the effect of modifying, revoking or nullifying the challenged act is being dealt with in the ordinary tribunals;
XV.   Against acts of authorities other than the judiciary when they should be officially revised in conformance with the law which governs them, or there is available against them some recourse, proceeding, or means of legal defense, by virtue of which they may be modified, revoked or nullified, provided that in conformance with the same law the effects of said acts are suspended by interposition of the recourse or means of legal defense by the aggrieved person without demanding greater requirements than those which the present law establishes for granting to the aggrieved person a definitive suspension [see arts. 122-36, *infra*];
XVI.   When the effects of the challenged act have ceased;
XVII.   When, the challenged act continuing to exist, it cannot produce any legal or substantial effect because the object or the substance of the same has ceased to exist;
XVIII.   In all other cases in which the non-allowability of the amparo proceeding results from any provision of the law. [*E.g.*, Article 27, par. XIV of the Constitution, dealing with the agrarian reform. — Ed.]

* * *

76.   Judgments pronounced in amparo proceedings shall be concerned only with private individuals or legal entities, private or official, who have requested amparo, being limited to defending and protecting them, if applicable, in the particular case giving rise to the complaint, without making a general declaration respecting the law or act which may have motivated the complaint.

A deficiency in the complaint may be corrected when the challenged act is based on laws declared unconstitutional by the Jurisprudence of the Supreme Court of Justice.

A deficiency in the complaint in penal matters and in the labor aspect of labor-law matters may also be corrected when it is found that there has been a manifest violation of the law which has left the aggrieved person without defense, and in penal matters, in addition, when he may have been judged by a law which is not exactly applicable to the case.

    * * *

77.   The judgments which are given in amparo proceedings must contain:

> I.   A clear and precise description of the act or acts challenged, and an evaluation of the evidence tending to show them as proven or not proven;
> II.   The legal foundations for discontinuing the proceedings, or rather for declaring the constitutionality or unconstitutionality of the challenged act;
> III.   The analytical points with which the judgments should conclude, making concrete, with clarity and precision, the act or acts for which the amparo is dismissed, conceded, or denied.

78.   In judgments given in amparo proceedings, a challenged act shall be considered as it may appear proven before the responsible authority; and there shall not be admitted nor taken into account evidence which was not given before said authority in order to prove facts which motivated or were the object of the challenged decision.

In the judgments there shall be taken into consideration only the evidence which proves the existence of the challenged act and its constitutionality or unconstitutionality.

    * * *

80.   The object of the judgment which grants amparo is the restitution to the aggrieved person of full enjoyment of the violated individual guarantee, re-establishing things to the state that existed before the violation, when the challenged act is of a positive nature and when it is of a negative nature, the effect of the amparo shall be to force the responsible authority to respect the guarantee in question and to fulfill on its part that which the same guarantee demands.

81.   Whenever in a proceeding of amparo a dismissal shall be ordered or the constitutional protection shall be denied because the complaint has been

interposed without cause, a fine of 200 to 1,000 pesos shall be imposed on the complainant or on his representatives as the case may be, on the attorney or on both.

For the purposes of this article, it shall be understood that a complaint was interposed without cause when, according to the prudent consideration of the official making the judgment, it appears that the amparo proceeding was interposed only for the purpose of delaying or obscuring the execution of the challenged act.

* * *

122. In cases within the jurisdiction of District Judges, suspension of the challenged act shall be declared officially or on the petition of the aggrieved party, in accordance with the respective provisions of this Chapter.

123. Suspension shall proceed officially [without request from the aggrieved party]:

> I. When it is a question of acts which involve danger of deprivation of life, deportation or exile or any of the acts prohibited by Article 22 of the Federal Constitution.
>
> II. When it is a question of some other act, which if it be consummated, will make physically impossible the restitution to the complainant of the enjoyment of the individual guarantee which is claimed.
>
> The suspension to which this article refers shall be declared clearly in the same order in which the Judge admits the complaint, being communicated without delay to the responsible authority for immediate fulfillment, by telegraph, under the terms of the third paragraph of article 23 of this law.

124. Apart from the cases to which the preceding article refers, suspension shall be decreed when the following requisites concur:

> I. That the aggrieved person so requests.
>
> II. That injury to the social interest not follow and provisions for public order not be contravened.
>
> It shall be considered, among other cases, that those damages follow or those violations are realized, when upon the suspension's being conceded, there continues the functioning of centers of vice, or of prostitution, the production of and traffic in enervating drugs; there is permitted the consummation or continuation of crimes or of their effects or the increase of prices of goods of primary necessity or necessary consumers' goods; the execution of means to combat serious epidemics is impeded, as well as measures to combat the danger of invasion of foreign diseases in the nation or the campaign against alcoholism and the sale of substances which poison the individual or degenerate the race.
>
> III. That the damages caused to the aggrieved person by the execution of the act are of difficult reparation.
>
> The District Judge, on granting the suspension, shall take steps to specify the situation in which matters are to remain and shall take pertinent measures to conserve the subject-matter of the amparo until the termination of the proceeding.

* * *

136. If the challenged act affects personal liberty, the effect of the suspension shall be only that the complainant remains at the disposition of the District Judge, only with respect to his personal liberty, remaining at the disposition of the authority which should judge him when the order emanates from criminal proceedings with respect to a stay [continuance] of the same.

When the challenged act consists in the detention of the complainant by administrative authorities or by the Judicial Police, as one responsible for some crime, suspension shall be granted if it may proceed without prejudice to the making of the appropriate deposit [similar to the filing of an injunction bond — Ed.]. If the suspension be granted in cases of orders for arrest, the District Judge shall order such means as he deems necessary to secure the presence of the complainant, so that he may be returned to the responsible authority if the amparo is not granted.

When the challenged act consists in the detention of the complainant by order of administrative authorities, he may be placed on provisional liberty with security measures and for the purposes which the preceding paragraph expresses.

In cases of detention by order of penal judicial authorities, or decree of preventive imprisonment, the complainant may be placed on bail in conformance to the federal or local laws applicable to the case.

Bail can be revoked when there are sufficient grounds to presume that the complainant is attempting to evade justice.

137. When there may be good evidence that the responsible authority is attempting to mock the right of the complainant to liberty, or to hide him by transferring him to another place, the District Judge may require the complainant brought before him in order to enforce said orders.

* * *

192. Whatever jurisprudence the Supreme Court of Justice may establish in its decrees of amparo can only refer to the Constitution and other general laws.

193. Whatever jurisprudence the Supreme Court of Justice functioning in plenary session may establish concerning interpretation of the Constitution and federal laws or treaties entered into with foreign powers, is binding on it and on the Divisions [panels] which compose it, the Circuit Courts [*Tribunales Colegiados de Circuito, Tribunales Unitarios de Circuito*], District Judges, State Courts, Courts of the Federal District and Territories and Boards of Conciliation and Arbitration.

The decrees of the Supreme Court of Justice functioning in plenary session constitute jurisprudence provided that the same decision is found in five decrees not interrupted by others to the contrary, and that they have been approved by at least 14 Justices.

193. Bis. The jurisprudence which the Divisions of the Supreme Court of Justice establish as to interpretation of the Constitution, federal

laws, or treaties made with foreign powers is binding for the same Divisions and for the [lower Courts and Councils listed above].

The decrees of the Divisions of the Supreme Court of Justice constitute jurisprudence, provided that the same decision is found in five decrees uninterrupted by any to the contrary, and that they have been approved by at least four Justices.

194. The jurisprudence established by the Supreme Court of Justice functioning in plenary session and by the Divisions of the same may be interrupted or modified.

In any case, the Justices may explain their reasons for requesting modification of the jurisprudence.

Jurisprudence is interrupted, ceasing to have an obligatory character, whenever a contrary decree is pronounced by 14 Justices if it is a question of matters decided in plenary session, and by 4, if it is in a single Division.

For the modification to affect the jurisprudence, the reasons for varying it must be expressed, and these reasons must relate to those which the Justices had in establishing the jurisprudence which is modified; furthermore, the requisites specified for establishing jurisprudence must be observed.

[Articles 195 and 195 Bis. establish procedures for bringing before the Supreme Court of Justice in plenary session any alleged conflicts in the jurisprudence of the lower courts, or conflicts among the Court's own Divisions. These questions are to be decided in the abstract, and the decision in such a proceeding cannot affect the rights of individual litigants.]

196. Whenever the parties to a proceeding of amparo invoke the jurisprudence of the Supreme Court, they shall do so in writing, expressing the meaning of the jurisprudence and designating precisely the decisions on which it is based.

197. Decisions of amparo and the particular votes of the Justices relating to them shall be published in the *Semanario Judicial de la Federación* [the official reporter for the Supreme Court of Justice], whenever the decisions are necessary to constitute jurisprudence or to contradict it; so also, those which the Court in plenary session or the Divisions may expressly require to be published.

AMPARO AND CASSATION IN MEXICO

Article 14 of the Mexican Constitution of 1857 contained a clause modeled after the "due process" provisions of the Constitution of the United States. In the 1917 constitutional convention, judicial abuses of this clause were criticized, and in its place the following language was adopted for article 14:

"No law shall be given retroactive effect to the detriment of any person whatsoever.

"No person shall be deprived of life, liberty, property, possessions, or rights without a trial by a duly created court in which the essential formalities of procedure are observed and in accordance with laws issued prior to the act.

"In criminal cases no penalty shall be imposed by mere analogy or by a prior evidence. The penalty must be decreed in a law in every respect applicable to the crime in question.

"In civil suits the final judgment shall be according to the letter or the juridical interpretation of the law; in the absence of the latter it shall be based on the general principles of law."

Literally, this language seems to establish a constitutional right to have all judicial decisions made according to law. Taken broadly, the article gives the Supreme Court the power to review state court decisions, whether or not they involve "federal" questions.

That is precisely what the Mexican Supreme Court has done with article 14, beginning long before 1917, and in the face of severe criticism. *E.g.* RABASA, EL ARTICULO 14 (1906). It has made the article into a means for appealing, by way of direct amparo, from the state courts to the national Supreme Court, in any case that the Supreme Court wants to decide. (The form remains that of an original action; in effect, this use of amparo amounts to an appeal.) This process has been called *amparo-casación*, to show its relation to the power of cassation (from the French *casser*, to quash) conferred on the highest reviewing courts in France and some other civilian countries. While the evaluation of facts is left to the state courts, every question of law has become a federal constitutional question.

Is such an interpretation consistent with a genuinely federal judicial system? What purposes may this use of the amparo serve, considering Mexico's political history? Is there a parallel in the English crown's early use of the King's Justice?

The effect of the development of *amparo-casación* in Mexico is much the same as if the United States Supreme Court were to be given jurisdiction as the highest common law court, establishing precedent for all kinds of questions and not simply for federal questions. While such a role is very different from the Supreme Court's present role, it was not unusual for the Court to assume the power to rule as the ultimate common law authority in its early years. *Martin v. Hunter's Lessee*, 1 Wheat. 304 (1816) is a famous example. There are even some who argue that from the beginning "the Supreme Court of the United States was meant to be head of a unified American system of administering justice." 2 CROSSKEY, POLITICS AND THE CONSTITUTION OF THE UNITED STATES 711 (1953). Professor Crosskey's reading of history on this question is part of his general thesis that the Constitution was adopted for the purpose of creating not a federal system but a unified, centralized government. (See Brown and Hart, Book Reviews, 67 HARV. L. REV. 1439, 1456 (1954) for two scathing attacks on Professor Crosskey's selection of supporting data and the conclusions drawn from the data selected.) What would John Marshall have made of a constitutional provision such as Mexico's article 14?

CLAGETT, THE MEXICAN SUIT OF "AMPARO"
33 Geo. L.J.* 418, 427-36 (1945)

A suit of *amparo* may be direct or indirect. The former is that in which the Supreme Court or any one of its four chambers takes original jurisdiction; and such a suit lies only against the final judgments in civil and criminal cases mentioned above, from which no further appeal is available. Such final judgments may include the decisions of the labor Boards of Conciliation and Arbitration. The Supreme Court of the Nation, composed of twenty-one justices, may sit either as a whole in certain cases, or divided into four *salas*, to hear either direct or indirect *amparo* suits. In the fourth *sala*, in which labor cases are heard, the *amparo* appeals come from the decisions of the labor arbitration boards. The indirect *amparo* cases are generally heard by the district courts. Relief is granted in such cases only when there is no other legal remedy which may be used to prevent the injury threatened by the acts or laws. A review of the judgments rendered by the district courts in *amparo* cases can be demanded *sua sponte* by the Supreme Court.
        * * *

Maurice Minchen[42] in a comparative work, devotes an interesting chapter to the comparison of the *amparo* suit with our various legal remedies, particularly with our writs of injunction and *habeas corpus*. Some of the points of similarity and difference between the *amparo* and the injunction to which he calls attention are the following: Our injunction can prohibit the authority who has violated the right in controversy from continuing his act, while the *amparo* merely surrounds the injured party with the protection of the Federal Government against the authority responsible for the invasion. In both countries, however, this public authority is liable to punishment if he should disregard this injunction order. The Mexican Constitution provides that:

> "If after the granting of the *amparo*, the guilty official shall persist in the act or acts against which the petition of *amparo* is filed, or shall seek to render of no effect the judgment of the Federal authority, he shall forthwith be removed from office and turned over for trial to the corresponding District Court."

Other points of difference are that the Anglo-American injunction will issue against a person whether he be a public official or a private individual,

---

42 Minchen, Comparacion General de las Constituciones de Mexico y los Estados Unidos del Norte (1923) 156-174.

while the *amparo* may be petitioned only with regard to violatory acts of public officials. Our courts may enjoin the continuation of a suit or they may order an official to perform a legal or an equitable duty, or desist from performing an act, the order being of a mandatory or prohibitory nature, while the *amparo* applies only to persons who have been injured by a violation of their constitutional rights. The injunction is a protection granted by a judicial power, which, in Anglo-American countries, may be either a federal or a local court; but the *amparo* is only a federal aid, an appeal created by the sovereign power of the Republic, regulated by the legislative power, and administered by the judicial branch. Such is the custom in Roman Law countries, which thus makes their courts administrative rather than independent and sovereign powers.

      * * *

Perhaps the greatest difference between the *amparo* suit and remedies employed in our country lies in the effect of the decisions rendered by the highest tribunals. As has been pointed out previously, in Mexico the relief granted is limited to the person requesting it, and no general statement of the validity or invalidity of the law or act in litigation can be made by the court. In this country, on the other hand, the effect is the outright repeal of the law which has been declared to be unconstitutional by the Supreme Court of the nation. As Ignacio Vallarta, one of the greatest authorities on Mexican constitutional law, has written:

"... the decision which grants the protection of the *amparo* against a law, does not necessarily bring about its immediate repeal by the legislative power, even though the law was not applicable solely to the person protected. This appeal merely nullifies the law in the special case in question, but does not oblige the legislator to revoke it. It is true that he is under a duty to do so when the judicial power by continual judgments has declared the law unconstitutional, because the legislator himself, in the enactment of the laws, is bound to respect the decisions of the supreme interpreter of the Constitution, and he would be rebelling against the Constitution itself if he persisted in promulgating or upholding laws which have been declared to be unconstitutional; but from this point to the one of imposing on the legislator by force the repeal of one of his laws, there is an incommensurable distance."[55]

Mexican authors in the field of constitutional law claim that one of the drawbacks in our system of judicial review is that in making the decision binding on all authorities, even those outside of the judicial field, the judicial power invades the legislative field. They maintain, moreover, that the summary repeal of a law does not always allow sufficient opportunity for that law to prove its good points, if any. They believe that this affects the stability of institutions and the order which is so necessary for peaceful administration. The corresponding drawback in the Mexican suit is that the effect of a favor-

---

[55] VALLARTA, EL JUICIO DE AMPARO V. EL WRIT OF HABEAS CORPUS (1881) 300.

able decision is merely to excuse one individual from compliance with the law, while it obliges other persons to bring analogous suits for similar violations for which the court, in its discretion, may or may not protect them against the law. As a matter of fact, there is nothing to prevent the same person from being injured anew by the same law. Under such circumstances he would have to petition another *amparo* for each injury, so long as the law itself is not repealed by the legislative branch of the government. Vallarta also illustrates this point by explaining that an individual, once given relief through an *amparo* appeal against the payment of a certain tax, will yet be obliged to bring a new suit to become exempt from the next or different payment exacted under the same tax law, while a second person, likewise aggrieved, must also bring a suit in his own name, and may not use as precedent the favorable decision of his predecessor. On the other hand, Vallarta points out also that in the event that an unfavorable decision be rendered in the trial court, the second and subsequent aggrieved persons are not prevented from petitioninig for relief and being successful in spite of the fact that it was refused in the first case.

QUESTIONS ON JUDICIAL PROTECTION OF THE CONSTITUTION IN MEXICO AND THE UNITED STATES

Mrs. Clagett's article contrasts the amparo practice in Mexico with constitutional litigation in the United States in a number of particulars. She notes that the remedy of amparo runs only against official violations of constitutional rights, and that our injunction can run against private persons as well. How much difference remains in *constitutional* cases when the "state action" limitation of the Fourteenth and Fifteenth Amendments is considered? Does the United States Constitution, as interpreted by the courts, contemplate private invasions of constitutional rights? In what particulars? When the amparo is sought against a judge, and the petition is based on a supposed failure to apply the law correctly in a suit between private parties (see Note, Amparo and Cassation in Mexico, p. 627, *supra*), does the amparo not truly run against private individuals? (And compare the *Contreras* case, p. 634, *infra*.)

Another contrast drawn by the article relates to the effect of a decision based on a constitutional determination. Is it true that "In this country . . . the effect is the outright repeal of the law which has been declared to be unconstitutional . . ."? May not a statute, or an administrative regulation, be invalid in one factual context and valid in another? Then are there any differences between Mexican and United States practice as to the effect of a determination of unconstitutionality?

How do you account for the express legislative invitation in the Law of Amparo to judicial lawmaking? Is there something in the nature of constitutional guarantees which makes them more appropriate for expansion and contraction in judicial decisions than the provisions, say, of the Civil Code? Do the provisions on the use of jurisprudence (articles 192-97 of the Law of Amparo) suggest a tentative inclination toward United States practice with respect to the effect of a declaration of unconstitutionality?

See generally GRANT, EL CONTROL JURISDICCIONAL DE LA CONSTITUCIONALIDAD DE LAS LEYES, ch. II (1963), Cabrera and Hedrick, *Notes on Judicial Review in Mexico and the United States,* 5 INTER-AM. L. REV. 253 (1963).

CORRAL
Supreme Court of Mexico
6 S.J.F.* 274 (1920)

[The complainant's land was attached by one Avila Godina in a private action against a third person. The complainant prosecutes this amparo proceeding, complaining of the illegality of the attachment. The defendants in the amparo proceeding are the judges of first instance who ordered and executed the attachment, and Sr. Avila Godina. The District Judge of the State of Durango has rejected the complaint.]

Considering: The illegality of the appealed decision is notorious, insofar as it concerns the amparo requested against acts of the Judges of First Instance of Canatlán and the Municipality of Tapahuanes, because the Constitution, in the ninth paragraph of article 107, expressly admits the allowability of the amparo with respect to acts of the judicial authority, affecting persons outside the lawsuit, acts such as those of which the complainant complains in the present case. But the same cannot be said respecting the amparo which, in the same complaint, is petitioned against acts of don Juan Avila Godina, because the amparo is allowable only against acts of the authorities, in accordance with article 103 of the Constitution, and the said Sr. Avila Godina does not have the status of an authority. Therefore, it is proper to modify the decision, affirming it insofar as it refers to the individual and reversing it insofar as it touches the authorities, so that the complaint may be processed in accordance with the law.

For the foregoing reasons, and based in addition on articles 68 and 92 of the Law of Amparo, modifying the appealed decision, it is resolved:

First.—[The decision was affirmed as to the private individual, and was reversed as to the defendant judge.]

---

* S.J.F. stands for Semanario Judicial de la Federación, the official reporter for the Supreme Court. All citations are to the Fifth Epoch (*Quinta Epoca*) unless noted otherwise. The Semanario is now in its Sixth Epoch, which began in 1957. — Ed.

Second.—Let the decision be made public; let the necessary fees be collected, and with the testimony of this decision, let the proceedings be remanded to the proper Judge, ...

Thus, by unanimity of eleven votes, the Supreme Court of Justice of the Nation, decided. The citizen President and Magistrates signed, with the Secretary as witness.—*E. Garza Pérez.*—*Antonio Alcocer.*—*Agtn. Urdapilleta.*—*José M. Mena.*—*Albo. M. González.*—*Patricio Sabido.*—*Adolfo Arias.*—*Ignacio Noris.*—*Benito Flores.*—*Gustavo A. Vicencio.*—*Enrique Moreno.*—*J.J. Orozco,* Secretary.

MEDRANO
Supreme Court of Mexico
9 S.J.F. 407 (1921)

Mexico, D.F. Full Accord of August 25, 1921.

The action of amparo of Isaac Medrano before the District Judge of Durango against acts of the Warden of "El Salto" [a prison, literally, "the jump"] having been examined on appeal — acts consisting of the Warden's having established a sawmill on lands owned by the complainant, violating the guarantees established in article 16 of the Constitution; the statement of the Public Minister before this Court, asking the dismissal of the action as unallowable, having been considered; and,

Considering: That from the record it appears that the person designated as the responsible authority is acting as a private individual, in the exercise of a right he believes legitimate, the amparo complaint to which this matter refers is not allowable, and, based on paragraph III of article 44 of the Regulatory Law of articles 103 and 104 of the Constitution, the action must be rejected and dismissed.

For the foregoing reasons, it is resolved:

First.—The decision of April 2 of this year, pronounced by the District Judge of Durango, is affirmed, dismissing the present action by reason of non-allowability.

* * *

[Eight judges voted in favor of this decision; the other three did not participate.]

In the case of *Cía. de Luz y Fuerza de Pachuca, S.A.,* 15 S.J.F. 192 (1924), the complaining electric company had cut off the electricity to some government buildings in the state of Hidalgo, and had commenced a proceeding in amparo against various state officials. While the company was successful in the lower courts in this action, the District Judge nevertheless ordered the company to reconnect the electricity pending a final decision. The company sought a direct amparo in the Supreme Court, and was successful, the Supreme Court pointing out that the action of amparo could not be prosecuted against the acts of private individuals, such as the electric company in this case.

CONTRERAS
Supreme Court of Mexico
15 S.J.F. 800 (1924)

Mexico, D.F. Full Accord of September 27, 1924.

[The complainant brought an action in amparo against the General Manager and the Board of Directors of the Mexican National Railways, complaining that they had abrogated a contract with the complainant granting him a concession to sell goods on board trains. The District Judge granted the amparo, including an order of *suspensión* (relief in the nature of an injunction).]

Considering: Since the persons designated by the complainant as responsible authorities are not carrying on public functions, but only acting as contracting parties in the agreement which was declared to be ineffective, it is not proper to grant the petitioned *suspensión*, since the action of amparo, according to the first paragraph of the first article of the Regulatory Law of articles 103 and 104 of the Constitution, has for its object the resolution of every controversy raised by laws or acts which violate individual guarantees; and the persons here designated as responsible for the acts said to violate individual guarantees not having the status of authorities, as is expressed above, it is evident that when the necessary elements do not concur there can exist no occasion for processing the action of constitutional guarantees.

[The decision of the District Judge was unanimously reversed.]

The *Contreras* case was the fifth decision of the Supreme Court to rely on the doctrine that the amparo was not allowable against the acts of private individuals. Therefore, under the terms of the Law of Amparo, this decision established "jurisprudence." It will be noted that the short opinion makes no reference to this fact. However, in the index to Volume 15 of the S.J.F., there is a section which indexes the various points of law on which jurisprudence has been established. At page 1627, the following entry appears:

"*Acts of individuals.*—They cannot be the object of an action of constitutional guarantees, which has been established in order to combat acts of the authorities that may be considered to violate the Constitution.

GUZMAN TERAN and MATUS
Supreme Court of Mexico
6 S.J.F. 377 (1920)

Mexico, D.F., February 24, 1920. Full Accord.

[The two complainants have been prosecuted in a military court for criminal battery. They complained against the judge of the military court, stating that he had refused to return the case to the chief of the garrison so that the latter, in view of the passage of the one year within which the offense must be tried (under article 20, par. VIII of the Constitution), might make the record available to the parties defendant; they also complained that the judge ordered the continuation of the proceedings against them. The District Judge denied the amparo.]

Considering: *Suspensión* of the act complained of would cause a prejudice to society and to the complainants themselves, for both the former and the latter are interested in having the said proceedings resolved in the shortest possible time, which could not be done if the requested acts were permitted to slow the proceedings. In addition, with respect to the refusal of the responsible authority to return the action to the chief of the garrison, the *suspensión* is not allowable, because, since the act is negative, its effect would be to leave things in the same state, which is contrary to the claim of the complainants themselves. Consequently, it is proper to affirm the decision on appeal, in conformance with article 55 of the Law of Amparo.

[The decision was unanimously affirmed by all eight ministers voting.]

[On April 6 and 10 of the same year, the Supreme Court decided three more cases, all of them announcing the same doctrine that the amparo is not allowable against "negative acts," that is, refusals on the part of the responsible authority to act. See 6 S.J.F. 959. These cases, along with others decided previously, established the jurisprudence of the court on this subject. See 6 *id.* 1105. — Ed.]

In the case of Valenzuela, 32 S.J.F. 1179 (1931), the complainant filed an action of amparo against the President of the Republic and the Secretary of Industry, Commerce and Labor, based on their refusal to confirm the concession of certain petroleum rights which he alleged had been granted to him. The responsible authorities raised the argument that the acts complained of were "negative acts," against which the amparo could not be granted. The court rejected that argument and granted the amparo saying: ". . . Although it is true that [the orders referred to] are negative in character, apparently, they are in their true nature positive or, at least, produce positive effects, and are not future or uncertain, as the lower court considered them in the decision on appeal, but present," and therefore the amparo was allowable.

Do not all "negative acts" always "produce positive effects"?

KERN MEX OIL FIELDS, S.A.
Supreme Court of Mexico
49 S.J.F. 238 (1936)

Considering: At pages 6-13, inclusive, of the *Diario Oficial* of May 30, 1930, appears declaration no. 88, and from its text it is seen that the stream called *Sanja Vieja* or *Arroyo Viejo* flows indirectly to the Pánuco River, therefore being included in article 10, par. VII of chapter 1 of the Law of Nationally Owned Waters presently in force, for which reason the President of the United States of Mexico declared that the waters of said stream are owned by the nation, along with its river banks, flood plains, banks and federal zones, in accordance with the provisions of article 2, chapter I of said Law. As is seen, the declaration complained of affects exclusively the ownership of the streams, lakes etc., included in its terms, since it refers to their waters, beds and banks. From the terms in which the complaint is conceived and the documents exhibited as proof, it is established that the complaining Company neither is the owner nor has it ever been, by virtue of the titles or contracts executed by it. It has only the right of exploration and exploitation; that right is confirmed, insofar as it touches the materials of the subsoil, which was made the property of the nation by article 27 of the Federal Constitution. As is seen, the exploitation and exploration of the subsoil are not affected by the declaration complained of, which neither says nor determines anything respecting petroleum or its derivative products. The declaration refers to ownership, and if as a consequence of that declaration there should be an act or agreement which might affect the rights of the complainant, it would then need to exercise its actions to complain of prejudice to them; but insofar as only the interests of the owner are affected, only he can complain for amparo in the terms of article 3 of the Law of Amparo. The prejudice [required by the Law] is not the indirect prejudice which arises from juridical relations of whatever kind, created between owner and tenant or beneficiary. In the action for constitutional guarantees, the word "prejudice" should not be taken in the terms of the civil law, as the deprivation of any lawful gain that might be obtained, but rather as a synonym for an offense to the rights or interests of a person, and it is surely in this sense that the word is taken in article 3 of the Law of Amparo.

Considering the foregoing, this action is not allowable and therefore should be dismissed under the terms of articles 43, par. VIII, and 44, par. II of the Law of Amparo.

[The decision of the lower court, rejecting the amparo, was unanimously affirmed.]

RIONDA
Supreme Court of Mexico
3 S.J.F. 778 (1918)

Mexico, D.F. Full Accord of September 12, 1918.

The Court having considered on appeal the decision of last July 24, by which the District Judge of Veracruz rejected the complaint in amparo filed by Gaspar Rionda against acts of the Inspector of Cattle of Córdoba; and

Resulting: In the complaint for amparo, the complainant says: that he bought in Veracruz 60 head of cattle to bring to this capital, and after the respective documents were obtained, the cattle embarked; but, on passing through Córdoba, they were detained by the Inspector of Cattle under the pretext that the documents were not in order, in his judgment; that since the cattle began to die, and the complainant had to rent a pasture and all this caused him damage, he took steps to secure the return of his goods and for that purpose gave a guarantee; but since the cited authority demands such a guarantee for the payment for only eleven head, the propriety of which demand is not well established, in his understanding, the complainant asks amparo and *suspensión* of the act, before the District Judge of Veracruz.

Resulting: That, the complaint filed, the District Judge of Veracruz rejected it wholly, saying that the act complained of relates to the guarantor, because it is the latter of whom the payment for the cattle is demanded by the responsible authority, and that, according to article 663 of the Federal Code of Civil Procedure, the amparo can be carried on and prosecuted only by the party who is prejudiced by the act, and in the conception of the Judge, the act complained of does not prejudice the complainant.

Considering: Although it is true that, according to article 663 of the Federal Code of Civil Procedure, the action of amparo can only be prosecuted and carried on by the party prejudiced by the act complained of, as in the present case, supposing that the guarantor corporation should be obliged to pay on behalf of the complainant, the latter would have to repay the guarantor what it had paid, since the money would have been paid on his account. It is evident that the one directly prejudiced is the complainant, and therefore, the amparo should be processed and carried on by virtue of his petition, in conformance with the cited provision. [The court unanimously voted to reverse the appealed decision.]

FRANCO EGARTE
Supreme Court of Mexico
3 S.J.F. 799 (1918)

Mexico, September 13, 1918. Full Accord.

The Court having considered, on appeal, the action of amparo which Lic. Carlos F. Uribe prosecuted on behalf of Pedro Franco Egarte on November 16, 1917, before the Second Supernumerary District Judge of the Federal District, against acts of the Third Judge (Civil) of this Capital, which he considers to violate article 16 of the Constitution, to the prejudice of his client:

Resulting: First: [Franco Egarte had given two notes to one Cano Ruiz on April 30, 1916. On December 14 of the same year, the government issued a decree establishing a general moratorium on debts. (It was debatable whether the two notes, which did not expressly promise payment in metallic money, were covered by the moratorium.) The following year, Cano Ruiz began an action against Franco Egarte, seeking to attach certain property of the defendant. Franco Egarte then commenced this action of amparo against the action of the civil judge in carrying forward the attachment proceeding, claiming a violation of the 1916 decree and of article 16 of the Constitution. The District Judge granted the amparo, and this appeal is taken by Cano Ruiz, the prejudiced third party who is permitted to appeal by the Law of Amparo.]

Considering: The complainant brings the present amparo against the decision of the Third Judge (Civil), who refused to suspend the preparatory proceedings in a commercial action of attachment, which proceedings consisted in the recognition of the signatures that support the documents on which the action of attachment is based, and the complainant considers that that decision will cause him prejudice, in case the complaint for attachment should be accepted and an attachment against him ordered. As is seen, the concrete act, performed by the Judge who is designated as the responsible authority, is entirely in accordance with law, since the proceedings preparatory to an action cannot constitute the exercise of an action in attachment for the collection of money, suspended by the law which established a moratorium on payments, to which the complainant refers and the prejudice that the latter maintains may be caused to him does not exist, since the mere apprehension which may be caused to him does not constitute the subject matter for the granting of the requested amparo, for which reason the appealed decision must be reversed and the federal protection invoked must be denied.

[All nine ministers present were in accord.]

GONZALEZ MATAMOROS
Supreme Court of Mexico
26 S.J.F. 1928 (1929)

[August 6, 1929.]

Considering: First: Fundamentally, the complainant in his amparo complaint states that the responsible authority is attempting to expropriate and demolish part of his urban real property at 606 Avenida Chapultepec, at the corner of Calle del 13 de Septiembre, of this Capital. Although the responsible authority in its justifying report denies the fact, alleging that it is not attempting to expropriate or demolish the said property and that, in case that it should come to consider expropriation necessary it would fulfill all the legal formalities, there is no doubt that the complainant, with the evidence presented at the hearing before the lower court, has demonstrated the existence of the act which he complains of in this action of constitutional guarantees. In effect, the notice directed to the complainant, in which it is expressed that its purpose is to discuss a matter related to the expropriation of the said property (probably indemnification, but what it is is not stated) already indicates the purpose of carrying the expropriation into effect. It cannot be admitted that the authority, in decrease of its respectability, should have attempted by means of the notice to bother the complainant without any object; besides, in the notice itself it is stated that it is to discuss a matter related to the expropriation of his property, which by itself admits the purpose of carrying expropriation into effect. But if there could be any doubt whatever concerning this, the letter directed to the citizen Treasurer General of the municipality in which it is expressly stated the amount which Srs. Fausto and Gutiérrez would pay for the extension of Calle de Agustín Melgar [a street] amounting to 12,670 pesos by way of deposit, to indemnify the complainant "for the demolition of part of his construction in the land which would be expropriated from him for the said purpose," constitutes proof that, effectively, it was a question of expropriating and demolishing the property of the complainant. Thus the fact that such action still may not have occurred cannot ground a dismissal, since, in any case, in the present amparo we are concerned with acts which are future but certain — not only because, considering the content of the quoted words of the responsible authority, it is taken as a fact that the expropriation will be made, but also because the acts themselves demonstrated by the two stated proofs, already constitute the beginning of execution of the acts complained of in this action of constitutional guarantees. Although future acts do not motivate the granting of amparo, according to a constant and reiterated jurisprudence of this Supreme Court, that jurisprudence refers to future and uncertain acts and not to acts which, as in this case, although they have not been executed, have the certainty that they will be executed, as the previously executed acts demonstrate. Consequently, for the purposes of the present amparo, the acts complained of should be considered to be certain.

Second: [The court found a violation of articles 16 and 27 of the Constitution, since the expropriation was not being made by a competent authority, and the expropriation had not been ordered on the basis of a determination and declaration of public utility. The decision of the court of 1st Instance, denying amparo, was unanimously reversed.]

GARCIA ALVAREZ
Supreme Court of Mexico
112 S.J.F. 586 (1952)

* * *

Considering: Sole paragraph.—The argument of the appellant authority [the President of the Republic, the Secretary of the Interior, the Chief of the Department of the Federal District, and the chiefs of certain offices of the District] is unfounded. Actually, in conformance with the jurisprudence laid down by the Supreme Court respecting the matter in question, "although the acts of expedition, promulgation, authentication and publication of a law are carried on in such form that they can no longer be made ineffective as a consequence of a decision of amparo (which by express constitutional provision shall be limited to protect individuals in the special case affected by the complaint, without there being any general declaration respecting the law or act which motivates it), it should nevertheless be kept in mind that the said acts are soon put into effect as law and the law in turn is applied to concrete cases, such as those complained of in the present action of amparo. And since those results of the law are imputable not only to the authorities who apply it but also to those from whom the law itself emanates or who have participated in the acts necessary to put it into effect, such results are susceptible of reparation in every concrete case. The unconstitutionality of the law can be complained of for this reason, not only against the Legislature which enacted it but also against the Executive which promulgated it and ordered it published, and against the Secretary of State who authenticated the promulgating accord and carried out the publication. Consequently, under the circumstances there is no application of the ground of non-allowability established by article 73, par. IX of the Law of Amparo." The foregoing is established in (among others) the decisions pronounced in the actions of amparo on appeal numbers 6991-50, brought by Raúl Moreno Hernández; 2479-51, brought by Diego

Alonso Hinojosa; 9043-50, brought also by the latter; and 2728-51, brought by Guadalupe Cuevas Vda. de García Salcho. Since the argument which the appellant authority has made is insufficient, the decision on appeal should consequently be affirmed.

For the foregoing reason, it is decided:

First.—The appealed decision is affirmed.

Second.—The Justice of the Union protects José García Alvarez from the acts which he complains of against the President of the Republic, Secretary of the Interior, Chief of the Department of the Federal District, and Chiefs of the Office of Licenses, Inspection of Regulations, and Censor of Infractions, subsidiaries of the Department of the Federal District, consisting in the enactment, promulgation, publication and authentication of the Regulation of the Bread Industry for the Federal District by the first three officers named and its application by the others, with respect to their delay in announcing the denial of a license to the complainant, and, therefore, in the possible closure of his bread distributorship, located in house no. 7 on Calle Soto in this city.

Third.—[The decision was unanimous, signed by all four judges of the second division of the Supreme Court.]

The doctrine of mootness, established in paragraphs IX and XVI of article 73 of the Law of Amparo, has its typical application in a case such as Segura, 19 S.J.F. (6a Epoca) 18 (1959). In that case the complainant was complaining in a direct amparo against the judge who had sentenced him to prison for a criminal offense. The amparo action originated in the First Division of the Supreme Court of Mexico, which dismissed the action on the ground that the complaining accused had already served his sentence.

HEREDIA
Supreme Court of Mexico
4 S.J.F. 862 (1919)

Mexico, D.F., Full Accord of April 17, 1919.

* * *

Resulting: First: The complainant, for himself and as representative of the political club "Melchor Ocampo," requested amparo and *suspensión* before the District Judge of Michoacán, against the decree of last December 23, given by the City Council of Maravatío, in which the council declared reelected as Alderman and Secretary of the said municipal corporation, José L. Mandujano, despite the fact that the State Constitution prohibits the re-election of members of the city council, and he considers that said act is contrary to the provisions of articles 8, 14 and 35, par. 5, of the Federal Constitution.

Second: The District Judge, considering that the prerogatives of a citizen, among which is that of being chosen to serve in popularly elected offices, are different from the natural rights of man, whose violation is the only one which may be the subject matter of the action of constitutional guarantees, rejected the complaint as not allowable, on January 2 of the current year.

Third: The complainant appealed against the decision, ...

Considering: That as the District Judge maintains, in the appealed decision the political rights which the complainant says have been violated do not give rise to the action of constitutional guarantees, in conformity with the first paragraph of article 103 and in the first rule of article 107 of the Constitution; and since, on the other hand, the infraction of articles 8 and 14, allegedly committed by the responsible authority, cannot be considered to have been violated in prejudice of the complainant Marcelino Heredia, the latter lacks the capacity to bring this action of amparo, considering the provisions of the first paragraph of the cited article 107 of the Constitution; and therefore, the decision of non-allowability, given by the lower court, must be affirmed, ...

[By unanimous vote of all eleven ministers, the decision dismissing the complaint was affirmed.]

ARAGON
Supreme Court of Mexico
14 S.J.F. 1109 (1924)

Mexico, D.F., Full Accord of March 28, 1924.
* * *

The Court has seen, on appeal, the decision dated last February 6, given by the District Judge in the State of Sinaloa which rejects as nonallowable the complaint in amparo formulated by Srs. Raymundo Aragón and Alfredo Campaña against acts of the State Congress of Sinaloa, consisting in the refusal to recognize their status as acting substitute Aldermen of the Municipality of Cosalá. . . .

Considering: The complainants refer in their complaint to the fact that the City Council of Cosalá, basing its action on article 26 of the Municipal Organic Law of the locality, called them to act in their capacity as substitutes in place of the regular alderman, . . . who had retired, and that, having taken the oath, they had taken office; that the legislature of the State of Sinaloa, notwithstanding the foregoing, refused to recognize said complainants as substitute aldermen, ordering that two other persons be named in their place. The complainants considered that the legislature's act violated the guarantees granted by article 14 of the Constitution, and they asked the assistance and protection of the Federal Judiciary. We consider that, in this case, the act is one which can be classified as a violation of individual political guarantees, signifying for the complainants the deprivation of their remuneration to which they have a right, and of the exercise of the office to which they were legally elected. It is proper, therefore, to consider such acts as included in the first paragraph of article 103 of the Federal Constitution, and to reverse the appealed decision, so that the complaint should be processed in the correct manner, and the proper decision rendered.

[The foregoing decision was joined by seven out of ten judges voting. The dissenters filed no opinion.]

PINEDA
Supreme Court of Mexico
63 S.J.F. 299 (1940)

Mexico, D.F., January 13, 1940.
* * *

Considering: The District Judge, in decreeing the appealed dismissal, considers that the complainant has not exhausted the administrative remedies to which the current Federal Fiscal Code refers in its article 160, paragraph V. This article provides that the Divisions of the Fiscal Tribunal shall hear actions initiated against the administrative proceeding of execution [for unpaid taxes or penalties] by persons who, having been affected by it, assert that they are entitled to attached goods, or that they are creditors preferred over the Treasury, ... The Judge also considers that since the complainant in the first case is able to resort to the said Tribunal in defense of his rights, (there existing consequently the ground for non-allowability to which paragraph XV of article 73 of the Law of Amparo refers), a dismissal of the action is required, in accordance with the provisions of paragraph III of article 74 of the the Law of Amparo which is invoked. The complainant alleges that in accordance with the thesis sustained by this High Tribunal in cases analogous to the present one, a person in his position has been able to resort to amparo, without having to exhaust previously the ordinary appeal referred to in the decision of the lower court. In reality the appellant is correct, having demonstrated . . . that he is a person outside the appealed administrative proceeding, ... And the tax officials admit that since they could not find the violator, Sr. Andrés González, they ordered the coercive power exercised against the complainant, in his status as owner of the building in which was located the bar where the infraction committed by González himself took place; all of which means that as a third person outside the cited administrative proceeding, the appellant had the right to resort to the action of constitutional guarantees.

The interpretation which this Second Chamber has given in that respect to Article 107 of the General Constitution of the Republic refers to those cases in which the laws expressly establish ordinary appeals or means of redress, which constitute the procedure to redress grievances considered to have been committed, those laws being at the reach of the affected party, since in such a case one should not resort to the action of amparo until after exhausting the defense established by ordinary laws. But it is not correct to accept these principles when the one who requests the amparo is a third person who does not have at his disposition those means or appeals. . . .

[The division unanimously voted to lift the attachment on the complainant's building. The court seemed inclined to establish some jurisprudence on this subject in a hurry. Within two months after the foregoing decision, the court had decided four other cases, on the same basis as that stated in this opinion. Thus the jurisprudence was established by March 13, 1940. See 63 S.J.F. 4742.]

R U I Z
Supreme Court of Mexico
48 S.J.F. 2956 (1936)

* * *

Considering: From the terms of the statement on appeal, it is inferred that there need be examined in this decision only the ground of non-allowability invoked by the appellants [the municipal president and the city council of the town of Tlalixcoyán, in the state of Veracruz], and which is said to consist in the fact that the complainant, before resorting to the action of constitutional guarantees, should have made use of the remedy established in article 12 of Law no. 208 of the State of Veracruz, which serves as the basis for the forced tenancy which is the subject matter of this action. The only argument described in the statement on appeal is thus groundless, since on numerous occasions this Division has established that there is no obligation to exhaust ordinary remedies established in the law [authorizing] the act, when the unconstitutionality of that law is asserted, since it would be contrary to the principles of law for the complainants to resort to that statute, insofar as it benefits them, and attack it insofar as it causes them some prejudice. And since in the case in question the complainant impugned as unconstitutional the cited Law 208 of the State of Veracruz, under which certain lands that he possessed were given in forced tenancy [to a group of petitioners], it is unquestionable that he was empowered to resort directly to the action of constitutional guarantees, without having to make use of the ordinary means of defense established in the same law. Therefore, as there is no question about the motives for which the amparo is granted, the appealed decision must be officially affirmed.

For the foregoing reasons and based on articles 103, par. I, and 107, par. IX, of the General Constitution of the Republic, it is decided [to affirm the decision of the District Judge granting the amparo and returning the land to the owner].

Although it may not be necessary to exhaust one's administrative remedy before resorting to an action of amparo that attacks the constitutionality of legislation, if the complainant does choose to pursue his administrative remedy, he runs the risk of later discovering he has consented to the application of the law through his very resort to the remedy provided. Such a case was Palomeque de Hermida, 5 S.J.F. (6a Epoca) 66 (1957), in which the Second Division of the Supreme Court of Mexico held that a landowner could not attack the constitutionality of the expropriation law of the State of Campeche in an action of amparo, since he had (unsuccessfully) pursued his administrative remedy established by that law. Cabrera and Hedrick, p. 632 *supra*, at 260, state that the Mexican Supreme Court "is presently reconsidering this doctrine." Until the doctrine changes, it might appear that the complainant must choose between attacking the constitutionality of a law which is applied to him and attacking its applicability, apart from constitutional considerations. In practice, that is not the result. The complainant attacks the constitutionality of the law (without exhausting the administrative remedies provided by the law) in a lower federal court. On appeal, the question of the law's validity is decided by the Supreme Court in Plenary Session. If the law is upheld, the case is then transferred to the appropriate intermediate appellate court or to the Supreme Court's Administrative Division (Chamber) for determination of the law's applicability. A more serious defect of this procedure is its inhibiting effect on the Court's ability to interpret laws to avoid constitutional difficulties. See Cabrera and Hedrick, *supra*, at 260-63.

BUSEY, LATIN AMERICA: POLITICAL INSTITUTIONS AND PROCESSES 39 (1964)

Mexican courts do not render judgments against the policies of the all pervasive PRI [the Partido Revolucionario Institucional, the government party]. Though gross examples of judicial subservence to PRI policy are not so evident today as they were at an earlier time (during 1934-1940, for example, when judicial terms were for six years and identical with that of the President and the Senate), it is clear that the courts never take a position contrary to that of executive policy. No writs of *amparo* issue against actions by the President, by members of his official family, by leading members of the PRI; or against federal legislation which has been passed by the Congress.

[It should be noted that the President is frequently made a party to an amparo proceeding, but only in a formal way; in such cases, the amparo may be granted, but it is clear that the judicial order runs only against lower officials. Does the failure of the judiciary to make a frontal attack on the chief executive signify the ineffectiveness of judicial review? — Ed.]

C. The Brazilian Writ of Security

EDER, HABEAS CORPUS DISEMBODIED:
THE LATIN AMERICAN EXPERIENCE
in XXth Century Comparative and Conflicts Law*
at 463, 465-69 (Nadelmann, von Mehren and Hazard ed. 1961)

Brazil was the first of the southern countries in our hemisphere to adopt habeas corpus. The lawyers who framed the Imperial Constitution of 1824 and the early legislation of the country, after independence from Portugal, were well versed in the law of England. That constitution, establishing a limited monarchy, followed the British pattern. The Penal Code of 1830, a progressive code for its day, made it a criminal offence for judges to refuse to issue or to delay a writ of habeas corpus, duly petitioned, or *ex officio* in a proper case (art. 183); for officers of justice to refuse or delay service of the writ; for the person to whom the writ was directed to refuse or delay presenting the prisoner at the time and place specified in the writ; to change the place of confinement or to hide the prisoner with intent to evade a writ of which the officer had notice, before service; to rearrest a person discharged under a writ for the same cause . . . .

These provisions were anticipatory of the provisions in the law of habeas corpus embodied in the Code of Criminal Procedure of 1832 (arts. 340-55). Every citizen who believes that he or another is suffering illegal imprisonment or restraint of his liberty is entitled to ask for an order of — Habeas Corpus — in his favor (art. 340). The petition should contain the name of the person under restraint and of the person causing it; the contents of the order of arrest or an explicit declaration that a copy was denied; the illegality claimed and signature and oath as to the truth of the allegations (art. 341). The writ contains an order to the detainer or gaoler to present the person before the judge or court at a stated time and place and to furnish a report as to the cause for

---

detention (art. 343). A judge reliably informed of an illegal detention is under a duty to issue the writ *ex officio* without a petition (art. 344). If the judge finds that the prisoner is illegally detained, he shall release him; or, if the offence be bailable, shall admit him to bail (art. 352). Imprisonment is deemed illegal when there is no just cause therefor; for failure to be brought to trial within the time required by law; when the process is manifestly void; for lack of jurisdiction of the authority that ordered the arrest or when the grounds justifying imprisonment have terminated (art. 353).

The provisions of these two codes, it will readily be noted, were adopted from the Habeas Corpus Acts of 1640, 1689, and 1816 and the British practice as expounded by Blackstone or other authorities.

The Brazilian legislation was a logical corollary of a provision in the Imperial Constitution declaring the inviolability of the civil and political rights of Brazilian citizens based on liberty, individual security and property (art. 179 (8)). The Brazilian writers state that habeas corpus was congenial to Portuguese law which had something similar in the *cartas de seguro.*

In Brazil, the writ was amplified by Law 2073 of 1871, extending the privilege to aliens, and, more important, including in its coverage *threats* to personal liberty, even where the petitioner had not yet suffered corporal constraint. This had already been established in practice by decisions of the courts. This was the first innovation. Under our law (except in cases of custody of children) actual imprisonment or restraint of freedom of movement is a necessary prerequisite to the writ. Other extensions of the scope of the writ were soon to follow. Continued in Decree 848 of October 1890 of the Provisional Government after the overthrow of the monarchy, the writ was incorporated as a constitutional guarantee in the first Republican Constitution (1891). Article 72 (22) provided:

> Habeas Corpus is given whenever an individual suffers or is in imminent danger of suffering violence or coercion by reason of illegality or abuse of power.

Illegality includes unconstitutionality and the writ was frequently used, and still is, for judicial review of the constitutionality of statutes and executive acts. The language of the article, under the arguments of ingenious judges and lawyers, notably Rui Barbosa, gave rise to a remarkable extension of the writ to cover deprivation, actual or threatened, of any of the constitutional liberties. The "Brazilian" doctrine of habeas corpus evolved to an extent where the English father would have difficulty in recognizing his transatlantic offspring. The nomenclature was maintained, but the institution was adapted to meet new social or political needs. It supplied the need, in the absence of other remedies in the procedural codes, for effective rapid measures to cope with abuse of the public power. By 1893, the competence of the judiciary to examine, by habeas corpus, the legality of the acts of the executive was established. In 1898, the Supreme Court asserted its right to examine the constitutionality of political acts. A period of conflicting decisions as to the scope of the remedy ensued. Habeas corpus was granted against invasion of the home by sanitary inspectors; it was denied to protect the freedom of movement of streetwalkers; it was granted to prevent examination of commercial books of account, to guarantee professional liberty, the exercise of elective officers, the practice of spiritualism, freedom of assembly. It was applied in civil family controversies to permit a wife to join her husband against the opposition of her parents. In 1909, in a leading case, the Supreme Court extended the writ to permit aldermen (*intendentes municipaes*) to attend meetings of the Municipal Council to which they had been elected. The opinion by Pedro Lessa, reinforced by his book, a classic of constitutional law, pointed out that the Brazilian habeas corpus bore only a slight resemblance to its English progenitor. It is a procedural remedy to guarantee every certain and incontestable right which is directly or indirectly connected with freedom of movement. By being barred by the executive authorities from access to the municipal council, the aldermen's freedom of locomotion was being interfered with.

Since almost every right can be indirectly connected with freedom of movement, it was a short step to a further extension of the scope of the writ. The Supreme Court in a decision of April 5, 1919, said:

> In effect, for the majority of the court, it is an accepted principle that habeas corpus is competent to protect the exercise of any right which is certain, liquid and incontestable.

Lessa maintained that freedom of locomotion being but a means to achieve an end, habeas corpus should be granted whenever the *end*, if lawful, presupposes freedom of locomotion and there is no reasonable doubt as to the petitioner's right to the action in question. Consequently habeas corpus became embodied in the law as a means to protect all political and electoral rights. It was used to reinstate the governor of a State who had been forced by federal troops to withdraw from the State House. The principle was frequently reiterated by the Supreme Court that habeas corpus was the proper remedy to enable duly elected deputies to assemble and exercise their functions. "Although a political question is involved, the Judicial Power cannot elude the duty to take cognizance of the justiciable question that is presented to it." This goes much further than our own Supreme Court has been willing to go.

Barbosa's theory went further; habeas corpus lies, irrespective of any question of locomotion, direct or indirect, in order to protect every certain and incontestable constitutional right. This became the view of the Court as we have noted from the above quotation. It was used not only to insure the right of elected officials to their office but also to protect the rights of peaceable assembly and freedom of speech, the right of Congressmen to publish their speeches, as well as to prevent the removal of a state judge in violation of the provision for tenure during good behaviour, and to prevent peonage. A lower court even granted the writ to allow minors, under parental power, to take part in Carnival festivities.

Lessa maintained, in contrast to Barbosa and the latter decisions of the courts, that habeas corpus was applicable only when freedom of movement was directly or indirectly but necessarily involved. There is no doubt that, as in the United States, the writ was abused. The courts were overwhelmed with habeas corpus proceedings. The President of the Republic urged reform. Lessa's theory was incorporated in the 1926 ammendment to the Constitution which provided that habeas corpus was applicable only where one suffers or is in imminent danger of suffering violence by imprisonment or illegal constraint in his freedom of locomotion. The gap thus created in the law for the protection of other constitutional rights was filled by the 1934 constitution in creating the writ of security (*mandado de seguranza*).

BRAZIL, CONSTITUTION OF 1946
(Pan American Union translation)

* * *

Art. 141.   The Constitution ensures to Brazilians and foreigners residing in the country the inviolability of rights concerning life, liberty, individual security, and property, in the following terms:

> § 23.   *Habeas corpus* shall be granted whenever anyone shall suffer, or shall be threatened with suffering, violence or restraint in his freedom of movement, by illegality or abuse of power. In disciplinary offenses, *habeas corpus* shall not apply.
> § 24.   To protect clear and certain rights not protected by *habeas corpus*, a writ of security shall be granted, regardless of what authority may be responsible for the illegality or abuse of power.

EDER, JUDICIAL REVIEW IN LATIN AMERICA
21 OHIO ST. L.J.* 570, 582-84 (1960)

The writ of security is a new institution in jurisprudence, typically and natively Brazilian, without a parallel elsewhere in the world. The principles of our writs of mandamus, prohibition, quo warranto and injunction are all embraced in the single Brazilian writ of security.

---

* Copyright ©, Ohio State Law Journal, reprinted by permission.

It is available for the protection of any certain and incontestable right or illegal. It does not lie for acts where an administrative appeal may be used which has the effect of a temporary stay, nor against judicial orders or decisions where an appeal or other procedural remedy is available, nor against disciplinary acts unless exercised by an incompetent authority or without due process.

The term "any authority" in the constitution was broadly interpreted both by the courts and by the implementing laws. Under the dictatorial constitution of 1937,* the writ did not lie against the President of the Republic or against members of the Cabinet. During the Vargas dictatorship, the use of the writ died out, to be revived without restrictions under the 1946 constitution. It lies against administrative and executive authorities of all ranks, high or low, and against legislative authorities. The writ (as in the case of the Mexican *amparo*) never lies against private individuals unless they are exercising public functions by delegation from the public power, *e.g.* public utility companies and trade unions which are deemed to be juristic persons of public, not private, law.

The writ must be asked within a term of 120 days; the defendant must present a report and defence within 5 days; the Attorney General's office is given 5 days within which to state its case and the judge must give judgment within 5 days thereafter. Theoretically the whole procedure takes only 15 days, but so great is the pressure on the courts this rarely happens.

A stay, suspension or interlocutory injunction may be ordered. The interlocutory injunction is of course of the utmost importance.

The documentary proof and other evidence must convince the judge beyond a reasonable doubt that the petitioner has a clear and definite right. There must be no uncertainty as to the facts. What constitutes a certain and definite right has been the work of the courts and the decisions are sometimes conflicting. Much is left to the discretion of the trial judge; the Supreme Court lays down only general standards and guides. The petitioner's clear right must be determinable *prima facie* without any examination as to the facts. The proceedings in this respect bear a resemblance to our motion for summary judgment. But the fact that questions of *law* are complicated and controversial does not prevent the grant of what the courts call the "heroic" remedy.

The writ has preference on the court calendar over every other action, except habeas corpus. The judge's order is enforced by a contempt proceeding if disobeyed. A stay may be granted if an appeal is filed. The denial of the writ is without prejudice to any other remedy the petitioner may have.

The writ does not lie to test the constitutionality of a statute *per se*, in the abstract. A concrete act on the part of a public authority violating or threaten-

---

* This constitution was never officially promulgated. — Ed.

ing directly a right of the petitioner is a necessary basis for the action. But a statute that is not truly legislative, but is in essence an administrative act may be attacked by the writ. The writ also lies when a statute is immediately self-enforcing or when, though in a general form, it is really directed against a single person. The tendency of the latest decisions seems to be, however, that a law or a tax may be declared unconstitutional, without concrete application, by means of the writ of security.

The law is not yet well settled as to the extent to which the writ of security can be used against judicial acts. The prior controversy was in part settled by Law 1533 of 1951. The writ does not lie against a court order or decision where there is a remedy provided by the procedural laws or the decision is open to revision. The statute has been broadly construed to allow the writ when the ordinary procedural remedy does not include a stay of proceedings.

The writ today (contrary to the rule in the United States) lies against the President of the Republic, but only in the Supreme Court. Against cabinet ministers, the Federal Court of Appeal is the competent court of first instance.

It is in the field of taxation that the writ finds its greatest application in today's practice, against unconstitutional or illegal taxes, *e.g.* interstate export taxes or violations of income tax exemption granted to journalists and professors. In tax matters, the courts have followed the maxim *in dubio contra fiscum* — a maxim we might well adopt. However, the constitutional provision that the salaries of judges may not be reduced was held not to exempt them from the incidence of the general income tax. Other tax cases also have given rise to conflicts of opinion and dissenting opinions are frequent. The courtesy with which the judges of the Supreme Court, with very rare exceptions, treat their colleagues might well set an example for our own judges. Progressive inflation in Brazil has caused increasing difficulties and the use of the writ of security enjoining collection of illegal or arbitrary impositions, instead of the older method of an action for restitution, has served to mitigate injustice.

[See also Marchant, *The Brazilian Writ of Security* (Mandado de Segurança) *and its Relationship to the Extraordinary Remedies of the Anglo-American Common Law: An Object Lesson in Latin American Law Making*, 19 TUL. L. REV. 213 (1944). A useful Mexican work is Fix Zamudio, *Mandato de Seguridad y Juicio de Amparo*, XVI (46) BOLETIN DEL INSTI-TUTO DE DERECHO COMPARADO DE MEXICO 3 (1963).]

D. The Argentine Amparo

In the years prior to 1957, the Supreme Court of Argentina recognized no generalized remedy in the nature of injunctive relief against unconstitutional official action. The writ of habeas corpus gave fairly rapid protection against illegal or arbitrary deprivations of physical liberty, but there was no comparable protection for other constitutional rights. Such protection was left to the ordinary course of judicial and administrative proceedings, in which constitutional questions might be raised in the manner that is normal in the United States. See LINARES QUINTANA, ACCION DE AMPARO 11-20 (1960); BIDART CAMPOS, DERECHO DE AMPARO 49-64 (1961).

The year 1957 saw a dramatic change in the Argentine jurisprudence, a change which may have reflected the judiciary's reaction to the 1955 overthrow of the Perón dictatorship. Beginning with the *Siri* case, which follows immediately, the Supreme Court has created a new remedy after the fashion of the Mexican amparo* and the Brazilian writ of security. (A similar remedy already existed in the courts of several of the Argentine provinces.) The following cases — some of them already established firmly as "leading cases" (they also use this term, in English) — show the Argentine courts struggling to create a coherent body of law out of the raw material of individual cases decided over a short period of time.

There have already been proposals for statutory embodiment of the Argentine law of amparo; a summary of one such proposal is printed after the opinions of the Supreme Court. Does this proposal make any important changes in the law of amparo as developed in the cases? What are the advantages and disadvantages of codification at this time? Would you favor such a proposal?

SIRI
Supreme Court of Justice of the Nation
239 Fallos 459, 1958-II J.A. 478,
89 La Ley 531, 223 G.F. 292 (1957)

Opinion of the Procurador General of the Nation.— ... [T]he closing of the newspaper "Mercedes," which gave rise to the present proceedings, has been made ineffective.

Consequently, since any decision of Your Honors in respect to the question brought up would only be abstract, I am of the opinion that the extraordinary appeal should be declared to have been improperly granted.—*Sebastián Soler.*

Opinion of the Procurador General of the Nation.—[The Procurador General, no longer sure that the case is moot, proceeds to consider the merits.]

In this concern I have already had the opportunity ("Fallos," vol. 236,

---

* For comparison of the Mexican and Argentine writs of amparo with United States remedies, see GRANT, EL CONTROL JURISDICCIONAL DE LA CONSTITUCIONALIDAD DE LAS LEYES (1963).

p. 41) to state my opinion that the recourse of habeas corpus protects only persons deprived of their physical liberty without the order of a competent authority. Therefore, if Your Honors decide to accept the allowability of the intended recourse, I believe it would be proper to affirm what has been decided, insofar as it is appealed.—*Sebastián Soler.*

Buenos Aires, December 27, 1957.—[Considering]: In the proceedings . . . the extraordinary recourse was granted against the decision of the Chamber of Appeals (Penal) of Mercedes (Province of Buenos Aires), declaring that the newspaper "Mercedes," under the management and administration of Angel Siri, had been closed since the beginning of 1956, "by police custody of the premises," which act violated the freedom of the press and of work as contained in arts. 14, 17, and 18 of the National Constitution, and arts. 9, 11, 13, 14, 23 and others of the Provincial Constitution. He [Siri] asked that, pending the report of the Police Commissioner of the District of Mercedes concerning the present reasons for the custody of the newspaper premises, he be accorded what was proper, consistent with the law and in accordance with the cited constitutional clauses.

[The Police Commissioner's report stated simply that, in accordance with an order from the Directorate of Security, Siri had been arrested and the newspaper closed down. No reasons for closing the newspaper had been given; neither the Police Chief nor the Minister of the Interior of the Province of Buenos Aires knew what the causes were or which authority had issued the order. Nonetheless the judge of 1st Instance rejected the complaint for habeas corpus on the ground that the writ protected only the physical liberty of individuals. The Chamber of Appeals (Penal) of Mercedes affirmed on the same ground.]

. . . In these conditions, it is clear that the right invoked by the petitioner to publish and administer the newspaper must be upheld.

[The plaintiff did not base his action on an expanded theory of habeas corpus, but simply relied on the guarantees of freedom of the press and of work.]

That this confirmation of the constitutional violation is sufficient reason for the judges to re-establish entirely the constitutional guarantee that is invoked, and it may not be alleged to the contrary that there is no law regulating the guarantee. Individual guarantees exist and protect individuals by virtue of the single fact that they are contained in the Constitution, independently of the regulatory laws . . . .

That in consideration of the nature and order of importance of the principles of the Fundamental Charter in relation to individual rights, this Supreme Court (in its present composition and in the first opportunity when it must pronounce on the point) departs from the traditional doctrine declared by the tribunal, insofar as that doctrine relegated to the ordinary proceedings (administrative or judicial) the protection of guarantees not strictly included in habeas corpus . . . . Constitutional precepts as well as the institutional experience of the country jointly demand the enjoyment and full exercise of individual guarantees for the effective maintenance of a state of law, and impose the duty of ensuring them upon the country's judges.

Therefore, the Procurador General having stated his opinion, the appealed sentence is revoked. And the proceedings are returned to the tribunal of origin in order that . . . the police authority [be directed to terminate] the restriction imposed on the petitioner in his capacity as editor-owner of the newspaper that was shut down.—*Alfredo Orgaz.*—*Manuel J. Argañarás.*—*Enrique V. Galli.*—*Benjamín Villegas Basavilbaso.*—Dissenting: *Carlos Herrera.*

[The dissent of Dr. Herrera relied on admitted precedent and argued that the Court had exceeded its jurisdiction. Dr. Herrera argued that the Court had no authority, in the absence of legislation, to create the new remedy.]

SAMUEL KOT, S.R.L.
[SOCIETY OF LIMITED RESPONSIBILITY] *
Supreme Court of Justice of the Nation
241 Fallos 291, 1958-IV J.A. 227,
92 La Ley 627 (1958)

2d Instance.—La Plata, July 8, 1958.—[Considering]: That the essential object of the recourse of "habeas corpus," as decided consistently by this tribunal and decided by the most authoritative doctrine, is the protection of personal or bodily liberty, and the recourse may not be extended to the protection of other rights claimed to be injured. Such rights must be exercised in accordance with the respective procedures created by the laws pertaining to the subject matter . . . .

This being so and the case at hand not being included in any of the suppositions of art. 415, Code of Criminal Procedure, the action of amparo brought by Sabatino Kot on his own behalf is rejected with costs (art. 428 of the cited Code). . . .

Opinion of the Procurador General of the Nation.— . . .

Here, . . . the petition firmly insists on the decision in the *Siri* case as a basis for the intervention of criminal tribunals in the question under consideration, although outside the aforementioned penal process.

Well, the decision of the *Siri* case is not applicable in the present case, in my judgment. There, . . . amparo was asked, not against an act performed by private persons but rather against an arbitrary act by an [official] authority,

---

* For comment on this case see CARRIO, RECURSO DE AMPARO Y TECNICA JUDICIAL (1959). — Ed.

and no clear remedy for this act existed in legislation, despite the fact that the act entailed the violation of individual guarantees assured by the Constitution.

As one observes, then, the situation is fundamentally different. In the first place, it is different because here it is not a matter of making an official act ineffective, since the workers occupied the factory on their own account; and in the second place because, contrary to what happened in the [*Siri*] case, the legislation of the state in whose jurisdiction this act took place provides a specific procedural remedy for resolving situations such as the one in this case . . . .

* * *

Buenos Aires, September 5, 1958.— . . . The firm of Samuel Kot (Society of Limited Responsibility), owner of a textile establishment situated in calle Arias 228 of Villa Lynch, San Martín (Province of Buenos Aires), has been involved in a conflict with its working personnel since last March 21. The strike by these workers was originally declared illegal by the San Martín Delegation of the Provincial Department of Labor on March 28, because of which the [employer] ordered the return of the workers to their jobs within 24 hours, with the exception of two union officials. A month and a half later, the president of the Provincial Department of Labor declared that decision of the San Martín Delegation to be void and suggested to both parties that work be resumed. The company refused to reinstate the two workers it had fired, and then these two and other workers occupied the factory on June 9 and have stayed there until now. [The factory has been prevented from being operated from that time, although the owners may enter it.]

[The business manager brought an action based on this usurpation of property, demanding the return of the immovable. The judge dismissed the action because the occupation by the workers was not made with the object of assuming ownership of the property, but only in the course of the labor dispute. This decision was appealed to the 3d Chamber of Appeals (Penal) of La Plata, which affirmed the final dismissal. On the same day the attorney for the firm sought from the same chamber relief in the nature of amparo (*not* habeas corpus) based on the *Siri* case. This relief was also denied in the court of 2d Instance (see the above-quoted decision).]

Considering: That, first of all, it is proper to set aside the basis expressed by the court for rejecting the argument of the complainant. He did not rely on the recourse of "habeas corpus" but rather on that of amparo, invoking the constitutional rights of freedom of work, of property and of free activity. That is, he alleged a different guarantee from the one protecting corporal freedom — one which, like "habeas corpus," obtains expeditious and rapid protection that comes directly from the Constitution. This Court declared it so in the decision of December 27 of last year, in the case of "Angel Siri" (Fallos, vol. 239, p. 450), with grounds which are here incorporated by reference insofar as they are pertinent.

That although in the cited precedent the illegal restriction on liberty came from the public authority and not from acts of individuals, such a distinction is not essential for the purposes of constitutional protection. If it is admitted that a tacit or implicit guarantee exists, protecting the various aspects of individual liberty (art. 33, National Constitution), no exception may be established that might exclude, absolutely and "a priori," all such restrictions imposed by private persons.

. . . There is nothing in either the letter or the spirit of the Constitution that might permit the assertion that the protection of "human rights" — so called because they are the basic rights of man — is confined to attacks by official authorities. Neither is there anything to authorize the assertion that an illegal, serious, and open attack against any of the rights that make up liberty in the broad sense, would lack adequate constitutional protection because of the single fact that the attack comes from other private persons or organized groups of individuals. (This protection, of course, is in the form of habeas corpus and the recourse of amparo, and not that of the ordinary proceedings. . . .) To attempt excessively technical constructions in order to justify this distinction means to interpret the Constitution in such a way that it would really appear to protect not basic rights, but open violations of those rights. The concrete facts of this case by themselves constitute a significant example.

This distinction is even less admissible, . . . considering the conditions in which social life of the past fifty years has developed. Besides individual persons and the State, there is now a third category of subjects, with or without a juridical personality, which past centuries knew only infrequently: consortiums, syndicates, professional associations, large businesses, which almost always accumulate enormous material or economic power. Often their forces are opposed to those of the State, and it cannot be disputed that these collective entities represent, with the material progress of society, a new source of threats for the individual and his basic rights.

If, considering these conditions of contemporary society, judges had to find that there is no constitutional protection for human rights against such collective organizations, no one could doubt that such a declaration would carry with it the loss of the great objectives of the Constitution and with that loss, the failure of the fundamental juridical order in the country. Plainly, that is not so. The Constitution does not foresake citizens in the face of such dangers nor does it necessarily require them to resort to the slow and expensive defense of the ordinary proceedings. Laws cannot be interpreted only from a historical viewpoint without considering the new conditions and needs of the community, for every law, by its nature, contains a vision of the future, and is intended to cover and govern acts that take place after its ratification: "Laws provide for the future," says art. 3, Civil Code, with a higher significance that is not exhausted, certainly, in the particular issue to which the precept is applied subsequently. With greater reason, the Constitution, which is the law of laws and to be found at the base of the entire positive juridical order, has the indispensable power to govern juridical relations born in social circumstances different from those that existed at the time of its ratification. This advance of constitutional principles, which is a part of natural development and not a contradiction, is the real work of the interpreters, particularly of the judges, who must have the intelligence that will best assure the great objectives for which the Constitution was written. Among these great objectives and even of first importance among them, is that of "assuring the benefits of liberty for ourselves, for our posterity and for all the men of the world who may want to live on Argentine soil" (Preamble).

[The court notes that the recourse of habeas corpus, which comes from the Anglo-American tradition by way of the Constitution of the United States, has been interpreted broadly to protect physical liberty.]

The same breadth should be recognized for the recourse of amparo, which this Court, in the aforementioned precedent [the *Siri* case], drew from the wise rule of art. 33 of the Constitution. . . . What habeas corpus and the recourse of amparo have in view primarily is not the "origin" of the illegal restrictions of any of the fundamental rights of persons, but those rights in themselves, for the purpose of safeguarding them. These guarantees do not apply unilaterally to the aggressors, in order to point out distinctions among them, but rather they apply to the injured persons, in order to re-establish their essential rights. The Constitution is irrevocably aimed at assuring to all citizens "the benefits of liberty" and this purpose . . . is weakened or damaged when distinctions are introduced that, directly or indirectly, become obstacles or delays to the effective fulfillment of rights.

[The court also cites the 1948 Universal Declaration of Human Rights of the United Nations.]

Consequently, whenever it is clear and obvious that any restriction of basic human rights is illegal and also that submitting the question to the ordinary administrative or judicial procedures would cause serious and irreparable harm, it is proper for the judges immediately to restore the restricted right through the swift method of the recourse of amparo. All that can be added is that, in such hypotheses, judges must take special pains in considering, and be very prudent — the same as in many other questions corresponding to their high position — so that they do not decide, through the highly summary procedure of this constitutional guarantee, questions susceptible of greater debate and which should be resolved in accordance with the ordinary procedures. . . .

[In the present case, the Court found that the striking workers made no claim of a right to continue to occupy the factory and that their occupation of the factory deprived the owners of their property and their right to work.]

* * *

In these conditions, it is not wise to require that the affected party claim the return of his property through ordinary procedures: if, every time that a group of persons physically occupied a factory, a private teaching institution, or any other establishment, in connection with a conflict, the owners had no other recourse for the defense of their constitutional rights than to allege a possessory action or one of ejectment, with many citations for each and every one of the occupants to appear in the action, with the power of each of the occupants to name his own attorney, to contest notices and documents, to offer and produce evidence, etc., then anyone can see how reduced would be the protection of rights given by the laws and how subverted the juridical order of the country would be. In such situations, of which the present case is one, judicial protection of constitutional rights does not tolerate or consent to similar delay.

[By a vote of three to two, the decision of the court of 2d Instance was reversed, and the granting of the amparo was ordered. The two dissenting judges argued that the amparo was available only against official invasions of constitutional rights, and not against invasions of similar interests by private parties. The dissenters further argued that the decision would introduce considerable insecurity into the law. They suggested that the extension of the amparo to actions between private individuals would create an excessive discretionary power in all the judges in the country to grant amparo — i.e., to decide private disputes — without using the normal means of hearing, proof, appeal, etc., which safeguard the rights of parties to ordinary litigation.]

GALVAN v. COUTO
Supreme Court of Justice of the Nation
246 Fallos 380 (1960)

[The plaintiff sought amparo against a private individual to secure fulfillment of his obligation to supply electricity. The lower court rejected the complaint.]

Buenos Aires, May 30, 1960.
        * * *

Considering: That as the foregoing opinion of the Procurador General points out, based on the jurisprudence of this Court, since the present case involves the nonfulfillment of a contractual obligation, the recourse of amparo is not allowable. The fact that it is alleged that in such a case the right to work will be infringed does not vary the resolution of the case. In effect, we deal with one form of exercise of that right, which presupposes the decision that there is a contractual obligation, and which, furthermore, is not unique. On the other hand [various procedural devices such as an order to maintain matters in status quo], possible in an ordinary action, provide proceedings suitable for the protection of the right [to work], which proceedings can be of assistance to the plaintiff.

Therefore, the Procurador General having given his opinion, the foregoing complaint is dismissed.

Benjamín Villegas Basavilbaso.—Aristóbulo D. Aráoz de Lamadrid.—
Luis María Boffi Boggero.—Ricardo Colombres.

The leading case standing for the foregoing proposition is *Buosi*, 244 Fallos 68, 1959-IV J.A. 36, 96 La Ley 709 (1959), involving a dispute over land and water rights. Similar rulings were made in the cases of *Magno Esquivel v. Corbiere de B.*, 247 Fallos 59, 99 La Ley 820 (1960) (contractual obligation to permit tenants to use an elevator), and *Precedo*, 253 Fallos 35, 1962-IV J.A. 334, 108 La Ley 328 (1962) (dispute over a labor contract).

MORIS
Federal Chamber of the Capital
(Contentious-Administrative Division)
1962-I J.A. 442 (1961)

2d Instance.—Buenos Aires, March 7, 1961.—Considering: [Following a minor disturbance at the headquarters of the Club Hípico Argentino, the plaintiff Moris, a member of the Club, was suspended from membership by order of the "intervenor," an official who had been appointed by the national government to manage the Club's affairs temporarily. (The propriety of the government's intervention is not in issue; all parties have treated the case as if the Club's own officers had suspended the plaintiff.) The plaintiff appealed from the decision of the intervenor to the Club's assembly, as he was entitled to do by the Club statutes. This appeal was permitted, but the suspension continued in effect pending the convening of the assembly. A successful appeal to the assembly, then, might simply wipe out the plaintiff's suspension after its period had terminated. The court of 1st Instance granted the amparo, ordering the intervenor to lift the suspension until the assembly next convened. The intervenor appeals to this court on several grounds, but particularly on the ground that the plaintiff's asserted constitutional right to freedom of association has not been injured.]

* * *

That ... it is necessary to point out that the guarantee of "association for useful purposes" contained in art. 14 of the National Constitution is not to be understood as referring only to the act of forming an association and drawing up its statutes, but that it must necessarily include also the power to exercise the rights that those statutes confer, and to make use of the association in accordance with its rules. Thus, when one of the members is deprived of prerogatives that explicitly or implicitly arise from the provisions that govern the organization, it cannot be maintained validly that the constitutional guarantee is unaffected.

That from the account of the foregoing acts, it transpires that in the present case a sanction was applied to the plaintiff by an authority that was not one of those selected by the [Club] statute. As no one has questioned the right of the [national] Executive Power to intervene in the affairs of the Club, we need not consider the matter. Besides, there is in the [Club] statutes a complete, regulated procedure for the application of punishments to the members, which in this case was not observed because of lack of leadership in the competent organs, as the intervenor affirmed. Neither is it proper to form a judgment in this respect, because within the Club the competent organ is provided to do it, that organ being the assembly of members. But a recourse exists before that assembly — and this the intervenor conceded — notwithstanding which, he ordered the execution of the suspension.

That accepting the legitimacy of this intervention, one cannot deny to the intervenor the power to adopt necessary means for maintaining the normal functioning of the Club. Among those means must be the minimum of disciplinary power indispensable to that end.

That in the present case it is not seen that the conduct of Moris could be of such seriousness as to compromise the normal functioning of the Club nor the decorum that should govern its development. It follows that it is arbitrary to require of him the fulfillment of a sanction imposed on him without the participation of any of the statutory organs provided for that object, and without awaiting the judgment of the assembly, which was the reasonable course. It is in this respect that one sees the illegality of the conduct of the intervenor, which illegality justifies judicial interference to safeguard the constitutional guarantee previously referred to ("Fallos," vol. 245, p. 542).

That, furthermore, judicial [protection] becomes necessary because, as the judge of 1st Instance says, the meeting of the assembly might be delayed until the total fulfillment of the punishment, or at least until a good part of it had been completed. This possibility shows that to turn the question over to the normal procedures can make an illusion of the constitutional guarantee that is endangered and cause Moris irreparable harm. And in this way the appellant is answered insofar as he maintains that judicial interference in the internal life of the Club endangers the constitutional guarantee of freedom of association.

For these considerations the appealed decision is affirmed, clarifying that the intervenor of the Club Hípico Argentino is ordered to hold in abeyance the fulfillment of the sanction applied to Gustavo A. Moris until such time as the assembly of members of the club may pronounce in this respect.—*Juan Carlos Beccar Varela.—Horacio H. Heredia.*—Dr. Gabrielli, who was on leave, did not participate.

The volume of amparo litigation in Argentina is reflected in the number of entries in the annual case digests published by *La Ley* under the title "Recurso de Amparo." Those digests contained very few amparo entries during the first year after the *Siri* case; after that, the volume increased very substantially, and then declined again:

1958	14
1959	90
1960	116
1961	170
1962	174
1963	110
1964 (9 mo.)	47

As you read the decisions that follow, consider whether they help you to explain these figures. See Bielsa, *El Recurso de Amparo*, 105 La Ley 1068 (1962).

LUMELLI
Supreme Court of Justice of the Nation
242 Fallos 300, 1959-III J.A. 410, 94 La Ley 210 (1958)

Buenos Aires, November 21, 1958.—Considering: That the Customs Administration of Bahía Blanca charged Omar Pablo Lumelli with illegally having brought an automobile into the country, . . . thus committing an infraction of the prohibitions established by [a 1957 law]. In virtue of this, the Administration ordered the seizure of the automobile and the detention of the accused. The latter's wife brought a "recourse of amparo," which was rejected by the Federal Judge of Bahía Blanca. She immediately appealed to the Federal Chamber of Appeals of that district, which ordered the release of the accused, but at the same time affirmed the decision of the court of 1st Instance "insofar as it did not grant the amparo against the order of seizure."

That the wife of the above mentioned Lumelli has filed an extraordinary recourse against the decision of the court of 2d Instance, the revocation of which decision she seeks on the ground that there has been a violation of the right of property and of various provisions of the National Constitution.

That, as the Procurador General shows with certainty, the plaintiff-appellant is not entitled to invoke the right of property. This circumstance obstructs the allowability of the claim of amparo, in the absence of any rule to the contrary such as that established by the procedural laws regarding *habeas corpus*. It is proper so to declare in this case, the more so since the owner of the seized automobile was himself in a position to act in the defense of his right, as the order of detention against him was inoperative before the commencement of the present recourse.

That, furthermore, the act against which the claim is asserted was executed by an administrative authority which, in the emergency, exercised jurisdictional powers given by [a 1956 law]. Because of this fact, the protection asked by the appellant could not be sought of agencies foreign to the case in which the seizure was ordered, but rather it had to be requested in compliance with the pertinent formal provisions of [the 1956 law]. These provisions, in principle, should be considered as excluding the exceptional remedy constituted by the claim of amparo.

[The amparo was held to have been improperly granted.]

GALLARDO
Supreme Court of Justice of the Nation
242 Fallos 434, 1959-I J.A. 635, 94 La Ley 749 (1958)

[Gallardo had applied for permission to operate a bus in the Province of Tucumán. Permission was denied on the ground that Gallardo had not shown that he was a permanent resident of Tucumán. There was a type of proceeding especially established to decide cases of this nature; Gallardo had not followed this special proceeding, but rather had brought an action of amparo in the Supreme Court of Tucumán. He was unsuccessful, and appealed to the Supreme Court of Justice of the Nation.]

Buenos Aires, December 10, 1958.—Considering: That the appealed decision . . ., insofar as it concerns substantially the competence of the provincial courts, decides questions outside the extraordinary jurisdiction of this Court.

That, furthermore, and as the statement of the Procurador General shows, the circumstances of the case differ from those exceptional circumstances contemplated in the precedents mentioned in that statement [particularly the *Siri* and *Kot* cases].

What is disputed in this proceeding is an administrative act, subordinate to and regulated by a provincial law, and respecting which the local institutions have established pertinent procedures for judicial inspection. This Court has declared that, in principle, the existence of a legal means for the protection of the disputed right, although the right may be based on the Constitution, excludes the use of the exceptional proceeding constituted by the complaint for amparo (*cf.* the case of Lumelli, Oscar Pablo, decision of November 21st last).

Therefore, and by reason of the statement of the Procurador General, the foregoing complaint is rejected.—*Alfredo Orgaz.—Benjamín Villegas Basavilbaso.—Aristóbulo D. Aráoz de Lamadrid.—Luis M. Boffi Boggero.—Julio Oyhanarte.*

EXHAUSTION OF NON-GOVERNMENTAL REMEDIES

The principle of the *Gallardo* case was later applied in a different setting by the Superior Court of the Province of La Pampa. In the case of Rodríguez, 1963-I J.A. 173, 111 La Ley 907 (1962), a member of the Costa Brava professional soccer team had been suspended by the league (Liga Pampeana de Fútbol) for 28 months, as punishment for a playing-field offense. He sought relief by way of amparo, alleging deprivation of constitutional rights to a fair defense, to carry on a lawful activity and to develop his personality by means of engaging in sport. Citing the *Lumelli* and *Gallardo* cases, the court affirmed a decision to reject the complaint. The chief ground was that the plaintiff had failed to pursue his gievance within the established procedures of the Argentine Football Association, of which the league was an affiliate. The existence of another means for securing the protection of the plaintiff's rights was considered to be a bar to the use of the "exceptional and summary" amparo procedure.

There is a parallel to this reasoning in United States labor legislation. One of the provisions of the "bill of rights" contained in the Labor-Management Reporting and Disclosure Act of 1959 prohibits a labor organization from limiting the rights of any union member to sue his union or its officers, or to commence administrative proceedings against them,

> *Provided,* That any such member may be required to exhaust reasonable hearing procedures (but not to exceed a four-month lapse of time) within such organization, before instituting legal or administrative proceedings against such organizations [sic} or any officer thereof . . . .

29 U.S.C. § 411(a)(4) (Supp. II, 1961).

PAMPINELLA
Federal Chamber of the Capital
(Contentious-Administrative Division)
1961-II J.A. 62, 102 La Ley 312,
231 G.F. 260 (1959)

2d Instance.—Buenos Aires, November 18, 1959.—Considering: Against the decision that allowed the recourse of amparo brought by Blas Pampinella, through which it was ordered that the Caja Nacional de Previsión para el Personal del Comercio y Actividades Civiles [a social security fund] readjust the pension benefit of the party named, in accordance with art. 2, Law No. 14,499, the aforementioned Fund brought this appeal, questioning the directed means.

The Fund argues ... that since, according to present doctrine and jurisprudence, the recourse of amparo has as its purpose the protection of individual rights and guarantees contained in the National Constitution, its viability demands as an inescapable condition that there be no other procedures established by law through which the rights claimed to be infringed might be protected. It maintains that, precisely for cases such as this, Law No. 14,236 instituted a specific procedure through which members may obtain a rapid and effective decision, without having to resort to other exceptional procedures, and that Pampinella has not followed this course.

In another line of argument, the appellant asserts that the recourse of amparo allowed in this case is also improper inasmuch as the alleged infringement of the member's right does not arise from an act contrary to the law committed by the Fund, since the Fund has completely complied with the rules of Law No. 14,499. That law compels it not to liquidate [its obligation to pay a supplementary amount equalling 82% of the base pension figure] until the Executive Power issues the relevant regulations. [The law required the issuance of regulations within 90 days after its enactment, but some two years later, at the time of this action, no regulation had yet been issued.]

In accordance with the doctrine established by the Supreme Court [citations to the *Siri* and *Kot* cases], as this tribunal recently noted ..., it is necessary, in order for amparo to be allowable in cases such as this: a) that there be an illegal act, the existence of which is clear and manifest; b) that one of the rights of liberty directly protected by the National Constitution have been injured by that act; c) that the injured person not have within his reach another legal means of defending his right or that the means provided by the laws be ineffective in avoiding a serious and irreparable harm.

In regard to this last requirement, the consideration of which offers particular interest, we should state, in accordance with the facts of the case, that while it is true that the Fund did not fulfill its obligation to readjust officially the pension of the petitioner Blas Pampinella, it is also true that the latter never complained of this conduct to the Directorate of the Fund, which is the organ in charge of "resolving all disputes concerning the granting of pensions," according to the function given to it in art. 11, par. d) Law No. 14,236. Had he proceeded in this manner, assuming that the Directorate should deny his petition, he then had the legal possibility (art. 13) of bringing a recourse of revocation in the same Fund, and of further appeal ... to the National Institute of Social Provision. Against the decision of the latter, he still had the recourse foreseen by art. 14 before the labor court.

Consequently, as a complete procedure regulated by Law exists to confirm petitions of the kind that has given rise to the present recourse of amparo, it is through that procedure and before the competent administrative and judicial authorities that the plaintiff ... should have defended his rights. He did not need to use an exceptional method such as the one chosen, which is recognized as legitimate only for those cases in which any defense could prove illusory in the absence of an adequate procedural system. . . .

* * *

By reason of these considerations, the appealed sentence is revoked insofar as it was the subject of this appeal.—*Adolfo R. Gabrielli.—Juan Carlos Beccar Varela.—Horacio H. Heredia.* (Sec.: Leandro Rodríguez Jáuregui).

[The Contentious-Administrative Court of the Capital, in a decision of 1st Instance which was not appealed, held that another pensioner had no right to amparo against the National Institute of Social Provision; this decision was made on the merits, on the ground that the pensioner was unable to show any constitutional violation. It seems to have been assumed that amparo would have been granted if such a constitutional violation had been shown. Scarpa v. Instituto Nacional de Previsión Social, 1960-I J.A. 581 (1959).]

TRAVERSO
Federal Chamber of the Capital
(Contentious-Administrative Division)
1961-II J.A. 53 (1959)

2d Instance.—Buenos Aires, November 23, 1959.—Considering: [Conrado T. Traverso had been in the foreign service of the Argentine government since 1922. In 1946 he was appointed, with the consent of the Senate, to the position of Ambassador Extraordinary and Plenipotentiary. In 1947 his "resignation" — which he had never submitted — was accepted by the government. After the 1955 overthrow of the Perón regime, Traverso sought reinstatement. In 1958 he was appointed Ambassador to Venezuela, and later in the same year he was transferred to the Ministry of Foreign Relations, again with the title of Ambassador Extraordinary and Plenipotentiary. In 1959 he was removed from this post by an executive decree. He brought an action of amparo against the enforcement of the decree, seeking restoration to his position as ambassador. He succeeded in the court of 1st Instance. The judge held that the decree which removed Traverso from his ambassadorial title was invalid, and that he must be reinstated. The effect of this decision was to leave him his title, but not to require the national executive to use him in any particular ambassadorial post.]

The *procurador fiscal* appeals and in this instance Conrado Traverso and the *fiscal* of the chamber explain their points of view in respective memoranda.

The case then, is ready for decision, and the first thing to be decided is whether or not the procedural route chosen is proper.

To this end, we should recall what the tribunal said recently — last September 17 — in the case of the Pieres Company [1961-I J.A. 133]: that, in accordance with the doctrine established by the Supreme Court, the following conditions had to be present in order for this procedural route to be allowable: [a] that an illegal act have taken place, the illegality of which is clear and manifest; and [b] that this act damage one of the rights of liberty directly protected by the National Constitution. The final condition is [c] that the injured person not have within his reach another legal means of defending himself or that the provisions of the laws not be effective to avoid his suffering a serious and irreparable harm.

It is a matter of establishing, then, whether the present case includes the stated conditions or whether, on the contrary, it lacks any of them.

a) As Ambassador Traverso asserts, the National Constitution provides that the Executive Power "name and remove plenipotentiary ministers and chargés d'affaires with the agreement of the Senate" (art. 86, par. 10). Article 30 of Law 12,951, in agreement with this higher rule, establishes: "The civil servant appointed with the agreement of the Senate will retain his employment during good conduct and his removal must be carried out in the same manner [*i.e.,* with the consent of the Senate]."

[Traverso had reached the age and level of seniority which entitled him to a pension upon his removal from office. He refused to accept the pension, however, because the acceptance might be considered a waiver of his objections to being removed without the consent of the Senate.]

The *fiscal* of the chamber compares the status of diplomats to that of judges and military people, maintaining that the ones who have true constitutional immunity from removal are the judicial magistrates. He says that military status does not hinder the retirement [by the government] of higher officers, for whose appointment the agreement of the Senate is necessary, and he says that this is the case of Ambassador Traverso, whose active functions only have been terminated.

However, it does not seem that these three positions in the constitutional system are very similar to each other. The Great Charter uses different rules in referring to each of them. ... [The Constitution expressly requires the agreement of the Senate for their removal as well as their appointment.]

* * *

Neither can the argument be accepted that only the active functions were taken away from this Ambassador, since that action involves depriving him of one of the essential rights belonging to a civil servant as the very effect of the juridical relation of public employment, *i.e.,* the right to discharge the duties of the office.

b) From what has been stated above, it is shown also that the second requisite for the allowability of amparo has been fulfilled in this case. And to that conclusion we should add that since the reform of 1957, the National Constitution assures the stability of public employment.

c) It is asserted that Traverso has within his reach the ordinary action to protect the rights he claims. But he invokes the circumstance of receiving neither salary nor pension, which circumstance creates a true economic burden for him. Likewise he says that if he agrees to retire it could be interpreted as renouncing the judicial action. He ends saying that the "economic pressure accentuated through the indefinite duration of an ordinary action would be transformed into a kind of moral violence, in order to force me to acquiesce in the arbitrariness of the Executive Power."

It is clear that if this gentleman obtains the pension due him, according to ordinary procedure, he will not be caused the serious and irreparable injury demanded for the allowability of the recourse of amparo. But to decide now that that attitude does not carry with it the renouncing of the action of which he might avail himself — in the event that it is believed that such was the case — would mean a prejudgment about a matter that would have to be decided at their convenience by the tribunals that would hear the relevant actions. Naturally, such an occurrence should be avoided.

Furthermore, in order to decide justly it is always correct to descend from excessively lofty postures and enter into the direct resolution of the live problem that requires solution.

The present case not involve complex fact situations that require the evidentiary amplitude of ordinary proceedings; neither is its juridical aspect intricate, so as to make a fuller debate indispensable. In such conditions it is practical and equitable to attenuate the rigor of the requirement ... and not to make dogmatic assertions for the sheer love of principles. This is clear on the condition that the illegality of the imputed behavior is undoubted, as in the present case.

For these considerations the appealed judgment is affirmed.—*Adolfo R. Gabrielli.—Juan Carlos Beccar Varela.—Horacio H. Heredia* (Sec.: Leandro Rodríguez Jáuregui).

[On April 7, 1961, the Supreme Court of Argentina reversed this decision, on the ground that the ordinary judicial remedies were available to Traverso. His assertion of "economic pressure" was said to be common to all litigants who seek economic relief, whether against private defendants or against the state. 249 Fallos 457, 1961-IV J.A. 503, 106 La Ley 415.]

COMMUNIST PARTY
Federal Chamber of Resistencia
1960-V J.A. 531, 101 La Ley 572, 576 (1960)

* * *

2d Instance.—Resistencia, February 25, 1960.—Considering: 1st. The decision of the court of 1st Instance, opposed by the *fiscal* of that instance, comes for consideration by this chamber; that decision allows the recourse of amparo brought by the Communist Party of Formosa [Province], which was injured by the resolution of the Ministry of the Interior of the Province, preventing the Party from carrying out public acts in the electoral campaign preceding the national and provincial elections of next March 27. The plaintiff Party takes the position that such a measure violates the complete letter and spirit of the National and Provincial Constitutions, the statute law regarding political parties, and the laws and decrees of the present electoral system. It adds that its request for permission to hold public meetings was rejected in accordance with decree No. 4965/59, which, it asserts, is "patently unconstitutional," since neither the state of siege now in force and from which this decree arises, nor the decree itself, applies in Formosa Province, nor does it have any remote justification.

* * *

2d. The federal judge of 1st Instance allows the requested jurisdictional protection, on the ground that because the Communist Party has electoral agents in Formosa — and that there is no final decision on the pending request for cancellation of its corporate personality — decree No. 4965/59 violates the decision of the electoral judge, which accords the appellant Party all electoral rights. For this reason the Party should be guaranteed by the judges in the enjoyment of rights arising from the National Constitution and from the laws . . . .

3d. That this chamber in a similar opinion opposed by the same Party has declared that it is clear from the presentation that the Party is trying to weaken or dispute the constitutional force of National Decree No. 4965/59 through the highly summary means of the recourse of amparo. And this tribunal established that such an aim is improper, since this exceptional method is to be used only when there is no procedure that might assure greater discussion . . . .

The demand of the appellant body that "our party be permitted to carry out public acts," and that "there be extended to all the public acts to be executed by the Communist Party of Formosa in the current electoral campaign, the decision ordering the authorization of the same acts on an equal plane with the other political groups," necessarily signifies a formal request for a declaration of unconstitutionality of a decree of the Executive Power. This issue cannot be determined through the very summary recourse of amparo, but rather through the normal means of the proper [ordinary] action, brought before a judge who is competent to hear the complaint.

Therefore, the *fiscal* of the chamber having been heard, the decision is revoked that allows the recourse of amparo, which recourse is declared unallowable.—*Leopoldo A. Virasoro.*—*Carlos V. Gallino Yanzi* (Sec.: Italo Chiapello).

ASERRADERO CLIPPER (S.R.L.)
Supreme Court of Justice of the Nation
1961-IV J.A. 108, 103 La Ley 315 (1961)

Buenos Aires, March 2, 1961.—Considering: 1st. [The plaintiffs have succeeded in both the 1st and 2d Instances in their action of amparo against the National Directorate of Customs, based on an alleged administrative violation of a legislative decree. The customs officials have refused to hand over certain merchandise until the plaintiffs pay certain charges that the plaintiffs consider to be illegal.]

2d. That, further, the court of 2d Instance considers it possible to set aside the requirement of prior payment of the duties questioned in this case, in exceptional instances in which the obvious illegality of the charge would make possible opposition to it, before payment, on constitutional grounds.

3d. That such a decision means a profound change of the system in force since the enactment of [a procedural statute], according to which there is no action for a declaration of unconstitutionality in the national procedural order. For, as this Court pointed out on a recent occasion (245 Fallos 552), "the application of the precepts of the laws of the Nation may not be hindered by an action for a declaration of unconstitutionality. This resolution corresponds, besides, to the presumption of validity that should be given to the acts of the constituted authorities and most particularly, to the laws enacted by the Congress of the Nation. It also arises from the fact that, in the national procedural order, the prosecution of actions such as those giving rise to this complaint has not been foreseen"; that is, the impugning of the constitutionality of a law by means of a declaration.

4th. That since the decision of this Court in the *Siri* case, the institution of the action of amparo by jurisprudential means has corresponded (as subsequent jurisprudence has repeatedly explained) to the necessity of giving due judicial protection to the human rights contained in the National Constitution, in those cases in which there is no legal means of according protection. Legitimate as this jurisprudence is when the lack to which it responds is authentic, on the other hand it is not legitimate if used to substitute another remedy that is subjectively considered more appropriate by the Nation's judges in place of the legislative criterion as regards the form and means of the defense of patrimonial rights. Such a substitution cannot be attempted without an obvious attack on the cardinal principle of the separation of powers and the pre-eminence ... of Congressional laws, insofar as they may be enacted in accordance with the National Constitution ....

[The Court notes that according to clear precedent, the only way to attack a tax or other public tribute is to pay it and then sue for its recovery. The Court also notes the seriousness of the problem of evasion of customs duties in Argentina, which problem requires prompt and effective administrative action for its solution.]

It is noted, consequently, that the action of amparo, the proceeding of which is most summary and does not permit sufficient discussion of the questioned tariffs, is able to upset the system that the legislator foresaw for the control of imports and the due fulfillment of the charges connected with them. ... If it were accepted that the action of amparo might serve to fetter the activity of the State in such hypothetical situations, the risk would be created that that claim, which is only a means for the protection of constitutional rights, could be converted to the opposite, that is, to the abandonment of the right of each and every person in the face of the behavior of those who deceitfully damage the national economy and offend the moral bases of the community.

* * *

Therefore, the *procurador general* having expressed his opinion, the appealed decision is revoked and the complaint rejected. Costs will be apportioned in all instances.—*Benjamín Villegas Basavilbaso.—Aristóbulo D. Aráoz de Lamadrid.—Julio Oyhanarte.—Ricardo Colombres.—Esteban Imaz.*

ASOCIACION BANCARIA (SECCIONAL REGIONAL DE TUCUMAN)
Supreme Court of Justice of the Nation
245 Fallos 86, 1959-VI J.A. 159, 103 La Ley 43 (1959)

Buenos Aires, October 23, 1959.—Considering: 1st. That, as the record shows, Arturo E. Zurita, secretary general of the [plaintiff association — a labor union representing banking employees], instituted a complaint for amparo against decree No. 4311/59 and subsequent orders issued by the Ministry of Labor and Social Security, providing for an administrative intervention into the union that he represents. ["Intervention" means that the Ministry takes over the management of the union, much as the government might seize a business. — Ed.] As grounds for the requested action, he invoked the constitutional provisions pertaining to the rights of property and of association, as well as art. 31 [vesting lawmaking power in the Congress] and art. 86, par. 2 of the Constitution [instructing the President not to alter the spirit of the laws by regulation], and the right to free and democratic union organization contained in Law No. 14,455.

2d.   That the intervention formally decreed was not carried out, because the administrative authority thought it prudent to "delay until the issuance of a new order" the taking of possession by the appointed intervenor, because of the resistance put up by the directors of the plaintiff Association.

3d.   That the judge of 1st Instance granted the requested amparo and consequently ordered that the "intervention and taking possession of the union hall and goods of the petitioner" be made ineffective.

4th.   That, this decision having been revoked by the intermediate appellate court, the plaintiff filed an extraordinary appeal, which was granted.

5th.   That, considering the nature of the right invoked and the lack of a procedural means capable of protecting it, the exceptional remedy of amparo utilized in this case is formally allowable. This is so, moreover: a) because the question raised is of pure law, there being no dispute as to the facts; b) because Law No. 14,455, after pointing out the recognized means of administrative control over labor unions, provides that against the application of those means there shall be a direct appeal before the Labor Chamber of the Capital [art. 37]. And this posibility of immediate judicial protection in situations when legal means of control may be used assumes a full support of amparo in cases such as the present one, in which the plaintiff claims to have been the victim of means of administrative control forbidden by law.

[On the merits, the court found the intervention to be manifestly illegal, and that the amparo should therefore be granted.]

Therefore, the *procurador general* having given his opinion, the appealed decision is revoked.—*Alfredo Orgaz.*—*Benjamín Villegas Basavilbaso.*—*Luis M. Boffi Boggero.*—*Julio Oyhanarte.*

BIDART CAMPOS, DERECHO DE AMPARO
361-63 (1961)

Although, in principle, a person who demands amparo must establish the existence of a certain and incontestable right, there are situations in which the existence of a mere legitimate interest suffices. . . . The notion of legitimate interest, rooted in administrative law, has served as the basis for a notable diffusion of the objective appeal or appeal or annulment [in judicial review of administrative action], and it is now called on in constitutional law as a basis for complaints in amparo. . . .

When in its decision of December 9, 1960, the Federal Chamber of Rosario accepted the amparo brought by the Dean of the Faculty of Medical Sciences of the University of the Litoral against the occupation of the building by students, the court based its decision on the ground that such an occupation impeded the Faculty from developing its specific activity, and caused harm, "in prejudice of professors and students, and to the right to teach and to learn that is consecrated in art. 14, of the National Constitution." Then it added "that it cannot be questioned that the Dean, as the indisputable authority over the mentioned Faculty, has the power to request the immediate reestablishment of the order which has been subverted, in order to make possible the normal functioning of the Faculty." (J.A., July 5, 1961.) In truth the constitutional right of teaching and learning was not something held by the Dean who asked amparo, but rather it belonged to the professors and students, because of which we maintain that the Dean was invested legally only with a legitimate interest, which was of itself sufficent to confer on him an active procedural personality in this summary action.

SPANGENBERG

Supreme Court of Justice of the Nation
256 Fallos 54, 1963-IV J.A. 103, 112 La Ley 527 (1963)

Buenos Aires, June 14, 1963.—Considering: [Four deputies to the national Congress filed a complaint in amparo, asking judicial relief against the continued execution of an Executive decree recessing the Congress. The decree had been issued shortly after the military had deposed President Frondizi in the spring of 1962 (see note, p. 677, *infra*); in addition to recessing the Congress, the decree had declared invalid the elections of March 18, 1962, in which the Peronists (the principal political antagonists of the controlling military group) had been unexpectedly successful. The deputies considered the provisions of the decree unconstitutional and the newly instituted Executive Power illegal. The specific acts complained of in this initial complaint involved the use of Federal Police to prevent the members of Congress from entering the Congress building. Other deputies joined as plaintiffs, along with certain private citizens, alleging the unconstitutionality of the cancellation of elections. The new government had also called new elections for the month of July 1963, to replace those cancelled. There were 27 plaintiffs in all.]

[The judge of 1st Instance held that he was incompetent to consider the legality of the portion of the decree ordering the Congress into recess, but he allowed the amparo with respect to the order setting aside the national elections. The court of 2d Instance reversed, holding that the decree by the de facto government had left the plaintiffs without any recognizable legal interest in the matter; the first decision had to be reversed, since it was in the nature of an advisory opinion, not affecting individual interests.]

[The Supreme Court of Argentina rejected the appeals of the plaintiffs, principally on the ground that they had been filed too late. In addition, by way of dicta, the Court made some general pronouncements on the purpose of the action of amparo.]

6th. That . . . the Court believes it fitting to add that the recourse of amparo was established though the jurisprudence of this Court in order to safeguard the human rights contained in the National Constitution . . ., that is, for the exceptional protection of individual rights, since the constitutional guarantees were given to individual persons and may not be invoked except by those entitled to them . . . . Consequently, this is not a question of an extension of judicial jurisdiction to include suppositions foreign to it, outside the specific material marked out.

7th. That, therefore, acts amounting to conflicts of governmental powers, outside the judicial scope within which their consideration might belong, cannot be treated through the said means of amparo.

8th. That in the present exceptional circumstances, and with the people of all the national territory gathered for the election of the Legislative and Executive powers and of the provincial governments, the [elections] should not be affected by judicial decisions that, with the reach of a mandamus, might interfere with them.

* * *

Therefore, the *Procurador General* having spoken, the appeals are declared not allowable.—*Benjamín Villegas Basavilbaso.*—*Aristóbulo D. Aráoz de Lamadrid.*—*Pedro Aberastury.*—*Ricardo Colombres.*—*Esteban Imaz.*—*José F. Bidau.*—Dissenting: *Luis M. Boffi Boggero.*

[Dr. Boffi Boggero argued in dissent that the plaintiffs' action had been dismissed on formal grounds, and that the persons affected had not had the opportunity to reply. He argued further that the Court's solution of the case denied the principle of a full and fair defense in court.]

[On the same day, the Supreme Court of Argentina rejected an appeal of the Popular Union Party — the party of Perón — in an action aimed at getting the party on the ballot for the imminent national elections (1963-IV J.A. 106). Once again, Dr. Boffi Boggero dissented, this time taking issue with the Court's reliance on the doctrine of political questions. Dr. Boffi Boggero cited the decision of the United States Supreme Court in the case of *Baker v. Carr.*]

PROJECTED LAW CONCERNING ACTION OF AMPARO OF CONSTITUTIONAL RIGHTS AND GUARANTEES*
Argentine Institute of Legislative Studies
1960-VI J.A., sec. doct., 3 (1960)

Art. 1.—This law shall govern:

a) Every place where the Federal Government has absolute and exclusive jurisdiction;

b) Whenever the act or omission to which reference is made proceeds from a federal authority, official or employee or from anyone who performs federal duties;

c) Whenever the act or omission affects persons within branches of the Federal Government or employees of a federal authority in the performance of their duties.

---

* For comment on this draft statute, see Bielsa, *El Recurso de Amparo,* 105 La Ley 1068, 1081-85 (1962). — Ed.

Art. 2.—Every person of manifest or ideal existence [*i.e.*, individuals, corporate bodies, etc.] shall have an action of amparo against any act or omission of a public authority, official, or employee, or of a private person, which seriously harms or threatens to harm in a serious and imminent manner, a right recognized by the National Constitution.

If the holder of the injured right should be prevented from exercising the action, a third person shall be able to bring it in his name.

Art. 3.—The action shall be equally allowable against the execution of judicial decisions that are given in clear violation of the guarantee of the right to a hearing.

Art. 4.—The action of amparo shall be allowable only when no other judicial or administrative procedures exist through which the same effect could be obtained or when, if such procedures exist, circumstances make them plainly ineffective for the protection of the affected right.

Art. 5.—Whenever an action of amparo is brought against an act or omission by an authority, any judge of first instance shall be competent to hear this action at the option of the injured person, provided that the judge has jurisdiction in the place where that authority is located, or where the act took place, or where the injured person's residence is located.

When the action of amparo is brought against judicial acts, the court of the appropriate level shall be comptent, and when it is brought against an act or omission of a private person, the court of the place of the act or of the residence of the injured person shall be competent.

* * *

Art. 8.—Upon commencing the action the plaintiff shall prove, by whatever means, the facts on which the action is based.

When an action is brought because of an act or omission by an administrative authority, the plaintiff in addition shall prove by whatever means that he has appealed unsuccessfully to the authority or to the latter's hierarchical superior. Proof shall not be necessary if the harmful effects have already begun.

Art. 9.—[This article provides for notice and hearing for the defendant parties.]

Art. 10.—At any time during the instance if there exists a grave harm or if it is imminent, the court, on petition of the party, may enact measures to prevent it or stop it. In such a case the court may demand a guarantee of the plaintiff corresponding to any damage that may be caused by those measures.

Art. 11.—[This article and article 12 provide for speedy decision: All evidence is to be taken within five days after the time for the defendant to answer, and the decision is to be given within 48 hours after the completion of the taking of evidence.]

* * *

Art. 14.—Only a decision that decides on the amparo, a decree that rejects the amparo without substantiation, or a decision that goes to the request referred to in Art. 10 shall be appealable. The appeal shall have devolutive effect [*i.e.,* the higher court may remand], but the appellate court may provide, on its own motion, for the suspension of the appealed decision.

In the action of amparo against acts of judicial execution, the decision shall be unappealable. Only the appeal of reposition [returning the lawsuit to its original state] shall be allowable against a decree rejecting the amparo without substantiation or a decision that goes to the request provided for in Art. 10.

* * *

E. Emergency Limitations on Judicial Controls

ARGENTINA, CONSTITUTION (1853)
(Pan American Union translation)

* * *

Article 18.   No inhabitant of the Nation may be punished without previous trial, based on an earlier law than the date of the offense, nor tried by special commissions, nor removed from the judges designated by law before the date of the trial. No one can be compelled to testify against himself or be arrested except by virtue of a written order from a competent authority. The defense, by trial, of the person and of rights is inviolable. The residence is inviolable, as are letters, correspondence and private papers; and a law shall determine in what cases and for what reasons their search and seizure shall be allowed. The penalty of death for political offenses, all kinds of torture, and flogging, are forever abolished. The prisons of the Nation shall be healthy and clean, for the security and not for the punishment of the prisoners confined therein; and any measure that under pretext of precaution inflicts on them punishment beyond the demands of security, shall render liable the judge who authorizes it.

* * *

Article 23.   In the event of internal disorder or foreign attack endangering the operation of this Constitution and of the authorities created thereby, the Province or territory in which the disturbance of order exists shall be declared in a state of siege and the constitutional guarantees shall be suspended therein. But during such suspension the President of the Republic shall not convict or apply punishment upon his own authority. His power shall be limited, in such a case, with respect to persons, to arresting them or transferring them from one point of the Nation to another, if they do not prefer to leave Argentine territory.

Article 24.   The Congress shall promote the improvement of existing legislation in all its branches, and the establishment of trials by juries.

* * *

Article 28. The principles, guarantees, and rights recognized in the foregoing articles may not be altered by the laws that regulate their exercise.

Article 29. Congress may not confer on the National Executive, nor the provincial Legislatures on the provincial Governors extraordinary powers, nor the whole of the public authority, nor grant them acts of submission or supremacy whereby the lives, the honor, or the property of Argentinians will be at the mercy of governments or any person whatsoever. Acts of this nature shall be utterly void, and shall render those who formulate or consent to them or sign them liable to be called to account and to be punished as infamous traitors to their country.

* * *

Article 32. The Federal Congress shall not enact laws that restrict the freedom of the press or that establish federal jurisdiction over it.

Article 33. The declarations, rights, and guarantees that the Constitution enumerates shall not be construed as a denial of other rights and guarantees not enumerated, but which rise from the principle of the sovereignty of the people and from the republican form of government.

* * *

Article 75. In case of illness, absence from the Capital, death, resignation, or removal of the President, the Executive Power shall be exercised by the Vice President of the Nation. In case of the removal, death, resignation, or disability of the President and the Vice President of the Nation, the Congress shall determine what public official shall act as President until the disability is removed or a new President is elected.*

* * *

Article 86. The President of the Nation has the following powers:
* * *

15. He is commander-in-chief of all the land and naval forces of the Nation.

16. He appoints the military officers of the Nation; with the consent

---

* As an implementation of Article 75 of the Constitution, the Congress enacted Law Nº 252 of September 19, 1868:

"Article 1. In the event that the Republic is without a head, due to the lack of a President and Vice President of the Nation, the Executive Power shall be vested in, first, the provisional President of the Senate, and secondly, in the President of the Chamber of Deputies, and if both of these are lacking, in the President of the Supreme Court.

"Article 2. Thirty days prior to the termination of the period of regular sessions, each Chamber shall select its president for the purpose of this law.

"Article 3. The official called upon to exercise the national Executive Power in the cases mentioned in Article 1 shall call for a new election by the people of the Republic of a president and vice president within thirty days following his installation in office, provided the incapacity of those who held those offices is permanent.

"Article 4. The official who is to exercise the Executive Power in the cases mentioned in Article 1 of this law shall, upon assuming office, take the oath prescribed by Article 80 of the Constitution, before Congress or, if it is adjourned, before the Supreme Court of Justice."

of the Senate for the higher offices and ranks of the army and navy; and by himself, on the field of battle.

17. He disposes of the military and naval forces and attends to their organization and distribution, according to the necessities of the Nation.

18. He declares war and grants letters of marque and reprisal, with the authorization and approval of Congress.

19. He declares, with the consent of the Senate, one or more districts of the Nation in a state of siege for a limited period in the event of foreign attack. In the event of internal disorder, he has this power only when the Congress is in recess, since this is a power belonging to that body. The President exercises this power under the limitations prescribed in article 23.

* * *

Article 94. The Judicial Power of the Nation shall be vested in a Supreme Court of Justice and in such lower courts as the Congress may establish in the territory of the Nation.

Article 95. In no case may the President of the Nation exercise judicial functions, assume jurisdiction over pending cases, or reopen those decided.

---

1. De Facto Governments

The cases which follow were the judicial culmination of an unhappy chapter in recent Argentine history. The administration of President Arturo Frondizi had permitted the Peronists to enter candidates in the congressional and gubernatorial elections of March 18, 1962. When the Peronists succeeded in winning a number of important offices, leading figures among the military began to press for cancellation of the elections. President Frondizi refused either to cancel the elections or to resign from office, and after two weeks of political scrambling he was escorted by the military leadership from the presidential home in Olivos and into imprisonment. The Vice President resigned rather than pretend to succeed to the presidency under such circumstances. Under the law of "*acefalía*" (headlessness), p. 676, *supra*, the next in line of succession was Dr. José María Guido, the Provisional President of the Senate. Dr. Guido was persuaded to take the oath of office as President, and a majority of the Supreme Court agreed to receive the oath. Dr. Guido served as President until his successor, Dr. Arturo Illía, took office in late 1963. Dr. Frondizi was arrested on March 29, 1962. Dr. Guido was sworn in as President on March 31. The Supreme Court lost no time in legitimizing the new government by formal judicial decision.

PITTO
Supreme Court of Justice of the Nation
252 Fallos 177, 1962-II J.A. 514, 106 La Ley 123 (1962)

Buenos Aires, April 3, 1962.
The Court having seen the record: "Petition of Luis María Pitto."
And considering: 1st) [The Court rejected the recusation of its members.]
* * *

3d) That in the case certain acts are attacked that were performed by this Court by virtue of the powers accorded to it in arts. 1 and 4 of law 252 [swearing in the new President]. It is asked, in addition, that the Tribunal place Dr. Arturo Frondizi back in the Presidency of the Nation.

4th) That both the oath received by the then Provisional President of the Senate, Dr. José María Guido, and the signature upon his assumption of command, are strictly juridical and appropriate. The first, because he is the next in line in case of "headlessness [acefalía] of the Republic" and in the absence of the Congress (arts. 1st and 4th of the law 252 [p. 676, supra]), it being proper to understand that said acefalía comes about because of the "lack of a President and Vice President of the Nation," and that it is not the place of the Supreme Court to make any pronouncement concerning the determining causes of this "lack." And, in turn, the signature objected to has been in a form adequate to confer full validity and firmness on the assumption of the office, in conformance with art. 4th of the cited law.

5th) That in addition, this Supreme Court, on performing the acts under examination, was carrying out a function invested in it, which function presupposes the duty of assuring the subsistence and continuity of the constitutional order, the only certain barrier against anarchy or despotism (Fallos: 205: 614; 248: 189).

6th) That, by reason of the foregoing, it is proper to add that the other petitions formulated are not allowable and, further, they are beyond the jurisdiction of this Court.

Therefore, the recusation interposed is rejected and the petitioned action is declared to be not allowable. And since the terms underlined in blue on [a page of the record] are gravely harmful to the decorum with which one must act before this Court, let them be expunged by the Secretary. Let there be applied to the one who signed [the document in question], by way of disciplinary sanction ... the maximum fine provided, of 500 pesos.—*Benjamín Villegas Basavilbaso.*—*Julio Oyhanarte.*—*Pedro Aberastury.*—*Ricardo Colombres.*—*Esteban Imaz.*—*Ramón Lascano* [the Procurador General].

[Dr. Luis M. Boffi Boggero had dissented from the acceptance of the oath of office from Dr. Guido, and did not participate in the decision of this case.

Dr. Aristóbulo Aráoz de Lamadrid, who had agreed with the majority to accept the oath of office from Dr. Guido, also did not participate in this case.]

FRONDIZI
Federal Chamber of the Capital (Penal Division)
1962-IV J.A. 404, 108 La Ley 682 (1962)

2d Instance.—Buenos Aires, June 15, 1962. [This is a proceeding in habeas corpus to obtain the release of Dr. Arturo Frondizi. From the time he was detained until the elections of July, 1963, Dr. Frondizi was kept under arrest. Both the court of 1st Instance and this Court rejected the petition for habeas corpus. In the course of its opinion, signed by all three judges, the Chamber made the following remarks. The opening paragraph refers to the *Pitto* case.]

. . . Such reasons, having been proclaimed by the highest tribunal of justice of the country upon fulfilling the provisions of art. 4, law 252, and exercising that high function, could be accepted as sufficient to reject the attack formulated by the appellants, as the judge of 1st Instance did in the appealed decision.

. . . In the judgment of this tribunal, nevertheless, the solution provided by law 252 for the case of *acefalía* of the National Executive only functions validly when there is given one of the suppositions contemplated in art. 75, Nat. Const.: sickness, absence from the Capital, death, resignation, or removal. It is impossible to hold, for obvious reasons . . . that the rule of our fundamental law foresees and permits the case of a removal by force, such as that presently seen in our country; but rather the rule refers to the removal by impeachment [*juicio político*] referred to by arts. 45, 51 and 52.

. . . The inapplicability of law 252 still does not deprive Dr. José María Guido of a sufficiently valid title to carry out the office of President of the Nation and consequently to act since such titles and their full validity derive from a rule, incorporated since ancient times into Argentine public law. In conformance with that rule, governments constituted in the country as a consequence of some act of force, and which find themselves in fact capable "of insuring the peace and order of the Nation, and therefore of protecting the liberty, life and property of persons" and which declare, in addition, their purpose of maintaining "the supremacy of the Constitution and other laws of the country," have sufficient title to "carry out validly the acts necessary for the fulfillment of the ends pursued" (Sup. Ct., Fallos, 158, 290). And based on this original situation of fact and in conformity with that jurisprudential precedent, the action of the present National Executive is also validated. In respect to that action the above-noted conditions are present and the government's titles, as the Supreme Court of the Nation said on the noted occasion, "cannot be judicially questioned with success by anyone," which leads, logically, to the recognition of full validity of the Executive's acts when they are performed within the orbit of its competence, to examine which the Judicial Branch is functioning, in the fullness of its powers.

. . . Whether one or another of the expounded reasons be accepted as the more appropriate ground, and as it is a matter in the present action of examining only the validity of an act of exclusive jurisdiction of the President of the Nation, it is proper to conclude that the current detention of Dr. Arturo Frondizi under decree 2887/62 is fully constitutional.

SANCHEZ VIAMONTE
Federal Chamber of the Capital (Penal Division)
1963-III J.A. 357, 111 La Ley 789 (1962)

2d Instance.—Buenos Aires, November 9, 1962.—Considering: That Dr. Carlos Sánchez Viamonte, . . . invoking his status as a member of the Argentine Socialist Party, asks protection [amparo] of his political liberty and his right to vote, both of which proceed from the representative form adopted for the Government of the Argentine Nation through art. 1 of the National Constitution. He asks this protection on the ground that the Executive Power affected that liberty and that right when it promulgated decrees 7162 and 7163 of this year. The decrees relate, respectively, to a new statute on political parties and the establishment of electoral courts, in such a way — he maintains — that they amount to a notorious usurpation of the constitutional prerogatives of Congress, for which reason they are unconstitutional "since they signify the destruction of the republican form of government and the annulment of the separation of powers."

That . . . the judge of 1st Instance rejected the amparo, the action having come to the attention of this tribunal by virtue of the appeal brought by the plaintiff . . . .

[The plaintiff does not claim that the decrees are invalid for reasons of substance, but only that they were issued by a government which lacked the power to issue them, *i.e.,* the Guido government.]

That, the extent of the requested amparo so defined . . ., its non-allowability is evident, since one cannot see how, for the sole reason of the origin of certain rules, concrete damage may be caused which might be rectified only through the summary means attempted by the appellant.

That, nevertheless, and accepting for argument the position maintained by the appellant that serious damage was caused to the rights mentioned above, still in the judgment of this tribunal it is not to be doubted that the present Executive Power is invested with the authority to issue the mentioned decree, since, as this chamber maintained last June 15 in the case of Arturo Frondizi (habeas corpus), it is an Executive Power de facto, sufficiently entitled to "carry out validly the necessary acts for the fulfillment of the ends pursued." Among those acts should be included, obviously, the enactment of rules that it deems proper for the purpose of "offering to the people of the Republic, to whom it is answerable, the conditions necessary for them to elect their constitutional agents in completely unobjectionable elections and with participation of democratic and democratically organized political parties," as one of the "whereas" paragraphs of decree 7162 affirmed.

For these considerations, the appealed decision is affirmed, rejecting, with costs, the amparo sought . . . by Dr. Carlos Sánchez Viamonte, with the costs of this instance in addition.—*Hernán Juárez Peñalva.—Enrique Ramos Mejía.—Ambrosio Romero Carranza.*

FOURNIER, COMMENT
in GOVERNMENT UNDER LAW*
at 83, 85 (Sutherland ed. 1956)

Finally, it might be interesting for you to know about a precedent that was recently established in my country [Costa Rica] in regard to these matters. In 1948, because of a revolution that we had against the Communists, the previous Constitution could not be enforced any more. The constitutional order had been broken. Then there was no constitution, and a *de facto* government was established. But that *de facto* government wished to limit its own authority and issued a decree declaring that the civil liberties chapter would remain in force until the new constitution was made. Then, some months after, one of the decrees of the same *de facto* government was challenged by somebody before the Supreme Court as unconstitutional. The government made the defense saying that it could not be unconstitutional because there wasn't any constitution. But the Supreme Court declared that as long as a government declares that there are certain fundamental principles of law which are superior, and that government had so declared, those principles were over any other law or decree, even though that second decree was coming from the same authority which had established its own self-limitations, and the court declared that second decree of the *de facto* government unconstitutional.

IRIZARRY Y PUENTE, THE NATURE AND POWERS OF A
"DE FACTO" GOVERNMENT IN LATIN AMERICA
30 TUL. L. REV.** 15, 33-36, 66-68 (1955)

. . . In two of the most important countries of Latin America, *de facto* governments have adopted the practice of asking the Supreme Court for recognition. The year 1930 was one of political crisis in Argentina. In September of that year, General José F. Uriburu sent a note to the Federal Supreme Court, informing it that he had established "a provisional government for the Nation" as a result of the triumphant revolution of the 6th of that month. The Court, on this as on other occasions, made its position known by means of an Accord (*Acordada*). In answer to General Uriburu's note, the Court said:

> "This government is in possession of the military and police forces necessary to insure the peace and order of the Nation, and therefore to protect the liberty, life and property of persons, and has declared, moreover, in public acts, that it will, in exercising power, maintain the supremacy of the Constitution and other laws of the country.
> "Such antecedents characterize, without doubt, a *de facto* government with regard to its organization, and of the nature of which the officials who form it at present or who may be appointed hereafter, participate, with all the consequences of the doctrine of *de facto* governments with respect to the possibility of accomplishing validly the acts necessary to carry out the purposes that it has in mind."

The Court went on to add that the provisional government just organized in the country was "a *de facto* government whose title cannot be judicially questioned with success by anyone, insofar as it exercises administrative and political functions derived from its possession of force as a measure of order and social security."

* * *

The practice of the Argentine and Brasilian Supreme Courts is open to serious criticism.

(1) The note or communication of a Provisional Government is not a judicial case, controversy or suit between parties, which is all that the Courts are authorized to determine according to the Constitutions and laws of their respective countries. The notes of these governments do not seek merely to bring a *fait accompli* to the attention of the Courts, but they seek a recognition by the Courts of such governments, that is, to put their "constitutional seal" of approval upon them through a declaration outside the scope of a judicial proceeding.

(2) The Courts cannot invoke a single constitutional or statutory provision in support of the practice of recognizing *de facto* governments. All they have been able to say is that:

> "It is within the scope of the functions of this Court to determine whether a government *de facto* is or is not in possession of the force necessary to maintain order and peace, for the purpose, in case it is, to state — for good of order and peace — that the credentials of said authority cannot be *judicially questioned* with success, and that just because a government

> *de facto* is involved, no impairment in the *judicial* protection of institutional principles and individual rights will be tolerated (Resolutions of September 10, 1930, and of June 7, 1943). But all opinions of a general political character about the ulterior conduct of said *de facto* authority are absolutely outside the function mentioned, as are also, according to the invariable doctrine of this Court, all questions of this character."

In other words, the Courts have undertaken to inquire into the strictly *political* question of the *de facto* existence of these governments and their possession of force, for the purpose of saying that their credentials cannot be successfully questioned in court by anyone. We feel justified in defending this practice only to the extent that the Courts have attempted to uphold a principle of juridical order by insisting on judicial control in the inevitable chaos of any revolution.

(3) The Courts have been drawn by the *de facto* governments into the orbit of national politics, contrary to their own traditional position that questions of a general political character are outside the scope of the Court's function. Their decisions in all these cases, to the effect that the Provisional Government is "a *de facto* government with respect to its organization," and "that its title cannot be judicially questioned," are strictly political. If the Courts have authority to declare at what stage a revolutionary government becomes *de facto,* the reverse must be equally true: they should have authority to withdraw recognition at that stage in a government's life when it fails to live up to the conditions that the Courts think are essential to a *de facto* status, such as the failure to observe "institutional principles and individual rights." Then, again, if the Courts are convinced that their function is to ascertain whether a government *de facto* is or is not in possession of the force necessary to maintain peace and order for the purpose of saying "that the credentials of said authority cannot be *questioned judicially* with success," they should also have authority to determine the stage at which a *de jure* government lacks that force, and to declare its credentials void.

The Courts have been lured onto dangerous ground and into questionable doctrine, fraught with ominous consequences for the independence of the Judiciary.[116]

---

[116] To illustrate: the impeachment proceedings brought by the Peronista Congress against certain members of the Supreme Court of Argentina in 1946, included, among others, the following specifications of charges: (I) taking part "in political matters, through the Accords of 1930 and 1943, which legalized the *de facto* governments, and which were issued as a general rule, without a proceeding or judicial case." 158 Fallos 290; 196 Fallos 5; (II) assuming "powers of a political nature, beyond the judicial function, to control and obstruct the fulfillment of the social ends of the revolution of 1943, and rendering judgments that involve political aims." J.A. 1946-I-89; (III) assuming "political functions in nullifying the creation of the Court of Appeals of Chaco." 201 Fallos 239; (IV) assuming "politico-administrative functions in setting aside the dismissal of judges, as ordered by the revolutionary government of 1943." 201 Fallos 245, J.A. 1945-II-372; (VII) "making up the annual list of co-judges of the Supreme Court from lawyers for foreign capitalism or who belong to the ruling class;" (XII) passing "on the constitutional question raised concerning the creation of the Labor Courts of the Federal Capital, thereby injuring the working classes by such delay." 48

The view that the Judiciary retains its *de jure* status in the *de facto* government, which we might call the "split-personality" theory of government, would lead to unavoidable conflicts between the *de facto* authorities and the Judiciary, that is, between the surviving organ of a defunct constitutional and legal order and a triumphant revolutionary legal philosophy seeking to alter the political and social structure of the State. This is precisely what brought on the conflict between the courts and the *de facto* authorities. This conflict was mild at first, when only political factors were involved, but it grew more serious later, as revolutionary movements accented profound social changes, as in Argentina during the 1930-1947 era. During that period the Supreme Court of Argentina took the position that it was the arbiter of the scope of the *de facto* government's powers, which were to be determined in the light of the National Constitution, and proceeded to hold that the *de facto* government was limited to acts necessary to keep the government functioning within the purview of the Constitution and to carry out the political purposes of the revolution. Consequently, it declared many of the decree-laws of the early *de facto* governments, that did not meet these conditions, unconstitutional in tax, criminal, judicial reorganization, wages and labor, and other matters. It soon became evident, especially as the social revolution under Perón got under way, that the limitations laid down by the Court would seriously obstruct the program of the revolution, since many of its objectives ran counter to the Constitution of 1853, which was then in force. Thus it is obvious that political considerations make it impossible to consider the Judiciary as other than a branch of the *de facto* government.

The tenure of office of the Judiciary in a *de jure* government should be presumed to have been voided by the fall of that government, and its tacit appointment by the *de facto* government should be presumed when it is allowed to continue in office as an agency of that government. The Judiciary's new title to office, though colorable, is sufficient for the extraordinary situation under which a *de facto* government functions, until its title is confirmed by the succeeding constitutional government.

We may infer from the fact that the Judiciary now admits that the powers of a *de facto* government are not limited by the Constitution, and that it upholds the validity of executive, legislative and judicial acts of *de facto* governments, that it no longer claims that the judicial function under a *de facto* government is to safe-guard institutional principles and individual rights. This change can be explained only on the theory that the Judiciary now regards itself as a *de facto* organ of a *de facto* government, required by the force of

---

La Ley 605. The judgment of the Senate, sitting as a Tribunal, was: "Article 1. To dismiss from office the following members of the Supreme Court of Justice of the Nation: Antonio Sagarna, Francisco Ramos Mejía, Benito A. Mazar Anchorena, and Attorney General of the Nation, Juan Alvarez." Mariano J. Drago, El juicio político como instrumento de opresión (Buenos Aires, 1947) 204-205. See González Roura, El "Affaire" de la Corte Suprema Argentina (Buenos Aires, 1950) 89-113.

events to concur in the policy of that government, notwithstanding any constitutional limitations, assuming that the Constitution remains in effect during the *de facto* period, that restrict the powers of government.

As long as the Judiciary claimed *de jure* status and its mission was to protect institutional principles, it could and did: (a) uphold the constitution, (b) define the limits of a *de facto* government, and (c) declare decree-laws unconstitutional. When it decided that a *de facto* government had legislative powers *in the measure necessary to govern* and that it did not have authority to declare decree-laws unconstitutional *by reason of their origin*, the Judiciary admitted, by implication: (a) that it is not, in the abnormal situation created by a revolutionary change, the vindicator of institutional principles of government and individual rights, (b) that it could not interfere with or obstruct the program of the revolution, (c) that it had become, qualitatively, a *de facto* agency of a *de facto* government, and (d) that the profession of a *de facto* government to support the Constitution, if that profession has been made, has become meaningless, and the Constitution itself non-existent for practical purposes.

In the case of Zarrain, 1959-VI J.A. 111 (1959), the plaintiff sought a writ of habeas corpus to free him from a three-year sentence for the crime of fraud. He asserted, and the Supreme Court of Argentina assumed for argument, that two of the three judges of the criminal Chamber of the Capital (the court of 2d Instance which had confirmed his sentence) had been "recommissioned" by the de facto government that succeeded the Perón government, without taking a new oath of office. The relevant statute required a new oath in cases of "new designations" of officers of the national government, including federal judges. The plaintiff argued that he had been convicted by judges who lacked jurisdiction.

The Supreme Court rejected this argument in an alternative holding. (The other ground was that habeas corpus was not the proper remedy; the Court followed its established doctrine, recently honored in the breach in the United States, that habeas corpus is not an appropriate substitute for appeal.) Four of the justices agreed that the judges who confirmed the plaintiff's sentence were de facto judges, and that "a de facto [governmental] agency, within the scope of its assumed function, possesses powers equivalent to those of the correlative de jure agency." The Court added that the two challenged judges, who had served as de jure judges during the period before the de facto government took office, were not "newly designated," but were simply continuing in office, so that no new oath was required.

LUTHER v. BORDEN
Supreme Court of the United States
7 How. 1, 12 L. Ed. 581 (1848)

These two cases came up from the Circuit Court of the United States for the District of Rhode Island, the former by a writ of error, and the latter by a certificate of division in opinion. . . . The jury [in the first case], under the rulings of the court, found a verdict for the defendants.

MR. CHIEF JUSTICE TANEY delivered the opinion of the court.

This case has arisen out of the unfortunate political differences which agitated the people of Rhode Island in 1841 and 1842 [Dorr's Rebellion — Ed.].

It is an action of trespass brought by Martin Luther, the plaintiff in error, against Luther M. Borden and other defendants, in the Circuit Court of the United States for the District of Rhode Island, for breaking and entering the plaintiff's house. The defendants justify upon the ground that large numbers of men were assembled in different parts of the State for the purpose of over-throwing the government by military force, and were actually levying war upon the State; that, in order to defend itself from this insurrection, the State was declared by competent authority to be under martial law; that the plaintiff was engaged in the insurrection; and that the defendants, being in the military service of the State, by command of their superior officer, broke and entered the house and searched the rooms for the plaintiff, who was supposed to be there concealed, in order to arrest him, doing as little damage as possible. The plaintiff replied, that the trespass was committed by the defendants of their own proper wrong, and without any such cause; and upon the issue joined on this replication, the parties proceeded to trial. . . . The existence and authority of the government under which the defendants acted, was called in question; and the plaintiff insists, that, before the acts complained of were committed, that government had been displaced and annulled by the people of Rhode Island, and that the plaintiff was engaged in supporting the lawful authority of the State, and the defendants themselves were in arms against it. . . .

The fourth section of the fourth article of the Constitution of the United States provides that the United States shall guarantee to every state in the Union a republican form of government, and shall protect each of them against invasion; and on the application of the legislature or of the executive (when the legislature cannot be convened) against domestic violence.

Under this article of the Constitution it rests with Congress to decide what Government is the established one in a State. For as the United States guarantee to each State a republican government, Congress must necessarily decide what government is established in the State before it can determine whether it is republican or not. And when the senators and representatives of a State are admitted into the councils of the Union, the authority of the government under which they are appointed, as well as its republican character, is recognized by the proper constitutional authority. And its decision is binding on every other department of the government, and could not be questioned in a judicial tribunal. It is true that the contest in this case did not last long enough to bring the matter to this issue; and as no senators or representatives were elected under the authority of the government of which Mr. Dorr was the head, Congress was not called upon to decide the controversy. Yet the right to decide is placed there, and not in the courts.

So, too, as relates to the clause in the above-mentioned article of the Constitution, providing for cases of domestic violence. It rested with Congress, too, to determine upon the means proper to be adopted to fulfill this guarantee. They might, if they had deemed it most advisable to do so, have placed it in the power of a court to decide when the contingency had happened which required the federal government to interfere. But Congress thought otherwise, and no doubt wisely; and by the act of February 28, 1795, provided, that, "in case of an insurrection in any state against the government thereof, it shall be lawful for the President of the United States, on application of the legislature of such State or of the Executive, when the legislature cannot be convened, to call forth such number of militia of any other State or States, as may be applied for, as he may judge sufficient to suppress such insurrection."

By this act, the power of deciding whether the exigency had arisen upon which the government of the United States is bound to interfere, is given to the President. He is to act upon the application of the legislature, or of the executive, and consequently he must determine what body of men constitute the legislature, and who is the governor, before he can act. The fact that both parties claim the right to the government, cannot alter the case, for both cannot be entitled to it. If there is an armed conflict, like the one of which we are speaking, it is a case of domestic violence, and one of the parties must be in insurrection against the lawful government. And the President must, of necessity, decide which is the government, and which party is unlawfully arrayed against it, before he can perform the duty imposed upon him by the act of Congress.

After the President has acted and called out the militia, is a Circuit Court of the United States authorized to inquire whether his decision was right? Could the court, while the parties were actually contending in arms for the possession of the government, call witnesses before it, and inquire which party represented a majority of the people? If it could, then it would become the duty of the court (provided it came to the conclusion that the President had decided incorrectly) to discharge those who were arrested or detained by the troops in the service of the United States, or the government which the President was endeavoring to maintain. If the judicial power extends so far, the guarantee contained in the constitution of the United States is a guarantee of anarchy, and not of order. Yet if this right does not reside in the courts when the conflict is raging — if the judicial power is, at that time, bound to follow the decision of the political, it must be equally bound when the contest is over.

It cannot, when peace is restored, punish as offenses and crimes the acts which it before recognized, and was bound to recognize, as lawful.

It is true that in this case the militia were not called out by the President. But upon the application of the governor under the charter government, the President recognized him as the executive power of the State, and took measures to call out the militia to support his authority, if it should be found necessary for the general government to interfere; and it is admitted in the argument that it was the knowledge of this decision that put an end to the armed opposition to the charter government, and prevented any further efforts to establish by force the proposed constitution. The interference of the President, therefore, by announcing his determination, was as effectual as if the militia had been assembled under his orders. And it should be equally authoritative. For certainly no court of the United States, with a knowledge of this decision, would have been justified in recognizing the opposing party as the lawful government, or in treating as wrong-doers or insurgents the officers of the government which the President had recognized, and was prepared to support by an armed force. In the case of foreign nations, the government acknowledged by the President is always recognized in the courts of justice. And this principle has been applied by the act of Congress to the sovereign States of the Union.

It is said that this power in the President is dangerous to liberty, and may be abused. All power may be abused if placed in unworthy hands. But it would be difficult, we think, to point out any other hands in which this power would be more safe, and at the same time equally effectual. When citizens of the same State are in arms against each other, and the constituted authorities unable to execute the laws, the interposition of the United States must be prompt, or it is of little value. The ordinary course of proceedings in courts of justice would be utterly unfit for the crisis. And the elevated office of the President, chosen as he is by the people of the United States, and the high responsibility he could not fail to feel when acting in a case of so much moment, appear to furnish as strong safeguards against a wilful abuse of power as human prudence and foresight could well provide. At all events, it is conferred upon him by the Constitution and laws of the United States, and must, therefore, be respected and enforced in its judicial tribunals.

A question very similar to this arose in the case of Martin v. Mott, 12 Wheat. 29-31. The first clause of the first section of the act of February 28, 1795, of which we have been speaking, authorizes the President to call out the militia to repel invasion. It is the second clause in the same section which authorizes the call to suppress an insurrection against a State government. The power given to the President in each case is the same, with this difference only, that it cannot be exercised by him in the latter case, except upon the application of the legislature or executive of the State. The case above mentioned arose out of a call made by the President, by virtue of the power conferred by the first clause; and the court said that "whenever a statute gives a discretionary power to any person, to be exercised by him upon his own opinion of certain facts, it is a sound rule of construction that the statute constitutes him the sole and exclusive judge of the existence of those facts." The grounds upon which that opinion is maintained are set forth in the report, and, we think, are conclusive. The same principle applies to the case now before the court. Undoubtedly, if the President, in exercising this power shall fall into error, or invade the rights of the People of the State, it would be in the power of Congress to apply the proper remedy. But the courts must administer the law as they find it. . . .

Much of the argument on the part of the plaintiff turned upon political rights and political questions, upon which the court has been urged to express an opinion. We decline doing so. The high power has been conferred on this court of passing judgment upon the acts of the State sovereignties, and of the legislative and executive branches of the federal government, and of determining whether they are beyond the limits of power marked out for them respectively by the Constitution of the United States. This tribunal, therefore, should be the last to overstep the boundaries which limit its own jurisdiction. And while it should always be ready to meet any question confined to it by the Constitution, it is equally its duty not to pass beyond its appropriate sphere of action, and to take care not to involve itself in discussions which properly belong to other forums. No one, we believe, has ever doubted the proposition, that, according to the institutions of this country, the sovereignty in every State resides in the people of the State, and that they may alter and change their form of government at their own pleasure. But whether they have changed it or not, by abolishing an old government, and establishing a new one in its place, is a question to be settled by the political power. And when that power has decided, the courts are bound to take notice of its decision, and to follow it.

The judgment of the Circuit Court must, therefore, be affimed.

[MR. JUSTICE WOODBURY dissented.]

In November 1946, Eugene Talmadge was elected Governor of Georgia. Mr. Talmadge died some seven weeks later, before the time for him to take office. The Georgia legislature then met to inspect the election returns, after which the legislature declared Herman Talmadge, Eugene Talmadge's son, elected Governor; the legislature acted under the terms of the state constitution, which gave it the power to elect a Governor by majority vote in the event that no "person" should have a majority of votes upon the inspection of the returns. That election was required to be made from among persons who had received votes, and it was proved that Herman Talmadge had received some 675 write-in votes. Herman Talmadge took the oath of office, and asserted that he was the Governor.

The outgoing Governor, Ellis Arnall, refused to vacate office, relying on the state constitutional provision which provided for the Governor to hold office until his successor was installed. When the incoming Lieutenant Governor, M. E. Thompson, took office, Governor Arnall resigned. Meanwhile, he had commenced an action against Herman Talmadge for a declaratory judgment as to the title to the office of Governor, and for an injunction against any invasion of the office. When Arnall resigned, Thompson was sworn in as Governor and moved to be substituted in Arnall's place. The motion was denied, and a general demurrer to Arnall's original petition was sustained. Arnall and Thompson appealed, and the case was argued along with an original action brought by Thompson for a mandamus to require certain state officials to give him information to which the Governor was by law entitled.

The Georgia Supreme Court, rejecting the argument of Herman Talmadge that the question was political and non-justiciable, reversed the trial court in the principal action, and stated that Thompson was "now entitled to perform all of the duties and exercise all the authority which by the constitution and laws are imposed upon the Governor of this State." The court found authority to act in the general language of the Georgia Constitution establishing the judicial power. Thompson v. Talmadge, 41 S.E.2d 883 (Ga. 1947). See Rutledge, *When is a Political Question Justiciable?*, 9 GA. B.J. 394 (1947), for a critical discussion of the decision.

---

2. The State of Siege and Martial Law

INTER-AMERICAN COMMISSION ON HUMAN RIGHTS (OAS), PRELIMINARY STUDY OF THE STATE OF SIEGE AND THE PROTECTION OF HUMAN RIGHTS IN THE AMERICAS* 1, 5-8 (1963)

During the decade 1950-1960, there were over one hundred occasions of the declaration or extension of a state of siege in the American states. During this period, the continent knew neither external war nor armed invasion. . . .

    * * *

The state of siege is a constitutional measure, designed to provide for the security of the state in times of emergency due to external attack or serious disturbances of public order which the government is unable to control by ordinary measures. It sanctions the temporary granting of extraordinary powers to the executive branch of government and permits the suspension or restriction of certain constitutional rights and liberties of the individual. In practice,

---

* Copyright Ⓒ, Pan American Union, reprinted by permission.

the institution suspends the separation of powers and temporarily invests the executive with discretionary powers ordinarily pertaining to the legislative and judicial branches. The execution of those powers must directly pertain to the maintenance of the public order. Several related institutions such as the state of assembly, state of emergency, state of national defense, or state of alarm, are essentially variations of the state of siege, and all will be treated here under the single generic term.

Although some commentators trace its origin to the time of the Roman Empire, in 501 A.D., when governmental powers were increased in the face of real emergencies, its modern history is generally dated to the French Revolution, to a law of July, 1791. As explained by the French Assembly, that law envisaged three different conditions: a state of peace, a state of war, and a state of siege. In the first situation, civilian authorities were completely independent of the military; in the second situation, the state of war, the civilian cooperated with the military; in the third, siege, the military dominated the civilian authority. Accordingly, siege was distinct from and more serious than the state of war and related directly to an armed attack on the territory of the nation. Article 11 of the original French law specified that the siege existed, "not only from the moment in which the enemy attacks commenced, but as soon as communications are severed, as a result of the encirclement, . . . to a distance of 1,800 *toises*."

Napoleon, amending the French Constitution in 1815, added an important provision clarifying the declaration of the state of siege. It stated that, "no place, no part of the territory can be declared in state of siege, except in the case of foreign invasion or civil disturbances. . . . In the first instance, the declaration should be made by an Act of Government . . . . In the second instance . . . it can only be declared by law."

Thus, historically, the state of siege is intimately related to the necessities of armed battle carried on within the territory of one of the warring parties. It was to be invoked only when a city or locale is under actual siege, or, as described by Sánchez Viamonte, "only in the case of the gravest risk which could threaten a nation . . . . The state of siege is so serious a measure that it is not . . . authorized in case of war but when there is a foreign attack within our territory." Its use against civil disturbances, as specified in the Napoleonic amendment, implied its use against the very people whom the government is supposed to represent. For a democracy, this raises a myriad of problems. Some of these problems were provided for at that time by allowing it to be declared only by law in case of internal disturbance, that is, only with the approval of the people's own representatives.

     * * *

The modern state of siege bears but little resemblance to its historical precedent. Carlos Sánchez Viamonte points out the eclectic nature of the modern Latin American institution which combines the French and American concept [suspension of habeas corpus] and amplifies both of them by extending, sometimes without limit, the right to suspend specific constitutional guarantees. What exists in Latin America today, in many respects, appears to be a unique institution. It is sanctioned in the constitution for everything from epidemics and public calamities to "dangers to the national sovereignty." It has apparently evolved to serve entirely new purposes, with a wholly new juridical content. . . .

KENNEDY, MEXICANS RENEW A LEGAL DISPUTE
N.Y. Times,* February 26, 1961, p. 32, col. 1

MEXICO CITY, Feb. 23 — One of this country's most controversial laws is coming under renewed attack as a result of a Mexican Supreme Court decision this week.

The law is Article 145 of the Federal Penal Code. It is popularly known as the Law of Social Dissolution. Under it David Alfaro Siqueiros, the muralist, was arrested last summer, and Demetrio Vallejo Martínez, a railroad labor leader, was arrested in 1959. They are being held without trial.

The law was originally passed in 1941 as a measure to counteract Nazi and Fascist activities in Mexico. At the end of World War II it was allowed to go into disuse but was resurrected in 1951 in the last part of the Administration of President Miguel Alemán. It was not put to its present use, however, until 1958, when it was invoked under the Administration of President Adolfo Ruiz Cortines in a strike of primary-school teachers.

Othon Salazar, head of the teachers' union, was arrested under the law. He was released on order of President Adolfo López Mateos when the President took office, in December, 1958.

Application of Law
Originally the law applied to the diffusion and activation by foreign governments of ideas considered inimical to the sovereignty of Mexico.

In 1951, however, the law was altered and was directed primarily toward incitement to rebellion, disunity and "the placing of obstacles to the legitimate aim of the Government."

In this reformed version, it was emphasized, the article applied to Mexican nationals as well as to foreigners. One lawyer, commenting on the reformed statute declared: "It is extremely ambiguous in terminology, but the most unfortunate part is that this ambiguity is subject solely to the interpretation of the state."

Ever since its enforcement the law has been under severe attack by constitutional lawyers and Leftist and Liberal labor leaders.

The attacks appear to have become more intense after the Supreme Court's unanimous ruling this week that the law is valid and constitutional. The court upheld a lower-court ruling in the case of Antonio Gómez Rodríguez, a member of the Railway Workers Union.

The unionist was convicted of threatening nonunion railway workers to prevent their return to work during a strike and of obscuring railway signals.

The Supreme Court ruled that the lower court was correct in interpreting this as a crime within the Social Dissolution Law. Heretofore the law was employed almost solely for the arrest of leaders and agitators in riots and other civic disorders.

Leading constitutional and criminal lawyers returned to their drive against the law this week immediately following the Supreme Court decision. The consensus was that the Supreme Court had evaded the questions of law in its consideration and had upheld the lower court merely on the basis of its conviction for a common crime.

DIARIOS "NORTE" Y "VOZ PERONISTA"
Supreme Court of Justice of the Nation (Argentina)
244 Fallos 59, 1959-VI J.A. 334 (1959)

Buenos Aires, June 15, 1959. Considering: That, according to the record, the attorney of Alberto Manuel Campos, attributing to the latter the ownership of the weeklies "Norte" and "Voz Peronista," brought an action of amparo in the court of 1st Instance, the Federal Criminal and Correctional Court No. 2 of the Capital. He maintained that the Directorate of Federal Coordination violated the constitutional guarantees of arts. 14, 17 and 18 of the National Constitution when it seized editions and prevented publication of the mentioned weeklies by setting up "police supervision" at the press named "The Standard," Calle Rivadavia 831 of this Capital. And, basing his request on the precepts of the same articles of the Constitution, he asked that the restrictions imposed on his client's right be declared ineffective.

[The federal police had closed down the two weeklies and seized editions of them on orders of the national Executive Power, given during a state of siege.]

That the amparo complaint filed was denied in all its parts by the federal judge of 1st Instance. When the proper appeal was made, the court of 2d Instance affirmed the appealed decision with respect to the seizure of the weeklies but decided to revoke it in regard to the police supervision of the press, "The Standard." . . .

That against the decision of 2d Instance, the plaintiff, invoking the aforementioned constitutional precepts, brought an extraordinary appeal. This appeal was granted to him, inasmuch as the *procurador fiscal* of the chamber gave his consent.

That with respect to the circumstances related above, the only question submitted for consideration and decision by the tribunal is that concerning the seizure of the copies of the periodicals, ownership of which is alleged by the appellant.

That, in this respect, the elements of judgment in the case are enough to prove the full validity of the questioned measures.

That, in fact, the seizure under consideration here was carried out in accordance with an order of the Executive Power intended to prevent the circulation of publications "of an insurrectional nature, which stimulate or foment strikes declared illegal, or that in any way may constitute a cause for disturbance of the general calm and public order." The competent authority, using powers that were proper and subject to the judicial control of reasonableness, considered that among those publications were included the ones giving rise to the present appeal. In such conditions, taking account of the suspension of individual guarantees resulting from decree No. 9764 of 1958 and laws No. 14,774 and 14,785 in accordance with art. 23 of the National Constitution, and complying with the reasons expressed by the members of this Court in Sofía, 1959-VI J.A. 98 (1959), ... which are incorporated herein for the sake of brevity, it does not appear doubtful that the impugned act of seizure is included within the scope of the exclusive powers of the Executive Power. And in this case, the seizure represents only a valid, that is, a reasonable manifestation of the police power. In consideration of the facts of the case and in view of the objective fact of the existence of publications classified as "insurrectional," the seizure constituted an adequate and proper means for the attainment of the goals of the aforementioned laws.

On its merits, the *procurador general* having made his statement, the appealed sentence is affirmed insofar as the appellant made it material.—*Alfredo Orgaz.—Aristóbulo D. Aráoz de Lamadrid.—Luis M. Boffi Boggero.—Julio Oyhanarte.*

The *Sofía* case, relied on by the Supreme Court in the foregoing opinion, is a leading Argentine case on the subject of the suspension of constitutional guarantees during a state of siege. In that case, the chief of the Federal Police had refused a license to the Argentine League for the Rights of Man to hold a public meeting in a Buenos Aires theater to "analyze the present situation in Paraguay, regarding the state of the rights of man." The refusal was based on the existence of a state of siege, which had been declared throughout Argentina as a result of a series of "insurrectional" strikes, led by Peronist-dominated unions against the government that had succeeded Perón. The judge of 1st

Instance denied the amparo sought by the League, and the Federal Penal Chamber of the Capital reversed, all within eight days after the refusal of the license.

On appeal, the Supreme Court, by a vote of 3-2, reversed once again, denying the League's right to amparo. The Court held, following established jurisprudence, that the decision to declare a state of siege was a political one, not susceptible to judicial review. The two opinions for the majority, however, agreed that during a state of siege the courts did have the power to review particular acts of the Executive branch, to determine whether they were, in the language of one opinion, "clearly and obviously unreasonable, [involving] methods that have no relation at all to the purposes of art. 23." The fact that the state of siege was originally declared with respect to labor unrest did not prevent the Court from taking notice of a more general political unrest which, the majority judges held, justified the suspension of the political rights which the League sought to exercise.

The two dissenting judges relied on the exceptional nature of the state of siege to argue that the suspension of guaranteess must be closely related to the particular circumstances which motivated the declaration of the state of siege. That relation, they argued, was not present on the facts of the *Sofía* case.

What effect does the requirement of "reasonableness" of Executive action during a state of siege have on the substantive content of constitutional rights? On the role of the judiciary in maintaining those rights? Are these two questions different?

TROSSI
Supreme Court of Justice of the Nation (Argentina)
247 Fallos 528 (1960)

Buenos Aires, August 26, 1960. [Twenty-eight plaintiffs sought release from detention by means of habeas corpus. They had been detained by the Executive under the terms of an act of Congress declaring a state of siege. The court of 1st Instance denied their petition.]

Considering: 1st) [In this extraordinary appeal], the appellants' counsel maintains that the decision of the judge of 1st instance infringes arts. 14, 14 bis, 18, 23 and 29 of the Fundamental Law, because there is no demonstration that the persons detained, in whose favor the present habeas corpus was filed, "were found in situations such as those foreseen by art. 23 of the Constitution," so that the arrests ordered in this case violate the constitutional precepts mentioned. He argues, also, the unconstitutionality of law 14,785 [declaring the state of siege].

2d) That, as the record shows, the persons whose liberty is sought by means of the prosecution of this action have been detained by order of the

President of the Nation, to "assure tranquility" and by virtue of the powers "conferred on him by the state of siege" [citation to the record].

3d)   That, taking account of this fact, the substantial impropriety of the appeal under examination is manifest, since, as has been consistently decided, in circumstances of the nature described judges are prohibited from substituting themselves for the President of the Nation in considering the truth or error, the justice or injustice of transitory measures of defense which he considers necessary to adopt in the exercise of the powers which art. 23 of the Constitution gives him exclusively. (Fallos: 243:504 and cases there cited.)

4th)   That neither can we accept the opposition to law 14,785, not only because that opposition lacks the foundation required by art. 15 of law 48, but also because the act in which the Congress declared the existence of the state of siege is, in itself, not justiciable. (Decisions cited in the foregoing paragraph.)

On its merits, and the *Procurador General* having stated his opinion, the appealed decision is affirmed insofar as it has been the subject matter of the extraordinary appeal.—*Benjamín Villegas Basavilbaso.—Aristóbulo D. Aráoz de Lamadrid.—Julio Oyhanarte.—Pedro Aberastury.—Ricardo Colombres.*

THE CASE OF RADIO RIVADAVIA

During the night of August 12, 1961, revolutionaries seized control of one of the centers of the Argentine National Radio. They broadcast over the network a revolutionary message. This message was carried not only by various government stations, but also by two privately-owned stations: channel LS4, called Radio Porteña, and channel LS5, Radio Rivadavia. Two days later, after the revolution had proved abortive, the National Executive issued a decree suspending transmission by both these private stations, on the ground that they had broadcast revolutionary messages. The closure of Radio Porteña was lifted soon after, but that of Radio Rivadavia remained in effect, on the ground that its managers had continued to broadcast the messages which came from the network center for a considerable time after the revolutionary character of the messages had been made clear.

The managers of Radio Rivadavia sought judicial relief in an action of amparo. The court of 1st Instance granted the amparo, ordering the return of the transmitter to the owners and managers, but the newspaper La Prensa reported — in the same story which noted the intention of the government to appeal — that a police guard continued to prevent the entry of the managers into the radio station. (October 10, 1961.)

On October 12, 1961, La Prensa printed an editorial in which it commented that in the United States and Great Britain judges were entitled to call on the assistance of the police or the army, or even individual citizens, to make their orders effective; it was suggested that the court use similar means to execute its decree in the case of Radio Rivadavia. (It will be recalled that La Prensa itself had been seized by the Perón government.) On December 28, 1961 the decision of the court of 1st Instance was reversed by the Civil Chamber of Appeals of Buenos Aires. There were two principal grounds: a) the managers of the radio station might have followed their ordinary judicial remedy, obtaining judicial review of the administrative action; b) the plaintiff had "abandoned" the action in the court of 1st Instance after the decision of that court and before the perfecting of the government's appeal.

On January 16, 1962, La Prensa ran another editorial complaining vigorously about the appellate decision. The writer commented that it was ironic that the court should have considered the case to have been abandoned by the plaintiff when the plaintiff was continuing to protest in all possible ways, including complaints to the Inter-American Society of Broadcasters and the Inter-American Press Association. The editorial stated, in part: "In the present case, obviously elastic interpretations have been resorted to for the purpose of slanting the importance of the problem. What is true — and public opinion knows it — is that the injustice continues, that a penalty of preventive character and excessive duration has been applied without a previous judicial decision, and that we have arrived at the curious paradox that while the victim protests in tones heard throughout the continent, justice declares solemnly the inexistence of such a protest." The editorial terminated with a call upon the Executive to permit the station to reopen.

On February 7, 1962, La Prensa carried a front-page story announcing that the decree closing the transmitters of Radio Rivadavia had been revoked the day before. After six and one-half months of suspension, transmission was resumed on March 1, 1962.

ASOCIACION CULTURA Y RENOVACION
Federal Chamber of the Capital (Penal Division)
1963-III J.A. 390, 111 La Ley 909 (1962)

2d Instance.—Buenos Aires, November 26, 1962. Considering: That Jorge Raúl Savransky, in his capacity as Vice President of the Asociación Civil "Cultura y Renovación," brings an action of amparo motivated by the closing of the headquarters of the organization, . . . and the seizure of equipment, documents and books belonging to the organization, during a meeting of the members on the night of May 4 of this year. After naming several purposes of the society, the complainant attacks as unconstitutional any decree or order that might be cited in support of the action, especially decree 4965/59, which he considers to violate express provisions of the National Constitution.

That . . . the judge of 1st Instance dismissed the complaint . . ., understanding that the National Executive Power, on issuing decree 3963 last May 4, acted in reasonable exercise of the police power based on the state of siege existing in the country, the case having come to the attention of the court by virtue of the recourse of nullity and the appeal brought . . . .

* * *

That, according to the heading and the "whereas" paragraph of decree 3963 of 1962 . . ., the acts against which the present action is brought were ordered by the National Executive Power as measures connected with the state of siege established by law No. 14,785, in accordance with the provision of decree 4965/59 and keeping in mind "the recrudescence of anti-democratic activities by the Communist Party and collateral associations."

That the Supreme Court of the Nation, exercising the legitimate power of judicial control, has distinguished between the power to arrest and transport persons given to the President of the Nation in art. 23 of the National Constitution, not susceptible to judicial review, and those measures of general order relating to the suspension of other constitutional guarantees, respecting which, as with those considered here, the Judiciary has not been denied the power to review for the sole purpose of establishing their reasonableness ("Fallos": 243, 504 and 247, 708).

That, in the present case the closing of the office indicated above and the seizure of the material mentioned . . . has taken place because the National Executive Power considered that the conditions required by decree 4965/59 were present. And, this being so, as is said in the appealed case, the measures attacked by the appellant are a reasonable manifestation of the police power that may be exercised during a state of siege, and thus it is proper to affirm the appealed decision. . . .

For these considerations and the concordant reasons of the appealed decision, the latter is affirmed insofar as it does not grant the amparo petitioned in favor of the civil association "Cultura y Renovación," with costs of both instances, rejecting the recourse of nullity.—*Hernán Juárez Peñalva.—Enrique Ramón Mejía.—Ambrosio Romero Carranza.*

JUDICIAL SALARIES AND JUDICIAL INDEPENDENCE: THE EFFECT OF A "FISCAL EMERGENCY"

Many Latin American constitutions, as well as Article III of the Constitution of the United States, provide against any reduction in the salaries of federal judges during their continuance in office.* Such a provision is contained in Article 96 of the Constitution of Argentina, which is taken from

---
* Compare Scheman, p. 61, *supra.*

Article III, Section 1 of the Constitution of the United States. Suppose that the national treasury is desperately short of cash, and that the Argentine Government, during a recess of Congress, issues a decree providing for the payment of the salaries of all government employees in bonds, redeemable in cash six months after issue. Should a judge be permitted to challenge the constitutionality of the decree by way of an action of amparo?

In Arias v. Gobierno Nacional, 254 Fallos 286, 1963-II J.A. 553 (1962), the Supreme Court of Argentina was required to face this question. The court of 1st Instance had granted the amparo to a Buenos Aires justice of the peace, ordering the Government to pay his salary in cash within ten days. On appeal, both the court of 2d Instance and the Supreme Court held that the amparo was not allowable. The Supreme Court admitted that a delay in payment of judicial salaries was not consistent with Article 96, but said that the violation could not be "attributed to the will" of the Government. Furthermore, the summary nature of the amparo proceeding would deprive the Government of *its* constitutional right to a full and fair defense in court. Would not this latter argument be equally applicable to all petitions for amparo? Were there, perhaps, non-doctrinal considerations which motivated the decision of the Supreme Court?

CONSTITUTION OF THE UNITED STATES OF AMERICA

Article I, Section 9, clause 2. The privilege of the Writ of Habeas Corpus shall not be suspended, unless when in Cases of Rebellion or Invasion the public Safety may require it.

[Article I establishes the Congress, and defines its powers. Article II, which vests the executive power of the United States in the President and establishes his powers, makes no reference to habeas corpus.]

EX PARTE MERRYMAN
17 Fed. Cas. 144, No. 9,487
(C.C.D. Md. 1861)

* * *

TANEY, Circuit Justice. The application in this case for a writ of habeas corpus is made to me under the 14th section of the judiciary act of 1789 [1 Stat. 81], which renders effectual for the citizen the constitutional privilege of the writ of habeas corpus. That act gives to the courts of the United States, as well as to each justice of the supreme court, and to every district judge, power to grant writs of habeas corpus for the purpose of an inquiry into the cause of commitment. . . .

    * * *

The case, then, is simply this: a military officer, residing in Pennsylvania, issues an order to arrest a citizen of Maryland, upon vague and indefinite charges, without any proof, so far as appears; under this order, his house is entered in the night, he is seized as a prisoner, and conveyed to Fort McHenry, and there kept in close confinement; and when a habeas corpus is served on the commanding officer, requiring him to produce the prisoner before a justice of the supreme court, in order that he may examine into the legality of the imprisonment, the answer of the officer, is that he is authorized by the president to suspend the writ of habeas corpus at his discretion, and in the exercise of that discretion, suspends it in this case, and on that ground refuses obedience to the writ.

As the case comes before me, therefore, I understand that the president not only claims the right to suspend the writ of habeas corpus himself, at his discretion, but to delegate that discretionary power to a military officer, and to leave it to him to determine whether he will or will not obey judicial process that may be served upon him. No official notice has been given to the courts of justice, or to the public, by proclamation or otherwise, that the president claimed this power, and had exercised it in the manner stated in the return. And I certainly listened to it with some surprise, for I had supposed it to be one of those points of constitutional law upon which there was no difference of opinion, and that it was admitted on all hands, that the privilege of the writ could not be suspended, except by act of congress.

    * * *

With such provisions in the constitution, expressed in language too clear to be misunderstood by any one, I can see no ground whatever for supposing that the president, in any emergency, or in any state of things, can authorize the suspension of the privilege of the writ of habeas corpus, or the arrest of a citizen, except in aid of the judicial power. He certainly does not faithfully execute the laws, if he takes upon himself legislative power, by suspending the writ of habeas corpus, and the judicial power also, by arresting and imprisoning a person without due process of law.

Nor can any argument be drawn from the nature of sovereignty, or the necessity of government, for self-defense in times of tumult and danger. The government of the United States is one of delegated and limited powers; it derives its existence and authority altogether from the constitution, and neither of its branches, executive, legislative or judicial, can exercise any of the powers of government beyond those specified and granted; for the tenth article of the amendments to the constitution, in express terms, provides that "the powers not delegated to the United States by the constitution, nor prohibited by it to the states, are reserved to the states, respectively, or to the people."

    * * *

The constitution provides, as I have before said that "no person shall be deprived of life, liberty or property, without due process of law." It declares that "the right of the people to be secure in their persons, houses, papers and effects, against unreasonable searches and seizures, shall not be violated; and no warrant shall issue, but upon probable cause, supported by oath or affirmation, and particularly describing the place to be searched, and the persons or things to be seized." It provides that the party accused shall be entitled to a speedy trial in a court of justice.

These great and fundamental laws, which congress itself could not suspend, have been disregarded and suspended, like the writ of habeas corpus, by a military order, supported by force of arms. Such is the case now before me, and I can only say that if the authority which the constitution has confided to the judiciary department and judicial officers, may thus, upon any pretext or under any circumstances, be usurped by the military power, at its discretion, the people of the United States are no longer living under a government of laws, but every citizen holds life, liberty and property at the will and pleasure of the army officer in whose military district he may happen to be found.

In such a case, my duty was too plain to be mistaken. I have exercised all the power which the constitution and laws confer upon me, but that power has been resisted by a force too strong for me to overcome. It is possible that the officer who has incurred this grave responsibility may have misunderstood his instructions, and exceeded the authority intended to be given him; I shall, therefore, order all the proceedings in this case, with my opinion, to be filed and recorded in the circuit court of the United States for the district of Maryland, and direct the clerk to transmit a copy, under seal, to the president of the United States. It will then remain for that high officer, in fulfillment of his constitutional obligation to "take care that the laws be faithfully executed," to determine what measures he will take to cause the civil process of the United States to be respected and enforced.

[Merryman was later released to the local United States District Court, in which he was charged with treason. After some continuances, during which Merryman was out on $20,000 bail, the prosecution was dropped. — Ed.]

KOREMATSU v. UNITED STATES
323 U.S. 214 (1944)

MR. JUSTICE BLACK delivered the opinion of the Court.

The petitioner, an American citizen of Japanese descent, was convicted in a federal district court for remaining in San Leandro, California, a "Military Area," contrary to Civilian Exclusion Order No. 34 of the Commanding General of the Western Command, U.S. Army, which directed that after May 9, 1942, all persons of Japanese ancestry should be excluded from that area. No question was raised as to petitioner's loyalty to the United States. The Circuit Court of Appeals affirmed, and the importance of the constitutional question involved caused us to grant certiorari.

It should be noted, to begin with, that all legal restrictions which curtail the civil rights of a single racial group are immediately suspect. That is not to say that all such restrictions are unconstitutional. It is to say that courts must subject them to the most rigid scrutiny. Pressing public necessity may sometimes justify the existence of such restrictions; racial antagonism never can.

In the instant case prosecution of the petitioner was begun by information charging violation of an Act of Congress, of March 21, 1942, 56 Stat. 173, which provides that ". . . whoever shall enter, remain in, leave, or commit any act in any military area or military zone prescribed, under the authority of an Executive order of the President, by the Secretary of War, or by any military commander designated by the Secretary of War, contrary to the restrictions applicable to any such area or zone or contrary to the order of the Secretary of War or any such military commander, shall, if it appears that he knew or should have known of the existence and extent of the restrictions or order and that his act was in violation thereof, be guilty of a misdemeanor and upon conviction shall be liable to a fine of not to exceed $5,000 or to imprisonment for not more than one year, or both, for each offense."

Exclusion Order No. 34, which the petitioner knowingly and admittedly violated, was one of a number of military orders and proclamations, all of which were substantially based upon Executive Order No. 9066, 7 Fed. Reg. 1407. That order, issued after we were at war with Japan, declared that "the successful prosecution of the war requires every possible protection against espionage and against sabotage to national-defense material, national-defense premises, and national-defense utilities. . . ."

One of the series of orders and proclamations, a curfew order, which like the exclusion order here was promulgated pursuant to Executive Order 9066, subjected all persons of Japanese ancestry in prescribed West Coast military areas to remain in their residences from 8 p.m. to 6 a.m. As is the case with the exclusion order here, that prior curfew order was designed as a "protection against espionage and against sabotage." in *Hirabayashi* v. *United States*, 320 U.S. 81, we sustained a conviction obtained for violation of the curfew order. The Hirabayashi conviction and this one thus rest on the same 1942 Congressional Act and the same basic executive and military orders, all of which orders were aimed at the twin dangers of espionage and sabotage.

The 1942 Act was attacked in the *Hirabayashi* case as an unconstitutional delegation of power; it was contended that the curfew order and other orders on which it rested were beyond the war powers of the Congress, the military authorities and of the President, as Commander in Chief of the Army; and finally that to apply the curfew order against none but citizens of Japanese ancestry amounted to a constitutionally prohibited discrimination solely on account of race. To these questions, we gave the serious consideration which their importance justified. We upheld the curfew order as an exercise of the power of the government to take steps necessary to prevent espionage and sabotage in an area threatened by Japanese attack.

In the light of the principles we announced in the *Hirabayashi* case, we are unable to conclude that it was beyond the war power of Congress and the Executive to exclude those of Japanese ancestry from the West Coast war area at the time they did. True, exclusion from the area in which one's home is located is a far greater deprivation than constant confinement to the home from 8 p.m. to 6 a.m. Nothing short of apprehension by the proper military authorities of the gravest imminent danger to the public safety can constitutionally justify either. But exclusion from a threatened area, no less than curfew, has a definite and close relationship to the prevention of espionage and sabotage. The military authorities, charged with the primary responsibility of defending our shores, concluded that curfew provided inadequate protection and ordered exclusion. They did so, as pointed out in our *Hirabayashi* opinion, in accordance with Congressional authority to the military to say who should, and who should not, remain in the threatened areas.

In this case the petitioner challenges the assumptions upon which we rested our conclusions in the *Hirabayashi* case. He also urges that by May 1942, when Order No. 34 was promulgated, all danger of Japanese invasion of the West Coast had disappeared. After careful consideration of these contentions we are compelled to reject them.

Here, as in the *Hirabayashi* case, *supra*, at p. 99, ". . . we cannot reject as unfounded the judgment of the military authorities and of Congress that there were disloyal members of that population, whose number and strength could not be precisely and quickly ascertained. We cannot say that the war-making branches of the Government did not have ground for believing that in a critical hour such persons could not readily be isolated and separately dealt with, and constituted a menace to the national defense and safety, which demanded that prompt and adequate measures be taken to guard against it."

Like curfew, exclusion of those of Japanese origin was deemed necessary because of the presence of an unascertained number of disloyal members of the group, most of whom we have no doubt were loyal to this country. It was because we could not reject the finding of the military authorities that it was impossible to bring about an immediate segregation of the disloyal from the loyal that we sustained the validity of the curfew order as applying to the whole group. In the instant case, temporary exclusion of the entire group was rested by the military on the same ground. The judgment that exclusion of the whole group was for the same reason a military imperative answers the contention that the exclusion was in the nature of group punishment based on antagonism to those of Japanese origin. That there were members of the group who retained loyalties to Japan has been confirmed by investigations made subsequent to the exclusion. Approximately five thousand American citizens of Japanese ancestry refused to swear unqualified allegiance to the United

States and to renounce allegiance to the Japanese Emperor, and several thousand evacuees requested repatriation to Japan.

We uphold the exclusion order as of the time it was made and when the petitioner violated it. *Cf. Chastleton Corporation* v. *Sinclair*, 264 U.S. 543, 547; *Block* v. *Hirsch*, 256 U.S. 135, 154-5. In doing so, we are not unmindful of the hardships imposed by it upon a large group of American citizens. Cf. *Ex parte Kawato*, 317 U.S. 69, 73. But hardships are part of war, and war is an aggregation of harships. All citizens alike, both in and out of uniform, feel the impact of war in greater or lesser measure. Citizenship has its responsibilities as well as its privileges, and in time of war the burden is always heavier. Compulsory exclusion of large groups of citizens from their homes, except under circumstances of direst emergency and peril, is inconsistent with our basic government institutions. But when under conditions of modern warfare our shores are threatened by hostile forces, the power to protect must be commensurable with the threatened danger.

* * *

It is said that we are dealing here with the case of imprisonment of a citizen in a concentration camp solely because of his ancestry, without evidence or inquiry concerning his loyalty and good disposition towards the United States. Our task would be simple, our duty clear, were this a case involving the imprisonment of a loyal citizen in a concentration camp because of racial prejudice. Regardless of the true nature of the assembly and relocation centers — and we deem it unjustifiable to call them concentration camps with all the ugly connotations that term implies — we are dealing specifically with nothing but an exclusion order. To cast this case into outlines of racial prejudice, without reference to the real military dangers which were presented, merely confuses the issue. Korematsu was not excluded from the Military Area because of hostility to him or his race. He *was* excluded because we are at war with the Japanese Empire, because the properly constituted military authorities feared an invasion of our West Coast and felt constrained to take proper security measures, because they decided that the military urgency of the situation demanded that all citizens of Japanese ancestry be segregated from the West Coast temporarily, and finally, because Congress, reposing its confidence in this time of war in our military leaders — as inevitably it must — determined that they should have the power to do just this. There was evidence of disloyalty on the part of some, the military authorities considered that the need for action was great, and time was short.

We cannot — by availing ourselves of the calm perspective of hindsight — now say that at that time these actions were unjustified.

Affirmed.

MR. JUSTICE FRANKFURTER, concurring.
* * *

The provisions of the Constitution which confer on the Congress and the President powers to enable this country to wage war are as much part of the Constitution as provisions looking to a nation at peace. And we have had recent occasion to quote approvingly the statement of former Chief Justice Hughes that the war power of the Government is "the power to wage war successfully." *Hirabayashi* v. *United States, supra* at 93; and see *Home Bldg. & L. Assn.* v. *Blaisdell,* 290 U.S. 398, 426. Therefore, the validity of action under the war power must be judged wholly in the context of war. That action is not to be stigmatized as lawless because like action in times of peace would be lawless. To talk about a military order that expresses an allowable judgment of war needs by those entrusted with the duty of conducting war as "an unconstitutional order" is to suffuse a part of the Constitution with an atmosphere of unconstitutionality. The respective spheres of action of military authorities and of judges are of course very different. But within their sphere, military authorities are no more outside the bounds of obedience to the Constitution than are judges within theirs. "The war power of the United States, like its other powers . . . is subject to applicable constitutional limitations," *Hamilton* v. *Kentucky Distilleries Co.,* 251 U.S. 146, 156. To recognize that military orders are "reasonably expedient military precautions" in time of war and yet to deny them constitutional legitimacy makes of the Constitution an instrument for dialectic subtleties not reasonably to be attributed to the hard-headed Framers, of whom a majority had had actual participation in war. If a military order such as that under review does not transcend the means appropriate for conducting war, such action by the military is as constitutional as would be any authorized action by the Interstate Commerce Commission within the limits of the constitutional power to regulate commerce. And being an exercise of the war power explicitly granted by the Constitution for safeguarding the national life prosecuting war effectively, I find nothing in the Constitution which denies to Congress the power to enforce such a valid military order by making its violation an offense triable in the civil courts. Compare *Interstate Commerce Commission* v. *Brimson,* 154 U.S. 447, 155 U.S. 3, and *Monongahela Bridge Co.* v. *United States,* 216 U.S. 177. To find that the Constitution does not forbid the military measures now complained of does not carry with it approval of that which Congress and the Executive did. That is their business, not ours.

MR. JUSTICE ROBERTS.

I dissent, because I think the indisputable facts exhibit a clear violation of Constitutional rights.

This is not a case of keeping people off the streets at night as was *Hirabayashi* v. *United States,* 320 U.S. 81, nor a case of temporary exclusion of a citizen from an area for his own safety or that of the community, nor a case of offering him an opportunity to go temporarily out of an area where his presence might cause danger to himself or to his fellows. On the contrary, it is the case of convicting a citizen as a punishment for not submitting to imprisonment in a concentration camp, based on his ancestry, and solely because

of his ancestry, without evidence or inquiry concerning his loyalty and good
disposition towards the United States. If this be a correct statement of the
facts disclosed by this record, and facts of which we take judicial notice, I
need hardly labor the conclusion that constitutional rights have been violated.

    * * *

    I would reverse the judgment of conviction.

    MR. JUSTICE MURPHY, dissenting.

    [In his dissenting opinion, Mr. Justice Murphy examined in detail the
asserted justifications for the exclusion order, and concluded that the order was
in fact based on community hostility more than on military necessity.]

    MR. JUSTICE JACKSON, dissenting.

    Korematsu was born on our soil, of parents born in Japan. The Constitu-
tion makes him a citizen of the United States by nativity and a citizen of California by residence. No claim is made that he is not loyal to this country.
There is no suggestion that apart from the matter involved here he is not
law-abiding and well disposed. Korematsu, however, has been convicted of an
act not commonly a crime. It consists merely of being present in the state
whereof he is a citizen, near the place where he was born, and where all his
life he has lived.

    Even more unusual is the series of military orders which made this con-
duct a crime. They forbid such a one to remain, and they also forbid him to
leave. They were so drawn that the only way Korematsu could avoid violation
was to give himself up to the military authority. This meant submission to
custody, examination, and transportation out of the territory, to be followed
by indeterminate confinement in detention camps.

    A citizen's presence in the locality, however, was made a crime only if
his parents were of Japanese birth. Had Korematsu been one of four — the
others being, say, a German alien enemy, an Italian alien enemy, and a citizen
of American-born ancestors, convicted of treason but out on parole — only
Korematsu's presence would have violated the order. The difference between
their innocence and his crime would result, not from anything he did, said, or
thought, different than they, but only in that he was born of different racial
stock.

    Now, if any fundamental assumption underlies our system, it is that guilt
is personal and not inheritable. Even if all of one's antecedents had been convicted of treason, the Constitution forbids its penalties to be visited upon him,
for it provides that "no attainder of treason shall work corruption of blood,
or forfeiture except during the life of the person attainted." But here is an
attempt to make an otherwise innocent act a crime merely because this prisoner is the son of parents as to whom he had no choice, and belongs to a race
from which there is no way to resign. If Congress in peace-time legislation
should enact such a criminal law, I should suppose this Court would refuse
to enforce it.

But the "law" which this prisoner is convicted of disregarding is not found in an act of Congress, but in a military order. Neither the Act of Congress nor the Executive Order of the President, nor both together, would afford a basis for this conviction. It rests on the orders of General DeWitt. And it is said that if the military commander had reasonable military grounds for promulgating the orders, they are constitutional and become law, and the Court is required to enforce them. There are several reasons why I cannot subscribe to this doctrine.

It would be impracticable and dangerous idealism to expect or insist that each specific military command in an area of probable operations will conform to conventional tests of constitutionality. When an area is so beset that it must be put under military control at all, the paramount consideration is that its measures be successful, rather than legal. The armed services must protect a society, not merely its Constitution. The very essence of the military job is to marshall physical force, to remove every obstacle to its effectiveness, to give it every strategic advantage. Defense measures will not, and often should not, be held within the limits that bind civil authority in peace. No court can require such a commander in such circumstances to act as a reasonable man; he may be unreasonably cautious and exacting. Perhaps he should be. But a commander in temporarily focusing the life of a community on defense is carrying out a military program; he is not making law in the sense the courts know the term. He issues orders, and they may have a certain authority as military commands, although they may be very bad as constitutional law.

But if we cannot confine military expedients by the Constitution, neither would I distort the Constitution to approve all that the military may deem expedient. That is what the Court appears to be doing, whether consciously or not. I cannot say, from any evidence before me, that the orders of General DeWitt were not reasonably expedient military precautions, nor could I say that they were. But even if they were permissible military procedures, I deny that it follows that they are constitutional. If, as the Court holds, it does follow, then we may as well say that any military order will be constitutional and have done with it.

The limitation under which courts always will labor in examining the necessity for a military order are illustrated by this case. How does the Court know that these orders have a reasonable basis in necessity? No evidence whatever on that subject has been taken by this or any other court. There is sharp controversy as to the credibility of the DeWitt report. So the Court, having no real evidence before it, has no choice but to accept General De-Witt's own unsworn, self-serving statement, untested by any cross-examination, that what he did was reasonable. And thus it will always be when courts try to look into the reasonableness of a military order.

In the very nature of things, military decisions are not susceptible of intelligent judicial appraisal. They do not pretend to rest on evidence, but are made on information that often would not be admissible and on assumptions that could not be proved. Information in support of an order could not be disclosed to courts without danger that it would reach the enemy. Neither can courts act on communications made in confidence. Hence courts can never have any real alternative to accepting the mere declaration of the authority that issued the order that it was reasonably necessary from a military viewpoint.

Much is said of the danger to liberty from the Army program for deporting and detaining these citizens of Japanese extraction. But a judicial construction of the due process clause that will sustain this order is a far more subtle blow to liberty than the promulgation of the order itself. A military order, however unconstitutional, is not apt to last longer than the military emergency. Even during that period a succeeding commander may revoke it all. But once a judicial opinion rationalizes such an order to show that it conforms to the Constitution, or rather rationalizes the Constitution to show that the Constitution sanctions such an order, the Court for all time has validated the principle of racial discrimination in criminal procedure and of transplanting American citizens. The principle then lies about like a loaded weapon ready for the hand of any authority that can bring forward a plausible claim of an urgent need. Every repetition imbeds that principle more deeply in our law and thinking and expands it to new purposes. All who observe the work of courts are familiar with what Judge Cardozo described as "the tendency of a principle to expand itself to the limit of its logic." A military commander may overstep the bounds of constitutionality, and it is an incident. But if we review and approve, that passing incident becomes the doctrine of the Constitution. There it has a generative power of its own, and all that it creates will be in its own image. Nothing better illustrates this danger than does the Court's opinion in this case.

      * * *

I should hold that a civil court cannot be made to enforce an order which violates constitutional limitations even if it is a reasonable exercise of military authority. The courts can exercise only the judicial power, can apply only law, and must abide by the Constitution, or they cease to be civil courts and become instruments of military policy.

Of course the existence of a military power resting on force, so vagrant, so centralized, so necessarily heedless of the individual, is an inherent threat to liberty. But I would not lead people to rely on this Court for a review that seems to me wholly delusive. The military reasonableness of these orders can only be determined by military superiors. If the people ever let command of the war power fall into irresponsible and unscrupulous hands, the courts wield no power equal to its restraint. The chief restraint upon those who command the physical forces of the country, in the future as in the past, must be their responsibility to the political judgments of their contemporaries and to the moral judgments of history.

My duties as a justice as I see them do not require me to make a military judgment as to whether General DeWitt's evacuation and detention program was a reasonable military necessity. I do not suggest that the courts should have attempted to interfere with the Army in carrying out its task. But I do not think they may be asked to execute a military expedient that has no place in law under the Constitution. I would reverse the judgment and discharge the prisoner.

RODRIGUEZ and RUGGERO
Supreme Court of Justice of the Nation (Argentina)
254 Fallos 116, 1962-VI J.A. 320, 108 La Ley 260 (1962)

Buenos Aires, October 24, 1962. The court having seen the record: "Rodríguez, Juan Carlos, Ruggero, Conrado Andrés, Tambascio, Juan Carlos — their prosecution for terrorist and subversive activities, public intimidation and other crimes."

And considering: 1st) That ... the Supreme Council of the Armed Forces affirmed the sentence ... of the Special Council of War No. 1, which condemned Conrado Andrés Ruggero, Juan Carlos Rodríguez and Juan Carlos Tambascio to the penalties of twelve years of imprisonment and absolute disqualification from civil rights, for the first two mentioned, and five years of imprisonment and disqualification for the latter. The defense counsel for Ruggero brought an extraordinary appeal, a hearing of which was granted .... The jurisdiction of this Court has thus been opened only with respect to the first of the named accused.

2d) That the act charged to Ruggero constitutes the crime of *estragos*, under art. 186 of the Penal Code, with the aggravating circumstance of par. 4th of the same, according to the appealed decision. That article punishes whoever "may cause a fire, explosion or flood" with "imprisonment of 3 to 15 years, if there may have been danger of killing any person." And the act consisted in the placing of a bomb in the cafe [*confitería*] at 1818-26 Santa Fé Avenue, on May 24, 1960, a bomb which exploded, producing considerable material destruction but no victims.

3d) That before this Court ... the defense counsel for Conrado Andrés Ruggero maintains the lack of jurisdiction of the military tribunals, based on the participation of military judges in the processing and the decision of the case, contrary to the National Constitution. At the same time he argues that the Code of Military Justice is unconstitutional and that law 13,234 is unconstitutional also, establishing "rules for organizing the Nation in time of war," and decrees 2628 and 2639 of 1960, whether they be based on the mentioned law or considered in isolation. These decrees (by means of which the "Conintes Plan" was put into execution — established by decree "S" 9880,

of November 14, 1958 — and which declared a state of grave emergency;
also, from March 16, 1960 on, submitting to military jurisdiction the crimes
which it lists, characterizing them as crimes of public intimidation and ter-
rorism, although perpetrated by civilians), he argues, would violate arts. 16,
18, 22 and 95 of the National Constitution. The defense affirms that the
so-called "martial law" is constitutionally unacceptable . . . . [There were also
some complaints about the rulings on evidence in the military courts, the
physical transfer of the defendant, the constitution of the Special Council of
War and the joint trial of this defendant with certain others.]
　　* * *

[The Procurador General argued for affirmance of the decision of the
military court, on the ground that the various decrees were justified by a state
of emergency.]
　　6th)　That it is proper to note, in the first place, that long-established
doctrine gives the State the power of self-preservation against attacks made
violently against existing institutions. [Citations to Roman law sources.] And
such powers include military powers, taking account of the fact that in exceptional conditions the ordinary legal authorities may be incapable of maintaining public peace and suppressing violence and depredation. Thomas M. Cooley, A Treatise on Constitutional Limitations, Boston, 1927, vol. 1, p. 637,
n.3. Thus it appears possible to assert that measures of defense adequate to
the magnitude of the danger, international or domestic, which requires their
adoption, must be considered valid in principle. For contemporary thought,
the condemnation or approval of such measures will depend, consequently
(apart from the proscription of iniquity), on the proportion they maintain to
the risk they adequately avoid, since the right to confront it effectively is not
questioned. Robert K. Carr, The House Committee on Un-American Activities,
Washington, 1952, p. viii. In the last analysis, and to the degree required by
exceptional circumstances, we find valid for the community, . . . the precept
in which classical wisdom made natural law concrete: "*Vim vi repellere licet*";
it is lawful to repel force with force.
　　* * *

[There is no need to consider the reach of state power to punish under
circumstances of extreme emergency without any judicial action.]
　　[The Court distinguishes between the use of military force as an auxiliary
to the civilian government, on the one hand, and the declaration of a state of
siege on the other. Although the two may coincide, they need not. This discussion is punctuated with numerous citations to North American authorities,
both to decisions of the United States Supreme Court and to treatises on constitutional law.]
　　11th)　That it follows that, as in this case, in conditions of grave and
violent internal disorder, there being no military operations, properly speaking,
the requirement of military assistance bears the character of aid to the civil

authorities, without substitution of the military for those authorities not perturbed by insurrection . . . .

12th) That it is proper to affirm, consequently, that arts. 23; 67, par. 23 and 24; 86, par. 15, 17 and 19; and 109 of the National Constitution and the pertinent provisions of the military laws, suffice to give a normative foundation to recourse to the army as auxiliary to the civilian authority, in the face of grave domestic subversion.

13th) That the accuracy with which the political powers appreciate the circumstances required for the validity of the auxiliary employment of the armed forces, cannot be reviewed by the courts of justice in a form which constitutes a free reconsideration of the exclusive powers of the political authorities. [This conclusion is even more required] in conditions in which, as in the present case, judicial review is requested in the course of an emergency and as an impediment to military action . . . . In principle, in effect, "the Court must conclude that it simply is not in condition to reject the assertion of the Executive as to the degree of military necessity." Earl Warren, the Bill of Rights and the Military, New York University Law Review, April 1962, p. 181. In a manner similar to what the Tribunal has declared respecting measures adopted during a state of siege, judicial review must not go beyond a determination of the inexistence of reasonableness in resort to military force. And provided that the existence and gravity of the state of subversion and generalized violence which motivated the issuance of the decrees in question is notorious, that which we have expressed suffices to reject, in this aspect, the constitutional attack on them.

14th) That it should, nevertheless, be pointed out that resort to the armed forces of the Nation ordinarily requires the consent of the Congress. For, although the President is Commander-in-Chief of all the armed forces, the latter are governed according to the laws and ordinances which the Parliament decrees (National Constitution, art. 67, par. 23). And because the establishment of a state of siege, to which it was an accessory, falls to the Congress (art. 86, par. 19) . . . . [The Court notes the possibility of a retroactive validating law which might ratify what the President had done in such a case.]

15th) It also seems clear that resort to the armed forces to put down insurrection is not limited to mere naked physical compulsion. The reasoning behind the foregoing paragraphs and their connection with a state of siege retain all their value when we analyze the tasks of investigation, arrest, participation of the Special Councils of War, the entry into domiciles and the adoption of the summary proceedings of the Code of Military Justice. Thus, it should also be concluded that during the emergency, it being a matter of acts related to it and means of investigation and security adequate to overcome it, no constitutional impediment exists for their validation by law, as law 15,293 effectively has done, on providing with greater breadth that "cases pending before the Special Councils of War constituted according to the provisions of decree 2639/60 shall continue their processing and shall be decided by the latter."

16th)   That there still is a problem, consisting in the existence of military penalties after the insurrectional movement which motivated the intervention of the armed forces has been put down. On the other hand, in this case there is no such problem concerning the fact of the termination of the insurrectional episode, because it appears unequivocally from decree 6495/61 dated August 1, 1961, which derogated decrees 9880/58 and 2628/60, concerning the execution of the "Conintes" plan. From August 1 of the mentioned year forward, there has been no more internal commotion of the State which would require the application of the mentioned plan.

17th)   . . . .

The exclusion of constitutional judges in the adjudication and final decision of criminal cases has no juridical justification after the subversive episode has been definitively overcome, even though a state of siege subsists, because the exceptional events which justify the implantation of military aid also limit its duration. . . . In these conditions, the invocation of the war powers of the National Government also fail to justify a continuing sacrifice of the fundamental rights of citizens, for such a sacrifice it not clearly necessary for national security. . . .

18th)   That it is a consequence of what has been said that although the action of the military tribunals in the matter, before the date of decree 6495/61, is valid as an exercise of an implied power, a corollary to the power of the civilian authorities to repress by military force the violence of an internal rebellion, . . . the extraordinary appeal must, nevertheless, be admitted. The constitutional guarantee of defense in trial, which includes that of resorting to justice for the protection of individual rights . . . would be seen to be frustrated in another manner if the appealed decision could be affirmed . . ., because "the right of every person, rich or poor, to resort to justice is essential for the rule of law to govern." International Commission of Jurists, "The Rule of Law in Free Societies," p. 27, Geneva, 1959. . . .

19th)   That, consequently, Conrado Andrés Ruggero must be tried again by judges who are members of the Judiciary of the Nation, according to the procedural laws which distribute among them jurisdiction over criminal matters. . . . It is proper, consequently, to provide that Conrado Andrés Ruggero be tried again before the judge in the Federal Criminal and Correctional Court of the Capital of the Republic.

* * *

Benjamín Villegas Basavilbaso.—Luis María Boffi Boggero (in partial dissent).—*Pedro Aberastury.—Ricardo Colombres.—Esteban Imaz.—José F. Bidau.*

[Dr. Boffi Boggero dissented only as to the grounds for decision. He was of the view that the Court should have considered the reasonableness of the various decrees founded on emergency conditions.]

DUNCAN v. KAHANAMOKU
327 U.S. 304 (1946)

MR. JUSTICE BLACK delivered the opinion of the Court.

The petitioners in these cases were sentenced to prison by military tribunals in Hawaii. Both are civilians. The question before us is whether the military tribunals had power to do this. The United States district court for Hawaii in habeas corpus proceedings held that the military tribunals had no such power and ordered that they be set free. The circuit court of appeals reversed, and ordered that the petitioners be returned to prison. 146 F.2d 576. Both cases thus involve the rights of individuals charged with crime and not connected with the armed forces to have their guilt or innocence determined in courts of law which provide established procedural safeguards, rather than by military tribunals which fail to afford many of these safeguards. Since these judicial safeguards are prized privileges of our system of government we granted certiorari.

The following events led to the military tribunals' exercise of jurisdiction over the petitioners. On December 7, 1941, immediately following the surprise air attack by the Japanese on Pearl Harbor, the Governor of Hawaii by proclamation undertook to suspend the privilege of the writ of habeas corpus and to place the Territory under "martial law." Section 67 of the Hawaiian Organic Act [1900], 31 Stat. 141, 153, authorizes the Territorial Governor to take this action "in case of rebellion or invasion, or imminent danger thereof, when the public safety requires it . . . ." His action was to remain in effect only "until communication can be had with the President and his decision thereon made known." The President approved the Governor's action on December 9th. The Governor's proclamation also authorized and requested the Commanding General, "during the . . . emergency and until danger of invasion is removed, to exercise all the powers normally exercised" by the Governor and by the "judicial officers and employees of this territory."

Pursuant to this authorization the commanding general immediately proclaimed himself Military Governor and undertook the defense of the Territory and the maintenance of order. On December 8th, both civil and criminal courts were forbidden to summon jurors and witnesses and to try cases. The Commanding General established military tribunals to take the place of the courts. These were to try civilians charged with violating the laws of the United States and of the Territory, and rules, regulations, orders or policies of the Military Government. Rules of evidence and procedure of courts of law were not to control the military trials. In imposing penalties the military tribunals were to be "guided by, but not limited to the penalties authorized by the courts martial manual, the laws of the United States, the Territory of Hawaii, the District of Columbia, and the customs of war in like cases." The rule announced was simply that punishment was to be "commensurate with the offense committed" and that the death penalty might be imposed "in appropriate cases." Thus the military authorities took over the government of Hawaii. They could and did, by simply promulgating orders, govern the day to day activities of civilians who lived, worked, or were merely passing through there. The military tribunals interpreted the very orders promulgated by the military authorities and proceeded to punish violators. The sentences imposed were not subject to direct appellate court review, since it had long been established that military tribunals are not part of our judicial system. *Ex parte Vallandingham*, 1 Wall. 243. The military undoubtedly assumed that its rule was not subject to any judicial control whatever, for by orders issued on August 25, 1943, it prohibited even accepting of a petition for writ of habeas corpus by a judge or judicial employee or the filing of such a petition by a prisoner or his attorney. Military tribunals could punish violators of these orders by fine, imprisonment or death.

White, the petitioner in No. 15, was a stockbroker in Honolulu. Neither he nor his business was connected with the armed forces. On August 20, 1942, more than eight months after the Pearl Harbor attack, the military police arrested him. The charge against him was embezzling stock belonging to another civilian in violation of Chapter 183 of the Revised Laws of Hawaii. Though by the time of White's arrest the courts were permitted "as agents of the military governor" to dispose of some non-jury civil cases, they were still forbidden to summon jurors and to exercise criminal jurisdiction. On August 22nd, White was brought before a military tribunal designated as a "Provost Court." The "Court" orally informed him of the charge. He objected to the tribunal's jurisdiction but the objection was overruled. He demanded to be tried by a jury. This request was denied. His attorney asked for additional time to prepare the case. This was refused. On August 25th he was tried and convicted. The tribunal sentence him to five years imprisonment. Later the sentence was reduced to four years.

Duncan, the petitioner in No. 14, was a civilian shipfitter employed in the Navy Yard at Honolulu. On February 24, 1944, more than two years and two months after the Pearl Harbor attack, he engaged in a brawl with two armed Marine sentries at the yard. He was arrested by the military authorities. By the time of his arrest the military had to some extent eased the stringency of military rule. Schools, bars and motion picture theatres had been reopened. Courts had been authorized to "exercise their normal jurisdiction." They were once more summoning jurors and witnesses and conducting criminal trials. There were important exceptions, however. One of these was that only military tribunals were to try "Criminal prosecutions for violations of military orders."[3] As the record shows, these military orders still covered a wide range of day to day civilian conduct. Duncan was charged with violating one of these orders, paragraph 8.01, Title 8, of General Order No. 2, which prohibited assault on military or naval personnel with intent to resist or hinder them in the discharge of their duty. He was, therefore, tried by a military tribunal rather than the territorial court, although the general laws of Hawaii made assault a crime. Revised L.H. 1935, ch. 166. A conviction followed and Duncan was sentenced to six months imprisonment.

Both White and Duncan challenged the power of the military tribunals to try them by petitions for writs of habeas corpus filed in the district court for Hawaii on March 14 and April 14, 1944, respectively. Their petitions urged both statutory and constitutional grounds. The court issued orders to show cause. Returns to these orders contended that Hawaii had become part of an active theatre of war constantly threatened by invasion from without; that the writ of habeas corpus had therefore properly been suspended and martial law had validly been established in accordance with the provisions of the Organic Act; that consequently the district court did not have jurisdiction to issue the writ; and that the trials of petitioners by military tribunals pursuant to orders by the Military Governor issued because of military necessity were valid. Each petitioner filed a traverse to the returns, which traverse challenged among other things the suspension of habeas corpus, the establishment of martial law and the validity of the Military Governor's orders, asserting that such action could not be taken except when required by military necessity due to actual or threatened invasion, which even if it did exist on December 7, 1941, did not exist when the petitioners were tried; and that, whatever the necessity for martial law, there was no justification for trying them in military tribunals rather than the regular courts of law. The district court, after separate trials, found in each case, among other things, that the courts had always been able to function but for the military orders closing them, and that consequently there was no military necessity for the trial of petitioners by military tribunals rather than regular courts.[4] It accordingly held the trials void and ordered the release of the petitioners.

The circuit court of appeals, assuming without deciding that the district court had jurisdiction to entertain the petitions, held the military trials valid and reversed the ruling of the district court. 146 F.2d 576. It held that the military orders providing for military trials were fully authorized by § 67 of the Organic Act and the Governor's actions taken under it. . . .

---

[3] In addition § 3 of a Proclamation of February 8, 1943, which returned some power to the civil authorities, had reserved a right in the Military Governor to resume any or all of the powers returned to the civilian government. In approving this Proclamation the President had expressed his confidence that the Military would "refrain from exercising . . . authority over . . . normally civil functions" and his hope that there would "be a further restoration of civil authority as and when the situation permits."

[4] We do not set out the other grounds of challenge since under the view we take we do not reach them.

... The petitioners contend that "martial law" as provided for by § 67 did not authorize the military to try and punish civilians such as petitioners and urge further that if such authority should be inferred from the Organic Act, it would be unconstitutional. We need decide the constitutional question only if we agree with the Government that Congress did authorize what was done here.

Did the Organic Act during the period of martial law give the armed forces power to supplant all civilian laws and to substitute military for judicial trials under the conditions that existed in Hawaii at the time these petitioners were tried? The relevant conditions, for our purposes, were the same when both petitioners were tried. The answer to the question depends on a correct interpretation of the Act. But we need not construe the Act, insofar as the power of the military might be used to meet other and different conditions and situations. The boundaries of the situation with reference to which we do interpret the scope of the Act can be more sharply defined by stating at this point some different conditions which either would or might conceivably have affected to a greater or lesser extent the scope of the authorized military power. We note first that at the time the alleged offenses were committed the dangers apprehended by the military were not sufficiently imminent to cause them to require civilians to evacuate the area or even to evacuate any of the buildings necessary to carry on the business of the courts. In fact, the buildings had long been open and actually in use for certain kinds of trials. Our question does not involve the well-established power of the military to exercise jurisdiction over members of the armed forces, those directly connected with such forces, or enemy belligerents, prisoners of war, or others charged with violating the laws of war. We are not concerned with the recognized power of the military to try civilians in tribunals established as a part of a temporary military government over occupied enemy territory or territory regained from an enemy where civilian government cannot and does not function. For Hawaii since annexation has been held by and loyal to the United States. Nor need we here consider the power of the military simply to arrest and detain civilians interfering with a necessary military function at a time of turbulence and danger from insurrection or war.[10] And finally, there was no specialized effort of the military, here, to enforce orders which related only to military functions, such as, for illustration, curfew rules or blackouts. For these petitioners were tried before tribunals set up under a military program which took over all government and superseded all civil laws and courts. If the Organic Act, properly interpreted, did not give the armed forces this awesome power, both petitioners are entitled to their freedom.

---

[10] *Moyer* v. *Peabody*, 212 U.S. 78; *Ex parte Milligan*, 4 Wall. 2, 125, 126; *Luther* v. *Borden*, 7 How. 1, 45, 46; see *Sterling* v. *Constantin*, 287 U.S. 378, 400; Fairman, The Law of Martial Rule, Chicago 1943, 209-218.

I.

* * *

[The Court found no express guidance in the language of the Organic Act.]

II.

Since the Act's language does not provide a satisfactory answer, we look to the legislative history for possible further aid in interpreting the term "martial law" as used in the statute. . . . [The Court found nothing in the legislative history to support the Government's argument.]

* * *

III.

Since both the language of the Organic Act and its legislative history fail to indicate that the scope of "martial law" in Hawaii includes the supplanting of courts by military tribunals, we must look to other sources in order to interpret that term. We think the answer may be found in the birth, development and growth of our governmental institutions up to the time Congress passed the Organic Act. Have the principles and practices developed during the birth and growth of our political institutions been such as to persuade us that Congress intended that loyal civilians in loyal territory should have their daily conduct governed by military orders substituted for criminal laws, and that such civilians should be tried and punished by military tribunals? . . . [Mr. Justice Black's historical review leads to a negative answer to this question.]

* * *

Courts and their procedural safeguards are indispensable to our system of government. They were set up by our founders to protect the liberties they valued. *Ex parte Quirin*, 317 U.S. 1, 19. Our system of government clearly is the antithesis of total military rule and the founders of this country are not likely to have contemplated complete military dominance within the limits of a territory made part of this country and not recently taken from an enemy. They were opposed to governments that placed in the hands of one man the power to make, interpret and enforce the laws. Their philosophy has been the people's throughout our history. For that reason we have maintained legislatures chosen by citizens or their representatives and courts and juries to try those who violate legislative enactments. We have always been especially concerned about the potential evils of summary criminal trials and have guarded against them by provisions embodied in the Constitution itself. See *Ex parte Milligan*, 4 Wall. 2; *Chambers* v. *Florida*, 309 U.S. 227. Legislatures and courts are not merely cherished American institutions; they are indispensable to our Government.

Military tribunals have no such standing. For as this Court has said before: ". . . the military should always be kept in subjection to the laws of the country to which it belongs, and that he is no friend to the Republic who advocates the contrary. The established principle of every free people, is that the law shall alone govern; and to it the military must always yield." *Dow* v. *Johnson,* 100 U.S. 158, 169. Congress prior to the time of the enactment of the Organic Act had only once authorized the supplanting of the courts by military tribunals. Legislation to that effect was enacted immediately after the South's unsuccessful attempt to secede from the Union. Insofar as that legislation applied to the Southern States after the war was at an end it was challenged by a series of Presidential vetoes as vigorous as any in the country's history. And in order to prevent this Court from passing on the constitutionality of this legislation Congress found it necessary to curtail our appellate jurisdiction.[22] Indeed, prior to the Organic Act, the only time this Court had ever discussed the supplanting of courts by military tribunals in a situation other than that involving the establishment of a military government over recently occupied enemy territory, it had emphatically declared that "civil liberty and this kind of martial law cannot endure together; the antagonism is irreconcilable; and, in the conflict, one or the other must perish." *Ex parte Milligan,* 4 Wall. 2, 124-125.

We believe that when Congress passed the Hawaiian Organic Act and authorized the establishment of "martial law" it had in mind and did not wish to exceed the boundaries between military and civilian power, in which our people have always believed, which responsible military and executive officers had heeded, and which had become part of our political philosophy and institutions prior to the time Congress passed the Organic Act. The phrase "martial law" as employed in that Act, therefore, while intended to authorize the military to act vigorously for the maintenance of an orderly civil government and for the defense of the Islands against actual or threatened rebellion or invasion, was not intended to authorize the supplanting of courts by military tribunals. Yet the Government seeks to justify the punishment of both White and Duncan on the ground of such supposed congressional authorization. We hold that both petitioners are now entitled to be released from custody.

Reversed.

MR. JUSTICE JACKSON took no part in the consideration or decision of these cases.

MR. JUSTICE MURPHY, concurring.

The Court's opinion, in which I join, makes clear that the military trials in these cases were unjustified by the martial law provisions of the Hawaiian Organic Act. Equally obvious, as I see it, is the fact that these trials were forbidden by the Bill of Rights of the Constitution of the United States, which applies in both spirit and letter to Hawaii. Indeed, the unconstitutionality of

---

[22] *Ex parte McCardle,* 6 Wall. 318. See also Warren, The Supreme Court in United States History, Vol. 2, 464, 484.

the usurpation of civil power by the military is so great in this instance as to warrant this Court's complete and outright repudiation of the action.

* * *

Such considerations led this Court in *Ex parte Milligan*, 4 Wall. 2, to lay down the rule that the military lacks any constitutional power in war or in peace to substitute its tribunals for civil courts that are open and operating in the proper and unobstructed exercise of their jurisdiction. Only when a foreign invasion or civil war actually closes the courts and renders it impossible for them to administer criminal justice can martial law validly be invoked to suspend their functions. Even the suspension of power under those conditions is of a most temporary character. "As necessity creates the rule, so it limits its duration; for, if this government is continued *after* the courts are reinstated, it is a gross usurpation of power." *Id.*, 127.

Tested by the *Milligan* rule, the military proceedings in issue plainly lacked constitutional sanction. . . .

* * *

The so-called "open court" rule of the *Milligan* case, to be sure, has been the subject of severe criticism, especially by military commentators. That criticism is repeated by the Government in these cases. It is said that the fact that courts are open is but one of many factors relevant to determining the necessity and hence the constitutionality of military trials of civilians. The argument is made that however adequate the "open court" rule may have been in 1628 or 1864 it is distinctly unsuited to modern warfare conditions where all of the territories of a warring nation may be in combat zones or imminently threatened with long-range attack even while civil courts are operating. Hence if a military commander, on the basis of his conception of military necessity, requires all civilians accused of crime to be tried summarily before martial law tribunals, the Bill of Rights must bow humbly to his judgment despite the unquestioned ability of the civil courts to exercise their criminal jurisdiction.

The argument thus advanced is as untenable today as it was when cast in the language of the Plantagenets, the Tudors and the Stuarts. It is a rank appeal to abandon the fate of all our liberties to the reasonableness of the judgment of those who are trained primarily for war. It seeks to justify military usurpation of civilian authority to punish crime without regard to the potency of the Bill of Rights. It deserves repudiation.

* * *

[Justice Murphy analyzed the reasons given for closing the civil courts in Hawaii, and found them wanting.]

MR. CHIEF JUSTICE STONE, concurring.

I concur in the result.

I do not think that "martial law," as used in § 67 of the Hawaiian Organic Act, is devoid of meaning. This Court has had occasion to consider its scope and has pointed out that martial law is the exercise of the power which resides in the executive branch of the Government to preserve order and insure the public safety in times of emergency, when other branches of the Government are unable to function, or their functioning would itself threaten the public safety. *Luther* v. *Borden*, 7 How. 1, 45. It is a law of necessity to be prescribed and administered by the executive power. Its object, the preservation of the public safety and good order, defines its scope, which will vary with the circumstances and necessities of the case. The exercise of the power may not extend beyond what is required by the exigency which calls it forth. ...

The Executive has broad discretion in determining when the public emergency is such as to give rise to the necessity of martial law, and in adapting it to the need. Cf. *Hirabayashi* v. *United States*, 320 U.S. 81. But executive action is not proof of its own necessity, and the military's judgment here is not conclusive that every action taken pursuant to the declaration of martial law was justified by the exigency. In the substitution of martial law controls for the ordinary civil processes, "what are the allowable limits of military discretion, and whether or not they have been overstepped in a particular case, are judicial questions." *Sterling* v. *Constantin, supra*, 401.

* * *

... I find nothing in the entire record which would fairly suggest that the civil courts were unable to function with their usual efficiency at the times these petitioners were tried, or that their trial by jury in a civil court would have endangered good order or the public safety. .... I can only conclude that the trials and the convictions upon which petitioners are now detained, were unauthorized by the statute, and without lawful authority.

* * *

MR. JUSTICE BURTON, with whom MR. JUSTICE FRANKFURTER concurs, dissenting.

With the rest of this Court I subscribe unreservedly to the Bill of Rights. I recognize the importance of the civil courts in protecting individual rights guaranteed by the Constitution. I prefer civil to military control of civilian life and I agree that in war our Constitution contemplates the preservation of the individual rights of all of our people in accordance with a plan of constitutional procedure fitted to the needs of a self-governing republic at war.

Our Constitution expressly provides for waging war, and it is with the constitutional instruments for the successful conduct of war that I am concerned. I recognize here, as elsewhere, the constitutional direction that our respective branches of the Government do not exceed their allotted shares of authority. The courts, as well as our other agencies of the Government, accordingly owe a constitutional obligation not to invade the fields reserved either to the people, the States, or the other coordinate branches of the Government. ...

* * *

It is well that the outer limits of the jurisdiction of our military authorities is subject to review by our courts even under such extreme circumstances as those of the battle field. This, however, requires the courts to put themselves as nearly as possible in the place of those who had the constitutional responsibility for immediate executive action. For a court to recreate a complete picture of the emergency is impossible. That impossibility demonstrates the need for a zone of executive discretion within which courts must guard themselves with special care against judging past military action too closely by the inapplicable standards of judicial, or even military, hindsight. The nature of judicial authority is largely negative as contrasted with the generally positive nature of executive authority, and it is essential that the opportunity for well directed positive action be preserved and vigorously used if the Government is to serve the best interests of the people.

For this Court to intrude its judgment into spheres of constitutional discretion that are reserved either to the Congress or to the Chief Executive, is to invite disregard of that judgment by the Congress or by executive agencies under a claim of constitutional right to do so. On the other hand, this Court can contribute much to the orderly conduct of government, if it will outline reasonable boundaries for the discretion of the respective departments of the Government, with full regard for the limitations and also for the responsibilities imposed upon them by the Constitution.

It is important to approach the present cases with a full appreciation of the responsibility of the executive branch of the Government in Hawaii under the invasion which occurred on December 7, 1941. The question is not shall the Constitution apply under such circumstances? The question is with what authority [have] the Constitution and laws of this country vested the official representatives of the people upon whom are placed the responsibilities of leadership under those extraordinary circumstances?

The vital distinction is between conditions in "the theatre of actual military operations" and outside of that theatre. In this case Hawaii was not only in the theatre of operations, it was under fire. If the Territory of Hawaii, on that date and during the immediately succeeding period, is recognized as the battle field it was, then under such circumstances of invasion and threat of immediate further invasion, the actions taken by the Governor of Hawaii and by the Commanding General of the Hawaiian Department, supported by the President of the United States, in suspending the writ of habeas corpus, declaring martial law and vesting in such Commanding General for those first several days the powers normally exercised by the Governor and by the judicial officers and employees of the Territory (at least to the extent that would be involved in the present cases if they had arisen at that time), were within the executive discretion of the officials who authorized the action. . . .

  * * *

Now that the war has been won and the safety of the Islands has been again assured, there is opportunity, in the calm light of peace, for the readjustment of sentences imposed upon civilians and military personnel during the emergency of war and which have not yet expired. It is important, however, that in reviewing the constitutionality of the conduct of our agencies of government in time of war, invasion and threatened invasion, we do not now make precedents which in other emergencies may handicap the executive branch of the Government in the performance of duties allotted to it by the Constitution and by the exercise of which it successfully defended the nation against the greatest attack ever made upon it.

One way to test the soundness of a decision today that the trial of petitioner White on August 25, 1942, before a provost court on a charge of embezzlement and the trial of petitioner Duncan on March 2, 1944, before a similar court on a charge of maliciously assaulting marine sentries were unconstitutional procedures, is to ask ourselves whether or not on those dates, with the war against Japan in full swing, this Court would have, or should have, granted a writ of habeas corpus, an injunction or a writ of prohibition to release the petitioners or otherwise to oust the provost courts of their claimed jurisdiction. Such a test emphasizes the issue. I believe that this Court would not have been justified in granting the relief suggested at such times. Also I believe that this Court might well have found itself embarrassed had it ordered such relief and then had attempted to enforce its order in the theatre of military operations, at a time when the area was under martial law and the writ of habeas corpus was still suspended, all in accordance with the orders of the President of the United States and the Governor of Hawaii issued under their interpretation of the discretion and responsibility vested in them by the Constitution of the United States and by the Organic Act of Hawaii enacted by Congress.*

---

* For additional treatment of some of the issues in this chapter, see DE VRIES AND RODRIGUEZ-NOVAS, THE LAW OF THE AMERICAS (1965).

TABLE OF CASES

INDEX

EDITORIAL
SUCRE
CARACAS